ART IN INDONESIA

Continuities and Change

ART IN INDONESIA

CONTINUITIES AND CHANGE

By Claire Holt

CORNELL UNIVERSITY PRESS · ITHACA NEW YORK

THE SOUTHEAST ASIA PROGRAM OF CORNELL UNIVERSITY AND THE ASIAN LITERATURE PROGRAM OF THE ASIA SOCIETY PROVIDED GRANTS THAT HELPED DEFRAY THE MANUFACTURING COSTS OF THIS BOOK.

CORNELL UNIVERSITY PRESS

FIRST PUBLISHED 1967
LIBRARY OF CONGRESS CATALOG CARD NUMBER: 66-19222

PRINTED IN THE UNITED STATES OF AMERICA
BY THE MAPLE PRESS COMPANY

ACKNOWLEDGMENTS

THE IDEA FOR THIS BOOK originated in 1952 when Dr. Charles B. Fahs, Director of Humanities of the Rockefeller Foundation at that time, suggested to me the value of discovering the effects of World War II, the revolution, and the attainment of independence upon the Indonesian visual arts. Dr. Fahs knew about my earlier experience in Indonesia, where between 1930 and 1938 I had worked as assistant to the late Dr. Willem F. Stutterheim in his archaeological research and had pursued my own studies of the Indonesian performing arts. To Dr. Stutterheim, my teacher and guide, I owe whatever basic insights I had gained into Indonesian culture and history; to his friend, the late Mangkunagara VII of Surakarta, at whose court the traditional arts flourished in the thirties, my introduction to the performing arts; and to Gusti Pangeran Aria Tedjakusuma of Jogjakarta, who instructed me with great patience, generosity, and humor, I owe my knowledge of the Javanese classical dance.

For two years Dr. Fahs's suggestion lay dormant, until in 1954 I applied for a Rockefeller Foundation grant and learned that Cornell University—in particular its Southeast Asia Program, then headed by Professor Lauriston Sharp—was willing to sponsor the project and participate in financing it. Thus with the institutional, moral, and financial support of the Rockefeller Foundation and Cornell University I was enabled to undertake the study, first in Indonesia (between 1955 and 1957) and later in Ithaca, New York, particularly at the Cornell University libraries, where the materials pertinent to Indonesian studies are of rare excellence.

When I began to organize my collected data, it became clear that the revolutionary changes which had occurred in the arts of postwar Indonesia could be discussed meaningfully only in historical perspective. Gradually the sections that were first intended as background expanded until the outline assumed its present shape, being almost equally divided among discussions of antiquity, the living traditions, and the contemporary modern art forms.

Five years later, the work on the manuscript, repeatedly interrupted by long periods of illness and by teaching commitments, had progressed to the point where publication became a definite possibility. Welcome encouragement came from The Asia Society in New York with an offer of a publication subsidy. Also, the Southeast Asia Program of Cornell University declared its willingness to make a contribution toward publication. These institutions furnished grants of support without which the book may not have materialized; for these I am deeply grateful.

My gratitude also extends to a great number of institutions and individual persons whose cooperation at various stages of my research and writing contributed to the present form of this volume. Not all of them can be mentioned here by name, but they may be assured that I remember their help with warm thankfulness.

In Indonesia, the courtesy and assistance of all authorities concerned paved my way in travel and research. I am particularly indebted to the then Ministry of Education and Culture and to the Archaeological Service of the Republic of Indonesia, in particular its Director, Dr. R. Soekmono, and his former assistant, Mrs. Jessie Oey-Blom. The Cultural Office of the Ministry of Education—especially its Division on Art Affairs in Jogjakarta, headed by Mr. Kusnadi—gave me invaluable help.

President Sukarno's cordial reception and encouragement of my work—allowing me free access for study and photography of his private, as well as the State's, art collections in the palaces of Djakarta and Bogor—are deeply appreciated.

In Bali, Mr. J. C. Krijgsman, Inspector of the Archaeological Service, was kind enough to show me the latest excavations and restoration work in progress. Mr. Rudolf Bonnet, the well-known painter then residing in Ubud, was on many occasions a gracious host and guide and, most important, placed at my disposal for study and photography his fine collection of Balinese paintings and sculptures, a few examples of which enrich this volume.

In Sumatra, travel and study would have been impossible without the generous assistance of the Cultural

Office's branch in Medan, directed by Mr. W. Simandjuntak, who arranged for my use of a pick-up truck. It became our *unta yang setia* ("faithful camel") hobbling along the potholes of Sumatra's ruined roads into some of the remoter areas that I had visited in 1938. Mr. Jusuf Said of the branch office of the Ministry of Information in Medan accompanied me into the lands of the Bataks as guide, interpreter, and ever helpful companion.

Above all, I am grateful to all the artists I visited in Java, Bali, and Sumatra, who allowed me to interfere with their work and take much of their time; without their helpful interest my study would have remained barren. Similarly, in the Art Academy (ASRI) of Jogjakarta and in the Fine Arts School in Bandung, directors, teaching staff, and students were helpful in many different ways.

As every writer who plans to illustrate his work well knows, he must have at least fifteen times as many photographs as are eventually to be published, but even then, some important items will be missing. So also with information collected in the field, supplementary data must always be sought *post factum*. Thus, when inevitably the need arose, I was fortunate in receiving unstinting cooperation from the photographic archives of the Archaeological Service, Republic of Indonesia; from Professor Allen Atwell, of Cornell University's Department of Art, who generously placed at my disposal his own fine photographs taken in Indonesia; from Professor Douglas Fraser, of Columbia University's Department of Art and Archaeology, who had photographed objects of primitive art in various museums of Europe; and from a number of institutions and museums in the Netherlands, Sweden, Germany, and the United States, whose courtesy is acknowledged in the Detailed List of Illustrations and Maps. My friend Alfred B. Hudson, before and after his anthropological field work in South Borneo, sacrificed many evenings drawing needed maps and photographing objects from my own collection as well as works of modern Indonesian artists which were exhibited in the galleries of Cornell University.

Much time and trouble were invested by friends in Indonesia who helped me supplement the biographical data on Indonesian artists. I am deeply indebted to Mr. Trisno Sumardjo in Djakarta; Mr. Sudjoko and Mr. Angkama of the Fine Arts School in Bandung; Mr. Kusnadi in Jogjakarta; and Mrs. Kay Hawkins, American painter, who at the time resided in Jogjakarta and helped convey and follow up my requests.

Certain parts of the manuscript have been read and commented upon by Professor Robert von Heine-Geldern of the University of Vienna; Mr. Sudjatmoko in Djakarta; Professor Joseph Campbell of Sarah Lawrence College; Professors George McT. Kahin, John M. Echols, and Robert B. Jones of Cornell University; and Mr. Soemarsaid Moertono, Mr. Pandam Siswoharsojo, and Mr. Benedict R. O'G. Anderson, former graduate students at Cornell. Dr. Louis Damais of L'Ecole Française d'Extrême-Orient, Paris, was especially helpful with advice and clarifications concerning some passages in ancient inscriptions cited in Appendix II. To all of these persons I am infinitely grateful for their thoughtful criticisms and suggestions, which are now incorporated in the manuscript.

Finally, not only enormous patience and hard work, but a number of excellent substantive suggestions were contributed by my assistants, Mrs. Judith Hudson and Mrs. Arlene Lev, both of whom had firsthand experience in Indonesia. Without their conscientious and stimulating cooperation the manuscript might never have been finished.

Three other persons, each in his own way, helped me greatly: Mr. Boyd Compton of the Rockefeller Foundation; Mrs. Bonnie R. Crown, Director of the Asian Literature Program of The Asia Society, New York; and Professor George McT. Kahin, Director of the Southeast Asia Program of Cornell University, who was ever responsive to my needs.

C. H.

Ithaca, New York
November 20, 1966

CONTENTS

DETAILED LIST OF ILLUSTRATIONS AND MAPS, WITH CREDITS

The following abbreviations are used in the plate credits:

DP Archaeological Service (*Dinas Purbakala*), Republic of Indonesia.

MN The late Mangkunagara VII of Surakarta. All photographs thus marked were taken between 1930 and 1938.

Where no credits are given, the photographs are by the author.

FIGURES

MAPS

NOTE ON TRANSCRIPTION, ORTHOGRAPHY, AND PLACE NAMES

IN TRYING to cope with the welter of variations in the spelling and transcription of Old and Modern Javanese, and Indonesian names and terms, I have, in principle, followed wherever applicable the prevalent Indonesian usage, which is largely based on Dutch spelling and transcription. Many names and terms derived from Sanskrit also appear in their Indonesian versions. Yet I was unable to resolve the problem of consistency and must beg the reader's indulgence. Dealing with pertinent names and terms in English, Dutch, French, and German scholarly works as well as in Indonesian texts where transcriptions may be consistent within one work but not necessarily from author to author, and having to quote occasionally from an original, I have had to sacrifice consistency and make some arbitrary decisions. Diacritical marks have been retained only in direct citations from works where they appear, and it is hoped that those readers accustomed to greater linguistic precision will find the means to clarify for themselves the possible ambiguities arising from the omission of diacritical marks.

To avoid confusion and *extreme* mispronunciation of Indonesian words and names, the reader should bear in mind the following: The letter *j* in Indonesian is equivalent to the English *y,* while the approximate sound symbolized in English by *j* is represented in Indonesian by *dj*. Thus *Djaja* is pronounced *Jaya* (with the *a* always sounding as in *father*); *Sudjojono* is pronounced *Sujoyono*. On the other hand, the English transcription has been used in names (*e.g.,* Surabaya, Majapahit, Srivijaya) which for a long time have so been spelled in English texts.

The sound *oo* as in *foot* is represented in our text in Indonesian names and words mostly with *u* but occasionally, when the Indonesian consistently retains in his name the Dutch equivalent *oe,* the latter has been used. Thus, Sukarno but Dr. Moerdowo. *In brief,* u *and* oe *are equivalent,* as sounds. Inconsistency in the spelling of one and the same name (as Sudjojono in the text and Soedjojono in the bibliography) is dictated by the need to cite the particular bibliographical reference precisely even though on other occasions the bearer of this name may spell it with a *u*. There are other such cases.

The sound *aw* (as in *law*), which occurs in many Javanese names and terms, is represented in Indonesia with either *a* or *o* (*e.g.,* Klana, Klono; Djaka, Djoko; bedaja, bedojo or bedoyo). Again, absolute consistency in adopting either one or the other method was impossible.

Finally, the letter *i* is never pronounced as is the pronoun *I* in English but is always either long, approximately as in *see,* or short as in *pit.**

In regard to geographical names, because most maps currently used in English-speaking countries do not yet show the relatively new Indonesian names for the islands of the Archipelago, their old names have been retained, such as Borneo (for the whole of the island including the Indonesian part called Kalimantan); Celebes, for Sulawesi; Moluccas, for Malukku; and West New Guinea, for West Irian.

* See *An Indonesian-English Dictionary* by John M. Echols and Hassan Shadily, Ithaca, N.Y., 1963, for detailed guidance.

INTRODUCTION

INTRODUCTION

Approaches: Art and History

THE RECORDED HISTORY of the Indonesian Archipelago began shortly before the onset of the Christian era with accounts in Chinese annals and in the first centuries of our era with the introduction of script from India. The contours of the distant past slowly emerge from the remains of early inscriptions made by rulers of the islands on stones or on copper plates and from later records engraved in palm-leaf books, which were eventually superseded by written and printed documentation on paper. While one region or one group of people became historical, however, elsewhere preliterate peoples remained nonhistorical. Among the latter some attained a considerable degree of cultural sophistication, but others in inland regions, isolated from the mainstreams of interinsular and international life by mountains and forests, persisted in their primitive ways of life and remained culturally "prehistoric."

Art in Indonesia correspondingly reflects an enormous diversity. Both geographical and historical factors have always precluded the development of a homogeneous art with a single line of evolution. Today a multitude of cultural phenomena coexist in the archipelago at quite different stages of their life cycles. Some are ancient but still very vital; others are old but are apparently dying or undergoing radical transformations; still others were born recently and are growing vigorously.

In the continuum of culture growth, old and new elements overlap, fuse, or exist side by side. Dates are only approximate dividers marking the introduction of new ideas or techniques without necessarily implying the disappearance of preceding beliefs and practices. Arts that developed in neolithic times do not disappear with the advent of the bronze age, nor do they vanish later. Sacred lore introduced in Indonesia with Indian religions survives in Java despite the subsequent spread of Islam. Religious ideas especially show great tenacity; it is easier to trace the time of their birth than to establish that of their death. One chapter does not close at any definite point of time in which a new one begins. Consequently, Indonesia's cultural history in general, and its art history in particular, cannot be easily fitted into neat chronological periods.

In this second half of the twentieth century, we see a bewildering array of old and new in all phases of Indonesian life. Traditional, highly stylized, and semi-ritualistic art forms, such as the shadow play, survive beside the modern secular art being created by contemporary artists, whose styles range from romantic naturalism to intellectually controlled abstraction.

My mission in 1955–1957, which was the initial stimulus to this study, was to discover how World War II, revolution, and independence had affected the visual arts in Indonesia. The study, as I envisaged it, was to be more a contribution to Indonesia's cultural history than an introduction to its art history from an esthetic viewpoint. Therefore, neither a complete discussion of its formal aspects nor a compilation of all knowledge about Indonesia's art seemed desirable, or feasible. Rather, I chose only a few examples to trace the main strands of continuities, discontinuities, and changes in the fabric of Indonesia's art history. In the pursuit of some strands I chose to range freely through time and space whenever a motif or an idea led from the past to the present or from the present back into the past. Nevertheless, the principal historical periods have been retained as solid bases from which such expeditions could be made.

In most studies devoted to Indonesia, Java inevitably remains the center of attention. Not only has it been through much of history the principal locus both of power and of converging insular and international commerce, but it has also provided the bulk of historical records. Moreover, because Java is the most populous of all Indonesia's islands (estimated to contain 70 million people), the number of its inhabitants alone tips the balance in its favor. Recent efforts to escape from historical "Javacentricity" have not been too successful. Finally, the arts of Java and those of neighboring Bali have received greatest attention from scholars and writers, and in this respect the present study will be no exception.

For those unacquainted with the archaeological and historical divisions of Indonesia's prehistory and history, a skeleton outline of the main eras follows.

I. PREHISTORY

Old Stone Age (Paleolithic), time span uncertain. Remains of this longest period (perhaps of several hundred thousand years) consist of crude chipped-stone implements such as choppers, pounders, and axes.

Intermediary Stone Age (Mesolithic), time span uncertain.

Objects of bone, shell, and horn appear. Paintings on rock walls, especially in the eastern parts of the archipelago, are ascribed to this era.

New or Late Stone Age (Neolithic), *c.* 2500 B.C.–

Estimated to have begun between 2500 and 1000 B.C. Neolithic technology is thought to have been introduced by migrants from continental Southeast Asia who were familiar with seafaring, agriculture, the use of the buffalo, domestication of dogs and pigs. Pottery, the making of barkcloth, and the shaping of wood and stone are developed. Implements include stone arrowheads, mortars and pestles, smooth adzes; adornments made of shells and animal teeth as well as of crude beads appear. Megaliths (large stones) in the shape of commemorative menhirs, ancestral seats, altars on terraced sites, cist graves and sarcophagi, and images and figures are hewn from large monoliths. Traces of ancestral cults and spirit worship are more clearly discernible than in the earlier periods.

Bronze Age, c. 300 B.C.–

The introduction of bronze objects from continental Southeast Asia and the development of skills in metal casting and metalworking mark this era.

II. THE SPREAD OF INDIAN RELIGIONS, FIRST OR SECOND CENTURY A.D.–SIXTEENTH CENTURY A.D.

During the first centuries A.D. small Hinduistic kingdoms existed, although little is known of them. Chinese reports indicate the presence of kingdoms in Java and Sumatra, and records confirm the existence of Kutei in East Borneo and Taruma in West Java in the fifth century and of an early Srivijaya kingdom in South Sumatra in the seventh century.

Central Javanese Period, c. seventh-tenth centuries. Hindu-Javanese culture attains a peak in Central Java under two rival ruling dynasties, one Buddhist and one Shivaite, between the eighth and the end of the tenth centuries. Their history has not yet been fully clarified. The famous propagators of Buddhism and builders of great Buddhist sanctuaries are the Shailendra (literally, "Lords of the Mountain") dynasty, a branch of which developed the kingdom of Srivijaya, based in Sumatra, into an empire. The kingdom of the Shivaite dynasty which supersedes the Shailendra in Java was known as Mataram.

East Javanese Period, c. tenth-sixteeenth centuries. Following the reigns of Kings Sindok, Dharmavamsa, and Airlangga (929–1047), three kingdoms rise successively as centers of power in East Java: Kediri (1045–1222); Singasari (1222–1292); and Majapahit (1294–*c.* 1520), which extends its suzerainty over other parts of the archipelago and exercises a strong immediate influence on the development of Balinese culture. Shivaism and Buddhism coexist and sometimes merge in syncretic cults strongly tinged by Tantric mysticism.

III. THE SPREAD OF ISLAM, *c.* 1250–

Beginning in Sumatra toward the end of the thirteenth century, conversion to Islam progresses in Indonesia, increasingly affecting the coastal regions of Java and of other islands in the fifteenth and sixteenth centuries. Ninety per cent of Indonesia's inhabitants are Moslems. In the early sixteenth century, sultanates on Java's north coast contest the power of Majapahit; on Java's west coast the Bantam sultans develop power. Toward the end of the sixteenth century in Central Java, a Moslem dynasty resurrects Mataram as a sultanate. In the eighteenth century, as Dutch political control penetrates, a reduced Mataram is divided into the principalities of Surakarta and Jogjakarta which retain largely nominal power.

IV. PENETRATION AND EXPANSION OF EUROPEAN TRADE AND POLITICAL DOMINATION, SIXTEENTH CENTURY TO 1945

After first contacts with Portuguese, English, and Dutch traders at the beginning of the sixteenth century, Indonesian rulers become enmeshed in the economic-political power drive of the Dutch East India Company (founded in 1602), which lasts until the Company's dissolution in 1799. At the beginning of the nineteenth century, Indonesia formally becomes a colony of the Netherlands, which up to the first decade of the twentieth century is engaged in the gradual expansion of its control in the islands other than Java. Occupied by the Japanese from 1942 until 1945, Indonesia proclaims its independence in August, 1945, following Japan's surrender, but the official transfer of sovereignty by the Netherlands follows only at the close of 1949 after protracted warfare and negotiations supported by the United Nations.

V. THE INDEPENDENT REPUBLIC OF INDONESIA, 1945–

The peaceful reconstruction of Indonesia as a sovereign country begins only in 1950, after four years of devastating struggle with the Dutch. From its inception, the Republic is headed by President Sukarno. The first decades of its existence are marked by a search for a national style in all phases of life.

Indonesia still awaits its new historians[1] who will illuminate much in its past that is unknown. The gaps in the mosaic of Indonesian history must be filled in with the vast array of bits and pieces that have been accumulated but as yet only partially correlated by many excellent scholars in the fields of archaeology, epigraphy, ethnology and linguistic, religion, customary law, literature, folklore, and the arts. Valuable insights gained by social scientists[2] during the last twenty-five years also await integration into the historical picture.

On the historical horizons now are ranged peaks of power—of the old Hinduistic kingdoms and empires in Java and Sumatra, of the Moslem sultanates in these and other islands, and of the administrations of the Governors-general of erstwhile Netherlands India—not unlike mountaintops whose lower slopes are enveloped in mist. Relatively little is known, or if known little mentioned, of the broad base of Indonesian society in antiquity and in more recent centuries. Throughout history, however, the villages, which are largely autonomous, have been the most important base units of Indonesia's political and economic life. Their produce and labor served the needs of ancient palace-cities and religious foundations, fulfilled the mercantile ambitions of princes in harbor towns, and made possible the agricultural export trade, through which their products flowed directly or indirectly into foreign markets, ultimately via Dutch channels. And the villages now lend stability to the still unstable order of the Republic.

Old Indonesia has usually been regarded as a land of peasants and princes (and marginally, of tribes), a generalization which may be justified in terms of Indonesia's old power structure. This view relegates to obscurity, however, all the various intermediary people on whose expert knowledge and skills both rulers and ruled must have depended. A number of terms and titles that appear in old inscriptions indicate the existence of a complex system of social life as early as the eighth and ninth centuries. An extensive royal bureaucracy administered the kingdom. Priests and monks supervised sacred foundations, temples, monasteries, and their sources of income. The village people were represented by their elders at great celebrations instituted by the ruler, and representatives from groups of merchants and of special craftsmen also appeared at these ceremonial gatherings.

Unfortunately we know too little of the organization and activities of such groups, which included architects and craftsmen. In short, we know too little of the "technical order of life," to borrow a phrase from Robert Redfield,[3] as contrasted with our somewhat clearer notions about the "moral order"—the nonmaterial cultural context within which the Indonesian arts developed and which they reflect.

A society's moral order determines many of the attitudes and actions of the people who live within its sphere. Through the ages changing moral orders have evoked the following predominant attitudes of Indonesia's people. A universe filled with energies which charge with life-power all existing beings and things, as conceived by peoples with a "dynamistic" view of life, required constant efforts to maintain the proper *balance of life potency* through magical means. A world dominated by unknown mysterious forces, spirits and ancestral souls, as conceived by peoples with an animistic view of life, called for *propitiation* of these forces. A cosmic order directed by high deities and reflected on earth by divine kings, as conceived in the Hindu-Buddhist era, demanded the preservation of *harmony* with this order. The recognition of the one and only god Allah, with the advent of Islam, demanded *surrender* to his Highest Will, but also *work* to secure His help and blessing. The constricting authority of alien colonial rulers, superimposed upon all preceding conceptions, strengthened the need for *adjustment* to the inevitable and *evasion,* patterns already developed under the old absolutism of native royal regimes. The new evolving ideologies of a democratic society in the independent Republic call for greater collective and individual *responsibility* for man's life on this earth. None of these attitudes and its resultant patterns of behavior have ever necessarily excluded any or all of the others. Today in both urban and rural Indonesia one is sure to find a mixture of all these attitudes in various combinations and proportions.

Viewpoints: Art and "Weltgefühl"

Works of art convey a special emotive mood which is undoubtedly closely linked with the moral order (or disorder, as the case may be) of a phase of history and of a cultural area. The Germans call this general feeling about the world *Weltgefühl* (literally, "world feeling"), as distinct from *Weltanschauung* ("world view"), which is a more conscious formulating of views on the universal order. The differentiation between these two concepts may have occurred when art and science parted ways.

The manner in which human beings have been depicted in Indonesia throughout the ages eloquently reflects a changing world feeling. In prehistoric times there were generalized, schematic representations of human beings differentiated mainly by sex characteristics (Pl. 2, Figs. 2, 3). In Hinduistic Indonesia a distinction appears which on the one hand stresses status, high and low (Pl. 96), and on the other the polarities, divine and demonic. In this era of deified kings, beauty is the attribute of gods and princes. Ordinary mortals have cruder features, naturalistic at first (Pl. 42) but gradually assuming ugly or amusingly grotesque forms (Pl. 71). In Islamic Java such typology persists in highly stylized puppets (Pl. 115) and masks. It is no coincidence that shortly before the Revolution the individualized person, unique as a character, emerges with force upon the Indonesian art scene (Pls. 193, 194, 195).

An awareness of the total cultural context within which an art work was produced doubtless aids in apprehending the world feeling it conveys, provided, of course, that the viewer's intellectual knowledge does not inhibit the free flow of nonrational response that also permits him to feel the impact of the expressive form and mood in a work of art. Since works of art are perceptions and feelings made visible, they testify to the one and indivisible realm of man *in,* rather than *and,* his universe.

The social applications of the arts also reveal a culture's values and sensitivities, or world feeling. Upon which structures does a society lavish the skills of its artists? Upon tombs, cathedrals, and palaces or on air terminals, banks, and sports arenas? To whom is most homage paid with images and monuments? To ancestors and saints or to generals, poets, and statesmen? What kind of deities or what kind of men are honored? What public functions call for visual symbols and spectacles that require the services of skilled artists? Celebrations of the agricultural cycle and cremations or national holidays, fashion shows, and performances which help promote commercial interests? Such questions yield fruitful answers concerning the ethos that characterizes a given culture.

In Indonesia's past, artistic creativity has served magic and religious ritual functions, has given visible form to myths, and has enhanced secular ceremonial life on all important occasions, whether at the courts of kings or in village communities. Death and fertility were the primary axes around which artistic creativity spiraled. The arts offer vivid testimony to the refusal of man, when confronted by death, to accept its finality: to his creation of beliefs and cults in order to assert the indestructability of his being, even at the risk in later religions of suffering the eternal tortures of hell. Early religious systems, however, were not concerned with an individual's rewards and punishments in the afterlife but served more fundamentally to ensure the perpetuation of human life in a continuum of eternity. Fear of death and of the dead made the dead live on. And, like that of other lands, much of Indonesia's immortal art has grown out of this assertion of immortality. It is only in twentieth-century Indonesia that art, devoid of its ancient functions, has embarked in part upon a self-conscious existence which breaks with traditions.

In present-day Indonesia the sociocultural context is directly observable. The country is in the midst of intense social change; new ideas and values are arising which variously affect the world view as well as the world feeling of both the society as a whole and of its individual members. While nationalist fervor impels the artist to seek a style symbolic of the collective national spirit, individualism as conceived in a modern democracy sends him in quest of highly personal expression.

Organization: The Spheres of Art

In this presentation, the arts of Indonesia have been conceived as belonging to three overlapping spheres superimposed on the chronological periods of Indonesian history.

The first of these spheres, labeled "The Heritage," embraces those art creations of Indonesia's prehistory and historical antiquity that have been preserved. These are works made of durable materials like stone, metal, and sometimes clay. Treasured in museums (in Indonesia and abroad), or guarded as national monuments in their original natural setting, they are visited by tourists, by school youth studying history, and by local and foreign art students.*

The second sphere, which I have designated "Living Traditions," embraces the plastic arts of Indonesia's non-Islamic regions (Bali, for instance) where traditional conceptions of form and content are perpetuated, even though often executed in a new medium. This sphere also encompasses the art of the dance in all parts of the archipelago. The living traditions also include such theater arts, intimately linked with chanted storytelling, as the ancient shadow play and classical dance drama of Java and Bali, Java's theater of three-dimensional rod puppets and the mask-plays. Finally, tradition is alive in the vast and rich field of the applied arts and crafts throughout Indonesia, which are not treated in this volume.

The third sphere encompasses contemporary "Modern Art," an urban phenomenon that has developed principally in Java. Its manifestations—separate from, but coexistent with, the vital traditional forms—appear most vigorously in painting, and less so in sculpture. Its developments parallel the growth of modern literature as well as of new trends in both stage and screen drama. A search for new dance forms has also begun.

If, from an imaginary "plateau of the present," we tried to sound the historical depths of the arts in these different spheres, we would find that the development of modern art has gathered its impetus during the past three *decades;* that the living traditional arts must have assumed their present forms during the last two or three hundred years after a slow evolution in the course of preceding *centuries;* that the plastic arts of historical antiquity had developed and undergone stylistic changes in the course of a *millennium.* Beneath the historical strata lie the many *thousands of years* of prehistory, during which the inhabitants of the Indonesian islands invented and perfected both their material culture and their forms of tribal or village organization and evolved ideas about man in nature and the forces operating in the universe.

Certain significant motifs recur in Indonesian art throughout the ages. Some of the designs applied by prehistoric painters and sculptors are still used today in the motifs that embellish Indonesian textiles and metal objects or in the wood-carved ornamentation of houses. And some of the concepts of magic that once underlay the creation of these designs are occasionally still in evidence on our imaginary plateau of the present, like old geological formations whose weathered surfaces stand out against a completely changed environment.

Despite the great diversity, one may ask if there are common, unifying elements which make these various art forms uniquely "Indonesian." Although political unity has not abolished cultural diversity, political unity and new technological advances—not least those in communications—have given all Indonesians greater access to their various regional art forms as well as to all currents, past and present, from the rest of the world. The tropical island republic certainly is eager to clarify its own cultural identity within the community of nations. There is a feeling that some deep, basic predispositions are shared by all the various ethnic groups that populate the Indonesian islands. Certainly there are many common factors: the tropical natural environment; physically similar peoples; the wide agricultural base of economic life; the direct or indirect repercussions from waves of cultural influences that have affected the life of the islands through the course of history; the shared experience of colonial rule; the upsurge during the revolutionary war that led to independence; and the progressive diffusion of one language. But can study of the arts help to discover the assumed common Indonesian characteristics? The extent to which unifying features can or cannot be discerned is of lesser importance perhaps than the fact that among Indonesians an urgent desire to find or create them is so actual.

In these pages we must limit ourselves to continuities and changes in the arts of Indonesia without trying to generalize about Indonesian art and, consequently, about the "national character" and temperament of the Indonesian people. Certain themes or decorative motifs do recur throughout the ages. We could regard these merely as confirmation of the permanence of the

* In the actual training of contemporary Indonesian art students, however, masterpieces of Indonesian antiquity play a much less vital role than do the reproductions of works of Greek antiquity or of the Italian Renaissance in the art academies of Europe and the Americas.

natural environment (the mountains, the sea), of the constancy of elements essential to an insular and agricultural people (boats, fish, buffalo, rice), or of the eternal fascination of man by woman. Yet the changing styles and moods of these recurring themes in art also reveal the changing conceptions and feelings of a society and its artists in different ages. And here the illustrations will speak eloquently of everything that the author has left unsaid.

Notes

1. For an illuminating discussion of problems of Indonesian historiography, see the contributions of Soedjatmoko, Resink, Mohammad Ali, and others to the symposium edited by Soedjatmoko *et al., An Introduction to Indonesian Historiography* (Ithaca, N.Y., 1965). Cf. also *Historians of South East Asia,* edited by D. G. E. Hall (London, 1961).

2. Such as Furnivall, Van Leur, Boeke, Schrieke, Wertheim, G. J. Resink, Burger, Kahin, Geertz, Soedjatmoko, Soekmono, and other contemporary Indonesian scholars.

3. Robert Redfield, *The Primitive World and Its Transformations* (Ithaca, N.Y., 1953), pp. 20–21.

PART I

THE HERITAGE

CHAPTER 1

Some Prehistoric Roots

Why do people carve their initials into the bark of old trees or scratch them onto rocks? What makes children retrace their steps in wet sand to look excitedly at their footprints, move a pencil around their fingers to create a contour of their hand on paper, or press a hand against a steam-clouded windowpane to produce its silhouette?

We say, "You recognize the hand *of the master." . . . Figuratively, the artist leaves to posterity an imprint of his hand. He transfers a part of himself onto matter, makes it visible, and gives it an existence apart from himself.*

In 1938 members of the Frobenius expedition, in search of prehistoric paintings along the west coast of New Guinea, discovered a multiude of hand silhouettes on a rock wall at Cape Abba near Darembang, on the south shore of the MacCluer Gulf. Like their European prehistoric counterparts, the stone-age inhabitants of Indonesia's Eastern Islands and New Guinea left to posterity pale shadows of their hands long since turned to dust. They pressed their outstretched fingers against the surface of the rock, daubed red paint around them, and thus produced lasting stenciled forms. The wild array of hand silhouettes on the Abba cave wall appears today like a flaming clamor across the ages. Somehow they are reminiscent of the outstretched hands of Bali's *ketjak* dancers which, illuminated by the flickering flame of an oil lamp, are thrust upward into the blackness of the night to the upsurge of humming or rhythmically chattering voices.

The discoverers, led by Dr. Josef Röder,[1] named the Abba rock *die Stammwand der Kulturen,* "the primeval wall of cultures." It is thought to contain the oldest surviving rock paintings of this area. On this "primeval wall" there are also silhouettes of footprints, several figures of men and sea animals, and various signs or symbols, among which are a crescent and other less ascertainable designs.

This painted wall was only one of many rock paintings found by Röder and Hahn as they explored caves and galleries that had been carved by the sea into the high coastal cliffs which form the south shore of the MacCluer Gulf and which were accessible only from the sea.

Not many prehistoric rock paintings have been discovered in other parts of the Indonesian archipelago. On some islands exposed rock formations and caves are rare; areas where cliffs and caves do exist may not have been sufficiently explored to yield their contents. So far, examples of rock painting are to be found mainly in the area of New Guinea's west coast, in the Kei Islands, Ceram, Celebes and Borneo. All were presumably made much later than the cave paintings of the bison and reindeer hunters of prehistoric Europe, with which, however, they have many aspects in common. Van Heekeren attributes the Indonesian rock paintings to the mesolithic era, but Röder conjectures that some may be only three or four centuries old, while the oldest may date back one thousand years.[2] In 1958, at the Niah caves in Sarawak, northwest

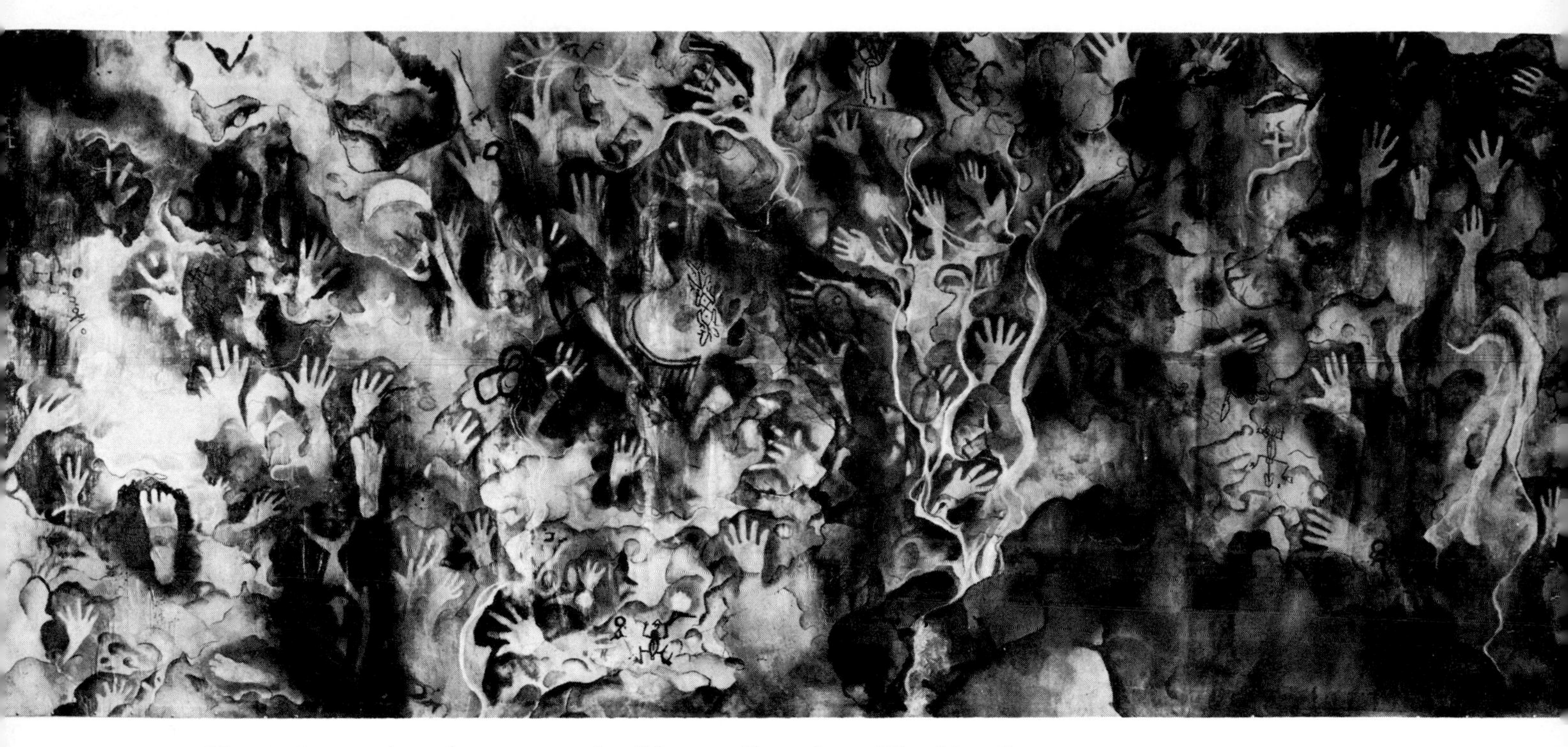

Plate 1. *Section of a rock painting in the Abba cave, Darembang, West New Guinea.*

Borneo, Tom and Barbara Harrisson discovered red rock paintings which offer interesting comparisons with some of those discovered by Röder and Hahn.[3] In a Dutch report on the Röder finds, the following comment appears:

The hand silhouettes, . . . the representation of genitals and of symbolic figures related to fertility and procreation, the anthropomorphic animals, and the 'X-ray' treatment of inner organs or body parts of animals, these and similar motifs we encounter likewise on the rock walls of Font de Gaume, Dordogne, Altamira and elsewhere in Europe of 18000 to 7000 B.C. It is an amazing thought that primitive man is basically the same kind of being, all distances in time and space notwithstanding, experiencing the same desires and reacting to life in the same spirit.[4]

Instead of bison, mammoths, deer and horses, whether isolated or together with schematized figures of human beings,[5] the prehistoric inhabitants of the tropical archipelago's eastern islands painted lizards, fish, turtles, birds and boats, together with symbols of celestial bodies, especially the sun and the moon. They also painted what are thought to be spirits in the shape of anthropomorphic reptiles, and schematized human figures, often depicted with exaggerated genitals.

Red, black, and white pigments were used. Röder discerned several different styles associated either with paintings in red ochre, or with linear drawings in black, or with figures traced in white lines. Whether this varied use of color is attributable to different groups of people or is characteristic of different ages has not yet been definitely established. Sometimes black or white drawings are superimposed over red paintings which are thus presumed to be older.

The range of styles in these and the few other prehistoric paintings found thus far in Indonesia is very wide. Within the group found by Röder are skillful, highly naturalistic paintings, particularly of fish;[6] there are astute simplifications of natural forms that render their essence, such as some figures of birds or reptiles, as well as mere linear schemes of sea animals and human beings. There are arresting stylized apparitions of hooded lizardlike spirits; there are human figures with large heads and small limbs, drawn in that expressive distorted manner found sometimes in pictures made by very young children. Some signs and symbols look like scribbles, while others are executed in gracefully sweeping lines drawn with great precision.

Today we may be struck by the seemingly haphazard agglomerations of figures and signs on the cave walls. To us they are not unlike separate words or cries uttered without any discernible connection. Yet there are also coherent visual statements where several elements are composed in a distinct thematic and formal relationship to one another. Such, for example, is a boat in which stand four human figures holding paddles, with a fish below and an elliptical (solar?) symbol overhead. To the right of this group is another coherent grouping of what might be two mythological beings: a larger human figure carries a smaller one on the palm of his raised right hand. Unfortunately we know nothing about the myths of the cave dwellers who painted these beings to give us a clue to the tantalizing pair. And we can only guess at the connections between figures and symbols that appear repeatedly in combination. In one case, however, there seems to be a clear relationship; Röder observes that near a lizardlike figure with pointed cap often appears a solar symbol. The local inhabitants, he reports, call this lizard figure *matutua,** or Great Ancestor, whose mythological origin is linked to the sun.[7] The matutua is also said to be the "Lord of the Fishes." Even today there are a few sites where offerings that include fishbones are brought to wooden matutua images to ensure that "the animals do not become less."[8] The distant ancestors of the present population* must have depended upon fishing for their survival. Thus fish and boats and the elements—the sun, the moon, the sea, and the winds—were paramount in man's consciousness, the sources of life and fertility. The rock paintings reflect an intense feeling for the close relationship of man with sea animals and the cosmos. The symbolic lizard becomes the link with the supernatural world. He is regarded as the Great Ancestor, the protector of fertility among the fish and hence the guardian of life for man.

Among the matutua figures of the MacCluer Gulf caves, there is one striking figure surrounded by hand stencils. This matutua has a masklike face crowned by a high gourd-shaped headdress, and he seems to be

* *Matutua* seems to be related to *atua*, the term used in by Tonga Islanders for their highest deities, who dwell in lizards as well as in a certain fish.

* The present population is a mixture of Papuan and Indonesian people, largely Moslem, especially along the coast. According to Röder, they (especially the Papuan members) still have traditions relating to their cave-dwelling predecessors and a "historical consciousness" of them.

Plate 2. *Rock painting from Risatot, Arguni Island, MacCluer Gulf, West New Guinea.*

Plate 3. *Rock painting from Risatot, Arguni Island, MacCluer Gulf, West New Guinea.*

dancing. One of his widely spread legs is raised; in one hand he holds up a boomerang and in the other a kite-shaped shield with a spiral design on its upper triangular part. A long, broadening, and decorated tail curves downward as if trailing on the ground.[9] This figure strongly suggests that the fisherfolk of the caves had their shamans, just as the prehistoric hunters of Europe and Africa had their conjurers whom we seem to recognize in dancing figures wearing animal heads.

The lizard has evidently retained its significance as a symbol of fertility in a number of Indonesian areas from prehistoric times to the present. It is to be found on a megalithic burial vat in Central Celebes[10] as well as on the beautifully decorated contemporary rice granaries of the Toba Batak in Sumatra. Having acquired a name of Hindu origin, *boraspati,* the lizard is regarded by the Toba Bataks as the earth spirit. On their granaries it is often represented heading toward breast-shaped knobs which the people refer to as *bagok*. The black dots near the matutua in Plate 4 may perhaps be the forerunners of the bagok, a female symbol complementing the male symbol of the lizard. Further the lizard often appears on the magic staffs of the Toba Batak

Plate 4. *Rock painting from Duri cave, Furir, West New Guinea.*

shaman (*datu*), in the stylized designs made of fiber strings woven into the matted-bamboo walls of Karo Batak granaries, as well as in the patterns of Batak shoulder cloths (*ulos*). When, in about 1954, new market halls were built in Balige (an important trade center on Lake Toba's south shore), the market gate was decorated with the undulating form of a lizard cut out of metal. In Borneo (Kalimantan) among the Dayak, in Nias, and probably elsewhere in the archipelago too, we find the lizard (sometimes the reptile is an iguana or a crocodile) in wood, stone, or, highly stylized, in ornamental design. In Java today, the lizard no longer retains a symbolic meaning. Among the various souvenirs offered for sale to tourists, however, are charming brass lizards, ranging in size from the little *tjitjak* to the full-grown *gekko* or *toké*, the ubiquitous residents of an Indonesian house. The gekko's deep throaty calls are counted, certain numbers in a series being interpreted as good or bad omens. Thus echoes of prehistory reverberate strongly in different parts of Indonesia in ancient symbols and customs that have been incorporated into the fabric of modern life.

In much the same way as the symbol of the lizard endures in the twentieth century, other motifs which appear in neolithic or bronze-age stages of culture can be traced from their prehistoric roots to the present. Among the fascinating continuities are those of magic signs—designs of knots, labyrinthine spirals, cross-hatched fields and other figures—that appear on the cave walls. As elsewhere in the world, they seem to have an extraordinary longevity and wide distribution. It is enough to watch a magician-healer-diviner, the Batak datu, draw his magic signs on the ground in order to realize how ancient is the esoteric art into which he has been initiated.

Unlike the deified lizards, fish, which are so conspicuous on prehistoric cave walls, do not retain a magic significance. In the MacCluer Gulf wall paintings, fish are variously represented: one may be a vivid naturalistic replica of the living creature in movement and another merely a schematic design of two curving lines that cross at the tail end.* These representations have a practical magical purpose as a propitiatory invocation or a charm to secure an abundant catch. On an Arguni Island cave wall each fish is a particular kind of fish and really "swims"; the impression of movement, as if under water, is enhanced by the diffuse weathered surface of the rock formations.

* Cf. Pl. 200 where exactly such schematic designs of fish appear on a modern mural.

Plate 5. *Section of a Toba Batak granary façade, Huta Sihotang, North Sumatra.*

In a very different environment, in Central Java of the tenth century, where Indian mythology had fused with earlier Indonesian animistic beliefs, we see imaginary fish filling the Indian Ocean. They are carved on one of the stone reliefs showing scenes from the *Ramayana** at the Shiva temple of Prambanan. In this particular relief the monkey army, which aids King Rama in his search for his abducted wife Sita, throws boulders into the water separating the land from the

* The *Ramayana* is summarized in Appendix I.

Plate 6. *Simalungun Batak* datu *drawing magic signs for a ceremony, Pematang Raya, North Sumatra.*

island of Langka (Ceylon). The monkeys want to build a causeway to march across to Langka. Indignantly, the population of the ocean—sea monsters, large and small fish, serpents, and other creatures—rises to thwart their efforts. The large fish are shown with boulders in their wide-open mouths, as if ready to swallow the stones. Expressions of malice, anger, and challenge permeate the scene. The wrath and actions of the sea creatures are marvelously anthropomorphized.

A thousand years later a contemporary artist in south Bali produced an ink wash showing an underwater scene which he called the "Conversation of Fish." Several fish hold their heads together, as if in gleeful gossip. Like the fish on the Prambanan relief, these have been endowed with human qualities. The same feeling animates both representations, although the mood of the Balinese is more playful. The Indian animal fables introduced into Indonesia with other ancient traditions have no doubt contributed heavily to the anthropomorphization of animals in Indonesian art. But when a contemporary Balinese painter wants to depict a fishing scene, the fish in the water and on the beach, although drawn with care and skill, are just ordinary fish, although a magical quality emanates from the fish-shaped boats made by the Balinese. It is only natural that to

Plate 7. *Rock painting from Mampoga, Arguni Island, MacCluer Gulf, West New Guinea.*

Plate 8. *Relief of the Shiva Temple, Prambanan, Central Java, 10th century.*

Plate 9. *"Conversation of Fish," ink wash by I. B. Nj. Rai, Sanur, Bali, 1956.*

Plate 10. *Rock painting from Wamerei (Jarak) Island, MacCluer Gulf, West New Guinea.*

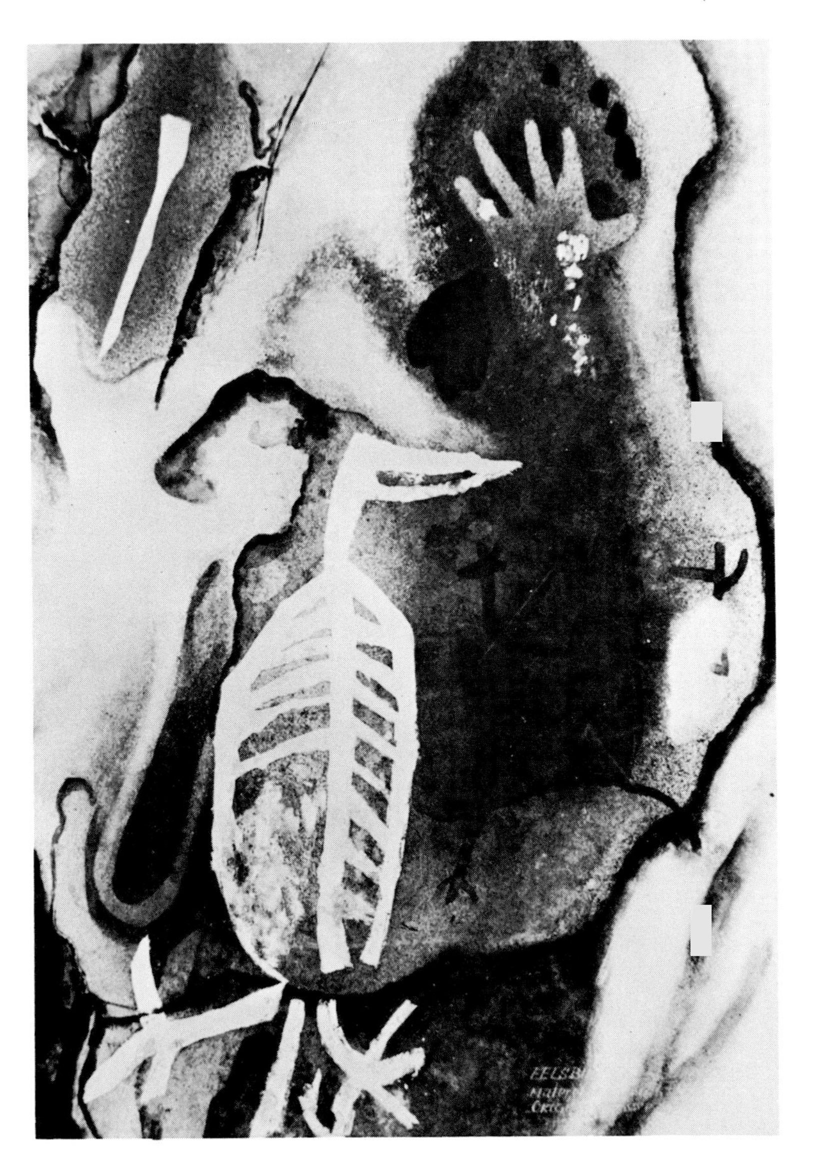

the modern urban painters of Java, who are far removed from the life of coastal fisherfolk, fish are no longer an attractive subject. Nor have they been influenced by their Indonesian-Chinese colleagues who, continuing in the tradition of their homeland's masters, paint playful carp in the translucent, softly rippling water of a pool. I found only one modern painter who had once painted fish: this was Henk Ngantung, who had done a still life—truly *nature morte*—of dead, dried, or decaying fish hung on an old wall with rusty nails. An exercise in dismal grays and yellows, it was Ngantung's first effort at painting in 1936.

An outstanding motif in all the traditional arts of Indonesia is the bird. Although Röder did not find many representations of birds on the rock walls around the MacCluer Gulf, there was a striking drawing of a hornbill found in one of the caves on the little island of Wamerei. The bird's silhouette is traced in bold white lines; its ribs are outlined, X-ray fashion, as they are in some of the leaf-shaped bodies of the matutua figures.

We find the hornbill in Indonesia's bronze-age art, for example, engraved on a bronze kettledrum where it is shown as figurehead on the stern of a ship.[11] Van der Hoop states that the hornbill was a symbol of the "god of the upper world" and that the vessel it adorns represents "a ship which carries the souls of the deceased to the hereafter." On the same plate in his book he shows the carved wooden bow of a Sembiring Batak

Plate 11. *Hornbill mask used in Simalungun Batak death rites* (huda-huda), *Pematang Raya, North Sumatra.*

Plate 12. *Iban Dayak ceremonial image of hornbill, Sarawak, Borneo.*

death-ship. Here the head of a hornbill juts out above a horse's head. According to Van der Hoop, the hornbill became a symbol of death and resurrection because, while sitting on her eggs, the female is immured in a tree hollow which is broken open when the young are hatched.[12] Stylized hornbill heads appear today in carved figureheads on some of the more elaborate boats on Lake Toba.

The hornbill's connection with death rites and the welfare of the souls of the dead has been maintained from prehistory into the twentieth century. In 1938 I witnessed performances re-creating the old funerary dances of Simalungun, Karo, Pak-Pak, and Toba Batak in Sumatra.[13] Hornbill masks, together with ghostlike human masks, were used in the funerary dances of the first three of the Batak groups. On the island of Samosir, however, a hobbyhorse dancer appeared instead of the stalking hornbill masks.

Among the Katingan Dayak of southern Borneo, the hornbill is mythologically associated with the creation of mankind and venerated as a symbol of the upper world.[14] In the northern part of the island, the Iban Dayak fashion a large stylized hornbill with a delicate curving bill. The casque, or horny protuberance above the bill, is elaborated into an intricate spiral. At the climax of earlier head-hunting rituals, the wooden hornbill was mounted on an enormous tapering pole, and as the pole was raised into a vertical position, the

Plate 13. *Batik designs, Central Java.*

warlike spirit of the hornbill was launched against the enemy, like "a primitive precursor of the guided missiles of the modern West," in Freeman's words.[15]

When the sun-bird Garuda, carrier of the god Vishnu and conqueror of the serpent, was introduced into Indonesia during the Hinduistic period, he became the most important bird in the traditional arts of Java and Bali. He appears, variously stylized, in wood, metal, and stone; he provides numerous designs for Central Javanese batik cloths. With the inception of the Republic, Garuda has become the emblem of the Indonesian state. There is little doubt that Garuda's ascendancy was facilitated by the old Indonesian veneration of birds, like the hornbill. Garuda's association with the sun made him supreme.

Apart from a variety of other birds, shaped by sculptors, painters, metalworkers, and weavers of Indonesia, one finds fantastic winged creatures. In Java and Bali, especially important are the winged lion, bull, and serpent. All three are mythologically significant and may have migrated eastward from the ancient "nuclear Near East" to India and on.[16] On popular contemporary prints sold in market places, Moslems can enjoy colored representations of the winged, crowned female centaur Burak, who carried the Prophet Mohammed on a miraculous voyage. Winged gates, found at some temples of Bali, were also known in Java. Two still stand at Sendangduwur near Tuban on Java's north coast where on of the island's oldest mosques was built on what may have been a pre-Islamic temple ground. Disembodied wings embellish many old designs of Javanese batik cloths and shawls. And, significantly perhaps, Java's classical dancers as well as the shadow-play puppets wear wing-shaped ornaments curving up behind their ears, a reduction perhaps of earlier bird-shaped or winged headdresses. One can hardly imagine a design more typical of Java's ornamental art than the upsweeping curves of wings.

Plate 14. *Rock painting from Sosorra Weru, Furir, West New Guinea.*

Among the arresting representations in the MacCluer Gulf rock paintings are those of boats and ships, which appear in a great variety of styles. Sometimes they are mere schemes drawn with two or three lines;[17] in many cases they are complex and dynamic configurations. A beautiful example of the latter is a charcoal drawing of a ship from the wall of a cave complex at Sosorra near the coastal village of Furir. This is only one of a number of well-preserved ship pictures found on a wall[18] situated behind two stalagmites (one of which is said to belong to the head of the village and the other, to its war chieftain). According to Röder's description, the whole site seems to have retained its worshipful, magical significance. At the entrance to the cave stands the sacred stone of Furir village; in its recesses there is a fresh water spring and pool. On the rock ledge east of the entrance are remnants of old repositories for corpses with their accompanying funerary gifts and an altar for burning offerings. To the west are niches in which women desiring children still place pairs of straw puppets, and where people anxious to prevent or cure illness deposit a single puppet. Like the cave drawings of human beings, these puppets have strongly expressed sex characteristics. Thus ritual preoccupations with the eternal trinity in the existence of man—death, procreation, and the preservation of life—visibly converge at this prehistoric site.

The ship reproduced in Plate 14 has been chosen because it contains most of the elements encountered in other ship depictions: the decorated, upcurving bow and stern; the mast; a more or less distinct figure of a man; and the recurrent, intersected circles, thus far unexplained, drawn in a lighter shade than the ship itself. Above the ship is the crescent of the moon; between the sickle-shaped stern and what might be an anchor appears the symbol of the (possibly) setting sun. Interpretation of the rest is impossible. From the whole design emanates an impression of movement, of a vital relationship between the vessel and the natural elements. Today, on the beaches and in the harbors of Indonesia's islands, one can still see fishermen's sailing craft as well as larger vessels with the same boldly upsweeping bow and stern serving commerce between islands. Gaily painted and graceful, they are naturally a constant attraction to modern painters seeking the picturesque. It is somehow moving to find that the well-known contemporary artist Affandi,* with his characteristically stormily sweeping strokes, unknowingly renders the same spirit of boats bound to the elements—the sea, the sky, and the land—as do the Sosorra cave paintings.

Throughout a long history, boats and boat-shaped objects (including coffins, sarcophagi, roofs of houses and granaries) have characterized ancient Indonesia's myths, customs, and rituals. The belief that the dead migrate by ship to the land of souls is illustrated in bronze-age art,[19] in the prehistoric cave paintings, and in the famous South Sumatran woven cloths that show representations of soul-ships. An old custom of putting the dead into boat-shaped coffins and placing these on the broad ledges formed by the tides could still be traced by Röder when he explored these dry galleries located high above the water on the cliffs of the islands Arguni and Bedore, and in a few other places along the coast. The boards of the coffins, following the silhouette of a boat, were decorated with carved designs.[20] Although this burial custom is no longer practiced (Röder surmises that it may have died out some 80 to 100 years ago), the Dayaks of southeast Borneo carve boat-shaped coffins for their dead. Similarly in Celebes the old weathered boat-shaped coffins of the Duri people are still visible, stacked in a gallery of an inland rock.[21]

The association of ships with death-houses is still found in parts of Indonesia. When traveling in south Celebes in 1938, we came across a Sa'adan Toradja death-house. The small structure which stood in the fields was covered by a large boat-shaped roof which jutted out at both ends so far that the gables had to be supported with poles. (Such roofs are typical also of the Sa'adan Toradja houses and granaries.) Through a small window one could see two effigies of the dead, seated as if ready for departure. They were fully dressed and were outfitted with satchels and baskets.

* See Plate 175.

Plate 15. *Toba Batak sarcophagus* (parholian) *on village plaza, Huta Pangalohan, Samosir, North Sumatra.*

Under the house, between the poles of its understructure and near a coffin, lay a boat with paddles.[22]

The shape of the boat is also reflected in the old stone sarcophagi of the Toba Batak called *parholian* (from *holi,* bone). Exhumed after preliminary burial, the bones of the high-ranking Batak dead were preserved in the parholian for many generations. The walls of these rectangular cists slant like the hull of a ship from a wider opening at the top to a somewhat narrower bottom. The heavy lid, its sagging ridge like the saddle-roof of Toba Batak houses, is also reminiscent of the boat shape. The protective "figurehead" at the "bow" of the parholian is a large monstrous head which is called *singa.* Beneath this there is often a squatting male figure; a female figure sits on the lid "astern." Seen from a distance, in a field or on a village plaza, a parholian seems to be floating: a minor sphinx adrift in time. And in some Batak or Toradja villages where houses and granaries stand in rows, one gets a strong impression of fleets of vessels, floating high. The shape of these roofs has led Vroklage to call them "ship-roofs."[23]

Among the Sa'adan Toradja of Celebes there are traditions about the origins of such roofs. The ancestors of the Toradja are said to have come in boats to Celebes from the West.* Their vessels, towed ashore, became the roofs of their dwellings. The souls of the Toradja dead then journeyed across the sea, returning to the land of their ancestors, the land of origin, and the cycle was completed.

* In other places legend says they had come from the rising sun, from the East. (Röder cites such a myth.)

In the village of Arui-Bab on the east coast of Tanimbar in the eastern part of the archipelago, Dr. Koentjaraningrat of the University of Indonesia found a long, boat-shaped stone platform on which members of the village council seated themselves for deliberations. Here the ancient custom of village elders or chiefs occupying ancestral stone seats seems to be combined with the idea of an ancestral boat.[24]

Reviewing the dominant motifs in the MacCluer Gulf rock paintings, we find in addition to hand and foot silhouettes representations of sea animals, especially fish and turtles, of boats, celestial bodies, some birds, human and mythological beings, a variety of signs and symbols, and, above all, the lizard and the lizardlike matutua. These motifs speak eloquently of an early culture oriented to the sea. None of the land animals prominent in the imagery and ritual life of Indonesia's various non-Islamic regions are present. Although the cave paintings may reflect a local, insular, and isolated cultural pocket from the relatively recent past, they also could be taken as testimony about Indonesia's coastal peoples during the so-called mesolithic era. Starting roughly with the second millennium B.C., however, important changes occurred in the people's mode of life as neolithic culture spread; their magico-ritual proceedings, too, must have undergone important transformations.

Subsistence became dependent upon grain cultivation and on the timeliness and abundance of rainfall; correspondingly, ritual was geared to the agricultural cycle. At the same time, in many regions the domesticated water buffalo (*kerbau*) became the principal sacrificial animal for death rites and other ceremonial feasts. In the twentieth century this tradition, harking back to the neolithic, presented the Dutch colonial administration with the serious and unresolved problem of preventing the slaughter of innumerable buffaloes, sacrificed annually by the Dayak in Borneo, the Toradja in Celebes, and, to a somewhat lesser degree, the Batak in Sumatra. The buffalo became in essence the dominant symbol of vital power. One can only

Plate 16. Singa *head of a* parholian *and old skull caskets in a field near Huta Pansur, Samosir, North Sumatra.*

Figure 1. *Painting on a cist tomb wall, Tanjungara, Pasemah, South Sumatra.*

guess at the prehistoric connections of the buffalo cult in Indonesia with the role of the bull in the ancient civilizations of the Near East and India.[25] The buffalo's head and horns, in either its real or artificial, stylized form, still appear today on the upcurving points of roofs in Sumatra or on the walls of Toradja houses[26] in Celebes. Also in ritual dances, the Sa'adan Toradja men wear either the heavy horns of a water buffalo as headdress or metal imitations of them. Similarly, among the Minangkabau (meaning victorious buffalo) of West Sumatra, the women's traditional ceremonial headdress is a turban with sharp conical protuberances, actually called horns (*tanduk*).

The earliest known representations of a buffalo in Indonesian art date from the bronze age. A striking example is a bold curvilinear painting found by C. de Bie[27] in the Pasemah region of South Sumatra. Traced in black, white, red, yellow, and gray bands, the painting is one of several discovered on the inner walls of a cist grave. Tremendous vigor is captured in highly controlled forms. A spirit of ferocity emanates from the frontal view of the animal's head and the profile of a forward-stooping, chinless, round-eyed and open-mouthed anthropomorphic figure. The latter's expression is reminiscent of the pugnacious warrior-riders of elephants and buffaloes, monumental monolithic sculptures, dating from the same period, and also found in the Pasemah region of Sumatra.[28]

The buffalo symbol, reinterpreted, became the symbol of the Indonesian nation when nationalism began to stir under Dutch domination. The head of the wild buffalo (*banteng*) is still the emblem of the Indonesian Nationalist Party. It has been said that Indonesia is like a buffalo: he could be led by the nose, but once aroused, he would go on the rampage. A famous painting by Raden Saleh, the solitary nineteenth-century precursor of Indonesian modern art, depicts a ferocious fight between a wild buffalo and a lion. Nationalists later saw this as an allusion to an oncoming struggle with the Dutch. The symbolism has been retained in a contemporary monument to the revolution at Madiun, Central Java, which shows a buffalo charging with an advancing armed guerrilla fighter carved in relief at the base of the monument.

Still visible today on our "plateau of the present" are upright menhirs and horizontal flat stone slabs with or

Plate 17. *Tall stone stele seen from chief's house in Bawomatalua, South Nias.*

According to Heine-Geldern, megalithic monuments were destined to keep alive the names of those who erected them or of those dead for whom they had been erected and as memorials of sacrificial feasts, to secure for their souls perpetual life in the hereafter.[30]

Throughout the world monuments continue to be erected to the glorious dead and to glorious deeds. In the depths of Celebes, or in a ceremonial place in Nias one can still find today a tall, carefully hewn obelisk-shaped pillar as imposing in its own surroundings as is the George Washington monument on the Mall of Washington, D.C. In our time throughout the Republic of Indonesia numerous monuments, often obelisk-shaped, have been erected to commemorate the fallen heroes of the revolution, the glorious dead, and the proclamation of independence in 1945, the glorious deed. Known as *tugu,* they can be found in most cities and towns, often at a special site which is the ceremonial place for speeches and wreath-laying on the anniversary days of the Republic.

During the first fifteen centuries of our era, when Indian religions spread to parts of the Indonesian archipelago, the upright megaliths merged with, or were superseded by the symbol of the god Shiva, his phallus —the *linga* rising from an altar-shaped pedestal with a spout, the *yoni,* female counterpart of the linga. Echoes of both, the prehistoric obelisk and Shiva's

without supports, which stem from megalithic cultural strata. The upright stones are unhewn, roughly hewn, or smoothly worked, tapering toward the tops or distinctly obelisk-shaped. Such stones (*simbuang*) were still being erected by the Sa'adan Toradja in 1938 for high-ranking dead before their corpses were finally deposited in a rock tomb. In Nias, Sumatra's small neighbor island to the west, a magnificent megalithic culture flourished into the twentieth century. Upright monolithic stelae, obelisks, massive stone benches, tables, elaborate seats for chiefs, even stone chests and drums, all carved with superb precision in a light grayish stone, can be found in front of a chief's house or along the wide stone-paved streets and on the ceremonial places of south Nias villages.[29] Ornamentation, if present, is sparse yet very strong, executed in clearly delineated motifs. In some mountain villages of Bali smooth flat stones laid horizontally on the ground, in front of another such stone set upright, form ancestral seats on which village elders sit at gatherings.

Plate 18. Linga *on* yoni *from Prambanan plain, Central Java.*

linga on its yoni, combine in the grandiose National Monument, the *Tugu Nasional,* scheduled for completion in 1967 on the great Freedom Plaza of the capital, Djakarta.

The sculptured human face, head, or entire figure —erect, seated, crouching, or in movement—realistic or fantastic, fascinated prehistoric carvers as much as they do modern artists. From time immemorial inhabitants of the Indonesian islands have fashioned images of ancestors, of dead chiefs, of deities or spirits in human or anthropomorphized animal shapes. Not many images can be ascribed with certainty to one or another period of time. Rather prehistoric art and contemporary Indonesian primitive art merge by virtue of the same dominant "magic" force that emanates from each and of the common intent and feeling that underlie their creation.

What has come down to us from presumably the first two millennia B.C. and from the early centuries of our era are naturally stone and metal objects. These include crude reliefs with human figures carved on the walls of burial cists, stone images, metal figurines, superb bronze ceremonial weapons and bronze drums with elaborate ornamental designs.[31] All wooden images and masks, which must have existed in profusion, have of course disintegrated. But one may assume that some of the wooden images found today in villages of the eastern islands of the archipelago, in the interiors of Celebes, Borneo, Sumatra, or the island of Nias, are not too remote in form and meaning from their prehistoric counterparts. Representative examples can be seen in some European and American museums, the best collections being in Amsterdam and Leiden.[32]

Among the striking examples of prehistoric stone sculptures are those described and photographed in Central Celebes by Walter Kaudern.[33] Together with other megalithic remains, such as monumental stone burial vats (some with the ubiquitous lizard carved in high relief on the lid), Kaudern found gigantic stone images unique in style. One such image, at Bada, 14.5 feet high, is typical. The semicylindrical mass of the body is topped by a huge elliptical chinless face with disks for eyes; sharp edges delineate a broad flat nose and branch upward into the equally sharply defined arches of the eyebrows. Carved in low relief on the body are short, thin arms with hands curving toward the erect male genital on the abdomen. Disk-shaped nipples mark the chest. The whole image has the enigmatic quality of an embryo.

Figure 2. *Giant stone image at Bada, Central Celebes.*

Images which are essentially upright, rigid forms without clearly differentiated limbs but with relatively large heads appear in scattered regions of the archipelago. In Nias there are such stone or wooden ancestral figures—armless slabs topped by a head usually adorned with a characteristic Niha headgear.[34] These primitive ancestral images foreshadow the erect and rigid posthumous statues of deified kings enshrined in elaborate temple-mausoleums during the so-called Hinduistic era of the first fifteen centuries of our era. Similarly, the stone reliefs carved with great artistry on the walls of these tomb-temples (*tjandi*) may have had prehistoric precursors in the decorated megalithic burial cists, such as the one found in Besuki, East Java, on whose outer wall are also carved human and animal figures.[35]

In style and expression the prehistoric free-standing images discovered by Kaudern in Celebes are worlds

Figure 3. *Wooden image of a deity(?), Nias.*

apart from the megalithic mounted warriors found in South Sumatra; and both are equally removed in style and feeling from the monumental art of Nias, which includes, for instance, the large figure of a woman, now headless, holding flat against her body a sprawling infant who clutches her conical breasts.[36] It is impossible to say now how far these images are separated from one another in time, just as it is impossible to say whether the powerfully carved stone group with a seated female figure holding two children, which now stands near the Simalungun Batak Museum of Pematang Siantar in North Sumatra, is a creation of a prehistoric megalithic culture, or the work of a carver who lived in the eighteenth or nineteenth century. Although all these images are massive, strong, and simple, practically devoid of ornamentation, with only the essentials of the body, sex, facial features, and clothing (if any) rendered, they do demonstrate that significant differences in style existed between the various ethnic groups in the distant past as they do today.

The great variety of wooden images found in the Indonesian islands are rarely more than 200 years old. Despite differences in style, they, too, convey a common feeling about the magical potency of supernatural or deified beings, and their symbolism extends across the world's continents. Thus, for example, from Luang Sermata (a small island group between Timor and Tanimbar at the eastern end of the Archipelago), the remarkable wooden image of a female figure (ancestral or divine) with outstretched arms seated before a bowl (Pl. 20) is related in conception and probably also in sacrificial function to some images known from Nias at the opposite end of the Archipelago. In addition, it brings to mind the "Serpent's Bride" and "The Consort of the Bull," goddesses with strong lunar associations discussed by Joseph Campbell in his volume on Occidental mythology.[37]

Our image from Luang Sermata has a coiffure in the shape of a coiled serpent; carved on the open palms

Plate 19. *Stone image of woman with twins, Tanoh Djawa, North Sumatra.*

Plate 20. *Wooden image of a deity(?), Southwest Islands.*

and painted under the breasts are double spirals, typical also of Nias ornamentation,* which may be stylizations of horns; and the crescent-shaped ornament on the chest is clearly lunar.

The human face alone appears in numerous forms —painted, engraved, sculptured in the round, or carved into a mask. Indonesians seem to share with the rest of mankind unlimited ingenuity in transforming human faces into supernatural apparitions or imbuing them with such intensity that human expression is transcended. Among the earliest depictions known in Indonesia of such "magically charged" faces (or perhaps masks) are those engraved between the handles of the large sacred bronze drum known as the "Moon of Pedjeng." Enshrined on an elevated platform in the village of Intaran (formerly known as Pedjeng) in South Bali, the drum is a superb specimen of bronze-age art. The intensity of the faces engraved on the drum is projected by the completely round eyes encircled by scored rims. The nose is narrow, and from large apertures in the earlobes disk-shaped pendants are suspended. Perhaps it is mainly the long narrow nose and the elongated ears with their pendants that bring to mind a wooden head hailing from an island of the Tanimbar group in the South Moluccas.

In such regions as Java and Bali, a slow evolution from primitive rites to theatrical arts has culminated in the production of finely carved, stylized masks for the stage, but in other regions, Borneo, for instance, a variety of masks are still used at death and fertility

Figure 4. *"The Moon of Pedjeng," prehistoric bronze drum, Pedjeng, Bali.*

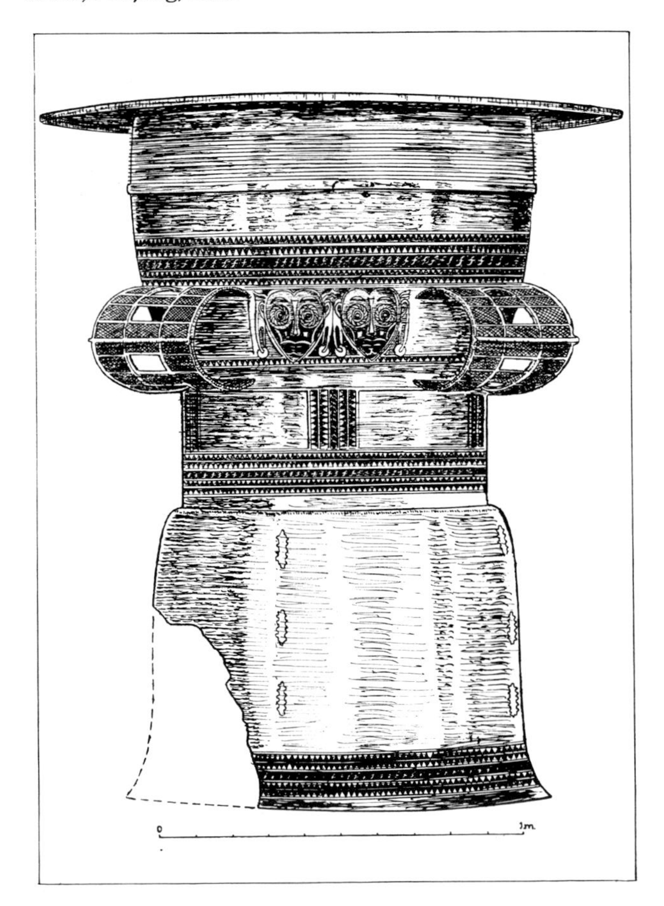

* Incidentally, the featherlike motif of a stalk with small leaves carved on the high, narrow back-piece behind the figure's head is also typical for South Nias art. And at agricultural ritual dances women of south Niha wear such ornaments at the back of their head.

Plate 21. *Head with ear pendant from Tanimbar, South Moluccas.*

rites. Masks of painted and decorated wood are worn by elaborately costumed dancers. One example is a bearded face, with short trunk entering its mouth, found in a mask used by a Dayak tribe of south-central Borneo at the great *tiwah* feast that concludes their death rites. Masked personages, presumably impersonating ancestral souls, appeared at death rites of some pagan Batak groups in North Sumatra (see pp. 105–106) until the first decades of this century. How deep into the prehistoric past does the mask lead us? We must consider ancient notions that the head is the most crucial part of the human body, the place where the greatest charge of life-power is concentrated. We must recall that this concept underlies that custom of preserving the skulls of dead chieftains, of filling out their features with malleable materials, painting and decorating them, which was still practiced in the recent past in some of the Melanesian islands to the east of Indonesia. This same notion justified the expeditions of head-hunters, whose trophies were installed with much ceremony and ritual incantation. The life-power of a head, whether of an ancestor or of a tribal enemy, could enhance the welfare of the community by infusing it with a new charge of life potency. The life of the remaining animistic groups in the Indonesian islands must be investigated—a task too vast for these pages—to trace the beliefs and customs in which masked figures play a prominent part. Just as in prehistoric times the mask may have served for the impersonation of ancestral or other spirits, we find today in a number of regions that it is intimately linked with death and fertility rites.

Having thus far examined separate themes in prehistoric art, we may turn to a generalized description of the religious orientation in pre-Hinduistic Indonesia, specifically of animistic Bali, given by Stutterheim:

> Daily life was directed by the souls of the departed ancestors who were supposed to be dwelling in the mountains. It was they who lived on at the hidden sources of the rivers, without whose waters no rice would grow. They were the founders of the village communities; they had established its customs and cared for its growth. These ancestors also disposed of the sources of magic life-power, the power which caused not only the life of man, but also that of animals and plants, even of the community of men—the mysterious *fluidum* without which no welfare was possible.[38]

As we have seen, in an earlier era or perhaps mainly in the eastern part of the archipelago the land of the ancestors was thought to be "across the sea" and the souls of the dead were thought to journey there in ships. Mountaintops, too, are widely believed to be the abodes of gods and ancestral souls. Also, high volcanoes are regarded to have a life and spirit of their own, and are venerated. Still in our times the ruling princes of Central Java send elaborate propitiatory offerings, including precious silk textiles, to be thrown into the craters of the towering Lawu, Merapi, and Merbabu volcanoes. In East Java, the Tenggerese hold annual ritual processions to the top of Mt. Bromo, making offerings at the edge of its crater. In Bali's temple courts, special shrines with a conical roof peaked by a spire of twisted fiber are erected for offerings to the island's highest volcano, Gunung Agung (literally, "Great Mountain"). The mountaintops, often wrapped in clouds and mist, were the mysterious abodes of ancestral spirits, and many sanctuaries were built high up in the mountains. Bali's most important temple, Besakih, is built on the slope of the Great Mountain, Gunung Agung.

Stutterheim comments further about religious beliefs and activities in pre-Hinduistic Bali:

It was perceived that through many causes the balance, the right amount of life-power of the community, could be disturbed. Some of the causes were known, and some were not to be discerned. Consequently there was a complicated and extensive system of acts and interdictions evolved for the eventual restoration of the disturbed equilibrium. . . .

The place where the sacred acts, intended to maintain the life-power of the community, were performed was the temple. It was a piece of ground surrounded by a wall for protection against unknown, and thus unmanageable, powers, on which special places were constructed as seats for the ancestors: upright stones for the male, and horizontal stones for female souls. For the soul of the ancestor-founder of the tribe and community, there was a whole pyramid built of stones. And lastly, the temple was provided with a stone-paved space for ritual dances.[39]

The terraced pyramid is a prototype for all the elaborate temple structures built in Java during the Hinduistic period; the design has been perpetuated in Bali's temple architecture. It is another almost universal architectural form, found in ancient Babylon, in the old civilizations of South America, and in evidence in Polynesia and throughout the South Asian continent. In fact, the pagodas of China and Japan, like the *meru* of Bali, are versions of the same basic principle.

One consecrated site of the megalithic era was found by Van der Hoop at Lebak Sibedug in South Sumatra.[40] It consists of a four-stepped pyramid facing west, about 20 feet high, with an extension of the lowest terrace in front. On this front terrace stands a massive upright stone (about 7.5 feet high and 20 inches thick) which rests on river stones piled up to form a base. Parallel to this structure, a flat, rectangular, two-stepped platform, measuring about 47 by 26 feet, is situated off to one side but forward of the front terrace of the pyramid. Between this platform and the front terrace of the pyramid four more upright stones were found. It is interesting to compare the plan of this prehistoric site with that of a contemporary Balinese temple, especially the location of its rectangular *balai* used for the installation of offerings in relation to the principal shrine.

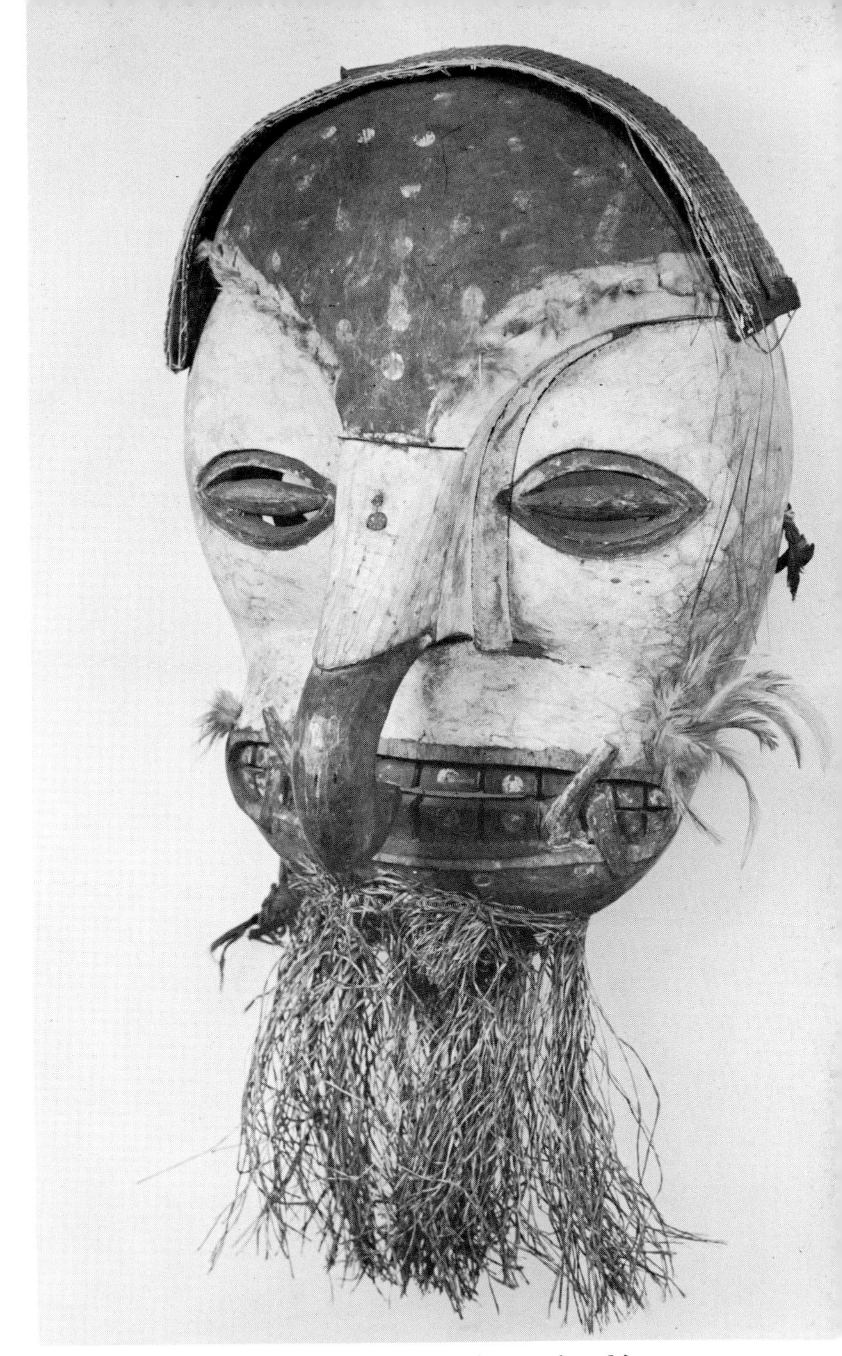

Plate 22. *Mask used at Dayak final death rites* (tiwah), *Sampit River area, South Borneo.*

Indonesian art historians generally speak of an "indigenous Indonesian spirit," which, after a period of assimilation of imported ideas and forms, breaks

Figure 5. *Prehistoric terraced sanctuary with menhir at Lebak Sibedug, South Sumatra.*

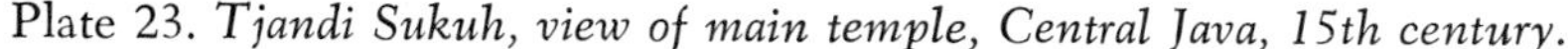

through, adapting and transforming the new ideas and forms to correspond with the old traditional conceptions. A spectacular resurgence of the total complex of ideas, forms, and feelings connected with the terraced pyramid and other related features of Indonesian megalithic culture is illustrated by the fifteenth-century sanctuaries of Sukuh and Tjeta in Central Java. The dates found on some parts of the sanctuaries place the construction of Sukuh between A.D. 1416 and 1459; that of Tjeta, between 1468 and 1475. Situated high on the slope of Mt. Lawu, these temples were built in the twilight of Hinduism, in an area far removed from the last crumbling Hinduistic kingdom, Majapahit, centered in East Java.

In both sanctuaries one might say that new wine had been poured into old vessels. The object of the cult to whom these temples were dedicated is Bima, the tempestuous and powerful hero of the ancient Indian epic, the *Mahabharata.** In this cult Bima appears to have symbolized magic potency and deliverance from the limitations of mortal life.[41]

Tjandi Sukuh is a large, unadorned, truncated stepped pyramid of rough-hewn stone. The trapezoid front slope is interrupted in the middle by two broad stone bands. These encase a narrow stairway which leads into a dark inner chamber beneath the flat rectangular top. Pylons and massive obelisk-shaped stones stand near the Sukuh pyramid, strengthening its association with archaic, megalithic monuments. The pyramidal temples of ancient Mexico and Peru come to mind as do the smaller pyramidal sanctuaries of Polynesia.

At both Sukuh and Tjeta,[42] symbols of fertility are strongly in evidence. On the stone floor of Tjandi Sukuh's entrance gate, a large phallus, opposite its female counterpart, is carved in relief. At Tjeta a large

* The *Mahabharata* is summarized in Appendix I.

Plate 23. *Tjandi Sukuh, view of main temple, Central Java, 15th century.*

Plate 24. *Obelisk at Tjandi Sukuh with figures from the* Garudeya *story at the base.*

Plate 25. *Image of Bima at Tjandi Tjeta, Central Java, 15th century.*

phallus lies similarly, pointing toward the tip of a horizontal triangular stone. Upon the phallus rests the figure of a lizard. Three toads surrounded by crabs and an eel are on the triangular stone, with lizards again in its corners.

The figures and reliefs of Bima found at Sukuh and Tjeta are stark, powerful sculptures. Their style has nothing in common with the images of Indian deities shaped during the preceding thousand years in Java. Although the hero's identity is derived from Indian sacred lore, his symbolism has been given a local but ancient interpretation. Similarly, Indian myths, Javanese mysticism, and ancient magic beliefs converge on a Garuda figure carved in relief on one of the pylons. According to a story (the *Garudeya*) the sun-bird had rescued his mother from slavery by stealing the nectar of life from the gods. The theme of deliverance, which had entered into the mystic and ritual life of Java and Bali during the Hinduistic period, here merged with the ancient conceptions about the liberation of the soul after death, for which special rituals were instituted. At Sukuh there are still other allusions to this theme. On a vertical stone slab there is a relief which shows three stages of Bima's life.[43] The last, at the top, is his meeting with a deity—the culmination of his search for the "water of life." Similarly, a coarsely sculptured scene from another story (*Sudamala*) depicts the liberation of the death goddess Durga from a curse.[44]

The powerful but crude sculptures and reliefs at Sukuh and Tjeta, such as the figure of Bima, stand out in strong contrast to the refined and ornate art that had flourished in Java's plains in the preceding centuries. Although Sukuh and Tjeta mark the end of the Hinduistic cultural period, stylistically they have nothing in common with its art. By association they carry us back to Indonesia's megalithic antecedents. The pyramid, pylons, and obelisks of Sukuh, with their unadorned monumentality and forceful sculptures, seem a distant offshoot from prehistory, separated from its roots by more than 1,500 years.

Notes

1. The results of the expedition have been published by Röder, in collaboration with Albert Hahn, in *Felsbilder und Vorgeschichte des MacCluer-Golfes West-Neuguinea* (Darmstadt, 1959).
2. H. R. van Heekeren, *The Stone Age of Indonesia* (The Hague, 1957). Röder, p. 85.
3. The Niah cave paintings are discussed by Harrisson in "The Caves of Niah: a History of Prehistory," *Sarawak Museum Journal,* VIII (1958), 549–595, and in "New Archaeological and Ethnological Results from Niah Caves, Sarawak," *Man,* LIX (1959), 1–8.
4. G. L. Tichelman and W. J. de Gruyter, *New Guineesche Oerkunst* (Deventer, 1944), p. 42. Extract translated by the author.
5. See H. Breuil, *Four Hundred Centuries of Cave Art* (Montignac, 1952).
6. Close observation and naturalistic rendering of animals and their movement is also apparent in a red ochre painting of a running boar with an arrowhead in his chest, which was discovered in 1950 on a cave wall in South Celebes. See Van Heekeren, *Stone Age,* pp. 96, 98, pl. 31. This plate is also reproduced in A. J. Bernet Kempers, *Ancient Indonesian Art* (Amsterdam, 1959), pl. 1. Cf. a red ochre rock painting of a wounded boar from Mirzapur, India, reproduced in A. H. Brodrick, *Prehistoric Painting* (London, 1948), pl. 51.
7. The lizard is venerated in many other parts of Polynesia, including Samoa and New Zealand where the ancestral souls, believed to enter very frequently into small green lizards, are called *atua.* G. A. Wilken, "De Hagedis in het Volksgeloof der Malayo-Polynesiers," *Bijdragen tot de Taal-, Land- en Volkenkunde,* XL (1891), 477–479.
8. Röder, p. 90.
9. Röder, p. 96, fig. 4.
10. See Walter Kaudern, *Megalithic Finds in Central Celebes* (Ethnographical Studies in Celebes, V; Göteburg, 1938), fig. 23c.
11. A. N. J. Th. à Th. Van der Hoop, *Indonesian Ornamental Design* (Bandoeng, 1949), pl. 73a. Cf. Röder, p. 155, fig. 8, for a drawing of a ship with a hornbill on the stern (bow?).
12. *Op. cit.,* p. 170.
13. As a member of the Rolf de Maré expedition for the recording of Indonesian dances. See Claire Holt, *Théâtre et Danses aux Indes Néerlandaises* (Paris, Les Archives Internationales de la Danse, 1939), p. 31 and figs. 200–204.
14. Hans Schärer, *Ngaju Religion: The Conception of God among a South Borneo People,* trans. by R. Needham (Koninklijk Instituut voor Taal-, Land- en Volkenkunde, Translation Series 6; The Hague, 1963), p. 13.
15. J. D. Freeman, "A Note on the Gawai Kenyalang, or Hornbill Ritual of the Iban of Sarawak," in Bertram E. Smythies, *The Birds of Borneo* (London, 1960), p. 102.
16. Cf. Joseph Campbell, *The Masks of God: Occidental Mythology* (New York, 1964).
17. For example, see Röder, p. 155, fig. 9.
18. Cf. painting with ships on the Niah cave wall in Sarawak, Borneo; Harrisson, "The Caves of Niah," pl. 1, pp. 586–590.
19. Van der Hoop, p. 172.
20. See Röder, p. 57, fig. 22; text, pp. 56–59.
21. See Claire Holt, *Dance Quest in Celebes* (Paris, 1939), p. 40 and fig. 23.

22. See *ibid.*, pl. 38, pp. 47–48. Cf. W. F. Stutterheim, "Some Remarks on Pre-Hinduistic Burial Customs on Java," in his *Studies in Indonesian Archaeology* (The Hague, 1956), illustrations on pp. 77, 84.

23. B. A. G. Vroklage, "Das Schiff in den Megalithkulturen Südostasiens und der Südsee," *Anthropos,* XXXI (1936), 712-757. See this article for the present distribution of saddle-roofs in the traditional architecture of the Indonesian islands.

24. Cf. B. A. G. Vroklage, "De Prauw in Culturen van Flores," *Cultureel Indië,* II (1940), 193–199, 230–234, 263-270.

25. See Campbell, *Masks of God: Occidental Mythology,* pp. 54–61.

26. See Holt, *Dance Quest,* figs. 31 and 32. See also Vroklage, "Das Schiff," for the buffalo and buffalo horns as a motif in other parts of the archipelago and the South Pacific.

27. C. de Bie, "Verslag van de Ontgraving der Steenen Kamers in de Doesoen Tandjoeng Ara, Pasemah-Hoogvlakte," *Tijdschrift voor Indische Taal-, Land- en Volkenkunde,* LXXII (1932), 626–635.

28. Heine Geldern notes the stylistic similarity of these South Sumatran megalithic sculptures with certain Chinese sculptures of the early Han Dynasty, in "The Art and Archaeology of Sumatra," in Edwin M. Loeb, *Sumatra, Its History and People* (Vienna, 1935), pp. 305–331. See also pls. 27–31 in Van Heekeren, *The Bronze-Iron Age of Indonesia* (The Hague, 1958).

29. See E. E. W. G. Schröder, *Nias, ethnographische, geographische en historische aanteekeningen en studien* (Leiden, 1917), and Heine-Geldern, "The Archaeology and Art of Sumatra," in Loeb, *Sumatra.*

30. Heine-Geldern, "Introduction," *Indonesian Art: A Loan Exhibition from the Royal Indies Institute, Amsterdam, the Netherlands* (Baltimore Museum of Art, 1949), p. 4. Cf. Harrisson, "A Living Megalithic in Upland Borneo," *Sarawak Museum Journal,* VIII (1958), 694–702.

31. See Van Heekeren, *The Bronze-Iron Age of Indonesia.*

32. See also Warner Münsterberger, *Sculpture of Primitive Man* (New York, 1955), pls. 60–73.

33. Kaudern, *Megalithic Finds,* p. 95. The large megalithic sculptures of South Sumatra mentioned above, on p. 23, which include warriors mounted on a buffalo or elephant, are atypical of ancestral images; no parallels to these have been found in other parts of the archipelago. It is interesting to note, however, that to the present day funerary sculptures for Toba Batak graves often show a male figure mounted on a horse.

34. More typical Niha images are seated or squatting figures with large, elaborately crowned heads. See picture 37, Loeb and Heine-Geldern, *Sumatra.*

35. Van Heekeren, *The Bronze-Iron Age,* pl. 17.

36. Münsterberger, *Sculpture of Primitive Man,* pl. 61.

37. Campbell, *The Masks of God: Occidental Mythology,* chs. II and III.

38. W. F. Stutterheim, *Indian Influences in Old-Balinese Art* (London, 1935), p. 2.

39. *Ibid.*, pp. 2–3.

40. A. N. J. Th. à Th. van der Hoop, *Megalithic Remains in South Sumatra,* trans. by W. Shirlaw (Zutphen, 1933), p. 65.

41. See Stutterheim, "An Ancient Javanese Bhima Cult," *Studies in Indonesian Archaeology,* pp. 107–143 and pls. 13–22. See also Mangkunagara VII of Surakarta, *On the Wayang Kulit (Purwa) and Its Symbolic and Mystical Elements,* trans. by C. Holt (Cornell Southeast Asia Program, Data Paper no. 27; Ithaca, N.Y., 1957), especially pp. 16–18, 23–24.

42. See pls. 329–338 in Bernet Kempers, *Ancient Indonesian Art.*

43. Reproduced in Stutterheim, "An Ancient Javanese Bhima Cult," as fig. 21.

44. See Bernet Kempers, pl. 331.

CHAPTER 2

The Impact of Indian Influences

CENTRAL JAVA

EIGHTH CENTURY TO TENTH CENTURY

IN THE FIRST CENTURIES of our era a new process started in the archipelago—the assimilation and adaptation of Indian culture. There are various theories about the manner in which Indian influences penetrated into Indonesia.[1] The oldest conjecture was one of colonization by Indians combined with intermarriage between Indian princes and daughters of local chiefs. It has also been thought that the dissemination of Indian religious ideas and technical skills may have been spread from settlements of Indian traders. Subsequently, stress has been laid on the role of Indian priests in introducing Indian religions to the archipelago. Conceivably, Indianization resulted from a combination of several of these means of penetration. The spread of Indian culture was undoubtedly stimulated by early trade, which involved exchange of cultural as well as material goods. To Indonesia came reports of India's religious life, the glory of its kings and palaces, as well as samples of Indian religious art. And conversely, accounts of the rich islands reached India: of their rulers, of the spices, gold, silver, and grain obtainable there, and of the nature of the local population in their villages, their well-developed agriculture, their skills in the working of wood, metal, and stone, and the excellence of their weaving. Such reports could not have failed to stimulate travel both ways. Indonesians may have gone to see for themselves the wonders of the fabulous land, to study there, and to acquire new skills. Among the voyagers to Indonesia may have been Brahmans from India who hoped to secure new, lucrative fields for their religious activities and for themselves. Van Leur suggests that priests from India may have come at the invitation of some of the islands' rulers.[2] Some evidence to support this theory appears in one of Indonesia's oldest known stone inscriptions found in East Borneo. Dating from about 400, it refers to a king named Mulavarman, mentions "priests who have come hither," and extolls the king's pious gifts to these priests.[3]

The migration of Indian gods to the Indonesian islands came about through the peaceful penetration of two religious systems: Brahmanism, especially its Shivaite aspect (although sporadically through the ensuing thousand years the cult of Vishnu was in evidence too), and Buddhism, which, after an initial appearance of the Hinayana school, soon was propagated overwhelmingly in its Mahayanist form, strongly tinged with Tantric elements. In time, both religious systems acquired some Indonesian traits, overlapped, and even merged into syncretic Hindu-Buddhist-Indonesian cults. The present religion of Bali is an offshoot of this syncretism. Thus when speaking of Indonesia's "Hinduization," or its "Hinduistic era," one subsumes the absorption and adaptation of both Brahmanism and Buddhism.

In outlying regions such as Borneo or Celebes, remains of early Buddhist or Shivaite images have been found, but Hinduization had a more lasting effect in South Sumatra, Java, Bali, and a few smaller islands adjacent to the latter two. The process of Hinduization, however, was slow, complex, and uneven; Coedès called it "osmosis."[4] A new priestly elite, probably largely Indian in the beginning, must have been active mainly in the immediate surroundings of powerful chiefs whom they converted to the new religion and then anointed as divine kings. These kings were supposed to be temporary incarnations on earth of various Hindu or Buddhist deities, and this practice gave rise to a cult of kings[5] in direct continuation of indigenous ancestral cults that had included the veneration of dead chiefs. It must be assumed that the religious practices introduced from India were known at first primarily in the palace-cities of Indonesian rulers. In the villages, ritual worship probably continued for a long time under the direction of priestly elders and conjuror-diviners who of old had been the mediators between the human and spirit worlds. The philosophical and mystical tenets of India's great religions remained for many centuries the prerogative of the priesthood, in monasteries and other sacred foundations for religious learning.

New ideas and practices, new institutions and techniques, not least script and scriptures, were introduced into the islands with a wealth of imagery. The gods and heroes of India's sacred lore, the masses of deities and the mythical creatures—animals, birds, serpents, turtles, and hosts of celestial beings, demons, monsters, and giants—mingled easily with Indonesia's own supernatural population. The new Indian deities met many congenial counterparts. The symbol of the supreme god, Shiva—the linga—lent a distinct phallic form to the sacred prehistoric upright stones. The linga's female counterpart, the yoni, was a more elaborate version of the horizontal female stones of the Indonesian ancestral seat; it served as pedestal for the linga itself as well as for commemorative statues of kings. The Indian World Mountain and abode of the gods, Mount Mahameru, was easily identified with certain mountains in the islands, where ancestral spirits had been thought to dwell. In legend the Mahameru itself was transplanted to Indonesia; the highest mountain of East Java bears the name of Sumeru. A description of the legendary transportation by the gods of the Sumeru to Java is given in a sixteenth-century East Javanese work, *Tantu Panggelaran*. An attempt to plant the mountain in the west caused the island to tip, so that for the sake of balance it was moved eastward. On the way pieces kept chipping off its lower rim, and thus the mountains Lawu, Wilis, Kelud, Kawi, Ardjuna, and Welirang were formed. The mountain's damaged foot made it difficult to steady it on the spot; it shook, and the top cracked off and fell away, becoming Mt. Penanggungan.

The many individual gods of the Hindu pantheon were readily understandable as new personifications of the elements: Surya for the sun, Chandra for the moon, Agni for fire, Shiva's consort Parwati for the earth, Wayu for the winds, and Indra for the sky. The carrier of the god Vishnu, the bird Garuda, now met the aerial carriers of ancestral souls, including the hornbill. Vishnu's spoked sun disk fused with pre-existing circular and spoked sun symbols. His consort Shri superseded the indigenous spirit of the rice; she became the goddess of the rice plant and of fertility in general.

The offerings these new gods demanded and the entertainments given for their pleasure merged with the old sacrificial rites, enhanced the performances of dances, and permitted the continuation of festive banquets following the slaughter of sacrificial animals. It is not surprising that the more austere Hinayana school of Buddhism, initially propagated in the fifth century in South Sumatra and perhaps Java, was superseded by Mahayana Buddhism with its rich pantheon of Buddhas and Bodhisattvas. And the magico-mystical practices of Tantric sects known to have influenced Buddhist cults in Indonesia[6] further contributed to the attraction of Mahayana in societies conscious of the mysteries of black and white magic.

The period between the seventh and tenth centuries A.D. is of particular importance for our knowledge of Buddhism and Buddhist art in Indonesia. During this period Buddhist art attained a peak of glory in Central Java, although, paradoxically, historical evidence of what appears to have been the greatest Buddhist center in the archipelago points to South Sumatra and the kingdom of Srivijaya. In its capital, which is believed to have been situated on the site of present day Palembang on the Musi River,[7] a renowned center of Buddhist studies flourished in the seventh century. The Chinese scholar-pilgrim I Tsing stayed there in 672 on his way to India and again on his return trip to China in 685. The scholars, monks, and pilgrims who congregated at Srivijaya—over a thousand of them at the time of I Tsing's visit—studied Sanskrit, and Sanskrit texts were being translated into other languages.[8]

Until its decline in the thirteenth century, Srivijaya had extensive relations, not all peaceful, with kingdoms in both the north and the south of India, with China, and with countries of continental Southeast Asia. Close ties were established with the heart of the Buddhist world in the realm of the Pala kings, especially the monastery city of Nalanda (in Bihar, east of Benares).

In the ninth century a ruler of Srivijaya, Balaputra, who was a descendant of the Central Javanese dynasty of the Shailendras—great patrons of Buddhism—founded a monastery in Nalanda probably as a hostel for pilgrims coming from Indonesia. A trove of bronze images unearthed from the ruins of this monastery disclosed a striking stylistic affinity with contemporaneous Hindu-Javanese bronzes; Nalanda is thus regarded as one of the important sources for Indonesia's Mahayana Buddhism as well as being important for the style of its highly developed bronze art of that period.[9]

One of Balaputra's successors in the tenth century is known to have founded a monastery in the south of India, at Negapatam of Colamandala, the realm of the Cola kings (the Coromandel coast in the area of present-day Madras), another region important to Indonesia's cultural contacts and trading relations with India.

The scanty testimony yielded by Sumatra is mystifying in comparison to the wealth of monuments and images preserved in Java from the flourishing period of Buddhism. Among the Buddhist remains in Sumatra are ruins of some stupas as at Muara Takus in the Padang Highlands, a huge granite image of the Buddha, and a few other stone images now standing in Palembang. A few bronze figures of Buddhist deities have been fished out of the Musi River and are now kept in the Museum at Djakarta (Pl. 26). The history of Srivijaya,[10] and its rivalries with Javenese kingdoms still awaits further clarification.

The institution of kingship in Indonesia had important consequences not only in the political and economic spheres but in the realm of the arts as well. For almost a thousand years masterpieces of architecture and sculpture resulted from royal construction projects. The erection of temples, monasteries, and monuments stimulated the development of a variety of styles in the plastic arts. It was the power of the priests, however, combined with that of the kings, which was decisive in causing the efflorescence of these arts.

One can gain an impression of the role of the priests from the text of a charter, engraved in stone in 778, which records the royal grant in freehold of the lands of the village of Kalasan near present-day Jogjakarta

Plate 26. *Bronze image of the preaching Buddha found near Palembang, South Sumatra.*

for the maintenance of a monastery and a Buddhist temple dedicated to the goddess Tara, presumably in honor of the founding king's deceased wife, who bore the same name. This temple, Tjandi Kalasan, one of the most exquisite examples of fine craftsmanship in Central Javanese art, still stands near the highway that connects Jogjakarta with Surakarta, although the central bronze image of the goddess, said to have been about 18 feet high, has disappeared. The tjandi's present exterior is not that of the original structure, but the result of a later renovation.[11]

The relevant passage of the charter's text reads as follows:

After the gurus* of the Çailendra-Lord Çri Maharājā dyah Pancapana rake Panangkarana had persuaded, they caused the building of a glorious Tārā temple. By order of the gurus an image of the goddess Tārā was made by experts, as well as a temple for her, and also an abode for venerable begging monks versed in the Mahayānā of the Winaya.[12]

The priests in this case played a persuasive as well as an organizational role. Thus an important phase of cultural development, including an efflorescence of the plastic arts, was furthered by the scholars and scientists of the age, the priests and monks. They must have possessed the Indian treatises (*shastra*) on the arts; some may have specialized as architects (*sthapati*) of religious structures and as master sculptors (*sthapaka*). These Sanskrit terms appear in the inscriptions of Java as they do in an old Indian treatise, *The Architecture of Manasara,* where we read:

The chief architect [*sthapati*] is said to be the creator [*prakriti*] and the sculptor [*sthapaka*] the life [of the images]; therefore they should work together in consultation with [lit., in company of] each other from the very beginning of the operation.[13]

The existence of such priest-architects is confirmed by an inscription of 832 (of Gandasuli) which contains the following passage: "Furthermore there is the Venerable Teacher named Dhalawa, an accomplished architect. . . ."[14] In a charter of 842, issued by a queen who assigned grounds for a sacred foundation, there is listed among the witnesses "the priest-architect of Kraunça."[15]

It is justifiable to assume that these learned priest-architects directed the construction of sanctuaries according to Indian manuals. And it is interesting to observe that a wood carver, referred to as *manapal* (*tapel* today means mask in Bali) in a charter of 850,[16] had no such high position in the religious hierarchy; his name, Ulihan, is prefixed by the term *Si,* indicating a simple man. He may have been a mask carver, but in any event his was an old, indigenous skill.

The priests must not only have trained Indonesian builders and carvers for the numerous and extensive construction projects in Java, but through them knowledge of the great Indian epics, the *Ramayana* and the *Mahabharata,* as well as of Buddhist legends and fables must have spread. This lore became an inexhaustible source for narrative stone reliefs which decorate Java's ancient sanctuaries and, not least, for the chanted recitals of storytellers. In time many of these works were translated into Javanese, in whole or in part.

Among the principal stone monuments of ancient Java, the majority are the so-called tjandi. Although this term is now applied to every Hinduistic sanctuary, Krom[17] suggests that it originally designated a monument erected over the ashes of a deceased person and that the word might be connected with *Tjandika,* one of the names of the goddess of death, Durga (a destructive aspect of Shiva's consort), who is still worshiped in special temples in Bali. The tjandi in Java and Bali are temple-mausoleums, or tomb-temples, in which the ashes of royal personages were deposited in a stone casket within a central pit. Above the pit was erected a commemorative statue of a king or queen in the shape of a Hindu or Buddhist deity.[18]

Designed along principles derived from the architecture of Indian temples, the forms of tjandi underwent modifications in Indonesia. Similarly, the major images enshrined in them, despite careful preservation of pertinent iconographic elements, acquired very different styles in Indonesia from those known in India. The images became increasingly rigid, mortuary statues of dead kings rather than of living gods. The "living gods," the deities of the Hindu pantheon and their hosts, were not enshrined within the principal chambers of the tjandi; they usually appeared in subsidiary chambers and in the outside niches of the sanctuaries. The walls were usually adorned with narrative and decorative reliefs. Where the scenes deal with life on

* *Guru:* spiritual guide, teacher, a word now embedded in the Indonesian language together with innumerable other Sanskrit terms.

Plate 27. *Southeast façade of Tjandi Kalasan, Central Java, 8th–9th century.*

this earth, they contain a wealth of information about architecture, utensils, clothing and ornaments, weapons, musical instruments and dance gestures, actions of priests, functions and attitudes of slaves or servants, human types, animals and plants of the Indian and Indonesian world. In scenes of the celestial world, the imagery, especially that of the Central Javanese structures, seems to be based more directly on conceptions and forms transplanted from India.

In Table 1 are listed the principal tjandi and other sanctuaries of Central Java, which are located on Map 1.

The plastic arts of the Hinduistic millennium, applied to the tjandi and their subsidiary structures, walls, and gates, were also employed on monasteries and holy bathing places which were sometimes combined with a tjandi. Casting, engraving, and chasing in bronze, silver, and gold were developed to a high degree. These processes were used for making sacerdotal objects such as vessels for holy water, bells for officiating priests, oil lamps, trays and a variety of ornaments[19] as well as for images. Most of the large bronze images, such as the former central image at Kalasan or the gigantic Buddha image known to have been enshrined at Tjandi Sewu, have vanished. They may have been smelted in later centuries for other purposes—to make weapons, utensils, or gongs, for example—just as many an ancient gold ornament or image unearthed by some *tani,* tiller of the soil, may have found its way into the crucibles of goldsmiths for the making of modern jewelry.

No archaeological evidence has been unearthed so far to indicate a slow stylistic evolution leading to the

TABLE 1

Principal Antiquities in Central Java

Tjandi or other antiquity	Religious Orientation	Century	Remarks
Kalasan (1)*	Buddhist	8th–9th	Though founded in 778, the temple's present structure is of a later date.
Dieng (2)	Shivaite	9th	Several groups of temples. Earliest inscription dates from 809.
Barabudur (3)	Buddhist	9th	Probably consecrated in 824.
Mendut (4)	Buddhist	9th	Assumed to be of the same period as the Barabudur.
Pawon (5)	Buddhist	9th	May commemorate King Indra, tenth ruler of the Shailendra dynasty.
Banjunibo (6)	Buddhist	9th (?)	
Sewu (7)	Buddhist	9th	Large temple complex.
Plaosan (7)	Buddhist	9th	Temple complex.
Pringapus (8)	Shivaite	9th	Remains of small complex.
Ratu Baka (9)	Traces of both Shivaite and Buddhist adherents	9th	Possibly remains of a fortified palace-monastery with hermitages in its vicinity.
Prambanan (10)	Shivaite	9th	Large temple complex.
Sari (11)	Buddhist	9th (?)	Possibly of the same period as Kalasan.
Ngawen (12)	Buddhist	9th–10th	Originally consisted of five sanctuaries.
Sukuh (13) and Tjeta (13)	Bima cult	15th	Drastic departure from Hindu-Buddhist style.

* Numbers in parentheses refer to the sites in Map 1.

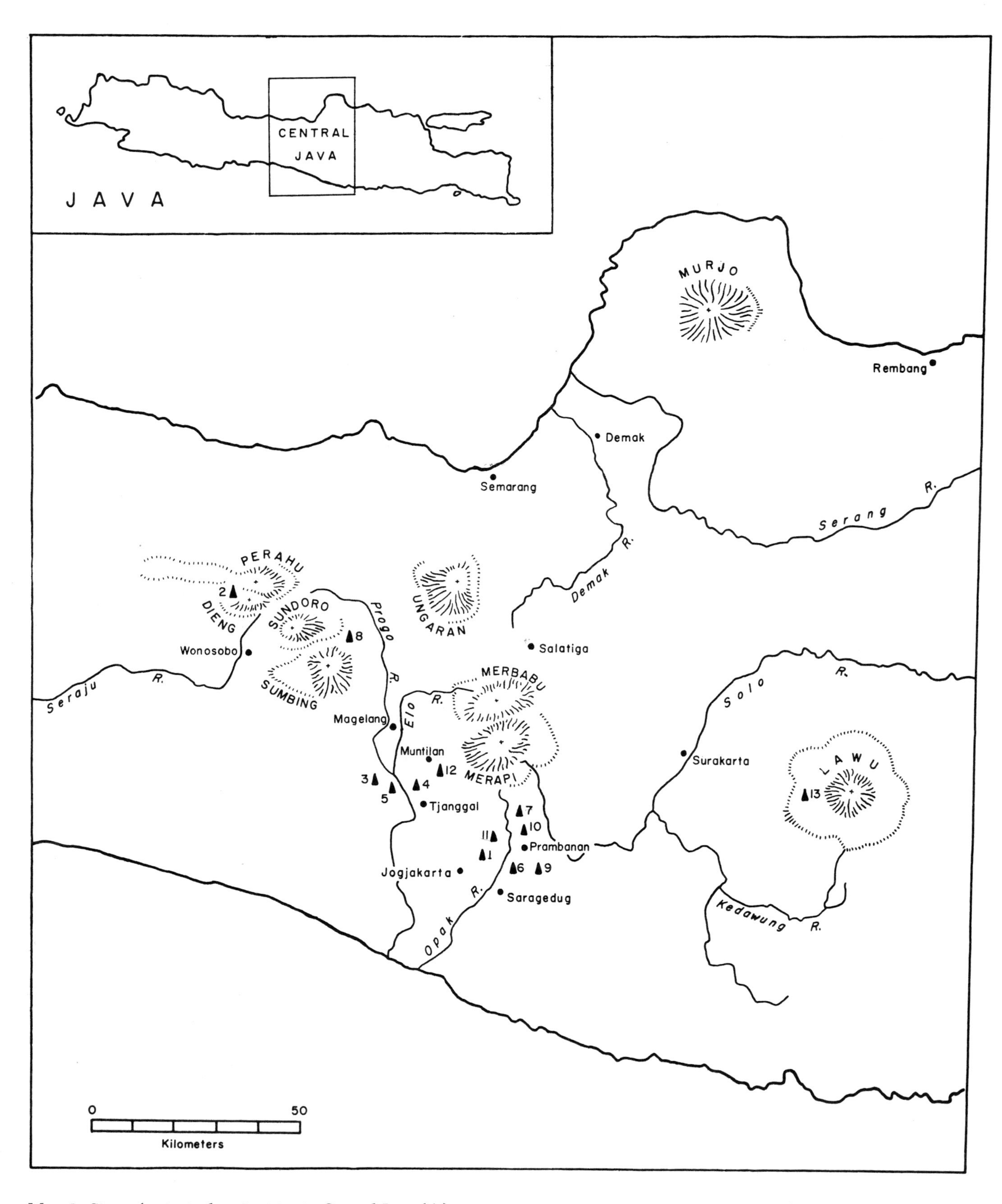

Map 1. *Sites of principal antiquities in Central Java* (▲).

highly sophisticated and delicate art of the Buddhist sacred structures which arose in the eighth century in the plains of Central Java. This art seems to have blossomed miraculously, as though from a void, with sudden luxuriance. Only a few sanctuaries in the plains and the remains of Shivaite tjandi (mistaken at first for the ruins of a city) on the remote, high plateau of Dieng (see pp. 52–53 below), predate the Buddhist monuments of Central Java. Among these are some which, until recently at least, have been regarded as purely religious structures without relation to the cult of kings, in other words, structures that were not intended as tjandi. An unequivocal example is the temple of Mendut (even though constantly referred to as *Tjandi Mendut*), a chapel related to the great stupa of the Barabudur. The large images of a seated preaching Buddha flanked by two Bodhisattvas enshrined at Mendut are clearly images for worship.

The Barabudur itself, a grandiose terraced monument crowned by a stupa, its silhouette a stupalike edifice, has always been regarded as a purely devotional Buddhist monument, erected to the glory of the Buddhist faith and as a site for meditation by Buddhist monks. De Casparis, however, has suggested the possibility that the Barabudur might be a tjandi as well.[20]

A detailed description of the Barabudur, with reproductions of its sculptured works, is contained in the monumental monograph of Krom and Van Erp.[21] An interpretation of its name, form, and significance given by Stutterheim[22] was significantly amplified in 1950 by De Casparis, who also gave a new reading of the monument's name, as cited below. Many other noteworthy writings discuss the various aspects of this rich monument.[23] A brief recapitulation follows.

The name Barabudur apparently derives from the second part of the original designation, Bhūmisambhārabūdara, "The Mountain of the Accumulation of Virtue in the Ten Stages of the Bodhisattva." This designation appears in a charter of 842, analyzed by De Casparis.[24] Apart from its overt meaning, as the embodiment in stone of the Buddhist doctrine, the name may contain two allusions: (1) to the architectural form of the monument—a *mountain* with an array of terraces, and (2) to the "Lords of the *Mountain*," that is, the Shailendra, during whose dynastic rule the monument was erected. The Shailendra dynasty may have been a continuation in Java of the "Lords of the Mountain" dynasty which ruled the kingdom Fu-nan in continental Southeast Asia until the first half of the seventh century A.D.[25] The founder of this dynasty in Java may have been glorified posthumously in the Barabudur, in the shape of a Bodhisattva on the threshold of Buddhahood. It is possible that the uncompleted Bodhisattva image originally found within the large crowning bell-shaped stupa of the monument was meant to symbolize the nearing, but still imperfect, state of Buddhahood of the Shailendras' progenitor.[26]

Early conjectures that the monument must have been erected between 750 and 850 are now being confirmed. It is now definitely known from stone inscriptions analyzed by De Casparis that the construction of the Barabudur was undertaken during the reign of a Shailendra king, Samaratunga, that it was probably founded in 824, and that in 842 a daughter of this king, designated as queen, had dedicated certain grounds with rice fields for the upkeep of the sacred edifice.[27] It would have been something of a miracle however if the erection of the basic architectural forms and the execution of all the images, reliefs, and other sculptured adornments of the monument would have been completed within the eighteen-year span between these two dates.[28]

The staggering statistics given by Van Erp in his archaeological description of the Barabudur[29] show, for example, that some 2 million cubic feet of stone (andesite) had to be hewn, transported, piled and carved; that the edifice, which rests upon a base of 403 square feet, contains 1,460 pictorial and 1,212 decorative panels, adding up to 27,000 square feet of stone surface carved in high relief. There are 504 Buddha images sculptured in the round, of which 72 are within the trellised *dagobas* (smaller stupas) of the circular terraces. Guardian lions, large spouts, ornate niches, decorated pilasters and antefixes, and the impressive gates need not be cited in detail. It should be added, however, that much intricate labor was involved in covering all the surfaces with a layer of hard stucco (so-called diamond plaster) for better preservation. Traces of this plastering have been found on Tjandi Kalasan as well. Such construction must have demanded armies of laborers, carvers, sculptors, and expert supervisors, working for decades with only human muscle power, rolling logs, ropes and levers, hammers, mallets, and chisels for hewing and carving. For comparative purposes it is interesting to note an estimate made by Groslier of the time and manpower that it may have taken to construct the Khmer sanctuary of Bantay

Chmar under King Jayawarman II, which is smaller than the Barabudur. Groslier concluded that under the conditions prevailing at that time it would have taken 21 years of work by no less than 30,000 stone cutters, 15,000 stone carriers, 4,000 builders, and 1,500 sculptors to accomplish the task.[30]

The Barabudur was constructed as a symmetrical mantle around a hilltop, the monument itself thus forming an artificial stone "mountain." Like so many other Buddhist sacred structures in South and Southeast Asia, it is essentially a stupa (dome or bell-shaped reliquary) placed on a stepped pyramidal base. Thus the ancient symbols of the circle (for the heavens) and the square (for the earth) are combined. The Barabudur's crowning bell-shaped stupa, 52 feet in diameter, rises above three descending tiers of circular terraces, each symmetrically studded with a ring of smaller stupas (or dagobas) with perforated walls.

Plate 28. *Aerial view of the Barabudur seen from southeast, Central Java, 9th century.*

Plate 29. *Staircase and gateway with* kala *head, leading to third gallery of the Barabudur.*

The entire circular superstructure rests on a monumental base of six stepped square terraces, the lowest forming a broad, flat rim that offers a wide path for the traditional circumambulation of the sacred edifice by the devout. A staircase in the middle of each of the four stepped pyramidal "slopes" ascends through four portals toward the free expanse at the top. From the lintels stare the monstrous *kala* heads[31] with bulging eyes and bared fangs, the protective guardians to repel evil forces, which can be seen on practically every sanctuary portal or niche harboring an image on Javanese tjandi. Upon the kala head several symbolic meanings converge: a monstrous emanation of Shiva, a solar symbol, and a sign of the upper world. Essentially a protective charm (see Ch. 4, p. 107 below), it is often combined with symbols of the underworld, the waters —two *makaras,* fantastic serpentine sea creatures with elephantine heads.

The monument has no inner space except one cell discovered inside the large, closed crowning stupa which may have once contained an unfinished Buddha image. Four of the square terrace floors are walled in to form passages, or galleries, under the open sky. These are invisible from the outside because the view is obstructed by high balustrades containing rows of niches with images of Buddhas. The galleries lead around the whole monument at successively higher levels. On the walls (formed by the body of the monument on one side and the inner side of the balustrade on the other) reliefs have been carved in endless sequences.[32]

The architectural plan of the Barabudur, the Buddha images in niches above the galleries,[33] and the themes of the reliefs are all symbolic of the monument's meaning, as is the absence of reliefs on the upper round terraces. "The ten stages of the Bodhisattva," the phases in the Buddhist Way of Salvation, are symbolized by the successively rising terraces, six square and three round, with the crowning stupa as the last phase. Stutterheim has divided these terraces into three spheres (*dhatu*). They represent the sphere of desire (*kamadhatu*) at the base, the sphere of form (*rupadhatu*) on the middle level, and the sphere of formlessness (absence of form, *arupadhatu*) at the top.

The lowest sphere, the kamadhatu, is symbolized by the so-called "buried foot" of the monument, the base terrace. Its outer walls have been carved with reliefs depicting the earthly existence (karma) of human beings in the power of desire, their good and evil deeds, and their corresponding rewards and punishments. For reasons not yet fully established, whether physical (sagging of the monument),* didactic (removal of this sphere from the eyes of the meditating monks),† or symbolic (closing off this sphere as unnecessary for the royal candidate to Buddhahood)‡ this series of reliefs has been hidden from sight by a heavy mantel of stones laid around the base terrace, incidentally widening the floor for the processional path.

The "sphere of form" (rupadhatu), symbolized by the four galleries above the base, contains all the visible reliefs. Their content, identified in part by Krom, basically follows certain Sanskrit texts.[34] From these and from the identification of certain figures or their contexts where texts could not be ascertained, espe-

* Theory of Krom and Van Erp.
† Theory of Stutterheim.
‡ Theory of De Casparis.

Plate 30. *View from the base of the crowning stupa of the Barabudur.*

Plate 31. *Buddha image originally enclosed within a perforated dagoba on a circular terrace, Barabudur.*

cially on the third and fourth galleries, it is clear that as one climbs to the higher levels, the more exalted the themes become. One rises, in fact, from the lower depths of earthly existence (karma) depicted on the "buried base" to the highest heavens of future Buddhas.

On the first gallery of the rupadhatu, the upper series of panels on the main wall depicts episodes from the life of Prince Siddharta Gautama, who as a sage became known as Shakyamuni, the historical Buddha. Below this series are scenes rendering the story of Prince Sudhana who became a Bodhisattva, and his beloved *kinnari* (a mythical celestial being, half-woman, half-bird), Manohara. On the balustrade side scenes from *Jataka* stories contain incidents from the previous incarnations of the Buddha. On the main wall of the second gallery the story of Bodhisattva Sudhana continues, as he visits ascetics, sages, monks, and high Bodhisattvas, worshiping at sacred places in quest of the highest wisdom. Jataka tales again appear on the balustrade side. Still higher, on the third and fourth galleries, there are scenes of Bodhisattvas and of ever higher heavens with Buddha figures enthroned in serene majesty. Then all representations end and with them, the "sphere of form" is left behind.

We emerge on the highest square terrace, upon which the three tiers of circular terraces rest, where no representations divert one's eyes, where "form" is absent or has been surpassed. Only the perforated bell-shaped dagobas arrayed in circles suggest invisible presences: within each a seated Buddha image is enclosed. The image cannot be seen from the outside, unless the visitor approaches close enough to peep through one of the square or diamond-shaped openings. Then he can glimpse a part of the image, with the tantalizing hint of the existence of the whole—a hint perhaps at the elusive essence of truth, in which only particles, never the whole, are revealed to the seeker.

No visitor to the Barabudur can help feeling a sense of release upon entering this upper sphere of the monument, where he is no longer hemmed in between the walls of the lower galleries with their profusion of representational forms. Pure space, the marvelous expanse under the dome of the sky which melts into the mountain ranges in the distance and the palm groves and rice fields below, creates a sense of extraordinary peace, the flow of infinity. He need not be a Buddhist, monk, or mystic to experience the grandeur of silence that reigns in this superb "void."

The Barabudur is a symbol of Buddhist cosmology, a hymn in stone to the Buddhist Way of Salvation. Its art could be described as classical Indian, and as a distant, tropical offspring of the Greco-Buddhist school of Gandhara which flourished in Northern India in the first centuries of our era.[35] In drawing a line connecting the Greco-Buddhist art of ancient India with that of Indonesia, Stutterheim observes:

I found among the remains of Nalanda some things that may be recognized as the immediate models of Central Javanese art, and it thus becomes possible to draw a line which leads from the art of Lara Djonggrang [Tjandi Prambanan], via that of the Barabudur, the temples of West India, Nalanda, to the renowned school of Gandhara, where the sculpture of stupas is linked with the Hellenistic sculpture of sarcophagi known to us from Asia Minor. This plastic art was adapted to the old Asian terraced pyramids; we find an offspring thereof in the Barabudur. This Gandhara sculpture is closely related to that of the old Christian sarcophagi, and therefore the art of the Barabudur is a distant relation of the altar reliefs and reliquaries of our medieval cathedrals.[36]

The adaptation and transformation of Hellenistic art on Asia's soil which spread throughout the Buddhist world from the Indus to the Yangtze and beyond to Japan produced among its numerous rich variations a distinct and unique style in Central Java. This style is naturalistic, with the element of idealization that enters into any efforts to render in concrete, plastic form the perfection of beauty or of the divine. The conceptions of beauty and the divine are Indian, but there is a quality of greater softness in the versions at the Barabudur than in Indian versions.

The different types of Buddha images which appear in the niches of the monument are of a grand simplicity, combined with subtlety. Detached serenity emanates from the classical faces. These stone images, through the magic of sculptured form, manage to impart that elusive quality or state to which the practitioners of *semadi* (skr: *samadhi*)* aspire—their "presence" denotes a "concentrated absence." In contrast, the elevated niches which shelter the Buddha images are elaborately decorated.

The great simplicity and stillness of the images is contrasted to the crowding forms on the sculptured panels along the galleries below. There is a smiling sweetness, a beatific blithesomeness that pervades these scenes, especially the ones that depict celestial or royal abodes with garlanded pavilions, bejeweled trees, and the musical grace of divine beings floating aloft. A mild benevolence seems to extend even to the covered representations of punishments in purgatory on the "buried foot." There are none of the terror-inspiring features that other arts have lent to hell. There is, for example, a rather cozy version of people being boiled in a tub with no more excesses than in an ordinary kitchen scene, but with trim trees in the background instead of pots and pans.[37] The foliage of the trees is conventionalized, with decorative rounded, triangular, or feathery masses crowning the trunks; the trees are reduced in size to fit the proportions of the laterally elongated panels.

Symmetry dominates the representations of meditating celestials and the scenes depicting the life of the Buddha. There is no tension or strong dynamic quality in these representations. The scenes are "appearances";

* The state of "absorption" as a final phase of meditation.

Plate 32. *Prince Siddharta cuts his hair, signifying his retreat from the world, Barabudur relief.*

the actions are gestures devoid of passion, without dramatic impact. A kind of detachment permeates the sweetness and lightness of graceful forms. A much earthier spirit appears in the folk scenes on the balustrade reliefs, depicting Jataka tales (Pls. 33, 34). Their liveliness stands in sharp contrast to the detached serenity of the Buddha images and the pious harmony of the scenes on inner walls.

The unknown sculptors of the Barabudur and of other Buddhist art of ninth-century Central Java at times achieved a degree of grace and soft inwardness rarely encountered. Outstanding examples are the two large-scale statues of seated Bodhisattvas—Lokeshvara and Vajrapani—in the high dusky chamber of Tjandi Mendut.[38] They flank a giant image of a seated preaching Buddha, too large to be easily perceived in its totality within the confines of the chamber or through the opening of its portal. The Bodhisattvas, although less grandiose, are of extraordinary beauty. Their still forms fill the space around them with that undefinable, timeless life which emanates only from the greatest works of art. The same is true of the Bodhisattva images which are still preserved in one of the ruined temples of Plaosan (Pl. 35). Their meditative stillness is enhanced by the attitudes of votive figures carved in relief on the walls nearby.[39]

In the case of Tjandi Plaosan there is a record describing those transcendental qualities which the sculp-

tors attempted to embody in stone. This large Buddhist temple complex is situated in the vicinity of Prambanan; it is attributed to a king of the ninth century married to a daughter of the last known Shailendra ruler of Central Java.[40] Plaosan is now largely in ruins, but some of the original images and reliefs, despite long exposure to the elements, are still in a remarkably good state of preservation. De Casparis gives an interpretative analysis of an inscription in Sanskrit verse engraved on a stone which comes from Tjandi Plaosan.[41] The verses extoll the images of the temple—the principal one, of a Buddha or a high Bodhisattva, and apparently of a number of other statues. It is said of them: "Twenty Jinas [Buddhas] are shining forth here, accompanied by Bodhisattvas."

From the similes of the ninth-century poet, which allude to the effects of Buddhist enlightenment and the transcendental qualities of Bodhisattvas, and simultaneously describe the stone images, we can gather something of the mood that emanates from their forms, in association with Buddhist conceptions. "The Brilliant One, as the incomparable sunrise in the form of an image adorned with the equipment of Dharma" is one reference to the principal statue. This image, the poet says, has "fallen into the temple by a miracle." In another strophe it is likened to a twilight cloud from which soft rain descends (as the exposition of the Doctrine cools the torturing heat of passions, De Casparis

Plate 33. *Lady carried in a palanquin, Barabudur balustrade relief.*

Plate 34. *Detail of three heads on a Barabudur balustrade relief.*

Plate 35. *A Bodhisattva in the north chamber of Tjandi Plaosan's southern temple, 9th century.*

observes).[42] Yet the image is radiant: "Owing to the blinding splendor of the crest of his head, from which radiant light, glittering from a hidden lotus in its interior, emanates, his excellent retinue, shining as the cool-rayed [moon]. . . ."

The "blinding splendor" emanating from a hidden source referred to as a lotus is here contrasted with the light of the soft, cool rays of the moon—another kind of radiance which pervades the images of subsidiary Bodhisattvas. Traces of a shaft at one side of the ceiling of Tjandi Mendut may indicate that the builders had tried to provide a special illumination for the principal image.

The sight of the Jina images in the temple, as "pure as the disk of the moon," dissolves the passions of lovers, stills anger, disperses "wrong views." A twentieth-century visitor to Plaosan may still find himself under the spell of one of these tranquil figures with their rich symbolic adornments, into whose forms was chiseled the soft, cool radiance of the moon.

These few selected examples demonstrate the form, mood, and meaning that art inspired by Buddhism achieved in Indonesia, as it spread dispassionate mildness and grace over the "magically charged" art of ancestral cults.

We now turn to Java's Shivaite art. Its supreme animating force was the god Shiva, creator and destroyer, whose phallic symbol, the linga, became the symbol of living Shivaite kings and of their power. A superb bronze image of the four-armed god (date unknown) found near Tegal on Java's north coast and now in the Museum at Djakarta eloquently expresses the spirit associated with this deity. A concentration of contained and yet outward directed energy emanates from this figure, so unlike the inward absorption of the Buddhist images that we have contemplated. The god's third eye in the middle of his forehead and his lower lip are gilded, adding to the force of his facial expression. Of his traditional attributes, the lunar crescent and a skull decorate his crown; a snake-shaped caste cord hangs from one shoulder across his chest; over his draped loincloth a tiger skin is wound around his hips; in his left hand he holds the fly whisk and, instead of the more usual rosary, a water jug, equally the symbol of an ascetic. The fine workmanship of the image, seen in

Plate 36. *Bronze Shiva found in Tegal, North Java.*

the modeling of the hands, the execution of the ornaments and the garments, testifies to the mastery attained by Java's ancient bronzecasters.

The oldest identified Shivaite sanctuary, whose scanty remains can still be seen on the Gunung Wukir plateau (south of Muntilan), dates from 732. It was erected by King Sanjaya, who reigned "in unbroken concord with his sister"[43] from approximately 732 to about 760. (Female rulers had been known in Java both before and after Sanjaya.) Sanjaya is regarded as the founder of the Shivaite lineage of kings who ruled Mataram until the first quarter of the tenth century. It is very probable that the sanctuary on Gunung Wukir originally enshrined a linga[44] which Sanjaya may have dedicated to mark the beginning of his reign or to consecrate the foundation of Mataram, or both. When I visited the site in the nineteen-thirties, all that could be seen were foundation stones protruding from the earth at the foot of a solitary tall tree which stood out against the sky, the grand panorama of Central Java's majestic volcanoes shimmering in the distance.

Much more has been preserved on the remote, high plateau of Dieng (about 6,500 feet above sea level), where a number of temple groups, dating probably from the beginning of the ninth century, lie amid volcanic pools and sulphurous fumes on the crater floor of a collapsed volcano. Eight from perhaps three times as many temples have been partly restored. These and numerous images assembled on the ground provide a good idea of the architectural and sculptural style of this temple city, whose population may have consisted primarily of priests and their assistants, guardians and servants attending to the sanctuaries and to the pilgrims who included royalty among their numbers. Compared with the plains' art of the following century, Dieng's architecture, ornamentation, and sculptured images are relatively simple and austere. The Shivaite pantheon is represented in profusion: Shiva alone or with his consort Parvati, Shiva's elephant-headed son, Ganesha, as well as the gods Brahma and Vishnu, lingas and yonis, a *naga* (serpent) crowned with a jewel are among the images found on the site. Peculiar to Dieng iconography are the anthropomorphic animal mounts of the principal gods; each rides on the shoulders of a

Plate 37. *Remains of three small* tjandi, *Dieng Plateau complex, 8th–9th century.*

seated human figure with the head of an animal—a bull (for Shiva), a goose (for Brahma), the bird Garuda (for Vishnu).

Each of the standing temples, and those which were seen by explorers in the past century but have since disintegrated (or whose loose stones have been carried off for various construction projects), have been given individual names, after the Pandawa heroes of the *Mahabharata,* their consorts, patrons, and attendants. Curiously, the same is true of the seventh-century Mamallapuram temples in southern India[45] similarly named for the Pandawa brothers. On the Dieng plateau one towering tjandi with a tapering five-tiered roof (formerly seven-tiered perhaps) contains horseshoe-shaped niches, each enclosing a head[46] stylistically unique for Java. This structure is known as Tjandi Bima in honor of that hero's mighty figure. In contrast, Tjandi Puntadewa (another name for the eldest of the Pandawa, Yudistira) is small and delicate; Tjandi Ardjuna is somewhat taller and more graceful; two smaller structures near it are named Tjandi Srikandi and Tjandi Sumbadra, for Ardjuna's wives; and an elongated, low rectangular structure is known as Tjandi Semar in honor of Ardjuna's hermaphroditic loyal servant and mentor who, incidentally, is an Indonesian and not an Indian creation. Reportedly there were also tjandi named after the twins Nakula and Sadewa, after Dwarawati (Kresna, king of Dwarawati), and after Semar's sons, Gareng, Petruk, and Bagong. It has generally been assumed by scholars that all these names, now officially listed with Indonesia's Archaeological Service, were given to the Dieng temples by the local population many centuries, perhaps a thousand years, after their erection. Thus it must be sheer coincidence that the same nomenclature had appeared at Mamallapuram. Nevertheless, the Dieng structures also share the most pronounced stylistic affinities with the temple architecture of south India. One might bear in mind, however, that a tradition which is followed in our own time perhaps may have been preserved by the population for a millennium or even longer without ever having been codified. The divine sons of Pandu from the ancient Indian epic have nonetheless been assigned temple-tombs on Java's soil, in the cool, misty heights of the Dieng, a proper abode for divine ancestors from whom Javanese kings eventually claimed their descent.

Plate 38. *Shiva mounted on his bull Nandi, Dieng style.*

The most magnificent of all Shivaite monuments in Indonesia is the temple complex of Prambanan, also known as Tjandi Lara Djonggrang. This group, dominated by a towering temple to Shiva, was probably built some time between the middle of the ninth and the beginning of the tenth centuries. Its founder belonged to the Shaiva dynasty descended from King Sanjaya (732–*c.* 760), which returned to power around the middle of the ninth century after having overthrown their rivals, the Buddhist Shailendra. Until recently it has been thought that King Balitung of Mataram (*r.* 898–910) was deified there in the shape of Shiva by his successor Daksa (*r.c.* 910–919). It seems unlikely, however, that the temple complex could have been built within the short span of Daksa's reign, so that the construction may have been inaugurated by Balitung himself. There are some indications, however, that the temple complex or at least its nucleus may have been built even earlier. An inscription of unknown origin describes a temple complex founded in 856 which corresponds in many respects to that of Lara Djonggrang.[47]

Legend ascribes the creation of the Prambanan temples to a demand made by Lara Djonggrang, a daughter of the King Ratu Baka.* As the price for her hand, the princess commanded an unwelcome suitor to erect these temples overnight. To prevent his accomplishing the task, she had the rice-pounding, signaling the end of the night, begun before dawn.† Cursed by her frustrated suitor, she was turned into stone. A stone image of Durga, Shiva's consort, which now stands in the northern chamber of the Shiva temple, has long been worshiped by the population as Lara Djonggrang, thus perpetuating the legendary connection between the temple and the Ratu Baka plateau.

Archaeologists have long been mystified by the monumental stone platforms of former pillared halls and gates, by the remains of chambers and of deep cisterns which lie apart from the main fortified area on the Ratu Baka plateau. These may be the ruins of a fortified monastery, perhaps once a retreat for a royal hermit. Apparently the site was originally Buddhist. The last of the Javanese Shailendra, Balaputra, after having taken refuge there, may have been routed from the plateau by a Shaiva king who then converted it to a Shaiva site.[48] A thousand years later, in another struggle for power, the fortified plateau was the scene for the defeat of a Dutch garrison, ensconced there after the Dutch occupation of Jogjakarta in 1949. The Indonesian guerrillas were guided by a member of the Indonesian Archaeological Service who knew the terrain well!

Reconstruction of the Prambanan temple complex (Fig. 6) shows that it was originally divided by walls into three areas. At one side of the central square the three main temples stand, facing east. The central temple to Shiva is flanked by smaller temples to Brahma and Vishnu. The bodies of these temples rise from an elevated terrace which is surrounded by a balustrade, forming a gallery. Facing these three temples are three smaller structures which originally enshrined figures of the gods' vehicles. Of these only the reclining life-size bull Nandi, Shiva's mount, magnificently carved of stone, has weathered the many centuries. Two small shrines stand near the northern and southern gates, facing toward the center of the square.

Around the central area originally lay three descending tiers of 156 symmetrically aligned shrines, which may have been votive buildings. The shrines were identical in size and general construction, but their details varied. Finally, within a third area between the second wall and third outermost wall, there may have been dwellings of priests, monks, ascetics, temple guardians, and abodes for pilgrims, all made of perishable materials. Possibly there were one or more bathing places here. Today all these have vanished, and rice fields have taken possession of the soil.

In the description of the sanctuary to Shiva erected in 856, one finds some features very similar to the layout of the Prambanan complex. Although in the inscription, analyzed and translated by De Casparis, many lines and words are missing or are undecipher-

* The name Ratu Baka, which in modern Indonesian may mean "Lord of Eternity" or "Eternal Lord" as well as "Ancestral King," is in striking congruence with the Hindu-Indonesian conception of god-king-ancestor. Moreover, this name perhaps also contains a part of Shiva's appellation Tryambaka, the Three-Eyed, the name which appears on one of the inscriptions found on the plateau full of ruins which is now called Ratu Baka. This site, only a few miles south of Prambanan, is believed to have been the site of Lara Djonggrang's father's palace. The memory of tradition is long, even if sometimes blurred!

† A similar legend exists in West Java, where, in the famous Sundanese *Sang Kuriang* myth, the creation of the truncated volcano Takubang Prahu is ascribed to an attempt by an unwelcome suitor to build the mountain overnight to meet the demand of the woman he coveted (she happened to be, unknown to him, his mother). She frustrated his labors by causing a cock to crow prematurely, signaling the arrival of morning.

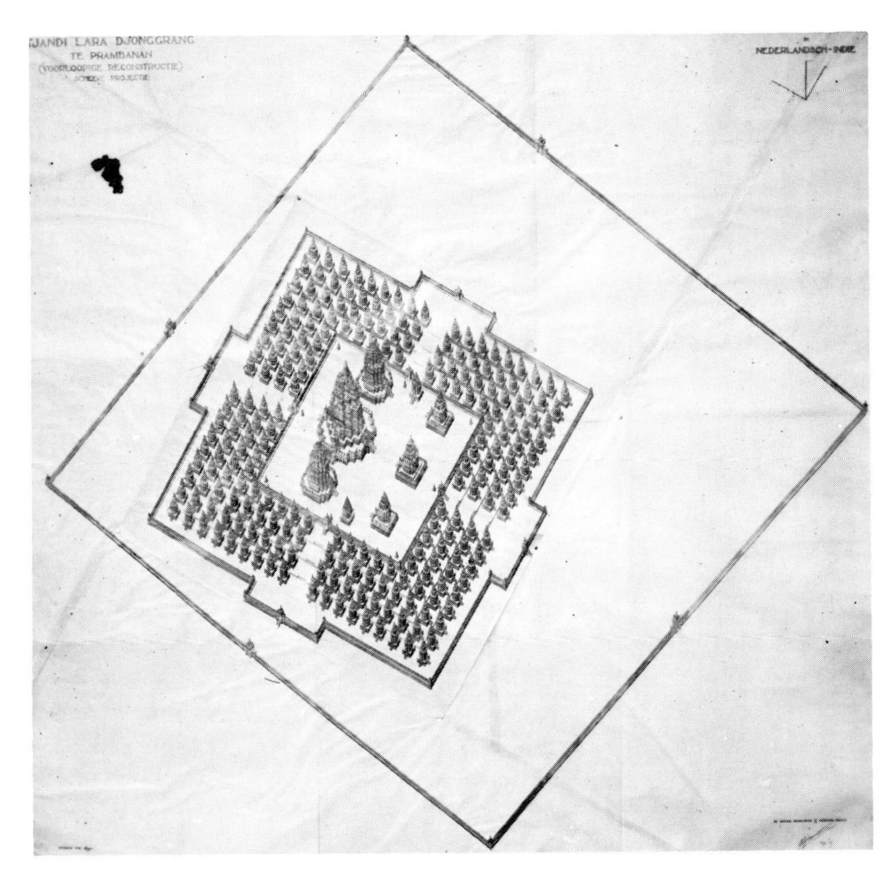

Figure 6. *Reconstruction model of the Prambanan temple complex, 10th century.*

able, a few quotations follow,[49] which not only illustrate the similarities between the sanctuary from 856 and the Lara Djonggrang complex, but also provide the flavor of the time.

> The young prince . . . , in possession of royal majesty [?], protected the country of Java, righteous and with . . . , majestuous in battles and in feasts [?], full of fervor and perfect, victorious but free from passion, a Great King of excellent devotion. He was a Çaiva in contrast to the queen, the spouse of the hero; exactly a year was the time of the . . . ; . . . stones heaped up by the hundreds for his refuge, a killer as fast as the wind . . . Balaputra.

The last lines seem to allude to the rout of Balaputra which may have taken place a year earlier.

The Shaiva king (known as Rakai Pikatan and identified also as Kumbhayoni) is referred to in the inscription as Djatiningrat. His name was changed when he handed his throne over to his successor Dyah Lokapala and retired, probably to a hermitage. The retiring king ordered funeral ceremonies, presumably for his predecessor (Rakai Patapān), but also, since "he could at last dispose of power and riches," "it was only natural that sanctuaries were built by him, the able one."

"The heart of the complex" was surrounded by a wall, the inscription says, and "fierce doorkeepers" guarded the gates. The principal temple is said to be "a beautiful dwelling for the god" and near its eastern side a miraculous Tanjung tree was planted—"the neighborhood of the Lord was the reason for its matchless growth. . . ." "At the gateways two small buildings were erected, different in construction," and there were many other small buildings, probably votive, which "were equal, of equal height, [served] the same purpose, [expressed] the same thoughts, [but] were each different. . . ." The temples with the gateways and images were completed "in a moment"—so eagerly and "cheerfully" did all the different people donate their gifts and labor with "surveyors working by the hundreds."

In referring to the main temple, the inscription says: "What would be comparable with this divine [building]: it was there for a deification; was this the reason why the spectators were overwhelmed and the [normal] sensations did not come back [?]?" Then, "on the day [fixed for] compulsory work on behalf of the Gods, the people in command performed the cere-

Plate 39. *Shiva Temple, Prambanan (Lara Djonggrang).*

monies. . . ." The inscription specifies the precise day in the Shaka* year 778, that is A.D. 856, when the statue of the god was finished and inaugurated. When the Shiva sanctuary had been completed "in its divine splendor," "the [course of the] river was changed so that it rippled along the grounds. . . ." Offerings to ward off evil spirits must have been made at the ritual consecration of the temple grounds, since the inscription says "there was no danger from the wicked ones, for they had all received their due; then the grounds were inaugurated as temple grounds. . . ." The inscription further mentions the size of the rice fields, including irrigated ones, now belonging to the Shiva temple. These fields were also consecrated, "fixed to remain a freehold that would belong to the God forever. . . ." "Those [in charge] were sent back with the order to worship, every day, without forgetting their duties; they should not be negligent in obeying the command of the gods; continuous rebirth in hell would be the result [if they were negligent]."

* Dates in the ancient Indonesian inscriptions of the Hindu-Buddhist period follow the Shaka era which begins in A.D. 78 and is named after the Shaka dynasty (of Scythian origin) who conquered parts of Northwest India.

At Prambanan, the best preserved images and reliefs are at the Shiva temple, although the structure itself had once crumbled.* This temple, now restored, towers impressively above all other structures, although in wider perspective it is dwarfed by the majestic, sharp-peaked cone of the fuming volcano Merapi, which dominates the landscape.

The image of Shiva is enshrined in the main eastern chamber, whose walls are decorated with patterned panels in flat relief, suggesting hangings of precious textiles.[50] The statue of Shiva is stately, erect, stiff, and frontal, and has an oval halo behind its head. The richly adorned four armed deity stands on a lotus, with a yoni as the pedestal. A skull studs his tiara, and kala heads decorate his armlets. Despite the broken nose, the purity of both the facial forms and the body shows the hand of a master sculptor. In the smaller southern, western, and northern chambers of the temple are enshrined respectively Mahaguru (Shiva's ascetic manifestation), Ganesha (Shiva's elephant-headed son), and Durga (the god's consort in her destructive form) as Mahisasuramardini, that is, as the slayer of a demon who had entered a bull.

The mastery of the Prambanan sculptors is manifested in three different sequences of high reliefs on the Shiva temple. Around the lower body of the temple are 24 Guardians of the Cardinal Points (*lokapala*). Some of these seated deities, flanked by attendants, are of extraordinary finesse and beauty. Another series, carved on the outer wall of the balustrade, consists of 62 groups of celestial dancers and musicians. The sense of animated movement and of sometimes ecstatic attitudes, based on the famous moments in the dance of Shiva, is so vital that the whole temple seems to be engirdled by their dance rhythms.† Each recessed group

* Its restoration, after that of the Barabudur, was one of the most ambitious projects undertaken by the Netherlands-Indies Archaeological Service. The work was interrupted in its final stages by World War II and completed during the first years of Indonesian independence.

† These have later counterparts on the walls of the twelfth-century temple at Cidambaram, South India, dedicated to Shiva Natesvara, King of the Dance. A comparison of the relief panels of the two temples eloquently corroborates the transplantation of Indian imagery to Java.

of dancers alternates with a group of three celestial beings posed in softly graceful attitudes. Finally, along the inner side of the balustrade wall which forms the gallery at the foot of the temple, is carved the story of the *Ramayana*[51] up to the moment when the monkey army led by Hanuman crosses the ocean to Langka (Ceylon). The story is continued on the Brahma temple, where the reliefs have unfortunately suffered extensive damage.

Although the reliefs of Prambanan have many stylistic affinities with those of the Barabudur, they are more dynamic in composition and more dramatic in mood. Here too an idealized naturalism derived from Indian art prevails. Nature—trees, rocks, waters—undergoes some decorative stylization, however, occasionally prefiguring the much stronger stylization that developed in the later art of East Java. Within the available space of the relief panels, the figures at Prambanan are of more generous proportions than those of the Barabudur; thus they give the impression of greater massiveness.

Plate 40. *Durga, north chamber of the Shiva Temple, Prambanan.*

Plate 41. *Group of dancers, relief on the outer wall of the balustrade, Shiva Temple, Prambanan.*

The scenes of the *Ramayana* sculptured at Prambanan are not "appearances" to contemplate, but high drama to witness and enjoy. The groupings, attitudes, and occasionally intense faces of the participants are all in expressive action. The servants and attendants or apprentices to hermit-priests, in their simple loincloths, are no mere adulating retinue; they appear to react to and comment upon the events that unfold before them. Their participation binds them closely to the richly adorned princes and princesses in high tiaras. Even the animals and birds sculptured in lively and loving fashion seem to take part in the events depicted. They add to the commotion; sometimes they are curious onlookers hidden in the foliage.

In contrast to the celestial blithesomeness that permeates many panels of the Barabudur, there is earthy humor at Prambanan. A good example is the great confusion during the rape of Sita, when an animal takes advantage of the contents of an overturned rice pot near a horrified servant girl, while another servant is accosted by a pet monkey. Instead of the detached inwardness of semidivine beings surrounded by piety and adoration, there is great vitality in the dramatic scenes. Exuberance, self-adulation, grace, and abandon emanate from the multitude of dancing figures on the balustrade's outer wall. In that high heavenly sphere there is not the stillness of meditating Bodhisattvas, but the activating power of exalted divine beings. In short, the plastic art of Java's two great monuments admirably reflects the systems of ideas and the moods attendant to Buddhism and Shivaism. The aspiration to ultimate stillness and merger with the Great Void of Nonbeing dominates at the Barabudur. At Prambanan everything speaks of generation of energies in the universe, the dynamism in the worlds of men and gods.

The sphere of the gods and its rich Indian imagery are rendered at Prambanan with both poetry and strength. An excellent example is the opening scene of the *Ramayana* relief series.* Here the god Vishnu is shown enthroned upon the world serpent Ananta, the Infinite. To his left a group of five figures in tiaras, including one priest, is seated. A large figure of an anthropomorphic, adoring Garuda, with a lotus flower in his hands, squats at Vishnu's feet to his right. The four-armed god reposes, his spoked sun disk and winged conch in two of his hands. His right elbow rests upon the head of the large serpent whose body coils upward around his knee. Beneath the serpent are waves from which large heads of fish and crabs protrude. The group of five, who may be supplicants entreating the god's help in combating the dangers posed by Rawana, King of Demons, slopes downward from the level of the god's elevation on a wavy mat. Everything floats in this sculptured scene.

In the background behind the squatting Garuda are cloudlike formations with some stylized foliage and rocks. In them a snake nestles, hypnotizing a bird; an animal that might be a weasel or lizard, two bushy-tailed rodents, and another small bird hide. And, playfully hidden within the configurations of this setting, another large head of a bird appears, echoing that of Garuda. The forms of the background are like those apparitions which we sometimes discern in the changing shapes of clouds. Animating nature by hiding some human, animal, or spirit forms in its elements was later developed to a much stronger degree in the art of East Java. Some of the older Balinese artists still take delight in this camouflage today, as if the atmosphere and the earth were inhabited by half-distinguishable apparitions. The strange owlish face that looks down from the foliage of a fruit tree at Rama, who is threatening a bird, is like an "invisible" grinning spook of whom the acting personage is unaware. In the same way, a

* It starts to the left of the main entrance and continues clockwise along the balustrade of the gallery.

Plate 42. *The rape of Sita, Ramayana relief, Shiva Temple, Prambanan.*

Plate 43. *Vishnu enthroned on the serpent Ananta, with adoring Garuda and supplicants: opening scene of the Ramayana reliefs, Shiva Temple, Prambanan.*

superciliously smiling "earth spirit" reclines under the kneeling demon-princess who meets Rama and Sita in a contemporary Balinese drawing. The spirit's forms merge with the stylized layers of the earth; in the right-hand lower corner a bird's head and that of a half-distinguishable small animal are also hidden. Camouflage of animals and occasional human figures also occurs in some recent wood carvings and batikked cloths skillfully made up of floral and foliage designs. This, however, is a circumvention of Islamic rules prohibiting the representation of living beings and is not the representation of spirits. Yet both fall into the general pattern of the Javanese predilection for "hidden meaning" (including chronograms) and for allusions, subtle metaphors, and puns.

The ideal of feminine beauty is perhaps best illustrated in the scene where captive Sita, attended by her devoted guardian and friend Tridjata, listens to Hanuman, who had found his way into Rawana's palace grounds in Langka. The white monkey, messenger of Rama, has emerged from his hiding-place and gives Rama's message to Sita. Seated on a pillow laid on a flower-strewn platform, her right arm resting on a rolled cushion, Sita gracefully leans her voluptuous, small-breasted body to one side. Her high tiara surrounded by a halo enhances the regal attitude of her slightly uplifted head, in contrast to the curly-headed Tridjata of the buta tribe (the monstrous subjects of Rawana) kneeling behind her. And the curve of the princess' left arm as it leans on her folded leg shows that a thousand years ago, just as today, the double-jointed elbow permitting the arm's inward curve was regarded as a sign of beauty and grace.

The reliefs of the *Ramayana* at Prambanan portray many intimate details from daily life. On the same panel with Rama and the bird (Pl. 44), large fruit hangs, looped by a cord to prevent its premature dropping. Suspended from a branch, there is a tray with red peppers hanging down for drying. In the scene of the rape of Sita (Pl. 42) we see near Rama's house in the woods a large water pot with a ladle and jug on the platform where food is stored, which testify to the antiquity of the style of pottery sold today in Java's market places. Vegetation is specific; a banana tree is in bloom near Rama's house, as it might bloom in any contemporary village courtyard. Birds, small rodents, and

Plate 44. *Rama threatens a bird who stole offerin gs, Ramayana relief, Shiva Temple, Prambanan.*

a monkey further enliven an already active scene. There is not a single panel in which the participating figures are isolated from their natural or man-made environment, a feature which continues in most narrative reliefs on the tjandi of later periods as well. Thus not only were themes and forms of Indian inspiration put into an Indonesian setting, but the whole representation was imbued with the Indonesian feeling of man's inseparability from nature.

The vividness of the sculptured version of the *Ramayana* at Prambanan may perhaps be taken as corroborative evidence that the epic had been translated into Old Javanese before the construction of the temple and was thus accessible as a guide for the Indonesian sculptors, even if it had been transmitted only orally. The depiction of the *Ramayana* on the Shiva temple of Prambanan would have been particularly appropriate if indeed King Balitung had been deified there and if, as suggested by Poerbatjaraka and supported by De Casparis, the translation of the epic had been made during his reign (898–910).[52] The dramatic stances of the heroes as well as the groupings of their satellites are echoed today in Java's classical dance drama (pp. 161–163 below), but otherwise the continuity has been broken. With almost as much suddenness as it had appeared, the "classical" style of sculpture vanished from Java, Bali, and Sumatra[53] sometime after the end of the tenth century.

Ironically, as always, the price paid by the village population for these religious works must have been enormous. Compulsory labor or taxation in labor for the building of temples must have been required of peasants already burdened with communal obligations for irrigation, road-building, and forest-clearance projects. It has even been surmised that the decline of classical Hindu-Javanese culture in Central Java after the tenth century was due in large part to the excessive labor demands for these vast building projects.[54] "Central Javanese royal culture was destroyed by its own temples," says Schrieke in concluding his essay, "The End of Classical Hindu-Javanese Culture in Central Java."[55]

In conclusion, one may ask what transformation Indian art had undergone in Java during this initial period of Indian cultural penetration. Use of the term "classical" for this period of Java's art history is based on the Javanese stylistic similarity to the highly developed art that flourished in India between the fourth and ninth centuries A.D. There are indeed striking examples of the nearly identical resemblance of Javanese works of art to some northeast Indian Buddhist art which was produced during the reign of the Gupta and Pala dynasties (for example, Sarnath, Nalanda). Similarly, there are close affinities between the Shivaite art of Java and that which flourished in south and southeast India under the Pallava and Chalukya dynasties (for example, at Aihole, Badami, Pattadakal, and Mamallapuram). But also in northwest India, in the cave-temples of Ajanta, Elura, and Elephanta,[56] one finds images which could have served as models for the sculptors of Java's sanctuaries. Representations of the Buddha on the Barabudur reliefs, for example, have strong affinities with Buddha figures in an Ajanta cave of 500–550. The marvelous seventh- and eighth-century representations of Shiva's cosmic dance at Elura and Elephanta have less magnificent but nonetheless very beautiful counterparts in the two-armed celestial dancers on the walls of the Shiva temple at Prambanan. No image of Shiva himself as Lord of the Dance appears at Prambanan or at any other of Java's sanctuaries. This may be significant for discerning differences between the worship of this deity in India and Indonesia. Strangely, the face of a door-guardian in the eighth-century Shiva Temple at Elephanta[57] brings to mind the face of the Bodhisattva Lokeshvara at Mendut. Numerous other examples could be cited. Yet, despite the very strong similarities in individual cases, despite the correspondences in symbolism, forms, and details (as in the dress and ornaments of sculptured figures, in the profilations of the architecture, in the shapes of pilasters and niches, or in floral designs), Java's sanctuaries are essentially Indonesian creations without exact counterparts anywhere in India.[58] From the Javanese sanctuaries, together with their sculptures, a vastly different world feeling emanates than from those in the land where their forms originated.

Plate 45. *"Rama and Sita encounter Rawana's Sister Surpanakha," ink drawing by G. Nj. Lempad, Ubud, Bali, 1956.*

The classical art of Central Java is understandably more homogeneous than that of India of the same and preceding centuries, since it was not scattered geographically over a vast subcontinent and did not result from a long historical evolution. It has been said that in India "nothing is destroyed and everything preserved." Thus, changing and overlapping art styles evolved over a long time span of intense, all-pervading religious life, and the accumulation of art works from different centuries at one sacred site creates the impression of turbulent diversity. Indonesia was able to pluck, as it were, the finest crystallized Indian forms without undergoing the pains of their birth and subsequent evolution.

A greater sense of order and harmony reigns in the Indian-inspired art of Java. True, there were no rugged natural rock walls in Java's plains, where the centers of power and cultural life had arisen, to stimulate the sculptors' limitless evocation of hosts of beings crowding on different levels and in varying depths, emerging at corners or half-vanishing in clefts, as on the rock walls of Mamallapuram or in the cave temples of northwest India. In Indonesia the carefully fitted, even tjandi walls functioned as the sides of the symbolic mountain. The reliefs were carved into well-proportioned framed stone bands or panels which engirdled the high base or the elevated body of the structure; they were composed to follow the curve of a stairway's wings. Images were neatly set into symmetrically distributed niches and chambers. Thus great harmony prevailed between the architecture of the temple and its adornments. Rich as the reliefs and other ornamentation of a Javanese tjandi may be, they never submerge, overwhelm, and suffocate a structure or its surface by boundless proliferation, alternation in proportions, and agglomerations of shapes as they do at

Plate 46. *Hanuman delivers Rama's message to captive Sita, Ramayana relief, Shiva Temple, Prambanan.*

some Indian sanctuaries. Everywhere their domains are delimited; they are distributed so as to enhance the architecture but not to overgrow it like jungle vegetation. Nor does one find in Indonesia the torrential force, the almost volcanic avalanche of imagery of India, perhaps epitomized by the "Descent of the Ganges" carved on a rock wall at Mamallapuram. Paradoxically, in the island of volcanoes, where erupting craters can send streams of glowing lava rolling down a slope with boulders, stones, and pebbles joining their thundering course, no elemental sweep of free-playing shapes appears in the plastic arts. No impassioned chaos is permitted or expressed. Within the demarcated framework of the relief panels, the proportions of human figures are kept in mutual balance, without extreme contrasts in size. In India, however, one finds the free intermingling of greatly varying sizes in statues or figures in high relief.

The basic idea that size reflects status certainly penetrated Indonesia also, but nothing comparable to the assemblages of sculptured beings of the seventh-century Ramashvara Temple at Elura,[59] for example, can be found in the art of Central Java. Order and harmony are achieved by using lesser images to flank a large central image symmetrically, as in the chapel of Tjandi Mendut. There the grouping of a large seated Buddha image flanked by smaller figures of two Bodhisattvas forms a well-balanced harmonious whole. Another solution to problems of harmony is to place the figure of higher status on a higher level, as on the relief panel at Prambanan, where Vishnu, enthroned on the serpent Ananta, is placed above his supplicants and Garuda.*

Another aspect which removes an Indian quality from Java's art is the absence of the ultra feminine forms and the cosmic sexuality that pervade much of Indian art. As in other lands of Southeast Asia inhabited by peoples of delicate build, the sculptors of Indonesia did not imitate the ideal Indian forms for female figures. If any doubts still linger as to whether the sculptors were Indonesians rather than Indians, this may help dispel them. The women of Indonesia have much narrower hips than do Indian women. With very few exceptions, Indonesian sculptors did not carve broadly curving hips that branch into long and heavy thighs under a very slender waist which, like a slim stem, supports the heavy fruit of round, laterally swelling, high-set breasts. One will also look in vain among Java's stone sculptures for deities uniting with their shakti or for celestial lovers in voluptuous embrace.[60] Unless every trace of such representations has been destroyed, it would seem that the old stress on potency, fertility, and vital power found full expression in the symbolism of Shiva's linga. Creativity epitomized in the sexual act, or sexuality conceived as an elemental force tending toward union, does not flow through Indonesian art as through Indian, although sensuousness is not lacking.

The same shastra that had guided Indian architects and sculptors must have been followed just as carefully, or perhaps even more carefully, in Indonesia. From these manuals the Indonesian builders learned many principles which determined the plans, techniques, and orientation of sanctuaries as well as the forms and placement of images. But neither the emergence of India's sublime masterpieces of deeply contained power, nor the overwhelming exuberance of its art, nor the mystery of its elemental frenzy can be ascribed to these manuals alone. Nor could the treatises prevent Indonesia's transformation of temples for the worship of living gods into tomb-monuments for deceased kings. It could not be foreseen in the shastra that a sense of humor would creep into representations on temple walls, or that cozy, familiar details like pots with ladles, or storage of food, or the planting of a banana tree would be among the self-evident preoccupations of Rama, Sita, and Lakshmana in their forest exile.

In general it would seem as if, in the warm humidity of the fertile tropical island, its lithe and sensitive people had softened India's imagery, mellowed its turbulence and impassioned power, and evolved a new and gentler harmony, with different physical proportions and other psychological dimensions. Man is rarely isolated from his natural environment which is lovingly depicted. It is said that while visiting Indonesia in 1927, Rabindranath Tagore once exclaimed: "I see India everywhere, but I do not recognize it."

Central Javanese art of the second half of the first millennium of our era shows a strong sense of—or strong desire for—a well-ordered, balanced, harmonious world. Its cosmic hierarchy culminates on the central peak of the World Mountain, where the highest

* It should be observed that in the typology of the Javanese shadow play, puppets representing the highest deities are smaller than those of the noble heroes, who in turn are smaller than their opponents. The largest puppets are those of the demons.

Hindu deities dwell, where the highest stage of Buddhist salvation is attained, or where on earth the highest king dwells in his palace. The World Mountain, with its various spheres derived from Indian sacred lore and imagery, is a guide for orientation in the universe. Everything that exists moves around it on various levels, as do the deities in their niches and the stories of gods, men, and animals on the reliefs around the base and walls of the tjandi-temples.

Not a trace of these ancient Indian-inspired forms and their mood can be found in Java's modern plastic arts, even though the conceptions from which they sprang are still a living force there, and Indian myths still animate the traditional stage of Java as well as Bali.

Notes

1. Summarized by G. Coedès in "Le Substrat Autochtone et la Superstructure Indienne au Cambodge et à Java," *Cahiers d'Histoire Mondiale,* I (1953), 368–377.

2. J. C. van Leur, *Indonesian Trade and Society* (The Hague, 1955), pp. 103–104.

3. N. J. Krom, "De Oudste Rijken (Eerste Tot Zesde Eeuw)," Ch. II of F. W. Stapel, ed., *Geschiedenis van Nederlandsch Indië* (Amsterdam, 1938), I, 124.

4. G. Coedès, "L'Osmose Indienne en Indochine et en Indonésie," *Cahiers d'Histoire Mondiale,* I (1954), 827–838.

5. For a fuller appreciation of the symbolic meaning of kingship in Indonesia's past, see Robert Heine-Geldern, *Conceptions of State and Kingship in Southeast Asia,* revised version (Cornell University Southeast Asia Program Data Paper no. 18; Ithaca, N.Y., 1956), and Coedès, "Le Culte de la Royauté Divinisée, Source d'Inspiration des Grands Monuments du Cambodge Ancien," *Instituto Italiano per il Medio ed Estremo Oriente, Serie Orientale Roma,* V (1952), 1–23.

6. See P. H. Pott, "Le Bouddhisme de Java et l'Ancienne Civilisation Javanaise," *Instituto Italiano per il Medio ed Estremo Oriente, Serie Orientale Roma,* V (1952), 109–156.

7. Dr. R. Soekmono, Director of the Indonesian Archaeological Service, in a paper entitled "Geomorphology and the Location of Çrivijaya," presented to the 9th Pacific Science Congress held in Bangkok in 1957, advanced a carefully reasoned theory that Srivijaya could have been situated in the region of present-day Djambi, along the coast northeast of Palembang. See his article, bearing the above title, in *Madjalah Ilmu-Ilmu Sastra Indonesia* (Indonesian Journal of Cultural Studies), I (1963), 79–92 (with sketch map).

8. G. Coedès, *Les Etats Hindouisés d'Indochine et d'Indonésie* (Paris, 1964), pp. 154–155.

9. See A. J. Bernet Kempers, "The Bronzes of Nalanda and Hindu-Javanese Art," *BKI,* XC (1933), 1–88; 33 illus.

10. See among others, J. G. de Casparis, "Bijdrage tot de Chronologie der Çailendra Vorsten op Java," in his *Prasasti Indonesia,* I: *Inscripties uit de Çailendra-Tijd* (Bandung, 1950), pp. 96–133; Coedès, *Les Etats Hindouisés* (1964); and O. W. Wolters, *Early Indonesian Commerce; a Study of the Origins of Śrīvijaya* (Ithaca, N.Y., 1966).

11. See Bernet Kempers, *Ancient Indonesian Art* (Amsterdam, 1959), p. 49, for the possibility that the present ruin may be of a later date than the original temple.

12. Quoted, in Dutch, by W. F. Stutterheim in *Het Hinduisme in de Archipel* (Groningen, 1951), pp. 27–28, and translated into English by the author. The interpretation of this inscription has met with considerable difficulties, hence the awkward placement in the translation of the words "had persuaded." The current assumption is that two rulers are involved: a (Buddhist) Shailendra suzerain (Çri Mahārājā) and a Shivaite vassal whom the former persuaded (through his priests) to build the sanctuary at Kalasan. See de Casparis, "Inscripties uit de Çailendra-Tijd" in *Prasasti Indonesia,* I, 100. Another record of interest with regard to the role of priests is an inscription from Ratu Baka which deals with the construction of a monastery. See de Casparis, "New Evidence on Cultural Relations between Java and Ceylon in Ancient Times," *Artibus Asiae,* XXIV (1961), 241–248.

13. Translated from the Sanskrit by P. K. Archarya (London, 1933), IV, 641.

14. De Casparis, *Prasasti Indonesia,* I, 65. De Casparis is not certain whether the Sanskrit term *sthapaka* here denotes a builder or a sculptor (p. 68, ft. 18) since, according to him, the general sense of the word is *erector,* and since the next sentence of the charter refers to an image: "They are making the statue of the divine King at the northern side of the *prasada* Sang Hyang Wintang. . . ."

15. *Ibid.,* pp. 86, 91, 94, fig. 12.

16. De Casparis, *Prasasti Indonesia,* II (Bandung, 1956), 239.

17. Krom, *Inleiding tot de Hindoe-Javaansche Kunst* (The Hague, 1923), I, 142–143.

18. See Stutterheim, "The Meaning of the Hindu-Javanese Candi," *Journal of the American Oriental Society,* LI (1931), 1–15.

19. There are fine examples of such metal objects in the museum at Djakarta. See also Stutterheim, "De Oudheden-Collectie van Z. H. Mangkoenagoro VII Te Soerakarta," *Djawa,* XVII (1937), 1–111, 60 pl. See also the description of the Collection Resink-Wilkens, in Stutterheim, "De Oudheden-collectie Resink-Wilkens," *Djawa,* XIV (1934), 167–197, pls.

20. De Casparis, *Prasasti,* I, 160–192.

21. N. J. Krom and Th. van Erp, *Beschrijving van Barabudur* (The Hague, 1920–1931), 2 vols., 692 pls. in 3 portfolios.

22. Stutterheim, "Chandi Barabudur, Name, Form and Meaning," in his *Studies in Indonesian Archaeology* (The Hague, 1956), pp. 3–62. (Translation of edition published in 1929 in Batavia.)

23. See also Paul Mus, *Barabudur; Esquisse d'une Histoire du Bouddhisme Fondée sur la Critique archéologique des Textes* (Hanoi, 1935).

24. *Prasasti Indonesia,* I, 199–204.

25. *Ibid.,* p. 204.

26. *Ibid.,* pp. 202–203, English summary.

27. *Ibid.,* pp. 175, 182.

28. Since this has been written, an *Antara* despatch published in the Djakarta newspaper *Berita Yudha* (August 30,

1965) indicates, presumably because some new fragments of the A.D. 824 inscription had been unearthed, that the name of the Barabudur's architect was Gunadharma and also claims that the monument's construction was completed in 17 years.

29. *Beschrijving van Barabudur,* II, 39. Cited in "The End of Classical Hindu-Javanese Culture in Central Java," *Indonesian Sociological Studies, Selected Writings of B. Schrieke,* II (The Hague, 1957), 298–299.

30. Cited in *ibid.*, p. 406, n.17.

31. F. D. K. Bosch, *The Golden Germ* (The Hague, 1960), 140–148, and E. B. Vogler, *De Monsterkop in het Omlijstingsornament van Tempeldoorgangen en -nissen in de Hindoe-Javaanse Bouwkunst* (Leiden, 1949), 35 illus.

32. Cf. Bernet Kempers, pls. 75–76.

33. For a more detailed description of the Buddhas and Boddhisattvas from the Barabudur, their distribution and symbolism, see Bernet Kempers, *Ancient Indonesian Art,* 43–45.

34. As identified by Krom, these texts are the *Lalitavistara* (story of the historical Buddha), the *Gandavyuha* (story of Prince Sudhana, a Bodhisattva), and stories known as *Jatakamala* and *Avadana.* These appear on the reliefs of the first gallery. On the second, the *Gandavyuha* is resumed, as are Jataka stories. The texts followed on the third and fourth galleries are not identified, although some of the exalted figures of Bodhisattvas and Buddhas represented on the reliefs are. See discussion in Krom, *Inleiding tot de Hindoe-Javaansche Kunst,* I, 366–387.

35. J. Ph. Vogel, *The Relation Between the Art of India and Java* (London, 1925), p. 31.

36. *Rama Legenden und Rama Reliefs in Indonesian* (Munchen, 1925), I, 215. Passage translated by the author. Cf. A. Malraux, *The Voices of Silence* (New York, 1953), pp. 131–273, "The Metamorphoses of Apollo."

37. See Bernet Kempers, pl. 70.

38. See Bernet Kempers, pls. 58–61.

39. See Bernet Kempers, pl. 136.

40. De Casparis, "Short Inscriptions from Tjandi Plaosan-Lor," *Bulletin of the Archaeological Service of the Republic of Indonesia,* no. 4 (1958), p. 20.

41. De Casparis, *Prasasti Indonesia,* II, 175–206.

42. *Ibid.*, p. 182.

43. Stutterheim, *Het Hinduisme,* p. 26.

44. Krom, *Inleiding tot de Hindoe-Javaansche Kunst,* I, 165–168.

45. See Vogel, *Relation between the Art of India and Java,* pp. 34–35, and H. Zimmer, *The Art of Indian Asia* (New York, 1955), I, 275–276.

46. See Bernet Kempers, pls. 25–29.

47. For this possibility, see de Casparis, "A Metrical Old-Javanese Inscription dated 856 A.D.," *Prasasti Indonesia,* II, 280–330. Yet he believes that further evidence is still needed to refute the previously accepted dating.

48. For a detailed discussion of these possibilities, see de Casparis, "Three Sanskrit Inscriptions from the Ratubaka Plateau," *Prasasti Indonesia,* II, 244–279.

49. Quotations are extracted from de Casparis' translation, "A Metrical Old-Javanese Inscription," pp. 316–330.

50. See Bernet Kempers, pls. 157–158.

51. For excellent reproductions of the reliefs, see Stutterheim, *Rama Legenden,* II.

52. See de Casparis, *Prasasti Indonesia,* II, 287.

53. For a discussion of Indian influence in Old Balinese art, see Stutterheim, *Indian Influences in Old-Balinese Art* (London, 1935); for a summary of Hinduistic art in Sumatra, see R. Heine-Geldern, "The Archaeology and Art of Sumatra," pp. 322–327, in E. M. Loeb, *Sumatra, Its History and People* (Vienna, 1935).

54. Schrieke, "The End of Classical Hindu-Javanese Culture," *Indonesian Sociological Studies,* II, 285–301.

55. *Ibid.*, p. 301.

56. See Zimmer, *The Art of Indian Asia,* II, esp. pls. 113, 141, 178, 231–232, 260–262, 299–304, which show Indian sanctuaries and sculptures mentioned on this and the following pages.

57. Zimmer, II, pls. 262–263.

58. See Krom, *Inleiding,* I, 127–142, for a detailed discussion of the question of the derivation of Java's Indianized art.

59. See pls. 227–234 in Zimmer.

60. Only one case of such an image has been reported, but the sculpture seems to have vanished. See de Casparis, *Prasasti Indonesia,* II, 269.

CHAPTER 3

The Emergence of New Styles

EAST JAVA AND BALI

TENTH CENTURY TO FIFTEENTH CENTURY

TOWARD THE END of the tenth century a new center of political power arose in East Java, and the history of Central Java receded into an uncertain background. With this shift to the east, a new chapter in Indonesia's cultural history began, the so-called East Javanese period, marked by the emergence of new trends in the art styles of Java in interaction with those of neighboring Bali.

Legend, corroborating historical fact, has contributed to the reconstruction of the East Javanese era as a dynamic and turbulent period. A number of large and small kingdoms vied for power. Victorious kings expanded their dominance and subjected lesser kings to vassalage. Dynastic intrigues and wars of succession led to the destruction of a palace in one place and the establishment of another palace-city elsewhere. Repeatedly, extended realms would be consolidated, only to be partitioned again or to fall apart under the pressures of rebellious vassals.

The principal kingdoms which rose to power were, in chronological order: (1) a kingdom of unknown name established by Sindok (r. 929–947), which, after having been ruled by several successors, was expanded and consolidated by the famous prince of Balinese origin, Airlangga (r. 1019–1047). Shortly before his death, Airlangga partitioned his kingdom; (2) the kingdom of Kediri (or Daha, 1045–1222); (3) the kingdom of Singasari (or Tumapel, 1222–1292); and (4) the kingdom of Majapahit (1294–1478?), which was the last of the Hinduistic Javanese realms. It may have lingered on up to the second decade of the sixteenth century. At its peak, Majapahit claimed suzerainty over most of the archipelago and beyond.

The process of East Java's Hinduization had begun much earlier than the tenth century, however. An inscription of 760 found at Dinaya (a place north of present-day Malang) refers to a king Gajayana who was "a benefactor of Brahmans, worshiper of Agastya."* The inscription says that Gajayana had erected a "lovely sanctuary for the Great Seer" with the help of citizens and a number of notables. Among the king's gifts to the sanctuary were land, cattle, slaves, materials necessary for offerings, a house for the Brahmans who were in charge of worship, and a guest house stocked with food and other necessities.[1] It is possible that the sanctuary discovered in the vicinity of Malang and known as Tjandi Badud, is the shrine to Agastya mentioned in the Dinaya inscription. The style of this structure, or what remains of it, corresponds to that of contemporaneous Central Javanese tjandi. It has even been suggested that the Shaiva rulers of Mataram were dynastically related to an East Javanese lineage, and that in a sense Sindok's kingdom was a "return" to East Java.

Starting with the end of the tenth century, the history of Java's neighbor island Bali became closely linked with that of East Java. Although knowledge of Bali's history is still dim, it is known that a royal dynasty, the Varmadewa, reigned there between the tenth and twelfth centuries.[2] Their seat of power may have been in the vicinity of the present-day villages of Pedjeng and Bedhulu in the south of the island. One of the Varmadewa kings, Udayana (r. 989–1001) married an East Javanese princess, the mother of Air-

* A seer-sage venerated in South India.

langga (*c.* 991–1049). In his youth Airlangga entered service with his father-in-law and later became one of East Java's great rulers. His younger brother governed Bali, possibly in Airlangga's name. Following Airlangga's death, Bali's kings regained independence. In 1284, however, the island was temporarily subjugated by Krtanagara, last king of Singasari, and in 1343 it finally became a dependency of Majapahit. Thereafter Bali was ruled by Javanese princes, vassals of Majapahit, who first made Gelgel their capital and later Klungkung. To the present the Klungkung dynasty, descended from Majapahit viceroys, retains the highest status among Bali's ruling houses, of which there are several (such as those of Karangasem, Gianjar, Tabanan in the south, Buleleng in the north, Djembrana in the west). While Bali's culture on the one hand had been heavily influenced by that of East Java, on the other hand the descendants of the Javanese viceroys were in time thoroughly "Balinized," as were the traditions and art forms their predecessors may have introduced from East Java.

During the six centuries of East Java's ascendancy, violent upheavals notwithstanding, there were protracted periods of relatively peaceful and continuous reign by both female and male sovereigns. Several of the East Javanese kings were distinguished by their statesmanship; some were known for their patronage of the arts.

Literature written in old Javanese, *kawi,* flourished at some of the courts. There is no doubt that the development of this literature exercised an important influence on the visual arts, supplying themes, visions, certain poetic moods, and perhaps even distinct styles. The literature included both transpositions of Sanskrit texts into Javanese prose or verse and new, original compositions. There were translations of purely religious texts, such as prayers (*mantra*), manuals in various fields of knowledge (*shastra*), and explanations of dogma (*tutur*). Prose transpositions of the *Mahabharata* (*parwan*) and Javanese poems in Sanskrit meters (*kakawin*) were more relevant for the development of the visual arts. Two important kakawin, derived from the *Mahabharata,* were the *Ardjuna Wiwaha* (Ardjuna's Wedding),* composed by Mpu Kanwa in 1030, and the *Bharatayuddha* (The War of the Bharatas), composed by Mpu Sedah in 1157. The latter deals with the climactic battles between the Pandawa and the Kaurawa.* These and a number of other long poems (such as the *Smaradhana, Krishnayana, Garudeya, Sudamala*) all inspired narrative reliefs on the walls of East Javanese tjandi. The Buddhist tales and animal fables (*Jataka*), earlier depicted on the reliefs of the Barabudur, were now more widely disseminated in their Javanese *tantri* version.

In the latter part of the East Javanese period, poems based on historical events and composed in Javanese meters (*kidung*) similarly became a source of inspiration for pictorial art in subsequent centuries. One of these, the tragic *Kidung Sunda,*† describes the fate of the King of Sunda who, in a fleet of festive vessels, brought his daughter from his domain in West Java to Majapahit for her proposed marriage to Majapahit's king. But instead of a glorious wedding there was a bloodbath: the king and his retinue were treacherously murdered and the princess committed suicide. A plot to annex Sunda had precipitated these events.[3]

Among the many other legends and romances set in old East Javanese kingdoms are included the story of *Tjalon Arang,*‡ the witch said to have been active during Airlangga's reign and whose destructive black magic had to be counteracted by the white magic of the holy seer, Mpu Bharada;[4] the romance of *Pandji,* laid in the period of Kediri, whose beautiful bride was stolen on the eve of their wedding; and the adventures of Damar Wulan, a youth of radiant beauty, prince by birth, but employed as a grass-cutter at the court of Majapahit, who, after many encounters with love and death, wins the hand of the maiden queen and thereby the kingdom.§ These tales have become embedded in the pictorial and dramatic arts of Java and Bali.

Finally we must mention the *Nagarakrtagama,*[5] a long panegyrical poem in which the court poet, Prapancha, glorifies the reign of King Rajasanagara, known as Hayam Wuruk (1350–1389). It is important for its historical value rather than for its influence upon the arts. The poetic descriptions of the *Nagarakrtagama* give an idea of the physical appearance of Majapahit's keraton (palace).[6] Despite the inevitable superlatives of the court poet, a vivid impression is conveyed of important ritual celebrations with their attendant entertainments for the people, of the detailed proceedings

* See synopsis in Appendix I.

* See Appendix I.
† See Appendix II.
‡ See Appendix II.
§ Synopses given in Appendix I.

at such rituals, of their participants, of the kind of spectacles that followed, and of the principal performers, who included royalty. These impressions become all the more lively if one has had some acquaintance both with court life in twentieth-century, prerevolutionary Central Java and also with ritual festivities in Bali.

During the six centuries of East Java's ascendancy, its religious life was marked by growing syncretism. Shivaite and Buddhist cults overlapped and fused, both strongly tinged by Tantric conceptions and practices, which aimed at deliverance by magic means. The Tantric Kala-Chakra sect has been identified as the source of strong influences during the Singasari period, especially during the reign of its last king, Krtanagara. Kings of that dynasty were deified in either Shivaite or Buddhist form, but sometimes in both. King Vishnuvardhana, for example, was deified as Shiva in Tjandi Mleri and as the Bodhisattva Amoghapasha at Tjandi Djago. Krtanagara was deified at Tjandi Djawi as "Shiva-Buddha." The fused religious systems, reaching down from the courts into village communities, were diluted still more if not overwhelmed altogether by old Indonesian beliefs and magic practices.

A similar process took place in Bali.[7] There the first traces of Buddhism date from the eighth century, perhaps introduced directly from India by missionary monks. In the following centuries, however, Buddhism appears to have been absorbed by Brahmanism, which here as in Java and other parts of Asia was infused with Tantric aspects. The old Balinese deities, the venerated gods of the mountains, the sea, and the lakes, joined the great Hindu-Buddhist pantheon, sometimes merging with the Indian gods. India's sun-god Surya, for example, became associated with Bali's sacred mountain, the Gunung Agung. A high ornate stone throne—a more elaborate version of the megalithic ancestral seat—stands empty in Balinese temples, in readiness for the sun-god when he is invoked to descend for offerings and celebrations; the back of this throne is always oriented toward the mountain. Thus the present syncretic Balinese religion came into being. Although there are still two kinds of high priests (*pedanda*) in Bali today—the *pedanda Bodha* and the *pedanda Shiva*—they both officiate at the same temples, sometimes simultaneously. The distinction between them is based more on the traditional adherence to them by certain families or on their external accessories and prayer texts rather than on substantive doctrine.

TABLE 2

Principal Antiquities in East Java

Tjandi or Other Antiquity	Religious Orientation	Century	Commemoration
Djalatunda (1)*	Shivaite	10th	?
Selamangleng (Tulung Agung) (2)	Buddhist	10th–11th	Cave-hermitage
Selamangleng (Kediri) (3)	Buddhist	10th–11th	Cave-hermitage
Belahan (4)	Vishnuite	11th	King Airlangga
Kidal (5)	Shivaite	13th	King Anushapati, 2nd king of Singasari
Djago (6)	Buddhist	13th	King Vishnuvardhana, 4th king of Singasari
Bara (7)	Shivaite	13th	(A giant image of a Ganesha)
Singhasari (8)	Shivaite-Buddhist	13th–14th	King Krtanagara, last king of Singasari
Djawi (9)	Shivaite-Buddhist	13th–14th	King Krtanagara, last king of Singasari
Sumberdjati (Simping) (10)	Shivaite	14th	King Krtarajasa, first king of Majapahit
Pantaran (11)	Shivaite	14th	State temple of Majapahit?
Surawana (12)	Shivaite	14th	A prince of Wengker
Tigawangi (13)	Shivaite	14th	Prince Matahun
Kedaton (14)	Shivaite	14th	?
Trawulan Museum (15)	—	14th–15th	(Majapahit art)
Selakelir and sanctuaries on Mt. Penanggungan (16)	Tantric-Shivaite	14th–15th	?

* Numbers in parentheses refer to the sites in Map 2.

The cult of kings existed in Bali too, but the nine tjandi found at Gunung Kawi (near Tampaksiring) are all deep façades hewn into a solid rock wall rather than free-standing structures enclosing one or more chambers.[8] The latest known posthumous images of

Balinese kings and queens date from the beginning of the fourteenth century. Thereafter Bali's subjugation by Majapahit may have precluded the deification ritual which was perhaps appropriate only for sovereigns.

Bali's walled temple courts, their gates, their stately meru—pagodalike structures built on high stone bases with thickly thatched pyramidally superposed roofs—their numerous shrines and balai (open pavilions for ritual purposes) provide a living picture of similar temples which existed in East Java and were made largely of temporary materials. There are depictions of such temple complexes on bas-reliefs of some of East Java's tjandi. In a relief on Tjandi Surawana (Pl. 60), for example, a meru can be clearly seen in the upper right, and a gate, whether to a temple or palace grounds, is visible at the far left. The remains of solid stone or

Map 2. *Sites of principal antiquities in East Java* (▲).

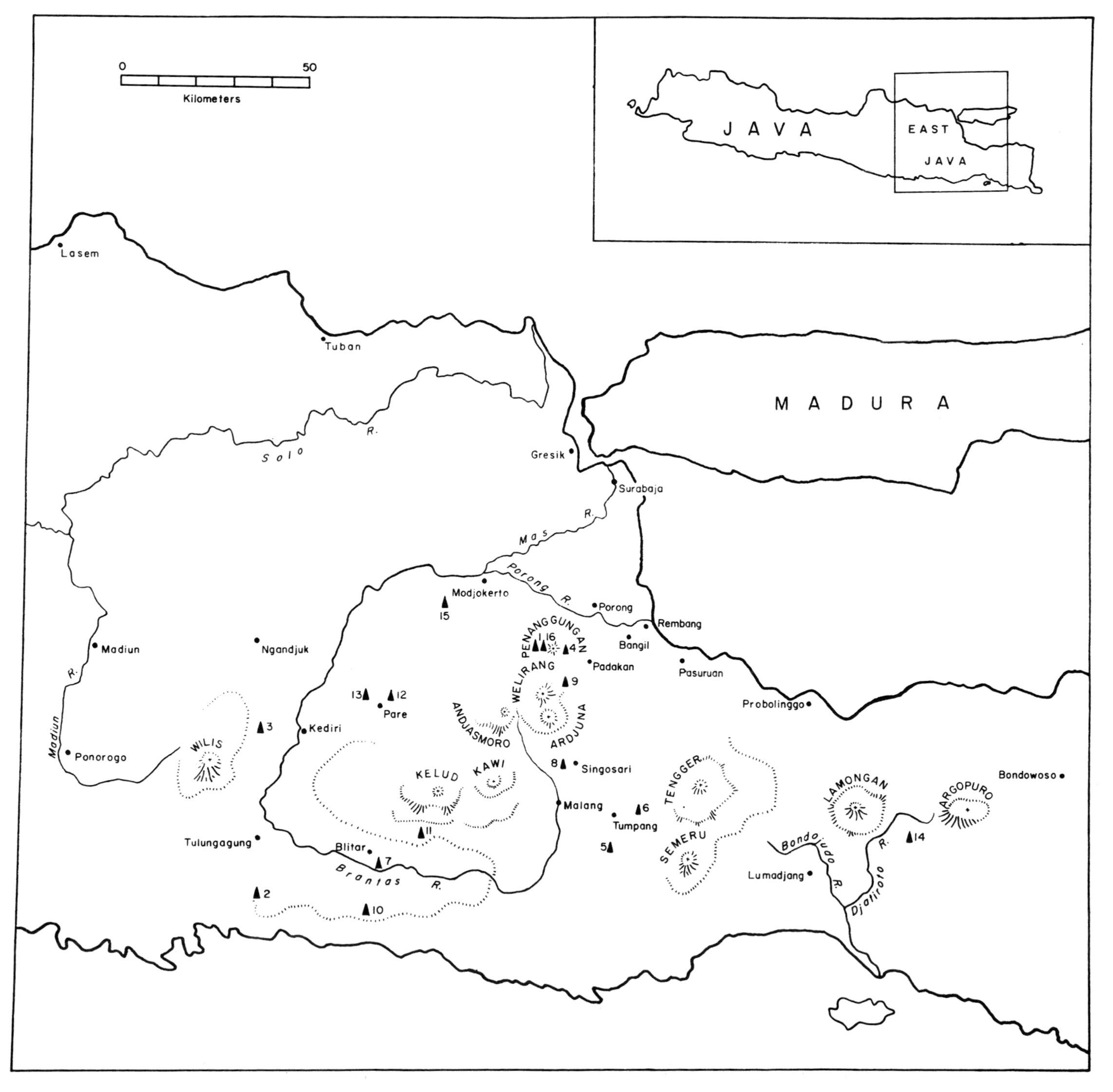

Plate 47. *Brick gate called* Badjang Ratu *near Trawulan, East Java, 14th century.*

brick structures in East Java consist primarily of funerary temples (tjandi), hermitages, sacred bathing places, and the gates and walls of vanished temples and palaces. In the fourteenth century, the author of the *Nagarakrtagama* listed 242 religious domains which during his time belonged to Majapahit's royal family and to different religious communities. According to Bosch, who compiled a statistical review of these domains on the basis of cantos 73–78 of the poem,[9] 27 of these domains were *dharma haji*—sacred ancestral grounds with royal funerary temples on them; and 215 were *dharma lepas,* or free domains. Of the latter, 43 were granted to Shivaite and 43 to Buddhist clergy; 50 to Buddhist lay orders; 7 to Brahmanic anchorites; 55 to a number of Shivaite, Buddhist, and Brahmanic sects; and 17 to Vishnuites. This list reveals the richness and variety of religious life in fourteenth-century Java, though Bosch mustered it mainly to argue that only 12 per cent of the religious domains appertained to royal funerary temples. Too much stress, Bosch maintains, had been placed by scholars like Stutterheim on the ancestral royal cult in connection with sacred structures built of permanent materials. The religious communities, he argues, must have had sanctuaries for worshiping gods, not kings. These surely could also have been built of stone, and thus not all surviving stone monuments should be regarded as tjandi. Whatever the case may have been, it is peculiar that of the *surviving* templelike sanctuaries in East Java, the most important and numerous ones are royal funerary temples, many precisely those listed in the *Nagarakrtagama.* The only imposing example to the contrary, also cited by Bosch, is Tjandi Panataran (see pp. 85–87 below), regarded as Majapahit's state temple. There are certainly some other stone or brick structures which may have been dedicated to the worship of deities rather than deified kings. The argument is, however, not crucial to our theme; some day it may be resolved with greater clarity. Meanwhile we turn to the visible remains of East Java's principal monuments and art, to discover what transformations took place between the eleventh and sixteenth centuries. A sketch map and a list above (Table 2) indicate the most important sacred sites of this period.

None of East Java's sanctuaries approaches the grandiose scale of such Central Javanese monuments as the Barabudur or the Prambanan complex. Conceivably East Javanese kings did not have economic or labor resources as great as those of the Shailendra and the Shaiva rulers of Mataram. The most imposing of East Java's temple complexes is Tjandi Panataran, which is located in the vicinity of present-day Blitar. Numerous dates carved on the tjandi itself or found inscribed on stones in the immediate vicinity show that from 1197 at the latest until well into the fifteenth century this site had been the scene of construction, renovation, and expansion. Of the principal sanctuary only three terraces of the substructure now remain. These, however, are so rich in architectural conception and ornamentation that one indeed feels that this temple must once have reflected the might and glory of Majapahit at the peak of its power, the time when this main structure was probably built.

With the possible exception of Panataran, however, both the size of other East Javanese tjandi and the themes and styles of their sculptural representations suggest that the "psychological distance" between these sanctuaries and the people was not nearly as great as it had been in Central Java. A greater intimacy may also have developed between the people and the royal courts whose priests perhaps no longer included many Brahmans and Buddhist teachers from overseas. Sanskrit, although assiduously studied by religious scholars, vanished as the official and literary form of expression, with the poetic form of Old Javanese becoming the bridge between the sacrosanct and the profane. Javanese priests, local poets, architects, and artisans now provided the religious and esthetic norms.

The local taste found expression in the more elongated form of East Javanese stone architecture. Tjandi structures acquired narrower bodies and taller roofs in relation to their elevated bases when compared with Central Javanese tjandi. The proportions of gates changed correspondingly. Symmetrical plans were no longer as prevalent as they had been in the tjandi complexes of Central Java. At thirteenth-century Tjandi Djago,[10] the principal sanctuary stands at the rear of the highest terrace rather than in its center, and the total effect is suggestive more of a terraced mountain slope than of a mountain peak (Pl. 48). Similar constructions on actual mountain slopes are found at Mt. Penanggungan's fifteenth-century terraced altar sites.[11] Bali's most important temple, Besakih, on the slope of the island's highest volcano, the Gunung Agung, is built on the same principle.[12]

The narrative reliefs on East Java's tjandi walls are executed in styles heretofore unknown. Two main trends develop: on one hand, an idyllic depiction of scenes from tales like the *Ardjuna Wiwaha* or the Pandji cycle is presented with soft grace in an almost romantic mood. The forms of human beings are very delicate, with slender limbs and simple attire. Details in the landscape retain natural forms. On the other hand, a "wayang" genre develops, a style in which human and superhuman beings are depicted in almost two-dimensional manner, their highly stylized shapes approaching those of shadow-play puppets. Surrounding these figures, nature becomes increasingly stylized,

Plate 48. *Tjandi Djago, East Java, 13th century.*

Plate 49. *Sahasranika (right), departing with his love Mrgavati, is cursed by the nymph Tilottama (left), relief from Tjandi Djalatunda, East Java, late 10th century.*

providing a magical, supernatural setting. In addition to these two principal styles, there are reliefs which combine some features of both, or which stand apart through peculiarities in their proportions or through their treatment of decorative details.

Despite the varied inventions in architecture and in the art of relief work, no correspondingly drastic changes occur in the sculpture of mortuary statues of deified royalty. Although East Javanese posthumous images acquired some local heraldry, more individual facial features, and on occasion modified body proportions, they remained basically similar to the images of Central Java's deified kings. As a kingdom's power began to decline, the images became smaller in size and cruder in execution.* Bali's posthumous images were all relatively small in size and showed a native development of distinct styles and iconography.[13]

On the whole, the East Javanese period of Indonesian cultural history was marked neither by a "degeneration" of the island's earlier classical forms (a view held by some scholars in the past) nor by a "resurgence" of indigenous Indonesian conceptions (a view which has superseded the earlier one). The art styles of East Java were a creative response of its architects, sculptors, and designers to the cultural climate of their time.

* Although posthumous images presumably were usually made of stone, three small figures, now in the museum in Den Pasar, South Bali, suggest that they may also have been made in bronze.

Such are, in broad generalization, some of the features that characterize the arts of the East Javanese period. We have noted the influence of literature, the close relations between East Java and Bali, and the emergence of new architectural and sculptural forms resulting from a stronger "Indonesianization" of both the courts and the priesthood. Upon closer examination, however, one also finds that works of art created under each successive dynasty—the kingdoms of Sindok, Kediri, Singasari, and Majapahit—possess distinct stylistic idiosyncrasies by which they can be identified as belonging to one or another time and locality.

The oldest East Javanese sanctuary with pronounced originality in construction and style is Tjandi Djalatunda. This monument, combined with a bathing place, is hidden in the forest high up on the slope of the Bekel, a western peak of the Penanggungan. Consecrated thirty years after Sindok's death, in 977, it was the repository for the ashes of an unidentified royal personage.

The principal elements of Tjandi Djalatunda are a wall, 16 feet high, erected against the mountain slope; a rectangular basin (about 50 feet wide and 40 deep) at the foot of this wall; and an elevated square terrace which stands in the basin but is connected with the wall at the rear. On this terrace once stood on a pedestal a nine-fold linga—one massive cylindrical stone with rounded top rising in the middle of eight shorter lingas, of alternate heights, and all engirdled at the base by a serpent. A spring issuing from the rocks behind the wall was captured into conduits and made to spout from openings at the tops of the linga's nine rounded cylinders. From the linga-fountain the water fell first into a tank at the foot of its pedestal and from there into the basin below, spouting through orifices drilled into sixteen stone panels which crowned the terrace.[14] Adjoining the principal basin at either side are two small walled-in pools, one with a naga head and the other with a head of Garuda as spouts. The nine-fold linga is no longer *in situ* but may still stand near the government resthouse at Trawas, a mountain resort below Djalatunda, where the linga had once been hauled. Stutterheim observes that the shape of the linga echoes the formation of Mt. Penanggungan with its subsidiary eight peaks. Both the natural mountain and the nine-fold linga in turn echo the traditional nine-peaked World Mountain, the Mahameru, whose top, according to legend, fell off to become the Penanggungan. Mt. Penanggungan abounds in terraced sanctuaries, hermitages, altars, and tjandi.

The Djalatunda site is now in ruins. The central linga has been hauled away; no trace has been found of the image that may have stood high up against the rear wall as the remnants of a round halo there now suggest. Of the original sixteen carved stone panels which crowned the terrace and functioned as spouts, three have disappeared completely, and the remaining thirteen, all heavily damaged, are scattered—a few still at Djalatunda, others in the Museum of Djakarta. Once, however, this sacred site with its waterworks softly murmuring in the stillness of the forest must have been an enchanting sight.

Despite their damaged and willfully mutilated state, the reliefs carved on the outside of the spout panels still offer much of interest. Bosch, with much ingenuity and erudition, has succeeded in reconstructing their meaning; he concludes that these reliefs depict incidents from the lives of leading members of the Pandawa lineage of the *Mahabharata,* over a span of nine or ten generations. Bosch found that the scenes depicted on these reliefs correspond to certain episodes described in the *Adiparwa* (the "prehistory" of the *Mahabharata*) and in a collection of tales called *Kathasaritsagara.* He lists the Pandawa on the reliefs, in genealogically descending order, as Palasara, Vyasa (probably), Pandu, Ardjuna, Abimanyu, Parikshit, Djanameya, possibly another intervening but unknown person, Sahasranika, and Udayana. Thus the line starts with Ardjuna's great-grandfather and ends with his grandson's (Parikshit) great-grandson, or even great-great-grandson. Whoever the prince commemorated at Djalatunda may have been, the reliefs seem to allude to his descent from the Pandawa lineage, and symbolize the presence of his ancestors who sanctify his tomb.[15]

The style of the Djalatunda reliefs does not convey the grand epic sweep of the Ramayana reliefs at Prambanan. In form and mood they are closer to intimate chanted poetry, a recitation of ancestral tales in the simple words of a familiar language. Only the strong stylization of rocks and clouds which provide the setting for the human figures and their dwellings lends the scenes an unearthly note. A very decorative element is

Plate 50. *Spout figure in Djalatunda style, East Java, 10th–11th century.*

provided in some scenes by umbrella-shaped trees whose foliage fits into the ogival top rim of the panel (Pl. 49). The figures depicted have none of the classic proportions found at the Barabudur or at Lara Djonggrang. The heads are large in proportion to very slender bodies; the female figures with their very thin limbs are of an ethereal grace. In comparison, Sita's figure on the Ramayana reliefs at Prambanan (Pls. 42, 46) seems overly robust and earthy. There is no trace of rich adornments—of the high tiaras, the elaborate jeweled ornaments on chest and arms, or the waistbands and caste cords—found in Central Java. Most of the male figures wear simple loincloths, while the lower garments of the female figures, flowing in long folds, suggest transparency. Instead of rich head adornments, there are skillfully shaped coiffures, coiled or tied up in a variety of Javanese styles; carefully traced grooves delineate the hair strands and curls which follow the main sculptural masses of the hairdresses. If, despite many affinities with Indian art, the reliefs of Prambanan were already far removed in form and spirit from their Indian counterparts, stylistically the Djalatunda reliefs, certain affinities notwithstanding, are equally distant from those of Prambanan.

Plate 51. *Airlangga's posthumous image as Vishnu carried by Garuda, from Tjandi Belahan, East Java, 11th century.*

The charming female spout figure in Plate 50 eloquently illustrates characteristics of East Javanese art of the tenth and eleventh centuries. Lithe and gay, this figure and its former companion piece (a male spout figure destroyed with the Netherlands Indies pavilion at the Paris Colonial Exhibition in 1931), whose exact provenance is unknown, have great stylistic affinities with some figures on the reliefs of Djalatunda.

Another combined tjandi and bathing place, which reveals the vitality of East Java's sculptures, is Tjandi Belahan. This sanctuary, dating from 1049, is located on the eastern slope of the Penanggungan. King Airlangga was commemorated there in the form of Vishnu carried by Garuda. Airlangga was of Balinese origin, and the prevalence of the Vishnu cult in his home island at that time may have resulted in his deification in the shape of Vishnu.

Like Tjandi Djalatunda, Belahan was built against the mountain slope; here, too, a spring was captured into conduits and spouts.[16] The image of Airlangga-Vishnu was originally installed in an elevated niche in the rear wall.* At either side, and below the central image, the figures of Vishnu's consorts, Shri and Lakshmi, were installed in niches where they still stand, mirrored in the clear water of the basin. From the breasts of one, and through a jug and flower in the hands of the other goddess, water spouted into the walled-in pool. Now a dreamy clearing in the jungle, the sanctuary may once have been attended by hermits and their apprentices. There is a Balinese counterpart to Belahan, the bathing place on the site of the "Elephant Cave" (*Goa Gadjah*), an ancient hermitage in Bedhulu (see Pl. 133), dating from the same period as Belahan. The bathing place, also with figures as spouts, has recently been reconstructed.

The Belahan image of Airlangga-as-Vishnu (Pl. 51) made at the very beginning of the eleventh century,

* The image is now in the Museum of Modjokerto, East Java.

contrasts strongly in both style and mood with the ninth-century statue of Vishnu at Tjandi Banon in Central Java (Pl. 52). The classical Banon image shows the god standing, a tall, calm figure, behind whose legs nestles a relatively small Garuda with symmetrically half-spread wings. In contrast, the half-kneeling anthropomorphic Garuda who carries Vishnu-Airlangga is a large, ferocious bird with asymmetrically and widely spread wings, ready to destroy anything that might threaten his divine burden—the slight, still, four-armed deity seated meditatively on a lotus against an oval halo.* The god's right foot rests on Garuda's shoulder; his detached tranquillity is accentuated by his carrier's fierceness. The bird's deep-set round eyes and half-open beak project menace and triumph, while his claws clutch the winding serpent underneath.

No significant stone monuments have been preserved from the kingdom of Kediri (1045–1222), which leaves a peculiar gap in our knowledge of what must once have been a flourishing culture. Conceivably Kediri's rulers had a greater interest in poetry than in the erection of impressive monuments. While literary works from Kediri's time continue to animate the other arts, they are unrivaled by the *Ardjuna Wiwaha,* composed during Airlangga's time, which became a favorite theme for pictorial works. The scene depicted most frequently, usually on the walls of hermitages, is Ardjuna's temptation by celestial nymphs sent down by the gods to disrupt his meditation in a grotto on the mountain Indrakila. In the poem, Ardjuna's meditation, or semadi, was undertaken in order to acquire special powers by which he could conquer the demon-king, Niwatakawatja, who threatened the gods.

Ardjuna's mystic exercise was successful, for, having withstood a number of trials including temptation by the nymphs, he received from the god Shiva a magic arrow (*pasopati*) which made him victorious. The existence of the high value attached by Javanese society to semadi, which persists to the present day,[17] is confirmed for ancient East Java by the presence of many cave hermitages as well as by frequent stories of royal recluses. Among East Javanese rulers there were

Plate 52. *Vishnu, with Garuda nestling at the back of the god's feet, from Tjandi Banon, Central Java, early 9th century.*

* Unfortunately a well-meaning official once undertook the restoration of the image's broken face, and regrettably no authority has so far initiated the expert removal of the cement additions, despite the obvious disfigurement and incongruity of the newly modeled features. No face at all would be preferable to such a "restoration."

Plate 53. *Relief depicting two scenes from the* Ardjuna Wiwaha: *cave hermitage Selamangleng near Tulung Agung, East Java, end of 10th century.*

several who became recluses. Airlangga was a hermit twice—once before he was installed as king, and again at the end of his reign. Similarly, Majapahit's Queen-Mother (*radjapatni*) retired to a hermitage. In Java, just as in India, legend often introduces the figure of a *rshi,* a holy sage and seer, who can work miracles and who is sometimes able to fly. Also the *wali,* legendary apostles of Islam in Java, were said to have been able to fly as well as to work miracles. The distant descendants of the ancient ascetics and seers are the contemporary Javanese guru, mystic teachers and practitioners to whom healing and oracular powers are attributed and who, on occasion, can have a powerful influence even on leading public figures.

There are two interesting cave hermitages which date from the Kediri period—one near the present town of Kediri and the other near Tulung Agung. Both caves are called Selamangleng. On one wall of the Tulung Agung cave, scenes from the *Ardjuna Wiwaha* are depicted. One sequence shows the beginning of the nymphs' descent from the abode of the gods to Mt. Indrakila. The deity (seated on a lotus in the scene to the left) had ordered them to disrupt Ardjuna's meditation, and they start off downward, moving among lush vegetation in which a deer and a monkey are hidden. The delicate figures of the nymphs are reminiscent of the female figures on the Djalatunda reliefs; there is a softness and grace in this intimate scene which carries no exalted mood. In fact, quite prosaically, one of the nymphs squats down in a stream, her skirt lifted, to relieve herself.

In the text of the *Ardjuna Wiwaha* the journey of the nymphs from their celestial abode to the grotto is described as follows:[18]

It was morning when they arrived there, and playfully they proceeded on foot along the path. The *tjamara* trees swayed on the slopes [as if] extending courteous greetings at the sight of the nymphs. The cinnamon trees, whose [glowing red] young leaves palpitated daintily, seemed to call out audibly, rivaling in loveliness and redness the nymphs' breasts and lips. The shapes of the beguiling trees of the forests were hidden in clouds, however; it was misty, one could hardly see; only that which was nearby was visible; as one moved away it was closed in again by mist. The yellow *sekara* trees had just grown young leaves; one tried to see the bees which hummed but remained invisible. Peacocks preened themselves, spreading their wings, standing opposite each other on the dead trunk of a *tjandana* tree.

The opening of the grotto [that served] as place for meditation was of white rocks, not unlike [someone] who approaches laughing with a salutation. . . .*

When the nymphs, upon arrival, rest and beautify themselves on the bank of a stream, the poet describes the scene as follows:

They went to rest there dragging [?] their feet; some among them started to quarrel; one of them dangled her feet in the water; [another] was fatigued and massaged her calves daintily. [One] rubbed her face; slowly she scooped up the water; another one still was arranging the coil of her hair. They mirrored themselves in the water, looking at their eyes, practicing how they would make [Ardjuna] [love] sick.[19]

A moment in the temptation scene is described thus:

Trustingly she laid her head [on his lap]. To calm him the others withdrew and only one stayed behind. The skirt-cloth was opened, and *it* looked as if *it* laughed through its power; then *it* looked as if it pressed together the lips, angered that it was not accepted.[20]

The moment of the seductive efforts of the nymphs as they accost the meditating Ardjuna appears in reliefs in several ancient Javanese hermitages. Through the centuries to the present, the subject has retained its fascination for the artists of Java and Bali. It has been carved in stone reliefs, painted on cloth, chased in metal, carved in wood, and drawn on paper. A detail of a traditional Balinese temple painting on cloth, from the beginning of this century, is one of many examples. To the present day the entire story of the *Ardjuna Wiwaha* is enacted in classical Javanese dance drama. But whereas the erotic elements of the temptation scene generally are vividly depicted in the sculptured or painted versions, only the faintest allusions to eroticism are given in the stylized gestures of the dancers.

In visual presentations only the actions of the heroes in the *Ardjuna Wiwaha* poem can be portrayed, as in our movie versions of some great novels, where the depth and beauty of mystical and philosophical components must remain confined to the text. So Ardjuna's beautiful prayer to Shiva, addressed to the god when he reveals himself, is found in the text alone:

"Om! May the homage of the helpless one be noticed by the Refuge of the three worlds. External and internal is your servant's homage, not otherwise. As fire from the wood, as butter from the milk art Thou who seemest to appear when there are people who speak about the good. Permeating everything, the core of highest truth, so hard to attain, art Thou. Thou who dwellest in being as well as in nonbeing, in the great as in the small, in that which is evil as well as in that which is pure. Thou art the creation, the existence and the passing away of the universe, even as the cause thereof. The origin and the destiny of the world, the soul of being and nonbeing art Thou.

"As the disk of the moon is to pots with water; does not one find the moon in those where it [the water] is pure? Likewise art Thou with regard to the creatures. Thou revealest Thyself in those who merge with the Lord.

"Thou art found by him who does not find thee; Thou art seen by him who does not see thee; Thou art grasped by him who does not grasp thee; Thou art the highest bliss without the slightest of veils."[21]

* As if showing his white teeth.

Plate 54. *Ardjuna's temptation by celestial nymphs, detail of a traditional Balinese cloth-painting.*

In turning now to some examples of thirteenth-century Singasari art, we cannot help recalling the history of its kings. This bloodstained dynasty was descended from a woman, Ken Dedes, who was coveted together with the throne by a notorious adventurer, Ken Angrok. His acts, including the murder of Ken Dedes' husband, placed him beyond good and evil. After a five-year reign Ken Angrok was murdered by his stepson, Anushapati, who after reigning for twenty years was slain in turn by his half-brother who died shortly afterward. Anushapati's son, Vishnuvardhana, who reigned for twenty years thereafter, escaped a violent death. His son and successor, Krtanagara, the last king of Singasari, was assassinated when his palace was overrun and devastated by his enemies. Krtanagara, who during his lifetime had sought salvation in cults of the Kala-Chakra sect, was also a man who had transgressed the sanctions imposed upon ordinary mortals.

Plate 55. *Prajnaparamita (thought to be posthumous image of Ken Dedes), Singasari, East Java, 13th century.*

Undoubtedly there were great tensions in the inner circles of the Singasari court, especially during the first decades of its existence and particularly in and around the person of Ken Dedes, whose son by her first marriage became the murderer of her second husband. Legend tells of her extraordinary beauty and describes her as a "woman with a flaming womb" whose magic would ensure its possessor's control over the throne.

An image of the Buddhist goddess Prajnaparamita was found in a sanctuary not far from the site of Tjandi Singasari, the most imposing monument of the period. This image is assumed to be the posthumous likeness of Ken Dedes. Its exquisitely chiseled cool perfection is not unlike that encountered in the work of a master jeweler. In form and style the statue is close to the classic Central Javanese images. It differs vastly in spirit, however, from the Buddhist sculptures of Central Java, such as those of the Plaosan Bodhisattvas. Not the slightest trace of mildness emanates from the precise, concentrated features of the goddess. If indeed this image represents Ken Dedes, the sculptor may have caught something of the queen's character in the lines of the hard mouth and in the tenseness of the beautiful, cold face.

Tjandi Singasari, partly restored, was never completely finished.[22] The most impressive remains in the vicinity are two gigantic (10′ 2″) squatting guardians, half-sunken into the earth at the place where perhaps a gate had once stood.[23] These fierce doorkeepers best illustrate the massive, monumental style of Singasari's sculptures. The tjandi itself, although much smaller than the Shiva temple at Prambanan, is similar in its basic arrangements. Singasari has four symmetrically placed chambers which face the cardinal directions and in which different manifestations of the god Shiva were once enshrined. There are two significant exceptions, however. First, the tjandi's tapering roof was hollow and contained two pyramidally vaulted chambers, one above the other. For this reason it has been called "the tower-temple" by archaeologists. The chambers in the roof may once have contained hidden images, possibly Buddhist. Secondly, the main, eastern chamber may have enshrined a linga on a yoni instead of a statue of Shiva.[24] In the three other chambers, as

Plate 56. *Tjandi Singasari, East Java, early 14th century. (The* kala *heads over the lower porticoes were never finished.)*

at Lara Djonggrang, stood a figure of Mahaguru, one of Ganesha, and one of Durga. The quality of these images surpasses by far that of their Prambanan counterparts. Superbly carved, monumental in conception, they combine great simplicity in their main masses with fine detail held subservient to the grand design of the whole.

The Durga *Mahisasuramardini* is much more expressive than the Lara Djonggrang Durga. Forceful yet restrained in movement, the six-armed goddess is firmly ensconced upon the head and croup of the reclining animal, her widespread legs in a semimasculine stance. She is armed with club and shield; some of her hands, now broken, must have held other weapons and symbols. With one remaining hand she grasps the hair of the small massive demon who is emerging from the head of the bull. This frequently repeated theme from the religious art of the Shaiva world has been re-created here in a peculiarly complex mood by a master sculptor. Great femininity is combined with power, and the goddess, calm and implacable, with her glance lowered, carries out her task with a detachment which nonetheless contains a trace of sadness or resignation. Bull and demon seem to accept, in an almost festive mood, the divine judgment.

The hand of the same sculptor who shaped the Durga can also be discerned in the other masterpieces of Singasari. Thus the elephantine son of Shiva, Ganesha, is again one of the finest of these images in Java.[25] He is surpassed in size and dynamic quality only by the famous Ganesha of Bara—a gigantic fourteenth-century image which sits in the landscape near the village of this name. On the back of this Ganesha a large monstrous Kala head is carved for protection.[26] The Ganesha of Singasari is a bulky, anthropomorphic ele-

Plate 57. *Durga from the northern chamber of Tjandi Singasari.*

phant, benign and childlike, who sits with his legs drawn up under his belly and his trunk dipping into a bowl which he holds in one of his four hands. His cushion, however, is made up of skulls; skulls adorn his conical crown-cap, form his earrings, and stud his bracelets. These macabre elements point to the general Bhairavist orientation of the Singasari court religion. The image of a naked, fanged, and skull-crowned Bhairava perhaps best expresses the demonic-erotic mood of a cult that seems to have held great fascination for the ruling and priestly circles of the time, Shivaite and Buddhist alike. Traces of a cult dedicated to Shiva in his monstrous and macabre emanation of Bhairava have been left not only in Singasari art but also in that of contemporaneous Bali and Sumatra.[27] A large stone Bhairava which significantly contains a small Bodhisattva image in the headdress has been found in Sungai Langsat, Central Sumatra. This Bhairava may have represented either Krtanagara or Adityavarman, a later ruler of the kingdom of Malayu who was related to the Singasari dynasty. Both were initiates of the Bhairava cult. An inscription which deals with Adityavarman's highest consecration eloquently documents, even if in somewhat veiled language, the macabre aspects of this cult. According to the inscription, the king was consecrated on a burial ground where he sat alone, on a pile of corpses, laughing diabolically and drinking blood, while the flames of a great human sacrifice spread an unbearable stench which, to the initiate, was like the fragrance of ten thousand million flowers.[28]

We need only to compare the Bhairava of Singasari (Pl. 58) with a posthumous image assumed to be Krtanagara's (Pl. 59) to see the difference between a living god identified with the king and a god-king who was dead. Iconographically the posthumous image tentatively identified with Krtanagara* is a *hari-hara-ardhanari*—a fusion of the gods Vishnu and Shiva (*hari-hara*)—whose attributes the deity holds up, the winged conch in the right hand and the rosary in the left hand. At the same time, he is half male and half female (*ardhanari*), having a full left breast and a flat right one. Stutterheim suggests that the image may represent Krtanagara together with his wife Sri Bajradewi.[29] At the right side of the figure lotus plants sprout from a bulb with exposed roots, typical for images of the Singasari dynasty.

Krtanagara is known to have been deified as Shiva-Buddha also at Tjandi Djawi and perhaps in a few other places as well, facts which illustrate the prevalent religious syncretism of his day. Whether Shivaite, Buddhist, or a combination of the two religions, East Java's mortuary images retain the stately rigidity first observed in the Shiva statue at Prambanan. The stamp of death is unmistakable. There is enough variety in the facial features of these images to suspect that they may have been portrait-statues. Such statues, however, were usually made and consecrated years after the rul-

Plate 58. *Bhairawa from Singasari, East Java.*

* Now in the Department of Indian Art of the State Museum, Berlin-Dahlem.

er's preliminary burial and subsequent cremation, so that the portraits must be only approximations, a somewhat idealized interpretation of the royal visage rather than a true likeness.

The poem *Nagarakrtagama* mentions the installation ceremony of a posthumous statue of the ruling king's grandmother, the Radjapatni.[30] The religious domain (*dharma*) in which the royal grandmother's tjandi was situated had been consecrated one year after her death. The posthumous image was not installed there, however, until the last post-cremation rites (*shraddha*) had been held. These rites, which aimed at the final liberation of her soul from all earthly bonds and ensured its entrance into heaven, took place twelve years after her death. Except for the royal pomp, the detailed description of the fourteenth-century shraddha rites is strongly reminiscent of contemporary Balinese post-cremation celebrations and attendant entertainments. And just as in Bali, where no death rites are complete without music, mask- or other plays and dances, so also the crowds of ancient Majapahit for seven days enjoyed alternating chanted storytelling, dramatic and martial dances.*

Plate 59. *Posthumous statue of Krtanagara in the shape of* hari-hara ardhanari, c. *early 14th century.*

The importance of deified dynastic ancestors to the living rulers is revealed in other parts of the *Nagarakrtagama.* The poet Prapancha, himself a Buddhist priest, accompanied the king (Rajasanagara, known as Hayam Wuruk) and his retinue on extensive journeys through the land. Thus his descriptions are those of an eyewitness.[31] During these journeys, or "Royal Progresses," the king visited a number of religious domains (dharma) in which tjandi were located and paid homage to his deified predecessors. Some of the tjandi mentioned in the *Nagarakrtagama* are clearly identifiable, others are not. Among the sanctuaries Hayam Wuruk visited, Tjandi Djawi, Simping (now known as Sumberdjati), Djago, Panataran, and Surawana still exist, some half-reconstructed, silent witnesses of the past. In Canto 37 Prapancha describes an unidentified dharma called Kagenengan and gives what may have been a typical picture of the tjandi and the king's worshipful actions.

A magnificent high gate and an engirdling wall surrounded the inner terraced court planted with beautiful flowering trees. There stood, "like the Mountain Mahameru," an imposing temple tower (*prasada*) in which was enshrined a consecrated posthumous image (*pratista*), designated in the poem as a "Shiva abode in Shiva's likeness." According to Pigeaud, the statue worshiped by the visiting king was that of the founder of his dynasty, the first king of Singasari, Ken Angrok (who took the name Rajasa), Hayam Wuruk's great-great-great-grandfather. In the poem, he is referred to as "lord Girinatha's Son" (Shiva's son), "a god materialized."[32]

* See Appendix II for the stanza in which the entertainments are described.

During one of his trips through the country, the king also visits a monastery where Prapancha steals away to walk about "pleasantly, lighthearted . . . free from work," exploring the site with its shady lanes and festively decorated dwellings. When he arrives at a sanctuary on a terrace, he stops to "read and re-read" with pleasure its carved reliefs illuminating a "literary gem, a kakawin."[33] A narrative poem depicted on a series of reliefs was thus a familiar adornment of a religious structure. Like the Balinese narrative scroll-paintings on cloth still executed in the twentieth century, the reliefs had to be "read."

Beginning in the thirteenth century, many narrative reliefs on East Javanese tjandi walls, balustrades, or bases acquired a strikingly new style—a "wayang style."* In this style the treatment of figures, and correspondingly of their environment, shows a flat, almost two-dimensional highly stylized patterning. The forms of figures closely resemble those of the flat leather-carved shadow-play puppets, especially of those from modern Bali, which are less elongated than the Javanese wayang puppets.

Some of the series of narrative reliefs on such tjandi as Djago, Panataran, Kedaton, and Surawana (Pl. 60) provide excellent examples of the wayang style. A feature common to puppets and wayang-style figures on these reliefs is the headdress; it either curves up both in front and back with curls worked into the upsweeping parts, or it is a cap decorated at the back with a protruding Garuda head—the *garuda mungkur,* that is, Garuda turned backward—which serves as a protective charm. The faces of the carved figures are shown either in profile, like those of the puppets, or in a three-quarter view in which both eyes are visible. Movement is restricted largely to the limbs; there is none of the suppleness of the unclad classical bodies. There is no depth; the treatment is flat and frontal. Concurrently,

* See Part II, Ch. 5.

Plate 60. *Scene from* Ardjuna Wiwaha, *relief at Tjandi Surawana, East Java, late 14th century.*

Plate 61. *Ardjuna, Balinese shadow-play puppet.*

natural elements become highly stylized. Trees and foliage are decoratively designed in low relief; they are combined with spiral and flame-shaped motifs which denote clouds and rocks and also fill the air. The filling of all space, animating it with dynamic configurations, is another important feature of the style. To the present day we see these general tendencies in the pictorial art of Bali.

Together with the wayang style appear on East Java's reliefs the figures of dwarfed, fleshy, and grotesquely malformed attendants of the heroes, the *panakawan* (see Pl. 64). They are even today indispensable figures in every form of wayang and all its related arts. How and when these grotesque beings entered the wayang world as foils for their noble or demonic masters is not ascertainable. Their prototypes may have been the buffoons who are mentioned in a number of early inscriptions.* Real dwarfs must have been in existence in ancient Java, as elsewhere in the world, and possibly they were employed as special semicomical servants in the households of the wealthy and the mighty. Under the palanquin of the traveling lady depicted on one of the Barabudur reliefs (Pl. 33) we meet such a dwarfed and seemingly gay creature. Also, dwarfs and other freaks, to whom an aura of supernaturalism clings, may have been protegés of the ancient royal courts as they still were in Central Java in the nineteen-thirties. Known as *polowidjo* (weeds), dwarfs, albinos, and other peculiarly deformed persons were special wards of the palaces, and on high ceremonial occasions they paraded in the retinue of the ruler.[34]

Beginning in the last part of the thirteenth-century at Tjandi Djago, shadow-play puppets provided a conventional scheme for the representation of figures in much of the pictorial arts of Java and Bali. For centuries to follow, human as well as superhuman beings have been shaped after wayang models. These figures were placed within a variety of settings, ranging from the highly stylized to the seminaturalistic.

A particularly forceful variety of the wayang style appears in scenes from the *Ramayana* carved on the walls of the base of Tjandi Panataran's principal sanctuary (Pl. 62). These scenes begin with Hanuman's mission to Langka as a scout, and end with the death of the giant Kumbhakarna, foreshadowing Rawana's final defeat. The action takes place almost entirely within the domain of the King of Demons and is thus fraught with danger. These reliefs are carved on vertical panels which are separated from each other by charming medallions, each with a different animal surrounded by stylized foliage. The reliefs thus do not have the continuity which the horizontally extended scenes create at Prambanan.[35]

In contrast with the naturalism and earthiness of the Prambanan reliefs, those at Panataran are permeated with supernaturalism. Upon careful examination one discovers monstrous kala heads, shapes of animals or spooky beings camouflaged in intricate motifs, so that the atmosphere appears charged with a life of its own. Thus, for example, on one panel (Pl. 63) which shows the monkey hero Hanuman defeating an elephant and routing his assailants in Rawana's domain, the space above the figures is filled with fantastic configurations that form, on the left, a monstrous, jawless face with what seem to be either long teeth or materialized breath issuing from its mouth, and, to the right, a figure in

* See Appendix II.

Plate 62. *Substructure of main temple of Tjandi Panataran, seen from southwest; East Java, 14th century.*

running motion, one arm uplifted and with a conch-like shape instead of a face; one of the scroll-shaped appendages forms a heavy pubic shield. On another panel (Pl. 64), showing Rawana's son Aksa, whose left arm was broken off by Hanuman (the arm is visible in the lower right corner), seated with an attendant who kneels before him, the supernatural apparition in the sky is more precise: a kala head gripping the celestial bow with stag heads at each end—omens of supernatural courage.[36] Such animation of the atmosphere is here much more pervasive than at Prambanan, where it occurs only occasionally. At Panataran naturalistic treatment is accorded only to "real" animals—to deer, birds, rodents, and monkeys—as distinguished both from the eerie animal forms camouflaged in the clouds or underfoot and from the stylized monkey heroes of the *Ramayana*.

Stutterheim called the emotive mood of the Panataran Ramayana reliefs "magicism." The flame motifs and radiations denote a surcharge of magic energies, he thought. He also believed that the fear of open spaces and the related fear of depth—presumably because the atmosphere was permeated by invisible, menacing beings or forces—may account for the avoidance of the third dimension and for the filling of all available space.

On the reliefs of Panataran, scenes of danger and conflict especially are filled with flaming scrolls and spirals; they are suffused with the partly distinguishable shapes of demonic beings. As Stutterheim observes, the demons were felt to be and to move like heavy clouds.[37] No Central Javanese reliefs, no matter how dramatic, were thus "magically charged." The destructive forces of the world were also represented in Central Java as demons and monsters, but there they appeared only as the foes of gods and heroes, not as pervasive presences.

The flaming energies depicted in the art of Java and

Bali starting with the East Javanese period have their counterparts in Tibetan art. Magic radiations envelop or emanate from divine as well as demonic figures, signify "white" as well as "black" magic. Bali's supreme deity, Tintiya, the unthinkable, the unimaginable,[38] is usually shown with flames issuing from his every joint (see Pl. 140), whereas the witch Tjalon Arang, her long tongue flaming, is surrounded by a blazing halo in traditional Balinese pictorial versions.

To return to Tjandi Panataran, this temple group is remarkable not only for its Ramayana reliefs. In its general plan and in the rich baroque effect of its principal sanctuary, the Panataran complex appears today like an old and gorgeous version of contemporary Balinese temple art. Panataran's reconstructed plan shows that originally the structures were situated within three areas, one behind the other, with access to each through a gate. The main sanctuary lies to the rear (Pl. 65). The remains of a number of smaller temples, shrines, and pavilions are comparable to those of a typical Balinese temple, even though their placement is more irregular. Among other substructures in the spacious front area, between the first and second gates, are two rectangular platforms, the larger about 44 feet long and the smaller about 31 feet long. These may once have been shaded by a fiber-thatched or tiled roof resting on pillars and, like the *balai agung* in Bali today, may have been used for ceremonial gatherings and banquets. Conceivably the larger one, with steps at either end in addition to a double set of steps in front, served for performances of dance-plays, the actor-dancers entering from the right and left sides as is still customary in Javanese classical dance drama performed in open pillared halls.

A late addition (1415) to the complex was a bathing place behind the main temple courts. It is decorated

Plate 63. *Hanuman in Langka throws a* buta *after defeating an elephant, Ramayana relief, Tjandi Panataran.*

Plate 64. *Rawana's son, Aksa, his left arm lost, after battle with Hanuman, Ramayana relief, Tjandi Panataran.*

Plate 65. *A part of Panataran complex with restored small temple dated A.D. 1369 (left) and substructure of main temple in the background.*

with figures and reliefs showing scenes from animal fables, in a style associated with late Majapahit art which has a certain gay intimacy.[39] Here very lively and naturalistic animals meet and act in a decoratively treated landscape which has no stylistic relation whatever to the ornate scrolls or spiral-shaped foliage motifs which surround the animals in the medallions between the Ramayana panels of the main sanctuary.

If we keep in mind that the whole site had been successively rebuilt, embellished, and expanded by the addition of new structures between the twelfth and fifteenth centuries, we are able to accept the different styles of sculptures on structures dating from the different centuries. Archaeologically it has been established that the present stone walls of Panataran's principal temple were built around an earlier brick structure. Nevertheless, even the new walls of the principal sanctuary, dated 1347, which could have been decorated in the course of a single decade, present a somewhat surprising contrast between the styles of its two main relief series. The high stylization of the Ramayana reliefs on the walls of the base, which forms the first terrace, has already been discussed. On the walls of the second terrace, however, we see reliefs of an altogether different style (see Pl. 62). There in long continuous horizontal bands, scenes unfold from the *Krishnayana* (the story of Krishna, king of Dwarawati, the divine mentor and helper of the Pandawa in the *Mahabharata* epic). Apart from a few episodes not directly related to the *Krishnayana,* the reliefs depict Krishna's romantic adventures in abducting the beautiful princess Rukmini on the eve of her betrothal to another suitor, with her full consent and connivance to be sure. As Krishna speeds homeward in a chariot bearing his love, he is pursued and attacked by the princess' enraged brother, which inevitably leads to armed clashes between the two parties.

With the exuberant, scroll-filled, demonic reliefs of the Ramayana below and flamboyant winged creatures along the walls of the third terrace above, the *Krishnayana* reliefs, despite the agitation of the battle scenes, suddenly appear rather tame and sweet in their almost naturalistic style which is held in flat relief. Here again one is tempted to speculate on the influence of a literary source on a style of pictorial plastic art.

The dynamic caryatids—winged "lions" and serpents—which protrude from the walls and corners of the third terrace remind one in shape and expression of the winged monsters at the foot of a Balinese cremation tower (*bade* or *wade*), a papier-mâché and tinsel version no less forceful than the stone supporters of the now vanished temple-tower of Majapahit's most important state sanctuary. Both the body proper and the superstructure of a presumably tall, tiered roof could not be rebuilt from the remaining stones. A tentative separate reconstruction of the lower part of the superstructure, however, discloses that in outside central niches in three of its walls there once stood images, surrounded by halos, of Brahma, Shiva, and Vishnu, each on his mount and flanked by his consorts in smaller niches. The central images have disappeared, although some of the consort images are still there.[40] At the corners were other deities, such as Indra, Agni, Wayu, and Kartikeya. Heavy serpents, their protruding heads hanging down, framed the niches of the principal gods. Small dwarfed caryatids at the foot of the temple body and other rich ornamentation suggest that the whole sanctuary must have presented a remarkable, although perhaps somewhat overladen effect. Again we must think of Bali, where dancing deities, monsters, and profuse ornamentation combine to echo, on a smaller scale, Majapahit's rich and lively art at the height of its power (see Pl. 134). The flamboyant baroque style of the middle Majapahit period is also in evidence in its bronze art. It is possible that the magnificent lamp standard (Pl. 66) with a coiled king-serpent (naga) as its foot and a Garuda head nestling in the loop of its body, though not dated, belongs to this period.

Not all East Javanese narrative reliefs in the wayang style are as surcharged with magic emanations as the *Ramayana* scenes at Panataran which, after all, are set in the danger-laden realm of the demon king Rawana. Other carved panels have exquisite poetic quality, as for instance on the walls of the base of fourteenth-century Tjandi Kedaton (Pl. 67). The slender and

Plate 67. *Samba, son of Krishna, led by the nymph Tilottama, relief at Tjandi Kedaton, East Java, A.D. 1370.*

Plate 66. *Bronze stand in the shape of a* naga, *possibly from East Java.*

Plate 68. *"Making a* Lontar,*" wise woman dictating a tale to scribe, ink drawing by G. Nj. Lempad, Ubud, Bali, 1956.*

graceful figures, probably Samba, son of Krishna and hero of the Bhomakawya story and the nymph Tilottama, preceded by a dwarf,* bring to mind some of the delicate illustrations to stories set down in old Balinese palm-leaf books, called *lontar.*† Text and illustrations are engraved on palm-leaf strips with a fine stylus and then darkened with the soot of burned palm-leaf spines rubbed into the grooves—a procedure still used in Bali by lontar copyists. A contemporary humorous drawing by a Balinese artist shows a wise woman who dictates a text to a lontar scribe (Pl. 68). As the lontar strips are only from about 1.5 to 2 inches wide and from 11 to 18 inches long, pictorial compositions must fit into horizontally elongated space much like the bands of reliefs on some of the tjandi walls or around the bases of platforms.

* Possibly a dwarfed female servant or a little girl.

† The strips of palm-leaf are cut from the leaves of the lontar palm from which the books derive their name.

In the later art of Majapahit a soft and lyrical genre appears in reliefs, often reflecting poetic themes and romantic tales. This style is already in evidence at Tjandi Surawana, where next to the *Ardjuna Wiwaha* story depicted in wayang style panels with scenes from the story of Sri Tandjung[41] present charming compositions in which the treatment of nature is among the finest in East Javanese art. The hero of the Sri Tandjung story does not have a wayang headdress, but wears an unadorned helmetlike rounded cap which is typical in representations of the hero Pandji* on other reliefs.

A stone head dug up in 1936 near Tjandi Selakelir on Mt. Penanggungan (Pl. 70), which fitted a trunk that had long stood headless on the grounds, shows this helmetlike headcovering. The statue, however, may have been the posthumous image of a prince. (The discovery of the head, curiously, was made in response to an announcement of a reward for its finder by the late Dr. Stutterheim who was eager to reconstruct the headless image of Selakelir. An old guardsman, who lived

* Pandji is not strictly a name; it also denotes a person of high nobility, somewhat similar to the term "knight" in the West.

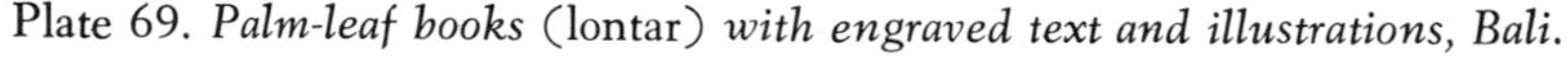

Plate 69. *Palm-leaf books* (lontar) *with engraved text and illustrations, Bali.*

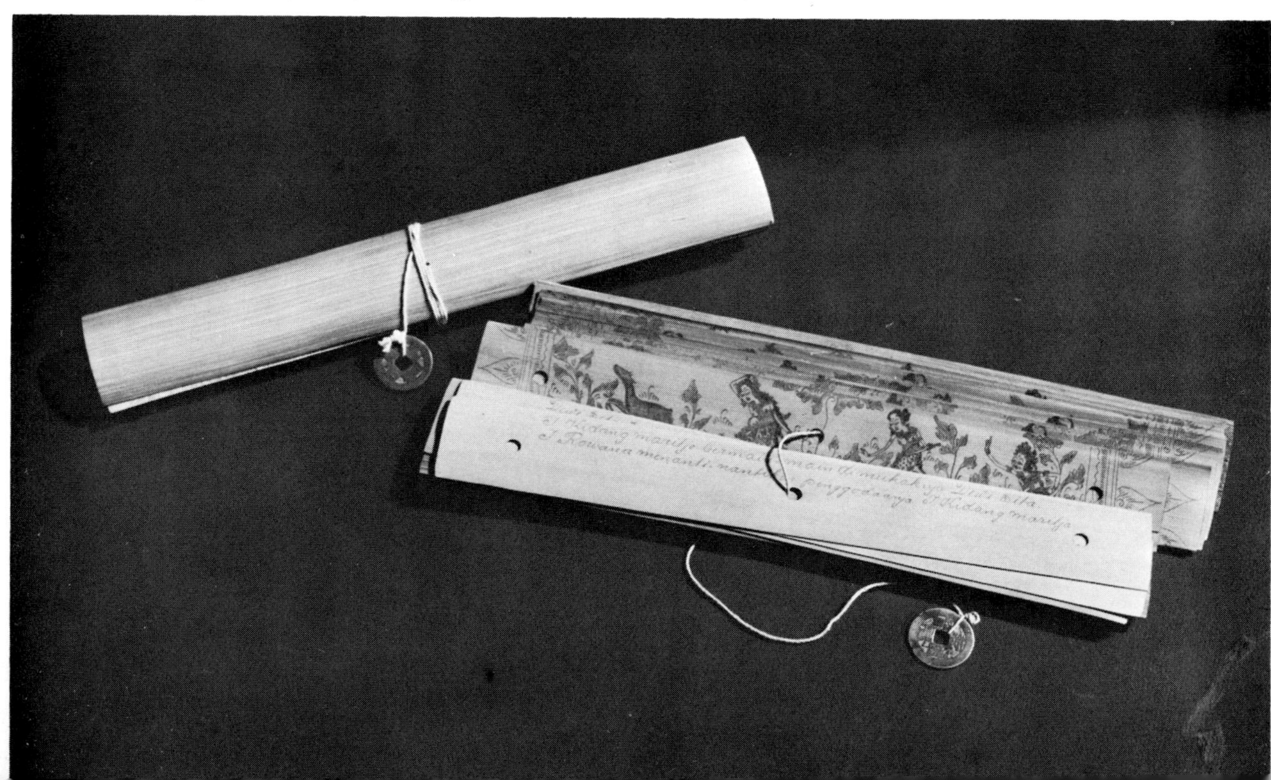

at the foot of the Penanggungan, claimed that the place where the head was buried was revealed to him in a dream one night, and when the next morning he climbed the mountain and started digging, his *patjul* (hoe) struck the nose of the head. The disfiguring cut was still quite fresh when it was brought down from the mountain slope.)[42]

Plate 70. *Head unearthed near Tjandi Selakelir, Mt. Penanggungan, East Java, 15th century.*

A scene showing an amorous pair dallying in an idyllic mountainous landscape, which decorates one of the fifteenth-century sanctuaries on the Penanggungan, may depict an incident from a Pandji tale (Pl. 71). The hero sits with his ladylove nestling languidly in his lap; he strums a long-necked musical instrument reminiscent of the Indian vina. The two-dimensional landscape is "naïve," and yet one can almost hear the splashing of water which streams from bamboo conduits into a pool, can almost walk along the stony path that winds up into the mountains past the resting pair. The forms of the mountains in the background are rounded; above them are gay bits of Chinese-style cloud bands. The foliage of the trees spreads gently; everything is soft, almost fluid. There is nothing of the angularity and sharply pointed designs or flame motifs which fill reliefs in the wayang style. The scene is laid on earth, in the familiar, beloved environment where no menacing, supernatural emanations disturb its peace. The ubiquitous panakawan of the hero is also present; he has something to say to the lady's female attendant, who is seated behind the amorous pair.

For lack of another label we might refer to the style which depicts romantic tales in a soft seminaturalistic manner as the "late Majapahit-Pandji style." By analogy with the differentiation now made in the style of puppets used for *wayang purwa* (plays based on the

Plate 71. *Amorous pair in landscape, relief at a terraced sanctuary (site 65) on Mt. Penanggungan, East Java, 15th c.*

Mahabharata) and for *wayang gedog* (plays based on Pandji legends),* it is conceivable that in the East Javanese reliefs a stylistic distinction was also consciously applied, as for instance at Tjandi Surawana.

From the Majapahit era there are remains not only of structures and stone sculptures related to the kingdom's official cults, but also of the period's informal art. There is no doubt that in earlier centuries in Central Java, objects of a secular nature were produced for the people's pleasure and play. Such objects may have been fashioned primarily of wood or clay, and pictures painted on cloth probably also existed. Although no trace of such objects has been found in Central Java, some of Majapahit's informal art has been preserved.

In the Museum of Modjokerto, for example, charming reliefs carved on stone socles are displayed, which show scenes of daily life, like one of a woman squatting in her kitchen (Pl. 72). One is reminded of Bali's secular sculptures, often placed within a temple court. As in Bali today, the nobles of Majapahit may have owned elaborately decorated weapons-stands; musical instruments may have had intricately carved and painted frames. Today's legacy, however, consists mainly of

* See Chapter 5 below.

Plate 72. *Woman in kitchen, relief on a stone socle found in the vicinity of Trawulan, East Java, late Majapahit style.*

ceramic objects, found in the area of the village of Trawulan, where extensive remains of walls and bases of structures have been discovered. It is assumed that the keraton of Majapahit was located there.[43] Innumerable clay objects and thousands of shards have been found in the earth; these have been assembled in a special museum at Trawulan where, for years, fragments have been studied and fitted together to produce an array of clay objects ranging from huge vats and jars to delicate clay figurines. Some of these are of exquisite grace (Pl. 73). Among the Trawulan finds is a whole clay landscape modeled in the round, showing a hermitage high up the side of a steep mountain where an ascetic is perched on a platform at the entrance to his cell. There is also a collection of small heads, obviously broken from little figures; some are of great loveliness and fine workmanship. The most famous among these is a very beautiful head of a young woman, possibly a likeness of a princess.[44] A few of the other heads show such distinct individualistic traits that they seem to be miniature portraits. One masculine face (Pl. 74) with heavy features and a stormy, grim expression has been identified—justifiably or not—as Gadjah Mada, Majapahit's renowned prime minister and empire-builder. An enlarged pictorial version of this face now graces the Gadjah Mada University in Jogjakarta, and a huge cement relief, duplicating the three-quarter view of the small Majapahit clay head, is now the centerpiece on the rear wall of the Military Police Corps Museum in Djakarta, where it is flanked by reliefs with somewhat less dynamic portraits of the Corps' outstanding leaders. The assertive face of "Gadjah Mada" is exceptional, however, among the otherwise gay and graceful clay creations found on the site of the old palace-city. The clay figurines may have been used as decorative objets d'art, but some, especially those of animals, suggest that they may have been toys.

With Majapahit's disintegration, which set in toward the close of the fifteenth century, art related to the cult of kings declined. The small size, cruder workmanship, and simplified iconography of Majapahit's latest posthumous images reflect this waning of power. Nor have any imposing stone structures remained from this late period; only the relatively modest terraced sacred sites on Mt. Penanggungan and some evidences of small sanctuaries built in the remote outposts of Majapahit domains in the easternmost regions of Java.

In surveying some of the principal sanctuaries and

Plate 73. *Terracotta figurine from Trawulan, East Java.*

art styles of the Hinduistic millennium, we have dealt mainly with Central and East Java, obtaining also some glimpses of ancient Bali. Within the same era, Hinduistic art also appeared in some of the other islands of the archipelago—in the very early kingdoms of Borneo, or in the ancient Sumatran kingdoms of Malayu and Srivijaya—but their significance for our knowledge of Indonesian art is not nearly as great as the developments in Java and Bali.

While the classical harmony of Central Javanese Buddhist and Shivaite art still bears the strong imprint of India's great art styles with their distant Hellenistic undertones, the highly creative East Javanese period provides examples of quite original works which in their styles convey purely Javanese conceptions of form and very different moods. There is little of the remote serenity and inwardness of Central Javanese Buddhist art; no longer is there the jubilant glorification of crea-

Plate 74. *Terracotta head of a man (associated with Gadjah Mada) from Trawulan, East Java.*

tion, echoed at some of the Shivaite sanctuaries. In East Java a dominant note is struck by Bhairava with his macabre dance; flaming energies and demons fill the Ramayana scenes selected for the adornment of Panataran. And while the stately images of kings retain their conventional mortuary character, the shadows of more distant ancestors emerge in the stylized supernatural setting of the wayang style. At the same time a soft poetic strain appears in reliefs based on lyrical poetry and romantic tales. The ancient myths gave rise to power-laden unearthly creatures within supernatural settings. Poetry and East Java's natural landscape—the mountains, rich vegetation, and winding rivers—inspire an art in which the sweetness and grace of beautiful human beings and the loveliness of this earth are conveyed.

The historical cycle of Java's art during the Hinduistic era closes, however, with the monumental pyramid of Tjandi Sukuh and the remains of Tjeta on Mt. Lawu, with the powerful figure of Bima as liberator. These monuments provide a concluding note not unlike the deep booming sound of a Javanese gong that reverberates at the end of a musical period. We do not know whether the spirit and style of Sukuh and Tjeta were symptomatic of a trend cut short after the fall of Majapahit, or whether it was a unique peripheral phenomenon. (Cf. Pls. 23–25.)

Threads that connect the Hinduistic millennium with the succeeding centuries fasten upon the shadow play, the dance, the themes of the great epics, East Javanese legends and poetry. But the broad strands of continuity in the plastic arts are broken with the onset of the sixteenth century, as the crescent and star of Islam begin to rise over Indonesia, and the cult of deified kings ceases. The abandoned tjandi fall into decay, their images and reliefs either defaced or buried in ruins under the cover of rapidly spreading vegetation. A gap of over four centuries ensues in the life of Java's representational plastic arts, and all artistic skills are channeled into ornamentation. During this interval, however, Bali perpetuates many East Javanese traditions, thus maintaining continuity with the Hinduistic past, while its arts are vitalized by a process of constant innovation.

Notes

1. W. F. Stutterheim, *Het Hinduisme in de Archipel* (Groningen, 1951), p. 32.

2. For a chronology of Bali's kings between the ninth and fourteenth centuries, see R. Goris, *Sedjarah Bali Kuna* (Bali, 1948). For a sketch of Hinduistic Bali, see Stutterheim, *Indian Influences in Old-Balinese Art* (London, 1935).

3. A traditional Balinese painting with an episode of the Kidung Sunda is reproduced in F. W. Stapel, ed., *Geschiedenis van Nederlandsch Indië*, II (Amsterdam, 1938), 85.

4. A good shortened version of *Tjalon Arang* appears in B. de Zoete and W. Spies, *Dance and Drama in Bali* (London, 1952), pp. 116ff.

5. See *Java in the Fourteenth Century: A Study in Cultural History,* The Nagarakertagama by Rakawi Prapança of Majapahit, 1365 A.D., translation and notes by Th. Pigeaud (The Hague, 1960–1962), especially vols. II, III, IV.

6. See Stutterheim, *De Kraton van Majapahit, VKI,* VII (1948).

7. See R. Goris, *Bali: Cults and Customs* (Djakarta, 1951), and Stutterheim, *Indian Influences in Old-Balinese Art.*

8. See Fig. 310 in Goris, *Bali.*

9. F. D. K. Bosch, "Uit de grensgebieden tussen Indische invloedssfeer en oud-inheems volksgeloof op Java," *Bijdragen tot de Taal-, Lanel- en Volkenkunde,* CX (1954), 1–19. Cf. Th. Pigeaud, *Java in the Fourteenth Century,* III, 86–91; IV, 219–250.

10. Stutterheim suggests a much later date for the existing structure at Tjandi Djago: A.D. 1343 rather than 1268, the commonly accepted date. For a discussion of this, see Bernet Kempers, pp. 84–85, 88.

11. See Bernet Kempers, pls. 323–324.

12. See Goris, *Bali,* pl. 419.

13. Seen Stutterheim, *Indian Influences in Old-Balinese Art.*

14. See Stutterheim, "Het Zinrijke Waterwerk van Djalatoenda," *Tijdschrift voor Indische Taal-, Land- en Volkenkunde,* LXXVII (1937), 214–250, for details of the technical and symbolic aspects of these waterworks. See also Stutterheim's article, "The Exploration of Mount Penanggungan in Eastern Java," *Annual Bibliography of Indian Archaeology for the Year 1936,* XI (1936), 25–30.

15. F. D. K. Bosch, "The Old Javanese Bathing-place Jalatunda," *Selected Studies in Indonesian Archaeology,* (The Hague, 1961), pp. 49–107.

16. See Bernet Kempers, pl. 200.

17. In an article devoted to the symbolic and mystical elements of the shadow play, the late Mangkunagara VII of Surakarta distinguished three kinds of samadhi (semadi): (a) for achievement of a destructive aim by means of (black) magic; (b) for the attainment of a positive goal through greatly enhanced powers; (c) for receiving a revelation about the mystery of existence.

See Mangkunagara VII of Surakarta, *On the Wayang Kulit (Purwa) and its Symbolic and Mystical Elements,* (Cornell University Southeast Asia Program, Data Paper no. 27; Ithaca, N. Y., 1957), pp. 13–16.

18. The passages (from Canto I, stanzas 12, 13, and part of 14) which are immediately cited and all subsequent extracts from the poem are translations by the author from the Dutch version by Poerbatjaraka, "Ardjuna Wiwaha," *Bijdragen tot de Taal-, Land- en Volkenkunde,* LXXXII (1926), 181–305.

19. Canto II, 5.

20. Canto IV, 6.

21. Cantos X and XI.

22. See the monograph by G. P. Rouffaer and J. L. A. Brandes, *Tjandi Singasari* (The Hague, 1909), for a detailed description of the site and its images.

23. Bernet Kempers, *Ancient Indonesian Art,* pl. 239.

24. N. J. Krom, *Inleiding tot de Hindoe-Javaansche Kunst* (The Hague, 1923), II, 80. As at Lara Djonggrang, the images of Mahaguru and Durga faced south and north respectively, but at Singasari the image of Ganesha faced east, since the main entrance of the tjandi is oriented toward the west.

25. See Bernet Kempers, pl. 235.

26. See Bernet Kempers, *Ancient Indonesian Art,* pl. 213.

27. R. Heine-Geldern, "The Art and Archaeology of Sumatra," p. 326. See also Stutterheim, *Indian Influences in Old-Balinese Art,* pls. 18, 20, 21, and Bernet Kempers, *Ancient Indonesian Art,* p. 87 and pl. 259.

28. Stutterheim, *Het Hinduisme in de Archipel,* p. 136.

29. *Ibid.,* p. 69.

30. Pigeaud, *Java in the Fourteenth Century,* III, Ch. 9ff. In the following, I have followed Pigeaud's interpretation and translation of the poem. All material within quotation marks is taken from his translation.

31. *Ibid.,* Chs. 7, 8, 10.

32. *Ibid.,* Canto 37, stanza 2; IV, p. 108.

33. *Ibid.,* Canto 32, stanzas 2–6.

34. Apart from our general acquaintance with court jesters from European history and folklore, I noted with interest that in ancient China jesters and dwarfs evidently were also constant members of a king's entourage. In Arthur Waley's *Three Ways of Thought in Ancient China* (Garden City, N. Y., 1956), p. 179, reference is made to "jesters and dwarfs who being always at his (the ruler's) side, have ample opportunity of studying his moods and fancies. . . ." The passage relates to the Realists' views of the ruler in the third century B.C.

35. For excellent reproductions of both the Prambanan and Panataran series and a stimulating discussion of both styles, see Stutterheim, *Rama Legenden und Rama Reliefs in Indonesien* (München, 1925).

36. Stutterheim, *Rama Legenden,* I, 185.

37. *Ibid.,* p. 197. Cf. H. Zimmer, *The Art of Indian Asia* (New York, 1955), II, pl. 40–41, "demons of the night subdued by the rising sun" at Bhaja, from the first century B.C.

38. See Stutterheim, "An Ancient Bhima Cult," in his *Studies in Indonesian Archaeology* (The Hague, 1956), p. 126, n. 45.

39. See Bernet Kempers, pl. 285.

40. N. J. Krom, *Inleiding tot de Hindoe-Javaansche Kunst,* II, 267, reports that an early visitor to the site saw a statue of Brahma which has since vanished.

41. Prijono, *Sri Tañjung, een oud Javaansch Verhaal* ('s-Gravenhage, 1938). See Bernet Kempers, pls. 299–300.

42. See also pl. 321 in Bernet Kempers, for a view of the head set on the torso.

43. See Stutterheim, *De Kraton van Majapahit.*

44. See Bernet Kempers, pls. 289–290.

PART II

LIVING TRADITIONS

CHAPTER 4

The Dance

Rhythms and Styles

Show me how you dance and I'll know where you are from. . . .

THERE ARE PROBABLY as many distinct dance styles in Indonesia as there are regional languages and dialects, and of these there are more than two hundred. Though mutually unintelligible, the majority belong to the Malayo-Polynesian family of languages. Similarly, one might think of Indonesian dances as belonging to a family of dances, with common roots and some persisting common characteristics. And just as in the course of history a multitude of foreign words—Sanskrit, Arabic, Portuguese, Dutch, and so forth—had been absorbed into the languages of Indonesia, so also has the dance vocabulary been enriched by borrowings which in time became Indonesianized. As in the plastic arts of Java and Bali, there has been a strong infusion of Indian elements into these islands' dances, enriching but not decisively shaping their style.

In broadest generalization, and always with allowance for exceptions, some of the common typical features of Indonesian dancing are described here.

Closeness to the ground is one of the most typical; the dancers tend to move more toward the earth than away from it. There are many kinds of dances and dance phrases in sitting, kneeling, crouching and half-crouching positions. When upright, a dancer often lowers his body on pliant knees.

Progress in space is largely accomplished in a variety of measured steps, with little running and virtually no hopping, leaping, or skipping. A general upward élan is missing. Exceptional are the martial dances of Niha men in south Nias who specialize in high jumps.

Conspicuous by its absence is spinning or whirling of the body around its own axis. Sinuous undulations of the body, as for instance in the Polynesian hula dances, are absent too. Back bends are rare as are other acrobatic features.

As in much of Southern Asia, the dance of hands is at least as important as that of the feet. Especially wherever Indian influences have affected dancing, the positions and movements of fingers are highly differentiated and are an important gauge of a dancer's artistry.

Of dance movements which discernibly derive from the imitation of animals, the most widespread perhaps are postures and motions based on those of birds and other winged creatures, unless a dancer explicitly impersonates a particular animal, as a tiger, monkey, elephant, boar, deer, or some animal-monster.

The tempo of dances is more often slow or moderate than rapid. Dance gestures in many areas tend to weave between rather than coincide with the accents of musical beats. In speed, the Balinese are exceptional as, for instance, in the scintillating rapidity of the *legong* dances performed by little girls (see Pl. 101).

Dancers as a rule do not transverse wide space while in motion. In many cases they remain practically in one place (see Pl. 83). There may be grandiose formations of many rows or of large circles, but the space within which each participant moves at any given moment is limited.

Choreographic formations are often in rows and files (see Pls. 78, 80). Big rounds in which the dancers either face the center or proceed in a circular file, and files moving in a serpentine course now occur mainly in islands outside Java and Bali. There are indications, however, that in Java, too, circular dances were known in the past.

The most common accessory of the dance is a scarf or a rectangular shawl either worn across one shoulder, draped over both shoulders, or attached around the

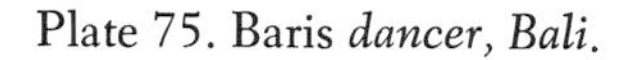

Plate 75. Baris *dancer, Bali.*

Plate 76. *Minangkabau dancers with tambourines perform* indang, *Matur, West Sumatra.*

waist. The free hanging ends of the scarf or shoulder cloth are picked up and manipulated by the dancers, enhancing the effect of their movements. The fan, used in several regions (Bali, South Celebes, South Sumatra), is less widely employed. Long artificial fingernails are worn in a few areas (Bali, South Sumatra) to add expressiveness to the hands.

Almost everywhere the dance costume, and especially the headdress, is of paramount importance and inseparable from the idea of dancing. The headdress can range from flowers in the hair (Pl. 78), to turbans tied in a special manner (Pls. 76, 83), elaborate, often precious diadems and crowns (Pl. 79), or frames supporting floral, metal, and other ornaments including horns, feathers, guilt leatherwork, and pendants of all sorts (Pls. 75, 81). Each headdress is peculiar to a specific kind of dance and each region has its own models.

Plate 77. *A Javanese dancer's hands.*

The over-all impression is that in Indonesia men dance more than women do. In any event, their dances are much more varied and, of course, more vigorous.

In the great majority of dances the participants are of one sex only. Male and female dancers appear together mainly in courting dances and in recreational group dances of young people. Dancer-actors of both sexes play together in dance dramas though it is known that in the past young boys played feminine roles in Java. In contrast, at one Javanese court, a prince introduced a dance-opera ("Langendriya") with an all-female cast.

Under no circumstances is bodily contact between male and female dancers admissible in the traditional sphere. Only with the adoption of some Western folk or ballroom dances, and, more recently, of choreography inspired by modern Western dance schools, has physical closeness of male and female dancers become acceptable.

These broad generalizations rest on a mosaic of dance styles, each with a shape and color of its own. The stylistic diversity in the dances of Indonesia is due, no doubt, as much to historical circumstances as to a

Plate 78. Djoged bung-bung *dancers, Tabanan, Bali.*

group's cultural temperament. It is a vast subject with many fascinating implications for a cultural anthropologist interested in kinesthetic idiosyncracies of cultural groups. All we can do here is to point to a few characterizing differences among the dance styles of various regional peoples.

Were a person thoroughly acquainted with Indonesian dances to be asked what visual image flashed up in his mind at the mention of "a Minangkabau dancer," "a Toba Batak dancer," "a Balinese dancer," "a Javanese dancer," an inevitably typical vision would appear on his mental screen. In some cases the images would differ from one another as much as those evoked at the mention of a "ballet dancer," "a jazz dancer," and "a folk dancer."

The image that arises in my mind at the thought of a West Sumatran Minangkabau male dancer is of a black-clad figure in wide pants and blouse assuming a broad stance on bent knees with his body inclining diagonally forward. His extended hands convey either challenge, defense, or attack; the attitude is strong and alert. The technique of Minangkabau male dancing is based largely on the stylized postures and gestures of *pentjak* (or *silat*)—the judolike art of self-defense with or without weapons, for which the Minangkabau are famous. The dance prelude to the actual encounter is an elaborate system of posturing with a pause after each effective stance or of a brief sequence of highly controlled movements. Every attitude into which the dancer momentarily freezes is precise and intricately balanced. The "pentjak style" of dancing is used even in Minangkabau narrative dances, as in the great round, *randai,* in which the dancers, to the accompaniment of chanted recitation, enact the episodes from the story of their culture hero, Tjindua Mato.

An image contrary in almost all details arises at the thought of another Sumatran dancer, a Toba Batak: his turbaned figure with a heavy, long shawl across one shoulder appears standing with legs held close together. His body bobs up and down and only the arms and turning hands provide variety in gesture. Compared with the broad, dramatic posturing of the Minangkabau, the dancing of the Batak male seems confined, tight, and almost obsessively repetitious. The dance of the *datu*[1]—magician-healer-priest of the non-Christianized Batak—is a typical and perhaps essential example of this style. Carrying his magic staff (*tunggal panaluan*), the dancer moves in tiny treading steps over the magic design he has drawn on the ground (see Pl. 6). But at the approach of the climax, when he pierces

with the sharp point of his staff an egg placed on the ground, he works himself up to a light skip and some hopping before the final thrust.

The feminine dance of the Minangkabau and the Batak similarly evoke contrasting visions. There is a soft grace in the dances of Minangkabau girls (even when danced by boys in feminine dress) and a rigidity in the dances of Batak women. Minangkabau girls' dances include the rhythmic and skillful juggling of objects such as plates or lighted candles affixed to saucers. These rest on the dancer's open palms and are made to describe in space semicircles, circles, and figure eights while the dancer inclines, dips, and rises, whether standing, stepping, turning, or kneeling. The melodious, even tenored folk tunes which accompany the dances are accented by clicks of rings (on the upper joint of the dancer's fingers) against the bottom edge of the plate. Dances with manipulated objects are also practiced by Minangkabau boys. In one, a whimsical courting dance, the boy swings and twirls an open parasol as he shades his girl partner while they are supposedly riding in a carriage. Chanted allusive quatrains (*pantun*), widespread in the Malaysian world, accompany the parasol dance.

The image of a Batak girl in a courting dance is one of an erect figure with downcast eyes. Although she occasionally shifts her feet sideways, essentially she remains in place. The most obvious movements are those of her hands (see Pl. 95). Yet the solemn simplicity of women's traditional dances in various Batak groups can be very impressive, especially when linked

Plate 79. *Javanese court dancer, Mangkunagaran, Surakarta.*

Plate 80. *Buginese* padjogé *singing and dancing, Pompanua, South Celebes.*

Plate 81. *Portrait of the late Ida Bagus Ketut, famous dancer of Mas, Bali.*

The Balinese, whose gorgeous robes are draped over a tightly fitting white shirt and trousers and tied under the armpits, is a startling and startled figure (see Pl. 75). Every part of his body is taut. His shoulders are drawn up so that the neck almost disappears between them. His tense face with wide-open eyes staring intently at an apparition visible only to himself is like an erratic thundercloud cut by lightning; the flash comes when the head abruptly jerks down and then up again as if in challenge and anticipation. One strained, arching hand laid on the chest adds to the projection of acute inquiry both timorous and self-assertive. After an outburst of a few sudden swaggering steps forward, the figure stops as abruptly as it had started.

The forceful Javanese dancer projects no such hypnotic and startling intensity. It is the very expansiveness and stately, regular rhythm of his gestures that make him an unrelenting force, impersonal, impassive. Since, apart from his crown and jewelry, his costume covers him only from the waist to the knees, the bareness of the limbs and torso emphasizes the power of his gestures. Our image of him in a short sequence of motions

Plate 82. *A Minangkabau* randai *dancer, Matur, West Sumatra.*

with ritual. A file of Toba Batak women in wide, flowing garments, each with one palm extended forward, slowly circling around a sacrificial buffalo is like an ancient frieze come to life. Or Karo Batak women, in heavy, broad turbans and tightly wrapped dark clothes, become expressive statuettes in slow motion when, standing in place, they slowly sink on deep-bending knees and rise again (Pl. 83). At intervals one arm curves upward so that a pointing finger can descend and touch the top of the dancer's head—a gesture which, to my knowledge, does not occur elsewhere in Indonesia.

There are many affinities between the dance techniques of the Javanese and those of the Balinese, especially dancing on out-turned bent legs and in the use of arching, turning, and palpitating hands. Yet spontaneous mental images of a Balinese male dancer in dynamic action and his Javanese counterpart again result in two very different visions.

Plate 83. *Karo Batak women in* mulih-mulih *funerary dance, Kaban Djahe, North Sumatra.*

is of a vigorous figure momentarily poised on one leg with the other leg raised sideways perpendicularly to the body but bent in a right angle at the knee; the dancer's head is turned toward an arm extended in the same direction as the raised leg; the other arm is lifted angularly behind the turned head. The next moment the sinewy raised leg stretches, descends, and as the foot is firmly implanted, heel first, on the ground, the weight of the dancer's body smoothly swings over to it in a broad diagonal motion while his head and arms reverse their position. Executed with almost gymnastic precision, the broad stance and successive wide shifts of weight with the alternatingly rising and extending limbs convey a sense of sustained power. Compared with the sudden outbursts of the hypertense Balinese dancer, the controlled poise of his Javanese counterpart seems an epitome of relentless steadiness.

The feminine dances of the Javanese and Balinese offer even stronger contrasts (cf. Pls. 100 and 101). Telling examples are the *serimpi* of Central Java and the Balinese *legong*.* The dance of the serimpi, embellished by the unfolding, falling, and fluttering of their dance scarves, is stately and restrained. The dancer's torso remains straight even when she inclines diagonally to one side. Her spine hardly ever bends and never arches. Her tightly wrapped hips shift subtly, almost imperceptibly; the spectator sees mainly the controlled movement of arms, the delicate play of hands and fingers, and the subtle rotations and shifts of the head. The glance of the dancer is constantly lowered, lending her performance a concentrated inwardness, or rather an almost trancelike "concentrated absence." At her fastest, in a figure called "flying," a serimpi glides tiptoe over the floor in tiny, even steps with one of her extended scarf-ends fluttering at her side.

In contrast, the lithe bodies of the Balinese legong are propelled in rapid staccato rhythms. In one hand the dancer holds a palpitating fan. Her spine is strongly arched; her hips shift abruptly from side to side as does her head and wide-open eyes. Instead of the delicate tiptoeing of the serimpi, the legong moves in a dust-raising lateral shuffle which sends her scooting in one direction and then in another. In slower, melodious passages, a legong dancer sinks and rises in place, and, in sign of lament, collapses forward, striking her knee with the fan.

* *Serimpi* and *legong* are names of dances as well as of the dancers who execute them. (For further discussion of these dances see pp. 117–119, also Pls. 100 and 101.)

Both dances involve a rigorous and difficult technique. But in Java controlled languor, a collected inwardness, and subtlety prevail. Paradoxical as it may sound, stillness pervades the serimpi and kindred Javanese dances. A renowned dancing master once said that a good dancer while executing serimpi feels no joy or exuberance; that in its mood is none of the brilliance of the sun, but rather the radiance of the full moon half-hidden by clouds; that inside the dancer is stillness but not a void, the stillness has a core, is "full"; and that the dancer sees nothing near or far because she looks "deep." If, in Java, the dance demands a gathering of the dancer's spirit into a kind of mystic state, the Balinese dancer seems to become "magically charged." Both dancers are instruments of "other" forces. This does not mean that either the Javanese or the Balinese dancer is taught to achieve a certain kind of inner concentration. Both receive only technical training. But it is the secret of the two styles that when technique has been transcended by full mastery a certain state is achieved in the dancer and a mood evoked in the spectator. Needless to repeat, there is a vast difference between the moods conveyed by the two styles.

Many more examples of stylistic diversity could be cited, not only from island to island but also from region to neighboring region. The Sundanese of West Java have characteristic movements which distinguish their dances markedly from those of the Javanese. In Celebes the dance styles of the Buginese and Makassarese in the south differ greatly from those of their neighbors to the north, the Toradja. This difference has been strengthened by the fact that the coastal Buginese and Makassarese have had more intensive contact with Java and the outside world than the inland Toradja. Throughout the Indonesian archipelago, one can find here and there echoes of Portuguese, British, and Dutch dances. Indeed, infusions of foreign influence, whether from Asia or from Europe, have through history contributed to the diversification of Indonesian dance styles.

Ancient Motives

The dance is one of the sturdiest threads of continuity in Indonesian culture. We may safely assume that the inhabitants of the Indonesian islands, like the rest of humanity, have danced ever since they discovered the secret of rhythmic movement springing from excitement, whether of desire, fear, or joy. The inherent "magic" of dance is its generation of vitality in both the dancer and the spectator. Born of exuberance and harnessed by skill, the dance from time immemorial has enhanced individual and communal life, especially its religious aspects. In a pagan world, the dance is a liberating incantation like hymns and prayers. It accompanies celebrations of all important aspects of life, not the least, death. And since life is reasserted with particular vigor in the face of death, and since the perpetuation of life means fertility, dances symbolic of fertility are as inseparable from pagan death rites as is resurrection from death in Christian faith.

Welfare and fertility are invoked with dances at planting and at the beginning of the new cycle after harvest; at feasts which accompany significant transitions in life, especially at weddings and funerals or cremations; at the inauguration of important projects; at anniversaries marking the founding of a community.[2] Whenever fertility and security are believed to depend on the protection of ancestral souls, on the benevolence of spirits of nature, or on the blessings of high deities, people dance to propitiate and honor them. The con-

Plate 84. *A Simalungun Batak mask dancer in* huda-huda *funerary rites, Pematang Raya, North Sumatra.*

tinuity of life is stressed by the presence of the protective ancestral spirits, impersonated by masked dancers, especially at funerary rites (Pl. 84). People dance around sacrificial animals or other offerings presented to the superhuman beings. Dancing priests and priestesses, often entranced, communicate with higher powers and transmit their will. And if chiefs or princes are regarded as the divinely endowed embodiments of a community's welfare, they are glorified and entertained by dances.

Dances also reinforce welfare and safety when they serve to expel or repel evil forces that cause sickness and other calamities. Dangerous spirits are often routed by dancers wielding weapons.

Trance dances play an important role in the communication with higher powers. They have various functions.[3] Sometimes they are initiated to counteract calamities such as epidemics and sometimes for oracular purposes. Often they are merely spectacles. The mysterious state of the dancers and their unusual behavior provide special fascination to the public. Trance dancers enjoy considerable prestige because when possessed they have become the instrument of a supernatural power.

We know from the preceding chapters that while in isolated areas of Indonesia the pagan or animistic view of life persists, in most areas the social order and world outlook have changed, partly from contact with other lands of Asia and Europe. The dance, like the other arts, has acquired new forms and functions. Thus, dancing shamanistic priests and priestesses gradually slip into the role of entertainers. In Hinduistic Bali, dancing is still an essential component of all ritual life, but it has also developed into a high theatrical art. Among the Islamic groups of Sumatra, some trance dancers are now associated with Islamic mysticism.[4] While echoes of ancient pagan rites still reverberate in the folk plays of Islamic Java, the shadow play has taken the place of ritual dances in times of crisis and festive climax. Dance and dance drama, which like the shadow play preserve the spirit and imagery of the Hindu-Javanese legacy, are today largely secular entertainment.

Thus, one of the great fascinations of the Indonesian dance world lies in the simultaneous existence of dances which in other places might be stages in a long historical evolution: from primitive dance rhythms accompanied only by chanting or drums, through complex rituals, to sophisticated theater arts with polyphonous music. In Indonesia, one cannot trace a general evolutionary line. All stages are present. Yet it is possible to recognize in some dances the transformations they have undergone, to discover that the content and function of certain dances are reinterpretations of older conceptions, and to follow the secularization of ritual.

To trace such transformations, the interested student can resort to analogies between dances of Indonesian nonhistorical and pagan groups (such as the Dayak or Toradja tribes in the interior of Borneo and Celebes) and those of a Hinduized people (the Balinese) and between both of these and dances practiced in Islamic regions, especially in Java and Sumatra. He can also turn to available historical documentation on dances of Indonesia's past.

The depth of tradition and the problems confronting a student trying to fathom it are best illustrated by a few concrete examples. The Javanese hobbyhorse dance is particularly challenging.

Known as *kuda kepang* (*kuda:* horse, *kepang:* plaited bamboo), this folk play is performed by men mounted on flat horses made of plaited and painted bamboo. The dancers' own legs create the illusion of the horses' movements. The play is also known as *kuda lumping* (in West Java where the horse is of leather, *lumping*), *ebleg* (in the southwest), *djatilan* (in the region of Jogjakarta), and *reyog* or *ludrug* (in East Java). Sometimes a single rider accompanied by a few musicians and a masked or unmasked man with a whip may trek through a town and stop at a street corner for a performance (Pl. 85). The usual combination, however, is four, six, or eight riders, several musicians, and one or more masked figures.[5] In a djatilan performance near Jogjakarta in 1956, four masks were present: a clown wearing a white half-mask, a man in a black mask, a red-faced "wild man," and a yellow-masked female being.* In addition, weaving about the eight dancing horsemen was a man who held with both hands a wooden crocodile head from which a long, twisted cloth trailed over his shoulder. In deep trance, he danced in a wide circle, unceasingly, obsessively, bending from side to side.

Entrancement is the principal event of a hobbyhorse performance. At the beginning, the dance is orderly;

* It is no accident that the colors of the four masks are black, white, yellow, and red. These colors have magical significance and are associated in Java as well as in Bali among other things with the four cardinal points.

Plate 85. *Stiffened hobbyhorse* (kuda kepang) *dancer whipped by "wild man," Solo, Central Java.*

in regular and persistent rhythms supplied by a small percussion orchestra, the horsemen "trot" in a circle. In some plays they are divided into two parties which engage in a sham battle. Gradually, the obsessive rhythms become more tense, and before long one of the dancers "becomes" (*djadi*), that is, becomes possessed. Sometimes trance is induced when the leader lashes a horseman with a whip believed to have been "charged" with magic power by means of a "filling" ritual. The entranced rider then starts behaving like a horse. He may run wild, wallow on the ground, eat grass or straw, and drink water from a bucket on the ground. His whole body stiffened, eyes unseeing, he may alternate wild charges in furious gallop with persistent treading, only to dash off wildly again or to stop abruptly before the troupe's spiritual leader. The latter, usually an old man and mystic teacher, calms him and eventually brings him out of the trance with incense and muttered incantations.

In the djatilan performance mentioned above, the red-masked figure carried a wooden weapon instead of a whip. Most of the time he remained apart from the other masks. The white-faced clown, advancing and receding in swaying steps, one arm swinging back and forth with each step, moved with the yellowish female mask on the fringes of the dance space. The black mask also remained unobtrusive. Yet their ghostlike presence lent the play that note of additional mystery which sets the imagination roving.

On one hand, we know of hobbyhorse dances with strikingly similar features, singly or in combination (masked fool, whip, feminine disguise, combats), in a number of countries,* from China to Spain.[6] On the other hand, a hobbyhorse dancer accompanied by two masks, one male and one female, figured in the funerary rites of the Toba Batak of Samosir in Sumatra before their conversion to Christianity several decades ago. As performed in 1938,[7] the "rider" of the *hoda-*

* Curt Sachs sees in these dances "well known defense and fertility motifs."

Plate 86. Singa barong *confronts Djoko Ludro, Ponorogo, East Java.*

Plate 87. Barong Kèkèt, *Bali.*

hoda dance (*hoda:* horse) pranced about holding the reins of his hobbyhorse while two white-robed masks danced nearby. Their bodies swayed from side to side and their hands, hidden by the sleeves, rotated wooden hands with straight upturned palms. In construction, the hobbyhorse was a simpler version of the ornate hobbyhorses used by the Cavallets dancers of Mallorca:[8] a cloth-covered frame attached around the waist of the dancer, with a wooden horse head in front and tail in the rear.*

To the north of the Toba Batak regions, among the Pak-Pak Batak, a funerary dance known as *kuda-kuda* also featured riders accompanied by masks. But instead of horses, effigies of hornbills served as mounts. Similarly, hornbill masks stalked among other dancers with painted masks in a Simalungun Batak funerary ritual called *huda-huda* (see Pl. 11). And among the Karo Batak, hornbill effigies were carried on the head of shrouded men accompanied by dancing monstrous masks.

Apparently horse and hornbill have merged in the funerary rites of these Batak groups. We have seen earlier that on bronze-age drums, the hornbill was associated with the conveying of souls of the dead to the hereafter. In contemporary Batak funerary art, commemorative male figures are often depicted on horseback. Did the horse supplant the hornbill when a horse cult was introduced perhaps from or via India? Are the hobbyhorse dancers of the Javanese folk plays, with the accompanying masked dancers (whose presence is as ghostly as that of the ancestral masks of Batak funerary rites), unknowing perpetuators of ancient death and fertility rites? And are they and the Sumatran riders of horses and hornbills both descendants of some more widespread death and fertility rites still echoed in the folk plays of other lands on the Eurasian continent?

The Javanese kuda kepang is an example of continuity as a living tradition, but in form only. Its original meaning and function have been lost; today it is a diverting spectacle. Sometimes the riders are said to represent a legendary king's cavalry clashing with an enemy force. The only hint of their possible ritual function in the past is the participation of hobbyhorse dancers together with a variety of masks in circumcision and wedding processions.[9]

In East Java, hobbyhorse dancers sometimes accompany, a red-masked hero known as Djoko Ludro who

* In the Madras region of South India, the *Poikkuthirai* hobbyhorse dancer's mount, similarly constructed, has a fanged animal head, a fantastic mixture of lion and tiger.

fights with a monstrous animal, the *singa barong*. Usually the singa barong puts the attacking horsemen to flight, but succumbs in the encounter with Djoko Ludro (see Pl. 86). This animal mask, like the hobby-horse dancers, is also a subject for much speculation.

Of all the Javanese animal masks (*barongan*)—tigers, boars, crocodiles, monkeys, elephants, dogs, buffaloes, deer, and a bird called Titit-Tuwit—the singa barong is the most impressive. Although *singa* means lion, the singa barong mask resembles or is distinctly a tiger (Pl. 86). It is crowned with a magnificent wreath of tall peacock feathers. The singa barong is impersonated by two men covered by a cloth attached to the mask. Pigeaud and Staugaard mention that the singa barong has been referred to as Radjawana (Javanese for King of the Woods, Skr. *rājavana*),[10] which is synonymous with the Sanskrit Vanaspati, Lord of the Forest.

In Bali, the most impressive of all barongs, which include tigers, boars, elephants, deer, dogs, goats, and horses, is the famous *barong kekèt*.[11] Like the singa barong, barong kekèt bears the title Lord of the Woods (Banaspati). His expressive, monstrous face (Pl. 87) is of no one particular animal but could be seen as a somewhat anthropomorphized combination of lion, tiger, cow, and goat raised to supernatural magnificence.* His mask and heavy fleece are kept in a separate shrine in the temple court and are considered sacred. When mounted on two dancers for a procession or a play, barong kekèt is truly regal. Gilt carved leather ornaments studded with glittering mirror or mica disks surround his head and decorate his body, and at the rear the tall, curving, and similarly adorned tail rises triumphant.

Barong kekèt has strong magic potency. His adversary is the witch Rangda, whose "black" destructive power he opposes with "white magic." Barong kekèt protects and restores fallen kris dancers who try unsuccessfully to attack the witch but are repelled by her and, in a state of trance, turn their daggers against themselves.[12] The present roles of singa barong and barong kekèt are different; while barong kekèt is magically protective and always victorious, singa barong is regarded as a ferocious and dangerous beast who is defeated in battle with his principal foe, whether Djoko Ludro or an opponent of another name. Yet they appear in adjacent and culturally related regions—East Java and Bali—and thus one is led to expect some link between them, especially since they both bear the title Lord of the Woods.

The title Banaspati belongs in East Java to the Kirttimukha head. In ancient Indian myth, it was the name of an emanation of Shiva's wrath, sprung from between the god's eyebrows, a monster of insatiable hunger, created to devour the demonic Rauh, an emissary of the Lord of Titans. When Rauh secured Shiva's mercy, Kirttimukha was, by Shiva's order, to consume his own body. He fed upon it until nothing was left but his leonine head, the "Visage of Glory," (kirttimukha). Shiva then ordained, perhaps as compensation, that Kirttimukha live in honor above the god's portals.[13] Thus it came to be that the monster's head appears above temple portals and niches in Java and Bali as a venerated guardian. In Central Java the guardian monster is known as Kala and in East Java it is referred to as Banaspati. Kirttimukha-Kala-Banaspati, as Bosch points out, is also associated with solar symbolism, especially with the sun at its zenith.[14] "Kala" is also the Sanskrit word for all-devouring "time."

The barong kekèt looks, in fact, much like the protective monster heads of the sanctuaries but complete with a bearded lower jaw. The gilded, carved leather ornaments around his head are akin to the winglike or flamelike motifs around the kala heads of the sanctuaries. Singa barong's wreath of tall peacock feathers, which rise from his head like a halo of rays, similarly, seems to point to solar symbolism. It is thus possible that the two barongs, both of whom are leonine and Lords of the Woods, were at one time somehow related to Kirttimukha-Kala-Banaspati, the devouring monster who became a protector of sanctuaries.*[15]

There have been suggestions however that the

* Barong kekèt like singa barong may have been in the past more distinctly a tiger. There is perhaps a vague hint of this in the statement of a Balinese priestess quoted by Jane Belo and summarized here: "Five generations ago," when a particular temple (*poera dalam*) was built, the god's "sitting place" *was at first a tiger barong* [author's italics] (*barong matjan*) and a Rangda (witch). "And it happened that the god was ashamed and there was utterance (in trance), to wit, that there should be a Barong Kètèt (Kekèt) as a sitting place for him, to be accompanied by a Rangda." Belo, *Trance*, p. 72.

The tiger is Indonesia's "lord of the woods"—there are no lions. Today the tiger is still mentioned with veneration mixed with fear in Sumatra, where he bears the title *datu*, and is said to preside over certain initiation rites.

* A parallel to this monster head is the Chinese *t'ao t'ieh*, "the glutton," whose face with gaping mouth but no lower jaw appears on early Chinese bronzes of the Shang Dynasty (1523–1027 B.C.).

barongs may have been introduced from China. Certainly, looking at a picture of a Chinese lion-dance (Pl. 88), one is struck by its similarity to a barong performance. The evil-repelling Chinese dragon, whose terrifying mask with long winding body appears also in Indonesia at Chinese New Year's celebrations, has been mentioned, too, as a possible source of the barong's origin.[16]

Joseph Campbell, authority on world mythologies, observes that "the barong looks to me like an Indonesian version of the serpent-lion motif, symbolic (one might say) of the spiritual power operative in nature. In most mythologies, this power is terrifying but life-productive—as is also spiritual illumination (cf. Mucalinda Buddha*). In the Biblical tradition (of which Islam is a product) this power is impugned and degraded; hence exhibits only its negative aspects (cf. Serpent in the Garden; barong in Muslim Java). . . ."[17]

The evolution of the barongs in Java and Bali is no doubt complex, and the strands connecting them with mythological monsters of other lands most likely cross and intertwine. Today in Bali barong kekèt retains the status of a protective deity, perhaps with lingering Hindu-Buddhist connotations. In Islamic Java, however, the singa barong could not retain any kind of divine status. If once the singa barong did indeed occupy a more exalted position, he has been brought down to that of a dangerous wild beast fought in the woods by emissaries of a legendary prince.

The Javanese hobbyhorse dancers and the barongs of Java and Bali are only two instances of many folk plays and mummeries which provoke tantalizing speculations on their origins. There are also the Javanese doll, Ni Towong, made to dance before a mirror at night[18] and a pair of male and female giants impersonated by huge dolls in Java and by men on stilts covered by costumes and topped by large masks in Bali.[19] Masked or painted clowns, grotesque, monstrous beings, and animals roam through the Javanese countryside. The performers are villagers, sometimes organized in small clubs just as the hobbyhorse dancers are. They appear upon invitation on special occasions, receiving some compensation in money and food. Unlike the small wandering troupes of mask-players or other actors who stage plays in the villages, they are rarely full-time professional performers.

* The meditating Buddha sheltered by the hood of the serpent-king Mucalinda. (See Heinrich Zimmer, *The Art of Indian Asia,* I, pp. 63–67).

Plate 88. *Lion dance, 19th-century woodblock print, Szech'uan, China.*

Plate 89. *Dancing drummers accompany a prince on his way to worship a stupa, relief on the Barabudur.*

Plate 90. *Dancing drummers, Tulung Agung, East Java.*

Dances in Historical Perspective

Historical documentation for dances in Indonesia relates mainly to Java. It consists of representations of dance scenes on the stone reliefs of the tjandi and other sacred structures; of royal inscriptions engraved on stones and copper plates which mention dances and other spectacles connected with certain ritual celebrations; and, beginning with the eleventh century, passages in Old Javanese literature which refer to or describe dance performances.* Scattered references to dances in Java and the other islands of the archipelago can be found in the writings of early Arab and European travelers.

This documentation is most valuable for information about nomenclature, circumstances in which the dances were performed, or the number and status of the participants; but it cannot yield information about the very essence of these dances—the sequence of their movements in time and space. Visual representations are more helpful inasmuch as one can glean at least a momentary attitude, a basic stance. They suggest certain dance techniques, typical postures and gestures.

* See Appendix II.

Plate 91. *Battle dance on a relief of the Barabudur.*

But tempting as it may be, one still cannot deduce with any degree of certainty whether the gestures were rapid or slow or how the depicted dancer would proceed in space. Thus, looking at one of the magnificent Indian bronze or stone images of the Lord of the Dance, Shiva Nataraja, and assuming its sculptor had a clear idea of the god's cosmic dance, one can only wonder whether the momentary attitude is a climax of a lively élan or a phase in slow posturing; how the suspended gesture would pass on to the next one; how the next one would look; and in what tempo the transition would be made.

Nevertheless, in studying visual representations of dances on Java's Hindu-Buddhist monuments, we can discover something about continuities and changes in their forms as well as functions. Among the reliefs that decorate the walls of the Barabudur appear a number of dance scenes which are especially instructive. Several dances are pictured in the context of popular life, others in a court environment. It is likely that at the time the Barabudur was being built the depicted dances were already traditional. Among them are some vivid prototypes of dances still performed in the twentieth century. For instance, in one scene we encounter a group of dancing drummers (Pl. 89) in company with a flutist and two other musicians with raised cymbals. They are part of the retinue of a high-placed personage who approaches a stupa with offerings. Traveling in East Java in the thirties, I encountered on the streets of Tulung Agung a procession of dancing drummers whose rhythms and whose steps may well have been very similar to those of the drummers on the Barabudur relief, perhaps identical. Dancing drummers are well known in India. In Java, they are also depicted on the reliefs at the Shiva temple of Prambanan.

Another scene on the Barabudur depicts two pairs of dancing men with swords, club, spear, and shields (Pl. 91). For the entertainment of the spectators nearby, they are apparently engaged in a danced sham battle. Martial dances for men are prominent in most Indonesian islands. Having grown out of man's combative spirit, war dances may once have been practiced in preparation for battle with human enemies and in celebration of victory. Varying in style from region to region, they are now mainly displays of valor and skill, an art and a sport. Some culminate in mock fights with a visible or invisible opponent. So, the Dayak of Borneo are famous for their solo sword dances; the Balinese for their magnificent *baris* dancers who appear in grand array at temple festivals, displaying lances, swords, or other weapons and shields of different shapes; the Javanese for their highly stylized danced battles of warriors often identified with heroes of a dance drama (Pl. 93); the Niha for their spectacular war-plays; the Minangkabau of Sumatra's west coast, for their half-danced, stylized *silé* (*silat*) combats.

If we compare the moment of the danced battle captured on the relief of the Barabudur with the stance and equipment of the contemporary Dayak sword dancer and with the attitudes of the Javanese combatants, we find some remarkable correspondences. The relief also shows that in the ninth century martial dances were already a popular entertainment. The excitement and amusement they created among the spectators in fourteenth-century Majapahit is described in the poem *Nagarakrtagama** and is further evidence of their uninterrupted popularity. Sham battles are ubiquitous climaxes of Javanese dance drama, and battle episodes are often isolated for separate performance. Javanese stage warriors are equipped with clubs, swords, spears, knives, round and oblong shields. Noble heroes fight with krisses and bows and arrows. In some special dances, as in those with lances, there seem to be lingering reminiscences of old tournaments and, perhaps, of temple rituals similar to the shield- and lance-bearing Balinese baris dancers who appear at temple festivals.

Still another Barabudur relief portrays a dance party (Pl. 94). Four pairs, each of a boy and a girl, dance to the rhythms of a *gambang* (a bamboo xylophone still used in Java and Bali) and two other instruments. They are apparently being encouraged by a gesturing, and perhaps chanting or shouting leader. The attitudes of the dancing boys are lively. They dance with turned-out and bent knees, raise their arms and incline the head. The figures of the young women are, in contrast, very restrained. Their straight legs are held close together; their bodies are erect, too. They look as if only their arms were moving as they tread in one place or perhaps move forward in small, delicate steps. The left hand of each female dancer is raised from the wrist with the palm forward, while the right arm is either extended sideways or moved across the body toward the left elbow. The restraint which typifies the girls of the Barabudur dance party still characterizes many indigenous dances for women. Thus, for example, in Simalungun Batak courting dances, the girls' demure attitudes are marked by impassive faces, erect bodies, relatively slow and small steps and gestures principally of arms and hands (Pl. 95).

The lively attitudes of the dancing boys on the Barabudur relief immediately suggest the style of dancing still exhibited by the male participants of a traditional Javanese dance party (*tayuban* or *tandakan*). On turned-out bent legs, head inclining to one or another side, and rotating the hands on angularly lifted arms, each dances around the female partner. Instead of each man having an individual partner, however, men dance (*ngibing*) in turns with one professional dance girl (*talèdèk* or *tandak*) especially engaged for the occasion. (The wife and daughters of the host and all female guests retire during a tayuban party into inner rooms and amuse themselves as best they can playing cards or gossiping.) The talèdèk is the heart of the celebration. She dances alone for a while and then approaches one of the guests offering him a dance scarf, an invitation to dance with her, or rather opposite and around her. To approach the dance girl at close range and try to touch her as she eludes is part of the fun. Sometimes the male dancer flourishes a gin cup from which he drinks when the dancing stops. In Bali, too, dance parties center around a single girl dancer

* See Appendix II.

Plate 92. *Kenyah Dayak sword dancer, Usal Djalong, Borneo.*

Plate 93. *Danced battle (Pandji Andaga against a Buginese warrior), Mangkunagaran, Surakarta.*

(*djogèd*) or a boy dancer in female dress (*gandrung*). They invite the male partner to ngibing by a tap on the shoulder with the fan. Ngibing is also the man's role at a Makassarese dance party in south Celebes, where the dance girl (*padjogé*), bowing, invites him to dance.

Whether and why and when dance parties of paired boys and girls (as depicted on the Barabudur) changed in Java into parties during which men danced in turn with one professional girl dancer is a moot question. It is possible that in ninth-century Java also, there were dances which were predominantly "stag parties" animated by one female dancer.

Another type of single female dancer in Java is the street-dancer, *ronggeng*. Unlike the talèdèk, a ronggeng does not invite partners but acts as popular entertainer. She wanders through the country with a small group of musicians and stops at a street corner in town or near a coffee shop in the rural areas to sing and dance for gifts of small change from the onlookers. The description of the ronggeng given by Raffles 150 years ago, apart from his esthetic biases, is still valid today. He said, in part:

> The rong'gengs accompany the dance with singing, the words being generally extempore to the music. . . . Their dress is coarse, but in other respects resembles that of the more select dancers. They do not, however, wear any tiara on the head nor armlets; bracelets are only worn occasionally. Their hair is dressed after a peculiar fashion, abundantly oiled, and ornamented with flowers of various kinds. . . . Their action is usually distorted, their greatest excellence seeming to consist in bending the arms and hands back in an unnatural manner, and giving one or two of the fingers a tremulous motion.

Of course what was "distorted" and an "unnatural manner" to him was and still is to the Javanese the measure of the dancer's skill and beauty—an arm curving at the elbow in double-jointed fashion and fingers subtly flexing from an upstretched hand. Farther on, probably alluding to Indian *nautch* dancers of his time, Raffles writes:

Plate 94. *Dance party on a relief of the Barabudur.*

Plate 95. *Simalungun Batak courting dance, Negeri Dolog, North Sumatra.*

Generally speaking, the rong'gengs do not descend to the performance of those disgusting and disgraceful postures and motions, which are stated to be so frequent on the continent of India, but they are not free from the charge of impropriety in this respect. Their song, though little esteemed and less understood by Europeans, sometimes possesses much humour and drollery; and in adapting their motions to the language, they frequently excite loud bursts of laughter, and obtain great applause from the native audience. . . .* It is not unusual for the performances of the rong'gengs to be varied by the action of a fool or buffoon. Mimicry is a favourite amusement, and beside imitating, in a ludicrous manner, the actions of the rong'-gengs, there are not wanting performers of this description, who occasionally direct their wit against all classes of society, and evince a considerable degree of low humour.[20]

Like the Indian nautch dancers, the ronggeng are reputed to be prostitutes but they are never despised or subjected to abuse. They may even marry a respectable member of the community. In fact, to the present day, these dancers have a somewhat protected position in Java.

Their profession is sanctified by a folk tale couched in Islamic terms. Three artisans, a wood carver, a goldsmith, and a tailor, were instruments of the divine will. The Lord Allah ordered the wood carver to make a statue of a beautiful woman and install it beside a little-traveled path. Passing by, the tailor took pity on the statue's nakedness and dressed it with his unsold wares, a *sarong,* a chest cloth, and a *kebaya* (blouse). Later, the goldsmith came by and adorned the statue with rings, bracelets, earrings and a necklace. All three, upon return home, fasted and prayed arduously that the figure might be imbued with life. After forty days, a *wali* (one of the nine legendary holy men who introduced Islam into Java) came upon the statue and to him Allah's will was revealed by an angel. The statue became animated. The wali led the beautiful woman to the house of the wood carver. The goldsmith and the tailor had already arrived here having been told by a *tjitjak* (household lizard) to do so. Each of the three men, seeing the lovely woman, recognized his share in her creation and claimed her for himself. But the wali ordered all three to accompany the woman, who was to dance and sing, wandering through the country. The wood carver was to play the *rebab* (one-string violin), the tailor was to beat the drum, and the goldsmith was to play the gong, *ketjrek,* and *ketuk* (all percussion instruments). They obeyed and the four wandered out and on to Majapahit.[21] And thus it was shown that the dance girl does not belong to one but to many.

Another story, of Indian origin, similarly elevates the dance girl's profession. Vishnu, incarnated as a young man, came to a village at night intending to test the charity of the people. He knocked at many doors but was harshly turned away by everyone, even by the Brahmans. At last he found a meal, hospitality for the night, and even entertainment in the poor hut of a dance girl. The god loved her and, departing in the morning, promised in gratitude protection to her and all her descendants. And since princes and kings are incarnations of Vishnu, they must love and patronize the descendants of the one *"qui fit pardonner la dureté des hommes."*[22]

The humble dance girls have more glamorous counterparts at the princely courts. The popular talèdèk, until the first decades of this century at least, had a more privileged sister, the singer-talèdèk (*pesinden talèdèk*) attached to the palace for select dance parties (*tayuban*). The counterparts of the common dance girl, the ronggeng, at the courts are female solo dancers who perform at festive receptions. The best known solo dance which originated at a court is the *golek.* It is a charming display of feminine grace with many of the stylized gestures alluding to self-beautification—a feature this dance shares with the famous love-dance for men called *kiprah* (pp. 164–165). The golek dance is also associated with a puppet (*golek*) who at dawn is made to dance in joyous epilogue to a shadow play to celebrate the victory of the righteous party.

We find on a Barabudur relief a single court dancer entertaining a royal couple seated on an elevation under a canopy, accompanied by musicians playing flutes, drums, cymbals and bells. Today one can find similar postures, though less dynamic, in the dances of some female court dancers, as in Plate 97. If her skirt were transparent, one could see that her basic stance is almost identical to that of the court dancer on the Barabudur relief.

On several other Barabudur reliefs we find single female dancers in less restrained attitudes. In addition to the expected musicians, they are often accompanied by one or two male figures who seem to participate in the performance (Pl. 98). Animated and jovial, they stand with hands extended toward the dancer either gesturing or marking rhythms with rattles, bells, or

* Compare with the hilarity provoked by the songs of the fourteenth-century dance girl. See p. 115 and Appendix II.

Plate 96. *Court dancer entertaining royal couple, Barabudur relief.*

small cymbals, possibly emitting vocal sounds, apparently supporting her dance. They are bearded and corpulent, the iconographical marks of a Brahman in Hindu-Javanese art. They may have been Brahman dancing masters of the court dancers. Even today the Javanese dancing master guides the dancers' rhythms, their changes and approaching pauses with audible signals during an actual performance as well as during training; he knocks these out with a wooden mallet on a hollow box called *keprak*.

The role of the ninth-century Brahmans may have gone beyond that of the dancing master. As Stutterheim pointed out, there may be a connection between the ninth-century Brahman dance directors on the Barabudur reliefs and sets of two officials who up to the twentieth century played an inexplicable, somewhat farcical role at certain court ceremonials.[23] At one court (where they wore artificial beards) they supported the dancers with shouts and clapping hands; at another court, their duties included the supervision of the pesinden talèdèk. Thus the Barabudur Brahmans may have combined the function of dancing masters with general supervision of the dance girls.

We have testimony of the existence of a dance girl

Plate 97. *Javanese court dancer, Mangkunagaran, Surakarta.*

very like the pesinden talèdèk at the court of Majapahit in fourteenth-century East Java. Her appearance is described in two stanzas of *Nagarakrtagama*.[24] In the course of seven-day celebrations held after the harvest to glorify the king and his palace as hub of the country's welfare, a female dancer called Juru i Angin appears upon the scene accompanied by one or more *buyut*. All we know about them is that they were called "great-grandfathers," that is, they were old men, but their role and relation to the dancer can only be guessed at. They may have been successors to the priestly or semipriestly dance directors shown on the Barabudur reliefs. They could have been the predecessors of the farcical supervisors of the royal dancers in the twentieth century. They could have also been simple clowns like those who accompanied the ronggeng in Raffles' time. Finally, all these Javanese functionaries—the Brahmans on the reliefs, the buyut in literature, the supervisors at the courts—may hark back to the buffoon (*vidûshaka*) of the classical Indian theater who was "a Brahman but ugly and ridiculous."[25]

The Juru i Angin sings as she dances, apparently in a humorous vein, since her words and acting cause laughter. In her song she alludes to choosing partners, which immediately brings to mind the pesinden talèdèk of the Central Javanese courts. After her dance, Juru i Angin is showered with gifts of clothing and thereupon is invited into the royal "Presence" to drink liquor in the company of various notables.

Pigeaud believes that the role of Juru i Angin may have been sacerdotal; that she may have personified an indigenous female deity whose name alone survives in Javanese folklore—Ratu Angin-angin.[26] Since *angin* means wind, she may have been symbolic of the west monsoon winds that bring rain and thus essentially a goddess of fecundity.[27] We know, however, that the pesinden talèdèk at the Javanese courts in the nineteenth and twentieth centuries was no more than a luxurious edition of the common talèdèk; she was a secular entertainer. And in the recent past there has been no female solo dancer at the courts who has had a sacral role.

Although ritual overtones have disappeared from the court dances of single female performers, an aura of

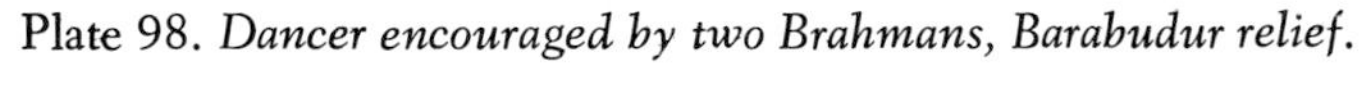
Plate 98. *Dancer encouraged by two Brahmans, Barabudur relief.*

sacredness still surrounds some group dances, especially the *bedoyo.* They have no counterparts on the reliefs of the Barabudur where the depicted court entertainers are either a single female dancer or a pair. The large groups of musicians and other groups of figures shown on the reliefs indicate that no technical difficulties would have prevented the depiction of groups of dancers had they existed at the ninth-century royal courts. There are, however, indications that groups of eight (or nine) dancers were customary at the court of Majapahit, though their function may have been different from that of the bedoyo.*

Before the Indonesian revolution depressed the status and reduced the means of the Central Javanese princely courts, bedoyo dancers, like sacred regalia, belonged to the innermost ceremonial life of a keraton.† Future bedoyo dancers were chosen by palace officials from among the children of villagers or keraton servants, who were taken to live in the palace where they were trained in the complex art of the dance and taught other skills. Eventually they might have become concubines of the ruling prince.

The most sacred of their dances in Surakarta was the *bedoyo ketawang* performed on the anniversary of the Susuhunan's ascension to the throne. It was believed that bedoyo ketawang was inspired by the Goddess of the Southern Ocean, Njahi (or Ratu) Loro Kidul. She was said to have appeared to the first ruler of the dynasty, Sultan Agung (1613–1645), and revealed her love for him in a song which she sang while dancing before him. The goddess was prevailed upon to teach her dance to the prince's dancers, so that he could always remember her. A performance of bedoyo ketawang was always preceded by offerings and the burning of incense to Ratu Loro Kidul who was said to be invisibly present during the dance.[28] At the keraton of Jogjakarta, bedoyo dances, including *bedoyo semang* and *bedoyo sinom,* were also linked to an encounter between Njahi Loro Kidul or one of her nymphs and a dynastic predecessor of the ruling sultan.[29]

The bedoyo traditionally appeared in a group of nine. Their costumes and adornments were those of brides. In the music and chanting that accompanied their slow dance a solo female voice usually preceded the choral parts. The text of the bedoyo ketawang songs was considered so sacred that its transcription was avoided for fear of desecration by errors. An example of the poetic content can be cited, however, from a 1924 bedoyo performance in which the theme was Ardjuna's glorification in Indra's heaven. After his victory over the King of Demons, Niwatakawatja, he was made for seven celestial "days" king of the universe and received as wife the most beautiful of all nymphs, Supraba:

> Of blinding beauty her face, she was enveloped in sumptuous robes, filling the vast hall of the heavenly city with her fragrance, all radiant light, enchanting in each of her motions. . . . The king [Ardjuna] ever more ardently pleads for her favors and tender love. In jest, she gives him a foretaste of the joys and delights that await him. And the heavenly beauties crowd her away, impatient in their desires.[30]

Though the themes of the bedoyo songs are often poetically erotic, there is little overt sensuality in the dance. The entrance and departure are solemn processionals. The beginning and the end of the dance proper consists, as in all other court dances, of the worshipful gestures of the *sembah,* addressed to a deity, the king, and the noble guests. In simple daily form, folded hands are raised to the level of the nose before a slightly inclined face. The dance version of the sembah is however an elaborate and beautiful sequence of head, arm, hand, and body movements while the dancers are seated on the ground. When they rise to dance, the bedoyo remain at first in one place, going through a series of softly flowing motions embellished by the subtle play of delicate hands which pick up and drop, spread and cast away the loose-hanging ends of their dance scarves. Most of the time they retain a lowered position on bent knees, as if they were half-seated in air. Gentle turns or rather half-rotations of the head follow the interplay of limbs, the body inclining to one side or the other. And as they slowly step to group and regroup themselves, the play of arms and hands continues as does the basic posture on half-bent knees.

The bedoyo dancers have been compared with little ethereal priestesses.[31] In spirit and form this esoteric court ballet indeed suggests a ritual. It brings to mind the *redjang* of girls or women in the temple courts in Bali[32] or the slow and solemn processionals (*mogaele*) of South Nias women held at harvest celebrations on the wide, stone-paved village plazas. Though there is no way to prove it, the bedoyo dance may well be the

* See Appendix II.

† The bedoyo dances, in contrast with other court dances, have never been popularized, and may be a dying institution, though they still linger on in the keraton of Surakarta.

latest and perhaps last version of an old fertility dance from the courts of Java. The Goddess of the Southern Ocean, like the elusive Goddess of the Winds, is undoubtedly symbolic of fecundity. In the keraton of Surakarta stands a tower where the Susuhunan is said to celebrate an annual mystic reunion with Njahi Loro Kidul, the creator of the bedoyo dances.

The royal courts where the bedoyo dancers were sheltered in seclusion are now crumbling or changing their internal order. Decay and defacement are in evidence in Surakarta where on the formerly immaculate whitewashed keraton walls unsolicited heraldics may include large black signs of the hammer and sickle. Choruses of young women, much sturdier than the bedoyo dancers, now entertain the public outside the keraton walls in dance intermezzi at the popular theater. To the accompaniment of songs, they mime in unison the actions of planting, reaping, stamping and winnowing rice without poetic allusions to mystical union of the head of the state with a goddess of fertility.

When a pair of dancers appears as royal entertainers or perhaps temple dancers on Barabudur reliefs, they are in identical attitudes (Pl. 99). The contemporary Javanese serimpi and the Balinese legong parallel the ninth-century dances inasmuch as they are essentially for one pair who move in unison during part of the dance.

The serimpi (Pl. 100) until about 1918 were exclusively girls of noble birth, nieces, grandnieces, and sometimes even the young daughters or granddaughters of the ruling princes of Central Java.* Their dances were the prerogative of the courts. Since 1918, however, when the dance school of the association Krida Beksa Wirama was established in Jogjakarta under the leadership of the son of the ruling sultan, Gusti Pan-

* Raffles said that the serimpi dancers were concubines of the prince. *History of Java,* I, p. 379.

Plate 99. *A pair of dancers in identical attitudes, Barabudur relief.*

geran Aria Tedjakusuma, the serimpi dance was taught to all female students enrolled in the school. Nowadays it is the basic classical dance for Javanese girls. At the courts, the serimpi usually appeared in a group of four but one pair was merely duplicating the dance of the other. At contemporary public celebrations—anniversaries of schools, for example—the serimpi is often performed by only one pair of dancers.

The legong dancers, who may originally have been temple dancers, were in the past also attached to the *puri* (the residences of the Balinese rajas now occupied by their descendants). Like the bedoyo of the Javanese keratons, they were selected for their beauty and promising grace from among the little girls of village families.[33] Though still often patronized by Balinese nobility, the legong dancers are now part of the general dance-club system of a village community. They perform on a variety of occasions—at temple festivals, at other celebrations, and commercially for tourists. Except for a prelude, in which a girl attendant (*tjondong*) performs an introductory dance, the legong is a dance of a pair and many of the formal figures are executed by the two dancers in unison. Like the serimpi in Java, legong is the classical dance par excellence of Balinese girls. Essentially the little trance dancers, *sanghyang*, who sometimes are thought to be possessed by celestial nymphs (*widadari* or *dedari* in Bali), also dance in legong style.

We have no way of knowing whom the paired dancers in synchronous movement on the Barabudur reliefs impersonated, or if they represented personages at all. Theirs may have been a dance without any dramatic content. The stories now attached to the legong and the serimpi dances may have been woven into formerly storyless performances of highly trained dance girls and the choreography enriched accordingly. One of the frequent themes of the legong dance is an episode from the story of the King of Lasem. The king holds captive a princess of Daha, Langkesari, whose return is demanded by her brother. As the result, a war ensues between Lasem and Daha. The principal episode in one of the many versions of the legong dance is the king's farewell to his wife and Langkesari before going off to war. The fateful outcome of the war is

Plate 100. Serimpi *dancers, daughters of the late Mangkunagara VII of Surakarta.*

foreshadowed by the appearance of a black crow—the bird of ill omen. As the story unfolds, the two dancers shift from one role to another. At various points, they may be Langkesari and the king, the king and his wife, the king and his prime minister, or both may simultaneously dance the part of the king.

Different stories are ascribed to the decorous dance of the serimpi, which culminates in a stylized and inconclusive duel, first with dainty krisses (daggers) and then with miniature bows and arrows. One interpretation is that the dancers portray a fight of two widadari, celestial nymphs, Supraba and Wilotama, who engage in a mock fight to amuse the gods.[34] In another, the combat of the two serimpi dancers is said to be a fight between two princesses involved in an intrigue woven around a king of Arabia. One of the princesses, impelled by love, schemes to liberate him from imprisonment but suspects the other of spying and trying to thwart her plans. This gives rise to the duel.*[35]

One should not. however, imagine the serimpi dancers as infuriated amazons. The prelude to their encounter is as exquisitely graceful, disciplined, and slow as that of the bedoyo. The same impersonal poise and subtlety is maintained even during the fighting or when one of the serimpi-princesses hovers, in tiny, even, rapid steps, around her temporarily smitten adversary who kneels on the ground.

Yet female warriors and amazons were known in Java's past. In the nineteenth century, Sultan Hamengku Buwana II of Jogjakarta had a troop of female cavalry (*pradjurit isteri*) who rode their horses with a skill that provoked amazement among the Dutch officials. When the Sultan was still crown prince, he had trained these amazons for dances to be performed at his coming coronation. This in turn brings to mind the eleventh-century relief of the Ramayana story on the Shiva temple of Prambanan where a female dancer with sword and shield appears at the coronation festivities held for Bharata, half-brother of the exiled Rama (Pl. 102). It would seem that no matter what stories are now attached to dances of women with weapons, they may well be, like so many other dances, of rather distant and now forgotten origin.

From the few examples cited so far, it is apparent that certain types of dance may have persisted over a long period of time. But it is also true that with the passage of time the style of some dancing underwent changes, responding to the introduction of new techniques and perhaps of whole new sets of dances.

To a choreologist interested in this evolution, the reliefs with dance scenes on the Barabudur are suggestive in several directions. First, there is a striking difference between the restrained mode of dancing girls of the common people, as in the dance party, and that of the court dancers. The former may be representative of an indigenous Indonesian manner. The latter style may have been an Indian mode of dancing introduced at the courts, and conceivably also into ritual. Among the Indian Brahmans and teachers in Java, some may have known the rules laid down in the treatise on acting and dancing, Bharata's *Natya Sastra,*[36] and some may have actually been dancing teachers.

Second, the reliefs of court dancers suggest which particular techniques had been introduced from India. One of them may have been the stance on turned-out, rhomboidally bent legs which is still basic to the classical Javanese dance tradition. Another imported element must have been the elaboration of finger posi-

Plate 101. *Balinese* legong *dancers, drawing by I Rudin, Sanur, Bali, 1955.*

* The late Paku Buwana X, Susuhunan of Surakarta, had his serimpi shoot toy pistols.

Plate 102. *Female dancer with sword and shield, Ramayana relief, Shiva Temple, Prambanan, 10th century.*

tions and hand gestures also preserved to the present. But, whereas in India numberless combinations of hand gestures with elaborately positioned fingers are a veritable sign language, the vocabulary of this language is far more limited in Indonesia and has lost much of its original meaning as well. Nevertheless, the dancers' hands have retained in their supple movements a great complexity and beauty. A Javanese prince once remarked that he could recognize a good dancer by her little finger!

Third, the Barabudur reliefs, like the series of panels with celestial dancers around the Shiva temple of Prambanan, suggest that not only certain techniques hailing from India but also the wider principles laid down in the *Natya Sastra* for dance and drama were adopted in Java. In a compendium of Bharata's treatise we read:

The sages speak of Nāṭya, Nṛtta and Nṛtya. Nāṭya is dancing used in drama (*nāṭaka*) combined with the original plot. Nṛtta is that form of the dance which is void of flavor (*rasa*) and mood (*bhāva*). Nṛtya is that form of dance which possesses flavor, mood and suggestion (*rasa, bhāva, vyañjanā*, etc.) and the like. There is a twofold division of these three, Lāsya and Tāṇḍawa. Lāsya dancing is very sweet, Tāṇḍawa dancing is violent.[37]

This classification is very useful even now when one tries to sort out dances for comparative purposes, whether within one culture or cross-culturally. The court dances of the girls depicted singly or in pairs on the Barabudur reliefs must have been nrtya. "Nrtya should be seen by a royal audience in the courts of kings," says the text based on the *Natya Sastra*.[38] So the dances of the bedoyo and serimpi, formerly the jewels of Javanese ceremonial court life, are also nrtya; they possess "flavor, mood, and suggestion" but render little of the dramatic content ascribed to their dances. Further, the reliefs clearly show that some of the dancers are in gently restrained and graceful attitudes, that is, dancing in the "sweet" or *lasya* mode, while the postures of others are forcefully expansive, corresponding to the "violent" *tandawa* mode. The division into these two modes is still basic today in the dramatic dances of men in Java and Bali, but it no longer applies to the dances of women. All of these are now delicate, "lasya," or, to use the Javanese term, *alus,* "refined," in fact so refined that they probably exceed even the demands of the Indian lasya. Is this, one wonders, the result of a gradual reversion in court art to the indigenous Indonesian style of restraint in feminine dances? Or did perhaps Islam's puritanical influence curb the expressiveness of the female dancer's body? No trace remains today in any Indonesian women's dance of the widespread knees or raised legs which characterize the more dynamic dancers of the Barabudur reliefs. True, some moments in the Balinese legong resemble the posture of the dancers shown in Plate 99; West Javanese dance girls in their alluring *dogèr* may feel affinity with the provocative attitudes of the dancers on yet another Barabudur relief; but nowhere, in or out of Java, will we find a dancing woman assuming as broad a stance as appears in Plate 98 or raise her leg as high as the dancers in Plate 99.

The Indian tradition of adherence to strict rules governing the execution of even the minutest gesture has had a lasting effect on the choreographic art of Java and Bali. As Coomaraswamy says, "Indian acting and dancing—the same word, Natya, covers both ideas—is thus a deliberate art. Nothing is left to chance."[39] In the two islands, just as in India, rules for the movements of the arms and hands, the positions of the fingers, the rotations and shifts of head and neck and the direction of the glance are no less important than those governing the stances, steps, and body posture. Some of these rules are based on Indian prescriptions, others, as precisely established and meticulously followed, are of local invention. Thus, just as in the plastic arts, the crystallized forms are as remote in style from the dances of contemporary India as are the islands' music, languages, and regional costumes.

We shall return to the canons governing dance gesture in another chapter, with the discussion of Java's classical dance drama, *wayang wong.* Although acting and dancing are synonymous in wayang wong and could be expressed with the Indian term natya, dance drama has been separated in this text from "the dance" (in the sense of nrtta and nrtya, treated in this chapter) because in form and content wayang wong belongs to a whole theatrical complex, "the wayang world," at the heart of which lies the shadow play.

Notes

1. See H. H. Bartlett, *The Labors of the Datoe* (Papers of the Michigan Academy of Science, Arts and Letters Reprint, 1930–1931), Parts I and II.

2. See A. W. Nieuwenhuis, *Quer durch Borneo* (Leiden, 1904); Claire Holt, *Dance Quest in Celebes* (Paris, 1939); Beryl de Zoete and Walter Spies, *Dance and Drama in Bali* (London, 1952).

3. For an excellent study of trance dances in Bali see Jane Belo, *Trance in Bali* (New York, 1960).

4. See R. L. Archer, "Muhammadan Mysticism in Sumatra," *Journal of the Royal Asiatic Society, Malayan Branch* XV (1937), 1–126.

5. For detailed descriptions see Th. Pigeaud, *Javaanse Volksvertoningen,* (Batavia, 1938), pp. 215–242; W. Staugaard, "Koeda Kepang," *Handelingen van het Eerste Congres voor de Taal-, Land- en Volkenkunde van Java* (Weltevreden, 1921), pp. 421–426.

6. Curt Sachs, *World History of the Dance,* trans. by Bessie Schonberg (New York, 1937), pp. 335–341.

7. This dance was demonstrated for a documentary film produced by Rolf de Maré in 1938, for *Les Archives Internationales de la Danse,* Paris.

8. See Curt Sachs, *Eine Weltgeschichte des Tanzes* (Berlin, 1933), pl. 15.

9. Pigeaud, *Volksvertoningen.*

10. *Ibid.*, p. 431; Staugaard, "Koeda Kepang."

11. De Zoete and Spies, *Dance and Drama in Bali,* pp. 90ff.; Jane Belo, *Bali: Rangda and Barong* (New York, 1949), pp. 32–33; R. Goris, *Bali: Cults and Customs,* (Djakarta, n.d.) p. 82, pls. 448–452; Jane Belo, *Trance in Bali,* pp. 72, 272.

12. Gregory Bateson and Margaret Mead, in *Balinese Character, A Photographic Analysis* (New York, 1942), have interpreted the barong kekèt as a benevolent and sheltering father image and the Witch as symbolic of the frustrating mother. See pls. 55–58, 62, 66, 67, especially.

13. Heinrich Zimmer, *Myths and Symbols in Indian Art and Civilization,* trans. and ed. by Joseph Campbell (New York, 1953), pp. 180–184.

14. F. D. K. Bosch, *The Golden Germ; An Introduction to Indian Symbolism* ('s-Gravenhage, 1960), p. 145.

15. See Schuyler Cammann, "Types of Symbols in Chinese Art," in Arthur F. Wright, ed., *Studies in Chinese Thought; American Anthropologist Memoir* No. 75 (1963), pp. 195–231.

16. Belo, *Bali: Rangda and Barong,* p. 33.

17. In a personal letter to the author. Cf. the lion-serpent motif as discussed by Campbell in *The Masks of God: Occidental Mythology* (New York, 1964), pp. 467–468.

18. W. H. Rassers, *Panji, the Culture Hero; A Structural Study of Religion in Java* (The Hague, 1959), pp. 31–34.

19. De Zoete and Spies, *Dance and Drama in Bali,* pp. 113–115; and Pigeaud, *Volksvertoningen,* pp. 163, 200, 206, 420.

20. Thomas Stamford Raffles, F.R.S., *The History of Java* (London, 1817), I, 382–383.

21. C. M. Pleyte, "De Eerste 'Ronggeng'," *Tijdschrift voor Indische Taal- Land- en Volkenkunde,* LVII (1916), 270–272.

22. Georges Groslier, *Danseuses Cambodgiennes; Anciennes et Modernes* (Paris, 1913), p. 140.

23. W. F. Stutterheim, "A Thousand Years Old Profession in the Princely Courts on Java," in his *Studies in Indonesian Archaeology,* (The Hague, 1956), pp. 93–103.

24. Theodore G. Th. Pigeaud, *Java in the Fourteenth Century; A Study in Cultural History; the Nagara-Kertagama by Rakawi Prapanca of Majapahit, 1365* A.D. (The Hague, 1960), III, Canto 91, stanzas 1, 2.

25. Anne-Marie Esnoul, "Les Traités de Dramaturgie Indienne" in Jean Jacquot, ed., *Les Théâtres d'Asie* (Paris, 1961), p. 25.

26. *Nagara-Kertagama,* IV, 315–322.

27. *Ibid.,* IV, 319. Cf. with the myth of Hainuwele from West Ceram in Joseph Campbell, *The Masks of God: Primitive Mythology* (New York, 1959), pp. 173–176.

28. See B. van Helsdingen-Schoevers, *Het Serimpi Boek* (Weltevreden, 1925), pp. 16–23; also P. A. Hadiwidjojo, "De Bedojo Ketawang," *Handelingen van het Eerste Congres voor de Taal-, Land- en Volkenkunde van Java* (Weltevreden, 1921), pp. 87–90.

29. J. Groneman, *In den Kedaton te Jogjakarta* (Leiden, 1888).

30. *Bedaya Dansen en Zangen;* Programma voor het Congres van het Java Instituut te Jogjakarta, 24–27 December 1924.

31. Helsdingen-Schoevers, *Het Serimpi Boek,* p. 12.

32. See de Zoete and Spies, *Dance and Drama in Bali,* pp. 46ff.

33. *Ibid.,* pp. 218–232, especially p. 228.

34. Helsdingen, *Serimpi Boek,* p. 19.

35. Groneman, *Kedaton te Jogjakarta.*

36. Nandikeśvara, *The Mirror of Gesture,* trans. by A. K. Coomaraswamy and Duggirāla Gopālakrishnāyya (New York, 1936). This text is a compendium of Bharata's *Natya Sastra.*

37. *Ibid.,* p. 32.

38. *Ibid.*

39. *Ibid.,* p. 18.

CHAPTER 5

The Wayang World

"Just as in a discussion of a whole culture, so in a discussion of wayang . . . there is no limit. While it is being analyzed, the subject keeps expanding; as soon as we believe that its outermost limits have been reached, new vistas open up. This is because wayang comprises all aspects of Javanese culture. It is fitting therefore that in order to explain our inability to cope with the subject in its entirety, we should borrow the words constantly used by the Venerable Dalang: 'To sum it up, one night does not suffice. . . . The characterization is incomplete—there are too many shades. Therefore we break off this . . . presentation. Enough.' "[1]

—Tjan Tjoe Siem

The Sphere

A WORLD OF SHADOWS, the wayang is the legendary world of the traditional (now "classical") Javanese theater. At its heart lies the shadow play.* Like the shimmering reflection of nature in a pool, the wayang world is the beguiling cultural twin of Javanese reality. It is populated by gods, noble and vile kings and princes, beautiful princesses, demons, giants, monsters, sages, servants, and clowns—all intimate members of the Javanese cultural family, tied to it by firm bonds of familiarity, love, and admiration.

In its narrowest sense the word *wayang* (literally, shadow) today designates the flat, leather-carved rod puppet of the shadow play. The Javanese puppet's own stylized shape exaggerates, like a shadow, the natural Javanese human form. One may say that a wayang's shadow—sharp and steady or diffuse and fluttering—is a shadow of a shadow.

In its widest sense the word wayang has come to mean a dramatic performance, a play, a show, whether the actors be puppets or human beings. When used alone, the word wayang thus means either a shadow puppet or a shadow play; in the designation of some other play, a second qualifying term always follows, as for instance, *wayang wong,* a play (dance drama) performed by man, that is by living actors.*

The "wayang world" embraces a variety of traditional Javanese theaters, the principal forms of which will be described below.

The first is *wayang kulit* (*kulit:* skin, leather): the complete generic name for the ancient shadow play, known and beloved not only in Java but also in Bali as well as in Javanese settlements in other regions. Both narration and dialogue are recited by the *dalang,* the storyteller, who manipulates all the puppets. The audience can sit either before or behind the screen and thus view either the actual puppets or their shadows.

* The Balinese theater is not as strongly influenced by the shadow play as the Javanese. Cf. Beryl de Zoete and Walter Spies, *Dance and Drama in Bali* (London, 1952).

* By extension, even a circus is sometimes referred to as *wayang kuda* (*kuda:* horse, thus "horse show"); and before the Dutch word *bioskop* was thoroughly entrenched in Indonesian usage, the cinema was called by villagers *wayang gambar hidup,* "living pictures wayang" or *wayang gelap,* "dark wayang."

A vast corpus of myths is perpetuated and disseminated by means of the shadow play. In their wayang kulit versions old Indonesian motifs alternate, intertwine, or merge with the mythology of India which in turn is expanded and embroidered often beyond recognition. According to the content of the performed plays, *lakon,* the Javanese wayang kulit is subdivided into:

1) *Wayang purwa** (*purwa:* primeval, original, ancient) with a repertory drawn from four groups of myths:[2] first, the so-called "Prehistory" based in part on the *Adiparwa* (prelude to the *Mahabharata*) and in part on ancient Indonesian mythology (plays based on this "prehistory" are usually performed only for exorcising and propitiatory purposes); second, the cycle of myths known as *Ardjuna Sasra Bau* dealing with the origins of some prominent figures of the *Ramayana* and in which through the figure of Kresna (who like Rama is an incarnation of god Vishnu) the connection between the *Ramayana* and the *Mahabharata* is established; third, the *Ramayana* proper;† fourth, the story of the Pandawa and the Korawa as related in the *Mahabharata.* Plays based on episodes of the *Mahabharata* or revolving around particular heroes of this epic are by far the most numerous and popular among all the varieties of shadow plays.

2) *Wayang gedog* (the meaning of *gedog* is unclear): its repertory of plays is based on the East Javanese Pandji legends; the leather puppets differ from those of wayang purwa in details of costume, especially of the headdresses; now relatively rare in Central Java but more popular in East Java where also the Damar Wulan legends enter into the wayang gedog repertory.

3) *Wayang madya* (*madya:* middle): its plays are based on nineteenth-century epic poetry of the poet Ranggawarsita, having as themes the reign of the East Javanese prophet-king Djayabaya; formerly confined to the court of the Mangkunagara of Surakarta, wayang madya is now probably rarely if at all performed.

In some Javanese writings the different kinds of shadow plays are made to correspond to successive periods of Javanese history—with a suitably constructed genealogy of kings—from the era of their mythological ancestors (wayang purwa) to modern times (wayang *Pantja Sila,** for example, which continues into the history of the Republic).[3] Some varieties of wayang are ascribed to individual rulers; others are remembered as inventions of individual dalangs. Because of their narrowly local or short-lived popularity, a number of wayang kulit varieties have not been included in the basic list above. Among them are *wayang kuluk,* introduced under Hamengku Buwana V (1822–1855), which dealt with the history of his Jogjakarta domain; *wayang dupara,* devoted to the history of Surakarta; *wayang wahana,* invented by Mas Sutarto under the pseudonym Rshi Wahana, and probably the first attempt in the twentieth century to use the shadow play primarily as a vehicle for airing contemporaneous social problems;† *wayang Djawa,* invented by a regent of Surakarta whose appellation (as dalang?) was Dutadilaga, glorified the deeds of Prince Diponegoro, hero of the Java War (1825–1830); *wayang kantjil,* created by the Solonese painter and wayang-maker Raden Mas Sajid, for performing stories about Mouse Deer (*kantjil*), hero of numerous popular fables; *wayang perdjuangan,* also by R. M. Sajid, for popularizing heroism in guerrilla warfare during the Indonesian revolution; *wayang suluh,* invented in 1947 in Madiun upon the initiative of a Youth Congress, in which naturalistic flat leather puppets of Indonesian leaders, officials, military and civilian personages as well as their opponents

* In Bali it is known as *wayang parwa* (*parwa* is possibly connected with the *parwan,* main divisions of the *Mahabharata*).

† Wayang kulit plays based on the *Ramayana* are sometimes classed separately as *wayang Rama.*

Plate 103. *Javanese* wayang kulit, *shadow-play puppets. From left: young Sumbadra and young Ardjuna.*

* See p. 202.

† Subtle allusions to current events and problems occur also in wayang purwa and other shadow plays, especially in the comical dialogues of the clowns and remarks by the storyteller.

(representatives of the Netherlands Government) and mediating foreigners (representatives of the United Nations), all in modern dress, appeared in plays about the revolutionary war and the subsequent United Nations sponsored negotiations; *wayang pantja-sila,* designed by Harsono Hadisoeseno for the political education of the masses, in which the five Pandawa brothers of the *Mahabharata* were made to symbolize the five principles of the Indonesian state proclaimed by President Sukarno;* finally, the shadow play acquired a special form and name in *wayang Adam Ma'rifat* in a district near Magelang, Central Java, where an Islamic mystic sect by that name used it as a vehicle for instruction.[4] I may add that personally I had learned in 1955–1957 of at least one case where wayang kulit was similarly used by a Christian mission in Central Java for dramatizing religious themes with one puppet representing the Blessed Virgin. These various modern attempts to harness the shadow play for propaganda are but shallow inlets compared with the deep, broad stream of mythology which has been captivating untold generations in the lands of Southern Asia—from India to Indonesia.

Traditionally, the function of the shadow play is bound up with exorcism, propitiation, and invocation of fertility. The appearance on the shadow screen of the gods and mythical heroes who fight their demonic adversaries was perhaps formerly tantamount to an invocation of ancestral spirits and powerful deities to promote welfare. Among the special plays of the "prehistory" cycle of wayang purwa which are regarded as particularly efficacious for ritual purification to avert evil—a ceremony called *ngruwat* in Java—the lakon (play) *Murwakala* is regarded as both magically dangerous as well as potent: Batara Kala (the wrathful emanation of Shiva) and Batari Durga (destructive form of his consort, Uma) appear in this play. Lakons about Dewi Sri, goddess of the rice, are performed to bless the rice crops and prevent their destruction by pests. The story of *Watu Gunung,* an unwittingly incestuous king whose mother-wife contrives to destroy him by sending him to the abode of the gods where he perishes, is said to be performed in East Java to secure rainfall. Occasionally the story of *Brayut,* so popular in Bali, about a couple with a horde of children, is performed in the shadow play at wedding celebrations.

At the same time, however, wayang performances are also highly prized secular entertainment. When they are broadcast in Java by radio, the public is content to enjoy only the voice of the dalang and the wayang music. But just as lovers of music invariably gather by special permit in a broadcasting studio in the West, so a small crowd of wayang lovers invariably gathers in a broadcasting studio in Djakarta or Jogjakarta to see the actual performance. But, whatever the occasion, the dalang never fails to lay down some offerings of rice and of flowers floating in a water-filled bowl and to light some incense with a short prayer before he opens the play. Sometimes he holds a few of the puppets over the rising smoke of incense and with an incantation propitiates the magically potent personages they embody: bringing down to earth deities and semidivine beings in name and image is not free from danger. The sacred nature of the shadow play and its magic efficacy are still strongly felt not only by the officiant dalang, but by the people as well.

There are two other puppet theaters related to the shadow play but performed without a shadow screen so that only the puppets themselves are viewed by the audience. But, as in the shadow play, the dalang, is both the narrator and speaker for all characters as well as manipulator of the puppets.

A second traditional form is *wayang klitik,* or *kerutjil* (both words indicate smallness): its flat wooden puppets are carved in relief and painted but the articulated arms are of leather; the repertory, in Central Java, consists of plays based on the Damar Wulan story; now rare in Central Java, it is still popular in East Java where Pandji stories also serve as themes for wayang klitik plays.

Wayang golek is a third form: it is performed with wooden, three-dimensional, costumed rod puppets (*golek*); the repertory in Central Java consists of plays based on stories about an Arabian prince, Amir Hamzah (an uncle of the Prophet Mohammad), whose adventures are related in the Javanese work *Serat Menak;* in West Java, Sunda, the heroes of the wayang golek stage are also those of the *Ramayana* and the *Mahabharata;* while very popular in Java (especially West Java and Jogjakarta in Central Java), the wayang golek theater is not known in Bali.

Very little has been written about wayang klitik and

* The Indonesian Communist Party also utilized the most popular hero of the *Mahabharata,* Ardjuna, endowing his all-conquering magic weapon, the arrow Pasopati, with the hammer and sickle insignia.

wayang golek[5] compared with the extensive literature devoted to the shadow play. Both lack the latter's depth of tradition and, although often performed semiritually in conjunction with family celebrations, they are not enveloped by as great an aura of mystery and sacredness. Also, in the absence of a shadow screen, wayang klitik puppets seem somehow more material and more limited in their effect than the shadow puppets. As for the round goleks, these are so realistic, except, of course, for the demonic characters, especially in Central Java, that they look like miniature human beings (about 18 inches high) dressed up for the stage (Pl. 104). Their expressive faces, like very good masks, have fluid smiles, fierce scowls, are sweetly dignified or riotously grotesque. In West Java the goleks' faces are much more stylized. The puppets' colorful costumes include replicas of Javanese court dress. Some male characters are attired in eighteenth- or nineteenth-century gold-braided jackets of European inspiration combined with caps or turbans, some in Arab style. But all puppets wear the Javanese long batik skirt to hide the dalang's hand which holds the puppet by its central rod handle.

The construction of a golek puppet is as simple as it is ingenious. The principal wooden components are: a roughly shaped truncated torso with a vertical hole drilled through its center; arms, in two parts strung together at the elbow and dangling loosely from the shoulders; a carefully carved and painted head, complete with headdress, with a somewhat elongated neck; finally, one pointed central rod, serving also as handle, and two thinner rods which are attached to the hands. The mechanism works thus: the central rod, passed freely through the torso and emerging between the shoulders, serves as pivot for the head, the neck of which is fitted tightly onto the rod's upper point; below the torso the rod broadens to prevent the trunk from slipping downward but with enough leeway to create the effect of the puppet panting, as after a fight, or of indignation, by repeatedly pushing the trunk up and letting it slide down again. By twisting the central rod, the puppeteer can make a golek's head turn in all directions which greatly enlivens its dance and other movements in conjunction with the arm gestures produced by the rods attached to the hands.

Wayang golek is probably the youngest and most secular of all Javanese puppet theaters. It may have been introduced into the island's interior from the northern coastal regions. The port cities along Java's north coast are centers from which Islam in the past had spread inland. Also, around these trading centers Chinese settlements had clustered for centuries. The Amir Hamzah stories, so prominent in the wayang

Plate 104. *Javanese* wayang golek *puppets from Jogjakarta. Center: Prince Machtal with Kuraisin faces the demonic Lokayanti.*

Plate 105. *Section of sixth* wayang bèbèr *scroll of Patjitan, South Java. Third scene: in the center, Sekar Tadji (Tjandra Kirana), attended by wise woman, receives her brother prior to her wedding with Pandji. (Figures to extreme left belong to preceding scene.)*

golek repertory, may have been brought, in Persian versions, by the carriers of Islam who presumably came from India. Among the Chinese settlers round puppets seem to have been known, but they were either hand puppets or string marionettes.[6] If the Javanese borrowed the idea of round puppets from the Chinese, it may have been natural for them to change the finger or string techniques to that of rods with which they were long familiar.

In West Java among the Sundanese, wayang golek is so popular that it takes precedence over the shadow play and includes the latter's repertory; plays based on the *Ramayana* and the *Mahabharata* (*purwa*) and the Pandji legends (*gedog*) are performed there as well as stories of the Amir Hamzah cycle.

There used to be still another manner of performing wayang stories known as *wayang bèbèr* (*bèbèr*: unfolding). It consisted of illustrations painted on long horizontal scrolls which the dalang unrolled, scene after scene, for the audience to see, as he recited the tale, speaking and chanting; the stories thus depicted and narrated included those of the purwa, gedog, and klitik repertories.

I met a wayang bèbèr dalang who may well have been the last of his kind in Java, with his old scrolls and his small group of musicians, in 1937, in the village of Gedompol in the Patjitan region of South Java. He had six scrolls, each divided into four scenes, painted on what seemed to be a sort of bark-cloth paper, badly frazzled at the edges and darkened by age to brownish-yellow tints. They were perhaps more than a hundred years old.* To my knowledge no one produces wayang bèbèr scrolls any more.† But it must have been a popular form of storytelling for centuries. Ma Huan, a Chinese Moslem who was secretary to an eminent

* See Appendix III for summary of the wayang bèbèr lakon depicted in these scrolls.

† From Benedict R. O'G. Anderson, Cornell University, who returned in 1964 from two years of field research in Indonesia, I learned that the wayang bèbèr scrolls here described still exist, are in the possession of a group of related families who keep them in turn each for a few months, and that performances are still being given for magic purification purposes. They claim that the scrolls have existed for twelve generations. Mr. Anderson also reported that excellent copies, painted on cloth, have been and are still being made of the wayang bèbèr scenes in Solo, not to be used for performances, but as paintings which seem to attract some connoisseurs.

admiral sent by a Ming emperor on a mission to Southeast Asia, wrote about Java in 1416:

There are a sort of men who paint on paper men, birds, animals, insects and so on; the paper is like a scroll and is fixed between two wooden rollers three feet high; at one side these rollers are level with [the edge of] the paper whilst they protrude at the other side. The man squats down on the ground and places the picture before him, unrolling one part after the other and turning it towards the spectator, whilst in the native language and in a loud voice he gives an explanation of every part; the spectators sit around him and listen, laughing and crying according to what he tells them.[7]

Finally, to our wayang world belong several forms of the human theater. *Wayang wong** or *wayang orang* (*wong* and *orang:* man, in Javanese and Indonesian respectively) is dance drama in which the dalang only recites and chants, and the dialogue is spoken by the actors themselves; the repertory of wayang wong plays is based on the *Ramayana* and the *Mahabharata* (thus a counterpart of wayang purwa). *Wayang topeng* (*topeng:* mask) is a dance–pantomime play by masked actors in which the plot is narrated by a dalang and the subject of which are plays based on Pandji stories (a counterpart of wayang gedog). *Langendriya* ("Joy of the Hearts") is a dance-opera with an all-female cast in vogue until World War II at the court of the late Mangkunagara VII of Surakarta. The plays were episodes of the Damar Wulan story (thus a counterpart of wayang klitik). In the last decade colorful performances of Damar Wulan plays have entered the repertory of the popular theater known as *Ketoprak.*

Thus the plays of the wayang theaters include themes drawn from the epics, the *Ramayana* and the *Mahabharata,* in versions made thoroughly Indonesian; a corpus of plays derived from indigenous East Javanese legends; and stories adapted from Arabian tales. In all the different theatrical forms in which these plays appear, whether the action is illustrated in static pictorial sequences as in the nearly defunct wayang bèbèr, or executed by puppets or by men, music elevates on its melodies and carries the imagery and words of the unfolding drama.

The link between these various forms of traditional theater, which makes them a part of what we have chosen to call the "wayang world," is not simply that they share the same stories, or that the dalang plays a central role in most of them, or that music is an integral element in the performance, or even that almost all of them are called wayang. What unites them is that they are governed by the same canons—in the structure of the plays (lakon) and in the typology of their heroes. Moreover, they all reflect the same shadowy yet glittering universe permeated with supernatural forces, ever charged with tensions, in which the plot always thickens like gathering thunderclouds that lead up to a climactic clash, the crucial battle between the protagonists of the "right" and those of the "left." They are all spiced by the farcical humor of grotesque servant-clowns, (known as panakawan in Java and parekan in Bali). And, not least, they all have been influenced, in Java especially, by the stylistic conventions of the shadow play, whose wayang style, as we have seen, had also strongly affected the style of the plastic arts in East Java and Bali from the thirteenth century A.D.*

* See Chapter 6 below, on dance drama.

* See Chapter 3.

Wayang Kulit, Its Origins

Just how and when the shadow play began to develop in Indonesia is still a matter of conjecture. The earliest record confirming the existence of a performance called "wayang" in Central Java dates from A.D. 907. A stone inscription issued by King Balitung mentions *mawayang,* performing wayang. It cannot be proven that this was indeed a shadow play but the possibility exists. Even the name of the story is given—the *Bimmaya Kumara*—possibly a story about Bima, hero of the *Mahabharata.* The inscription states that the performance was given "for the gods." The occasion was a ritual dedication of a freehold for the benefit of the god of a local monastery. The various entertainments that followed the consecration rites were held "for the welfare of the sacred foundation and of all subjects."† The inscription clearly proves that at the beginning of the tenth century some form of wayang together with dances, music, songs, and buffoonery and also the recitation of the *Ramayana* and the *Mahabharata* were part of ritual celebrations held by ruling princes and that a "wayang" was in the nature of an offering to the gods and an invocation ensuring the people's welfare.‡ One may assume that in King Balitung's time the mawayang practice was not new, but

† See Appendix II, p. 282.

‡ Cf. Appendix II, p. 287.

how much earlier it existed there is no way of ascertaining.

Shadow plays are known to exist or to have existed in many parts of the world, from Eastern Asia to the Mediterranean. The oldest is presumably the shadow play of India which Pischel traces back to the time of "the very old" Pali canon, the Buddhist *Therigata,* which may have been composed in the first century B.C. When a nun named Subha, while promenading in a mango grove, was accosted by a *Taugenichts* (good-for-nothing), as Pischel says, she reprimanded him in the following words:

You throw yourself, oh blind one, upon something non-existent
even as upon a mirage evoked before your eyes,
upon a golden tree appearing in a dream
a shadow play (*rupparūpakam*) amidst a human crowd.[8]

As in Indonesia, where through the centuries different terms appear for "shadow play," so in India through the ages different words were used which are now interpreted to mean "shadow play" or "shadow-play puppet." Following the *rupparūpaka(m)* of the Pali canon, the term *rupōpajīvana* appears, which, according to Pischel, at least, incontrovertibly refers to a theater with leather puppets. This word is found in a passage of the twelfth book of the *Mahabharata* and is commented on by Nilikhanta (in the seventeenth century) as follows: "*Rupōpajīvana* is known among the people of the south as *jalamandapika.* In it, after a thin cloth has been spanned, the doings of kings, ministers, etc. are brought before the eyes [of the onlookers] by means of figures [made] of leather."[9]

The term most often cited for the ancient Indian shadow play is *chayanataka,* translated as shadow drama. It appears in a thirteenth-century literary work, the *Dutangada,* "Angada as Envoy," a dramatized episode of the *Ramayana.* Its author, Subhata, expressly introduced his play as a chayanataka. Pischel notes that in Thailand, too, a playscript based on the *Ramayana* was marked with the word *nang* (leather), the name of the still-flourishing Thai shadow play. Because of this analogy and for other reasons he surmised, in 1906, that the Indian chayanataka was a continuation in *literary* (italics ours) form of what once must have been a shadow-puppet folk theater.[10]

There is evidence, however, that the Indian shadow play actually exists (or at least existed in 1935) in South India, in a region of Kerala* among the Nayar, a matrilineal warrior caste famous for its specialization in the heroic *Kathakali,* dance-drama performances of the *Ramayana* and *Mahabharata.*[11] An interesting eyewitness account of the Kerala shadow play appears in an article by Stan Harding.[12] His description is worth bearing in mind for later comparison with the Javanese wayang kulit.

The performance described by Harding was given by a small troupe of players, headed by a guru, that always went on tour during February, March, and April. The performance took place near a banyan-shaded road close to a little Nayar village community. It was the last day of an extensive festival, not further defined. A procession of the puppets carried by their manipulators and accompanied by Brahmans and a *vellichapad* ("through whose mouth a goddess is supposed to utter oracles when he danced himself into frenzy"[13]), went from the temple to the playhouse. On Harding's photograph the playhouse appears as a small, rectangular thatched structure with a half-wall along the visible long side of the house. He mentions that during the play the manipulators of the puppets were hidden behind the half-wall and projected the puppets' shadows on a white screen which, presumably, spanned the opening between the half-wall and the roof above them. The source of light was camphor and incense burning in a hollow bamboo about one foot in length. (Several camphor torches were used in an effective scene of conflagration, as when Sita undergoes her ordeal by fire.)

Harding says that the shadows of the puppets were far more beautiful than the figures themselves; some were rather dilapidated and may have been between sixty and a hundred years old; others were new. They were made of perforated deer skin (cows being sacred). Silhouettes of four puppets are reproduced with the article: one is of Hanuman, the white monkey-hero of the *Ramayana,* in profile—an isolated standing figure with one articulating hand extended forward. The other three are seated figures: Rama on a throne, three-quarter face, with one articulating arm; Rawana, likewise enthroned, full face, with one or two articulating arms; Sita, seated in a bower with a bird perched on a branch before her. Her one articulating arm was removed for the photograph because it was disproportion-

* Since writing this, I have learned from Dr. Joan Mencher, anthropologist who did field research in Kerala, that the shadow play is known in adjacent Andhra.

ately long and clumsy, probably a recent poor substitute for the original arm. During the performance, apart from battle scenes, the puppets often remained stationary, gesticulating only a little with the right or left hand (as also happens in Java). The story was recited by two singers who chanted either in unison or in response to each other. The words of the song were from Kambar's *Ramayana,* of which Harding saw two palm-leaf manuscripts, one in the possession of the guru, and the other carried in a basket along with the puppets. The poet Kambar was said to have lived a thousand years ago at the court of a Chola king who had commanded him to tell the story in songs. But like many of his illustrious colleagues through the ages the poet preferred drinking and singing to writing; so, to save him from disgrace, the goddess of the arts, Sarasvati, herself wrote the songs for him.

Harding stated that a shadow play lasted at least seven nights, but that a "normal run" was twenty-one nights; and that, "under very favorable circumstances," it might continue for forty-one nights. Each night at the beginning of the play, the shadows of two Brahman pilgrims were cast on the screen and they recapitulated the events of the preceding nights. They also appeared at other times commenting on the developments of the play.

As will be seen later, there are notable elements in this South Indian shadow play which have parallels in Indonesia: an aura of sacredness; the theme of the play (*Ramayana*); chanted recitation; the type of puppets, (rod puppets made of leather); and the presence of commentators (in Kerala, two pilgrim Brahmans, in Indonesia, servant-clowns). Features unlike those of the wayang kulit in Java and Bali include: more than one performer manipulating the puppets; the absence of instrumental music and of spoken narration and dialogue; the style of the puppets in general, and in particular the occurrence of seated figures (all wayang kulit puppets are standing figures*).

Comparing the South Indian shadow puppets with those found east and west of India, a student of the shadow theater is confronted with the question: parallel invention or diffusion? In each area, the style and composition have some elements common to one or more of the others. To the west, plays with shadow figures which are not really puppets but rather static silhouettes of human figures in a "landscape" (similar to the Kerala figure of Sita in a bower) are known in Egypt, where they can be traced back to the twelfth and thirteenth centuries A.D.[14] In Turkey, articulated flat leather puppets, closer to that of the Kerala Hanuman, are used in the ribald Karagöz plays[15] which have spread along the North African coast as far as Algeria.[16] To the east, Indonesia is the outstanding land of the shadow theater and presumably Thailand borrowed this art from Java. Comparison between the Kerala figures, especially the seated ones, and the Thai *nang* silhouettes of seated beings within decorative floral frames may perhaps, however, suggest a different theory.

The origin of the shadow play in Thailand, according to H. H. Prince Dhaninivat, is however of comparatively recent date. The earliest authentic mention of the nang is found in the Palatine Law of King Boromatrailokanath enacted in 1458. A less dependable source historically, a romance written in the eighteenth century, includes the shadow play among the arts practiced at the thirteenth-century court of Sukhothai.[17] Thus the distinctive style of the Thai nang must have developed in the course of the last five centuries. The nang figures, large, elegant, often leaf-shaped and static configurations, are held up by half-dancing performers and thus sway and move in space *in toto*. Despite the divergence in the style of figures and technique of performance, it is generally accepted that Thailand's nang play was originally inspired by the Indonesian wayang kulit which had spread to the Malay Peninsula and thence northward to Thailand.[18] A parallel development was the spread of Pandji tales, known in both Malaya and Thailand where they have provided a rich source for both literature and drama.

Situated between Indonesia and Thailand, the northern parts of Malaya have shadow plays known as *wayang Djawa* and *wayang Siam*. The flat leather figures are cruder versions of the Javanese wayang puppets and of the Thai nang silhouettes, respectively.[19]

Gesturing shadow-play puppets, translucent and multicolored, delight audiences at shadow plays in China. The origin of the Chinese shadow theater, known as *ying-hsi* (also transcribed as *ying-yi*), is ascribed in a Chinese encyclopedic work to the beginning of the eleventh century.[20] The pertinent passage as quoted by Jacob reads: "Only at the time of Jn-tsung (1023–1064) of the Sung dynasty could one find among the market people narrators of the history of the three states . . . ; some of them extracted stories

* To indicate that they are seated, the puppeteer lowers them so that their feet disappear.

from it, embellished them [farther] and made up shadow people (*ying-jn*). It was then that for the first time figures (*hsiang*) were made of the battles of the three states, Shu, Wei, and Wu."[21]

Jacob also mentions an interesting episode reported by the Persian, Dshuwani, connected with "wonderful Chinese plays, never seen before by anyone, behind a screen." It was performed before the Mongol ruler Ogotai, third son and successor of Jenghiz Khan. In one scene an old, turbaned man, attached by his long beard to a horse's tail, was being dragged along the ground. When Ogotai asked who he was, the visiting Chinese explained that he was "one of those rebellious Moslems whom the soldiers bring in this manner from the towns." Ogotai ordered the show to be suspended.[22] Up to the nineteen-thirties at least, Chinese shadow plays were performed in Mongolia, but always by Chinese and in the Chinese language.[23]

So far scholarly opinions remain divided or noncommittal[24] as regards the origin of the Javanese wayang kulit. If the shadow play indeed was not known in China before the Sung dynasty, a theory that it was introduced to the Indonesian islands from China would be untenable. A reverse process might even be considered since by the tenth century sea traffic between China and Indonesia was already fully developed.

As originally surmised by Krom, India remains the most likely source of the shadow play that spread to Indonesia, developing, significantly perhaps, only in the two pre-eminently Hinduized islands, Java and Bali.[25] And if the Kerala shadow play may be taken as an indication of a long persisting regional tradition, it suggests that South India in particular may have been the source of its transmission to Java. Is it perhaps no mere coincidence that in the Old Javanese charter issued by Maharaja Sri Lokapala in A.D. 840, three kinds of performers—*atapukan, aringgit,** and *abañol*—are mentioned in one breath with "servants of the inner apartments hailing from Champa, Kalinga, Aryya, Ceylon, *Cola, Malabar* [my italics], and Karnataka?"†

There are three arguments in favor of the independent invention of the shadow play in Indonesia: the theory of Rassers that it has evolved from ancient indigenous initiation rites[26]; the fact that all parts of the wayang's technical equipment are designated by indigenous and not by Indian terms[27]; and the presence of the strikingly original figures of the servant-clowns who have a very prominent role in wayang plays but no counterparts in the Indian epics. These clowns are thought to be purely Indonesian mythological divine beings (seemingly demoted to the status of servants but actually powerful) who preceded the Indian epic heroes on the shadow screen.[28] One should remember, however, that while such semicomical satellites do not appear in the *epics,* they do appear on the ancient Indian *stage* as the *vidushaka,* "a Brahman but ugly and ridiculous."*

The shadow play, wherever performed, is a superb medium for storytelling. In each of the countries where it exists, it has acquired its own repertory and a distinct technique and style of its own. And the myths, semihistorical tales, romances, or satires that are brought to life on the shadow screen are at the very core of the people's culture. Thus, wherever its technique may have originated, the Indonesian wayang kulit also is a uniquely Javanese and Balinese creation—in the form and content of its plays, in the style of its extraordinary puppets, and in the manner of presentation by the storyteller, the "Venerable Dalang."

The Dalang and His Theater

The dalang is the central force of the wayang world. Playwright and producer, principal narrator and conductor, he is the creator and prime mover of the illusory shadow world. He transports his audience into the realms of ancient lore by the sounds of his voice, as he chants of remote kingdoms, the strivings of the heroes, or poetically evokes sweet, strident, or ominous moods. He brings to life the puppets in his hands, making them seek, wander, grieve, and rejoice, and he speaks for each in ever changing timbres and accents. The Javanese poet R. M. Noto Soeroto in his "Wayang Songs" has likened God to a Supreme Dalang.[29]

The art of the dalang, formerly passed on from father to son and from master to apprentice, but nowadays taught also in special schools in Central Java, demands much knowledge, high skills, and great disci-

* *Ringgit* is the term used in the eleventh-century Old Javanese poem *Ardjuna Wiwaha* for a leather-carved shadow puppet; this meaning has been retained in modern "High" Javanese (*kromo*). The front veranda of Javanese houses, within the inner doorway of which the wayang screen is customarily installed, and which thus serves as place for shadow-play performances, is called *paringgitan*.

† See Appendix II, p. 281.

* See p. 115.

pline. What a dalang must know is listed by one expert,[30] himself an eminent dalang, in the following order:

Tambo (history), that is knowledge of the old stories, the history of kings [not least their genealogies], etc.

Gending (music): a truly deep understanding of the melodies, modes and phases, songs, etc. required for the accompaniment of a wayang performance.

Gendèng (recitation): mastery of the chanted recitation accompanied by the music of the *gamelan* [orchestra of Javanese instruments] as well as of the spoken recitation linked with the gamelan's sounds.

Gĕndeng (detached daring): "to behave like a person unruffled by anything," to be "self-forgetful," without embarrassment or fear of playing the fool.

Bahasa (language): mastery of various "levels" [modes] of speech appropriate to the status of each wayang figure.

Ompak-ompakan (eloquence): "exaggeration"; "the dalang must be able to describe the beauty of all creation in eloquent words which enhance it beyond mere reality and this in a way proper to *pawayangan* [art of shadow play]."

Ilmu batin (spiritual knowledge): "to be able to expound the essence of this knowledge, when, for example, the dalang speaking for a priest gives advice to a ksatriya. Spiritual knowledge here does not refer to religion (*agama*), but to the perfection of the soul and to magic power (*kesaktian*)."

These requirements do not even touch upon the dalang's other essential accomplishments, especially his techniques in the art of puppetry (*sabetan*). The writer seems to take these for granted. The stress is on the art of storytelling, its relationship to the music, the ability of a dalang to dramatize his narration in a state of "self-forgetfulness," and on "spiritual knowledge"—the metaphysical teachings of priests and sages, knowledge of charms and the magic powers of deities and demons.

There are striking parallels between the qualifications demanded of a dalang and those that were required, on the one hand, of the Indian *sutradhara,* director and producer of classical drama and, on the other, of a shaman who officiates today in a Dayak community of Central Borneo.

About the sutradhara of ancient India, Jeannine Auboyer writes:

The director of the troupe was simultaneously the architect of the theater . . . the producer of the play, the teacher of his comedians and the leading actor. His duties were demanding and the qualities he had to possess were worthy of high officials. Judge for yourselves—he had to know everything that concerned musical instruments, the technical manuals, the numerous dialects, the art of conducting, the commerce of courtesans, the writings on poetry, manners and fashions, eloquence, dramatic acting, the crafts, versification, the planets and the lunar zodiac, colloquial speech, the world, the countries, the mountains, the inhabitants, ancient history, the genealogies of kings.[31]

From contemporary Borneo, where a team of young anthropologists were recently studying a Ma'anjan Dayak village, comes the following report:

The *wadian* [shamanistic priestess] must be able to go into trance, for trance is the door to the spirit world where, especially in healing ceremonies, the causes and cures for sickness must be sought. She must be an expert dancer, must possess the stamina to see her through a ritual that may last between an hour and nine days, and above all she must be able to master verbatim the countless chants which accompany the ceremonies she will be called upon to perform. In addition to her function as a religious practitioner and healer, the *wadian* also fills the role of local historian. Among her chants is a complete recounting of the origins and wanderings of the Ma'anjan people, the whys and wherefores of their customs and traditions, the names of their heroes and the genealogies of their great families. Finally, the *wadian* provides the village with its primary source of entertainment. All *wadian* performances are "open to the public," and it is a quiet week when there is no *wadian* ceremony in one of the villages of Padju Epat. The people of Telang, regardless of religion, will indeed travel for miles to watch a famous *wadian* in action.[32]

In the continuum of dramatic art—from shaman to stage director—the dalang, like the wadian of Borneo, is both officiant of a magically efficacious ritual and entertainer; and, like the Indian sutradhara he is the organizer, creator, and conductor of a dramatic play as well as its leading performer. Wayang kulit, having grown out of sacred rites, is thus no exception in the general history of the theater. Still strongly linked to its ritual beginnings, wayang kulit has also attained the ultimate stage of a sophisticated theater art.

The meaning of the word "dalang" is interpreted in two ways. One of the given meanings is "itinerant," suggesting an itinerant performer.[33] The other connects the title to concepts of creativity and ingenuity, suggesting that the dalang is a man having skill in creation, also wisdom, the title thus having a connotation that inspires respect.[34] Dalangs are indeed highly respected members of their communities; they are referred to with the honorific Ki (abbreviation for Kyahi), or Venerable, as shown by the motto of this section.

The dalang is obviously a superior person. Apart from his skills, he must have great endurance; traditionally a wayang kulit performance starts after sundown and lasts without interruption until sunrise, with the dalang as sole performer, never leaving his place. During the whole night he sits cross-legged on his mat before the white screen (*kelir*), illuminated by a lamp which hangs above and a little forward of his head. The flickering flame of an oil lamp, *blentjong* (*damar* in Bali), used to create a much warmer and more animated atmosphere than the cold steady light of an electric bulb which is increasingly coming into use. Two banana stems, penetrable but firm enough to support a puppet stuck into the pulp by the pointed end of its handle, are attached horizontally along the lower edge of the screen and thus serve as "podium." To the dalang's left, within reach of his right foot, stands a wooden chest, *kotak*,* on which he knocks out with a wooden mallet warning accents at some dramatic moments and signals to the musicians at transitions to new melodies or rhythms. The musicians are ranged behind him or at his side, seated on mats behind their instruments, the mere names of which reflect the gamelan's sonorities: *gendèr, bonang, saron, kenong, kempul, gong* or the duller accents of a *ketuk*.[35] The plaintive sounds of the *rebab* (one-string violin of Arabo-Persian origin) and the playful or nostalgic voice of a flute (*suling*) insinuate themselves into the gamelan's chiming fugues. From time to time the dalang adds jarring sounds of clashing metal plates, *kepyak*, suspended from the wall of the wooden box; he strikes them with a cylindrical hard knob wedged between the toes of his right foot to simulate the clamor of war and to provide harsh accents to the blows and counterblows of battling heroes. Thus, in the motions of his arms, hands, fingers, feet and voice, the dalang must maintain, often simultaneously, differing rhythmic patterns.

Often a dalang carves his own wayangs. But whether or not he produces them himself, he has the most intimate knowledge of their iconography which, as we shall presently see, is a vast field. The number of variations in the wayangs' fantastic shapes is astonishing. The puppets themselves are the product of infinite care and meticulous skill. Their silhouettes are first carved out of buffalo parchment and then the features and adornments are perforated in fine lines, dots, hair-thin curves and scrolls until, viewed against the light, some parts are like exquisite filigree.[36] Painted and

* A set of wayang puppets is referred to as a *kotak*, i.e. "chest (of puppets)."

Plate 106. "Wayang Kulit *Performance," ink wash, anonymous, Batuan, Bali,* c. *1955.*

gilded identically on both sides, the puppet is inserted between the gripping halves of a split, upward-curving, and tapering stem (*gapit*) which grows out of a solid handle with a pointed end. Most puppets have in addition two manipulating rods (*tjempurit*) attached to their hands. The only points of articulation are the elbows and the shoulder joints. But motion is not restricted to the arms since the whole puppet can be tilted, made to advance or recede, dance, fight, fall and rise, turn, hover, or descend from heights.

There are many gradations in quality. The finest puppets are masterpieces of lacy leatherwork and have stems and rods made of horn. The cruder ones lack the great finesse of the openwork, have coarser coloring and wooden stems and rods. At the sight of a fine wayang puppet, a warm glow of recognition, appreciation, and affection suffuses a Javanese who has known its shape since childhood. "Ah, Gatutkatja!" The puppet of the flying hero (Pl. 107) is lovingly held by its handle, the ends of the other two rods are gathered between the connoisseur's fingers to give the puppet's arms appropriate angles, and then the wayang is raised, admired for a moment, made to hover, soar, and then swoop down like a hawk. A warm glance and a happy smile. Or, "Hah, Bima!" (See Pl. 116.) Recognition is instantaneous, although in a glance all iconographic details have been verified; the checkered loincloth, the long nail of the thumb protruding from a closed fist, the upturned nose and round eyes of the round face straining forward as if pulling ahead the whole wide-stanced, impetuous figure. A lay bystander may receive an explanation: "This is Ardjuna during ascesis, you see, his hair grown long." Identification of wayangs usually releases long discussions of their genealogy.

Plate 107. *The flying hero Gatutkatja,* wayang kulit, *Java.*

The manual dexterity of the dalang matches his vocal versatility. In agitated scenes, as of fighting, he holds one wayang in each hand and makes them threaten, clash, stab with a dagger, or shoot off an arrow. The gestures of each puppet are produced by the nimble fingers of only the hand that holds it; to an untrained person, even holding up a wayang in one hand and manipulating its two rods with the other is a problem. The dalang also varies and enhances the effects of the puppets' shadows by placing them at certain angles to the screen so that the shadows become distorted and more diffuse than the sharp, dark silhouettes of the figures standing flush against the screen. Thus blacks and grays, sharpness and diffusion, immobility and a wide range of movements are in constant interplay.

When the dalang has set up his stage, he sticks into the center of the banana-stem "podium" the symbol of the wayang world, the *kayon* (or *kekayon*), also known as *gunungan* (Pl. 108). Kayon is derived from *kayu,* tree, and *gunungan* from *gunung,* mountain. The symmetrical leaf-shaped figure is thus a combination of tree and mountain or predominantly one of the two. Indeed its outline suggests a peaked mountain and within its confines the principal perforated and painted figure is a tree with spreading branches and with a flaming kala head in its crown. Birds, monkeys, and other creatures nestle in the tree. Below, the tree trunk is flanked by two beasts—two tigers, a lion and an elephant, two wild bulls, or others. At its foot there is often a closed, winged portal, guarded at each side by a ferocious armed doorkeeper. It looks like a gate to a sanctuary, or perhaps heaven.

Much has been written about this fascinating figure.[37] Though the elements of its internal design vary, they are always mythological symbols of the eternal. The mountain is the Mountain of the gods, the World Mountain; the tree is the Tree of Life, the Celestial Wishing-Tree of myth, bearing a solar symbol. Unlike the puppets, the kayon's figures are painted on only one side. The reverse, usually turned toward the screen, is all red—it is fire. The kayon-gunungan stands for the cosmic order, the realm of the gods, the universe.* It places the shadow play within a sacred world. It has in fact a parallel (or perhaps prototype) in ancient India where a lavishly decorated tree trunk called *jarjara* was placed on the stage and worshiped during the prelude to a dramatic play. This jarjara was a version of "Indra's staff," or banner, known as *Indradhvaja*, a decorated tree trunk around which the lord of the sky and King of Gods was worshiped with offerings, dances, songs and plays and "all other things generally attending the festive homage to a mighty god."[38]

When in the course of the shadow play there is an ominous commotion in nature (*gara-gara*), a sign that the cosmic order is being threatened, the kayon's agitated, fluttering shadow streaks across the screen indicating portentous storms; it inclines to horizontal position to suggest the waters, or, turned red side out, becomes a conflagration. Sometimes the kayon represents a tree or a whole forest; often it is a mountain. But its main symbolic function is to create the divine setting for the play when, immobile and mysterious, like an oracle, it occupies the center of the screen before a performance begins. It appears there again between the play's major periods, and finally at the conclusion of the show. Its reappearance seems to imply that "the World Order is stable and reigns supreme." "*Tantjeb kayon*"—"implant the kayon"—is the equivalent of *finis* at the termination of every shadow-play script.

The shape of the Balinese kayon (Pl. 109) differs from that of the Javanese as does the style of Balinese shadow-play puppets.[39] In Bali, the kekayon has a rounded top and the lush foliage of the tree fills most of the figure. But here too beasts flank the trunk and the waters or underworld are symbolized by serpents at the foot of the tree. The style of Balinese wayangs, which are somewhat more naturalistic, less elongated, and strongly resemble the figures on East Javanese reliefs carved in "wayang style,"† is generally considered

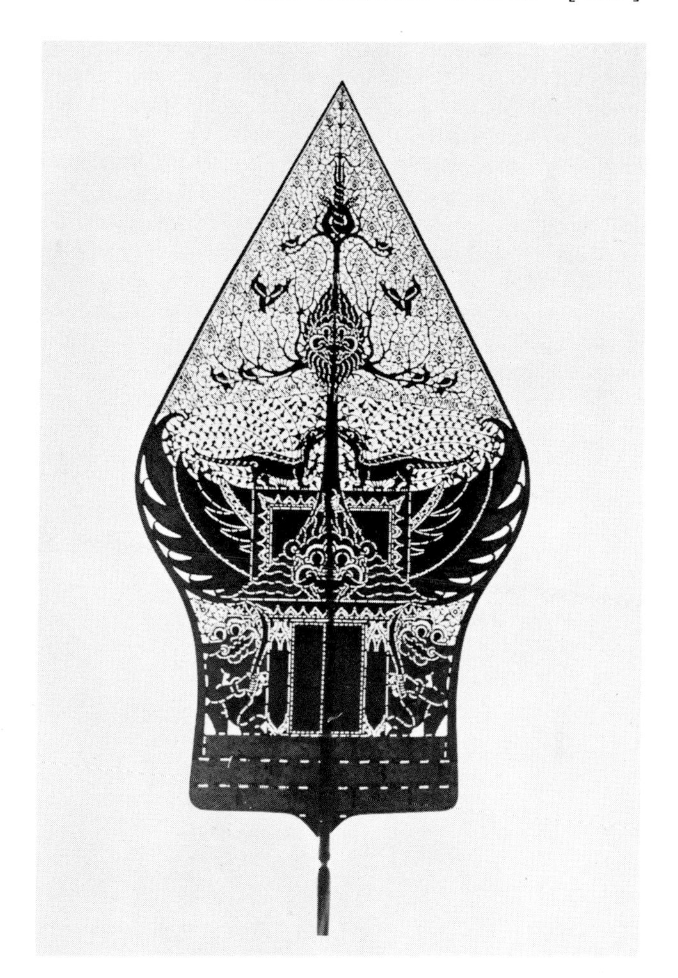

Plate 108. Kayon, wayang kulit, *Java.*

older than that of the Javanese wayangs. There are also more puppets in Balinese sets with unarticulated arms, by the way, than in Java; in addition, some of the figures have affinities with South Indian ones. The extreme stylization of the Javanese puppets may have evolved in the last two or three centuries. Whether it was stimulated by the desire to remove them still farther from any human semblance because of Islamic proscription of image-making, or whether it was merely an attempt to perfect their forms to enhance the effect of their shadows and expressiveness of their gestures is not certain. Stutterheim suggested still another possibility. Speaking of the wayang-shaped figures on the *Ramayana* reliefs on the main temple of Tjandi Panataran, he said:

The formal treatment of these heroes is intimately related to their representation in the shadow play, *wayang*. In it,

* The kayon's shape and symbolism bring to mind the silhouette and identical symbolism of the ancient Javanese temple-mausoleums built for deified kings, the tjandi (see Part I). Many of the tjandi were decorated at their base with stone reliefs depicting ancestral stories (e.g. the *Ramayana* at Tjandi Prambanan and Panataran; scenes from the life of the Pandawa progenitors at Tjandi Djalatunda; episodes from the *Mahabharata* at Tjandi Djago, etc.). These stories are also performed in the shadow play and there are put into cosmic context by means of the kayon. Thus wayang imagery perpetuates the ancient conceptions of a dominant world order symbolized by the World Mountain—conceptions which in centuries past had similarly been expressed in stone architecture.

† See Chapter 3, pp. 82–83.

too, the figures must have undergone a peculiar development that made them into disembodied schemes, incomprehensible to those who try to discern in them human beings. Their strange traits have evolved out of the continuing process, which lasted for centuries, of developing ever farther the ancient Indian conceptions regarding physical features associated with perfection. All the deviations from the natural forms of the ordinary mortal human body are based upon the teachings about "signs of good fortune," the science of omens. The bodies of the wayang figures are model charts of such traits that denote supernatural prerogatives, propitious qualities, and signs.

No conscious alteration has ever taken place, no self-willed imagination has ever participated in the creation of these wondrous forms. They just grew in the course of centuries.

Plate 109. Kayon, wayang kulit, *Bali*.

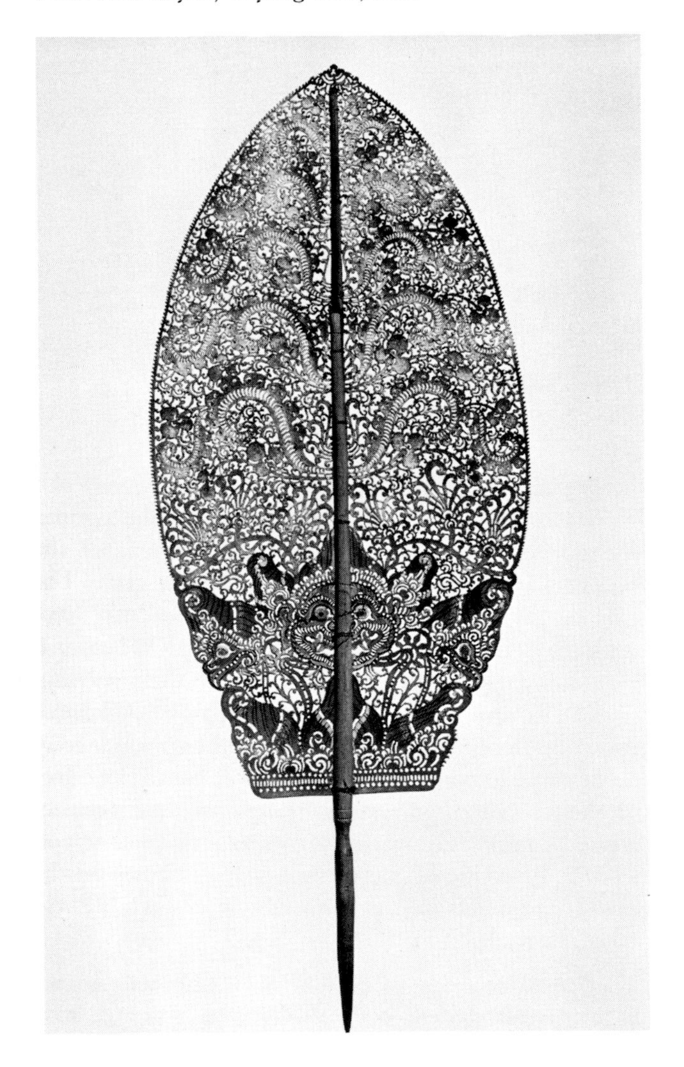

Stutterheim then pointed out that one of the striking features in the shape of the wayang heroes is their long arms. Now it is known, he said, that in ancient India *dīrgabāhu* [long-armed] was an honorific and a sign of high qualities; that in the *Citralakṣana* it is stated that one of the signs of perfection (*lakṣaṇa*) of the universal ruler (*cakravartin*) is the possession of very long arms which reach to the knees; that in the same lakṣaṇa we find the origin of the very thin waist, the "lion's waist." The eyes of the cakravartin according to the Citralakṣaṇa, are "long-drawn."*

And further:

> The more strongly these heroes are felt to be the spirits of ancestors and are assigned a special world in which their stories take place, the more the supernatural† and exceptional qualities are stressed and the farther their forms depart from human insufficiency and imperfection. Norms of beauty and the teachings about physical traits auguring good fortune in this case become identical.[40]

In the opinion of contemporary Javanese, the long arms, long noses, and other exaggerated features are explicable primarily as effective means for expressive shadow staging.

The Play

The plays, lakon, of the shadow theater, and for that matter of all other types of the Javanese traditional theater, are not literary works as are old Indian stage plays or Western dramas. Seldom are they written in a complete form that includes the dialogue.[41] Aside from the improvised dialogue, a shadow play has extensive narrative and descriptive parts recited by the dalang. Some of these, like his chants and certain stereotypes in speech, follow a traditional pattern; some are of the dalang's own creation.

The approximate meaning of the word lakon is "course (of events or action)" and this is what a lakon script essentially provides: it is an organized listing of successive scenes (*djedjer* and *adegan,* that is, "arrays" and "stances") of a play. It specifies for each scene the

* The Buddha is also "long-armed," "lion-waisted," etc.

† In Celtic mythology, Joseph Campbell (in a personal communication) notes, there is "Lug of the Long Arms." He also draws attention to the long rays ending in hands of the Solar Disk (*aton*) in the depictions of Ikhnaton in ancient Egypt (1377–1358 B.C.). Cf. the long arms of the Rice Goddess on Balinese *lamaks* (see p. 176 and Pl. 198).

place where the action occurs, the names of the participating characters, and what they talk about and why, but without citing their precise words. As in the draft of a scenario, only the gist of the story and the development of its plot are thus outlined.

The structure of a lakon is more or less standard. The play which traditionally lasts ten hours* is divided into three principal phases, each containing a number of scenes.

During the first phase, which lasts from about eight o'clock in the evening until shortly before midnight, the situation is defined. From the dalang's description and narration, and from the conversations of the representatives of the parties involved in the plot, the cause of conflict—and there is always conflict—becomes clear. The conversations usually take place in the palace hall of first one and then the other opposing monarchs. In their reception halls the kings (or gods, or demons) gather in council with their sons, prime ministers, army commanders, and so forth to discuss their problems or intentions and reach a decision on a course of action. The plot may center around a beautiful princess coveted by rival princely suitors; the search for a magically potent object (a jewel, a weapon), the possession of which is often a precondition to winning a princess; the fate of the realm may be at stake with the need to discover the secret of an enemy's invulnerability; the recovery of a mysteriously vanished son or daughter may be involved. In subsequent scenes of the first period, preparations for action are made outside the palace—envoys are sent out, troops gather, allies appear, or wedding preparations are made. Later, somewhere en route, representatives of the opposing parties meet and engage in an inconclusive fight, *perang gagal*. During this first phase the music of the gamelan is of a special tonality called *paṭet nem*,[42] usually of the five-tone, *sléndro* scale.† The tempo is moderate, quickening only during the fighting. Softly chiming cadences accompany speech. The alternation of the dalang's chanting, narrative, and dialogue calls for constant changes in the music. Moreover, each of the principal types of hero who set the mood of a scene has his own melody played at his appearance.

At midnight, the eagerly awaited second phase commences. It is introduced by "ominous manifestations" in nature, gara-gara, from which this phase derives its name. The gamelan switches to the *paṭet sanga* tonality. The principal hero (for example, Ardjuna or one of his sons) comes up with his loyal panakawans (servants-mentors-clowns) (see Pl. 115). Often the scene is laid in a dense wild wood and as a rule the hero is burdened and sorrowful as the critical stage of his adventures nears. For quite a while his followers try to console and amuse him and thus delight the audience with their pranks, comical songs, and nonsensical quarrels. They also offer the hero good advice. The turning point of the story is reached when a crucial battle, *perang kembang*, develops in the woods between the hero and giants (*raksasa*) or monsters (*buta*). This battle is the dalang's chance to display his virtuosity.

About three o'clock in the morning, the denouement

Plate 110. *Balinese* wayang kulit *puppet of a princess.*

* Shorter versions are now also given.

† The other, seven-tone, *pélog* scale is used in a variety of other plays.

begins. The gamelan switches to the third tonal mode, *paṭet manyura,* and the higher-pitched music increases in tempo as the final resolution of the plot is nearing. The principal antagonist is slain in "the battle of the lakon," *perang lakon,*[43] after which subsidiary battles, *perang sampak,* are fought to clinch the victory. In the end, just as when after a storm the glittering constellations reappear in the firmament, so the noble heroes reassemble in their full glory at their home palace, and then sunrise is at hand. The triumphal dance of a hero, Bima, for instance, may conclude this scene. Otherwise, after the kayon has been implanted, a lovely round puppet of a dance girl (golek) executes a joyous epilogue to the animated chimes of the gamelan.

Lakons are classed into *lakon pokok* (stem lakons),* *lakon tjarangan* (branch lakons) and *lakon sempalan* (detached lakons).[44] As their names suggest, the first are basic stories, or rather plays, which follow closely the traditional versions of classical tales and their separate episodes, as described in such works as the *Bharata Yuddha, Ardjuna Wiwaha,* or the Javanese version of the *Ramayana.* The second, derived from the lakon pokok, are highly embroidered elaborations of episodes constituting essentially a new story with newly invented adventures of some of the personages. The third are completely independent creations in which only the names of the well-known heroes, their salient characteristics, and familial relationships are borrowed from the original myths, but none of the situations, intrigues, or adventures resembles anything found either in the Javanese versions of the Indian epics or in the old Javanese legends. Some lakon *tjarangan* and *sempalan* may have been created to allude more specifically to circumstances surrounding the occasions for which a wayang performance has been commissioned. Wayang lakons are creations of generations of dalangs and many of them have been laid down in so-called *pakem,* manuals for dalangs that contain a collection of lakons interspersed with detailed technical instructions concerning the music, the chants with old fixed texts, and so forth. Lakons have also inspired a whole wayang literature in the form of so-called *wawatjan* with wayang stories written in prose, but more often in poetry, sometimes recited on festive occasions.

The spellbinding art of a good dalang hinges largely on his recitation and chanting. The spoken narration (*kanda* or *kotjap ing pagedongan**) is a flowery, poetic description of places and persons and situations. The chants, *suluks,* in Old Javanese verse often so transformed by oral tradition that the words become incomprehensible, are captivating melodies which create a special mood, obliterating reality; the suluks are the magic carpets on which the audience can float from scene to scene. A dalang's opening narration may run as follows:

Swuh rĕp data pitana: may silence reign.

There was a country, a famous country, which will form the beginning of this tale. Even though there were many states on this earth, spanned by the sky and surrounded by the ocean, there was none like Mandraka. This kingdom serves as starting point of our story because among a hundred other countries there were not two, and among one thousand there were not ten, that could compare with it. Naturally, this kingdom was constantly talked about: it was a state of highest rank, a land backed by mountains, bordered on the left by irrigated rice fields, by rivers on the right, and it faced a great port. All that was planted was fruitful, all that could be purchased was cheap, and the countryside was peaceful; proof of this was the continuous flow of traders passing along the roads in safety by day and by night. Mandraka was populous, the houses of its inhabitants stood roof to roof—sign of the land's prosperity.

The villagers tilled the soil, raised water buffalo, cows, ducks, and chickens, without penning them, without tying them up; during the day the animals scattered on the pasture and at night returned themselves, each to its own enclosure—because there were no thieves. The tranquillity of the country was ensured since it was free from enemy attacks; the king's subjects never grumbled but, ever in concord, upheld the king's commands.

So Mandraka was respected by all other countries. Truly its power was great, its glory shining brilliantly, its radiance spreading everywhere, its fame reaching to distant regions. Not only kingdoms in Java, but also overseas countries bowed to it. At certain fixed times princesses sent as tribute arrived, and other goods were dispatched from foreign lands as signs of loyalty.

Now it should be told that the name of Mandraka's king was Prabu Narasoma; this name means that he was patient with his subjects. He was also called Salya, or "the wise"; Mandraripa, or "the famous"; Mandrakeswara, or "the well known"; Somadanta, "the righteous one" whose soul is like

* Also known as *lakon djedjer, lakon dapur, lakon ladjer,* or *lakon lugu.*

* *Kotjap ing pagedongan* means literally "spoken inside the house" and brings to mind the Kerala shadow-play house as a contrast to the unenclosed installation of the shadow-play performer in Indonesia. The term may possibly imply a previously different arrangement.

that of a priest. Therefore many countries submitted to him not as the result of conquest, but because they were dazzled by the power of the wise king, a king who constantly distributed alms, gave clothing to the naked, food to the hungry, who comforted those in distress, provided a cane to those walking in slippery places; no one could find fault with the generosity of Mandraka's king. It is impossible to describe in one night the full extent of His Majesty's excellence and munificence; so may this suffice.

On Thursday, His Majesty entered the audience hall, sat on the royal jewel-studded lion-throne set on perfumed carpets strewn with all kinds of flowers and crowded with young girls and their attendants—His Majesty's retinue bearing all the regalia made of solid gold. The peacock-feather fans on his right and his left wafted His Majesty's fragrance in all directions until he seemed like the god Batara Sambu descended to earth accompanied by all the celestial nymphs. Not a voice was heard, no one moved; the wind was still; only the calls of the engkuk bird and the djalak bird perched on the roof of the audience hall were audible, and the alternate knocking of the court blacksmiths, gong-makers, and goldsmiths at work reached the audience hall, indistinctly, adding to the luster of the hushed world.[45]

The story goes on. The dalang recounts that the king's daughter Herawati, betrothed to Kurupati, had mysteriously vanished without a trace. The heart-broken king had to suspend the wedding agreement until she was found. Would Kurupati be able to recover her? . . . And then, before the dialogue between the personages assembled on the screen begins, the dalang's voices rises into a soaring chant, with archaic words in meters of the old kawi poetry, casting a spell upon what has been said and what is to come.*

The dalang's chants, suluks, provide the audience with the highest esthetic enjoyment, especially if a dalang has a good voice. They are ritual incantations raised to the level of a high art. They fill the whole atmosphere around the wayang play, envelop it by a swell of sacred words and sounds that nothing can penetrate or dispel. They can create an emotionally warm or chilling atmosphere; project the "inner voices" of a hero; forebode the clouds of gathering disaster; convey the longings of a lovelorn heart or the lamentations of sorrow and bereavement. Suluks intervene when a situation is pregnant with doubts and dangers. They are also chanted by the dalang at the appearance and disappearance of certain heroes and at transitions from one scene to another.

* See Appendix III, pp. 293–296, for a summary of this lakon.

Tjan Tjoe Siem observes that "tragedy is evaded on the Javanese stage by means of the suluks."[46] This may not sound true to a Javanese spectator who sits with tear-filled eyes absorbed in the hardships of a noble hero. Even a Westerner who understands the dalang's words and, above all, is familiar with the characters of the play and the wider context of the lakon can be deeply moved. So, a young friend of mine[47] wrote: "I remember seeing a beautiful example of this [sadness, *rindu*] in Solo: gara-gara; Abimanyu [son of Ardjuna] in the woods in despair because of the failure of his search for a kris which Kresna had told him to find; very dark and quiet; the dalang then had him say quietly in a heartbroken sob, 'Petruk . . . Petruk. . . .'—just that, summoning Petruk, but you felt hearing it that your heart would break." There are even more truly tragic moments in some lakons, especially in episodes connected with the *Bharata Yuddha,* the "Great War of the Bharatas": the same Abimanyu takes leave of his beloved Sitisundari before going off to the battle in which he is to die; Kunti's meeting with her heretofore unacknowledged son, Karna, who will fight her other sons; the deaths of the Pandawas' great and venerated teachers Bhisma and Durna, and many more. But on the stage, the fateful moments of a hero's agony are not portrayed in full force, and in that sense, the suluks are the lightning rods of the dramatic structure. According to Tjan Tjoe Siem they are also spells that neutralize "a danger-laden atmosphere created when magically potent figures emerge from darkness onto the lighted screen and then retreat from light back into the darkness."[48] Some suluks, he says, especially those derived from verses of the *Bharata Yuddha,* are so *sekti* (charged with magic power) that only a sekti-endowed person, who is like a priest or a deity, may recite them, and such a person is the dalang—for, wasn't Lord Içwara himself the first dalang?*[49]

It is difficult indeed to separate in wayang the magical and esthetic elements that permeate the play and all its component parts. I vividly remember my perturbation when the director of a university museum decided to exhibit some wayang puppets purely as *objets d'art* in total disregard for their symbolic meaning or their status in the polar hierarchies. It was impossible! A noble hero's profile *could not* in a certain combination be shown on the left; a deity, though small, *could not* appear on a level lower than a prince. I

* See Appendix II, p. 287.

could imagine the dismay of an Indonesian visitor to this exhibition. A group of wayang puppets obviously is meaningful *and* beautiful only if in their order they reflect the laws of the wayang universe. Arbitrariness spells disruption; and such disruption causes uneasiness in the beholder; and uneasiness precludes enjoyment. The viewer responds acutely to the totality of form and meaning. The totality dictates the grouping no less than the individual wayang's elaborate iconography.

Iconography and Ethos of the Wayang World

The immutable laws of the wayang world are elementary and universal. Even as the atom's colossal dynamics is hidden in the positive and negative charges of its particles, so the wayang's cosmic order is unthinkable without a constant interaction of positive and negative polarities. It is a stable world based on conflict. And just as a painter cannot create an effect of light without some dark masses and vice versa, so also darkness and light are felt as inextricably complementary in wayang. God Shiva embodies both creation and destruction. In religious and ethical systems high virtue is recognized only when seen against human baseness, saintliness against sin. And so the "right" (*tengen*), or positive, and the "left" (*kiwo*), or negative, realms, into which the shadow screen or classical stage is divided by an invisibile vertical line down the center, are the electrodes that spark the wayang world into life. But the polarization is not total. For, on both sides there are characters who possess qualities which typify their antagonists. Such characters lend poignancy to any total conflict, add subtle shades of grays to a black-and-white situation; just as in any total war, "the enemy" is known to include innocent and even noble individuals who by force of circumstances must remain loyal to their nation no matter what its leadership.

Both the beings who belong to the realm of the right and those of the realm of the left (Pls. 111, 112) are ranked hierarchically and within each hierarchy are differentiated: (a) by their function (for example, princes, sages, army commanders); and (b) typical temperamental characteristics. The iconography of the wayang puppets externalizes functional role, hierarchical status, and temperament, and, sometimes, also a hero's age, state, or mood. A group apart are the clowns to whom we shall return later.

A full set of wayangs may include as many as three or even four hundred puppets. The smallest is about

Plate 111. *Heroes of the "left," the Korawa and an ally. From right: Durna, priestly teacher and councilor; Kurupati (Duryodana in youth), eldest of the Korawa; Karna, Ardjuna's half-brother; Dursasana, a very aggressive Korawa.*

9 inches high, the tallest sometimes close to 40. Apart from the kayon, the largest figures are those of giants (of which Kumbakarna of the *Ramayana* is the biggest) and monstrous demons; the smallest are of some high deities and of women. Size is not a sign of greatness but rather of great physical power (Bima) or of monstrosity, violence, and uncontrolled passion as opposed to self-mastery (Pl. 113), hence spiritual power and refinement.[50] The majority of larger figures belong to the left, with the right party having relatively more of the smaller figures. But notable exceptions occur on both sides.

While size might indicate whether a figure is to be attributed to the positive or negative category, it alone is not decisive. In wayang iconography as in graphology, no one trait can be interpreted in isolation; each feature must be related to other significant idiosyncracies in order to arrive at a meaningful characterization. There are in wayang a number of typical syndromes whose principal elements are stature, posture, shape of eye, shape of nose, shape of torso. Taken together, these physical traits and attitudes indicate a hero's basic constitution. Functional role and status are indicated by the costume, ornaments, and attributes. Since in the dynamics of the wayang world the heroes' inner qualities are paramount, we shall discuss the physical features and their meaning first.

The face is of primary significance among them. Especially the shape of the eye and the nose. There are at least thirteen different shapes for eyes and as many for noses. There are three basic types of heroes, who have the following combinations of traits:[51] (1) The "finest," or noblest, characters have an elongated narrow eye, as if half-closed (*lijepan*),* and a long, pointed (*lintjip*) nose. A small and slender (*andap alit*) body complements this configuration (see Pl. 103). (2) A range of intermediary types has a "soybean-shaped" eye (*kedelèn*), rounder but still oblong, combined with a "well-proportioned" (*sembada*) long nose with a slightly turned up tip. Their bodies are medium sized (*pideksa*) (see Pl. 114). (3) The crude, physically powerful, or violent beings have "round-pupiled" (*ṭelengan*), wide open, circular eyes; the upturned nose is bulbous (*dempok*) and the body heavy and tall (*ageng inggil*) (see Pl. 113).

Both eyes and noses have still other intricate variations for old sages, the clowns, or different demonic

* Other perhaps more common designations for this type of eye are *djaitan* ("stitched together") and *gabahan* ("rice-grain shaped").

Plate 112. *Heroes of the "right," the five Pandawa brothers. From left: Puntadewa (Yudistira), Bima, Ardjuna, Nakula, and Sadewa.*

creatures. There is also a range of at least a dozen shapes for mouths and snouts to lend variety in expression.

Another variable for the three basic types listed above is the posture of the head, also signifying a temperamental attitude. The bowed (*tumungkul*) head denotes that the hero is patient (*sabar*), dedicated (*mungkul*), and unperturbable (*sareh*)—three of the highest virtues. The extreme opposite—impatience, aggressiveness, excitability—is denoted by an upturned (*langak*) face. The intermediate, straight (*longok*) position of the profile stands for more neutral traits with a variety of shades. Often very young heroes are depicted with faces leaning forward as if their pointed noses were sniffing the wind; deities as well as demons can have straight forward-looking faces. The combination of a puppet's eye shape with one of the three head postures determines the tone and pitch of the dalang's voice when he speaks for it; he thus has for the basic types alone nine tonal variations.

Another set of variables is that of the puppets' facial colors.[52] Basically they are black, white, gold, and red. Shades of rose and purple are considered varieties of red. Blue is perhaps a variation on black; brown and gray are also used, mainly for animals and some monsters (butas). There are conjectures that the four basic facial colors are associated with the cardinal points (black for North, red for South, gold [yellow] for West, and white for East) and that this is the oldest, cosmological reason for their use. It is difficult, however, to discern any consistent correlation between the various heroes and their facial colors and the symbolism of the cardinal directions. Perhaps in some distant past these associations were valid, but the symbolism seems to have been lost just as the symbolic meaning of Indian hand postures (*mudra*) is now blurred in the classical Javanese dance. Although the use of colors may be becoming more arbitrary, there is still considerable consensus about their meaning. Black is supposed to indicate inner maturity, adulthood, virtue, including

Plate 113. *Ardjuna (right) meets a giant* (raksasa). Wayang kulit, *Java.*

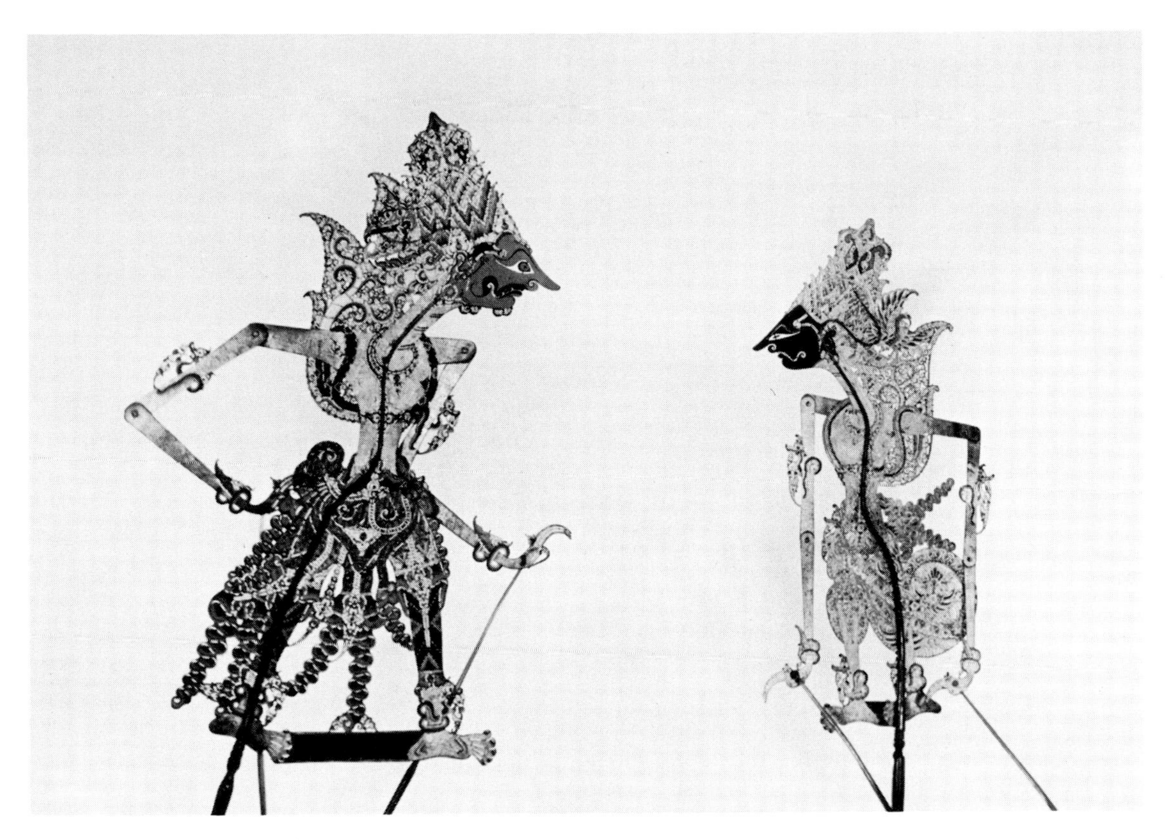

Plate 114. *The royal brothers, black-faced Kresna (right) and rose-faced Baladewa (left).* Wayang kulit, *Java.*

calmness. Red, on the other hand, denotes uncontrolled passions, desires. Gold has a double function: it may denote beauty (of the hero), royal or princely status, glory, but may also reflect the desire of the maker or owner of the puppet to make the wayang itself as beautiful as possible. White is said to indicate noble descent, youth and beauty, too, but its use is ambiguous. Some say that beings with blue faces are cowardly. Relatively few wayangs have white faces; the prevalent facial colors are black, red, and gold. In the course of one play the same character may appear at one time with a golden face and at another with a black face to indicate different aspects of the hero or stages in his life.

From this brief review of leading variables it becomes clear that whereas in some combinations the significant iconographic features are mutually complementary and reinforcing, they modify one another in other configurations. Thus Ardjuna (Pl. 103) is always depicted with the narrowest type of eye, a long, downward-tending pointed nose, as his head is usually bowed; his face, depending on his age or mood, is either white, gold, or black. Reinforcing his subdued attitude is the stance of his closely adjoining legs. His tempestuous brother Bima (Pl. 116), however, who is an outstanding member of the "right," has a towering stature, an aggressive wide stance; his eye is round and his upturned nose semibulbous; he also has a curly beard—sign of his virility? Bima is impetuous like the demons, a true son of the wind god. But he is thin-waisted and his face is black. And his checkered loincloth (a sacred pattern) signifies his magic potency as does his phallic thumb with its long nail. On the other hand the Pandawas' divine mentor Kresna and his elder brother Baladewa (Pl. 114) are clearly differentiated by stature and facial color as members of the right and left respectively. Kresna's face is always black, his eye narrow, nose pointed, but his head is straight. Baladewa, an ally of the Korawas, is taller, has a "soybean-shaped" eye, a "medium" nose; his face is red or rose. Thus the red or rose facial color, like large size, immediately suggests some quality separating the character from the party at the right. By "reading" these and other iconographic clues one is helped to identify a hero's inner constitution.

To determine the hero's functional role and status,

the most helpful clue in his costume is the headdress. Headdresses range from a simple tuft of hair (for clowns) to gorgeous tiaras (for some high kings, queens, and certain deities). Between these two extremes there are more than two dozen varieties of stylized coiffures and headgear, enlivened by wing-shaped ear ornaments, which are among the most graceful and elegant creations of generations of wayang designers. A priest can be recognized by his conchlike turban; a princely regent by his helmetlike crown; members of the Pandawa clan, by their coiffures rising scroll-shaped at the back.

Some puppets are bare from the waist up. Some are fully clad, especially gods, seers, and older women. Physically vigorous types have curly short beards under the chin or on the throat; monsters are hairy with heavy bristling eyebrows and hair in the nostrils.

The highly stylized garments of the lower body consist of a rich variety of patterned loincloths and *dodots*—large rectangular ceremonial cloths draped around the hips, formerly the court dress for princes and high officials. The cloths are short for young men, long for women; they have bustles for royalty; they are tucked up to do battle. Long trousers and short pants are in evidence too, topped by either a hipcloth or by a long jacket. Deities and sage-priests are depicted wearing long coats and *shoes* with upturned toes. All garments and adornments have a variety of designs, but these are fortunately not always iconographically significant.

Ornaments include rings (on the hand, which may have nine different finger positions); bracelets, armlets, anklets, necklaces with decorative pendant plaques. Special attributes are caste cords and pubic shields. They are the same adornments found on the statues of deified kings enshrined in the old Javanese tjandi. The presence or absence of certain attributes is sometimes relevant. The wing-shaped *praba* ("glow," "radiance"), equivalent to the halo of glory, is reserved for some kings. In the case of the flying hero Gatutkatja, who is likened to lightning, the praba probably also represents wings (Pl. 107). It is difficult to determine, however, why certain princes have prabas and others not. It is also not clear whether the presence or absence of the *Garuda mungkur* ("Garuda looking back") protective charm at the back of some heroes' head has a special significance. Originally these attributes may have been systematically given only to those figures thought to possess special divine endowments or grace. Today they merely help to identify heroes already known to possess them. The most precisely identifiable wayangs are those of the *Mahabharata* and *Ramayana* lakons. For derivative or freely composed plays, in which many characters appear under new names, standard puppets are selected to fit the type.

The great majority of wayangs are executed in the decoratively elaborate and iconographically intricate "wayang style" which lends their appearance a certain unity, but there is one notable exception: the silhouettes and treatment of the figures of the "clowns." Their fantastically grotesque flat shapes are outlined in strong and simple manner; there is no lacy openwork in the scanty garments, not a single ornament on the tufted bare heads. The short-legged, fat, hermaphroditic old Semar is flat-nosed, with a hypertrophic jaw, a wise, tired eye, an enormous rear part, a bulging paunch, and heavy, almost feminine breasts. His sons are the tall, long-nosed Petruk and the little, limping and frightened Gareng. (His third son, Bagong, who used to appear but rarely, now is reportedly becoming very popular.) Semar is a mysterious figure with a visible sign of sacredness, his checkered hipcloth. This is how a dalang introduces Semar and his two sons (Pl. 115):

> Why is he called Semar? . . . Semar is derived from the word *samar* (dim, obscure, mysterious). Indeed, Kyai Lurah* Semar may well be called mysterious. Designate him as a man, his face looks like a woman's; say that he is a woman, his appearance is that of a man. How does Kyai Lurah Semar look? He has a turned-up nose, but it is lovable; watering eyes but lovable; puffed cheeks, also lovable; he is potbellied, but lovable; in short, everything about him is lovable. Kyai Lurah Semar is indeed a mysterious personage, for in reality he is not a human creature, but a deity of the Suralaya, named Sang Hyang Ismaya. Kyai Lurah has two sons: the elder's name is Kyai Lurah Nala-Gareng, the younger one's Kyai Petruk. Why is he called Nala-Gareng? *Nala* is hard, *gareng* is dry; Nala-Gareng has a dry heart, he is always sad. How does he look? His eyes are squinting; his lips don't close well; his arms are crooked (having been broken); he limps and walks like a cripple since his feet are full of yaws. And Kyai Lurah Petruk? His body is long; his nose is long; his eyes are long; his lips are long; his neck is long; his legs are long; his steps are long; and long are his hands. What is his nature? He is mischievous . . . ; if he steals, he is praised for it; if he deals out blows, he is rewarded for it.[53]

Semar is not only loved, but revered and regarded

* Honorific: the Venerable Chief or Head.

by some as the most sacred figure of the whole kotak, or wayang set. He appears on the screen precisely at midnight, preceded by the gara-gara, "omnious manifestation," when danger is greatest, the distress of his master deepest, and when help is essential. Some writers on the wayang conjectured that Semar and his sons are old indigenous Indonesian deities who have been demoted to the status of servants with the ascendancy of the Hindu gods and the semidivine ksatriya heroes of the epics.[54] Another interpretation is that the panakawans are "the people"[55] not otherwise represented in the palace hierarchies. They are the voice of the simple village folk, with all their strength, misery, and wisdom. Without them a princely master is unthinkable; without their support, advice, and succor, he may be lost. Semar, who is never in the wrong, is particularly powerful. Of all the wayang heroes he alone dares, in some lakons, to remonstrate with the gods, even with Batara Guru (Shiva) himself and the feared Batari Durga; he demands from them some decision or intercession in no uncertain terms, and may even force them to act or desist. Whether deity or deified symbol of the people, Semar combines his role of servant-mentor with that of a mediator between his masters and the gods. Some demonic heroes have two grotesque servant-clowns of their own, Togog and Sarahita (or Sarawita), who is supposed to be Semar's brother. They are not the bravest of creatures.

Wayang typology has exercised a powerful influence on the daily attitudes of the Javanese. Almost automatically people incline to look upon a heavy-set man with round eyes, a heavy nose, and a loud voice as inferior; a slender, not very tall person with elongated eyes and subdued manner a priori may be superior. But just as in the wayang itself, there are always exceptions. So, for instance, the late P. V. van Stein Callenfels, the noted archaeologist and the oversize *enfant terrible* of the Netherlands Indies administration, had won the hearts of many Indonesians. A bearded, corpulent giant, whose heavy bulk ensconced on a palanquin had to be transported sometimes to an archaeological site by a dozen or more carriers, he was likened to Kumbakarna, the noble giant of the *Ramayana*. (When news of Stein Callenfels' death, which occurred in Ceylon, spread in Java, it seemed to many quite appropriate that he should have met his end where he belonged—in Rawana's kingdom, Langka).

Ideal conduct in the wayang world corresponds to the highly stylized etiquette of Javanese courts which permeated Javanese society before the revolution and still persists in the older generation. To past generations, wayang, apart from serving as a character chart by which to judge other people, provided one with a choice of ideal types to be emulated. Just as Sita became the ideal of a devoted wife for the women in India, so many a young Javanese used to aspire to

Plate 115. *The* panakawan, *noble hero's servants. From right: Semar, Gareng, and Petruk.* Wayang kulit, *Java.*

achieve a steadfastness like Ardjuna's, or the swift courage of Gatutkatja. When American "westerns" reached the open-air movie screen in Java, Tom Mix soon attained immense popularity perhaps because he was a hero, swift on his flying horse, impetuous, gallant and brave, like Bima's son.

If the wayang has educational value for the young as has always been claimed by their wayang-loving elders, what kind of virtues does it stress? The virtues are embodied in the Pandawa brothers and their allies. Ideally, purity, righteousness, and compassion (Yudistira) are the highest virtues; but self-mastery and dedication to duty (Ardjuna) are the aim of most aspirations. The other prized qualities are strength and courage directed toward positive aims (Bima and his son Gatutkatja), loyalty (the twins Nakula and Sadewa), wisdom paired with transcendental knowledge, clairvoyance, and magic powers (Kresna, ascetic-sages).

Obviously for children—who always constitute a considerable portion of the audience—wayang plays are fascinating adventure stories spiced by the jokes of the beloved panakawans. As they grow up, the repertory becomes a sort of family history and they follow with particular interest the behavior of their favorite heroes in new circumstances created by the dalang. It is almost like observing the conduct of friends, neighbors, and relatives in critical situations.

To adult spectators, depending on their degree of sophistication and their religious orientation (often influenced from childhood on by the wayang), shadow plays have a variety of meanings. Like all myths the lakons are susceptible to interpretation on different levels.[56] Below the rippling and shimmering surface of the tale, meanings of cosmic as well as human import seem to be hidden; the nature of the world order and the laws governing all creation are thought to be mirrored in the wayang.

Among the themes of which wayang lakons are regarded as symbolic are the eternal contraposition of light and darkness and nature's cycles of generation, decline, and renewal. Another view is that a lakon's hidden meaning is a portrayal of man's development, from childhood to maturity. His stamina is first tested when he engages in youth in the inconclusive battles of the first phase; he attains adult status when in the confusing wilderness, his own heart, he conquers the demons or monsters, his passions. With the passions mastered, he can attain the victories necessary to his own and his community's welfare. (The hero's progress is beset by temptations and tests suggestive of initiation rites.)

Mystically inclined Javanese discern in wayang plays mystic teachings, including encouragement of the spiritual exercise known as *semadi*. "One can learn about the way of *semadi* from what the dalang recites about it," wrote the late Mangkunagara VII of Surakarta, quoting the dalang:

> Now is described the fierce battle between the middle one of the Pandawas, Raden Ardjuna, and his adversary. . . . Despair is in his heart, for, again and again, he is at the point of suffering defeat. Suddenly he halts the contest; he seats himself for the semadi and turns to the purification of his heart and mind. He folds his arms, one over the other, and stretches his legs straight forward, closely joined. He suspends the functions of the nine openings of the body. Sounds do not penetrate to him; forms are not distinguished by his eyes; his attention is fixed only upon the inhaling and exhaling of his breath while his gaze is kept upon the point of his nose. He concentrates his thoughts. The Lord of the World hears his prayer and simultaneously there appears before him the arrow Pasopati like a blue radiation (*daru*) from heaven."[57]

A semadi practitioner aspires to a state in which he can experience divine revelation, or, in other terms, apprehend his own inspired insight. In relation to wayang lakons, the Mangkunagara distinguishes three kinds of semadi, or rather three of its aims: the first is to grasp the meaning of life, to comprehend its origin and purpose (in wayang lakons this theme appears as the hero's search for his father whom he does not know); the second is to actuate higher powers within oneself, to overcome frustration and obtain mastery over the order of things (Ardjuna's ascesis is an example of semadi undertaken for such a purpose); the third, less frequently reflected in a lakon, is semadi undertaken to secure "higher powers" for black magic (as when a hero wishes to bewitch a princess he covets, or his rival).*[58]

There are special lakons which more than others probe into the spheres where mystics like to dwell. One of them is the lakon *"Bima Sutji"* ("Bima Purified"), in which the hero seeks the "water of life." Bima's quest is interpreted as a desire for initiation into "True

* The Prince does not mention a possible fourth purpose, to attain ultimate enlightenment and salvation, or deliverance in the Buddhist sense. Apparently, in wayang plays, this completely mystical goal recedes before the magico-mystical aims of semadi.

Knowledge" and its motivation as a longing for self-identification, for "oneness" or wholeness. He rejects his relatives' warnings about the danger of his undertaking; indeed, he seems to feel that even death is preferable to uncertainty.[59] First, searching for the water of life, he rips asunder the mountain Tjandramuka and is suddenly confronted by two giants whom he fights and defeats. They then assume their true shape; before him stand the gods Hendra (Indra) and Bayu (Wayu). (Bayu, we must remember, is Bima's father.) They inform him that the water of life cannot be found in the mountain and advise him again to consult his guru, Durna. This time Durna tells Bima that the water of life is in the vast depths of the ocean. Again Bima's brothers and friends try to restrain him, but he rushes off with steps that are "seven times as far as the gaze of an elephant reaches" and arrives at the ocean's shore. Knee-deep in the water, he is seized by a serpent but, with his long thumbnail (*kuku pantjanaka*), he pierces the monster entwining him and then plunges into the unfathomable depth. On the bottom of the ocean he encounters a diminutive being, Dewa Rutji, who in appearance is a tiny replica of Bima himself (Pl. 116). Upon the little deity's invitation, Bima, perplexed but willing, enters into Dewa Rutji through his ear and thus, mystically interpreted, fuses with his own newly discovered "spiritual self." Bima's thumbnail here symbolizes his will power and the serpent, his breath which he dares to cut off. (The successful semadi practitioner's breath is said to fail him just before the moment of revelation when, in the words of Javanese mystics, he enters "the world filled with light and no shadows.")[60]

Moreover, to a mystitc, the Mangkunagara wrote, the wayang performance itself suggests the practice of semadi. So, the gamelan music accompanying Bima's vertiginous journey provides sensations akin to those experienced by a semadi practitioner just before and after his "spiritual self" emerges; the dalang's knocks of the mallet against the wooden wayang chest are like his accelerated heartbeats when that moment nears; and the *ayak-ayakan manyura,* pulsating melodies played during Bima's emergence from the ocean and his return to his brothers, are said to render completely "that indescribable feeling of returning from the semadi state to full rational consciousness."[61]

Some dalangs may be mystics themselves and may either overtly or covertly encourage the appreciation and practice of semadi. Regard for it has persisted in Asia ever since the first Indian yogi discovered the secrets of controlled breathing and absorption in meditation. The fruits of semadi, immortalized in the

Plate 116. *Bima (left) meets Dewa Rutji.* Wayang kulit, *Java.*

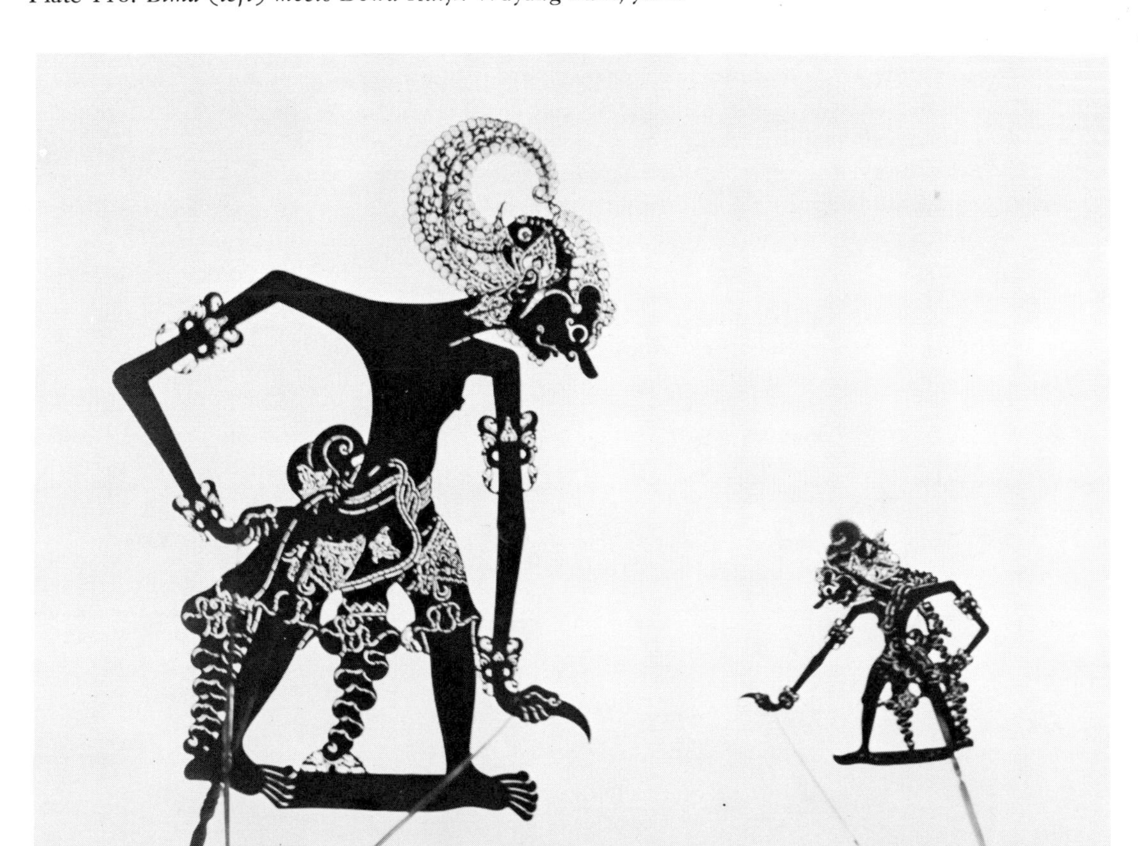

eleventh-century Javanese poem *Ardjuna Wiwaha,* are still sought today by some Indonesian leaders—directly, or indirectly through mystical gurus—to enhance their insights or their influence and temporal power.

To many young Javanese and to some intellectuals of the older, revolutionary generation, the wayang world is a soporific anachronism. Nor is wayang favored by Javanese who are devout Moslems, but their reservations are influenced by religious rather than intellectual considerations. Yet its attraction is powerful. To turn their backs on it completely is for some truly a *tour de force.* A telling example of ambivalence is the confession of a young writer that he was *afraid* of wayang as well as of gamelan music. Seeking an Indonesian "national identity"* as well as individual self-realization in the modern world, the new generation turns to the creative spirits of their own time—not the dalangs, but the new poets and writers whose world is shot through with social and personal conflicts, with revolt against deep-rooted traditions.

In wayang lakons a hero rarely has inner conflicts. The one outstanding exception, deriving from India's sacred literature but muted in the shadow play, is Ardjuna's moral dilemma, which is so beautifully expressed in the *Bhagavad Gita,* The Song of the Lord.[62] On the eve of the great battle with his cousins, he turns in distress to his divine mentor, Krishna (Kresna): he does not want to fight and to kill, feeling that his own death is preferable to slaying his kin. But the pain and doubts of this great conscientious objector of Indian mythology are overridden by Krishna's exposition of the mystique of caste duty (to a ksatriya, "there is nothing nobler than a righteous war"[63]), and by the divine teacher's metaphysical doctrine. All worldly experience is illusory; the universal Self is eternal, imperishable, only the body in which it dwells perishes. But when a warrior slays, he must do so with detachment, without hate.

> But he whose mind dwells
> Beyond attachment,
> Untainted by ego,
> No act shall bind him
> With any bond:
> Though he slays these thousands
> He is no slayer.[64]

On those rare occasions when the "War of the Bharatas" is actually brought upon the shadow screen, the dalang may chant briefly about Ardjuna's hesitations, but there is no evidence that this humanistic trait of the hero's character is widely associated with his image in the mind of the wayang-conscious public—his adherence to the ksatriya's duty and his irresistibility in love overshadow all. The external battles that rage on the wayang screen are inevitable within the established world order in which everyone has his allotted place, role, and fate. Virtually all lakons end in the victory of the "right" party. It is a rare play indeed that culminates in the destruction of its heroes and, when this happens, retribution is close at hand. If a wayang play is never a tragedy in the Western sense, neither is it ever truly a comedy. Farce, satire, comical confusions of identity are practically never the essence of a plot, though humor is not lacking.* It is mainly the panakawans in their interludes who amusingly bring the audience down to earth with their folkish ways, jests, and pranks. Few of the other characters have a sense of humor. Demons can roar with malicious laughter; some monsters are very funny even if they don't mean to be; but the principal figures have little gaiety. Wayang plays, like good stories, to paraphrase Isak Dinesen, are neither tragic nor comic, but "marvelous."

The heroes of the wayang world act and move like the planets with their satellites, inexorably following their predestined course, each according to his nature, his fate, his karma. Their cosmic space is that of myth. They are part of the divine world order—"A static eternity of estates and castes" with "minute and detailed laws of conduct . . . a gigantic as well as a minute order," in which men are given "ceremonial identities set apart by extravagantly differentiated roles and costumes." These phrases were used by Erik H. Erikson[65] to characterize the stylized conception of the world order in the life of medieval Europe, but they are also singularly apt for characterizing the wayang world.

But whereas man in medieval Europe was burdened by a consciousness of sin and the constant injunction to repent and reform, to sin in the wayang world is mainly to kill a member of one's own family or a holy person. When it is done, it is more often than

* See Part III, p. 215.

* Reportedly in recent years (1963–1965) there has been a trend toward an increasing share of farce and satire in both wayang kulit and wayang wong—a sign of the times?

not by accident. Though the slayer is seized by grief and remorse, he also knows that retribution is inevitable. So when Gatutkatja in a fit of temper strikes his uncle Kalabendara and the latter dies, Gatutkatja, overcome by sorrow and self-reproach, tries to embrace the corpse. But the corpse vanishes with a warning that Gatutkatja's "debt" will be settled in the Great War, the Bratayudda. On the battlefield, Gatutkatja, fully aware that his death is imminent, volunteers to fight his half-uncle Karna allied with the enemy. Karna's arrow comes short of hitting the flying hero but the dead uncle's spirit catches the deadly missile and propels it to its mark. Retribution by fate is full accepted; the divine balance sheet is ever squared. There is nothing man himself can do except submit to providence. In wayang lakons no crushing conscience ever continues to torture a hero and he can reform no more than a stream inundating a village or a volcano spewing fire and ashes. The overriding morality is the duty of the ksatriya—the code of knights—and laws of behavior appropriate to each estate.

No doubt in many lakons the dalang makes his heroes quite human. Ardjuna may have an outburst of temper and later make amends; an ascetic sage may be sarcastic; intrepid Gatutkatja is struck with shyness at the sight of beautiful Pregiwa, his cousin*; King Kresna indulges in wit. These charming embroideries do not, however, obscure the patterns of destiny. Decisive in this destiny is the quest for and possession of magically potent resources—be it knowledge of a magic formula, the boon of invisibility or invincibility, the gift of a miraculous weapon, or the accumulation through spiritual exercise of supernatural powers. The enchanting but often elusive princess around whom so many lakon plots revolve is herself like a coveted charm. Disguises, transformations, and resurrections abound in wayang plays: a young ascetic may turn out to be a princess; tigers or giants are transformed gods; the death of a hero is not necessarily final. Everything is fairy tale, symbolism, or mysticism. Just as in dreams, there is no room for rationality.

And so, today as in centuries past, the shadows of heroes, whose fate is known to deities and seers, come to life in wayang dress on the white screen. The shadows' faith is acceptance of the immutable order of things; the shadows' will strives to enhance their power, to gain possession of the desired mate, to defend their domain, to make their universe secure. These primordial, almost innate, drives are transcended when they seek to probe into the secrets of their origin and destination, to realize the essence of their own being. And, as in nature, darkness is always dispelled by sparkling light, and morning, literally, always dawns—till sunset is at hand again. The tensions will persist forever, the fortunes of the heroes swing back and forth, and the quest, beset by storms like nature's cycles, continues in the timelessness of myth.

* See Appendix III, p. 306.

Notes

1. "Anoman Trigangga," in Koentjaraningrat, ed., *Tari dan Kesusateraan di Indonesia* [Dance and Literature in Indonesia] (Jogjakarta, 1959), p. 35. Extract translated from Indonesian by the author.
2. J. Kats, *Het Javaansche Tooneel* (Weltevreden, 1923), pp. 85, 87–98, 159.
3. See Harsono Hadisoeseno, "Wayang and Education," *Education and Culture* (Djakarta), No. 8 (October, 1955), 9; cf. J. Kats, "Wayang Madya," *Djawa* (Bijlage, Mangkoe Nagoro number, September, 1924), 42–44.
4. Harsono Hadisoeseno, pp. 3–5.
5. See H. H. Juynboll, "Wajang Kelitik oder Kerutjil," *Internationales Archiv für Ethnographie,* XIII (1900), 4–17, 97–119 and pls.; Amir Sutaarga, "De Wajang Golek in West-Java," *Indonesië,* VIII (1955), 441–456.
6. L. Serrurier, *De Wajang Poerwå* (Leiden, 1896), p. 141; Sutaarga, "De Wajang Golek," pp. 444–445.
7. W. P. Groeneveldt, *Historical Notes on Indonesia and Malaya; Compiled from Chinese Sources* (Djakarta, 1960), p. 53, reprint of article in *VBG,* XXXIX (1880).
8. R. Pischel, "Das altindische Shattenspiel," *Sitzungsberichte der Koeniglich Preussischen Akademie der Wissenschaften* (Berlin), XXIII (1906), p. 488. The passage has been translated into English by the author.
9. *Ibid.,* p. 487. Translated by the author.
10. *Ibid.,* pp. 494–498; also Georg Jacob, Hans Jensen, and Hans Losch, "Das Indische Schattentheater," no. 2 in Georg Jacob and Paul Kahle, ed., *Das Orientalische Schattentheater* (Stuttgart, 1931), pp. 31-145. Jacob includes a translation of the *Dutangada.*
11. Beryl de Zoete, *The Other Mind* (London, 1953), pp. 90–98.
12. Stan Harding, "The Ramayana Shadow-Play in India," *Asia,* XXXV, No. 4 (April, 1935), 234–235.
13. *Ibid.,* p. 234.
14. Paul Kahle, "Der Leuchtturm van Alexandria," no. 1

in Jacob and Kahle, eds., *Das Orientalische Schattentheater,* p. 11.

15. Denis Bordat and Francis Boucrot, *Les Théâtres d'Ombres; Histoire et Techniques* (Paris, 1956), pp. 27–51.

16. Wilhelm Hoenerbach, *Das Nordafrikanische Schattentheater* (Mainz, 1959), p. 3.

17. H. H. Prince Dhaninivat, *The Nang* (Bangkok, 1956), p. 6.

18. *Ibid.*, pp. 5–6.

19. See Jeanne Cuisinier, *Le Théâtre d'Ombres à Kelantan* (Paris, 1957).

20. Georg Jacob and Hans Jensen, "Das Chinesische Schattentheater," no. 3 in Jacob and Kahle, eds., *Das Orientalische Schattentheater,* pp. 2–4.

21. *Ibid.*, pp. 2–3. Translated by the author.

22. *Ibid.*, pp. 3–4.

23. *Ibid.*, p. 4.

24. Cf. G. Coedès, *Les États Hindouisés d'Indochine et d'Indonésie* (Paris, 1964), pp. 26–27, r. 8.

25. N. J. Krom, *Hindoe-Javaansche Geschiedenis* (The Hague, 1926), p. 47.

26. W. H. Rassers, "On the Origin of the Javanese Theatre," in *Panji, the Culture Hero* (The Hague, 1959), pp. 95–215.

27. G. A. J. Hazeu, *Bijdrage tot de kennis van het Javaansche tooneel* (Leiden, 1897), p. 3.

28. Kats, *Het Javaansche Tooneel,* p. 41.

29. H. H. Mangkunagara VII of Surakarta, *On the Wayang Kulit (Purwa) and Its Symbolic and Mystical Elements,* trans. by Claire Holt (Ithaca, N.Y., 1957), pp. 4–5.

30. Ki Reditanaja, *Kartawijoga,* trans. from Javanese into Indonesian by R. Hardjowirogo (Djakarta, 1951), pp. 3–4; cf. Kats, *Het Javaansche Tooneel,* pp. 33–34, for what a dalang must know and do, and not do.

31. Jeannine Auboyer, "Le Théâtre Classique de l'Inde," in Jean Jacquot, ed., *Les Théâtres d'Asie* (Paris, 1961), p. 16. Translated by the author.

32. Alfred B. and Judith M. Hudson, "Telang: A Ma'anjan Village of Central Kalimantan," in Koentjaraningrat, ed., *Villages in Indonesia* (Ithaca, N.Y., 1966), pp. 90–114.

33. Hazeu, *Bijdrage tot de Kennis van het Javaansche Tooneel,* p. 23.

34. R. A. Kern, "De Beteekenis van het Woord Dalang," in *BKI,* XCIX (1940), 123–124.

35. Kats, *Het Javaansche Tooneel,* lists the instruments for a small and for a large gamelan accompanying wayang kulit and provides illustrations. See also J. Kunst, *Music in Java; its History, its Theory and its Technique* (The Hague, 1949); and Colin McPhee, "The Balinese Wayang Kulit and Its Music," *Djawa,* XVI (1936), 1–50.

36. See R. L. Mellema, *Wayang Puppets; Carving, Colouring and Symbolism,* trans. by Mantle Hood (Amsterdam, 1954).

37. For additional illustrations and discussion of the kayon see: Kats, *Het Javaansche Tooneel,* pp. 23–24; A. N. J. Th. à Th. van der Hoop, *Indonesian Ornamental Design* (Bandung, 1949), pp. 274–281; F. D. K. Bosch, *The Golden Germ* (The Hague, 1960), pp. 178–186, 227–228, 244–249, and pls. 66–69, bibliography.

38. Bosch, *The Golden Germ,* pp. 152–153, 179.

39. Cf. McPhee, "The Balinese Wajang Koelit and Its Music," pp. 1–50; Miguel Covarrubias, *Island of Bali* (New York, 1950), pp. 236–244.

40. Willem Stutterheim, *Rama Legenden und Rama Reliefs in Indonesien* (Munich, 1925), I, 200–201. The quoted passages are translated by the author.

41. A good example of a complete lakon is given in Tjan Tjoe Siem, *Hoe Koeroepati zich zijn Vrouw verwerft* [How Koeroepati acquires his wife] (Leiden, 1938).

42. See Mantle Hood, *The Nuclear Theme as a Determinant of Patet in Javanese Music* (Groningen and Djakarta, 1954), pp. 126–129, for a discussion of *patets* in Javanese wayang kulit.

43. Ki Reditanaja, *Kartawijoga,* p. 6.

44. Cf. Kats, *Het Javaansche Tooneel,* pp. 85–86.

45. Extract, translated from Indonesian by the author, is based on Ki Reditanaja, *Kartawijoga,* pp. 7–8. A different version is given in Tjan Tjoe Siem, *Hoe Koeroepati zijn Vrouw verwerft,* pp. 3–6.

46. Tjan Tjoe Siem, *Hoe Koeroepati,* p. 248.

47. Benedict R. O'G. Anderson, in a personal communication.

48. Tjan Tjoe Siem, p. 248.

49. *Ibid.*, p. 249.

50. Cf. the giant demons and small gods in the Jain mythological system described in Joseph Campbell, *The Masks of God: Oriental Mythology* (New York, 1962), pp. 228–231.

51. R. M. Sulardi, *Printjening Gambar Wayang Purwa* [Specifications of Wayang Purwa Figures] (Djakarta, 1953).

52. Cf. Kats, *Het Javaansche Tooneel,* pp. 8–21, analytical tables of principal iconographic features of 37 wayang purwa puppets; Mellema, *Wayang Puppets,* pp. 61–63, lists the facial colors of 155 puppets, some duplicates, of 94 characters.

53. Budihardja, "Grepen uit de Wajang," *Djawa,* II (1922), 22–23.

54. J. Kats, "Wie is Semar?" *Djawa,* III (1923), 55.

55. H. O. "Petroek als Vorst," *Djawa,* II (1922), 169–172.

56. Cf. H. H. Mangkunagara VII of Surakarta, *On the Wayang Kulit;* Clifford Geertz, *The Religion of Java* (Glencoe, Ill., 1960), pp. 261–282.

57. H. H. Mangkunagara VII, *On the Wayang Kulit,* p. 14.

58. *Ibid.*, p. 16.

59. *Ibid.*, p. 23.

60. *Ibid.*, pp. 17–18.

61. *Ibid.*, p. 18.

62. Among several of the existing translations, see *The Song of God: Bhagavad Gita,* trans. by Swami Prabhavananda and Christopher Isherwood (New York, 1954).

63. *Ibid.*, p. 38.

64. *Ibid.*, p. 122.

65. Erik H. Erikson, *Young Man Luther* (New York, 1962), p. 186.

CHAPTER 6

Dance Drama

In defining the wayang world (in Chapter 5), we have said that at its core lay the shadow play. In part this is true because during the last century the shadow play has influenced the traditional human theater so strongly that dramatic dancers have increasingly acquired the characteristics of wayang puppets. Although especially true of Javanese *wayang wong* (dance-plays without masks), it applies to some extent also to *wayang topeng* (dance-plays with masks) and such other varieties of dance drama as the operatic *Langendriya.*

In the vast insular realm of Indonesia, the art of dance drama has been fully developed only in Java and Bali. Since excellent descriptions of Balinese theatrical forms are available to the English reader in the work of Beryl de Zoete and Walter Spies,[1] the focus here will be on the less frequently discussed classical drama of Java.[2]

Before World War II, dance drama, like music and dances, was cultivated and perfected at the princely courts of Central Java. That the nobility's preoccupation with the performing arts is of long standing is attested by the description of court festivities given in the fourteenth-century poem *Nagarakrtagama.* During the colonial period this interest may have become even more intense, since the ruling princes, deprived of many of their former powers and yet possessing considerable wealth, were able to display the glory of their courts mainly on ceremonial occasions that included elaborate spectacles.

Between the eighteenth and twentieth centuries repertories were expanded, costumes enriched, and dance techniques perfected. Many innovations were introduced into the style of court performances, which is probably why Javanese traditions ascribe the "invention" of wayang wong to one or another ruler of the eighteenth century.[3] The "initiation" of mask-plays, however, is credited to the sixteenth-century religious leader Sunan Kalidjaga[4]—a coastal prince revered as one of the seven wali, the miracle-working apostles of Islam.

That mask-plays are undoubtedly of far more ancient origin has already been indicated. Practices in Bali, where to the present mask-plays often enter into post-cremation celebrations, suggest a possible role for masked dances in pre-Islamic Java. The attribution of Javanese mask-plays to Sunan Kalidjaga was perhaps motivated by the need of the Islamic courts to sanction heathen but continuingly popular customs.

As for plays without masks, they may have developed from pantomimic war dances or chanted recitals of myths which were accompanied by illustrative dance-mime. If we are to accept Pigeaud's interpretation of the nature of the *raket* plays in Majapahit as described in the *Nagarakrtagama,* these may well have been a form of dance drama. On the other hand, the raket might have been specifically a mask-play as was previously thought by other scholars. The likelihood, however, is that certain elements of the present *style* of both wayang wong and wayang topeng were initiated only about eighty or ninety years ago and then further elaborated and perfected.

Of the four courts in the two capitals, Solo and Jogja, of the so-called Princes' Lands (*Vorstenlanden* in Dutch nomenclature) located in the heart of Java, the highest in rank were the keratons of the Susuhunan of Surakarta and of the Sultan of Jogjakarta. The keratons—actually small walled palace-cities with several thousand inhabitants—harbored some of the best dalangs, musicians, dancing masters, and a variety of artisans who produced the finest wayang puppets, masks, and dance costumes in existence in Java. The other two smaller courts, each with its own contingent of experts in the arts and crafts, were the *istana* (palace) or *astana* of the Mangkunagara in Surakarta and the Paku Alam in Jogjakarta.* All the titles of the hereditary rulers perpetuated the ancient conception of the monarch's cosmic role; his keraton, a microcosm of the universe, was the center of the world. Thus the Susuhunans of Surakarta bear the title *Paku Buwana,* Spike (or Axis) of the World; the Sultan's honorific is *Hamengku Buwana,* He Who Cradles the World in His Lap.

Each of the princely courts tried to develop a theatrical specialty of its own. Thus the most sacred of the bedoyo dances (see pp. 115–117) were brought to perfection in the Susuhunan's keraton in Surakarta; the dance-opera "Langendriya" ("Joy of the Hearts") with its all-female cast was the specialty of the Istana Mangkunagaran; the Sultan's keraton in Jogja was famed for its grand-scale wayang wong performances, while at the lesser court of the Paku Alam, gamelan music and singing were assiduously cultivated. Moreover, the dance styles evolved at each of the courts were distinguished by either striking or subtle differences. Rivalry between the two capitals led to mutual scoffing. The Solonese smirked at the "stiffness" and drilled precision of Jogja dancers, while the Jogja partisans, with insidious smiles, alluded to Solonese "laxity." Mutual derogation is gleefully maintained in the two capitals to the present day.

Some of the princes took a direct personal interest in the production of plays and dances. Eminent among such rulers was the late Mangkunagara VII of Surakarta who reigned from 1915 to 1944. A great lover of all traditional Javanese arts, he personally selected the casts, chose the color schemes for the dancers' costumes, supervised rehearsals, and directed the choreography.

Many of the finest dancers were members of the aristocracy. The courts' dancing masters and mistresses, often old, wrinkled men and women of amazing vitality and suppleness, trained young princes and princesses as well as children of high dignitaries related to the

* These courts were referred to as *Mangkunagaran* and *Paku Alaman.*

Plate 117. *Detail of a* wayang wong *scene from "Hanuman as Envoy." Rawana (center) listens to pleas of Tridjata on behalf of captive Sita; Hanuman (left) overhears them, Mangkunagaran, Surakarta.*

ruler, to whose education proficiency in dancing was essential. The dancing masters and their assistants also trained contingents of dancers selected from the lowlier families of the keraton population for the subsidiary roles in plays. While some dances, like the bedoyo, remained the prerogative of the courts, others, especially the dramatic ones, seeped from court-trained servants—and everybody below the ruler was a servant (*abdi*)—into the popular sphere. This seepage grew to a small stream with the foundation in 1918 in Jogjakarta of the dance school *Krida Beksa Wirama*. Sponsored by the keraton, the school was given permission to teach all pupils dances practiced at the court, including the serimpi dances for girls. For almost fifty years the principal dancing master of this school has been Gusti Pangeran (Prince) Aria Tedjakusuma (a brother of the late Sultan Hamengku Buwana VIII), himself an accomplished dancer. Through these decades Pangeran Tedjakusuma, lithe and nimble, patient and humorous, has personally conducted the heavily attended dancing lessons and rehearsals for plays. The lessons are given in the spacious, pillared, open reception hall (*pendopo*) of his residence (*Tedjakusuman*) to the accompaniment of gamelan music. Seated cross-legged on a mat, the Prince knocks out the guiding signals for the dancers with a wooden mallet on the slit wooden signal box known as *keprak*. At intervals he demonstrates some movements to an awkward student. Hundreds of alumni of the school remember their lessons at the "Krida" as the most gratifying hours of their youth. Some of them, especially sons and daughters of aristocratic families, have remained accomplished amateurs while others have themselves become dancing masters. Some students from humbler families have become professional dancers, joining theatrical companies.

Invariably during the lessons and rehearsals young children gather silently at the edge of the hall, intently watching the dancers in action. When the time comes for them to learn the dances, they have already absorbed the form and spirit of the movements, just as from their earliest conscious days they have known the identities and peculiarities of the shadow-play puppets.

In Surakarta, too, a dance school conducted in the thirties under the auspices of the Mangkunagara VII produced a number of professionals. Thus court art inspired the popular stage. Wayang wong companies gave performances at night fairs and in amusement parks, competing with Wild West films and other entertainments. But instead of imitating the open pillared hall devoid of all sets, the plays for popular audiences were performed on an elevated stage complete with curtain and props. Realistically painted backdrops and wings depicted the interior of a royal hall, a palace gate and courtyard, a road with rice fields and mountains in the distance, or a dense wild forest reminiscent of the settings for children's performances of Little Red Riding Hood. Against these stage sets the stylized, wayang-like figures of classical drama, incongruous as they might have seemed to a Western spectator, strode, danced, fought and fled in the grand style of the classical tradition learned from court dancing masters, whether first, second, or third hand. The dancing was not as exquisitely perfect as in the princely pendopos, the costumes less gorgeous than those of the courts, being of inferior craftsmanship and cheaper materials, the groups less imposing for lack of space on the stage, but to the audience the spectacle was nevertheless enchanting.

Plate 118. *Gusti Pangeran Aria Tedjakusuma guiding dancers with knocks on the* keprak, *Jogjakarta, 1936.*

In the case of mask-plays, wayang topeng, interaction between court and folk art was almost the reverse. For, following the establishment of Islam in Java, mask-dances, banned from ritual life, may have fallen into disfavor at the Moslem courts, but they were preserved in folk plays presented to villagers by strolling mask-players. Thus when mask-plays returned to favor as they apparently did at the court of Kartasura and later in Surakarta, in the eighteenth century, it was more a popular than a court tradition. After a period of vogue at the courts, mask-plays apparently declined again, perhaps as a result of the ascendancy of wayang wong. In any event, in the first half of the twentieth century it was a rare occasion indeed when one could witness a full-fledged wayang topeng performed by court dancers. The art of mask-carving declined too. In 1956 I was able to locate only one mask-carver in the vicinity of Jogjakarta, although there may have been one or two more. In Bali, however, the production of masks goes on unabated.

Just as in all other aspects of art and life, the style of Balinese masks differs markedly from that of Javanese masks. In Java iself there are distinct stylistic idiosyncracies in masks from different regions, but practically all Javanese masks have taut faces, tapering toward a delicate chin (in Central Java the basic shape of a mask is almost triangular), sharply ridged and pointed noses, and relatively small mouths (Pl. 119). Most Balinese masks, in contrast, have full, oval faces with broad, rounded noses and relatively heavy lips. There are exceptions, of course, notably the masks of the ethereal *sandaran*.[5] In Java the range of comic masks is standard and limited, but there seems to be no limit to the number and range of wild grotesqueries which the Balinese invent for their comic characters.

Plate 119. *Mask of Ragil Kuning, Pandji's sister, Jogjakarta.*

Plate 120. *Mask dancer in Balinese* wayang topeng, *Mas, Bali.*

In all regions, older masks—from the past century or even perhaps two centuries—can be recognized by their stronger sculptural quality: eyebrows and moustaches as well as hair curls or strands, diadems, and other ornaments are carved in high relief. In masks made more recently these parts have become flatter, are sometimes engraved, or even merely indicated by a painted design. Old Javanese masks are also identified by the leather tag attached to the mask's inner side at mouth level. Formerly, the actors, who remained mute, gripped this tag with their teeth to hold the mask in place. Today the masks are strapped to the head. In order to see, a mask-dancer must tilt his head back a little, since the mask has only rather narrow slits along the lower eyelid. His head does not long remain motionless, but is kept moving slightly even when the rest of his body is still. This lends the masked dancer an eerie and somewhat birdlike quality, especially when his slightly uplifted head turns to the side and his nose points upward. The mysterious fluid quality of the mask is enhanced by the half-open mouth on which an elusive smile seems to hover.

The Javanese masks, like the make-up of wayang wong dancers and the heads of the round wayang golek puppets, follow the same iconographic principles as do the flat leather puppets of the shadow play. Thus when one sees the dreamy mask of the hero Pandji—his smooth white (or green) face, narrow, elongated eyes, the finely chiseled straight and pointed nose, the delicate half-open lips showing pearly teeth—and then looks at the red mask of his rival, Klono, who stares out of round, wide-open eyes, his long upturned nose protruding defiantly, one knows immediately which is the noble and which the violent, demonic character.

While mask-dances were rare in the capitals of Central Java before World War II, interest in them has somewhat revived since the establishment of the independent Indonesian Republic. Moreover, some masks and half-masks have always been used for certain monstrous and animal characters in wayang wong plays. Such personages as the monkeys of the *Ramayana* wear either masks or half-masks to bring their lower jaw forward (see Pl. 117); the King of Demons, Niwatakawatja, of the *Ardjuna Wiwaha* wears a magnificent mask in wayang wong plays performed in Jogjakarta. Masks also appear in some shorter dances which depict only a single episode from either a wayang wong or a wayang topeng play.

Javanese dance drama may well have reached a pinnacle of perfection and splendor in the period from 1900 to 1940. The long process of expanding and polishing form and content culminated in the crystallization of a grand, monumental style unmatched elsewhere in Indonesia. In the decades preceding World War II, grandiose wayang wong performances, such as those given between 1925 and 1938, which lasted from two to four days, were given at some of the princely courts. Such spectacles, held in a glittering court setting before princes, exquisite court ladies, high dignitaries and elegantly attired invited guests, now belong largely to the past. Yet for the history of the Javanese classical theater some knowledge of dance drama as it used to be performed in the court setting is essential. (How we wish today for more details about the various spectacles at the court of Majapahit than can be gleaned from the *Nagarakrtagama.*)

The plan in Figure 7 shows the innermost courtyard of the keraton of Jogjakarta with its Golden Hall (*bangsal kentjana*). It is a magnificent version of the

Plate 121. *Klono, Pandji's adversary,* wayang topeng, *Jogjakarta.*

Plate 122. *Pandji,* wayang topeng, *Jogjakarta.*

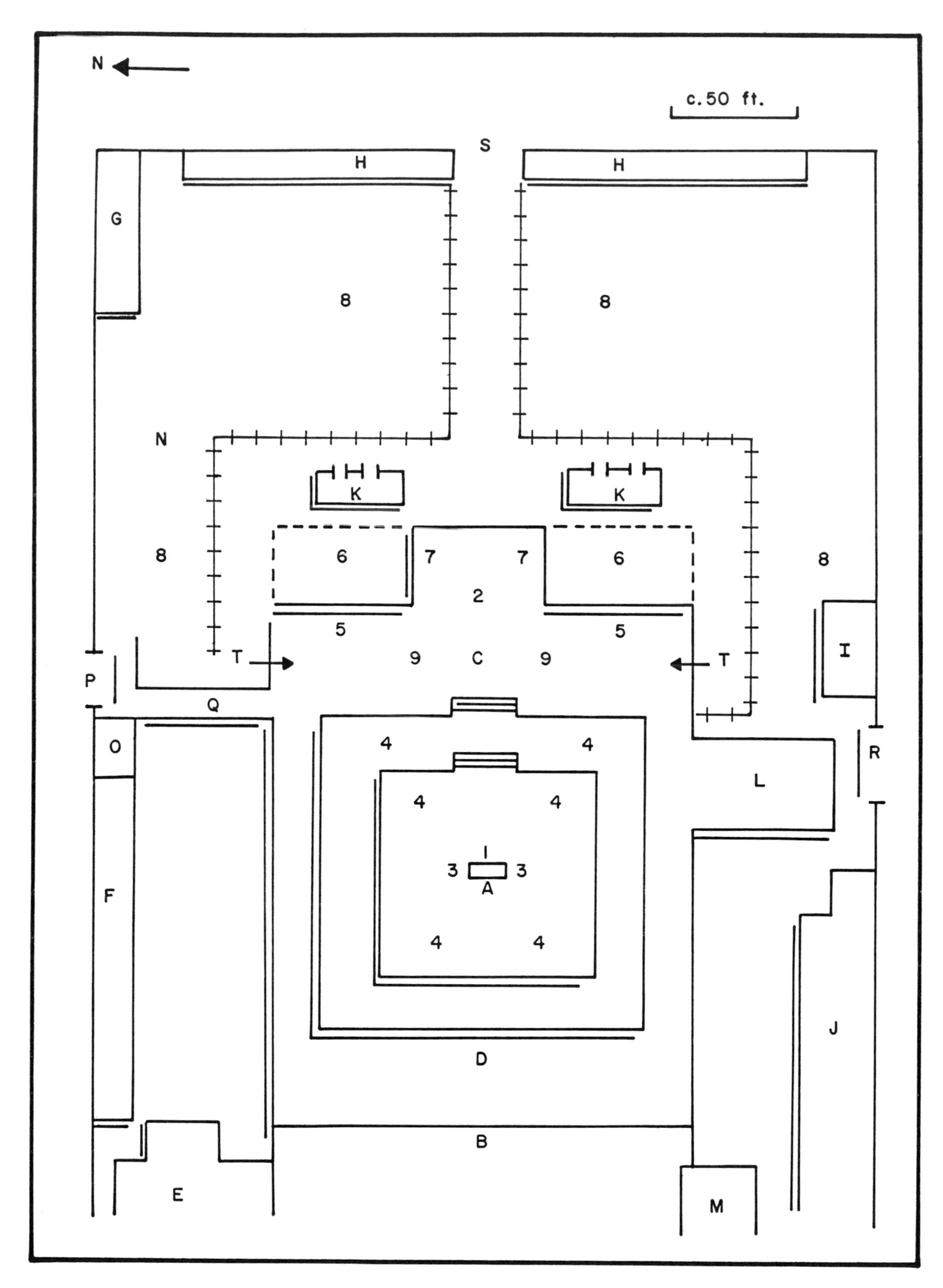

Figure 7. *Plan of innermost courtyard, Keraton of Jogjakarta.*

LEGEND TO FIG. 7

A Bangsal Kentjana, *the "Golden Hall"*
B Prabajaksa, *hall where sacred objects* (pusaka) *are installed*
C Tratag wetan, *Western tratag, the stage*
D Tratag Kulon, *Western tratag, (where female relatives of the ruler are seated)*
E Gedong Kuning, *"Yellow House," private quarters of H. H. the Sultan*
F Purworetno, *private office of H. H. the Sultan*
G *Offices of keraton personnel*
H *Structure where gamelan instruments are kept*
I *Room for preparation of drinks*
J *Rooms for female keraton attendants*
K Kotak, *"chest," actors' waiting room*
L Bangsal Manis, *"Sweet Hall": buffet*
M Bangsal Pengapit, *inner chamber*
N *Pavilion for Western music band*
O *Toilets*
P *Northern gateway (guests' entrance)*
Q *Passage*
R *Southern gateway*
S *Eastern entrance (actors' entrance)*
T *Points of actors' entrance upon stage, the tratag.*
1 *H. H. the Sultan*
2 *The Dalang*
3 *Very important persons*
4 *Invited guests*
5 *High officials*
6 *Lesser officials*
7 *Gamelan musicians and singers*
8 *Masses of standing spectators*
9 *Dancers on-stage*

------ *temporarily roofed space*
——— *permanently roofed space*
||||| *temporary low bamboo fence*

traditional pendopo—the open-air pillared pavilion with its low, overhanging pyramidal roof—found in front of every Javanese nobleman's house built in traditional style. The pendopo serves for audiences, receptions, and celebrations accompanied by entertainments. In the royal Golden Hall, red and gold carved pillars support the beams of the roof, and the softly gleaming white marble floor is laid in three ascending levels. As the plan shows, the wayang wong plays were enacted on the eastern *tratag*. It is a rectangular space of marble flooring, about 130 feet long and 20 wide, sheltered by an extension of the hall's overhanging eaves from which the space derives its name. On the days of the performances, the Sultan, Hamengku Buwana VIII, appeared from his inner apartment at eight in the morning, and the assembled guests approached to greet him one by one. From then until late in the evening when the day's performance ended, the Sultan did not leave his throne on a platform in the center of the hall's highest elevation. At his side sat the Dutch Governor of the Jogjakarta territory. High Javanese and Dutch dignitaries sat in rows to the right and left of the elevated throne, with other high-ranking personages seated at right angles to them on either side of the hall. Behind the throne an assemblage of exquisitely attired and adorned court ladies sat in semicircular rows, while in front along the edge of the tratag, but on a lower floor level, there were rows of guests of lesser rank. Seated on mats across the tratag were the dalang, master of the play, in the center, and one or two assistants at a little distance to his left and right. Behind the dalang were ranged on mats the gamelan musicians at their instruments and the singers. To the right and left of these there were again rows of high Javanese officials seated on chairs and facing their ruler with his entourage in the Golden Hall.

Throughout the long day refreshments were served to all guests: at noon, files of waiters distributed the courses of an elaborate luncheon, the guests being provided with small tables at their seats. By three in the afternoon many of the European guests left for a rest and change of clothes, inevitably missing a part of the performance. They returned toward sunset to follow the continuing spectacle, or to play cards in some adjoining quarters, and to enjoy the fine food served at dinner.

Outside under the open sky along the courtyard walls west of the Golden Hall stood crowds of lowlier keraton inhabitants and some privileged townsfolk. They could catch a glimpse of both the stately assemblage presided over by the Sultan in the hall and the drama unfolding on the tratag. Those in front could also see at close range the gorgeously attired dancers as they first arrived in the inner courtyard and later when they emerged from the two sheds serving as

Plate 123. *Rawana, king of demons,* wayang wong, *Mangkunagaran, Surakarta.*

Plate 124. *Rama, hero of the* Ramayana, wayang wong, *Mangkunagaran, Surakarta.*

"backstage" and filed slowly past the crowd to their points of entrance at either end of the tratag. The actors' waiting rooms are called *kotak* (chest), the same term used for the wooden chests in which the dalang stores his wayang puppets. Here the parallels with the shadow play begin.

First, the kayon (or gunungan), symbol of the tree of life and the world mountain: before the day's play commenced and after its conclusion, a three-dimensional kayon was placed in the middle of the dance space. It was built of two flat painted panels tapering toward the top and intersecting at right angles so that it formed four wings and looked a little like a simplified Christmas tree decorated with ancient Asian symbolic motifs.

Second, the dance space, tratag: like the shadow screen, it was elongated and relatively shallow. And as on the screen, an invisible vertical line cut across the center of the "stage" separating individuals or groups as they appeared on the scene. This line either divided the party of the "right" from that of the "left" or, if all the characters belonged to the same party, it separated individuals and groups who faced each other, as when a king attended by his retinue addressed a group of his commanders and warriors ranged opposite him. Furthermore, the placement of the audience in front of and beyond the tratag was in a way similar to the placement of the audience at a shadow play, before and behind the shadow screen. Finally, the dancers always took positions in profile to the spectators, enhancing their resemblance to the wayang puppets. (In Jogja, the angularity and precision of the gestures tended to create a stronger wayang-like effect than in Solo, which prided itself on greater subtlety.)

Third, absence of decor: generally there was no scenery at the court performances of wayang wong; as on the shadow screen, the figures moved in unencumbered space. During the twenties and thirties, however, a deplorable trend to provide aid to the imagination developed at the keraton of Jogjakarta. Buckets with artificial decorative trees were used to create a palace garden for some captive princess to roam in, or a papier-mâché rock with a grotto was shoved onto the tratag to accommodate the meditating Ardjuna. Taborets were brought for a king and his princes to sit on while their subjects sat or knelt on the floor, and so forth. Fortunately, these efforts at realism, which marred the purity of the wayang wong style, were limited even in Jogja; the less grandiose but beautifully produced wayang wong plays at the court of the late Mangkunagara VII of Surakarta remained relatively untouched by this trend.

Fourth, iconography: the stature, make-up, and costumes of the dancers were analogous to the corresponding puppets of the shadow play. The principles governing their gestures as well as vocal expressions are basically the same, although vastly elaborated kinesthetically, as those followed by the dalang when he brings the puppets to life. Every dancer has an additional attribute, a dance scarf, the *sampur,* a long, wide shawl attached to the waist so that its two free ends hang from the center of the female dancer's waist and from the hips of the men. These scarf-ends, about 25 inches long, are picked up at one edge, tossed aside or over the wrist, extended sideways like sails during "flight" and manipulated in a variety of other ways, lending to some dancers additional grace and lightness, to others, force (see Pls. 124, 126, 129, 131).

From the moment a male Javanese dancer commences his training he usually must choose or be assigned a particular system of dancing, determined largely by his physique. If he is small, of average height, slender, has an oblong face, almond-shaped eyes and a narrow ridged nose, he is the ideal type for the "fine" or *alus* system. It is characterized by restrained, slow, and subtly evolving gestures; the dancer may never bend or extend his limbs at an angle of more than forty-five degrees to his body; his glance may never be raised but must remain fixed on the ground at a certain predetermined distance from his feet; the rotations and shifts of his head are smooth and subtle; when he speaks his voice is soft, his speech is even and dispassionate. If the aspirant, in extreme contrast, is tall and vigorous, or heavy-set and round-faced, he is destined to dance in the "forceful" or *gagah* manner, which has expansive and aggressive gestures. His limbs rise at right angles to his body; his arms shoot out and are swung up to the level of his head or even above it; his eyes are wide open; his head shifts and rotates violently with abrupt stops; the voice of the gagah dancer ranges from loud to booming or shouting, from thunderous rolling to stuttering crowing. In the gagah system there are several modes, depending on the character whom the dancer impersonates: the forceful Bima dances in a mode whose details differ from that of a demonic king; and the mode of either is different from that of a monster, buta. Some monsters like the famous fanged *buta tjakil* have their own characteristic mode, but all are essentially gagah.

There are, of course, a number of potential dancers who do not clearly fit into one or the other of the two basic systems. They may specialize in one of the subsidiary or mixed modes. Each mode is governed by systematic rules that determine every pose and the slightest movement, literally from fingertips to toes.

Plate 125. *The monstrous* buta tjakil *in a threatening posture,* wayang wong, *Mangkunagaran, Surakarta.*

The same basic division into "fine" and "forceful" dances for dramatic actors is known in Bali under the names of "sweet" (*manis*) and "rough" (*kasar*). These terms seems to echo more closely than the Javanese the ancient Indian classification, as described in the *Natya Sastra,* into lasya, which is "very sweet" and tandawa, which is "violent." In India today as in the past, however, women as well as men may dance in either a softly graceful or a forcefully expansive manner.[6] Feminine dances in Balinese wayang wong and all dances of women in Java (except the dance of old grotesque female attendants) are alus, even more alus than the finest dance mode for men. This means that a girl dancer's knees are kept closer together, her arms remain closer to her torso much of the time, and her steps are smaller. This and other details are reflected in the general designation of feminine dances as *ngentjeng,* "close-fitting," "tight." At the keraton of Jogjakarta young boys used to be trained in the feminine dance modes. In wayang wong performances given there in the thirties such boy dancers played the roles of young princesses. The opposite was true of the Mangkunagaran, where girls were trained to dance in both the masculine alus and gagah styles for the operatic Langendriya plays with episodes of the story of Damar Wulan. Today, there is an increasing tendency in Surakarta's popular productions to cast women in the roles of young princes.

Plate 126. *Scene from* Langendriya: *Damar Wulan (left) fights Menak Djingga, Mangkunagaran, Surakarta.*

By analogy with the iconography and gestures of the wayang puppets, it is evident that the alus dancers impersonate the noble characters of the play, and that arrogant princes, demons, giants or monsters are impersonated by dancers whose movements follow the rules of one of the several gagah modes. And just as in the shadow play, where modifications and combinations of iconographic traits reveal a hero's mixed qualities, so also the kinesthetic typology of dance drama is systematically elaborated to render various shades of temperament or spiritual qualities. In fact, it is the principal function of the dance in wayang wong to externalize a hero's inner qualities. Even the expressions of emotion or mood are governed by the particular mode of the dance and thus remain "in character." For example, the famous love-dance, *kiprah,* in which an infatuated prince mimes his ever-growing passion, can be performed in either an alus or gagah manner.

Thus a wayang wong dancer is no less fixed within his system of gestures than is a wayang puppet in its design and movements. But again, as in the shadow play, the heroes' panakawans are not subject to the rules governing the stylized behavior of their masters. The clowns provide hilarious foils to the elegance or magnificent ferocity of the principal characters, and for this reason they, especially Semar and his sons, are at least as important to the public at large. Old Semar, the most sedate of the panakawans, has his own typical posture and gait: his fat body leans forward, one hand lies palm up on his back, the other, with a downward-pointing forefinger, is extended partly forward and moves down and up. Each of his sons, too, has a typical manner of walking: Gareng limps, Petruk steps with a finger pointing forward (Pl. 127). But after their entrance, they become quite relaxed and realistically expressive during dialogue and slapstick pranks. Their mode of dancing is called *getjul,* a direct allusion to pranksters.

A sampling of wayang wong plays produced in the decades preceding World War II in the princely capitals of Central Java shows that the majority were inspired, as were shadow plays, by the *Mahabharata.* The Ardjuna Wiwaha story, in full or in part, was the favorite. Heroes and heroines of the *Mahabharata* appeared in such lakons as "The Death of Samba," "Srikandi Learns Archery," "Sumbadra's Predicament," and "Pregiwa and Pregiwati,"* to name only a few.

* See scene-by-scene summary in Appendix III.

Plate 127. Wayang wong *scene from "Pregiwa-Pregiwati": Angkawidjaya, son of Ardjuna, meets Pregiwa and Pregiwati; Gatutkatja (left) contemplates the girls; Semar, Gareng, and Petruk (right) share the surprise of their master, Mangkunagaran, Surakarta.*

Among plays derived from the *Ramayana,* "Hanuman as Envoy"* was one of the favorite plays at the court of the Mangkunagara of Surakarta (see Pl. 117). In recent years the whole story of the *Ramayana* has been performed in a week-long series of plays at the annual dance festivals held in the newly built open-air theater at Prambanan.

To return to a performance of the thirties, without attempting to describe any one particular play as it unfolded scene after scene in the course of several days, we will try to convey some impressions of typical moments that were highlights in a play.

The fully costumed royal dancers were fabulous apparitions. Golden-yellow paste (*boreh*), dried into an even, dull, aureate surface, covered every visible part of their skin—the bare torso, arms, legs, neck, and face where it served as the base for other make-up. The actors became golden-yellow beings, some exquisitely delicate and completely removed from any everyday association. Sparkling against the dull gold of their bodies were glittering crowns and diadems, wing-shaped ear ornaments with dangling tassels, crescent-shaped plates on the chest, armlets, bracelets, rings. Black accents were provided by caps imitating upswept coiffures or by the women's own long hair, by blackened eyebrows and eyelids or a painted moustache. A male dancer's tightly fitting kneepants, his broad sash and flowing dance scarf were made of precious multicolored woven silk fabric (*tjindé*) and his hipcloth,

* Summarized in Appendix III.

Plate 128. *Gareng "shaving,"* wayang wong, *Mangkunagaran, Surakarta.*

draped over the pants, of a stately brown batik pattern on an ivory field. The elegant handle of a kris stuck at an oblique angle into the belt at the back, protruded under the right arm. The shoulders of female dancers were bare; a cloth passing under the arms covered the breasts; the torso was tightly bound with a long waistband into cylindrical shape; a belt secured the dance scarf which fell over the tightly wrapped ankle-length skirt with a draped train. Thus a group of dancers moved in a shimmering of gold and black, in the rich, mellow colors of batiks and silks.

As soon as the dancers reached the sides of the tratag and ascended its marble floor, either from the right or the left or from both sides simultaneously, they sank to the ground, seating themselves—the men cross-legged, the women with knees close together and drawn up to the chest—to make the obeisance, the *sembah*. This is addressed primarily to the ruler on his throne, but also to his guests, to the sacred shrine of the goddess of fertility, Dewi Sri, in the interior (*dalem*) of the royal residence,* and to all higher powers. The moment they are seated in this posture they become transformed. The bodies are "charged" from within; the erect spine, relaxed yet straight shoulders, lend the torso a stately poise. The faces assume a masklike immobility. Some of the dancers bow their heads very slightly, their eyes downcast; others face straight ahead with a fixed, open glance. The force of every precise attitude, the expressiveness of every gesture flows toward the dancer's fingertips, his toes, in the direction of his fixed glance—as in a vessel filled to the brim the fluid flows into every recess.

After the obeisance, the group rises and "walks" toward the center of the dance space, each member eventually freezing into a static pose at his appointed place. While advancing, each dancer proceeds in his own stylized gait (*tayungan*). Every step is an intricate interplay of legs, arms, hands and head. Throughout, the alus characters retain a lowered position on the rhomboid base of their out-turned legs, gliding slowly forward: the advancing foot touches the floor heel first and gradually flattens as the weight of the body shifts onto it; the other leg, bent angularly, is raised and sinuously stretched for the next step forward, while the opposite arm with a hand exquisitely poised is slowly brought forward. (For a Western dancer the most difficult aspect of the classical Javanese technique is the discipline of extraordinarily slow and smooth motion.) Hypnotically, the soft flow of the alus dancer's onward movement progresses against the heroic strides of the gagah dancers whose flexing arms cut into space as they turn their heads and fix their gaze first to one side and then to the other in alternating preparation for each new stride.

There are as many stylized gaits as there are dance modes, and, in addition, certain subsidiary semicomical or animal characters have their individual manner of stepping. Hermits' apprentices, for instance, advance with a slight hop from one out-turned and bent leg to the other, while swinging out one bent arm with raised thumb first to the side and then upward past the chest. Old female attendants in a royal retinue take two small springy steps forward and immediately recede in tiny steps, their arms swinging. Back and forth and yet advancing, four of their mincing steps occur within the time span needed for one step by other dancers. Thus slow, fluid progress, portentous, brusque advance, furtive treading, gay staccato steps, and stately, floating movement (of women) all interlace, weaving between, and at intervals coinciding with, the beats of gongs that punctuate the musical phrases. The effect of this group movement can be likened to the contrapuntal intertwining and blending of individual instruments in a grand musical ensemble.

Were a knowledgeable spectator to attend a rehearsal in which the players were not wearing make-up and costumes, he would instantly recognize by the manner of stylized walking, the type, if not the identity, of the various characters. In many wayang wong scenes these highly controlled and diverse modes of advancing are the principal elements of dance. Throughout the play, the audience observes not so much what the players do but how they do it, and above all, they relish a dancer's mastery.

When the dancers have reached their appointed places and have arranged themselves—perhaps for the scene of an audience with a legendary king—they form a tableau. On the right side the king stands, his female retinue sinking to the ground behind him. The group he faces is composed of standing, half-kneeling, and seated figures, perhaps his sons, viceroys, ministers, commanders, and a priestly counselor. If Bima, the indomitable second of the Pandawa brothers, is in a group, he usually remains standing, legs wide apart, one hand on his hip, head turned in profile—a constant challenge of poised self-sufficient power. Complete im-

* This shrine is a sumptuous nuptial bed; in wedding ceremonies bride and bridegroom sit in state at its foot.

mobility reigns while the dalang chants. Only when the dialogue begins does the person speaking extend one hand forward, as do the puppets on the shadow screen. A ruler's hand when addressing a subject has delicately differentiated fingers, some curving as in the hand of the preaching Buddha; a subject expresses reverence and submission by pointing forward with a stretched thumb, the other fingers pressed into the palm (see Pl. 117). The timbre, pitch, and rhythm of the voice is determined by the dance mode; a quiet, hardly audible flow of words (of an alus dancer) may be countered by a thunderous response (of a gagah dancer).

Similar to that of a shadow-play lakon, the opening scene is almost always one of a royal council. Action in this scene is restricted to the processional arrival of the court, the formation of static groups, the dialogue and the departure of all participants. Such a scene might be enriched by the sudden arrival of an envoy, a scout, or an ally. With the following scenes, as the intrigue develops, movement becomes increasingly varied and lively. Battles between different antagonists highlight the play's progress, each combatant fighting in his own style.

There is always a prelude to the actual encounter. The rivals face and scrutinize each other, exchange information as to their provenance and identity, insult each other. Expressive movement begins with the challenge: the adversaries brace themselves for the fight, circle around each other, test the opponent with preliminary feints. Then they finally come to grips.

The battles demonstrate with particular eloquence the symbolic import of the dance modes. In many cases they illustrate the confrontation of uncontrolled, brutal force with the superior discipline of the mind which subdues the body but does not weaken it. The clearest of such symbolic confrontations is an encounter between Ardjuna and a buta—a bearded, monstrous creature with dark red, blue, or brown face and fangs, jerky gestures, and a stuttering voice. While the monstrous adversary fumes with threatening gestures. Ardjuna remains imperturbable; when the former attacks with furiously swinging and darting arms, Ardjuna, without losing his poise, evades the blow in a swift smooth turn and then sends his opponent reeling with a mere flip of his dance scarf. In a way the play can be likened to the wild assault of the maddened bull on the self-possessed matador who deftly eludes it. Unlike his assailant, Ardjuna never yells, never jumps or leaps, does not roll on the floor when knocked down. If temporarily disabled, he sinks to the ground, head bowed, and remains still to gather new strength. While the gestures of the buta are in fact technically highly controlled, they nevertheless convey a boundless, futile expenditure of physical energy in the face of superior force attained by spiritual endeavor and self-discipline.

Battles are never fought in groups. A war is a succession of single combats. Martial music, dominated by the low-pitched gongs, charges the atmosphere with a dark spell, obsessive premonitions of impending crisis. At no time, whether during the lightning-quick attack, or the moments when the opponents are locked in each other's grip, or at the moment one of them is felled, are the clear-cut plastic attitudes of the dancers blurred. Every moment can be fixed into a static sculptured relief like those on the walls of the ancient tjandi. And many of the stances are almost identical with the heroic postures of figures depicted on the reliefs a thousand years ago (compare Pls. 125 and 44). But instead of gray porous stone, there are the patterned batik loincloths, colorful, fluttering dance scarves, the glitter of gold, and the sounds of battle music. When a hero falls, a male chorus bursts into a long-drawn "aaaaaaoooooouuuuuu," which slowly fades out.

Among the most expressive moments of the wayang wong play is the triumph after battle. I once saw an unforgettable scene in which the monkey Hanuman danced around a buta he had beaten. The monkey crouched near his prostrate victim, contemplating him from under a hand which shielded his eyes and alternately inclining his head to left and right. Then, still crouching, he hopped sideways and stopped to look, his head wagging. He thus circled around the victim in uncanny, silent triumph, with only his anklet bells marking the rhythm of the light side-jumps.

Other moments of particular beauty occur with the appearance of a flying hero such as Gatutkatja. Enacting flight, he moves high on tiptoe in semicircular curves, reversing the direction as he advances; his small, rapid steps are so even that the body is carried forward without rise or fall. The effect of flight is enhanced by the fluttering scarf-end extended to one side; the other is raised across the chest toward the shoulder. Sometimes the hero is supposed to hover at great heights from which he scans the landscape below—in search of a lost kinsman, to guard a friend in danger, or to seek out an enemy. Spying his target, he stops in "mid-air," shields his eyes with one arching hand, stretched

Plate 129. *Gatutkatja and Pregiwa in a love scene,* wayang wong, *Mangkunagaran, Surakarta.*

fingers palpitating incessantly, inclines his head obliquely, birdlike, at an angle that depends on the height of his "ascent." I discovered this latter nuance from a remark by a Javanese lady who observed, "Gatutkatja was flying rather low today."

Emotions in wayang wong are expressed with great restraint through stylized, allusive gestures often employing the dance scarf: a princess lost in the woods, her head bowed, lifts a scarf-end to her eyes and gracefully drops it, to signify her sadness. Unlike a Kabuki actor, a wayang wong figure can never become grief incarnate. His masklike face never participates in the expression of emotions. In love scenes it is the tension between lovers, never an embrace, that is conveyed. When, during a performance at the keraton of Jogjakarta, Ardjuna wooed a ravishing princess impersonated by a frail boy dancer, the princess remained motionless. She stood watching Ardjuna approach in his slowly flowing stylized gait, his head inclined to one side beseechingly, his curved arms stretched forward as if in anticipation. As he came close, he circled slowly around the immobile figure of the princess, then lifted her lithe body and carried her off—a stiff statuette perched on one arm of her disappearing lover. Ardjuna's attitudes, up to the moment of lifting the princess off the ground, were essentially a slow, ennobled version of the wooing gestures of male dancers at a tandak dance party with a dance girl. In another love scene, between Gatutkatja and the beautiful Pregiwa, as enacted at the Mankunagaran, the lovelorn pair, facing each other at some distance, kept "looking" at each other—she, as if hiding her face behind a lifted scarf-end; he, as if trying to get a clearer view of her by cutting out the light with one raised hand and clutching at his scarf with the other (Pl. 129). The fixed glances maintained the tension. It was broken when Gatutkatja, unable to cope with the situation, drew his kris to kill himself. Pregiwa grasped his wrist—a rare moment of physical contact.

The most exciting dance of passion is performed by a single male dancer without the presence of the object of his love. A king or a prince is enamored; the thought of the princess he desires is overwhelming and obsessive. This is the essence of the dance, but it lasts nearly an hour. The hero begins by beautifying himself, then imagines himself to be with his beloved, and finally falls into a hallucinatory state. The original version of this love-dance is said to be the dance of King Klono (Pl. 130), Pandji's rival in the mask-play, when he gives vent to his passion for the princess of Kediri in the presence of his astounded attendants. The dance is therefore known as "Klono," but in its wayang wong version, it is known as *kiprah,* a word that probably connotes joyful exultation mixed with anticipation. Both versions are magnificent and often one of them is performed as an independent event in a mixed dance program.

The rhythmic gestures of the kiprah dance depict the following phases.[7] First the king or prince repeatedly sways in place over his widely implanted and bending legs, playfully tossing his scarf-ends which fly up at his sides. Then he looks into the distance, shielding his eyes, as if in anticipation of the arrival of his beloved. The rhythms are persistent, the movements repetitive as they are executed first to the right and then to the left. He then makes counting motions with his nimble fingers—counting his troops for an eventual fight to win her. He strides off to one side, claps his hands as if in impatience or to give orders, and then begins to adorn himself. His whole body possessed by the rhythms of the music, he goes through the gestures of smoothing his moustache, of setting a crown on his head, arranging the hair on his forehead, and spreading the folds of his dress. Now the ear pendants are fastened; the hands stretch and turn as precious rings are inspected. The lovelorn prince takes on proud and elegant attitudes, preens himself like a peacock. With noble gestures he begs the beloved to accept a gift. He raises his arms, angularly bent at wrists and elbows, to his head; they are like the antlers of a deer, symbol of beauty and pride. Now he inclines his head, begging his beloved to fasten a flower in his hair and then, holding a scarf-end up by two corners, he gazes, always dancing, as if inspecting himself in a mirror. The dance becomes faster, more restless. A high, sweet flute-like voice rises above the sounds of the gamelan in a song of longing. As if in a trance, the prince, oblivious of his surroundings, sways from side to side. He stops, turns, and looks at a pillar in the distance. Head inclined, his arms outstretched, he slowly advances toward the pillar where a vision beckons. Before long the illusion is broken, he turns away, but from another corner a new vision lures him. Again the trancelike advance with a short hesitation after every step, again the eager wooing, and again the shattering frustration. Completely possessed, he now moves unseeing, almost stumbles over one of the frightened attendants who quickly scrambles away. Then, as if under the spell of the persisting seductive song, the dancer-king recommences his swaying motions until, exhausted, he falls to the ground. A good rendering of Klono or kiprah is thought to be one of the highest accomplishments a dancer can achieve.

Because of the compelling unity that the rules of a dance mode impose upon a dancer's expressions, he cannot, stepping out of his framework, externalize in gestures conflicting emotions, as for instance a change from self-possession to abandoment, or the alternation

Plate 130. *The dance of Klono: the moment of admiring finger-rings, Mangkunagaran, Surakarta.*

of lyrical and strident moods. The hero he impersonates retains a relatively homogeneous temperament, and in every situation acts "in character." Inner conflicts, such as those dramatically danced by Martha Graham,[8] are at most indicated in the dalang's chanted recital. It was an interesting departure from tradition when in 1956 a dance association in Djakarta, with a considerable membership of university students, confronted the problem. They staged the "Penitence of Ardjuna," which includes the temptation scene. The producers apparently decided that though Ardjuna, according to the story, remained steadfast, he must have had some moments of weakness. How to portray ambivalence in wayang wong style? So they split Ardjuna into two: he was impersonated by twin dancers, identically costumed, moving in unison. But when the celestial nymphs displaying their charms accosted the double Ardjuna, the pair tended apart: one leaning toward the temptresses, the other drawing away from them. Eventually they regained their harmonious unity. This innovation was not as offensive as some others that undermine the grand style of wayang wong in modern productions.

Wayang wong, once primarily a court endeavor, is now becoming mainly a commercial theater art. Professional companies, such as the Ngesti Pandawa in Semarang, the older Sriwedari troupe in Solo, and one or two companies appearing in the capital, stage traditional lakons for the paying public. As in wayang kulit, the plays rarely have a script. The Sriwedari actors for instance, are given an outline of the plot (often on the morning of the performance day!) with lists of the participants and their actions in each successive scene. It is their responsibility to furnish the dialogue, which they frequently improvise right on stage.

The productions of the amateur dance associations, often taught by members of the nobility, are purer in style and, performed in a pendopo, retain more of the quality of the court spectacles. Patronage of the arts has now passed from the courts to the state. Dance associations and schools proliferate. But while there are still many lovers of the classical traditions, dance schools are developing where boys and girls in leotards go through exercises very similar to those practiced in Western schools for the modern dance. A leading spirit in this direction is Bagong Kussudiardjo, a graduate of the Krida Beksa Wirama and a superb dancer in the classical tradition. After studies in the United States and extensive study tours to other parts of the world, he has introduced in his school body feelings entirely

Plate 131. *A prince dances* kiprah: *the moment of smoothing moustache, Mangkunagaran, Surakarta.*

new to Javanese dancers; boys and girls now leap and jump, arch and twist their spines, collapse on the floor, whirl in space; they no longer concentrate on the dainty play of fingers, no longer depend on the fluttering dance scarves, and the girls' limbs are freed from the confining tightness of waistbands and long batik wrap-around skirts. Each dance is a new creation, barbaric as it may appear against the overrefined wayang wong style polished by generations of dancing masters.

In Djakarta there is an academy for the theatrical arts, and on the modern stage one can see Western plays in translation as well as modern plays written by Indonesian authors. This modern drama is largely divorced from music and dance, unlike some varieties of folk theater. It would take us too far afield to attempt even a quick survey of the latter, but it deserves a study in its own right.

The shadow play and wayang wong are the most important Indonesian theatrical forms, which reflect in their iconography and meticulous systematization of expression significant aspects of traditional Javanese culture. It is against this background—of glamorous mythological setting, systematized symbolism, overt magic and hidden mysticism that Western ideas and art forms have made their entry into Java. Reality became the concern of twentieth-century artists who emerged from the anonymity of courtiers and craftsmen to win recognition as individuals. Instead of the well-ordered mythological world of the past, the present and future with all their problems and uncertainties have become the sources for contemporary inspiration.

Plate 132. *Bagong Kussudiardjo impersonates a monkey, Jogjakarta.*

Notes

1. Beryl de Zoete and Walter Spies, *Dance and Drama in Bali* (London, 1952).
2. See J. Groneman, *In den kedaton te Jogjakarta* (Leiden, 1888); Stella Bloch and Ananda Coomaraswamy, "The Javanese Theatre," *Asia* (July, 1929), pp. 536–539; Th. B. van Lelyveldt, *De Javaansche Danskunst* (Amsterdam, 1931); Th. Pigeaud, *Javaanse Volksvertoningen* (Batavia, 1938).
3. See the controversy between B. Schrieke and Th. Pigeaud in their articles, "Wayang Wong," *Djawa,* IX (1929), 5–6 and 7–13.
4. Pigeaud, *Javaanse Volksvertoningen,* pp. 41–42.
5. Cf. De Zoete and Spies, *Dance and Drama in Bali,* pl. 40.
6. See Beryl de Zoete, *The Other Mind: A Study of Dance and Life in South India* (London, 1953).
7. See A. J. Resink-Wilkens, "De Klana-dans," *Djawa,* IV (1924), 99–100, illus.
8. See Claire Holt, "Two Dance Worlds," *Impulse 1958* (San Francisco), 17–28, illus.

CHAPTER 7

Bali's Plastic Arts: Traditions in Flux

BALI'S UNIQUE PLACE in the wide panorama of Indonesian culture as well as the extraordinary creativity of its people is by now commonly accepted. To the cultural historians of Indonesia, Balinese society has long been of special interest because, unlike Javanese Hinduistic cults, which had practically vanished with the spread of Islam, Hindu-Buddhist ritual life in Bali has continued to flourish without interruption into the twentieth century. Thus Bali provides many clues for the reconstruction of Java's former religious life, especially that of East Java. In some cases Bali could even yield data of interest about India's past religious life, because some things may have been preserved in old Balinese sacred texts that have been lost in India itself.

Nevertheless, time does not stand still in Bali. On the contrary, as we enter the second half of the twentieth century, we may note enormous changes that have taken place during the last three decades. Thirty years ago a process of change, especially in the arts, was in full swing, while life in general had become vastly different from the days of Bali's final conquest by the Dutch in 1905. And so it surely must have been throughout the island's history, though not necessarily at such a rapid pace.

Balinese history, like that of Java, begins to acquire discernible outlines with the advent of Indian script, when the Balinese began to absorb into the matrix of their indigenous culture (which must have already been an amalgam of Malayo-Polynesian cultural strains) Buddhist and Brahmanic teachings. These were brought directly to Bali from India by proselytizing priests and monks and were also diffused through contacts with neighboring Java's Hinduized kingdoms. Contacts with China and some regions of Farther India (possibly those of the Khmers and the Chams[1]) may have contributed to the conglomerate of Bali's culture and its arts. Despite the incursion of these religions, the all-pervading spirit of Bali's cults and customs is pagan in the best sense; it is a worship of nature, its gods and spirits, the celebration of man's existence in nature, of life as well as death.

No visitor to Bali can fail to perceive the scintillating quality of the Balinese scene—the colors, shapes, sounds, and smells and the expressive forms into which its people cast their rituals and spectacles. He may not realize at once the secret of the island's less direct impact upon his intoxicated senses. It lies in the rare harmony between Bali's lush tropical nature and equally lush art. Gamelan music, dances, paintings, and sculptures are full of animation; the architecture of temple complexes, the exuberant ornamentation of their gates, walls, and shrines rival the dense and varied flora; the pyramidal roofs of dwellings and pagoda-shaped temple structures echo the mountains. The dancing figures of deities at the temples seem to have emerged from the sun's radiance or the gold of the rice fields; the monstrous guardians of gates and shrines, from the deep gorges or the dark recesses of an old banyan tree. In Bali, nature and man's creations seem to have fused to an extraordinary degree.[2]

We do not know whether in the past the Javanese were as sensuously pagan as the Balinese today, or whether the Balinese have always been more effervescent than their neighbors to the west. In discussing Tjandi Panataran we were repeatedly reminded of Bali. But one may wonder whether it was Bali that inherited its ornate and flamboyant art from Majapahit, or whether in some of the structures of Majapahit's erstwhile state temple, traces of Balinese influence perhaps had been at work.

Plate 133. Goa Gadjah, *cave hermitage near Bedhulu, Bali,* c. *11th century.*

Despite its small size (about 2,100 square miles), Bali is not a homogeneous cultural area. Volcanic mountains separate the north from the fertile south, the valley of Bali's principal rivers, the Petanu and the Pakerisan, where since antiquity the most important cultural centers have flourished. The barren western part of the island, where stretches of jungle still harbor tigers, is relatively inaccessible; in remote mountainous areas, nestling in the vicinity of crater lakes, Bali Aga villages (supposed to be communities of "original" Balinese inhabitants untouched by the Hinduized culture of the plains) follow customs unknown in the lowlands.[3] The oldest examples of Balinese Buddhist and Shivaite art have been found in the south, especially in the area of Pedjeng and Bedhulu,[4] where the ancient kings of Bali may have had their capital.

Near Bedhulu lies the "Elephant Cave" (*Goa Gadjah*), a Shivaite cave-hermitage, probably dating back to Airlangga's times with its adjacent holy bathing place, recently restored. An older, very beautiful holy watering place, Tirta Mpul, is located at Tampak Siring, in the vicinity of which, along the Pakerisan river, nine rock-hewn tjandi and traces of a monastery have been found. Stutterheim tells a remarkable story in connection with Tirta Mpul. The people of the nearby village of Manukaya carry the sacred stone enshrined there on the full-moon day of the fourth month of the year to be ritually bathed in the holy waters of Tirta Mpul. The content of the stone's weathered inscription was unknown to the villagers. Upon deciphering it, Stutterheim found that it was the charter of Tirta Mpul's foundation, in the fourth month, on the day of the full moon, of the year A.D. 962![5] For a thousand years the observance of the precise day had been preserved by tradition.

Archaeological research into Bali's Hinduistic era has disclosed a gradual evolution from strictly Indian-derived sculptural forms to increasingly idiosyncratic Balinese forms. Stutterheim divided old Balinese art into three periods: (1) a Hindu-Balinese period, from the eighth to tenth centuries A.D., "during which, owing to direct influences from India (Buddhism), or influences from Java, or both, sculptures of decidedly Indian character were created"; (2) an Old Balinese period, tenth to thirteenth centuries, "in which the Indian influences were adapted and incorporated into an art which became distinctly Balinese and inevitably more primitive in the beginning than that of the preceding period"; and (3) the Middle Balinese period, which flourished during the thirteenth and fourteenth centuries, forming a transition to the modern art of Bali.[6]

Mortuary sculpture for deified royalty—erect or seated male and female figures—of which a number of examples have been preserved,[7] was produced in Bali as it was in Java, and the same frontal, rigid forms prevail. But apart from this distinctly funerary style, another evolved, beginning in the thirteenth century, which has led up to what we now call "traditional Balinese art." To characterize this style, we can do no better than quote Stutterheim once more. He comments on the Balinese "national character," as contrasted with that of the Javanese:

> The Balinese, in contrast with the Javanese, especially those of Central Java, have a strong predilection for the baroque and for redundancy. . . .
>
> . . . In contrast with the Javanese, who is bent on mysticism and relishes above all a profound discourse, the Balinese has a preference for things concrete, and is, for instance, a great lover of a hearty meal. The ideal of the Javanese is the refined knight, who bears misfortune and even injustice without flinching, but who also, in joy and triumph, is master of his emotions. He seeks the refined, even the subtle and spiritual, and his arts are marked by reserve and finesse. The Balinese, on the other hand, likes the more coarsely expressive in jest and earnest; he is lavish with gilt and bright colors; his music, though rich and melodious, is characteristically explosive; and sudden outbursts of rapid, jerky movements typify his vigorous dance-rhythms.

And further, noting the "baroque, wild, flaming" style of some sculptures of the Middle Balinese period, he says:

> These characteristic baroque traits finally lead to the peculiar contemporary art of Bali, whose coloured wooden figures of dancing gods are the purest expression of the Balinese soul and phantasy. Everybody knows them now —their demoniac features with bulging eyes, their brawny limbs and over-ornate dress. Sparkling with gold and with shining red, blue and green colors, they lead as it were a

Plate 134. *Monsters clutching serpent, detail of ornamentation at base of temple gate, North Bali, contemporary.*

round-dance, flashing with their eyes, stamping and snorting. This is the way the Balinese also likes his gods best, not as pale ascetic lords, but as vigorous super-Balinese.[8]

This, we must remember, was written thirty years ago, and some of the generalizations valid then are no longer wholly valid today. The *ideal* Javanese character persists, it is true . . . in the wayang world and among those Javanese who still adhere to its ethos. But no one can assert with assurance that it is still the ideal of the vastly expanded educated sector of the population. Stutterheim's "contemporary" Balinese art is now contemporary only in part, since it applies mainly to traditional temple architecture but no longer to the expanded sphere of secular sculptures and paintings. One should also note that the robust deities or mythological beings Stutterheim has in mind, whose animated forms grace the exteriors of temples—affixed to the walls of shrines, standing on the pilasters of walls or balustrades, or flanking a staircase to a temple gate —are not the principal Balinese gods. These remain free-floating and only descend to earth temporarily when invoked to be worshiped, feasted with offerings, and entertained with music and dances. Their seats, or receptacles, are often small and dainty effigies into which the gods enter for the duration of the ritual celebration, only to depart to their lofty realms thereafter.[9] Otherwise, like Surya, the sun-god for whom an elevated throne is always in readiness, they remain invisible.

Bali's sumptuous ornamental and figurative art is applied mainly to its temples and palaces. Gates, walls, and the high, decorated bases of shrines, built of relatively soft limestone (*paras*), are constantly in need of renovation. In the mountain regions villagers, often at great cost, engage stone carvers from the plains to decorate their rebuilt sanctuaries. Thus in the middle fifties stone carvers from the Gianjar district in the south executed the rich ornamentation on the entrance gate of the Batur temple (near the highest point of the Kintamani Pass). New limestone panels were set into the old brick body of the gate, on which were carved the figures of the heroes of the *Mahabharata* in traditional wayang style. The unfinished pilasters and antefixes of the temple wall had to wait until the villagers could save enough funds to have the work continued.

The *puri* (palaces) of Bali's rulers (whose power was formerly absolute, then reduced to semiautonomy under the Dutch administration, and now curtailed by

Plate 135. *Priest with bell seated on mythical animal, stone sculpture on temple grounds, North Bali.*

the Indonesian Republic through elective councils) were in the past as lavishly decorated as were the temples (*pura*). In some of them both sculptures and paintings in traditional style have been preserved. Similarly, in some houses of high-caste Balinese, the pillars and beams of pavilions are carved, painted, and gilded; crowning a pillar or enlivening the top surface of a cross beam, are wooden polychrome figures—of Vishnu carried by Garuda (Pl. 137), of a fantastic animal, bird, or some such representation. Finally, excellent examples of Balinese traditional art, sculptures as well as paintings on cloth, can be seen in the Bali Museum at Den Pasar, established in the late twenties or early thirties when it became clear that some neglected pieces of fine sculpture standing in or near certain temple sites needed to be preserved and that new fashions in both painting and sculpture were threatening to wipe out the old traditions.

As has been noted by several observers, Balinese artists are quick to pick up and imitate any innovation that strikes their fancy, especially one that has met with success. Success is judged by two criteria: when an original work has elicited the approval or admiration of local connoisseurs, and when works imitating the new style find a ready commercial market. As elsewhere in the world, there are only a few inventive spirits or innovators, and a host of imitators. During the last three decades Bali has increasingly become a factory—or workshop—for tourist souvenirs which fill the gift shops from Hong Kong to New York, from Amsterdam to Singapore. What is decisive for our discussion, however, is first, the art the Balinese produce for themselves, and second, that part of their art which, although produced for foreign consumption, is significant stylistically, displays superior craftsmanship, and, its foreign market notwithstanding, reflects changing conceptions of form and content—in short, works which are expressions of the artists' changing feelings about the world and Balinese humanity within it.

Plate 136. *Ardjuna, relief in wayang style on gate of Batur Temple, Bali, contemporary.*

Plate 137. *Vishnu on Garuda, polychrome and gilded wood carving, decorating interior of pavilion in courtyard of G. Nj. Lempad, Ubud, Bali.*

Before attempting to trace the process of change that has occurred in Bali's visual arts within our lifetime, we must examine some of the latent predispositions that undoubtedly have paved the way for new trends.

As we have seen in the case of Majapahit, an informal and playful art existed side by side with the elaborate, official temple art—a juxtaposition, one must assume, that has always existed, given man's faculty for play. So in Bali, on the grounds and walls of some temple courtyards or on structures belonging to a puri, expressive and often humorous secular figures enliven the ornate ceremonial environment. In the absence of art galleries and museums, these were the only places where such creations belonged. Thus, wandering around a temple, one could meet on the terrace of some shrine the figure of a pregnant woman or that of a mother with a child—a plain woman of the people, not a divinity, in her most vital aspect of procreator, stressing the theme of fertility. The utter simplicity and earthiness of the group of mother and child in Plate 138 contrasts vividly with more official ornate figures such as the priest seated on a regal mythological animal (Pl. 135), or the image of Rangda, the witch (whose representations in stone are close to that of the death-goddess Durga), enshrined in a profusely decorated niche (Pl. 139). Among many examples of secular sculptures there is a charming set of humorous musicians—a flutist, rebab player, drummer and others—which originally were perched on a wall of the Klungkung palace, but are now on view in the Bali Museum at Den Pasar. Furthermore, among the temple reliefs one can discover scenes of anything but divine or magical significance—in spirit, as strictly twentieth-century karma, they would belong to the "buried base" of the Barabudur. Covarrubias has illustrated a few of these reliefs[10] which show Netherlanders drinking beer or riding in automobiles, as well as Balinese engaged in rousing sexual fun. One may assume that the interlarding of temple decorations with earthy and humorous depictions is not new in Bali.

In traditional paintings on cloth, too, the style varied according to the subject. Mythological themes with rep-

Plate 138. *Mother and child, Bali Museum, Den Pasar.*

Plate 139. *Rangda enshrined, Ubud, Bali.*

resentations of gods, epic heroes, and other legendary figures were depicted in the Balinese version of the wayang style. The figures, elaborately costumed and wearing the stylized coiffures and headdresses of wayang figures, were shown mainly in profile but with both eyes visible, their thin arms often angularly poised; the environment—trees, mountains, pools—was decoratively conventionalized (Pl. 140). As in wayang, the figures of the retainers and servants had vulgar and grotesque shapes.

Narrative cloth paintings (of which the oldest are on barkcloth, the later ones on homespun or manufactured cotton) were used for the festive decoration of temple structures and for the embellishment of the pavilions or inner chambers of Balinese nobles. Some (called *ider-ider*) had the shape of long bands from 1 to 1.5 feet wide on which, as on the horizontal reliefs of Javanese tjandi or the scrolls of Javanese wayang bèbèr, a story was depicted scene by scene, each separated by a flame, tree, or mountain motif. These scroll paintings, some as long as 12 yards, were suspended during temple celebrations along the eaves of a temple shrine or a pavilion serving ritual purposes. The other type of narrative painting appeared on large rectangular cloths, on which separate scenes had to be read along variously divided areas. Rectangular cloth paintings (the smallest about 5 feet by 6 feet) served as backdrop curtains (*parba*) in temple pavilions or as hangings (*langsé*) at the sides of princely bedsteads. Finally, large painted cloths of trapezoid shape spanned the pyramidal ceiling between the bamboo rafters of a pavilion, creating the effect of an overhead "mural" (Pl. 140).

The carefully designed figures and decorative motifs were colored with locally made paints applied to sized cloth. The range of colors was limited to black, white, Chinese red, blue, yellow and browns, made of such substances as soot, powdered bones, indigo, and mineral pigments mixed with a liquid containing fish-glue. The tradition of coloring linear designs has persisted: old as well as new Balinese paintings are essentially all colored drawings.

Plate 140. *A scene in the realm of the gods, painting in traditional style, Klungkung, Bali.*

Plate 141. *"Peasant with Bullocks," drawing by G. Nj. Lempad, Ubud, Bali, 1931.*

On traditional narrative cloth paintings appeared stories from the *Mahabharata*, the *Ramayana*, the *Malat* tales (the Balinese term for Pandji stories) and other Balinese legends. There were also pictorial renderings of the popular *Tjalon Arang* story in which the flaming figures of the witch and her apprentices dominated many scenes. The favorite story of Ardjuna's temptation by celestial nymphs (*Ardjuna Wiwaha*) was similarly a frequent subject for a langsé (see detail in Pl. 54 above). Unlike the stately and static group of gods in Plate 140, battle scenes were full of movement, with spears and arrows flying between fighting heroes and speeding charioteers. Hunting scenes showed wild commotion—fleeing animals, hunters knifing a boar or a wild bull, servants shaking their rattles, and frightened birds taking to the wing. Nor were amorous scenes missing: as of a hero's bliss in a pavilion where his ladylove languorously nestled in his arms.

In contrast to the fantastic and highly stylized representations of legendary figures on traditional cloth paintings, there were also depictions of folk scenes treated in a simple, naively realistic manner. The best examples of such paintings appear in the squares of Balinese pictorial calendars, also painted on cloth, in which the propitious days for certain activities are illustrated. A fisherman in his boat, a man harvesting rice, placing offerings at a shrine, ploughing his field, or going to market with his produce: such simple themes of daily village life were thus also known in Balinese pictorial art before its more intensive secularization in the twentieth century. A drawing of two peasants with bullocks made in 1931 is typical of this style (Pl. 141).

There is one more sphere in which certain antecedents of Bali's modern style can be discerned—its rich and imaginative "temporary art." This includes the sumptuous ornamentation of cremation towers, the animal-shaped sarcophagi in which exhumed remains of corpses are burned, the intricately composed and decorated temple offerings, and the endless variety of objects created by women out of ingeniously cut and folded strips of young palm-leaf to be used for ritual purposes—little effigies, decorated containers for sweetmeats, fronds, and rosettes for the artfully stapled offering-cones of fruits and cakes which women carry on their heads to the temples. From palm-leaf women also make long rectangular panels, called *lamak,* which on festive days are suspended from the front edge of temporary bamboo altars or from permanent stone shrines.

The central lamak motifs most frequently found are a stylized tree (kayon) and an equally stylized feminine figure, called *tjili,* with a fan-shaped solar headdress. These could easily be Balinese versions of the Tree of Life (or the Tree of Heaven) and the Great Mother Goddess known so widely in the cults of the world's most ancient civilizations. The goddess of the earth and fertility is here identical with the Rice Mother, or, in Hinduistic terms, with the goddess Shri. Stutterheim, in his incisive article on the emergence of new styles in Balinese carving and painting,[11] drew attention to this tjili figure on the lamaks as one of the traditional forerunners, or predisposing factors, for the adoption by Balinese artists of slender elongated forms. On the lamaks, when the flat outline of the goddess is not transformed into a completely abstract design, it often appears as a geometrically precise, elongated, high-waisted, hourglass-shaped body with a triangular (or semicircular or heart-shaped) disk for the face surrounded by the radiating crown and connected with the body by a thin straight strip for the neck. The arms are very long and thin, ending in comb-shaped or fan-shaped hands. The example on Plate 198 below shows a typical tjili design, but there are innumerable other versions, some much more elongated and of very elegant proportions.

Thus, though it seemed to be an accident that sparked the emergence of a new style in Balinese wood carvings in 1930, some latent predispositions were there. In that year, Walter Spies, the German-born and Russian-educated musician and painter[12] who loved Indonesia and settled in Bali, where he established an intimate and fruitful relationship with the Balinese art community, had commissioned a wood carver to make him two statuettes from an elongated piece of fine wood someone had given him. After a while, the carver, I Tegelan of the village of Belaluan (adjacent to Den Pasar), brought back a single figure of a girl dancer with a peculiarly lengthened torso (Pl. 142). "It was a pity to cut this beautiful piece of wood into two," he said to Spies, "so I made one *togog** out

* A figure carved in the round.

Plate 142. *Girl dancer, by I Tegelan, Belaluan, Bali, 1930.*

of it." Spies was surprised but also delighted and as he was a "significant person" in the Balinese art community, his opinion counted. The Balinese were also impressed by the Mexican painter and author, Miguel Covarrubias, who in 1930 lived and worked in Belaluan collecting materials for his book on Bali. Both Spies and Covarrubias were much interested in lamak designs, not least the tjili motifs which they copied for their collections of Balinese art materials. Each of them in his own way tended to exaggerate by further elongation in his own paintings the slenderness of the Balinese physique. Thus a mutually stimulating process may have developed between the Balinese, who themselves are delicately built and the European and Mexican artists who emphasized the slenderness of Balinese figures in their drawings and paintings, which were, in turn, seen by Balinese artists, including the wood carver of Belaluan. However the development began, from this moment on other Balinese wood carvers followed suit. But much more happened than mere imitation of I Tegelan's elongated torso of an otherwise traditionally clad and adorned figure. Soon ornamental

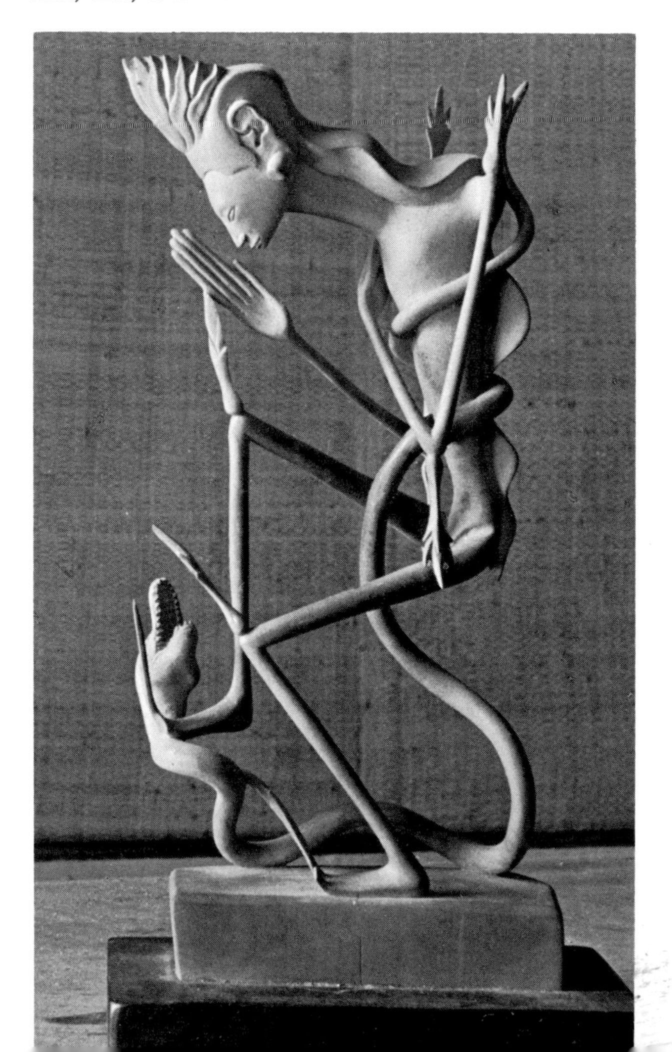

Plate 143. *Earth Goddess with serpent, by I. B. Njana, Mas, Bali,* c. *1936.*

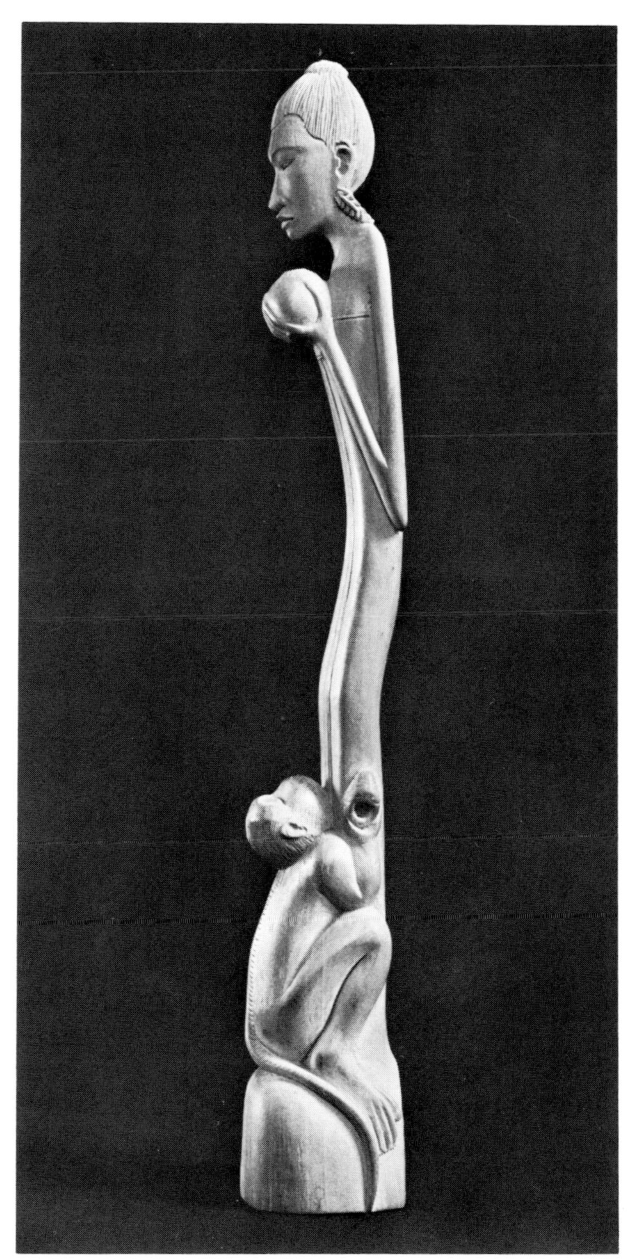

Plate 144. *Priest and monkey, anonymous, Mas, Bali, 1956.*

details were simplified; strongly delineated and angularly composed masses disappeared. In the village of Mas, still an important art center, the most fantastic sleek, fluid, elongated, and sometimes even spidery figurines appeared. A fantastic example is the carving of the Earth Goddess, Sang Hyang Pertiwi, entwined by a serpent (Pl. 143). It is the work of one of Bali's finest wood carvers, Ida Bagus Njana of the village of Mas. Unlike the traditional colored and gilded wood sculptures of flaming fantastic creatures or elaborately adorned human figures, the smooth carvings with flowing lines were of highly polished natural wood.

Not all carvers, however, followed the new fashion of elongated shapes. In some villages, such as Njuh Kuning, wood carvers specialized in very realistic figures of animals and birds, whose forms and motions they rendered with admirable faithfulness to nature, even when treated humorously like the slightly anthropomorphized frog shown in Plate 145. Others, like the famous I Tjokot of the village of Djati, remained devoted to unworldly monsters, forcing some to serve as supports for pots or lamps (Pl. 146). But the general trend toward fantastically elongated shapes continued and by the middle fifties seemed to have reached its optimal possibilities. Some figures became veritable needles, made of ebony or other hard wood, whose

Plate 146. *Spooks* (léyaks) *supporting lamp holders, by I Tjokot, Djati, Bali, 1956.*

Plate 145. *Frog in dance posture, by Wajun Ajun, Peliatan, Bali, 1954.*

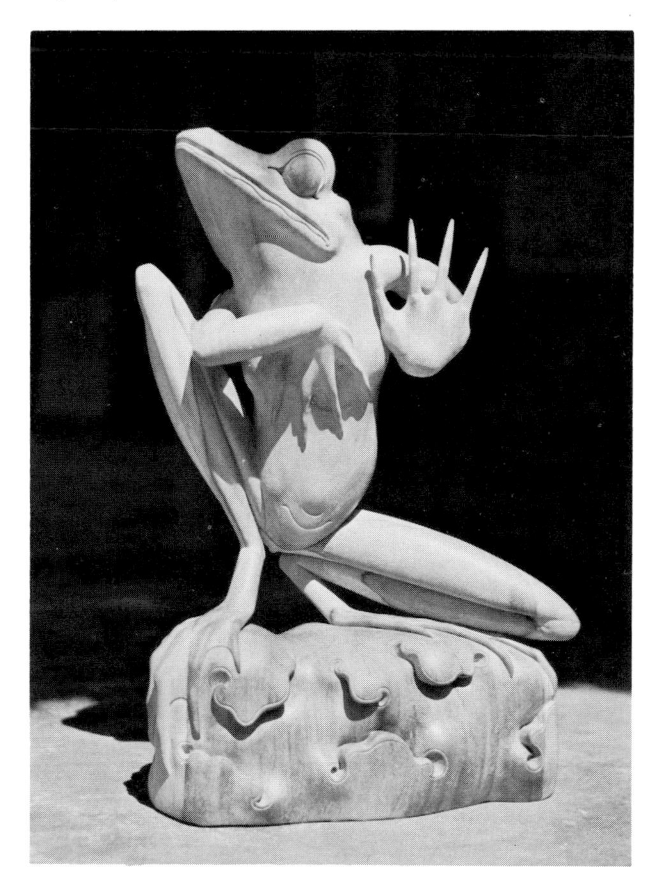

subtly turning surfaces reflected light in a most sophisticated manner; the only relation to reality remained in the narrow, often exquisitely chiseled faces.

In the midst of the persisting fashion of elongation in the middle fifties, Ida Bagus Njana, took to creating fat, squat, often flattened figures, some of which were vaguely reminiscent of the compact Japanese *netsuke,* though much larger. Boldly simplified, completely closed masses, Njana's sculptures have rounded lines and gently waving, highly polished surfaces in which the grain of the wood is masterfully utilized to enhance the flow of movement and the texturing of forms (Pl. 148). Whether Njana's new style, initially followed only by his son, is again stimulating a host of imitators, I do not know. The fact that his carvings command the highest prices on the tourist market and the scarcity of them would indicate such a development, but it is doubtful that any other carvers could rival Njana's masterful hand.

Somehow, the delightful aspect of the story of Bali-

Plate 148. *Squat figure, by I. B. Njana, Mas, Bali, 1957.*

Plate 147. *Elongated figure, anonymous, Mas, Bali, 1956.*

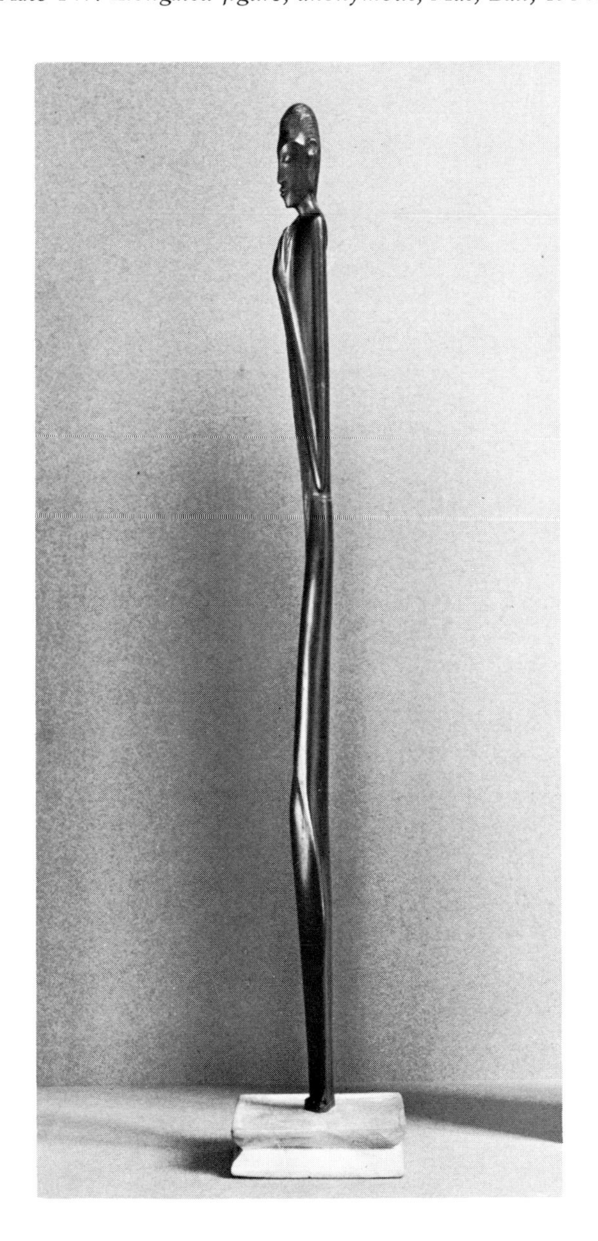

nese wood carving during the last three decades is the matter-of-factness with which the artists themselves treat their own or others' sometimes truly stunning inventions. As of old, the carvers continue to pursue their craft without pretension, without any theory of their art. No critics analyze, praise, or deride their work publicly, though undoubtedly the carvers discuss one another's work among themselves. The idea of critical selection had been introduced, however, in the thirties with the establishment in Ubud of a cooperative society for the advancement of Balinese art known as Pita Maha. To counteract the vulgarizing effect of the tourist trade on Bali's art products, the late Walter Spies and some of his friends including the painter Rudolf Bonnet, both residents of Ubud, took the initiative in its establishment. A small jury, composed of these two European and two leading Balinese artists, selected from numerous submitted paintings and carvings those of highest merit and worthy of exhibition by the Pita Maha. With the onset of World War II in 1942 the Pita Maha was dissolved. But in 1954 the painters of Ubud organized the association *Golongan Pelukis Ubud* (Society of Ubud Painters), which in 1956 had between 45 and 50 members, painters as well as carvers. As a new member joined, he had to contribute his pro-rata share in the treasury and each member was obliged to submit annually "two meters" of paintings for exhibition and eventual sale with the treasury retaining 6 per cent of the price obtained. The society's gallery was located in one of the subsidiary structures on the site of Walter Spies's former residence, Tjampoean (Confluence).

To a Western observer the daring inventiveness and enviable skill of the Balinese artists are a constant source of amazement, even though he may deplore the mass production of second-rate and third-rate togogs that fill the gift shops of the world. But then how much chaff blows around our own galleries and is even discussed in abstruse language as serious art? Once one dismisses the strictly souvenir variety of Balinese wood carvings, the question remains whether the trends toward simplification of forms as well as of surface treatment, toward less fantastic (nonmythological) subjects in more fantastic shapes, toward smoothly flowing instead of angular forms, toward fluidity bordering on the sleek and even effete in the hands of lesser masters are significant symptoms for the spirit of the times in Bali.

Stone sculpture has remained unaffected by the trends in wood carving, in part because the material does not lend itself to workmanship of thin and fragile forms. Furthermore, stone is neither easily transportable nor, most important, exportable by purchasers from overseas. The style of stone carvings, applied mainly to the decoration of temple walls, gates, and shrines, basically retains its lush decorative quality and sturdy flamboyancy.

Innovations in the style of painting, which also began to occur in the nineteen-thirties, include some of the elements manifested in wood carving but, because of the wider representational scope of paintings, the implications of the change can be diagnosed more explicitly. As already mentioned earlier, the great majority of traditional paintings on cloth were narrative. The imagination of the Balinese is so filled from childhood with numberless stories, so vividly are they aware of the heroes and their fates, that a painter is never at a loss for subject matter. Of any random scene, the artist as well as the viewer knows the antecedents and sequel as unerringly as does a good Christian recognize the context of a Biblical scene. But whereas on the traditional cloth paintings one could "read" a sequence of scenes related to some episode of a story, or even a whole story, narrative painting in the thirties gradually became restricted to a single scene. This was partly a result of the introduction of Western materials —precut pads of drawing paper suitable for ink, water color, and tempera. In Ubud, the outstanding master, Gusti Njoman Lempad, filled whole drawing pads with sequences of scenes from the *Ramayana* (see Pl. 45 above) in the traditional ornate wayang style, and scenes of the story of Men Brayut and her husband, the couple with a host of clamoring children,[13] which he depicted in a riotously humorous and realistic vein similar in treatment to the scene of the old wise woman dictating to a lontar scribe (Pl. 68 above). His ink drawings were often embellished with specks of gold and red. Despite advanced age (he was reportedly born in 1873), his hand was still steady, and in the late fifties he was productively engaged not only drawing but also carving in his courtyard a large wooden figure of Men Brayut.

For painting, the Balinese mainly adopted imported tempera colors, which were closest to their own homemade glue-based paints. The size of cloth was now limited by the novel idea of *framing* a picture, something the Balinese had never done for themselves. The tourist demand for paintings either framed or suitable for framing in time changed not only format and technique but also affected the content of paintings. From the realm of the gods and mythological heroes, from the dramatic episodes out of epics, so close to their own hearts, the painters increasingly turned to Balinese life on this earth—to scenes of planting and harvesting, fishing, market life, ritual celebrations and dramatic spectacles. In fact, as depicted by the Balinese, life in Bali itself became a grand spectacle—idyllic or full of *ramai* (commotion, crowded "doings"), detachedly decorative—as much a "world of appearances" as the Barabudur reliefs of scenes on this earth. In the early stages of the departure from the traditional style, the strong magic "charge," the fearsome tensions so typical of Bali's magic-laden atmosphere persisted as did some riotously humorous and, possibly to us, obscene themes.

To appreciate the full scope of the new departures, we need only look first at one of the many paintings which decorate the stately ceremonial pavilion in Klungkung (Pl. 140). The scene is laid in the realm of the gods (the standing figures surrounded by haloes) where Bima (the prostrate figure in the checkered loincloth at the lower right), attended by two panakawans, has been punished for remonstrating with the deities (possibly demanding the return of Pandu, father of the Pandawas, who had died). Incidentally,

Bima's own begetter, the wind-god Wayu, is among the other Hindu gods (second from the left); he wears the same checkered loincloth and displays the same long phallic thumbnails as his impetuous son. The treatment of the ornate figures of the Hindu gods and the group kneeling at their feet, of Bima and his grotesque servants is typical for the traditional wayang style. The exception is the full-face figure on the right, representing the ineffable, purely Balinese supreme deity, Tintiya, who is separated from the other gods by a mountain motif.

Again, as in the case of wood sculpture, Walter Spies may have played an oblique role in stimulating some local Balinese painters to new forms of expression. In 1933–1934, the very gifted and sensitive painter Dewa Gdé Meregeg, of the village of Padangtegal (which almost fuses with Ubud where Spies lived), produced exquisite ink drawings and paintings which, though more decorative, echoed some of Spies's works. Another painter who also lived in Ubud, Rudolf Bonnet, born in the Netherlands and trained in Italy, played a stimulating role in Bali's art life during the thirties[14] as well as the fifties. Like Spies he was a discerning critic and collector of Balinese art,[15] helped the artists procure materials, and taught them certain skills. His own style of painting was more academic than Spies's, and even though he conscientiously tried to avoid influencing the style of Balinese artists directly, those in his immediate environment adopted certain of his manners in figural representations, especially in the postwar period.

During the thirties the village of Batuan (a lively art center next to Mas, Ubud-Padangtegal, and Sanur on Bali's south coast) experienced a veritable explosion of creativity. Sheaves of paper were covered with fantastic pictures in what might be termed the "Batuan style of the thirties." Usually painted on a black background, the pictures were often sultry, crowded representations of either legendary scenes or themes from daily life, but they portrayed above all that fearsome

Plate 149. *"The Little Mists," by Walter Spies, Iseh, Bali, 1938.*

nocturnal moment when grotesque spooks, freakish animal monsters, witches and vampires accosted people. Their spirit was reminiscent of the hellish fantasies of Hieronymus Bosch, although not as sadistic as they.

Not a trace of the wayang style remained in these Batuan paintings. Human figures and their faces were drawn frontally as well as in profile. Attempts at some depth were made through naively distorted perspective drawing (possibly learned from drawing teachers in the schools). But the treatment of nature—mountains, trees, their foliage, and often gigantic flowers—remained as decoratively stylized as in the traditional paintings.

Among the Batuan painters there were some bold spirits who ventured into the new media with daring conceptions of composition. A water color by Ida Bagus Togog illustrates a moment from the story of a goldsmith who once saved the life of a tiger, and to whom the beast in gratitude brought a golden neck ornament (Pl. 151). The receding avenue of trees was a strange new element in the otherwise traditional, decoratively treated environment, as were the relatively large areas of unfilled space. The usual tendency of most Balinese artists is to fill all available space, in fact to overcrowd it with figurative and decorative elements.

More typical of the Batuan style of the thirties are

Plate 150. *"Cowherd," by D. G. Meregeg, Padangtegal, Bali, 1933.*

Plate 151. *"Goldsmith and the Grateful Tiger," by I. B. Togog, Batuan, Bali, 1934.*

the ink washes shown in Plates 152 and 153. Both have black backgrounds and both are filled to capacity with crowding forms. The scene in Plate 152 is of a funerary procession along a village street, in which a long-armed *léyak* (vampire-spirit) accompanies the bier. Fear is the dominant note. Two water carriers, in the background, scamper away. The pallbearers and the villagers with them seem to hurry on, as if aware of the uncanny presence. From the twisting high trunks (one with a round birdcage hanging from it) spreads dense, decorative foliage, hiding the houses and shuttered granaries below. To the left, the fence and houses seem to topple, but this is merely the painter's expedient for making space for the street. Two birds, one of them hypnotized by a snake, and a dog enliven the scene.

In the painting shown in Plate 153 the focal figure is of a dramatic baris (*baris melampahan*)[16] dancer, whose intensity is stressed by his large size. The scene is nocturnal, within a festive shed, as indicated by the three lamps suspended from the roof beam. In accord with the custom of real performances, the hero is shown entering between two tall umbrellas held by standing men. Before the dancer, two other actors, recognizable mainly by the handles of their krisses protruding above their right shoulders, sit on the ground. To the dancer's left, in the background, four musicians seated

Plate 152. *"Funeral," by I Tombelos, Batuan, Bali, 1934.*

in a row play the *trompong* (an instrument with horizontally suspended kettle gongs), and facing them are two drummers. The head of a spectator emerges behind the trompong-player at the right end of the row. In the foreground a group of five women are seated on the ground, the two in front holding infants.

In both paintings unsuccessful attempts at creating depth are discernible, but in both some foreground figures are smaller than those behind them. Patterns of repeated movement, whether in the figures or the decorative elements, appear in both. In form and mood the paintings are strong and expressive, showing distinct stylistic idiosyncracies.

Compared with such Batuan paintings, the later increasingly naturalistic or decorative paintings produced during the fifties are weak and often insipid. Idyllic paintings of cockfights, dancers, villagers in the fields and at markets are no longer charged with tension. Legendary subjects have lost their original force except, of course, for depictions of such figures as the witch Rangda and her apprentices or the frightful léyaks and other spooks. This trend is especially true of the present Batuan output and of the commercial art from the Ubud area, although there are always exceptions. One of Ubud's leading and most skillful painters, Anak Agung Gdé Soberat, a veritable chameleon in his capacity to change styles, has in the course of 25 years (1930–1955) covered with remarkable mastery and agility the whole range from traditional to contemporary styles in all their variations. He was the first painter, to my knowledge, who in 1956 took to oil paints.

Two painters of deserved repute—Ida Bagus Madé Nadera of the village of Tegallingga, and Ida Bagus Madé of Tebesaya—have retained vitality and originality, each in his own way. Nadera, whose market scene appears in Plate 154, probably has an unconscious penchant to portray himself in both the male

Plate 153. "Baris *Performance," by I Tupelen, Batuan, Bali, 1938.*

and female faces which appear on his canvases. Thus the faces of the three central seated figures (of a woman vendor and two men) are all variations of what essentially is Nadera's face. The desire to portray oneself has never consciously percolated to the surface among Balinese painters and sculptors, and up to the late fifties in Bali I never encountered a self-portrait, or any portrait at all. In the visual arts of Bali, unlike those of Java, the individual person has not been recognized—as yet. In Balinese paintings, human faces are often mere schemes, seldom differentiated and, if so, only as generalized types. In this respect, Nadera's painting is already somewhat exceptional.

As for Ida Bagus Madé, in 1956 he startled me by displaying a large canvas entitled "Atomic War in Indra's Heaven." The idea of the atom has, in his case, supplanted all the demons and monsters of his world. Unfortunately, at the time of my visit to Tebesaya, my supply of film had been so affected by tropical heat and humidity that I could not capture a semblance of his painting with any degree of success. The painting itself expressed not only a fusion in the artist's imagination of an atomic explosion with a cataclysm in the realm of the gods, but its treatment too was a mixture of traditional Balinese pictorial conceptions with elements derived from the West. Westernized, or perhaps merely secularized, were the nude, very human, beautifully delineated and modeled light brown bodies of the nine intertwined figures—a group somehow reminiscent of Laocoon, though entwined by their own limbs instead of a python. The figures were suspended, half-drowning, in mushrooming whitish clouds from which red flames issued. Small patches of deep blue sky around the edges were echoed by the bluish-black hair of the figures. Central was a large male of somewhat darker body hue than the rest, with a demonically intense profile and backward fluttering locks. Between his legs and spread arms, amid the clouds and flames, clung the intertwined figures of a woman and boys, some climbing, some toppling, and all holding on to one another in an irregularly circular configuration. This was unmistakably the last judgment, strangely Balinese and yet un-Balinese. The bodies could have been drawn by an Italian painter of the Renaissance, but the clouds and flames were strictly Balinese, as was the muted quality of the flat paint. And, again, the profile of the central figure, despite its demonically burning gaze, was that of the artist himself.

Meanwhile, in Batuan, Ida Bagus Madé Widja fills

Plate 154. *"Market," by I. B. M. Nadera, Tegallingga, Bali,* c. *1954.*

canvas after canvas with the grand spectacle of Balinese life on earth. His paintings are the epitome of crowded appearances, a synthesis of the people's activities amid their houses and fields, temples and shrines all merging with the tropical vegetation. Men, beasts, plants, mountains and clouds, and man's work are all one. No longer a story, as on the old cloths, to be read scene after scene in a definite sequence, but the simultaneous existence of a multiplicity of phenomena in the feast of life. To the viewer the surface of Widja's painting in Plate 155 is like a jungle. To find his way in it, he may, scanning the whole, rest his eyes on a clearing, off center to the left, where a legong performance is under way. Behind the two girl dancers, five musicians are seated, two of them drummers, one with small cymbals (*tjeng-tjeng*), and behind him one playing a big gong suspended from an ornate frame. Six more musicians are ranged to the dancers' left, playing *gendèrs* (percussion instruments like xylophones with resonant metal plates). From here on the viewer can take off in any direction and especially in the foreground meet groups which, if cut out, would form independent pictures in the same vein as Nadera's market scene in Plate 154. Thus, in the lower right-hand corner, women sell clay pots, pumpkins, bananas, and papayas, with a customer possibly haggling over the pot held up by its vendor. Behind them a woman, carrying a tall offering to the temple, stops to chat with a friend who clutches a piglet in her arms. Ornate shrines in a walled courtyard are visible to her right; behind them a child is climbing a tree in which birds are perching; to her left an official seated on a chair hands a document to a man laden with coconuts and followed by another with two filled baskets on a carrying pole, obviously en route to the market. To the left of them again a food vendor at her low stall is in lively altercation with a heavily moustached customer who holds up both his hands, while an old man in the gate tries to scare away two dogs fighting in the street. There, a man who is carrying a whip while riding on a buffalo stops his mount for a drink at a waterhole. Still farther to the left, a man with a blowpipe and accompanied by a child aims at something up in the air behind a temple compound, where, half-hidden by the foliage, two priests sit in a pavilion. On the corner of its base-platform stands an ornate statue of a dancing deity. A woman selling bottled drinks and bananas sits near the high, elaborately carved throne of the sun-god Surya while children play at its foot, one climbing on the wall . . . and so one can go on and on, until he has seen all the temple gates and shrines; the terraced rice fields; the coconut palms, banana trees, sugar

Plate 155. *"Life in Bali," by I. B. M. Widja, Batuan, Bali, 1954.*

Plate 156. *"Birth," by I. B. Rai, Sanur, Bali, 1956.*

palms, and fruit trees; the white festive streamers and high *penyors* (tall curving bamboo poles with palm-leaf decorations suspended from their tips) which line Bali's streets at New Year's celebrations; all the women carrying offerings on their heads; all the orchids, birds, rodents, priests, villagers and their children; the small patch of billowing white clouds above the conical mountains in the far background.

Perhaps the Balinese artists who live inland, where no grand vistas or far horizons open to the eye, are more prone to crowd their paintings than those who live by the sea. In the village of Sanur on Bali's south coast, a few painters like I Regig or Ida Bagus Rai create pictures far less crowded than those of Batuan or Ubud. In Sanur the sea is dominant. The far line of the horizon is interrupted only by the silhouette of the small island of Nusa Penida or the occasional sail of a fisherman's fish-shaped boat. In the thirties some painters of the Sanur area depicted submarine life, various sea creatures, turtles, crabs or bathing scenes. From Sanur comes the ink drawing of conversing fish by Rai shown earlier in Plate 9. The same painter, in a new realistic vein, depicted a woman in childbirth assisted by her husband who massages her belly as she is supported by two other women. The door of the chamber is bolted, an oil lamp burns overhead. The themes of fertility, procreation, and the continuity of life at the moment of birth-giving are rarely depicted so explicitly in the art of the Western world. In Bali, whether festive or fearridden, farcical or solemn, religious or secular, art is inspired by exuberant life. The traditions of Balinese art are now in flux. Sculptural and pictorial styles change in different regions and with individual artists. But the tradition of *practicing* the arts—music, dance, painting, and carving—so far continues unabated in this essentially peasant society.

Yet the progress of the modern historical process affects Bali, too. Will the growing number of educated Balinese in time be alienated from their traditional ways and views of life? Will modern politics, already infused into the villages and disrupting the old communal cohesion, affect the heretofore harmonious ritual life and undermine all the temple arts? Will communities still be willing and able to spend fortunes on lavish ceremonies, on subsidizing their music and dance clubs, on commissioning sets of new masks, gorgeous costumes for their actors, or for the making of a magnificent new barong when population growth may force a reorientation in economic life and relegate these activities, still felt to be necessities, to the realm of luxuries? Does the establishment of a museum for Balinese modern art (*Puri Lukisan*) in Ubud, which was opened in 1956, signal the beginning of the divorce of the arts from communal religious life with which, in large measure, they are still organically connected?

Whatever direction art life in Bali may take in the future, it would seem that the strongly developed Balinese sense of form, the inventiveness and skill of its artists and craftsmen hold promise for new surprises to come.

Notes

1. See W. F. Stutterheim, *Indian Influences in Old-Balinese Art* (London, 1935), text to pl. IV and p. 38.

2. See illustrations in R. Goris, *Bali: Cults and Customs* (Djakarta, 1951), and Miguel Covarrubias, *Island of Bali* (New York, 1950).

3. Cf. Walter Spies, "Das Grosse Fest in Trunjan," *Tijdschrift voor Indische Taal-, Land- en Volkenkunde,* LXXIII (1933), 220–256.

4. See Stutterheim, *Oudheden van Bali* (Singaradja, Bali, 1929), 2 vol., illus; and his *Indian Influences in Old-Balinese Art.* See also Goris, *Bali: Cults and Customs,* pp. 80–84, pls. 301–316.

5. Stutterheim, *Indian Influences in Old-Balinese Art,* pp. 28–29.

6. *Ibid.,* p. 35.

7. *Ibid.,* pls. VI, VII, X, XII, XIII, XIV.

8. *Ibid.,* pp. 36–37.

9. See Jane Belo, *Bali: Temple Festival* (New York, 1953), pp. 11, 29–31.

10. See Covarrubias, illustrations between pp. 202–203.

11. Stutterheim, "Een Nieuwe Loot aan een Ouden Stam," *Elsevier's Geillustreerde Maandschrift* (1934), pp. 391–400.

12. See Hans Rhodius, ed., *Schönheit and Reichtum des Lebens Walter Spies* (The Hague, 1964); also Covarrubias, pp. xxi–xxiii.

13. See C. J. Grader, "Brajut," in *Orientatie,* No. 37 (October, 1950), pp. 3–19, for the story with 8 illustrations by Gusti Njoman Lempad.

14. See R. Bonnet, "Beeldende Kunst in Gianjar," *Djawa,* XVI (1936), pp. 60 ff.

15. Numerous objects of the Bonnet Collection were exhibited in the Netherlands, in 1961 at the Municipal Museum of The Hague, and in 1962 at the Central Museum of Utrecht. On both occasions, excellent descriptive and illustrated catalogues with scholarly introductions were published. See *De Kunst van Bali, Verleden en Heden,* Haags Gemeentemuseum (1961) which also contains reproductions and descriptions of several traditional Balinese cloth paintings from the Th. Resink Collection; and *Hedendaagse Kunst van Bali,* Centraal Museum (Utrecht, 1962).

16. See Beryl de Zoete and Walter Spies, *Dance and Drama in Bali* (London, 1952), pp. 165–174.

PART III

MODERN ART

CHAPTER 8

The Setting

Before Independence

WHEN THE PORTUGUESE, the first Europeans to appear in Indonesian waters, conquered Malacca in 1511, delegates came from neighboring kingdoms to pay tribute to the victorious Albuquerque. Reportedly among the envoys was one from the "leading king of Java" (the ruler of Majapahit), who brought with other gifts "a cloth as long as a *beirami** on which were drawn all his battles, his chariots with wooden castles drawn by horses, and elephants with such castles, and the king with four flags in these chariots, and so natural that it could not have been better."[1]

We thus have confirmation that in the beginning of the sixteenth century were experts in painting at the court of Majapahit. These artists evidently produced paintings on long pieces of sized cloth, a technique perhaps similar to that used by the Balinese well into the twentieth century. In terms of style, considering the reaction of a European that the representations were *"so natural* that it could not have been better," one surmises that they were not as stylized as the Balinese cloth paintings with legendary themes.

Furthermore, the sixteenth-century epic poem, *Kidung Sunda,* tells of a portrait painter who was sent from the court of Majapahit to West Java to paint a Sundanese princess renowned for her beauty. When the painter returned and offered the portrait, wrapped in yellow silk, to the king, the latter was "entirely enraptured with it. The longer he looked at it . . . , the greater an impression it made on him . . . it was as if she had taken possession of his innermost self, as if she were hovering before his eyes; and he could not get his fill in caressing her as if she were already sitting in his lap."[2]

* A piece of Cambay linen.

Of the painting itself, the poem says that the painter "caught her likeness in the most minute detail," and that it was a "beautiful portrait."[3] Of course the superlatives of the poem give no real clue as to the style and technique of the portrait. There is, moreover, no analogy to be found in Balinese traditional art (see p. 185). Thus, we actually know little more than that paintings on cloth and portraits existed in sixteenth-century Java.

Western influences on art in Indonesia may have started with a trickle of pictures brought by agents of the Dutch East India Company as presents to local rulers on whose benevolence successful trade depended.

"Some poor paintings of ships, mounted horsemen, naked individuals, Moses, Aaron, David, Salomon and similar patriots of the Old Testament, all of no value, to be used as presents for the great ones who have earnestly requested these things." Thus reads the description of a group of objects in the cargo of a Dutch ship that landed in Batavia in A.D. 1637.[4] One of the "great ones" who had requested such pictures was the Sultan of Martapura in Borneo.

Among other reported gifts of pictures were a painting of a large Dutch ship presented to a radja of Bali, and a view of the Amsterdam harbor, given to the Sultan of Palembang from the East India Company's Governor General Jan Pieterszon Coen. There is a record that the Susuhunan of Surakarta received a present of five paintings from Holland.[5]

These paintings, undoubtedly curios in the palaces, could not have failed to attract the attention of the court painters. The *djuru sungging* (painters) who during the subsequent centuries worked in the keratons of Javanese Moslem princes, although sometimes illustrating and decorating court chronicles and other manuscripts, were largely restricted to designing decorative motifs or coloring wayang puppets. Java's pictorial art had declined to the point that early in the nineteenth century, during the brief interlude of British rule, the admirable Sir Thomas Stamford Raffles, then Lieutenant-Governor of Java and its dependencies, while inquiring into all phases of Javanese culture, could find practically no evidence of pictorial representations in Java. In his *History of Java* he writes:

> The Javans have made no progress in drawing or painting; nor are there any traces to be found of their having, at any former period of their history, attained any proficiency in this art. They are not, however, ignorant of proportions or perspective, nor are they insensible to the beauty and effect of the productions of other nations. Their eye is correct and their hand steady, and if required to sketch any particular object, they produce a very fair resemblance of the original. They are imitative, and though genius in this art may not have yet appeared among them, there is reason to believe that, with due encouragement, they would not be found less ingenious than other nations in a similar stage of civilization. They have a tradition, that the art of painting was once successfully cultivated among them, and a period is even assigned to the loss of it; but the tradition does not seem entitled to much credit.[6]

Raffles was also skeptical about—or at least left the question open—whether the Javanese themselves had designed the magnificent edifices of antiquity, while he admired "the high degree of perfection in which architecture and sculpture were at one period practised in that island." At his time, he states, the art of sculpture has been entirely lost, and the only modern buildings of any architectural importance were the keratons, or palaces of the rulers.[7] Raffles' observations pertained only to Java. The state of the arts in Bali and other regions, where neither Islam nor the East India Company had penetrated, must have been quite different.

Throughout the nineteenth century, as the Dutch colonial superstructure became increasingly consolidated in Java under an efficient centralized administration, enterprises owned and managed by Westerners grew, and the number of Dutch residents increased. Among them were some artists who brought the habits and practices of their homeland with them. Western education, at first the privilege of some sons of the Indonesian nobility, gradually became accessible to children of other well-to-do families as well. By the beginning of the twentieth century a group of Indonesian intellectuals had formed who started to activate nationalist sentiments which eventually led to the end of the colonial era.

The first Western-trained painter of significance appears in the nineteenth century—Raden Saleh (1816–1880), a man of great talent who won international recognition.* He was well educated, widely traveled, and spoke fluent Dutch and French and could also converse in German and English. During his stay of over twenty years in Europe he was strongly influenced by the works of Delacroix, whose romantic art and new color harmonies had startled the contemporary French art world. Like Delacroix, who drew upon impressions of North Africa for novel effects in color and light, Raden Saleh too was influenced by the African scene when he accompanied Horace Vernet, a well-known painter of animals, to Algiers. And like Vernet, Raden Saleh created magnificent paintings of animals, particularly of ferociously fighting beasts. Later, when he settled in Djakarta (then Batavia), he maintained a small zoo to facilitate his animal studies.† In addition, Saleh was a fine landscape and portrait painter.

When Raden Saleh returned to Indonesia, he was a celebrated painter, knighted at several European courts, with the title of Royal Painter to the King of Holland. In Europe, he had become accustomed to contacts with famous artists and their princely patrons; his colonial motherland was like a desert to him. "Café et sucre, sucre et café, sont tout ce qu'on parle ici. C'est vraiment un air triste pour un artiste,"‡ he is quoted as having said to William Barrington d'Almeida,[8] who visited him in Java.

Raden Saleh had no fellow artists among his compatriots and virtually no stimulating contacts among the Dutch officials, planters, and merchants. Of aristocratic descent himself, he was received at the courts of Central Java and spent a few years in Jogjakarta, where he painted portraits of the Sultan and his family. Yet despite his great talent and achievements Raden Saleh died without having initiated a new school of Indonesian painting. Nonetheless no Indonesian writings on the development of modern art fail to mention him as the solitary precursor of those now regarded as the "fathers" of the present modern art movement. More

* For a biographical sketch of Raden Saleh and of some other painters discussed in this chapter, see Appendix IV.

† Djakarta's zoo, located near Raden Saleh's former residence, is now called the "Raden Saleh Garden."

‡ Coffee and sugar were, of course, among the principal products exported by Dutch merchants.

Plate 157. *"Eruption of Mt. Merapi at Night," by Raden Saleh, 1865.*

than half a century elapsed after Raden Saleh's death before such a movement got under way.

During this interval, however, several Indonesian landscape painters had emerged. Some had even surpassed their teachers and models, Dutch and other European naturalists who had come to the islands to paint "the beautiful Indies."

One outstanding representative of this genre was Abdullah Surio Subroto (1878–1941), who studied at the Academy of Fine Arts in Holland, where he had initially gone to study medicine. A resident of Bandung in West Java, Abdullah "the Elder" trained a number of students; his artistic descendants are the commercial landscape painters who flourish in Bandung to the present day. His son, Basuki Abdullah, is now a well-known painter. Another early figure was Mas Pirngadie (*c.* 1875–*c.* 1936), an exquisite draftsman who was employed by the Royal Batavian Society and the Archaeological Service of the Netherlands Indies in Batavia for making reconstruction drawings of ruined antiquities and archaeological finds. Mas Pirngadie also collaborated with Jasper in the production of five elaborate volumes on Indonesian applied arts.[9] Pirngadie painted landscapes as well as folk types. His was a delicate, meticulously precise art with great finesse in form and feeling. Its spirit is reflected in a windswept landscape of Java's south coast, painted in 1927 (Pl. 158).

Still another artist now considered a member of the old generation of landscape painters is Wakidi. Like Abdullah the Elder and Pirngadie, Wakidi had been taught by a Dutch painter. He now lives and works in West Sumatra, where he paints the gorges, mountains, streams, and fields of the area around Bukit Tinggi. These landscapes are permeated with golden browns and yellows; the effect is strongly reminiscent of the pre-impressionist school of eighteenth- and nineteenth-century European painting, whose canvasses are suffused in the mellowness of such tints. Few of Wakidi's numerous students have followed his style. Instead they have turned to bolder brushstrokes and to more vigorous colors. And, as in the case of Abdullah the

Plate 158. *"Pelabuhan Ratu," by Mas Pirngadie, 1927.*

Elder, some of Wakidi's students are among the successful commercial landscape painters who work in Sumatra's capital city, Medan.

Thus in the first decades of the twentieth century Westernized art was equivalent to naturalistic landscape painting, and several Indonesian artists had attained high skills in this genre. Later rebellious Indonesian art leaders sarcastically alluded to these landscape painters and their Dutch preceptors as "the painters of the beautiful Indies." Many of these "beautiful Indies" paintings were purchased by Dutch residents, for whom they were more than a picture to embellish a wall—the landscapes were also catalysts for their nostalgia, that slightly painful love for the sun-drenched, lush, and humid land, its glorious mountains, its shimmering inundated rice fields, slender feathery palms, flowering trees, a land which was theirs and yet not theirs. For sooner or later they would return to their flat northern homeland.

The cultural life of Indonesia's Dutch community before World War II was insulated from that of the Indonesian intelligentsia. The Dutch *Kunstkringen* (lit., art circles, that is, art associations) provided its members with concerts, exhibitions, and lectures by local or visiting artists and speakers, but these events were restricted to the Kunstkring membership. Few if any of the significant art events of European origin were open to the Indonesian public. In contrast, all major Indonesian art events (such as the gala performances of classical dance drama at the courts of Javanese princes) were eagerly attended by invited Dutch dignitaries, their wives, and other high-ranking non-Indonesian guests. Similarly, to the delight of tourists, all dances and spectacles at temple feasts or cremations in Bali were open to anyone who cared to witness them. (It is interesting to note that an attempt to establish a commercial moving-picture theater in Bali during the nineteen-thirties failed, since the Balinese saw no reason to pay admission when their own performances, financed by the community, were always open and free to everyone.)

There was considerable interest in the indigenous arts and crafts among the Dutch and other European residents of prewar Indonesia. A number of collectors prided themselves on their acquisitions. Some specialized in textiles, some in masks, puppets, wood carvings, or in ancient bronzes whenever these eluded the Netherlands Indies Archaeological Service. This agency had been established in the early twentieth century to preserve, restore, and study Indonesian antiquities.

The Archaeological Service was directed by excellent scholars. In cooperation with the Royal Batavian Society for Arts and Sciences, it built up the rich collections now housed in the museum at Djakarta and in a few regional museums. It studied, restored, and preserved sacred structures of Indonesian antiquity; it conducted archaeological research and developed a vast body of literature on Indonesian art and archaeology. The names of such scholars as Rouffaer, Brandes, Krom, Van Erp, Bosch, Van Stein-Callenfels, Stutterheim, Van der Hoop, and De Casparis are too well known to be stressed. But the results of their work were never published in local languages. The great body of studies on all aspects of Indonesian culture, past and present, was written largely in Dutch, but also in French, English, and German. The language barrier and the high prices of these publications thus made the literature relatively inaccessible to Indonesians. In 1948, Goris wrote in his preface to a sketch of Bali's history that until then the Balinese had been unable to read about their own history because everything had been written in Dutch.[10] The legacy of these scholars now awaits further development by Indonesia's scholars.

Neither the intensive concentration on the art of the past nor the extensive ethnographic work and cultural studies developed by Dutch scholars throughout the Indonesian archipelago could nourish the creative impulses of Indonesia's twentieth-century young people. Those endowed with artistic gifts were now seeking new modes of visual expression. There was not a single specialized art school in the Netherlands East Indies public educational system before World War II. Indonesian art teachers, educated at teachers schools and colleges as instructors for the public schools, at best trained good draftsmen and copyists who later could find employment as teachers, as draftsmen in such governmental offices as the Archaeological Service, in publishing firms, or occasionally with an architect. The colonial government's program to revive traditional crafts, as in silver work and leather tooling in the vicinity of Jogjakarta, stimulated mainly the copying of old designs.

An important impetus toward the development of creative and original pictorial expression began in 1922 with the inauguration of a nongovernmental school system by the admirable educator, the late Ki* Hadjar Dewantara. His school in Jogjakarta, called *Taman Siswa* (lit., Pupils' Garden), gradually became headquarters for a widespread network of similar schools and teacher training centers in both Java and other islands. In a sense the Taman Siswa was an Indonesian version of progressive education, a mixture of concepts of Montessori and the Dalton system, tinged with the anthroposophic teachings of Rudolf Steiner and the ethical-esthetic approach of Rabindranath Tagore. To this Dewantara added his own Javanese spirit. He created an educational system based on the concept *among* (lit., loving care). Instead of making children follow a teacher, they were to be guided, figuratively "from behind," in a manner not unlike our image of a guardian angel appearing behind his ward. The teachers, addressed as *ibu* (mother) and *bapak* (father), were to foster in the children a free, humane, creative, and at the same time nationally conscious attitude. While their initiative and self-reliance as individuals were encouraged, the pupils were also led to take pride in their Indonesian cultural identity.

* Abbreviation of Kjahi, an honorific term.

The arts, especially painting, were an important feature in the Taman Siswa curriculum as an outlet for the pupils' inner impulses. In a spirit similar to that of Taman Siswa, Mohammad Sjafei subsequently established an Indonesian-Netherlands School at Kaju Taman near Padang in West Sumatra. A painter himself, Sjafei also stressed the importance of art at his school.

A number of Indonesia's contemporary painters, among them Sudjojono, Basuki Resobowo, Rusli, and Alibasjah, at one time or another had been students, teachers, or both at a Taman Siswa school. Beyond doubt the seeds planted at Taman Siswa contributed to Sudojojono's later initiation of a new movement in art.

Writing in the late thirties, Sudjojono agitated for change:

> The paintings we see nowadays are mostly landscapes: rice fields being plowed, rice fields inundated by clear and calm water, or a hut in the middle of a ripening rice field with the inevitable coconut palms or bamboo stools nearby, or bamboo groves with blue-shimmering mountains in the background. Similarly there are paintings of women who must have red shawls fluttering in the wind, or, shaded by an umbrella, wear a blue jacket—everyday *lebaran** poetry.
>
> Everything is very beautiful and romantic, paradisical, everything is very pleasing, calm, and peaceful. Such paintings carry only one meaning: the beautiful Indies . . . for . . . foreigners and tourists. . . .
>
> The mountain, the coconut palm, and the rice field are the holy trinity in the scenes of these painters . . . and like the painter, so the public, . . . And should a painter dare to paint something different than this trinity, . . . the art dealer will tell him, "Dat is niet voor ons, meneer."

* The celebrations which follow the great one-month fast (Ramadan, called *puasa* in Indonesia) when people customarily get new clothes.

("This is not for us, sir.") What he really means is, "This is not for the tourists or the pensioned Hollander, sir." And such a painter, if he does not want to become tubercular, might better become a teacher or look for a job as a statistical clerk. . . .

This is not a healthy situation, respected reader. What are its causes? First, the majority of painters here are Europeans, foreigners, who remain here two or three years only and are thus in a sense tourists themselves. Second, our local painters only want to serve the tourists (i.e., they are only after money). Third, our painters only imitate the works of these foreign painters and serve the needs of tourists because they do not have enough force to create anything original. . . .

. . . They are people who live outside our real life sphere. But fortunately a new generation is coming up, a generation which carries the living seeds of a people who will live and who, together with other peoples, will soon arise, a generation with new and fresh ideas.

. . . Who will show the world: "Look, that's how we are." A generation that will dare to say, "This is how we are," which means this is our condition of life now, and these our desires, . . .

The new artist would then no longer paint only the peaceful hut, blue mountains, romantic or picturesque and sweetish subjects, but also sugar factories and the emaciated peasant, the motorcars of the rich and the pants of the poor youth; the sandals, trousers, and jacket of the man on the street.

. . . This is our reality. And the living artist . . . who does not seek beauty in antiquity—Majapahit or Mataram—or in the mental world of the tourist, will himself live as long as the world exists. Because high art is work based on our daily life transmuted by the artist himself who is immersed in it, and then creates. . . .

Art may not follow some group of moralizers or become the handmaid of this or that party. It must be absolutely free, liberated from all moral bonds or tradition in order to be fertile and vital. . . .

Painters of Indonesia!

If there is still any of your own blood in your breast, carrying seeds of visions from your Goddess of Art, leave your tourist-like sphere, break the chains that restrain the freedom of your blood, so that the seeds I have spoken of become a large Garuda with strong wings who can carry you up to the blue sky, where, hovering, you will perceive and absorb the beauty of the world, of the moon, the stars and the sun, the world created by the Lord. Probably you will suffer, be burned by the heat of the sun, as your aching chest gasps for breath, or hunger gnaws at your insides . . . but when you die you'll not journey in vain to the palace of the Goddess of Art in the land of eternity; you will dare to knock at her gate, saying: "Goddess, I have come." And the Goddess will open the door and joyfully invite you herself to enter. . . . And you will further be able to say: "Have I sacrificed enough to prove my love for you, Goddess?"

"Enough, enough, enough."[11]

The above extracts and some of their context, too long to quote here, reveal Sudjojono about 24 years old, raised in an atmosphere of mounting nationalism, with a general socialist outlook and bitter about the hothouse atmosphere of the colonial Indies which was choking the Indonesian creative spirit. He appeals to his fellow artists to depict "reality" and "truth" in their work, thus establishing their identity as Indonesians. He turns his back on the past (Majapahit, Mataram) which is dead, and pleads that the artists root their expressive impulses in the present daily life of their society. Significantly he rejects the subjection of art to any moralistic or ideological doctrine ("Art may not follow some group of moralizers or become the handmaiden of this or that party . . ."), a problem he himself confronted again in his later years when he apparently renounced this credo. The theme of the artist's immortality and of his work's enduring for eternity enters too. This is expressed by Sudjojono, the poet, in very Javanese terms. The legacies of the Hinduistic tradition ("Garuda with strong wings will carry you up to the sky . . ."), Javanese religion ("the world created by the Lord . . .") and mysticism (the suffering and sacrifice needed to attain a divine goal) are all reflected in his concluding plea. This combination in Sudjojono of a rebellious spirit at once nationalistic and socialistic, bent on self-assertion, with deep poetic mysticism is in a way typical of many individuals in contemporary Indonesia, especially in Java. President Sukarno's speeches eloquently reflect the same cultural fusion. And all the points Sudjojono touches upon here have remained important ingredients in the great debate which continues to rage over the future of art and culture in Indonesia.

One important problem is that of an "Indonesian style," which is discussed by Sudjojono.[12] Why, he asks, do the works of our painters not have a distinctly Indonesian style, while the old traditional paintings of Java and Bali do have one? He answers that Indonesian culture had ceased developing and was in a state of stagnation, "as if dead," and that no new culture had yet developed to harmonize with the new trends in Indonesian life. He then recommends the study of Western art "from Leonardo da Vinci . . . to Picasso,"

Plate 159. *"Before the Open* Kelambu,*" by Sudjojono, 1939.*

and everything in between. Not only should Western techniques be studied but also the Western philosophy of art. This, he says, would lead to the study of primitive art in different lands which, in turn, would open the eyes of Indonesian artists to the spirit and styles of their country's different regional arts—those "of Bali, of the Bataks, the Menangkabau, Dayaks, Papuas, Javanese and others." The Indonesian artist may then become interested in the collections of the Djakarta Museum, Sudjojono continues, but these, he warns, should be regarded only as vestiges of the past, not relevant for the present. Their only merits are as reminders of Indonesian creativity in the past. It is more important, he thinks, to study the life of the common man in the villages and the colored pictures made by primary-school children who are not yet spoiled by the drawing lessons of their teachers. Theirs, he says, is a living and fresh art; theirs are the colors of the villages and their people; they render the color feelings of Indonesians, which may seem strange and "exotic" to Dutch connoisseurs but nonetheless are "our colors." Thus, he concludes, the Indonesian artists first are forced to "turn to the West in order to go East" where they will find their own style, their own identity.

In 1937, Sudjojono and the painter Agus Djajasuminta launched the *Persagi* (abbreviation of *Persatuan Ahli Gambar Indonesia,* Union of Indonesian Painters, although literally, "of picture experts"*) which soon counted around twenty members. The first efforts of the Persagi group to emancipate themselves from the triteness of the naturalists evidently were not too successful. "Just look at the Persagi exhibition arranged at Kolff's† in Djakarta," Sudjojono wrote soon afterward:

Can we say that this is an exhibition of Eastern art, or of Indonesian art? No! The things and themes depicted are Indonesian, but the character of the brushwork and the color feeling are still Western. . . . The compositions are indistinguishable from those of Adolfs, Locatelli, Jan Frank, Sayers and of other European painters who live here. . . . Because we still follow the style of others—starting with Raden Saleh, the elder Abdullah, Pirngadie up to our present-day painters—our original indigenous way of painting is inhibited, it is rusted and cannot come forth, it remains inside, hidden, alone, like a beautiful maiden turned toward a Western wall who is a stranger to the young artists of today. The maiden awaits the daring suitor. . . . Painters of Indonesia! Seek the key that will open the door for that beautiful maiden, seek it each your own way.[13]

Sudjojono thus believed that genuine Indonesian feeling and style were latent in its artists and were merely waiting to be released. He himself had studied painting with Pirngadie and also with Yazaki, a Japanese painter residing in Java. In 1939 Sudjojono produced what is perhaps his best painting to date, "Before the open *kelambu**." In theme and expression it was certainly unprecedented on the Indonesian art scene. A dejected figure of a woman, her hair hanging loose, perches on a wide armchair; her passionate pale face, dark eyes, and set mouth are a mixture of sadness, reproach, questioning and perhaps hate. Her expression is in stark contrast to the gay, fluffy whitish mass of the ornate mosquito netting over the iron bed behind her, as is her dark skirt with its dramatic scalloped red border flowing down along her thighs and legs. The treatment is free and imaginative; the colors are strong yet subtle. A deeply human feeling emanates from the whole work.

In the next year Sudjojono produced another painting new in both theme and style. Called "Tjap Go Me†," it represents the riotous abandon of a crowd at Chinese New Year celebrations. A grinning dancing girl, white-faced clowns, masks, and other figures crowd together, like an avalanche descending upon three white flowerpots on high stems in the foreground.

Ten years later, however, Sudjojono's daring, his freshness in form and feeling were lost. Almost compulsively he now adopts near-photographic rendering of what he terms reality. The painting "Neighbor" (Pl. 160) made in 1950 shows the transformation. By that time Sudjojono was espousing the brand of social (or socialist) realism preached by the Communists.

During the last years preceding World War II, the *Bond van Kunstkringen* (the union of the Dutch art circles) extended its activities, and, stimulated by the patronage of the industrialist P. A. Regnault, who owned paint factories in Indonesia, arranged for exhibitions of original paintings by such masters as

* The word *gambar,* picture, had later become a denigrating term for a painting, as I discovered in 1955. A painting was then referred to as *lukisan,* and a painter as *pelukis. Lukisan* was art; *gambar* was tripe.

† A bookstore where art exhibitions were occasionally held.

* *Kelambu:* mosquito net which forms a tent over the bedstead.

† Name of the Chinese New Year celebrations in Indonesia.

Gauguin, Utrillo, Chirico, Chagall, and Van Dongen as well as of lithographs by Daumier, Corot, Gavarni, Millet, Pissarro, Toulouse-Lautrec, Dérain, Rouault, Kandinsky, Picasso, Toorop, and others.[14] Thus a great range of styles and techniques was represented. It is to be assumed that at least some of the Indonesian painters gained access to these exhibitions, for by 1938 the Kunstkringen began admitting Indonesian artists to its events. Prodded by the local Dutch artists, the Kunstkring of Batavia in 1941 arranged an exhibition of paintings exclusively by Indonesian artists. Among the artists represented were Sudjojono and Agus Djaja, the founders of Persagi, Emiria Sunassa, R. M. Sumitro, R. M. Surono, and several others. At this time a Dutch critic characterized Sudjojono's "Before the open kelambu" as vacuous and formless; he was equally harsh on the others. Essentially, the critic's advice was that the Indonesian painters should learn more about craftsmanship from Dutch artists.[15] It is quite plausible that the exhibited works suffered from great technical deficiencies when compared with works of European masters or, for that matter, with those of Raden Saleh. But what the Indonesian painters probably needed then, in addition to constructive criticism, was some encouragement and recognition of their potentialities.

Plate 160. *"The Neighbor," by Sudjojono, 1950.*

This encouragement came during the Japanese occupation, which for the artists was an exciting although difficult period. Shaken from the ruts of Dutch colonial existence, they were treated with relative mildness and consideration by the Japanese. Artists were given increased opportunities for development, especially through the official recognition accorded them by the Cultural Center (*Keimin Bunko Sidhosjo,* known in Indonesian as *Pusat Kebudajaan*), which had a separate art division that the Japanese used for propaganda purposes. Agus Djaja headed the division under the supervision of the Japanese painter Yosioka. A number of painters whose names are prominent today soon assembled there. Among them were Affandi, Sudjojono, Basuki Abdullah, Otto Djaja, Basuki Resobowo, and some younger painters who had studied with one or another of the above (such as Kusnadi, Nashar, Trubus, Zaini, Sjahri).

Like their political leaders who had found it expedient to collaborate with the Japanese while pursuing their own national goals, the artists of the Cultural Center were confronted by a dilemma, when the Japanese demanded their services for purposes detrimental to their people. The Japanese authorities, for example, were recruiting *romusha,* the forced laborers who were sent to build roads in Burma and other parts of Southeast Asia under subhuman conditions; great numbers of them perished. The Japanese invited the artists to submit paintings for an exhibition intended to stimulate recruitment. Reportedly, Affandi's contribution depicted emaciated skeletons in dismal surroundings. Needless to say, his painting was not included in the show.[16]

During the occupation, however, the Japanese permitted many exhibitions, and prizes were awarded for the best works. The resulting publicity and the attraction of a large Indonesian audience stimulated artistic activity. Furthermore, with the internment of the Dutch, higher educational facilities had been disrupted, and the many Indonesian students who found themselves with enforced leisure time turned to educating themselves, often devoting attention to the study of art.

Paradoxically, as Wertheim has pointed out, it was during the Japanese occupation that Western music and painting acquired an enthusiastic following among young Indonesians and Chinese-Indonesians.[17] In con-

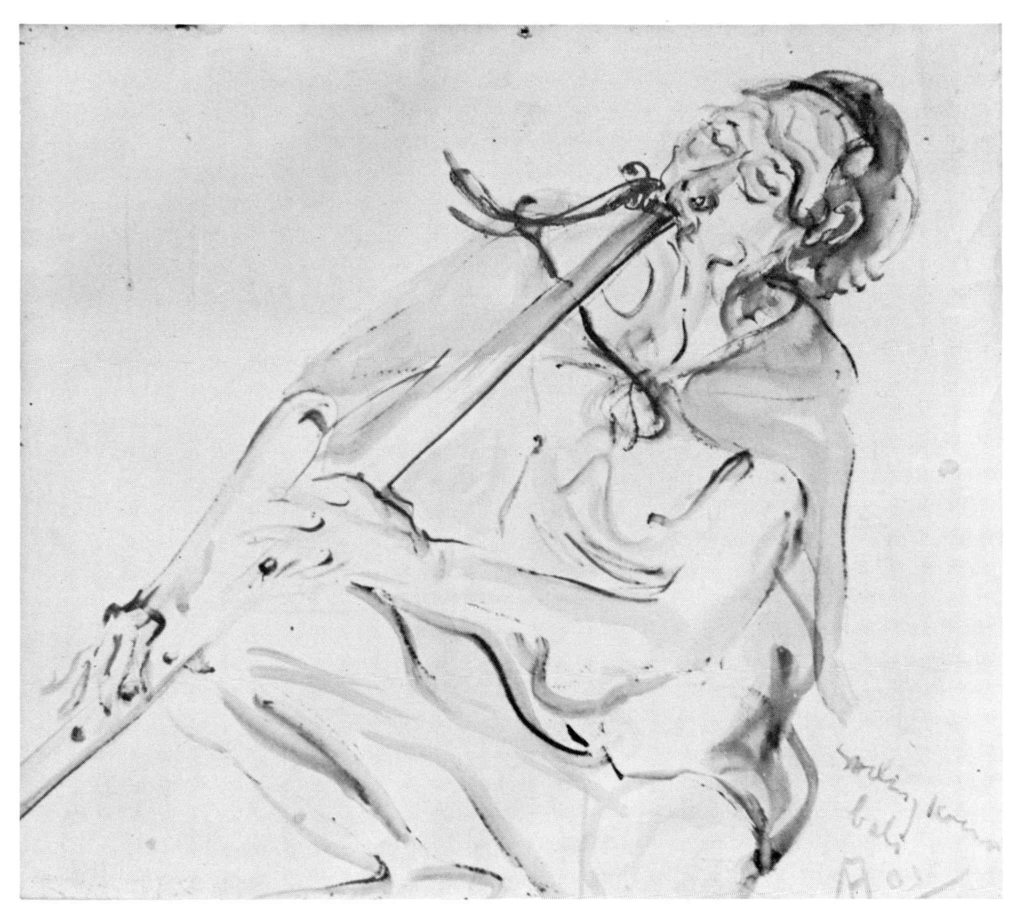

Plate 161. *"Bali Flutist," by Affandi, 1943.*

trast there is little clearly identifiable Japanese influence discernible in modern Indonesian art. Traces of such influence today can be found only in one work by Affandi and in a few by Hendra. In the case of Affandi, Japanese brush techniques stimulated a work of remarkable quality—a watercolor called "Bali Flutist." When I once expressed admiration for the bold and expressive brushstrokes of this fine composition, Affandi said that he himself did not like the work, that, in fact, he was "afraid of it." Pressed for further comment, he explained that as the result of exercises in brushstrokes under the guidance of a Japanese painter, his "hand became so skillful that it could catch what he saw with just a few strokes." This hand of his, acting as if independent of his own will and consciousness, was what had frightened him—the hand had become "too skillful." Affandi did agree, however, that the "Bali Flutist" was among the best of his "very few" good works which have *isih* (substance, essence, content), yet it was almost "too good," being "too complete in itself." It showed "no struggle," left no potentialities, and there seemed "nowhere to go from there." Affandi eventually gave this work to a friend.

The lack of greater Japanese influence can perhaps be explained by the probability that the Japanese painters who accompanied the occupation forces to supervise its pictorial propaganda program had already been affected by Western ideas at that time. They did not carry the traditional Japanese art styles to Indonesia. Moreover, the Indonesian artists may have been reluctant to follow Japanese models of whatever style when their initial enthusiasm for the Japanese regime dampened. Above all, the duration of the Japanese occupation, about three and a half years, was not long enough to leave a lasting imprint.

During the second half of the occupation period, greater freedom for artists was afforded by the cultural organization known as *Putera* (an abbreviation of *Pusat Tenaga Rakjat,* lit., "Center of the People's Strength" or Energy) established in 1943. Headed by Sukarno, Hatta, the educator Ki Hadjar Dewantara, and the religious leader Kjahi Hadji Mansoer, this purportedly all-Indonesian organization also had its own art section, directed by Sudjojono. When an exhibition was held in Djakarta in May, 1943, under Putera's sponsorship, as many as sixty painters participated. One-man shows were also held, and thus a number of modern painters became well known during the Japanese interregnum. An intimately related group at that time, the painters later went their own ways. The group included not only the older painters (Affandi, Hendra, Sudjojono) but also young talent (such as Kartono Yudhokusumo, Mochtar Apin, and Henk Ngantung).

It was during the Japanese occupation that the impetus first given by Persagi began to accelerate. By the time the revolution broke out in August, 1945, the number of Indonesian painters was perhaps double, possibly triple that of prewar days. And they were ready to throw themselves headlong into the stream of revolutionary activities.

After Independence

For Indonesians, modern history begins on August 17, 1945, the day when, in the wake of Japan's surrender, their leaders Sukarno and Hatta proclaimed independence and raised the red-and-white flag. Since then the celebration of August seventeenth has annually punctuated the life of the island-republic. Efforts to build a peaceful orderly existence could not begin before 1950, however, since the land had been ravaged by eight years of war, Japanese occupation, and revolution. After the withdrawal of the Japanese, four years were spent in bitter armed struggle with the Dutch. Having re-entered Indonesia in the train of the British-led Southeast Asian Allied Command, which was to arrange for the surrender of the Japanese, the Dutch had hoped to re-establish their civil administration and control over Indonesia, despite the proclamation of independence. During their efforts to pacify their former colony, they established a number of puppet-states in areas under their control. The Dutch resorted to military campaigns, called "police actions," endeavoring to destroy the newborn republic. They were hoping for the creation of a Federal Indonesian state within a Netherlands commonwealth. The tenacity of Indonesian resistance and United Nations' intervention after the second Dutch "police action" eventually led to the official transfer of sovereignty from the Netherlands to Indonesia.

During these four years of strife, thousands of people, both fighters and refugees, were uprooted. The country was splintered into Dutch-controlled areas and the ever shrinking territories of the Republic. Eventually, by 1947, the Dutch had succeeded in reducing the Republic's control to scattered areas in Java and Sumatra. A small enclave in Central Java, with Jogjakarta as capital, became the Republic's stronghold.

This was a time of great brotherhood, when prince and peasant, teacher and schoolboy, intellectual and trader, men and women from all walks of life were thrown together. All class barriers fell under the sheer weight of emergency, the common cause against a common enemy. Around the embattled enclave, the land was being ruined by the Indonesians' own scorched-earth policy, which left nothing to the advancing Dutch forces. The villagers, torn between blandishments and threats, first from the Japanese and then from the returning Dutch, assisted their own freedom fighters and sometimes at night turned into guerrillas themselves.

The upheaval caused by the war for independence was still very fresh in the memory of the people in the late fifties. Whether government officials or politicians, teachers, students, railroad workers, traders or artists, this period lived on in their consciousness as the high point of their existence, the time when life had attained unprecedented intensity and high purpose. The mere recollection of the revolution still sets a participant's whole being aglow. And in practically every contemporary Indonesian artist's life there have been unforgettable experiences when, carried by the revolutionary tide, he lived through a heroic time. As narrated by some Indonesian artists, however, their individual exploits rarely appear heroic. Moments of high comedy enter into sorrowful episodes; terror and cowardice, freely confessed, are mixed with great or even reckless courage; moments of despair flash through prolonged periods of extreme privation and danger, yet they are alleviated by the warmth of comradeship. Danger germinated endurance and cunning, and the resolve, come what may, to fight or go under, made the young especially feel more alive and alert than ever before. At stake was the fate of both the newborn Republic and their own survival. The artists may have been guerrillas hiding in the mountains, members of the more or less regular Republican armed forces, or just ordinary townsmen or villagers. In Dutch-occupied territories some risked their lives daily, when under cover of some innocuous occupation they carried out missions on behalf of the besieged Republic or provided food and a hiding place for a fighting patriot. The late Kartono Yudhokusumo, a child prodigy who started painting at the age of six, was a charcoal peddler in Jogjakarta. For long hours every day he bicycled through the city and could only paint in his scanty leisure time. When the Dutch occupied the capital in December, 1948, after their parachute attack, their military forces imposed strict controls on the Indonesians' activities. Once Kartono was stopped by a patrol and brought to a military post as a suspected smuggler. Kartono decided, "I have to make them laugh—once they laugh, I am saved," and so he played the fool. The Dutch found his remarks and his naiveté excruciatingly funny and let him go.

Kartono's *joie de vivre* even in such dark hours was the extreme opposite of the sentiments expressed during the revolutionary war by a young poet, the late Chairil Anwar, who wrote:

On the march, I do not know what time will bring.
Agile lads, old men with sharp eyes,
The dreams of freedom and the stars of certainty
Keep me company as I guard this dead area of my beat.
I am one with those who dare to live,
I am one with those who enter the night,
The night made sweet with dreams, without dust.
On the march. I do not know what time will bring.[18]

Despite the upheaval in the early days of the revolution, the artists found time to organize several associations. In Jogjakarta the *Pusat Tenaga Pelukis Indonesia* (lit., Center of Strength of Indonesian Painters) was established under the leadership of Djajengasmoro. Sudjojono gathered a group of painters together in 1946 in Madiun, where they formed the *Seniman Indonesia Muda* or *SIM* (lit., Young Artists of Indonesia). This association subsequently moved first to Jogjakarta, then to Solo, and in 1948 returned once more to Jogjakarta. SIM's members produced anti-Dutch and revolutionary posters which they often distributed behind the enemy lines. A similar organization, *Seni Rupa Masjarakat* (lit., Plastic Arts of the Community), had been founded in Jogjakarta by Affandi and other artists, and it was merged with SIM. Later, in 1947, Affandi and Sudjojono parted ways once more, when Affandi joined Hendra in founding the *Pelukis Rakjat* (lit., People's Painters) at Jogjakarta, an association which under Hendra's leadership remained one of the most active art groups in Indonesia until 1957.

To bolster the morale of the combatants and to fire the imagination of the population, the artists engaged in the feverish production of posters using the scanty materials at hand. Members of the Pelukis Rakjat decided to paint documentary scenes of the revolution, although to their great regret these collections were destroyed in the general upheaval. The paintings from the 1945–1949 period that have survived are generally dark and stormy. (When I once commented on the dark palettes of that period and their congruence with the revolutionary atmosphere, however, one painter drily remarked, "We couldn't get zinc white then!")

Artists like Affandi continued working in Jogjakarta, trying to fix the grim reality of the times onto canvas. Affandi relates that once in 1946 when he sat painting at a market place where, because of shortages in food and clothing, people went about starved and half-naked, a young man threw dirt at him, splashing his canvas and saying, "This artist is mad. While our people are naked he paints them on canvas and even makes a bad painting which we cannot understand."[19]

Following the Dutch occupation of Jogjakarta in December, 1948, feelings of defeat and despair were overpowering. At this time another young poet, Rivai Apin, reflected the mood of Indonesia's youth in his poem "Elegy," which opens with these lines:

What we now feel we need not tell;
What we now think, we need not say,
But be not sad, strive on,
And we'll proclaim the Truth to the stars and the earth.

The concluding lines say:

You, the younger brother who will come,
and you, the elder brother who has gone,
Let us bear this cracked soil, this scorched-up land;
The heaviness of the burden, the pain in the shoulder,
the bitterness of defeat within the heart
Will intensify love for the faith that we profess.[20]

During the final period of the revolution, the painters portrayed scenes around them: guerrillas in their hideouts or in action, as in Sudjojono's "The Hour of the Guerrilla," fleeing refugees, and burning cities.

With the transfer of sovereignty and the advent of freedom (*merdeka*), the Indonesians joined in enthusiastic mass demonstrations giving vent to surging pride and their new sense of national identity. The revolution had given them an unprecedented opportunity to express emotion; it also opened the way to a new torrent of artistic activity.

Together with the political revolution, a period of intense social change had been initiated. It was as if the Indonesian people had to turn about 180 degrees psychologically; they had to face the future rather than the past which heretofore had been relied upon for guidance and security. In the new society the leaders exhorted the people to continue the "struggle" instead of demanding their acquiescence. The new society called for ability to make decisions rather than acceptance of fate. The old social order, in which an individual's status and role had been more or less fixed, was dissolving. The fluid base of the new society allowed mobility to each individual. Some were pushed up the new social ladder by the events of the revolution, while others could now begin to climb on their own. From the isolation and the stuffy protection of a paternalistic colonial regime, the new nation emerged, glaringly exposed to international scrutiny.

After 1950, the revolutionary turbulence gradually subsided, leaving residual enclaves of armed bands who terrorized the countryside in several regions. The strong bonds forged by the upsurge of militant nationalism sagged. The revolutionary leaders, having won the battle for independence, had to find new direction; they were faced with the need to evolve new policies for the reconstruction of their country. The ideological differences between the various political parties, which had already been simmering before the revolution, now broke out into the open. The contest for leadership was reflected in the rise and fall of successive cabinets. The magnificent vision of a "cooperative state," propounded by President Sukarno in 1950, was still to be realized, as was the harmonious collaboration of the principal political blocs whose diverging ideals the President tried to reconcile within the *Pantja Sila,* the five principles of the Indonesian state—Faith in God, Nationalism, Humanism, Democracy, and Social Justice. While a new political elite emerged at the top of the social pyramid, a wave of innovations spread below it as a new bureaucracy was formed. Countless new organizations came into being. Urban centers, especially the capital Djakarta, were filled with those seeking new opportunities. In the provinces too the changing social organism demanded new institutions and new procedures which required numbers of trained workers who were then unavailable.

In all layers of society, people's interests and loyalties increasingly were drawn into spheres which transcended familial ties and regional borderlines. The mobility of the individual was vastly expanded through opportunities for service in the armed forces or the police, the spreading educational system and modern communications, the lure of trading opportunities or urban employment in and out of government. Within the community itself, an individual's intersecting and radiating affiliations, whether political, religious, trade unionist, or all of these, multiplied and widened in the succeeding years. But the greatest trek of all was that of youth to schools in the urban centers, following their elementary schooling in the village. Without great fanfare an enormous amount of school construction, teacher-training, and textbook printing had been achieved during the first decade following the revolution, and still continues. Millions of children now attend elementary and intermediate schools; they will form not only a vastly swelled literate population but also a layer of self-conscious and alert young people with a common language. They already have gained widened national and even international horizons. They no longer speak Dutch as their parents may have, but assidiously study English. Although nationalism remains the prime motivating force of the revolutionary generation, many of these young people are now in search of other focal values to "illuminate" and lend conviction to their strivings.

The many thousands of students from all parts of the archipelago, who appear to be, by the way, taller and huskier than their parents, crowd Indonesia's universities and are becoming a new force that will press upon the older revolutionary leadership. The hundreds of Indonesians who go abroad annually for study and technical training in time will exercise influence in their society which, during the colonial era, had almost been insulated from the mainstreams of international life.

Indonesia now is exposed to influences from all parts of the world, from the Western Atlantic nations, the Eastern socialist countries, the Arab world and the neutralist Afro-Asian bloc it has joined. The nation is open to such a variety of influences and pressures that some thoughtful Indonesians are fearful that their country will not have a chance to work out its own destiny in peace and at its own pace. To this possible interference are added all the internal problems, as yet unresolved, of economic advancement further compli-

Plate 162. *"The Hour of the Guerilla," by Sudjojono, 1949.*

cated by a rapidly increasing population. It is a country where the son of a village magician-healer may be training to be a microbiologist in a hospital laboratory, or the son of a prince to be a teacher, a playwright, or a radio announcer—this in a land where the rhythms of a ponderous oxcart must mesh with an airplane's humming engines. "We live in several ages simultaneously," an Indonesian friend once said to me, "and social ferment will not abate for a long time to come."

While social orders and cultural climates have been changing in Indonesia—in our century at a greatly accelerated rate—nature has changed but little. The island world is still enveloped in humid warmth and covered with lush vegetation, as it was thousands of years ago. The warm humidity mellows the majesty of the high volcanoes with their awesome craters and the threatening denseness of the jungle. Indeed, it seems to mellow everything, even the slow persistence of toil or the dire poverty of the most barren, desolate areas of Java's southern mountain ranges.

Although not visible inland, the sea is always present. At the low northern shores it washes sandy beaches and their coves which harbor graceful fishing craft, or it penetrates deep mangrove swamps. The high cliffs of the islands' southern coasts are immersed in the turquoise depth of the vast Indian Ocean, which pounds wildly against eroded rocky walls. Rice fields in all stages of maturation carpet the fertile plains or form terraces along the slopes of hills. Where trees cluster into islandlike masses amid the fields, one may be certain that a village is hidden in their shade. Ethereal *pinang* palms, the feathery foliage of the coconut, the darker, shorter sugar-palm, large-leafed banana trees, and bamboo groves are present wherever the soil's fertility has supported human habitation.

Dry and rainy seasons alternate regularly, and the

change of the monsoons affects the hues of the many greens. The dominance of these greens is the despair of painters who seek the interplay of rich colors. Day and night, constantly of almost equal length, are ushered in by very brief transitional periods during which the landscape assumes extraordinary beauty. At dawn, as the blue-gray haze still envelops the land, and the lower mountain slopes are hidden in white low-hanging clouds, the peaks of volcanoes, deep purplish-blue, seem to float above the earth, almost reaching the sky. With the first rays of the sun the dew-moistened foliage breaks out in a softly jubilant scintillation, each leaf with glistening edges and sparkling points. After the glaring light and heat of midday subsides, before sunset there come again fleeting minutes of magic transformation. Gold then enters into the greens, the skies blaze in all colors of the rainbow, and there is a hush before the swiftly falling darkness. It is the cool radiance of the moon, not the brilliance of the sun that enraptures Indonesian moods, however.

The animal world is as rich as the plant world. Sharing the villagers' courtyards amid chickens and ducks are gray ponderous water buffaloes, brown bullocks and cows, or the white humped *zebu* with mild, black-rimmed eyes. In non-Moslem areas dark-gray or black pigs with sagging backs are bred. To the delight of the ubiquitous lizards of various shapes, insects abound. Herons stalk in the rice fields. In East Java at sunset one can see flying foxes (huge bats) leaving their hide-outs to raid fruit trees. In the forests on the mountain slopes are deer and wild boars, rodents, snakes, monkeys and occasional tigers. The tantalizing calls of jungle birds, some soft and low, others in high-pitched staccato, only accentuate the great stillness. In the plains there are birds loved for their sweet cooing, trilling, or richly modulated calls. In Java during the day one can see birdcages hoisted into the air on high bamboo poles. The bird markets are an inexhaustible source for contemporary artists' sketches and paintings. The growth of towns and cities and the widespread network of roads and busy highways on an island such as Java, however, have removed the animal world from the daily awareness of the people, and urban artists of Java are no longer observers of animals, not even of those they see daily in their own environment.

In outward appearance Indonesian cities and towns still bear the marks of former Dutch colonial economic, administrative, and social life. Nevertheless, the agglomeration of Indonesian, Chinese, and old or modern European-style structures (sometimes with mixtures of Dutch and Indonesian, Dutch and Chinese, or Indonesian and Chinese architectural features) lends them a character all their own. The old palace-cities, of which Surakarta (Solo) and Jogjakarta (Jogja) in Central Java are good examples, have grown around the keratons. Large plazas, *alun-alun,* to the north and the south of the palace-complex, where the sacred old *waringin** trees still receive offerings, serve as sport-fields and grounds for large annual fairs, and parades. The alun-alun is a feature in most old towns, and in Java the mosque is usually situated at its eastern side, facing west, toward Mecca. The old harbor towns that formerly were busy participants in the Asian sea trade, such as Bantam, Tuban, or Gresik, have fallen into relative obscurity after the rise of the modern ports of Surabaya, Medan, and Djakarta.

Every large city also has its *kampung* areas—either villagelike enclaves hidden behind the house façades that line the main thoroughfares, or shantytowns on the city fringes inhabited by the poor working population. Many an artist is a kampung dweller. Bicycles, pedicabs, pony carts, autolettes, buses, motorcars, jeeps, and trucks crowd the streets in addition to the heavy oxcarts which, following routes of their own, assemble near the market places. In Jogjakarta, which since 1950 has been transformed into a university town, a steady stream of bicycles, often five deep, flanks the car traffic on either side of its main street. The network of buses connecting towns and villages increasingly removes from the roads the walking, half-trotting market-bound villagers with their loads. The general rhythm of life has been markedly accelerated since World War II, as have the movements of people who are increasingly adopting Western-style clothing in which they feel "released," especially the girls who traditionally have worn tight jackets and ankle-length batik skirts which restrict free motions.

The age-old life of markets, and peddlars continues in the villages and towns. And people, as ever, congregate at the eternally recurring family events—birth, puberty, marriage, and death—as well as at high religious holidays or at the beginnings of planting and harvesting. Each group marks these events in its own way; all appeal to the Higher Powers, whether in mosques or temples or churches, or in the shade of an old tree on the village square.

New traditions are forming and taking root, too. To

* A wide-spreading banyan tree with air-roots.

the list of public holidays new ones have been added, pre-eminently the August 17th Independence Day and the commemoration of fallen heroes of the revolution.

Although twentieth-century technology is in evidence everywhere to some degree, the industrial age is fully reflected in only a few scattered places, where oil wells and tin mines are exploited on a large scale or where a rubber factory, a modern sugar or textile mill is in operation. There are no agglomerations of smokestacks at the approaches to any of the large cities, signaling the presence of concentrated machine-industry, apart from an electric-power station, radio towers, or water-supply works. The cities are mainly administrative, military, service, and trade centers. Indonesia is still predominantly garden, market, and workshops and, increasingly, school.

The cosmopolitan, hot, and hectic capital, Djakarta, with its overloaded telephone wires, congested traffic, and busy airport—a veritable melting pot, not only in the figurative sense—is the hub of political, mercantile, and modern cultural life. Here all Indonesians can lose their ethnic-regional identities, which fifty years ago would have been conspicuous were it only for the distinctive traditional costume now supplanted by uniform Western dress. "Unity in Diversity," the national slogan, is slowly being realized for the ethnic groups, although political factionalism is still rampant.

Attainment of independence and the changing social order have drastically affected what we may call the "esthetic order" of Indonesian society in human appearance and behavior. Formalized behavior and appearance are usually strongest in hierarchical societies and in the ritual life of a tradition-bound community. The sense of esthetic ordering is still evident in Bali's ritual or secular processionals or in some Javanese princes' entourages where court traditions today remain hidden behind palace walls.

Here is the recurrent dilemma of modern times: pageantry is too expensive in terms of money, labor, and time; colorful tradition vanishes into uniform grayness. The leveling process is reflected in mass-produced garments as well as in the abolition of outward signs of status and provenance. The gorgeous traditional costumes of different ethnic groups, donned on high ceremonial occasions will gradually become stage-costumes. From family treasure they may devolve into museum pieces within the next two generations. The disappearance of these colorful costumes and the highly stylized, codified behavior stemming from the ancient royal-cosmic order is deplored by conservative members of the older generation and foreign visitors, not least the numerous tourists whose avid cameras are set to record exotic sights. Yet the disappearance of the "feudal order" (as Indonesians always refer to their traditional past), inevitably including its esthetic aspects, is hailed by youth and political leaders. To them the substitution of sober functional structures for ornate traditional architecture symbolizes progress, as does the appearance on sportfields of girls in shorts. And yet it is likely that for a long time to come, while modernizing at home, the Indonesian national and cultural identity will be stressed abroad, at international fairs, on propaganda publications, or good-will missions, with all the forms and colors animating Indonesia's old traditional arts and institutions.

Art and the State

From the very inception of the Indonesian Republic, its leaders envisaged the State as playing an active role in the development of the arts. The Provisional Constitution explicitly stated that "the authorities shall protect cultural, artistic, and scientific freedom" and that "upholding this principle, the authorities shall promote the national development of culture and of the arts and sciences wherever they are able to do so."[21]

One of the first significant steps toward the furtherance of art was the foundation in January, 1950, of the Indonesian Academy for the Plastic Arts at Jogjakarta, commonly referred to as ASRI (an abbreviation of *Akademi Seni Rupa Indonesia*). The conditions for establishing the academy were ripe. A number of art associations active in Jogjakarta, each with its own group of students, had been hoping to pool their resources and students to form a school. One organization, led by the painter Djajengasmoro, the *Pusat Tenaga Pelukis Indonesia* (lit., Center of Strength of Indonesian Painters), exercised particularly strong initiative. With the support of the national government, their dream came true. The academy was housed in makeshift quarters, a large old house with an inner court. The back veranda and open galleries became crowded classrooms for painting and sculpture. Another eight years passed before ASRI acquired a building constructed especially for its own purposes.

Of the Academy's five divisions—painting, sculpture, handicrafts, the graphic arts, and the training course for art teachers—the divisions of painting and art education were the most heavily enrolled from the start. For admission, all students were required to have completed senior high school.* The competence of ASRI's teachers in the various divisions was uneven. In 1956, only 2 of the 16 regular and 35 visiting teachers had received academic training. Whereas excellent draftsmanship was common to a number of the older instructors—a skill acquired under the Netherlands Indies regime—painting was a relatively new art. Sculpture, a long forgotten field, was being rediscovered.

In ASRI's crafts division, where metalwork, leather carving, wood carving, and other applied arts were taught, old master craftsmen skilled in their traditional ways were the instructors. They could train good copyists, and there was little creativity. In the graphic arts the teachers were younger, more imaginative, and had a greater awareness of the changing times and its needs. In 1956 the academy had about 200 students.

The first director of ASRI, R. J. Katamsi, who retired in 1958 and was succeeded by I. Djumadi Hadisawarno, had been an experienced art teacher before World War II. A conscientious, mild, and tolerant man, trained in the Western academic tradition, he admired Indonesia's ancient classical art. Yet he recognized and supported budding talent among his students, no matter how unorthodox its expression. Thus in 1956 the old gentleman proudly displayed on his front porch a huge and very moving sculpture by the young Amrus Natalsja. Amrus himself worked and slept in Katamsi's backyard where he hewed giant tamarind tree trunks into violent, pathetic figures.

Apart from ASRI, the Republic inherited another specialized art school in Bandung, West Java. Its history differs from that of ASRI and is relevant to a degree for understanding some of the antagonistic undercurrents and rivalries which existed between the two schools in their early years. In 1947 the Fine Arts School of Bandung came into being as a drawing-teachers' training school added to the long established Bandung Technical Institute, where, incidentally, President Sukarno had studied construction engineering in the late twenties. In 1948 Bandung became the capital of the short-lived State of West Java (known as *Negara Pasundan**), one of several semiautonomous states created in territories occupied by the Dutch.

In 1950, after the transfer of sovereignty, a new Department of Architecture and Fine Arts was established at the Bandung Technical Institute when it became affiliated with the University of Indonesia. In 1958, however, it regained its independent status. S. Sumardja, formerly Secretary General of Pasundan's Ministry of Education, was the art school's first director. An academically trained art teacher, Sumardja came to head a largely Dutch staff. Although very different in most other respects from the director of ASRI, Sumardja had the same conscientiousness, tolerance, and readiness to encourage young talent. In the late thirties he had been the first to recognize Affandi's gifts.

As of 1957 both schools, which were under the direct or indirect jurisdiction of the Ministry of Education and Culture,† appeared to enjoy complete freedom in seeking and pursuing their own ways. There was no trace of a nationally prescribed art ideology; there was no interference with or pressure on either staff or students in so far as subject or style was concerned. Consequently, in both schools one could find a great variety of conceptions in the works of both teachers and students. This situation does not seem to have altered radically in the succeeding years.

In addition to supporting the art schools, the Government, through the Ministry of Education, provided subsidies to some art students as well as to some general university students. In 1956 the subsidies ranged between 150 and 250 rupiah a month, then enough to cover bare subsistence. In return the recipients, upon termination of their studies, were committed to work for the Government for as many years as these scholarships ran, plus an additional two years. To an indigent art student the ensured subsistence was a great inducement to launch into this otherwise hazardous profession.

The Government's concern with the promotion of the arts was further channeled through the Cultural Office of the Ministry of Education and Culture.‡ The Cultural Office (*Djawatan Kebudajaan*) had branches

* In 1958 an art school (*Sekolah Seni Rupa*) at the high-school level was added, and it shares the Academy's newly built premises.

* *Negara:* State; *Pasundan* derives from *Sunda.* The region is predominantly inhabited by the Sundanese.

† See Figure 8, governmental organizations concerned with the arts.

‡ This ministry was later split into two departments. See Figure 8.

in all provincial capitals. In addition some provinces and municipalities had their own cultural offices. In Jogjakarta, for example, which is an extreme case, four cultural offices coexisted in the middle fifties, each with overlapping functions: the Art Division of the Central Government's Cultural Office; the Cultural Office of the province of Central Java; the Cultural Office of the "Special Territory of Jogjakarta" (*Daerah Istimewa Jogjakarta*), the domain of the Sultan of Jogjakarta; and Jogjakarta's municipal Cultural Office.

The location in Jogjakarta of the Art Division (*Bagian Kesenian,* now *Urusan Kesenian,* Art Affairs) of the Cultural Office inevitably weighted its activities somewhat in favor of the needs and interests of Central Java rather than those of more remote regions. The Art Division was divided into six specialized sections—literature, music, plastic arts, dance, "dalangship" (the art of conducting shadow and other puppet plays), and *pentjak,* the stylized art of self-defense. The functions of the Art Division have been officially defined as follows: (a) to conduct research into the art treasures of the past; (b) to protect, develop, and propagate the existing arts in society; (c) to find new norms in every art field, in harmony with the growth of the present Indonesian society; (d) to acquaint the international world with Indonesian art.[22]

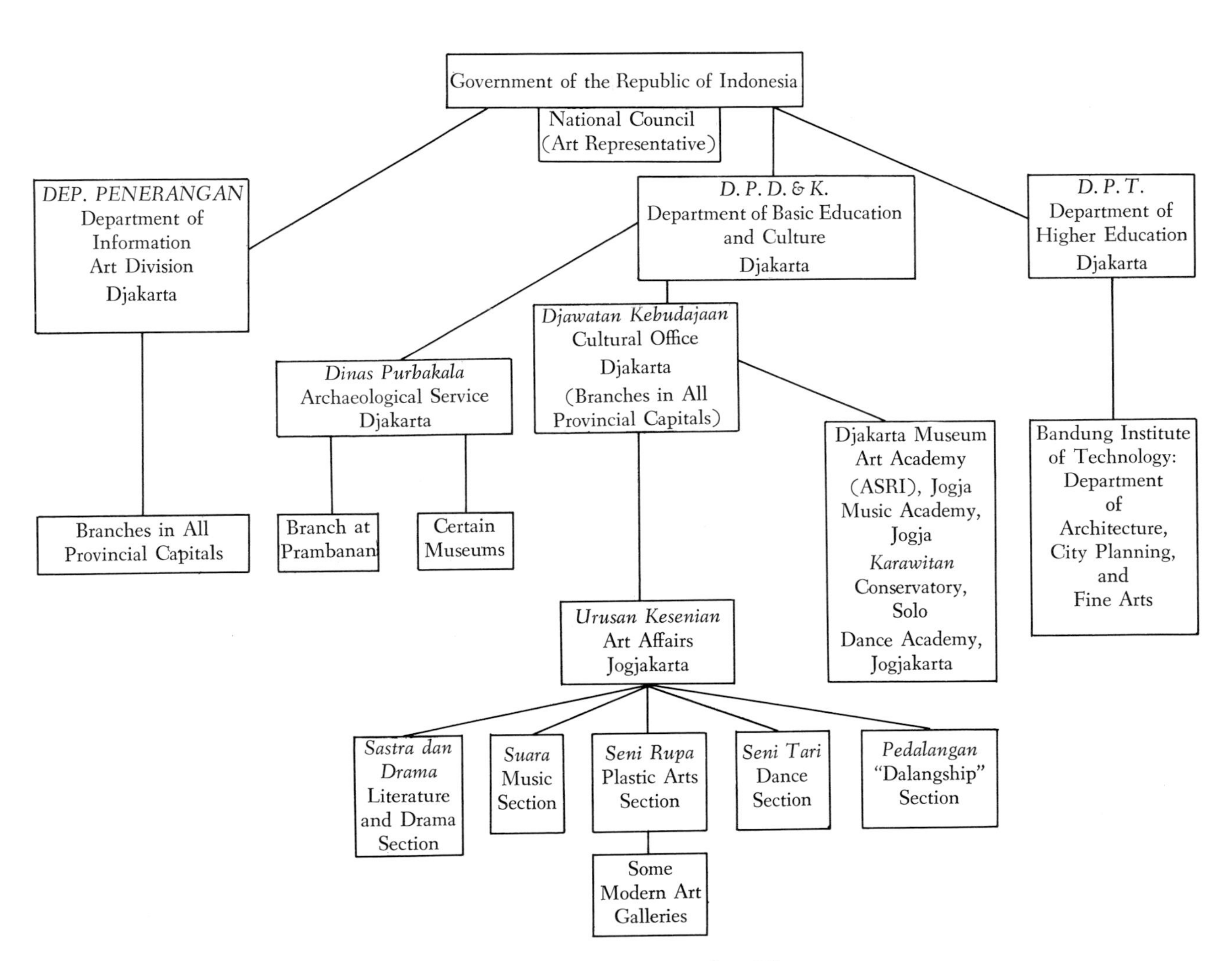

Figure 8. *Governmental organizations concerned with the arts (as of 1963).*

The first of these activities—research into the art treasures of the past—is in largest measure the task of the Archaeological Service.

In the promotion of existing arts the Art Division was very active. It organized a variety of art events, including exhibitions, purchased paintings for a special collection for showings at home and abroad, promoted conferences and published an illustrated magazine, *Budaya* (Culture). Of great importance was the Division's local administration of government subsidies to legitimate art organizations, especially to those which offered training courses and had a substantial body of students.

The third task—finding new art norms for modern Indonesian society—was furthered by the Art Division by encouraging experimentation and the exposure of artists in various fields to new art trends. On the one hand, it sponsored intra-Indonesian art exchanges and. on the other, lent support to artists' applications for studies abroad, which had to be approved in Djakarta by the Cultural Office and the ministry of Education and Culture.

Similarly, in acquainting the international world with Indonesian art, the Art Division dealt with cultural missions of artists, musicians, dancers and puppeteers who were sent to various countries from Indonesia and with foreign groups visiting Indonesia in return.

Government subsidies to art associations, channeled through the Cultural Office, contributed in no small degree to the proliferation of such associations in every field—not least in painting and the dance. The Indonesian predisposition for associative life and work, for forming clubs, leagues, cooperative or rather mutual assistance (*gotong royong*) organizations, is well known. The Government's financial support has sometimes led existing associations to split into separate units, each of them claiming a subsidy. Economic considerations, of course, were not the only cause for the multiplication of associations. Factionalism based on political ideological grounds, the clustering of ethnic groups, professional interests, personal rivalries or ambitions of potential leaders all played a role too.

The Government's subsidies similarly contributed to the multiplication of dance associations. In some measure such subsidies alleviated the plight of some members of impoverished higher aristocracy traditionally given to the patronage of music and dance. Their open, spacious, pillared reception halls (*pendopo*) have come to function mainly for the conducting of dance classes and of performances.

The Indonesian Government offered some fellowships for international cultural exchange and also approved fellowships granted to Indonesian artists by foreign governments or private foundations. Between 1954 and 1956 some thirty Indonesian artists and art students studied and worked abroad, in India, Italy, the Netherlands, France, the United States, and Japan. At the same time there was a lively exchange of cultural missions—groups of artists or dance companies exchanging visits with those from such countries as the People's Republic of China, the Soviet Union, Czechoslovakia, Malaya, India, Pakistan, and the United States.

Beginning in 1948 the Netherlands government Foundation for Cultural Cooperation, known as STICUSA,* with headquarters in Amsterdam and an office in Djakarta, was very active in Indonesia. Between 1950 and 1957, the year when STICUSA withdrew from Indonesia, the foundation granted a number of fellowships to Indonesian artists for study in Holland and helped them to hold exhibitions there. In Amsterdam, STICUSA published a monthly journal, *Cultureel Nieuws—Indonesië,* in which articles from the Indonesian and Dutch press on Indonesian cultural subjects were reprinted. In Djakarta a number of Indonesian periodicals devoted much space to cultural developments, especially in literature and the visual arts.[23]

Another ministry concerned with the arts, the Department of Information, served mainly as an outlet through radio broadcasts, for the performing arts, both traditional and modern. Its English publications, addressed to the foreign community in Indonesia, to visitors, and for publicity abroad, often illustrated and described a variety of Indonesian art works. This ministry had an art department of its own, a collection of modern paintings, and an archive of photographs.

Finally, the State in the person of President Sukarno, who is an avowed art lover and collector, provided a strong stimulus to artists. In the absence of a national museum for modern art, the presidential palaces substituted as such, although the collections were not acces-

* An abbreviation of the Dutch title, *Stichting voor Cultureel Samenwerking,* which in full is followed by *tussen Nederland, Indonesië, Suriname en de Nederlandse Antillen* (between the Netherlands, Indonesia, Surinam and the Dutch Antilles).

sible to the public at large. The Istana Merdeka (Freedom Palace) in Djakarta, the alternate palace in Bogor, and the presidential mansion in the resort of Tjipanas, are filled to capacity with collections of paintings and other art objects. These belong in part to the State; in part, they are the President's private possessions. Though predominantly composed of works by postwar Indonesian artists, the collections also include works by foreign artists who have lived and worked in Indonesia (as, for example, the Austrian painter Ronald Strasser; the Dutch painters W. G. Hofker and Rudolf Bonnet, one-time residents of Bali; the Italian Romualdo Locatelli; and the formerly popular Dutch painters who lived in Java, Adolfs, Dake, and Sayers). There are also examples of modern Indian, Vietnamese, Filipino, Japanese, and Chinese paintings, including some by the Djakarta painter Lee Man Fong.

The curator of these collections in 1956 was the painter Dullah, who was close to Sukarno. He lived in a wing of the palace in Djakarta, and often accompanied the President on his trips at home and abroad. It was Dullah who selected the 206 paintings from Sukarno's private collection which Chinese experts photographed and then reproduced in the de luxe, two-volume, oversize monograph[24] given to President Sukarno by the People's Republic of China on the occasion of the 1956 state visit. The text, including a preface by Sukarno and an introduction by Dullah, is in four languages: Indonesian, Chinese, English, and Russian. Not only was this magnificent gift, including many hundreds of sets, geared to one of Sukarno's cherished avocations, but its publication also proved a boon to those artists whose paintings appeared in the monograph. Each received 2,000 rupiah from the Chinese authorities for every painting that was reproduced. The painter best represented, with 26 canvasses, was Dullah himself. Whether this presumption contributed to his release or not, Dullah is no longer in charge of the President's art collections.

Impressive architectural projects emanated from the Presidential Palace, reflecting Sukarno's sense of history and of national pride as well as his personal predilections. Whether it was the shape of the projected National Monument, or the construction of the imposing modern Hotel Indonesia, or perhaps the Indonesian pavilion for the 1964 World's Fair in New York, the President found time to examine personally sketches and plans, and more often than not to advance his own suggestions.

Plans for a competition for designs of the National Monument (Tugu Nasional) on Djakarta's Freedom Square (Medan Merdeka) were announced in 1955 by a committee headed by the President. The specifications were that the monument should be 64 meters high in commemoration of the year 1945 ($19 + 45 = 64$), when Indonesian independence was proclaimed. Several groups and individuals submitted plans the following year, but none won the final approval of the jury. After several more rounds, a compromise plan was adopted. Construction was inaugurated in 1961 and may be completed in 1967.

The performing arts too enjoyed patronage of the presidential palace. A great display of regional dances was held there annually in celebration of Independence Day on August 17th. From time to time a shadow play was performed at the palace for invited guests, with the President himself attending throughout the night.

The performing arts, especially the traditional ones, were further stimulated by the Council on Tourism which in the fifties was headed by the Sultan of Jogjakarta. Among its various activities, the Council helped promote the construction of a large open-air amphitheater near the famous Prambanan temples.

Thus, it was very clear in the fifties, that the study and practice of the arts in Indonesia were substantially stimulated by the Government's direct and indirect financial support to organizations and individuals. There were, of course, a number of relatively prosperous and independent artists. Others remained independent despite poverty or earned their living from salaried work. But there were also many who distinctly looked to the Government for support and, moreover, felt that they were entitled to it.

As for the official art policy, spokesmen, not least the President himself, stressed the need to develop a "national art." The President often criticized a film, play, or an art style by saying, "It is not Indonesian enough." In fact, after 1959, the concept of "national identity" had become one of the guiding principles of the state.

While Indonesia's traditional regional arts have distinct styles of their own, there is the desire to somehow synthesize or generalize them into all-Indonesian art forms. The Government's general policy was to "foster the creation of an Indonesian art out of elements of local arts." Therefore interregional exchanges in art exhibits or dance performances were encouraged. Yet, while the Government positively pursued its policy of trying to develop a national art, it took practically no official action to prevent or counteract Western or other foreign influences. As the following pages will illustrate, Indonesia's plastic art world in the fifties was a wide open field where each artist could be his own prophet.

Notes

1. *Encyclopaedie van Nederlandsch Indie,* 2d ed. (The Hague, 1917–1921), III, 718. The author is indebted to Harsja Bachtiar, whose research for an unpublished term paper, "The Social History of Indonesian Painting," Cornell University, 1958, has been utilized in part in this section.
2. C. C. Berg, "Kidung Sunda; Inleiding, Tekst, Vertaling en Anteekeningen," *Bijdragen tot de Taal-, Land- en Volkenkunde,* LXXXIII (1927), 67, stanza 18a. Extract translated by the author from the Dutch version.
3. *Ibid.,* p. 62, stanza 4b.
4. S. Kalff, "Inheemsche Schilderkunst op Java," *Oedaya,* II (1925), 202.
5. F. de Haan, *Oud Batavia* (Bandung, 1935), p. 506.
6. Thomas Stamford Raffles, *The History of Java,* I (London, 1817), 472–473.
7. *Ibid.*
8. William Barrington d'Almeida, *Life in Java* (London, 1864), II, 288–289.
9. J. E. Jasper and Mas Pirngadie, *De Inlandsche Kunstnijverheid in Nederlandsch Indie,* 5 vols. (The Hague, 1912–1927).
10. R. Goris, *Sedjarah Bali Kuna* (Bali, 1948), p. 2.
11. S. Sudjojono, "Seni Loekis di Indonesia sekarang dan jang akan datang" ["The Art of Painting in Indonesia Now and in the Future"], in *Seni Loekis, Kesenian dan Seniman* [Painting, Art and the Artist] (Jogjakarta, 1946), pp. 1–9. Extracts translated by the author.
12. Sudjojono, "Menoedjoe Tjorak Seni Loekis Persatoean Indonesia Baroe" ["Toward a Unified Style in the Painting of New Indonesia"], *Seni Loekis,* pp. 10–15. Extracts translated by the author.
13. Sudjojono, "Menoedjoe Tjorak," pp. 12–13.
14. W. H. van Helsdingen and Mr. Dr. H. Hoogenbert, *Hecht Verbonden in Lief en Leed* (Amsterdam, 1946), p. 176.
15. J. de L., "Indonesische schilders (Kunstkring te Batavia)," *de Fakkel,* I (1941), 686–688.
16. Cited in an article, "Indonesie Schilders: Affandi," in the Djakarta daily, *Het Inzicht,* I, no. 29 (3 August 1956), 4.
17. W. F. Wertheim, *Indonesian Society in Transition* (The Hague, 1946), p. 299.
18. This poem, "Night Watch," appeared in translation in the anthology *The Flaming Earth, Poems from Indonesia,* edited by Ahmed Ali (Karachi, 1949).
19. "Affandi's opinion about painting," *Indonesian Affairs,* III (April-May 1953), 56.
20. From Ahmed Ali, ed., *The Flaming Earth, Poems from Indonesia.*
21. Provisional Constitution of the Republic of Indonesia, 1950, Section VI: "Fundamental Principles," Article 40.
22. *Pewarta K. P. P. & K.* (Bulletin of the Ministry of Education and Culture), April, 1953, p. 4.
23. Among them were: *Orientatie, Gema,* the literary section of the journal *Siasat* called *Gelanggang, Konfrontasi, Sastra,* and *Basis* as well as the monthly journal *Indonesia.*
24. *Paintings from the Collection of Dr. Sukarno, President of the Republic of Indonesia,* compiled by Dullah (Peking, 1956), 2 vols.

CHAPTER 9

The Great Debate

Whither Indonesian Culture?

THE DEVELOPMENT of modern art in Indonesia, as a facet of cultural change, is, of course, a part of the broader question about the future direction in which Indonesian culture would develop. This question has been passionately debated by the country's leading intellectuals for more than three decades. At the roots of the debate is the confrontation of the "East" with the "West." Is modernization equivalent to Westernization? Does the adoption of Western technology mean acceptance of Western cultural values, institutions, art forms? Could the "good" elements in Western culture be assimilated and everything harmful or debasing be rejected? Would it be possible to select only certain needed techniques to improve material welfare without forgoing Indonesia's spiritual heritage? Isn't Indonesia in danger of losing its cultural identity?

Writers, poets, scholars, educators, and politicians participated in what is known as the "Polemics on Culture" (*Polemik Kebudajaan*), which burst into print in 1935.[1] Essentially the same debate is continuing now, in changing circumstances and with new participants. The issues are obscured, first, because the debate unfolds against a background of Indonesia's own internal cultural diversity, largely disregarded by the participants, but sometimes reflected in their own modes of thought. Second, outside Indonesia, that crucial part of the world lumped under the general term "the West" has been growing more complex and diverse especially with the advent of the cold war. Third, Islam, to which many Indonesians look for guidance, has been affected by reformist movements. In addition, many of the propounded concepts and ideas are loaded more with emotion than with precise meaning. But the debate itself was and is significant and inevitable under the pressure of cultural change.

In the debate of the thirties (1935–1939) Takdir Alisjahbana opened the argument and then answered his opponents as they expressed their views. His opening salvo was a call to transform Indonesia's "static" society into a "dynamic" one by adopting Western attitudes and techniques. Takdir took the position that everything that preceded the development of a national consciousness was not actually *Indonesian,* but "pre-Indonesian"—that there was a vast difference between the localism of ancient cultures and the modern aspiration for an all-Indonesian national culture. (The debate excluded political visions: a national state could not be mentioned since disapproval by the Netherlands Indies government could have cut short the polemics.) Takdir pointed to foreign cultural influences in the past, from India, from the Arab world, which had enriched rather than impoverished the culture of the Indonesian islands. "And now the time has arrived," he said, "when we turn our eyes to the West." It was due to Western education and contact with Western ideas, in fact, that the concept of national unity was born in Indonesia, he claimed. He foresaw that Western influences would play an even stronger role in Indonesia than Indian and Islamic ones had in the past.[2]

In answer, the writer Sanusi Pané pointed to continuity in history. It was not possible to create a new culture suddenly, he held, the present leans on and is built out of the past. As for the potential influence of the West, "European culture flourishes on materialism, intellectualism, and individualism," he said. "Its economy expands by developing industry, trade, and modern imperialism. . . . Individualism breeds boundless competition in the economic sphere. In art, the goal is *art pour l'art.*" Yet, with all of Europe's attainments in economic development, "There are people with overabundance and people who are hungry." Pané further argued that "in the East . . . materialism, intellectualism, and individualism are not needed so much. Man is not forced to combat nature in trying to master it. He feels himself in unity with the world around him. . . ." The highest attainment aspired to in India as well as in Indonesia, Pané held, was mystic: "Man in unity with the universe denies his physical desires and purifies his spirit." The West, stressing physical welfare, forgets the spirit, "it is like Faust." The East cherishes the spirit, forgetting the body, "it is like Ardjuna meditating on Mt. Indrakila."[3]

In reply to these and similar contentions, Takdir Alisjahbana vehemently and repeatedly tried to shatter the old clichés about East and West. He complained, for example, "we have not yet developed the habit of conducting polemics which would penetrate to the very roots of an issue." He continued:

> . . . Such phrases as "imitating the West" and "traditions of the East" have become stereotypes, used lightly and without the slightest notion of their true meaning. While the word "West" seems to be associated with cruelty, greed, selfishness, and materialism, "East" is a sacred (magic) word containing all fine qualities, peacefulness, humanism, religiousness, and practically everything that is beautiful and noble. People indeed forget that since time immemorial good and evil existed in equal measure everywhere; that greed, selfishness, war, oppression, and other evils are not exclusively a Western monopoly and that, in reverse, fine sensibilities, peacefulness, religiousness, etc. are found not only in the East. For that matter, up to the present, the twentieth century, there still are in India, which is much admired by many Indonesians, eighty million people who are despised and oppressed in a manner that would be difficult to find in the colonial history of the West. People also forget that the Western technology and science they want cannot be separated in any way from Western philosophy, art, customs—in short, from the Western way and view of life. It is not likely that airplanes, well-equipped hospitals, efficient banks, or rationalized agriculture would spring from such spirits as Gandhi's or Tagore's.[4]

Between these two extreme positions, other, milder voices spoke up. The scholar Poerbatjaraka, urging the study of Indonesian history, believed that full orientation to the West was dangerous. He summed up his argument by saying: "Don't be obsessed with our ancient culture nor intoxicated by the West. Get to know both well, and choose from each that which is good so that we can apply it successfully in times to come."[5]

Similarly, the newspaper editor Tjindarbumi, while welcoming the debate as a healthy and much needed airing of views, warned that "the Westerners know not patience and never enjoy peace of heart." While studying the West's philosophy and adopting some of its techniques, a people can still retain their cultural originality and need not go through the bitter experiences of the West. Mockingly, he pointed out that in European schools, where individualism and patriotism are stressed, children are encouraged to become outstanding people, heroes. Indonesian children are taught in schools about Dutch heroes. Will they strive to become a second Jan Pieterzoon Coen or a second Van Heutz?*[6]

The educator, writer, and editor Raden Sutomo, pursuing the subject of education, stressed the difference between schooling, *pengadjaran,* and guidance in conduct and values, or upbringing—*pendidikan.* Western teaching, he held, does not provide moral guidance but the two must go together. The result of Western education is an uprooting of the individual. He cited several leading personalities—Tjipto Mangunkusumo, Sukarno, Tjokroaminoto, and Hadji Agus Salim—who, he said, after painfully experiencing rootlessness as the result of Western education, had to retrain themselves, "their spirits," as Easterners:

> Tjipto, for instance, "slept" with the Bhagawad Gita. And in his daily life he always displayed the virtues of a true ksatriya.
>
> Sukarno, while making propaganda, reveals his "Javanism" by citing examples from Wayang Purwa, so much so that people in other islands get annoyed.
>
> The late Tjokroaminoto and Agus Salim based their ideas on Islam, while Samaun and Muso, the Communist leaders, very much like to be ascetics and gurus. . . .

Acquisition of Western knowledge may easily lead to superficiality, Sutomo warned. "Looking ahead" is fine, provided one first "looked back."[7]

Adinegoro, journalist and editor, making a distinction between "culture" and "civilization," asserted that "the culture of the East cannot be changed to resemble that of the West, but the civilizations of the two can become the same." Japan, he thought was a good example of a combination of an Eastern culture with Western civilization. Indonesia's leading intellectuals must become "culture-philosophers," he thought. They must discover a way, that is, to preserve harmony in these circumstances.[8]

* A governor of the East India Company and a Dutch general who ruthlessly conquered and pacified parts of Indonesia.

Harmony is the keynote of Javanese philosophy of life. The late Ki Hadjar Dewantara believed that human desires are but cogs in the Universal Machine. The individual's will is subject to "the laws of cause and effect," which he identified with the Indian conception of Karma. Change is inevitable and, confronted with it, people are always ambivalent—deploring loss of the old, yet welcoming the new as a liberation. Though man is only a small part of the universal will, he still can give direction to the era, participate in shaping his world. "God is within us." With these cosmological premises established, Dewantoro goes on to say that the future of Indonesia must be heeded lest its culture become petrified. While admitting that he leaned toward Pané's outlook, he thought that his differences with Alisjahbana could be bridged.[9]

Dr. M. Amir, physician and psychiatrist, had similar views. He said:

> I myself was a student of a Western school . . . from the first to the last grade. I was able to study Western society not only in our country but also, for many years, in Europe. No one could accuse me of despising Western science, art, and culture. Yet I am convinced that the spirtual development of our people—though our minds be sharpened in laboratories, in the Western manner—will progress along its own lines as in Japan, China, and India. There, though Western-oriented, the culture in essence certainly retained its own Eastern base. Once more, it does not matter if we use spoons and forks, machines and tools from the West. It's no mistake to read Shakespeare, Dante, and Goethe. It's very beneficial to admire the figures of Rembrandt and Da Vinci. We are delighted to hear the music of Beethoven and Wagner. Yet we must seek an art of our own, a culture of our own, a literature of our own.[10]
>
> As long as national ideals live on in the East, moving toward the West is not dangerous.[11]

Takdir Alisjahbana tirelessly analyzed and refuted his opponents' arguments, pleading for a more positive orientation. Then the prospects of World War II and its actual outbreak interrupted the cultural debate in print. It continued, however, among the intellectuals, in thoughts and conversations during the Japanese occupation. After the war, the debate was resumed at meetings and in print.

With the establishment of the Indonesian Republic, the conservative Moslems insisted that the state and its culture be based on the precepts of Islam. This contributed a heavy strand of argument to the general debate and indirectly was relevant to the visual arts, since orthodox Moslems could not possibly sanction "the making of images." An interesting footnote in this connection is a remark by a young painter, who was a leader of a Moslem student organization. He observed that abstract art was very congenial to the Islamic spirit.

Communist ideology presented a greater challenge than before. The establishment of the Communist-sponsored cultural organization Lekra, in 1950, quickened the penetration of Communist influence into the art world. Voices arose condemning Western influences as harmful since they introduced cosmopolitanism as opposed to nationalism, and individualism as against a social consciousness.[12] They demanded that art be in the service of social enlightenment, especially of peasants and workers, and be rooted in folk life, depicting social reality.

Marxist-socialist terminology was used in Indonesia not only by the Communists. President Sukarno used it himself and so did his followers. So the poet Sitor Situmorang, who represented the artists in The People's Provisional Consultative Congress (*Madjelis Permusjawaratan Rakjat Sementara*), speaking in 1960, condemned "bourgeois and individualist esthetics." He praised social realism, which, he claimed, provided an answer to the problem of art dedicated to national development. He said: "The ideal of great art is a longing for a National Tradition."[13]

Actually, the longing Sitor spoke of preoccupied not only the followers of Sukarno. The phantom of a "national spirit" hovered over everyone concerned with Indonesia's future since the beginning of the revolution. The visions of Indonesia's ancient, traditional arts, distinctly identifiable in content and form as Indonesian, were haunting. Why couldn't a modern art be evolved that would also be distinctly Indonesian?

Even Takdir Alisjahbana eventually responded to this longing. No longer the young, intrepid challenger of his compatriots, especially the traditionalists, he felt free in 1960 to recognize openly that Indonesia's cultural character should be preserved. He wrote:

> Indonesia's traditional artistic skills, her sense of form and colour, and her unique cast of thought can all be used to give life to the abstract ideals and values of the new era, though these uses may well be very different from and even in conflict with the values and ideals of the past. . . .
>
> The core of the problem is to shift our cultural patrimony and pick out those elements which can be fully in-

tegrated into a new modern culture, which will itself produce new values, new attitudes to life, new perspectives, and new ways of thinking and acting. From another angle one could describe the processes as smuggling new concepts and ideals into those old "forms" that are still relevant to the modern age: or more simply still, we must reinterpret our traditional heritage.

And specifically about art, he says:

In the field of art, the range of experiment is enormous. There are so many skills, styles, and materials inherited from the older culture which can be turned to successful use in the new. I am thinking in particular of the craftsmanship of the Balinese sculptors and carvers, the dances of Bali and Java, the vivid colour sense of the Toradja, the art of batik, the wayang puppets, etc. If these traditional arts and crafts can be taught in the schools alongside the scientific knowledge, and the values and mental categories developed by modern culture, there is every reason to hope that the two cultural elements will produce in the talented and gifted student a synthesis of the artistic trends of our times flavoured with something peculiarly Indonesian.[14]

This view seems fairly close to the official government policy and even exceeds it by suggesting that traditional arts be taught in the schools. Alisjahbana was still thinking in wide international perspective but crystallizing his attitudes in favor of unity *and* diversity in the world. The views of ultranationalists, in contrast, were turned inward.

After the attainment of independence, the extreme nationalists clung for guidance to the political philosophy of the state. For them it was no longer a matter of "East" and "West." Instead of discussing the culture of the East they now focused narrowly on "Indonesianism." They used President Sukarno's Five Principles of the State, the Pantjasila, and later his other formulations, as the guidelines for cultural discourse. During a cultural congress in 1951, Mr.* M. Nasroen asserted that "Indonesianism" is urgently needed in art as well as in art criticism: "All art criticism, subjective as it may be, must be based nevertheless on nationalism and Indonesianism." It was the duty of the government, Nasroen held, to promote this "nationalism in art."[15]

Yet nobody can clearly state what national modern art is or ought to be. What are the criteria? Is it subject? Decidedly not. For didn't or do not some painters, foreign as well as Indonesian, paint local scenes and types with an utterly "un-Indonesian" effect? Such paintings, though ethnographically correct, might have that sentimental flavor against which the Persagi group revolted. Furthermore, there are, for example, the works of some Chinese artists resident in Indonesia who paint local themes. But in their works there is a distinctly Chinese flavor—in the composition, lines, and colors. A scene of Bali by the renowned Lee Man Fong seems enveloped in sandy dust instead of lush tropical greenery. Are the colors a criterion? Perhaps. Didn't Sudjojono say "these are *our* colors" though he didn't specify which? Indeed, there are outspoken predilections for certain colors among Indonesians. Many will agree that they are magenta pinks, purples, aquamarines, and orange-yellows, apart from those colors traditionally preferred in regional costumes.

There seems to be another, less tangible ingredient. When the painter Salim, who lives and works in Paris and is for all purposes a Parisian artist, came to Indonesia in 1956 for a visit, he exclaimed reproachfully, "There is not a drop of Indonesian emotion in your work!" He was addressing young painters of the Bandung school. And the question came up—what is this specifically Indonesian emotion?

Sukarno's reaction, "This is not Indonesian enough," or uprooted Salim's yearning for "Indonesian emotion" in art is very understandable. They long for an art that couldn't happen elsewhere but in Indonesia; an art permeated by that elusive component that would make viewing it a homecoming, give them a feeling of "yes, this is mine," which would strike a chord of deep recognition and yet be more—a revelation.

The problem of style in the arts is intimately linked with the quest for a national cultural identity; the controversies about the direction which art in Indonesia should take become clearer in the light of the general cultural debate. The exhilaration fired by the sense of national cohesion which the revolution had produced seemed to promise, perhaps to include, a self-understood Indonesian national image. Indonesian society in the post-revolutionary period, however, gradually entered a sort of vacuum where it could only cling to the same, but now ebbing, *élan* of revolutionary nationalism. But the focus around which revolutionary cohesion and ardor had once formed—the enemy—had disappeared. Freedom notwithstanding, there were no new positive values sufficiently crystallized to nourish or support the individual more than the generalized and vague principles of the Pantja Sila (see p. 202 above). President Sukarno probably diagnosed and

* Mr. is not Mister but the Dutch title *Meester* held by attorneys-at-law.

voiced the greatest need of young Indonesians in this acute stage of transition from an old to a new order, when in 1959 he elevated the concept of *kepribadian nasional* (national personality or identity) as the central principle for the state's policies (see below, p. 248). The assertion of the Indonesian state's identity has probably been the mainspring of the President's international policies. Internally, the whole cultural debate, including the problems besetting the field of modern art, revolved around this point.

Many artists, however, pursued their own ways without consideration of the ideological or philosophical premises discussed by their intellectual compatriots; some others tried to work in consonance with the convictions they had espoused. The principal centers where modern art was evolving were the cities in Java, pre-eminently Djakarta, Bandung, and Jogjakarta.

Jogjakarta

The city of Jogjakarta, or Jogja for short, is permeated with a sense of national pride. Its people feel that they are heirs to a glorious past whose traditions are still alive in their midst, that they were heroic participants in the Indonesian Revolution and that they are actively building the future.

Historically, Jogja is a palace-city and lively trading center, the capital of the domain or "Special Region" of the sultans of Jogjakarta. Its present autonomous ruler is H. H. Hamengkubuwana IX. Under his predecessors, Jogja was famed, as it still is, for the cultivation of traditional arts and crafts. During the war for independence, Jogja was the refuge and temporary capital of the embattled Republic from which its leaders directed resistance to the Dutch. Nationalist fervor was not confined to the Republican leaders, Sukarno and Hatta, and their followers; the Sultan also espoused the nationalist cause and thus a feudal prince and socialist-oriented revolutionaries were united in a common struggle. Guerrilla fighting, propaganda, and scorched-earth tactics were the Republicans' means; disdain and defiance of the Dutch were the princely ways.* In the person of the Sultan, his subjects see not only a traditional, hereditary lord of the domain, but also a modern statesman who participates in national affairs. In his own "Special Region" he is concerned with efficient administration, the spread of education, development of industry, and the cultivation of the arts.

The first university created by the Republic was in Jogjakarta, the University of Gadjah Mada, which opened in 1946. Young people soon flocked there from all parts of Indonesia, and Jogja became a city of students. Lacking other quarters, the university, at the invitation of the Sultan, was housed mainly within the palace walls until, in 1958, it moved into buildings of its own. Another institution of higher education of which Jogjakarta is proud is the academy of fine arts, ASRI. The University and the Academy were lacking in trained staff and equipment compared to the University in Djakarta and the art school in Bandung, inherited from the Dutch. But in the eyes of Indonesians, the Jogja institutions had the supreme virtue of being their own. The tenfold multiplication of secondary schools[16] added enormously to the influx of youth.

The pace of "cultural life" in the narrower sense, that is, activities devoted to the arts, had reached an amazing intensity in 1955. In a city of roughly 270,000 inhabitants and some 8,000 university students, 74 art organizations were listed officially. Of these, 14 were of a general nature and with mixed interests, including associations formed by students of common ethnic origin for the practice and display of their particular regional arts. Dance and music had 17 and 16 associations respectively, and 12 groups were devoted to drama, from shadow play to modern stage and film productions. Apart from these, the university students had their own literary and dramatic clubs. As for the plastic arts, there were 7 associations, some with an extended membership and prominent leaders. It was estimated that in the mid-fifties about two-thirds if not three-quarters of Java's painters lived in Jogjakarta. With its art academy, its painters' associations, the presence in Jogja of the government's Art Division of the Cultural Office, and of several luminaries of the Indonesian modern art world, Jogjakarta was the Mecca for many aspiring young artists, who came from different regions, and an attractive place for established artists to live and work in a stimulating and congenial atmosphere. The

* A story circulating about the Sultan of Jogjakarta is that, when the Dutch occupied Jogjakarta in December, 1948, the Sultan locked himself up in his keraton and refused to negotiate with them. When, finally, he did consent to meet with their delegation, he emerged on top of the palace wall, for all the people to see and hear, and literally talked down to the delegates who stood at the appointed spot on the ground below.

intense activity of the painters was not an isolated phenomenon. Around them and sometimes interacting with them were the groups of young actors, playwrights, poets, and dancers. The folk theater with the help of the young artists developed a new vitality. The wayang world, with its highly stylized forms, however, remained a world apart. The modern artists turned away from it even though quite a few of them had started their careers by drawing and coloring shadow-play puppets in their childhood.

If you asked knowledgeable Indonesians in 1955–1957 to name the country's leading painters, they invariably mentioned first among five or six names those of Sudjojono, Affandi, and Hendra.* During these years, all three were living in Jogjakarta. Sudjojono headed the Young Artists of Indonesia, SIM, and Hendra was the leader of the People's Painters, the Pelukis Rakjat. Affandi, an old friend of Hendra, though affiliated with the People's Painters, was first and foremost Affandi—a solitary phenomenon, a dynamic painter concerned mainly with his own art.

Some highlights of Sudjojono's views and activities have been mentioned in the preceding chapter. He was rightfully considered the founder of the Indonesian modern art movement and his reputation rested on the recognition of this role rather than on his work in the years after Indonesia's attainment of independence. Sudjojono was a man torn between art and politics. He had had a good education under the Netherlands Indies regime and was well-read in European philosophy and literature. After the war, he espoused communism as the ideal system for achieving social justice. He believed that artists should be politically conscious and cited Picasso and Diego de Rivera as good examples. Art, he held, should be dedicated to the social and political struggle. He felt that he must participate in politics even if it prevented him from devoting his time to painting, hoping that his art would meanwhile mature and gain depth.

A lithe, vivacious, and eloquent man, Sudjojono, 43 years old in 1956, was grappling as an artist with a compulsion to "paint out," in every detail, what he saw. When I first met him, he was perched on an elevated bamboo platform installed in a rice field behind the house of the painter Trubus. Trubus, a teacher at the ASRI academy, lived on the slope of one of the foothills around the volcano Merapi. He had a magnificent view of the "fire-mountain" whose different moods he constantly painted. Sudjojono had come to paint the Merapi, too, on commission from President Sukarno. As he clambered down from his platform, he complained of feeling obliged to paint meticulously each leaf of the tobacco plants in the foreground. Evidently the conversion from his earlier free approach to near photographic naturalism somehow bothered him. At home, he had batches of excellent ink sketches which showed not only his skill but also that the freshness of his perception had not vanished. A number of these had been made during his extended trip in 1951 with an Indonesian art delegation to East Berlin, Rumania, the Soviet Union, and across Siberia to China. A short poem or an aphorism was inscribed on some of the sketches. While Sudjojono freely acknowledged his personal preferences for such unfettered masters as Cézanne and Van Gogh, he dogmatically forced himself to espouse social realism.* Yet Sudjojono had a keen appreciation of Java's ancient art. The writer Sitor Situmorang said about him: "He opened my eyes to the beauty of Prambanan."

Founded in Madiun in 1946, the art association which Sudojono headed was one of the oldest artists' organizations to which, at one time or another, most of Indonesia's prominent painters belonged, including Hendra, who left SIM in 1947 to form the People's Painters. In the mid-fifties, however, SIM had few artists of distinction with the exception of Sudjojono himself, its secretary and teacher Harijadi, and Suromo, one of ASRI's best teachers. At SIM's studio, political discussions if not indoctrination were probably as important as exercise in art.

Harijadi, a gifted and sensitive person, embittered by poverty but addicted to motorcycle racing, lived nearby in a modest house. The house was full of children, six or seven of them. His wife, in addition to caring for the family, tried to contribute to their livelihood through commercial efforts of her own. All the walls were covered with paintings, large and small, and many others were stacked on the floor.

One of Harijadi's paintings, in the collection of President Sukarno, perhaps reflects best this artist's feelings in the fifties about himself and his society. It was painted in 1953 and is entitled "Gathering Clouds

* Other names most frequently mentioned in various combinations were Ngantung, Kartono, Rusli, Basuki Resobowo, and sometimes, Wakidi.

* Since this was written, Sudjojono has been expelled from the Indonesian Communist Party because the party disapproved of his second marriage.

Plate 163. *"Gathering Clouds and Parting Roads," by Harijadi, 1953.*

and Crossing Roads." It seems to be asking "where to?" —a question similar to that which underlay the cultural debate and yet in a very different mood. The gathering darkness above is heavy with menace; beneath it, small forlorn figures peer into the clouds as if hoping for light; one has turned away; one, in the middle, reflecting perhaps the artist's state of mind, seems to be asking, "What am I to think and do?" Perplexity is the dominant mood (Pl. 163), but also the separateness of human beings, groping in their insecurity. Harijadi eventually left, or was expelled from, SIM, reportedly because of a disagreement concerned with fees earned for a commissioned work which he had refused to share with the association.

Hendra, unlike Sudjojono, was not dogmatic or given to cerebrations. The difference between these two men was perhaps best illustrated by the story of their separation in 1947, a split in SIM that resulted in the establishment of the Pelukis Rakjat. It was said that this split was caused by a disagreement between Sudjojono and Hendra on the manner of distributing the association's monthly governmental subsidy. Sudjojono apparently insisted on allocating it to SIM's members according to merit. He proposed to divide them into four classes—A, B, C, and D—depending on their achievements and standing as artists, a procedure reminiscent of the official classification of artists in the Soviet Union. Hendra's position was that the only valid distinction was whether a member had a family or not. If married, Hendra claimed, an artist was entitled to 200 rupiah a month, and if single, only to 100, regardless of their respective merits as artists. In general, however, Hendra's ideology was close to Sudjojono's; he and his group agreed that art must be dedicated to the people; be inspired by them and also be understandable to them. Nevertheless, in the mid-fifties at least, few of them were willing to paint in the social realist style prescribed by the Communists who courted them and with whom they cooperated.

The People's Painters were at that time the most active and numerous group in Jogjakarta and included several highly respected artists among its members. The organization's slogan was "Art for the People" and its philosophy encouraged communal living and cooperative work. The People's Painters arranged periodic shows in the capital and in other towns, which were usually very well attended, and received commissions from different organizations. Until 1957, under Hendra's leadership* the group as a whole was very productive. It therefore attracted many young aspiring artists from different parts of the country, more in fact, than their community could absorb. The applicants were young people who did not wish to enter the academy, or could not afford to, or could not meet its requirements. By joining the Pelukis Rakjat, a young man also acquired a home; he could live and work together with other members in the association's communal establishment, their *asrama,* on the outskirts of Jogjakarta.

The asrama consisted of a large main house and several smaller structures nearby. In the main house, Hendra, his wife, and little son occupied one of the bedrooms which also served as his private studio. A spacious, high-ceilinged front room served as the community's gathering place, lounge, and art gallery. At a large round table in the hall consultations were held and projects were discussed. Whenever possible, the Pelukis Rakjat acted as a body; commissions for a sculptured panel, a mural, or a monument such as the Tugu Muda in Semarang, were usually executed cooperatively by several members of the group. It was in their paintings that they asserted their individuality.

Many a visitor, always cordially received, has spent time in the hall of the Pelukis Rakjat where he might have found Hendra at work on some project, looked at the latest paintings displayed on the walls, and chatted with some of the artists drifting in and out. They worked hard, especially in preparation for a large exhibition or when a commission came their way. Evidence of their activities was everywhere, in the hall, in their rooms, and outside in the courtyard strewn with more or less successful attempts at sculpture in stone and cement. Because sculpture, apart from decorative wood carving, had become an almost forgotten art in Java, Hendra tried to revive it. To initiate his students into the techniques of chisel and mallet, Hendra sought out a stonecutter whom he found among the makers of Islamic tombstones.

To sketch and paint, the Pelukis Rakjat artists often went out singly or in small groups and installed themselves either in the fields, at some river bank, in town on a street corner or at the market place. Sometimes they trekked to distant beaches or mountainous regions to paint landscapes. If they used models, it was mainly for portraits. Studies of the nude were not in evidence. Sketching nudes is a problem in the Indonesian art world wherever the puritanical spirit of Islam makes such a practice reprehensible, and this certainly is the case in Java and in Sumatra.

The sale of paintings was effected mainly at exhibitions, especially those held in the capital. Among special patrons of the People's Painters at the time were an art-loving colonel of the Military Police Corps, a Djakarta business man and collector, some trade unions which requested their services, and some foreign residents who bought their paintings. President Sukarno was favorably inclined toward them and from time to time purchased paintings by Hendra and other members of the association for his private collection or for that of the state. The Communist-sponsored People's Cultural Institute, Lekra, lent them promotional support. A number of Pelukis Rakjat members have been selected for travel abroad with cultural missions to the USSR, the East European countries, and the People's Republic of China.

* He was succeeded by the painter Sudarso.

When a painting was sold, a certain percentage of the price was retained for the benefit of the communal household. In certain cases, however, Hendra imposed restrictions. For example, he would not permit the sale of a small painting of a peasant's courtyard with resting cattle (Pl. 164), which was the work of Tarmizi, the youngest member of the group, a deaf Minangkabau boy in his late teens. The painting, of rare delicacy, had a special, luminous serenity. It was the best painting that Tarmizi had produced so far, Hendra explained, and it could not be sold until the boy had produced a better one. The same principle applied to everyone, he said. So long as a successful work had not been superseded by a better one, it had to remain hanging on the wall of the community house. A portrait of a seated girl in pink, by Trubus, also awaited a worthy successor (see Pl. 182 below).

I first met Hendra in October, 1955, in Djakarta where 21 participating members of the Pelukis Rakjat opened one of their periodic exhibitions. Of the 44 works shown, there were only two by Hendra himself. He talked about his paintings mainly in terms of their meaning. In one painting, "The Fair," Hendra expressed the tenderness of a young mother for her children. With colorful toys in their hands, they sit gazing at the fair in the deep blue distance, its lights and bustle (Pl. 165).

Affection and tenderness, toward and between women and children especially, was a major theme in Hendra's life as well as his art. One had only to see him take his little son into his arms to feel the gentleness and warmth flowing into the child from his whole being. He himself was reared without a mother or other loving feminine care. In his paintings, he dwells in the world of women. A wistful quality often emerges from his characteristic elongation of the forward-tending neckline coupled with receding contours of chin and forehead. Another characteristic feature is Hendra's

Plate 164. *"Cows," by Tarmizi, 1955.*

tendency to paint women's and children's hair in loose wisps or disheveled and flowing. While the colors of "The Fair" are deep and strong, many of Hendra's other paintings of women place them in a world of delicate aquamarines.

Hendra claimed that compassion for the poor and downtrodden motivated his art. In his youth, when he became homeless after a violent quarrel with his dissolute father, he wandered through villages where it was the poorest who fed and sheltered him. Later, as a comedian, he entertained simple folk in the Sunda lands of West Java. This undoubtedly strengthened his lasting fondness for the colorful popular stage.

"The People" meant to Hendra the burdened women who carry heavy loads tied to their bent backs, vendors at the roadside and their customers, women and children. The burdened women plodding along Central Java's roads to and from markets had become the ubiquitous symbol of poverty and degradation in many of the Pelukis Rakjat paintings. Hendra's huge unfinished "The Poultry Vendors" (Pl. 166) is perhaps the most expressive example of this theme. The large, clumsy feet of the poultry vendors, along the central axis of the canvas and set off against a light background, are the heroes of the painting. The cackling ducks and chickens form a dense, oppressive cloud above the women's forward-straining heads. The paint is especially thick in this upper part of the canvas, adding to the effect of weight. The colors are opaque; the lines and shapes, crude. One of the marching women stuffs a betel quid into her mouth, so like a beast of burden snatching at a leaf. The moving grotesqueness of the procession is strengthened by its juxtaposition with the relaxed group of women gathered around a large tray of food, and by the casual glance of one of them toward the passing vendors and their noisy burdens. Hendra's credo of art for the people, or more correctly, *about* the people, was emotionally motivated and not compulsive dogma; it was not "painted out" with the meticulous, near-photographic precision adopted by the former leader of SIM.

Hendra moved in several stylistic directions simultaneously. The style of "The Poultry Vendors" offers strong contrast to the translucent colors and fine calligraphy of such paintings as "Delousing" (Pl. 167). The tightly knit group in tilted space, of two women and a child with a puppet, is a poetic statement of a prosaic subject—the friendly service of picking lice out of a companion's hair. Black hair, in masses, wisps, long flowing strands and a curly shock, dominates the composition and stands out against the delicate aquamarines like a unifying landscape. There is languor in the soft faces and long delicate fingers of the women, and poetry in their light-hued, gaily flowered garments. The child's sullen face, surmounted by tousled hair, and her grinning, grotesque puppet clown with his mischievous eye provide whimsical notes to the lyricism of the composition. Still other Hendra paintings have flat opaque surfaces and massive, clearly defined shapes evoking reminiscences of Gauguin.

There were still other sides to Hendra: on the one hand, a love for the microcosms in nature, small colorful flowers, a little world of goldfish which he lovingly cultivated; and on the other, a predilection for large size, heroic works. He preferred large canvasses whenever he could afford to procure them and indeed painted some huge ones. They were not, however, among his best works, perhaps because he had to spread them on the floor of his cramped bedroom and crawl around to paint them.

Addiction to size often led the Pelukis Rakjat under his leadership to set up incongruously large and clumsy works in unsuitable surroundings. For example, they carved a gray cement relief, 8 by 12 feet, depicting five sturdy workers for a miniscule lobby of the Public Workers' Union (SEBDA) building at Madiun. They also produced gigantic portraits in relief for the Djakarta Museum of the Military Police Corps housed in an old, graceful colonial mansion. Along the back wall of its central exhibition hall a "portrait" head of Gadjah Mada,* 8 feet high, is flanked on either side by two 6-foot high reliefs of military police corps colonels. Another memento of Pelukis Rakjat endeavors in monumentality was Rustamadji's stone bust of the Sultan of Jogjakarta, which was over 4 feet high. It stood forlorn and neglected on the ground in the lane leading to the People's Painters asrama. Evidently, neither the subject of the portrait nor any one else was interested in allocating to it a more dignified place.

When I once touched upon this "affliction by gigantism," as I called it, Hendra retorted, "This is to protest against all those puny buildings, the lack of space, the lack of boldness in building and thinking."

In 1956, Hendra was deeply involved in designing a second version of the National Monument his first plan having failed in the competition. His ground plan,

* Gadjah Mada is the famous Prime Minister and empire-builder of fourteenth-century Java.

Plate 165. "Sekaten " (*The Fair*), *by Hendra Gunawan, 1955.*

cross-sections, and clay model showed a tall, heavy, conical pillar tapering to a spire and decorated with ornate flaming motifs. It rose from the middle of a huge platform shaped like the spread-eagle outline of the Garuda bird. Recessed from the edges of this high platform were buildings whose shape followed the curving outlines of wings and tail. Ornamentation of the balustrades, porticoes, and stairwings echoed that of the Hindu-Javanese tjandi, but instead of makaras at the end of the banisters, there were elegant snails—symbols of poverty according to Hendra. The effect of the whole was somewhat like a combination of nineteenth-century Grand Opera, Sans Souci, Hindu-Javanese architectural elements, and Soviet Russian heroic sculptures. The statues represented revolutionary heroes, the People on the March, including sailors and soldiers with fixed bayonets. The days and nights spent by Hendra on this project, which impaired his health and drained his resources, remained, however, unrewarded by success.

When, in earlier years, Hendra carved in cement a statue of Indonesia's revolutionary hero, General Sudirman, it was neither oversize nor overtly heroic. On the contrary, the pathetic character of the statue erected in front of the People's Council Building in Jogjakarta implies in itself heroism. A man with an emaciated face, wearing a Javanese turban and a long, heavy overcoat stands gazing ahead into space. One hand clutches the edge of his coat as if to protect him from a cold wind, the other rests on a cane. This is the way the much admired and very ill Sudirman looked leading the revolutionary army before he succumbed to tuberculosis in 1948.

Of the younger painters who participated in the 1955 Pelukis Rakjat exhibition in Djakarta, Batara Lubis, Djoni Trisno, Alibasjah, and Tarmizi drew one's attention. Alibasjah, an art teacher, was represented by a few well-composed and expressive landscapes. Djoni Trisno, an actor as well as a painter, showed a portrait of a sturdy girl, "Red Blouse," with the symbolic figure of a burdened woman and an oxcart in the background. In a skillful self-portrait, the handsome and easy-going Trisno depicted himself looking like a sorrowful apostle. Behind his head, extended a dreamlike background —an empty iron bench on a deserted road and a house behind a tortured, leafless tree, reminiscent of surrealist

Plate 166. *"Poultry Vendors," by Hendra Gunawan, 1956 (unfinished).*

painting. Trisno's versatility is reflected in one of his pastels (Pl. 168) which shows the abandoned gaicty of slum dwellers at a dance party, "Dogèr." The people's amusements had also served as theme for a charming painting by ASRI's and SIM's Suromo. In his "Ketoprak" the illuminated stage of the popular open-air theater is surrounded by the deep, still night (Pl. 169). In the shadows below the stage the public is assembling. Before the curving wall with signs announcing the play, "The Golden Mask," people are lined up to purchase tickets. The ubiquitous vendors of snacks are gathered at the gate. This bright little world is depicted with sophisticated naiveté; the encircling lighted outlines of the wall, of the theater roof with the monstrous kala-head on its gable, and of the musicians' shed, lend the composition a gentle and yet unequivocal unity.

Batara Lubis, who had given up studying at ASRI, had a distinct style of his own, though he had borrowed certain mannerisms from Hendra. His patterned paintings were characterized by dark, heavy outlines and strong if not brash colors. In some paintings steel-gray tones created a dusky atmosphere which was strangely outspoken. He liked to light up his paintings

Plate 167. *"Delousing," by Hendra Gunawan, 1954.*

Plate 168. "Dogèr," *by Djoni Trisno, 1956.*

with bright decorative elements. Lubis came to Jogja from Sumatra and one wondered whether his style was influenced by his native environment. Indeed, this thought appeared justified when I saw his native village in Sumatra (Huta Godang in South Tapanuli) where his father, the Radja Djundjungan, had been the titular lord of the village and head of the clan (*marga*).* In Huta Godang, old and venerated *adat* buildings were still intact: the ceremonial house, repository of sacred heirlooms and symbol of age-old customs; the chief's house, occupied by aged relatives; and a pavilion on high, heavy posts, blackened by age, where the ceremonial drums were beaten. These structures had high roofs covered with a thick layer of dark fiber that stood out amid the greenery in heavy towering masses. The plaza in front of the chief's house was dry and stony. Despite the scorching sun, the setting was harsh and dark. Lubis, himself an expert drummer, arranged for the old drums to be brought out. They were suspended from the railing of the pavilion, hanging nine in a row outside under the heavy eaves of the roof, while, standing inside, several men including Batara, belabored them with sticks. The drummed pieces had names which reflected their powerful, dark, and sometimes furious rhythms: "Rolling Boulders," "Thundering Storm." The dark, rapid, intertwining and syncopated beats unrolled into frenzy, hands and hair of the drummers flying. The rolling boulders be-

* By 1955, he had become the regent (*bupati*) of South Tapanuli and lived in the port town, Sibolga.

Plate 169. "Ketoprak," *by Suromo, 1950.*

came an avalanche, the drums thundered until the beats set one's blood pulsing in response and fire filled one's eyes.

A carved, wooden bracket which once adorned the post at the foot of the pavilion's staircase was kept among the relics in the ceremonial house. It represented a "child- and woman-eating" monster which Batara Lubis lovingly copied on paper. Here, unmistakably, were the sources for the winding designs that characterized many of the painter's decorative vignettes. He painted differently in Sumatra than in Central Java—with simpler shapes and harsher colors. In Jogjakarta, in the Pelukis Rakjat asrama, he was in very different surroundings, in a softer land, among people with different customs, clothing, mentality. In the asrama, he was "Batara Lubis." In Huta Godang, he was "Sutan," the title given the chief's son. In the asrama, he was a member of collective organization with many social obligations and little privacy. At home, he was a prominent member of his clan, with little privacy and many social obligations, of a different sort but equally taxing. It was a strange parallelism of demands upon an individual in two social units belonging to entirely different worlds—the traditional organization of a Batak clan and a modern collective or communal art organization. Placed between these two worlds, Batara Lubis espoused no particular social philosophy and did not strain, as a few of his colleagues did, to depict social reality. His main preoccupation remained the interplay of color effects aided by his facile decorative patterning.

Compared with the enterprising People's Painters and the heavily politicized SIM, Jogjakarta's other two art associations of the day appeared less dynamic. They were organized later and none of their leaders enjoyed a reputation approaching that of Sudjojono or Hendra.

The PI (*Pelukis Indonesia*) or Indonesian Painters, was founded in 1950, and PIM (*Pelukis Indonesia Muda*) or Young Indonesian Painters, in 1952.

Kusnadi, one of the founders of PI and formerly a member of the People's Painters, headed the association in 1955. He was also head of the Plastic Arts Section of the government's Cultural Office. According to its leader, the PI was established to provide associative opportunities to artists who did not wish to participate in extreme left political activities as they would have to in SIM, or be involved in a politically "colored" organization like the People's Painters. In his official capacity, however, Kusnadi, while influential in many ways, maintained cordial relations with these two associations and sought their cooperation for government-sponsored projects, as for instance the big art exhibition held in conjunction with the Asian-African Conference in Bandung in 1955 or exhibitions sent with cultural missions abroad.

PI's relatively small membership included some other artists employed at the Cultural Office. One of them was Bagong Kussudiardjo, an outstanding dancer who devoted considerable time to painting. Bagong was no exception in possessing several talents and practicing more than one art. So, for example, a young student, Dating Boestami who came to Jogja to study law at Gadjah Mada University, was known at home in West Sumatra as the talented painter and poet Motinggo Boesje.

PI's activities were restricted to occasional exhibits. The association had no headquarters of its own. Kusnadi's office and home probably served as central gathering place. In contrast, PIM—the Young Indonesian Painters—started out by raising funds for a house which they built in the middle of rice fields on the border of the city. Its founders and most of its members were teachers and advanced students of ASRI. Widajat, a versatile painter and teacher in the Academy, was one of PIM's leading spirits, whereas the promotional and administrative cares were in the hands of Sajogo. PIM's spacious and bright hall provided excellent facilities for exhibitions, gatherings,

Plate 170. *"Oxcarts, Jogja," by Batara Lubis, 1956.*

and classes. After three years of struggling to establish itself, this association was ready to expand its activities. It was envisaged as an apolitical organization of ASRI alumni, but reportedly it disintegrated in the early sixties and was replaced in part by a new organization called *Sanggar Bambu* (Bamboo Studio).

As for ASRI itself, students were packed into its cramped quarters and could be found there at work at all times. ASRI's teachers, like Hendra, were busy re-

Plate 171. *"The Dispossessed in Twilight," by Amrus Natalsja, 1955.*

discovering sculpture. Models served mainly for portraiture in clay; the nude human body was not studied from life. Among the students of sculpture Amrus Natalsja was the most forceful and original. His home was in Sumatra and several of his earlier wood carvings were reminiscent of the magic staffs of the Batak magician-healers, the datu, on which, like totem poles, figures were carved one on top of another. Amrus had carved several upright or curving poles in this manner but his winding and entwined figures did not have the stark rigidity of the magic staffs. His later groups had a savage force. "The Dispossessed in Twilight," hewn out of a heavy trunk of an old tamarind tree, and finished in boldly chipped surfaces (Pls. 171, 172), conveys the pathos of human existence with a power rarely encountered in the works of other Indonesian artists. Here again, as in the case of Lubis, the artist's work seems to carry echoes of his homeland's imagery. A tempting juxtaposition with Amrus' group is the stone mother with two children by an anonymous Batak carver of an unknown period (see Pl. 19). Though charged with an impersonal force, the primitive Batak image does not, like "The Dispossessed in Twilight," project human pathos.

Among the other sculpture students was one, Arby Sama, who was moving in a very different direction. He was experimenting with semiabstract shapes which at that time was quite unusual at ASRI and for Jogja in general. Although he was neither encouraged nor guided in this direction, evidently there was no explicit disapproval of his compositions.*

In the painting classes the array of regular and visiting teachers offered the students a great diversity of approaches, relative skill and competence in instruction. Djajengasmoro, Suromo, Widajat, and Saptohudojo were among the regular teachers. They were joined by the sculptor Edie Sunarso when in the late fifties he returned from studies abroad. Among the visiting teachers were several members of the People's Painters including Trubus and Sudarso who devoted much time to ASRI, also Hendra and Affandi who visited the students less regularly. Apparently none of the teachers imposed on the students a distinct discipline or style of painting and many a student felt that he must seek his own way—*tjari sendiri*†—as they ex-

* I am told that during the sixties the trend at ASRI had changed from realism to semiabstract and even abstract forms in both sculpture and painting.

† Lit., "search for yourself."

Plate 172. *Detail of "The Dispossessed in Twilight."*

pressed it. Yet the critcisms of the teachers, especially of Affandi when he came, were highly prized.

Affandi, though he firmly and importantly belongs to the Jogja scene, has had much experience abroad and enjoys an international reputation. His art is addressed to the world at large.

A mild man with a bold brush, when asked into what school of painting he places himself, he replies: "I am told that I am an expressionist." Some Westerners associate his style with Van Gogh's; others liken him to Kokoshka, with whom, indeed, he has affinities. His earlier works were executed with much greater re-

Plate 173. *"My Mother," by Affandi, 1941.*

straint. The contrast between the fine portrait of his aged mother painted in 1941 (Pl. 173) and "Mother Sleeping," painted in 1960 (Pl. 174), dramatically illustrates the evolution of Affandi's style. During these twenty years his vivid brush had given way to the palette knife and then to the tube out of which he squeezes winding strings of pure color directly onto the canvas. Sometimes these thick strings of paint are flattened with the tube's nozzle or a finger. The background and larger areas of color are rubbed in with the palm, sometimes spread so thin as to resemble a brushed wash. Many of his recent paintings have to be viewed from a great distance. Affandi himself is very farsighted and it is astounding that he can judge while painting the projected effect. Thus, only from a considerable distance can one discern the shapes of his typically stormy painting of beached outrigger boats in Bali. Here the fish-shaped bows appear as flaming, toothed, monsters like crocodiles under the agitated masses of deep blue which form the shoreline and mountainous shapes in the background. The reds in the teeth of the open jaws on the left, surmounted by a fiery branching mast, create a veritable conflagration.

In 1956, Affandi lived in Kota Gdé, an old town near Jogja, renowned for its ancient and holy cemetery of former rulers visited by pilgrims, and for its silversmiths. His daughter Kartika, married to the academician Saptohudojo, followed in the footsteps of her father as a painter. One of Affandi's startling and moving paintings was produced when his first grandchild was born. It shows a stark naked, somewhat pot-bellied Affandi with a baby in his arms under a deep blue starry sky. Affandi explains that, holding the newborn child, he suddenly felt himself as naked and as helpless in the vast universe.

Through the years Affandi produced many self-portraits in different media—ink, oil, clay (see Pl. 193). Several of these are whimsical. In his self-portraits one can find Affandi crouching, scowling, sulky or just being himself; while in the United States he humorously depicted himself in a bright red costume against a snowy landscape. He says that often, when he is frustrated by a painting he is working on, he ends up by filling the canvas with a portrait of himself.

After twenty years of painting, Affandi's style shows a growing boldness and daring in the choice of colors and the application of paint. Basically, however, his art has consistently retained the same character of strong linear movement and expressive tension. This may be the reason why among his colleagues there is the feeling that "Affandi will always remain the same." His art is not unanimously acclaimed in his homeland,

Plate 174. *"Mother Sleeping," by Affandi, 1960.*

Plate 175. *"Balinese Fishing Boats," by Affandi, 1961.*

though his reputation is. President Sukarno freely admits that he does not appreciate Affandi's art, but the effect of his direct and dynamic style is felt to be liberating by a number of artists. The late Chairil Anwar, Indonesia's celebrated poet, declared in a poem entitled "To Affandi, the Painter":

> One day when I have lost the gift of words,
> When I have lost the courage to enter my own home,
> When terrored on the threshold I stand irresolute
> Because of the decay, the instability
> To which all things are born—
> (For I know, I know—Death must come to all—
> My hands must stiffen before the work is done;
> Without soul, without hope I must suffer. I have seen it in the dream)—
> Then, give me a little room
> In the high tower where you have gone before.
> Where you have turned away
> From the world's noise and show—so glorious from outside,
> So false in form. There where you will be praying
> Give me a little room
> Till the encircling darkness has vanished and the gloom.[17]

Affandi's "bamboo house" and studio are now a landmark in Jogjakarta and attract visitors from near and far. In consonance with his international orientation and sound commercial sense, Affandi in the early sixties inaugurated in Jogjakarta an International Association of Plastic Arts known as I.A.P.A. of which he was himself the chairman, the painter Rusli vice-chairman, and Sukarno Hadian secretary.

Rusli, too, is a distinctive figure on the Indonesian art scene. His art, contrasted with Affandi's, is of exquisite delicacy. He had spent several years at Rabindranath Tagore's educational center, Santineketan, finding there, unlike Affandi, an atmosphere very congenial to his own spirit. Rusli's watercolors are poetically suggestive. His calligraphy reflects on the one hand affinities with the art of Dufy, and on the other with Chinese traditions. Often the red imprint of his thumb becomes an integral part of his composition (Pls. 176, 177). In 1955–1957 Rusli was not settled in Jogjakarta but visited there periodically.

There were in Jogjakarta a number of other promising painters—too numerous to be discussed here. To mention only a few names, such painters as Nasjah, Handrijo, and Suromo (see Pl. 169) commanded attention in their own ways.

In sum, Jogjakarta's modern art community in the mid-fifties was composed of a wide range of personalities who worked in a great variety of styles. The paintings produced there, despite the lack of discipline and of technical accomplishment, had a freshness born of enthusiasm combined in some cases with helplessness. Even the opponents of "Jogja"—a term which came to stand for its agglomeration of painters, especially the People's Painters—always acknowledged this freshness. And despite the contrasting styles and underlying ideologies or absence of them, the dominant feeling among the majority of Jogja's painters was that their art was "national," indigenous, genuine, Indonesian. This belief had little to do with the pursuit of—let alone achievement of—a certain style in painting that could be identified as being distinctly Indonesian. It stemmed mainly from the painters' emotional or dogmatic identification with the land and its people. By painting Java's mountains, rice fields, markets, oxcarts, village courtyards, or the people's toils and amusements, by painting portraits of others and themselves, they were national inasmuch as their art was devoted to Indonesian life, and inasmuch as they did not consciously imitate contemporary Western art but "tjari sendiri," searched for themselves. The formal aspects were a matter for each individual to resolve. And here, as the students of the Bandung art school pointed out, "Jogja" had nevertheless wittingly or unwittingly adopted Western conceptions of painting, starting with natural-

Plate 176. *"Semarang Harbor," by Rusli, 1956.*

ism and stopping short with the postimpressionists. With a few rare exceptions, there was no experimentation with abstract or nonobjective art in the fifties. Hendra, scanning an illustrated catalogue of a large exhibition held in New York in 1955, kept repeating "*gila, gila, gila*"—"this is mad, mad, mad. . . ." And a young art teacher, fresh from several years in Italy, said: "You see, we are still very close to nature."

In discussing the "Jogja" artists as artists, we have introduced some of their personal traits, their ideals, and social behavior. This kind of study flowed naturally from the artists' own views of themselves; they do not separate their artists' consciousness from their social conscience—a conscience which binds some of them to doctrinaire ideologies and politics, others to vague and emotional nationalism or "Indonesianism." They would never say, "The picture is the thing," but would insist that it has a social significance. The majority of Jogja's artists were or were trying to be, in this sense, moral men. Sudjojono was destroyed as an artist by his commitment to communism, his particular kind of morality. Affandi, in contrast, consistently pursued his art with complete concentration on the expressiveness of his work, without regard to any social ideology that could affect his choice of subject or style. In fact, he has that nonmoralistic attitude which belongs to all artists intent only on perfecting their creation. The "Indonesianism" of Jogja's painters, whose orientation lay between these two extremes, was not only focusing on their land and its folk but also a dedication to them. Implicitly it, too, was colored by a cherished sense of morality.

This was the situation in the middle fifties. It would seem that in the succeeding years, with the emergence of some new leaders, the art associations, though changed in name and composition, were still divided into politically (Communist) oriented and apolitical organizations. Thus in the place of the defunct PIM, there was the *Sanggar Bambu* composed of graduates and senior students of ASRI; and, displacing the old SIM, a younger set led by the sculptor Amrus Natalsja, created the *Bumi Tarung* ("Fighting Grounds," or perhaps "Arena"), supported by the Communist art institute, Lekra. In ASRI itself, however, the former absence of a central philosophy, despite the continuing multiplicity of direction by staff and students, apparently had been filled by the government's proclaimed stress on national identity.

Plate 177. *"Hut in the Valley," by Rusli, 1956.*

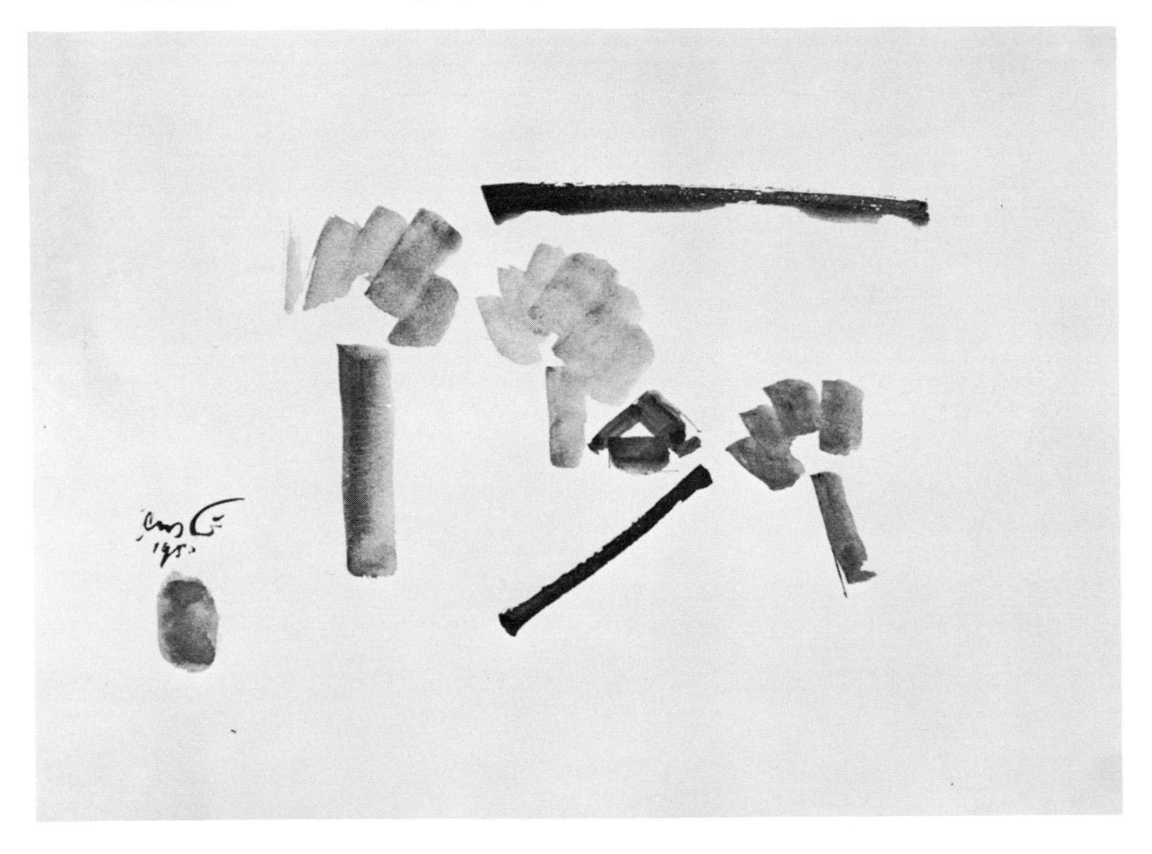

Plate 178. "Perahu *in Bali," by M. N. Mulder, 1950.*

Bandung

Bandung's history and its cultural climate strongly contrast with those of Jogjakarta. The capital of West Java, which had a population almost triple that of Jogja in the mid-fifties, had developed into a modern urban center largely through Dutch initiative. Its high altitude and pleasant, cool climate made it a highly desirable residential site and a resort where Europeans once could find new vigor after a prolonged stay in the hot and humid plains.

The population of the region in which Bandung is located is largely Sundanese. They have a dialect of their own and are generally considered more lighthearted than the Javanese of Central Java. The Sundanese themselves regard the Javanese as "ancient and tired people." Reinforcing this claimed difference in disposition, the Sundanese prefer batik skirts of light tints with large and free patterns, often floral, in contrast to the traditionally subdued, dark brown and dark blue tones of Central Java's batik garments with their smaller and more regular designs. (Since the revolution, however, gayer colors and freer patterns have appeared in Central Java, too.)

Among the Sundanese aristocracy, unlike that of Surakarta and Jogjakarta, there were no ruling princes during the colonial period. Its top-ranking members were the regents, but for all practical purposes, they were Netherlands Indies civil servants. Bandung's historical role during World War II and the Indonesian Revolution is associated mainly with the March, 1942, Dutch surrender to the Japanese,* and with the short-lived, Dutch-sponsored autonomous state of Negara Pasundan of which Bandung was the capital. Although there had been intense revolutionary activity in Bandung, no dramatic light was ever fixed upon it. Thus

* Surrender was formalized at Lembang, a hill resort near Bandung.

neither ancient palace traditions nor pride stemming from a recognized role in the revolution has animated the spirit of the city's inhabitants.

Dutch culture has left a strong imprint on Bandung's physical appearance and on the life of its upper-class Indonesian inhabitants. There are no enclaves of kampung-dwellers hiding behind the big, modern hotels, the office buildings, or on the wide avenues where content, whitewashed residences are set off by neat front gardens. No sidewalk vendors enliven the shopping section and one has to get away from the city's center to find a little coffee shop, or *warung*. Bamboo houses and huts are relegated to the city's outskirts.

As a center of learning and research under the Dutch administration, Bandung was oriented toward science and technology. Located there were the Department of Mines and Geological Survey, the Volcanological Service, the Pasteur Institute, and the Technical Institute where students could specialize in different branches of engineering. The presence of the postal and railroads administrative headquarters and the proximity of the military training center at Tjimahi contributed to Bandung's Western style.

Bandung's art school, too, was a legacy of the Dutch. It was begun as a training school for drawing teachers and not for creative artists but gradually its character changed. When taken over by the Indonesian government, several Dutch art teachers were retained. Among these, an important figure with a lasting influence, was M. N. Mulder. A painter with an academic training in Holland, Mulder (affectionately referred to by his students as Ries, his nickname), had studied and worked independently in Paris before coming to Indonesia in 1948. His own works unmistakably reflect the strong influence of Jacques Villon. He left Bandung in 1959, having trained a group of gifted students who regarded him as an excellent teacher and who, in turn, became teachers at the Bandung school themselves.

Plate 179. *"In the Waiting Room," by A. Sadali, 1953.*

The Bandung art school or "Seni Rupa," "Plastic Arts," as it is briefly referred to, was not surrounded by vigorous art associations. Besides the St. Lucas Guild, which had a considerable Dutch membership from 1948 until its dissolution in 1953, there were two associations founded by young Indonesian artists: *Jiva Mukti* (Free Spirit), organized in 1948 by Barli, Karnedi, and Sartono; and *Tjipta Pantjaran Rasa* (Creativity, Fountain of Feeling), or TPR, formed in 1953 by R. Walujo, Abedy, and Angkama Setjadipradja. Unlike the Jogja associations, whose leading members exercised an influence upon ASRI students either as visiting teachers or by sheer proximity, the Bandung organizations were overshadowed by "Seni Rupa." Its strong leadership in methodology and esthetics influenced the associations indirectly and also directly through teachers and students who had become association members. So, for instance, Mochtar Apin, then a student, was chairman of Jiva Mukti in 1951–1952, and the teacher Angkama Setjadipradja was one of the leading spirits of TPR.

Completely outside the school's sphere of influence, and independent of all other organizations, stood the *Sanggar Seniman* (Artist's Studio) of the late Kartono Yudhokusumo. On the Bandung art scene, Kartono was in a way the counterpart of Affandi in Jogja; he was equally independent and original, though his style was very different from Affandi's. With Kartono always set apart, the term "Bandung" was used in Indonesian art circles to denote principally the "Seni Rupa" school and more specifically the group of evolving painters around Mulder.

Compared with the improvised rugged and cramped quarters of ASRI, the Bandung school in the mid-fifties was strikingly modern and comfortable. The classrooms, the teachers' studios, and the office of the director, Mr. Sumardja, were spacious, bright, and equipped with handsome, functional furniture built locally after designs made by the architecture students. Compared with ASRI, Bandung's "Seni Rupa" had fewer students and also, proportionately, a much smaller faculty —80 students and 10 teachers in 1956. The teaching of art history was better developed in Bandung. Indian, Indonesian, Islamic, and European art history were taught. The only common point of the two schools was their weakness in the teaching of sculpture, and among the Bandung students no striking talent had

Plate 180. *"Self-Portrait," by But Muchtar, 1956.*

emerged to rival Amrus Natalsja. It was very different in painting.

The leading lights in painting among the senior students and the recent graduates who were working as instructors were Sadali, But Muchtar, Srihadi, Popo Iskandar, Subhakto, and Angkama Setjadipradja. Studying in Paris, after a period in Holland, was another talented Mulder student, Mochtar Apin.* Because Mulder's influence on the painting style of his students was notable (though several remained immune to his Villon-like qualities) and because no ideological content appeared in "Bandung" art, it was branded by "Jogja" as Western and un-Indonesian.

* Since 1956 most of these painters have spent some time abroad, especially in the United States, and all are teaching at the Bandung School of Fine Arts.

Plate 181. *"A Girl Named Ira," by Srihadi Sudarsono, 1955.*

The Bandung group countered these accusations by asserting that art was international; and, moreover, that "Jogja" had also borrowed its art styles from the West, the only difference being that "Jogja" had not gone beyond representationalism, having stopped short with Post-Impressionism.

Ries Mulder, deeply devoted to his task as teacher, but constantly obliged to defend his approach to teaching, once wrote:

> My method of teaching is to provide an introduction to the language of form in the widest possible sense—the possibilities of line, tone, color, form, and space and their use in art expression as applied in various epochs and different parts of the world. . . . When criticizing the work of my students, aside from purely technical advice, I restrict myself to the improvement of what they themselves try to achieve in their work. I am fully conscious, of course, that an element of personal influence remains inevitable. But no one with inside knowledge of the situation here would deny that I have managed to keep this influence in bounds so that it can operate indirectly. The students influence one another to a stronger degree than they are affected by my direct influence.[18]

These passages appear in a letter to Salim, an expatriate painter settled in Paris who was then visiting Indonesia. Mulder's long exposition was provoked by Salim's disapproving public remarks about the un-Indonesian character of painting at the Bandung school. Mulder also wrote: "You . . . have been free to seek and find yourself without hindrances or prejudices or sentiments, without daily insistence that you be 'Indonesian.' Why do you want to withhold this freedom from others?—the freedom to orient oneself, unimpeded, to the language of forms and to find one's convictions in the slow process of acceptance and rejection."

This slow process of acceptance and rejection, of the gradual crystallization of the young painters' personalities, continues to the present. Despite the similarity in general approach, there were, in the mid-fifties, marked differences among them. Sadali's works, with their webs of delicately delineated geometrical shapes and cool, subdued colors, created an effect of lightness and space. "In the Waiting Room" (Pl. 179) is a good example of his harmonious layering of planes with juxtaposed nuances of light shades. The painting creates a feeling of expanse going beyond the confines of the suggested waiting room and, strangely, also one of suspended time. A very different spirit emanates from But Muchtar's "Self-Portrait" (Pl. 180) where the planes are balanced more impetuously and the colors are stronger. Finally, "A Girl Named Ira" by Srihadi (Pl. 181) is a highly patterned, mosaic-like composition of sharp, angular planes, each with a hue of its own, in which strong accents of bright red (as in the jacket) and black amid gray, green, and yellowish tones lend a very vivid character to the whole. Yet the painting retains a certain brittle delicacy. This portrait by Srihadi, when viewed next to "Young Girl" by Jogja's Trubus (Pl. 182), dramatically illustrates the difference in all conceptions between a good young painter of the Bandung school and one from Jogja. Trubus conveys the adolescent grace and shyness of his subject in softly flowing forms of iridescent pinks and grays.

As suggested by the small selection of paintings shown here so far, there was also a difference between the Bandung and Jogja painters in the choice of their themes. In Bandung, scenes drawn from folk life were conspicuous by their absence. Neither their picturesqueness nor their social implications seemed to attract the painters' interest. Few portraits and practically no self-portraits, so abundant in Jogja, were in evidence. They painted, rather, landscapes, still lifes, and com-

Plate 182. *"Young Girl," by Trubus, 1955.*

positions with figures, often exercising in limited palettes. They always seemed to place primary value on the esthetic ordering of shapes and colors; subject and meaning were not so important to them. They could have asserted with ease that "the picture is the thing."

To the revolutionary and romantic generation of artists assembled in Jogja, Bandung art appeared alien and cold, even meaningless. One thoughtful Indonesian observer remarked that were it not for the existence of the Bandung school, Jogja's "Indonesianism" might never have been formulated. "Jogja's quest for "nationalism in art," he thought, was less a positive conviction and more a reaction to the intellectualism and estheticism of the Bandung painters, to the unmistakable influence of a Dutch teacher, a reaction, in fact, to "Bandung's" westernism.

The conceptions and technical skills of the Bandung group as a team were demonstrated when, in 1956, they decorated the mess hall of the University of Indonesia in Djakarta with a series of fourteen murals, which were to symbolize the various arts and sciences taught at the University. The project was completed in less than a month by the four painters who designed the murals. Each was assisted by one or two students. But Muchtar painted "Prehistory," "Cultural Growth," and two murals on the Arts; Srihadi's murals depicted "Agriculture," "Medicine," "Architecture," and "Industry"; Popo Iskandar designed "Music," "Law," "Fishing," and "Mining"; while two panels by Subhakto depicted "Nature." Subhakto was one of the few Bandung students who did not adopt the geometricized, highly structured style inspired at the school by Mulder. His murals of nature, free, gay, and light, gave one wall of the mess hall an entirely different, smiling character.

Symbolizing the new scientific era, on the "Agriculture" panel Srihadi designed austere elongated figures whose tall, slender, dark forms suggest scholars in academic gowns (see Pl. 200 below). They stalk amid the fields, providing dark vertical counterpoints to the horizontal planes. The dark masses of a suggested structure on the left may be a fishery research station with hints of nets above and two little fish below. The sheds with dark roofs in the background may indicate plantation agriculture, perhaps tobacco, which requires such installations for the drying of the leaves. Srihadi used the same devices in his other three panels, each a unified, well-balanced, serene composition.

Esthetically and technically, all the young painters had admirably met the essential requirements of their commission. They created with their murals a decorative, cheerful, and meaningful setting for the university students' canteen. Unfortunately, the basement in which the canteen is located later proved rather damp and reportedly the murals are disintegrating.

It was these murals which had provoked Salim's reproach that the Bandung artists lacked "Indonesian emotion." And yet, Mulder reminded Salim, the construction workers who were busy finishing the canteen while the murals were being painted greatly admired Srihadi's panels. "If there be no trace in them of any Indonesian emotion, how would you explain this liking?" Mulder queried. He wondered whether Villon's style had not struck a congenial chord in the predisposition and temperament of his young Indonesian followers. Indeed, there was so much in Srihadi's and Sadali's work which was clearly their own that Villon's style might have been more a prop than an alien imposition.

And, as foreseen by Mulder, this prop eventually fell away. By 1960, But Muchtar, while retaining intellectual control, relaxed his former rigidity in the delineation of shapes, achieved greater cohesion in his compositions, and a greater fluidity in color composition. In the paintings produced while he was studying in the United States, the colors are far from compartmentalized—freely fusing, they become a vibrant force permeating background and figures alike.

Srihadi, who spent a year and half at the Fine Arts Department of the University of Ohio where he obtained an M.A. degree in 1962, abandoned completely the Villon-like precision of geometrically delineated forms with their delicately balanced color planes creating space. While preserving his subtlety, he turned to less defined, almost biological shapes, to agglomerations of colors reminiscent of geological formations, and to veritable explosions of luminous reds and blues, as in the painting he called "Dance II" (Pl. 183). The flaming reds, which Srihadi seldom used during his Bandung student days, "came upon him," he said, while he was on the plane en route from Indonesia to the United States; somehow they were connected in his feelings with his tropical homeland.

This turning toward Indonesia was strengthened during the time he and Muchtar were studying in the United States. It is a truism, but too often forgotten, that going abroad as a student, or even as a visitor, does not only mean learning foreign skills or getting an insight into foreign culture. It also, more importantly

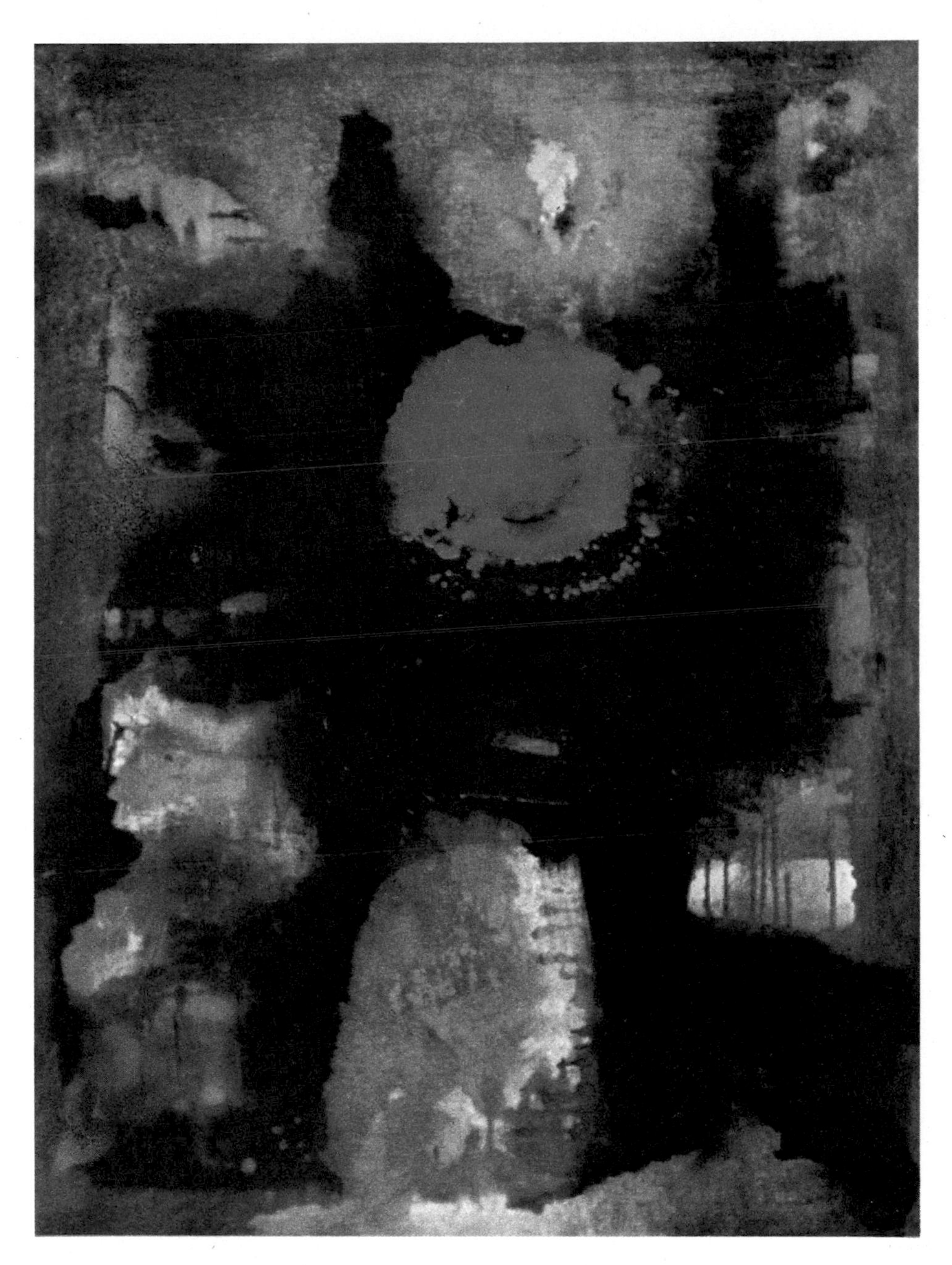

Plate 183. *"Dance II," by Srihadi Sudarsono, 1961.*

perhaps, means obtaining a perspective on, gaining new insights into, and re-evaluating one's own commitments to the homeland.

"Bandung" in the mid-fifties was a center for a new Western-influenced esthetic. No works of the Bandung school of painters were in the collection of President Sukarno or of the State. Neither had any been purchased by the Art Division of the Cultural Office which has a collection of its own. But, despite its unpopularity, no pressure was exerted to change the school's style and educational methods. When Mulder left in 1959 the young artists he had trained took over. By that time appreciation for their work was beginning to grow. They were receiving commissions for murals and favorable comments on their exhibitions; they were selling their paintings and finding a growing demand for their services in interior and furniture design. They had been designing pottery at a small ceramics factory in Bandung since their student days, and by 1959 its products had become very popular and were sold in most major cities. Thus, the Bandung artists are becoming the direct or indirect source for Indonesia's modern design. Emancipated from the classroom, and enriched by experiences abroad, they can now continue to crystallize their predilections.

Bandung had another vital art institution in the person of the late Kartono Yudhokusumo. On the Indonesian art scene, he was discussed in the same breath with art associations and schools. His Sanggar Seniman (Artist's Studio), built in 1952, nestled at the edge of palm-dotted rice fields along the Siliwangi Road skirting the town. It was a compact structure with a dark exterior; but when one entered it, the world expanded and burst into color.

When I first visited Kartono's studio in 1955, on one easel stood an arresting canvas in brilliant colors, an exotic fairy tale with no heroes other than the fantastic plant world (Pl. 184). The painting, called "Orchids," evoked simultaneous associations with work by Rousseau and Walt Disney. It had, however, neither the massive cohesion of the former nor the slickness of the latter. It was difficult to dwell on the total effect of the carefully painted blossoms and foliage. The eye was immediately impelled to wander from cluster to cluster and tempted to try to penetrate the restless flowering jungle, to a turquoise pool and beyond.

On another easel, there was a large painting, a jubilant vista. Recessed from a mass of deep purples in the foreground, terraced rice fields cascaded from two sides into a valley bounded in the far distance by bluish mountains overhung with clouds (see Pl. 199 below). This subject has been depicted by Java's landscape painters over and over again ever since Abdullah the elder painted his soft panoramas. But Kartono's landscape sparkled with color and was wedded to light rather than to the humid haze of the tropics. It was not any one particular landscape, but rather a synthesis of the island's glories made young. Kartono was not satisfied with his "Rice Fields"; its foreground perplexed him. Evidently, he could not solve the problem, since he later literally covered up these "Rice Fields" with another flowering jungle, although a very different one from the "Orchids." He was having a similar problem with the "Orchids." "My focus always seems to be 'beyond,'" he remarked, "so I have trouble with the foreground." And, as if to console himself, he once observed, "The world is never 'finished,' why should a painting be?"

At the age of thirty-one, Kartono had close to 25 years of painting experience, since he had been a child prodigy who painted landscapes and street scenes at seven. Encouraged by his father, an art teacher, he painted continuously. Unlike most artists in Jogja, who were largely self-taught or who had studied with older self-taught Indonesian painters, Kartono was trained by schooled, professional painters, Dutch and Japanese. It was the Indonesian painter Sudibio, however, who had made a lasting impression on him. Kartono, always spoke of Sudibio with affection and admiration, unreservedly acknowledging an indebtedness to him. His favorite European painter was, of course, Rousseau.

A slender young man with a large vivid face surmounted by a mass of wavy black hair, lit up by flashing teeth and the gleaming whites of his eyes, Kartono wore an air of childish ingenuousness. Sometimes one was not quite certain whether his artless frankness, naive questions, and complete freedom in discussing his appetites were unadulterated expressions of his nature or whether they were, perhaps, tinged with shrewdness. It was certain, however, that Kartono had a great appetite for life, a tremendous capacity for enjoyment. At the same time, he was able to get along on very little money when, periodically, his resources dwindled. He accepted life as it came and as it was: "I am never disappointed because I never expect anything." With this lack of expectations and illusions went a kind of impersonal modesty; at times his presence was no more obtrusive than that of a pebble or a plant.

The image of Kartono, in the minds of all who knew him, was inseparable from his motorcycle, his greatest treasure, an adored steed decorated like a circus horse. Painted red at one time, it was promptly repainted pea-green when two other red motorcycles appeared on the Bandung scene. To Kartono, his motorcycle meant movement, speed, access to the beautiful countryside, in short, freedom. Riding it, he met his death.

Kartono cannot be grouped with any of his contemporaries, so strongly does his style set him apart. His later style was described by most of his colleagues as "decorative." Indeed in such a painting as "Orchids," the decorative element, which asserted itself in ever stronger measure from 1949 on, is dominant. But many of Kartono's paintings convey far more than pleasure in artfully composed shapes and colors. For instance, his delight in nature and his joy of life pervade the painting "Dieng." It expresses an emotional state, an exuberance, better perhaps than most of his subsequent paintings. The naive joy is accentuated by the holiday mood of the figures—the painter himself in primrose pants, blue blouse, and golden straw hat, his wife sketching nearby, the bicycles (predecessors of the motorcycle), and the children under the pines (Pl. 185).

"Dieng," painted in 1949, combines two different styles, reflecting Kartono's transition from naturalism to the more spectacularly decorative. The carefully painted pines in the right foreground have a very different "tone of voice" than the rest of the painting, the bold masses of gay cloud formations, the iridescent crater walls, the luminous turquoise lake.

After crystallizing his "decorative" style, Kartono continued to study nature, constantly sketching and painting outdoors. He drew upon these studies for his more stylized studio compositions. Of his students he expected not only a love of their art but above all a love of nature. His own naturalistic paintings were very competent and by far superior to the products of the commercial landscape painters who abounded in Bandung. He used them as potboilers—they sold easily and kept him alive while he took infinite care and a very long time to complete what he considered his "real paintings." It was typical of Kartono that there was not a trace of snobbery in his attitude toward the commercial landscape painters. On the contrary, he felt

Plate 184. *"Orchids," by Kartono Yudhokusumo, 1955.*

Plate 185. *"Dieng," by Kartono Yudhokusumo, 1949.*

respect and affection for them, regarding them as honest and skillful craftsmen without pretensions. He was less tolerant of Sudjojono with whom he had grown up* and had once admired. "I always hoped he would become a great man," Kartono said. "It is difficult to accept what happened to him—we cannot be friends any longer."

Although Kartono knew well and had been associated with many of Jogja's leading artists, he had little in common with their approach to art. Social content in painting did not interest him in the least. He seldom painted people. Apart from a few portraits, people appear in his paintings, as in "Dieng" or in a gay composition called "Bandung," only as parts of the landscape in almost the same spirit as do the human figures that populate a Balinese painting. In fact, Rousseau and other influences notwithstanding, Kartono's art was perhaps closest in spirit to that of some young Balinese painters who depict the loveliness of their world with naive freshness.

* See Appendix IV for details.

The intellectual constructions of semiabstract compositions as practiced at "Seni Rupa" were just as alien to Kartono as was "Jogja's" socially oriented art. What he did have in common with the "Seni Rupa" school was a very conscious appreciation of craftsmanship and the basic conviction that the picture is the thing.

Before Kartono was killed on a slippery curve which his speeding motorcycle failed to negotiate, he had had one near-fatal accident. Upon returning home, he painted a landscape, the title of which retains his feelings, "I'm So Glad to Be Alive." How Kartono's art would have developed had he lived cannot be guessed, but in him Indonesia has prematurely lost a sincere and gifted artist. Out of loyalty and affection, the group of young teachers at "Seni Rupa" have cooperatively taken over Kartono's Sanggar Seniman. It continues to be a studio for private students in memory of the artist.

As mentioned earlier, Kartono was devoted to and admired the painter Sudibio, and we shall stop here for a glimpse of this artist even though he does not actually belong to the Bandung scene. In fact, Sudibio

Plate 186. *"Panorama," by S. Sudibio, 1953.*

does not belong to any art community in the three cities which we are visiting, but lives in relative isolation in Madiun, half-incapacitated by a depressive state and cared for by his sister. His closest companion there is the painter Ismono who lives nearby. A sensitive, mild-mannered but courageous and formerly devil-may-care character, in the early fifties he fell into a state of melancholia, yet continued to paint. His penchant for surrealism which already appeared in an early self-portrait (see Pl. 194 below) became stronger in time, as his fantasies grew darker and more morbid.

In 1953 Sudibio painted the charming "Panorama" (Pl. 186) where, between the foreground and the conical mountains at the back, there are a number of little worlds to be explored. As in some Chinese paintings, the eye is made to follow a road curving inward and upward. A whimsical (or perhaps half-mystical) note emanates from the fantastic round, sunlike trees which sprout from the mountaintops—a startling transformation of volcanic fire and smoke into smiling symbols of life and growth that guard the land below. Like delicate lacework, the painting has a general undulating movement and falls into separate clusters of self-contained units.

A crowd of village women in the foreground to the left, with their backs to the spectator, are recognizable by their shoulder scarves and heavy hairknots. Entering the tree-lined road that leads into the picture, one meets first a peasant woman carrying a child and accompanied by a girl. Following the curving path, one then overtakes a man with a pitchfork and, a short distance away, two villagers with baskets suspended from shoulder poles. At this point the road forks. Ahead lies a wider roadway; it leads up to a mansion fronted by a reception pavilion (*pendopo*) with the tall pyramidal roof typical of East Java. To the left lies another complex—a small house half-hidden by trees with an adjoining shed where several women are at work. Behind this house another tree-lined road winds from left to right into the distance, toward the foot of the mountains and past two more pairs of small houses where tiny figures, one of a man and one of a woman, approach their dwellings.

A loving involvement and delicacy emanate from the landscape with all its minute details. The different varieties of trees are alive, expressive. The architecture of the houses is carefully delineated and even the roof tiles are painstakingly drawn. The soft cadences of the movement of the terrain, with the staccato of scattered dark dots suggesting stones develop into idyllic tunes as one reaches the little worlds around the houses.

A last glimpse of Kartono—the mountain landscape he painted in 1955 (Pl. 187) is practically the opposite of Sudibio's in every respect. As in a piece of fantastic achitecture, the complex elements of Kartono's composition form a massive unity. The painting evokes the remoteness of a petrified world on the tops of volcanoes. The sharply defined, jagged outlines of the crater walls with their clearly modeled folds, the pointed peaks and flattened tops, stand out starkly against a soft sky with

Plate 187. *"Craters," by Kartono Yudhokusumo, 1956.*

billowing clouds. The sky's diffuseness enhances the abruptness and precision of the rock formations. In color, reddish browns and grays of the petrified masses are enlivened by the light turquoise of two crater lakes surrounded by the rock walls. The whole scene is bathed in brilliant, hard light. Like Sudibio, Kartono too seems to pay homage to the power of creation, but not in its benevolent promise of fertility. He depicts awesome desolation, the forbidding aspects of nature, the eternity of hard rock that guards under the sun the mysteries of dark crevices and luminous pools.

In 1954 Sudibio transmuted his personal agonies into a romantically surrealistic painting (Pl. 188) he called "Inspiration." Perhaps his unhappy love life made him depict female figures holding weapons in their hands. In "Inspiration" a paint brush and a tube of paint are the muse's attributes. Behind her haloed, floating figure looms the painter's own head—half face, half skull, which can also be read as two adjacent profiles. Transparent, stunted trees seem to sway in the indeterminate setting of wind-blown drapes and little clouds. At the feet of the muse rises a miniature dream city with flat, rectangular, semicircular and towering structures, some with lighted pinnacles. It is like a construction made of matchsticks in its meticulous execution, as obsessively precise as the hair-fine pattern on the woman's jacket. From behind the dream city emerges a large disembodied hand holding a crystal ball. A grotesquely large, painted vase emerges in the upper right corner. The helpless little flames that flicker symmetrically in the trail of the muse, the little lights on the spires of the toylike city, and the luminosity of the crystal ball do not dispel but rather enhance the gloom of his fantasmagoria.

Djakarta

Like any metropolis, Djakarta is a great market place, a central exchange for all variety of goods, services, and ideas—from peanuts to automobiles, from garbage removal to high political office, from expertise in cosmetics to connoisseurship in paintings. The capital is the nation's literary center, home of a budding motion picture industry, a modern theater academy, and of the most knowledgeable art critics. In Djakarta are the headquarters for the nationwide mass media and for national organizations in every conceivable field. The city has the most luxurious establishments in the country and its worst slums. Its inhabitants include the most highly educated and enlightened citizens and the most dejected, ignorant urban proletariat. Between the palace of the President, or the air-conditioned de luxe Hotel Indonesia, and the shanties of the kampungs lies Djakarta's commercial, administrative, and residential body, a vast, sprawling organism.

In the mid-fifties, the hectic traffic of the capital was enlivened but also made more hazardous by thousands of tricycle pedicabs, the *betja,* which were carriers not only of passengers and their bundles but also of a special kind of urban folk art, a betja art. No betja was complete without a painting on the back of its carriage.*

The majority of betja paintings were stereotype Chinese landscapes produced by Chinese or copied by Indonesians from models supplied by Chinese entrepreneurs who hired out their fleets of vehicles to Indonesian drivers. But there were also among the betja paintings colorful original panels—naive depictions of pretty girls, of fantastic winged horses with blond female riders, a circus scene, or a landscape with an idyllic mountain lake. The betja paintings were produced with great speed (I have seen one completed within 35 minutes) for fees ranging between 15 and 25 rupiah.† On a flat, usually sky-blue background prepared in advance, often by a child or an aged relative, the betja painter outlined the figures and colored them with amazing dexterity and without any model before him.

On the prestige ladder of Djakarta's artists, betja painters were below the lowest rung. At its top were the relatively wealthy salon or "palace" painters. Nevertheless, a betja decorator, settled in his modest little house in a kampung, could be better off than the young artist struggling for recognition who also lived in a kampung but in direst poverty. Between a painter like Dullah, who had a suite in the palace as curator of the Presidential and the State art collections, and an artist like Nashar, who barely survived in a hut, were the many salaried professionals. Some, like Oesman Effendi and Baharudin, worked as illustrators and

* New regulations prescribing solidly colored betja bodies and the introduction of motorized betjas (*bemo's*) in the sixties have practically abolished "betja art."

† Similar prices were charged in 1955–1956 in Jogjakarta's market shops for the paintings on glass made by folk artists. In the same year, 1956, oil paintings by the People's Painters were priced between 1,000 and 10,000 rupiah.

designers with publishing houses and the press; others, like Basuki Resobowo and Zaini, specialized in the design of stage decors. The country's best cartoonists, "Sibarani," S. Soeharto, and "Ran" among them, also were employed in the capital. Dukut Hendronoto, an exceptionally gifted film-cartoonist also working in Djakarta, given the resources, might have emerged as Indonesia's Disney. In 1963 he was giving drawing lessons to children on a Djakarta television program.

Large art shows were held in Djakarta's only permanent art gallery, the *Balai Budaya* (Hall of Culture), and also in the Hotel des Indes (now *Duta Indonesia*), in the former Dutch club *Harmonie* (now *Wisma Nusantara*), and in the Youth Building (*Gedung Pemuda*). A new art gallery, run by the Foundation for Indonesian Art and Design (*Jajasan Seni dan Design Indonesia*), was established in the suburb Kebajoran in 1958. By exhibiting in Djakarta an artist hoped to come to the attention of the most important patrons and possibly sell a painting to them—first of all President Sukarno, then the well-to-do Indonesian and Chinese art collectors, the foreign embassies, individual members of the diplomatic corps, and other foreign residents of the capital. As anywhere in the world, an artist might have to incur heavy debts in order to finance an exhibition in the capital. Thus, a one-man show by

Plate 188. *"Inspiration," by S. Sudibio, 1954.*

Harijadi in 1957 called for an outlay of close to 25,000 rupiah but only about 12,000 rupiah were realized from the sale of three paintings. It was not clear who covered the deficit.

From Djakarta radiated country-wide influences affecting the life and work of artists in the provinces. From the provinces, in turn, came impulses to which the capital responded through its various central organizations, each a sort of cultural switchboard. The organizations most directly concerned with the arts were the Cultural Office of the Ministry of Education and two nongovernmental, rival art federations—the Council on National Culture, or BMKN (*Badan Musjawarat Kebudajaan Nasional*) and the Institute for People's Culture, or Lekra (*Lembaga Kebudajaan Rakjat*).

The BMKN, founded in 1952, was an apolitical body subsidized by the Government. Lekra, established in 1950, was distinctly Communist-oriented with apparently adequate funds, the sources of which could not easily be traced. Both organizations collected membership dues and, in both cases, these could not nearly meet their expenses.

The membership of BMKN consisted of organizations as well as individuals. At its inception in 1952, it counted among its members 120 art associations in Java, Sumatra, and Borneo, about a dozen cultural and educational bodies, including the P.E.N. Club, the Taman Siswa Schools, Jogjakarta's Art Academy (ASRI), and regional foundations. Lekra was also a member of the BMKN. BMKN's individual members were concentrated in Djakarta. They were leading intellectuals—writers, journalists, painters, musicians, and dramatists—and also doctors, lawyers, and high-placed officials interested in cultural affairs. BMKN was thus a variegated agglomeration of persons and organizations with widely scattered interests in the arts and sciences and often competing ideologies.

Lekra had established 18 provincial branches headed by representatives who recruited local members and directed their activities. Its membership was gradually being molded into a homogeneous body closely tied to Lekra's ideology. In some cases, a Lekra branch seemed to coincide with an existing local organization, as with SIM in Jogjakarta. The heads of Lekra's provincial branches were usually well-known artists or writers—at one time Sudjojono and later Suromo in Jogja, the painter Mohammed Hadi in Solo, and the writer Bakri Siregar in Medan. At headquarters in Djakarta, the painters Henk Ngantung and Basuki Resobowo, who succeeded the former in the sixties, played leading roles. The branch leadership adhered to central directives for recruitment and for the development of their substantive programs. Each branch was divided into separate sections devoted to literature, drama, painting, and dancing. In addition, the branch had one section called *realis dinamo,* translated as "the realist-dynamo" or perhaps "dynamic realist." This was a group active in the production of entertaining popular shows interwoven with propaganda. Lekra was thus more tightly organized than the BMKN.

BMKN's goals and programs were all-encompassing, their central aim being the development of the nation's culture. Such an aim could provide only diffuse guidelines. The federation was envisaged as an all-sheltering "roof organization" which would coordinate the cultural life of the country and direct it toward a national orientation. With a few notable exceptions, however, especially in the literary field, BMKN's wide-ranging aims were rarely implemented with concrete, detailed, and systematic programs of action.

BMKN's achievements lay principally in the promotion of contemporary literature. The organization's leadership coincided in part with the editorial staff of its monthly journal, *Indonesia,* which at one time or another included such prominent writers and essayists as Achdiat K. Mihardja, Armijn Pané, and Boejoeng Saleh. Trisno Sumardjo—author, translator of Shakespeare's plays and other English works into Indonesian, art critic and painter—worked for years on BMKN's secretarial and editorial staff. Oesman Effendi was active in the preparation of the periodical too. Apart from essays on art and literature, domestic and foreign, *Indonesia* published poetry, short stories, plays, and articles concerned with Indonesia's cultural problems. Sketches and paintings by Indonesian artists were printed on the cover and interspersed with the text. BMKN also contributed written materials for use by the mass media, the radio, the daily press or magazines, and sponsored art classes in the gallery Balai Budaya.

Furthermore, the biannual cultural congresses organized by BMKN were the principal forums for the continuing debate on the prevailing condition and future of Indonesian culture. At these congresses resolutions were passed to stimulate both governmental and nongovernmental support of the arts. The congress reports are significant documents, reflecting the problems and recording the controversies that highlight Indonesia's modern cultural history.

Lekra, on the other hand, in conjunction with its vaguely formulated declaration of general principles, had very concrete programs of action for each separate art field, and these were systematically implemented by its branch organizations. The declaration of its aim included the following statements:

> . . . Lekra gives active support to everything that is new and progressive, Lekra actively assists in the demolition of the remainders of colonial "culture" which has left a part of our people in dark ignorance, with feelings of inferiority and with weakness of character. Lekra accepts our ancestral heritage critically and studies carefully all its aspects, just as it does the classical creations of other peoples anywhere, and thus creatively endeavors to further the great tradition of our history and our nation, directing it toward a new culture which is rational and scientific. Lekra proposes to its members, but also to other artists, scholars, and cultural workers who are outside Lekra, that they study . . . the actual truth in life, and be faithful to truth and reality.
>
> In the arts, Lekra supports creative initiative, creative daring, and Lekra agrees with every form, every style, etc., so long as it is faithful to truth and meets the highest standards of artistic beauty.
>
> In short, in repudiating the antihuman, antisocial character of the culture that is not-of-the-people, in repudiating the violations of truth and beauty, Lekra helps shape a new society capable of self-advancement, a society developing its individuality which is both multifaceted and harmonious.[19]

Demanding "firm adherence to the people," Lekra's declared working principles were "reciprocal help, mutual criticism, and comradely discussion of the problems of creativity."[20] To members interested in painting, Lekra offered: a local studio, art materials, discussion meetings, exhibitions of their works along with other Lekra members from all parts of the country. The wording of the Lekra statement cited above suggests that nonmembers might participate in local exhibitions under Lekra's auspices but not in Lekra exhibitions on a national scale.

The distribution of art materials to professionals and students alike was a great inducement for joining Lekra since supplies were scarce and very expensive. Successful promotion of artists, however, was perhaps Lekra's greatest attraction. In sponsoring exhibitions, Lekra offered to artists coveted opportunities, especially the distinction of being shown in the capital. It also paid the high costs of transporting paintings and sculptures to the place of exhibition. Thus, in 1957, Amrus Natalsja's huge wood sculptures were shipped from Jogja to Djakarta with Lekra's help. In 1956–1957, it had also launched a fund-raising campaign to build a House of Culture in Djakarta, perhaps to serve as a permanent exhibition hall to augment if not to rival the facilities offered by the Balai Budaya which at that time was administered by BMKN. This hall opened August 16, 1959, just in time for the Republic's Independence Day celebrations.

While Lekra maintained art centers and studios in all provincial capitals, BMKN's only directly sponsored art classes were conducted beginning in 1957 in the Balai Budaya. BMKN could not offer its members the same range of facilities as Lekra. It had no proper apparatus for organizing local activities or for the distribution of art materials even if it could have obtained a supply through purchase or as a gift from some donor. BMKN's funds were rather limited. Apart from membership dues it depended largely on the Government's subsidy* which often lagged and at one point in 1956 was six months in arrears. Sporadic fund-raising schemes were discussed but more often than not remained in the talking stage. Because it was devoted to seeking a *national* culture, BMKN could not accept financial help from foreign sources either.

BMKN lingered on, but its activities were almost paralyzed. Its journal *Indonesia* continued to be published by the Foundation for Cultural Publications (*Jajasan Penerbit Kebudajaan*). BMKN's decline was due to a number of causes, its financial problems and organizational defects among them. But in large part it was also due to the BMKN leadership's inability to meet and counter Lekra's aggressive tactics. While Lekra initially was a member-association of BMKN, it soon became its worst enemy. A number of Lekra's active members, having retained membership in BMKN as individuals, often outtalked and outvoted BMKN's other members at its congresses, causing disruption and disaffection. Several succeeded in gaining seats on the BMKN executive board and effectively obstructed its activities.

Another reason for the decline of BMKN lay in the

* The monthly subsidy in 1956 was 15,000 rupiah.

changing focus of the Great Debate. BMKN's leadership was regarded by the authorities as insufficiently nationalistic while official policy was hardening in favor of an explicitly nationalistic art. In mid-1959, the Indonesian Nationalist Party (P.N.I.), in a bid for cultural leadership, formed the Institute for National Culture (*Lembaga Kebudajaan Nasional* or LKN) with the writer and poet Sitor Situmorang as chairman.* Not surprisingly, less than six months after Lekra's 1959 Congress in the Sriwedari amusement park in Solo, LKN held its first congress in the same place. Two months later, on August 17th, President Sukarno proclaimed his "Manipol-Usdek" doctrine.† With this political manifesto, the President redefined the state philosophy. Its basic principles were to be the 1945 Constitution, Indonesian Socialism, Guided Democracy, Guided Economy, and National Personality. It is the last principle, with its stress on national identity, that became the guideline for the development of the arts. And thus, theoretically at least, the Great Debate was settled in favor of a national-oriented art. The Debate could continue only as regards the particular forms appropriate to expressing Indonesian "National Personality."[21] In the BMKN-LKN-Lekra triangle of the early sixties, BMKN became a somewhat impotent residue of the "liberal" orientation toward the arts; the LKN became the proponent of the official nationalist line and a rival of Lekra; and Lekra itself, while subscribing to the principle of "National Personality," continued to promote Communist ideology. Further politicizing the art sphere, the left-wing socialist party Murba and the conservative Islamic party *Nahdatul Ulama* (N.U.) had also established their own cultural organizations.

It seems fairly clear that the competition for "the soul of the artist" directed from the capital will continue. In reality, however, the organizations have more influence on the artists' social and economic circumstances and their political outlooks than on their art.

In the mid-fifties among Djakarta's painters, the "big names" were Basuki Abdullah, Lee Man Fong, and Henk Ngantung. Their reputations rested on very different foundations.

Basuki Abdullah was the salon painter par excellence. Many a society woman dreamed of having her portrait painted by Abdullah, certain that she would appear glamorously lovely. Abdullah also painted large landscapes, heroic subjects, and legendary themes. His romantic and flamboyant style appealed to many members of the Indonesian upper and middle classes and was favored by the President. A painting by Abdullah hangs behind the President's desk. It depicts the Indonesian national hero, Diponegoro, in a storm-blown white mantle, mounted on a fiery black stallion against a blazing background suggestive of a conflagration. The majority of Abdullah paintings in the President's private collection[22] portray beautiful young women; one depicts the rape of Sita, and another the goddess of the Southern Ocean, *Njahi Roro* (or *Loro*) *Kidul.* She emerges from the depths amid dark stormy waves, not unlike a lovely bejeweled society hostess in evening gown, somewhat drenched. The painter's craftsmanship in his particular style is superb.

Lee Man Fong was dean of the Chinese-Indonesian painters who were organized in the *Yin Hua* art association founded in 1955 and which in 1959 had 124 members.*

The major function of the organization has been to arrange exhibits for its members, which have been held frequently in Djakarta hotels or in their own gallery, "Tati," located on Prinsenpark in Djakarta. Following a large exhibition by Yin Hua artists, the association was invited to send a delegation to the People's Republic of China. In the latter half of 1956, Lee Man Fong led a selected group of Chinese-Indonesian artists to China, where they visited for about five months, arranging exhibits in Peking and Canton.

Despite his European schooling, Lee Man Fong has retained an unmistakable Chinese flavor in his art. He left China when still a child but may have absorbed its culture during his youth in Singapore. Nevertheless, having made Indonesia his homeland and painting prolifically there, he has developed a unique stylistic syncretism.

It is a curious sensation to see an Indonesian food vendor through Lee Man Fong's eyes (Pl. 190). In his painting "Saté Vendor," two worlds converge to create a new one. The subject is Indonesian: a vendor fanning the fire and roasting tidbits before his portable bamboo stall. His figure is harmoniously elongated and

* Reportedly he was no longer heading LKN in 1964.

† Manipol is an abbreviation for Political Manifesto; Usdek are the initial letters of the five principles enumerated below.

* Another Chinese-Indonesian art center was the *Mung May* association in Malang, East Java, where the painter Lim Kwee Bing conducted an art school with predominantly Chinese students.

Plate 189. *"Portrait of Mrs. A. K. Gani," by Basuki Abdullah, 1952.*

the fragility of his limbs is stressed. His air of concentration is mixed with an "awayness" and spreads into the stillness which dominates the painting. The "Chinese space" behind the vendor augments this feeling. It is deepened by the jagged branch with tender leaves above the stall which echoes the calligraphy of the Chinese characters on the left. The quality of the whole composition is one of delicate tenuity.

Some of the other Chinese-Indonesian painters have also developed a syncretic style of their own; some, like the Djakarta painter Lee Siang Yun, pursue two distinct styles simultaneously. Lee Siang Yun paints goldfish or lotus leaves with dragonflies in traditional Chinese manner while picturesque Djakarta street corners and portraits are painted in sturdy, naturalistic Western fashion.

The third prominent figure on Djakarta's art scene, Henk Ngantung, owed his reputation partly to his competence as a painter and partly to his influential position. He was chairman of Lekra's central committee and sat on juries which selected works for exhibitions at home and abroad. In 1954, he led a cultural mission to the People's Republic of China which took a selection of 95 paintings for exhibition. In 1955, Ngantung was elected to Parliament. In 1961, he became vice-mayor of Djakarta and his career as an artist was overshadowed by his administrative functions.

Ngantung painted landscapes and waterfront views in vigorous fresh colors and these were probably closest to his heart. He also painted betja drivers (Pl. 191), cowherds, portraits of friends and the people of Bali. Like some of his colleagues, he painted in more than one style. His portrait sketches are dynamic and expressive. In one composition with three figures of Balinese girls the treatment, is free, has living movement, and a distinct, mellow mood. In contrast, a painting of a Balinese girl in the President's collection is a static, bland, near-photographic rendering of a picturesque subject.

Plate 190. "Saté *Vendor," by Lee Man Fong.*

The activities of Djakarta's other artists were more submerged in the daily bustle of the capital. None of them had the influential position of Henk Ngantung and few of them came to public attention with grandiose one-man shows such as were instituted from time to time by Basuki Abdullah. But some were actually or potentially more significant artists.

Between 1948 and 1958 many of Djakarta's artists belonged to the now defunct League of Indonesian Painters or GPI (*Gabungan Pelukis Indonesia*), of which Affandi was one of the founders and which was headed by the art teacher and painter Sutiksna. At GPI's modest headquarters, its members gathered for painting classes and maintained a small exhibition of their works. A group of young painters split off from GPI in 1957 and formed their own art association, *Matahari* (The Sun), under the leadership of Mardian.

Of the Matahari group only Mardian came to public notice in the mid-fifties with an exhibition at the Balai Budaya, though some of his associates such as Wakidjan, Wetik, and Nashar were known to be promising artists. Mardian himself was evolving an agitated style in riotous colors applied in dots and daubs with practically no delineation of shapes. One of his paintings, "Indonesia in 1956," is a coherent expression of disorientation which one is tempted to compare with some cave paintings that seem to be incoherent statements about orientation in the world. After four years in Jogjakarta, where he was a student of ASRI and a member of SIM working under Sudjojono, Mardian moved to Djakarta in 1954. Thereafter his work appears to have shed every trace of his Jogjakarta schooling and ideological indoctrination. The only principle he seemed to espouse was the need to "seek for oneself"; his paintings showed this in full measure.

Of the older and more mature artists, Oesman Effendi and Trisno Sumardjo not only practiced art but also thought and wrote about it. Neither of them had enough time and resources to exhibit his works in the years 1955–1957. The only works by these artists which

Plate 191. "Betja *Driver," by Henk Ngantung, 1947.*

I had a chance to examine and photograph were among the series of forty paintings of historical scenes intended as visual aids in the teaching of Indonesian history in secondary schools.* This series was prepared by them together with Zaini and Basuki Resobowo. Since the style of these paintings was necessarily conditioned by their intended use in the classroom, they could not be regarded as representative of the artists who painted them. They have historical interest and, in addition, they demonstrate the artists' skill in presenting scenes of Indonesian history in a manner acceptable to schools.

* These paintings were on view on the premises of the publishing house FASCO in Djakarta, which produced the color prints for use in schools.

Under the leadership of Gaos Harjasumantri of the BMKN, Oesman Effendi, Trisno Sumardjo, and Zaini founded in 1958 the *Jajasan Seni dan Design Indonesia* (Foundation for Indonesian Art and Design), which has developed one of the best art galleries in Greater Djakarta.

The isolated figure of the late Emiria Sunassa also belonged to the Djakarta art scene. She was the only renowned woman painter of the older generation. A daughter of the last Sultan of Tidore, an island domain in Eastern Indonesia, she took up painting when she was over forty. Shortly before World War II, her works were exhibited by the Union of Art Circles (*Bond van Kunstkringen*) and elicited favorable comments. She continued to paint during the Japanese occupation and afterward. A few of Emiria Sunassa's works show flashes of power and originality. One of her best canvasses is "Dayak Wedding," an unhesitating, strong, and integrated statement with a tribal ceremonial as subject. The array of five figures behind a festively decked table with a row of gongs at its foot is simple and static. Yet the painting, with its deep shadows and contrasting light surfaces, conveys an intensity similar to that of a heroic tale of bygone ages or of the deep voices of tribesmen chanting. The painting must have been inspired by Emiria Sunassa's personal contact with Dayak life in Borneo in the nineteen-thirties. Later, as the impact of her impressions there faded, she turned to other subjects, some imaginary and symbolic, but none comparable in strength and cohesion to "Dayak Wedding."

Finally, though not living in the capital, the brothers Agus and Otto Djaja* are significant figures, each connected with Djakarta in his own way. Agus is an "old timer"; in 1934, he was already teaching art and in 1938 he was, with Sudjojono, a founder of Persagi. For many years thereafter he was in the forefront of the Indonesian modern art movement. In the late forties, he earned recognition abroad when he spent two years in Europe with his younger brother Otto. While there, he painted one of his best canvasses, "Kuda Lumping I." It portrays the wildness of an entranced hobby-horse dancer. The agitated scene is full of tension accentuated by the highlighted staring eyes of the dancer and of his flat bamboo horse, by the impetus of his stiffened body, and by the flashing undulation of the whip. There is great spontaneity and daring in line and color. The brothers Djaja influenced each other very strongly. Some of Otto's renderings of folk life very much resemble those of his brother; they have the same agitated quality. Nocturnal glee pervades his painting of a fighting dance in which costumed girls posture in the light of a torch. In the mid-fifties, the brothers parted ways. Agus retired to Bali and became a glamorous painter of the "last paradise," appealing to the ready tourist market. Like that of Sudjojono, his reputation is based on past rather than present achievements. Both Agus Djaja and Sudjojono had once given up their earlier expressionist styles in favor of more literal manners, but for diametrically opposed reasons: Sudjojono for the sake of social protest and propaganda, Agus to escape from politically infested urban Java to a house on the beach and the color-drenched theatricalism of Balinese life.

Otto Djaja settled in Semarang on Java's north coast and maintained close contact with Djakarta. Unlike his brother, he has a sense of humor which lends a piquant touch to some of his paintings. In the riotous sketch, "Family Outing," Otto reveals himself as a skillful caricaturist. He depicts the exultation of "Sunday drivers" on a bicycle, which in Indonesia serves as pack mule and family car (Pl. 192). He is also an excellent illustrator, and has provided delightful color illustrations for a booklet called "Pasundan."

In Semarang, Otto Djaja has given great encouragement to the barber-painter Sugianto, in whose shop he sometimes exhibited his paintings. "Yanto" was one of Java's rare naive painters whose art was sincere and very touching. Otto Djaja seemed to have recognized this and had not undertaken to become his teacher.

Among the amateurs a significant group were members of the Indonesian Armed Forces, who were encouraged by higher officers to practice the arts in their leisure time. In November, 1954 the Association of Armed Forces' Amateurs of the Fine Arts was formed, which published a bulletin devoted to the study of painting and modeling. In the years 1955 and 1956 the association held at least four exhibitions in Djakarta as well as in Bandung. The associations's secretary, Lieutenant Colonel Ashari, himself an amateur painter, was particularly active in promoting these efforts, as was Lieutenant Colonel Widya. The works of the military artists were offered for sale and in 1956 the prices for their paintings ranged from 200 to 4,000 rupiah.

The catalogue of an exhibition held, following Armed Forces Day, in early October, 1955, in Bandung listed 82 paintings by 27 participants, among whom were officers of the Army, Navy, Air Force, and Military Police Corps, and a few civilians. A few pastels and watercolors appeared, but the majority of the paintings were oils. The subjects were treated naturalistically for the most part, and the paintings were executed with various degrees of competence. They included landscapes, portraits, a few still lifes, folk scenes, two representations of dancers (one Dayak and one Balinese), and two of animals—a wild buffalo and a cat. The only mythological subject was a depiction of Dewa Rutji, the little replica of Bima symbolizing the towering hero's spiritual self.

* Their full names are Agus Djajasuminta and Otto Djajasuntara.

Plate 192. *"Family Outing," by Otto Djaja, 1956.*

On the back of the catalogue was printed a quotation from Plato: that soldiers should be trained in the arts as well as in sports for the attainment of a balanced physical and spiritual development; that exclusive concentration on physical prowess might produce a coarse, callous and even cruel character, whereas exclusive preoccupation with art might be conducive to weakness; that a soldier, to be brave and intelligent, must harmoniously combine strength with delicacy, courage with humility.

Returning to Djakarta's professional art community, it was not dominated in the fifties by a particular trend, school, or philosophy. Djakarta was most strikingly the market place with a constant coming and going of artists from the provinces.[23] In the capital, the artists were more split up than in Bandung or Jogja; they belonged to different social strata, led very different lives, and congregated in small groups. While in Jogja and Bandung even the youngest artist felt confident, the metropolis, although buoyant for the famous, weighed heavily on its other artists.

Thus, Jogja, Bandung, and Djakarta as art centers each in its own way participated in the great debate on the future of Indonesian culture. Jogja, in the mid-fifties, stood for "Indonesianism" and an art devoted to the people. Bandung defended a purely esthetic approach and the position that art was international. Djakarta was the arena for the continuing debate where the intellectuals and politicians advanced their conflicting theories. The conflict between BMKN and Lekra was related to the issues of the debate but was more a struggle for power between a "liberal" and a Communist organization. Between these two, the LKN endeavored to steer the country's art into nationalist channels. In Djakarta, the artists' own commitments, if they had any, were drowned in the floods of intellectual and political speculations. In Jogja and Bandung, the artists' commitments were reflected in their works. Their mutual antagonism was sharpest in the mid-fifties, but since then reportedly has mellowed. Students and teachers from both centers have studied abroad and have returned with new approaches to painting and teaching. Jogja may be gaining in technical proficiency and sophistication; Bandung may be acquiring a broader esthetic perspective and may be reassessing its relation to Indonesian culture. One thing is certain: the debate will continue, although with a new focus of controversy. The basic issues on the political level are seemingly resolved for the time being but on the esthetic level they are hardly susceptible to conscious or speedy resolution.

Notes

1. Achdiat K. Mihardja, ed., *Polemik Kebudajaan* (Djakarta, 1950). All excerpts from the *Polemik Kebudajaan* have been translated by the author.

2. S. Takdir Alisjahbana, "Menudju Masjarakat dan Kebudajaan Baru Indonesia" ["Toward a New Indonesian Society and Culture"], *ibid.*, pp. 13–21.

3. Sanusi Pané, "Persatuan Indonesia" ["Indonesian Unity"], *ibid.*, pp. 22–26.

4. S. Takdir Alisjahbana, "Djiwa dan Pendjelmahan; Isih dan Bentuk" ["Spirit and Creation; Content and Form"], *ibid.*, pp. 136–145.

5. Poerbatjaraka, "Sambungan Zaman" ["Times to Come"], *ibid.*, pp. 31–34.

6. Tjindarbumi, "Mentjari Verhouding" ["In Search of Proportions"], *ibid.*, pp. 56–58.

7. R. Sutomo, "Perbedaan Levensvisie" ["Difference in Vision of Life"], *ibid.*, pp. 66–73.

8. Adinegoro, "Kritik atas Kritik" ["A Criticism on a Criticism"], *ibid.*, pp. 80–86.

9. Ki Hadjar Dewantara, "Pembaharuan Adab" ["Cultural Renewal"], *ibid.*, pp. 115–117.

10. M. Amir, "Menjambut Karangan S. Takdir Alisjahbana" ["In Answer to the Article of S.T.A."], *ibid.*, pp. 131–135.

11. Amir, "Pertukaran dan Pertikaian Pikiran" ["Exchange of Ideas and Controversy"], *ibid.*, pp. 96–114.

12 See A. S. Dharta, writer and member of Lekra's executive committee in "Het Cultureel Congress te Solo" ["The Cultural Congress in Solo"], *Cultureel Nieuws; Indonesie 1955,* (Amsterdam), no. 45, 17–18.

13. *Pikiran Rakjat* [*The People's Thoughts*] (Bandung), November, 1960.

14. Takdir Alisjahbana, *Indonesia in the Modern World,* trans. by Benedict Anderson (New Delhi, 1961), pp. 191–194.

15. Mr. M. Nasroen, *Kebudajaan Indonesia* [*Indonesian Culture*] (Djakarta, 1951), pp. 14, 15, 20.

16. Selosoemardjan, *Social Changes in Jogjakarta* (Ithaca, N.Y., 1962).

17. From *The Flaming Earth, Poems from Indonesia,* trans. from Indonesian by Ahmed Ali (Karachi, 1949).

18. Translated from Dutch by the author and quoted with M. N. Mulder's permission from an unpublished letter dated 1956.

19. From a mimeographed statement accompanying application for membership, Lembaga Kebudajaan Rakjat, Tjabang Medan (Medan Branch, Lekra), Statement No. 003/ku/ Lekra; Lampiran: = 1 =. Dated June 15, 1956. Translated from Indonesian by the author.

20. *Ibid.*

21. See A. H. Johns, "The Genesis of a Modern Literature," in Ruth T. McVey, ed., *Indonesia* (New Haven, 1963), pp. 410–437.

22. Twenty-five of Basuki Abdullah's paintings are reproduced in color in *Paintings from the Collection of Dr. Sukarno,* Vol. II.

23. Even though there were a number of serious and skillful painters outside the three main centers in Java, Jogjakarta, Bandung, and Djakarta, none of them had attained national stature. The peripheral groups are significant nevertheless as they indicate the widespread interest in modern painting. In Java itself, there is a sizable group of artists in Surakarta (Solo) who in 1949 under the leadership of Dr. R. Moerdowo formed the association, which is also an art school, known as *Himpunan Budaja Surakarta* or HBS (Cultural Association of Surakarta). In Sumatra, the most important organizations are in Medan, the *Angkatan Seni Rupa Indonesia* or ASRI (Fine Arts Group of Indonesia), active since 1945; and, in Bukit Tinggi, the *Seniman Muda Indonesia* or SEMI (Young Indonesian Artists), created by Ali Akbar in 1948 and led in the late fifties by Zetka.

CONCLUSION

CONCLUSION

In conclusion, we may return to the question which initially stimulated this study: what was the effect of the war, revolution, and attainment of independence on the visual arts of Indonesia?[1] In trying to summarize, we become aware of a further question: are the observed trends in Indonesia uniquely local or have similar developments occurred also in other countries with a colonial past, especially in those countries of South and Southeast Asia which have in common with Indonesia an ancient Hindu-Buddhist cultural heritage? It would be far beyond this author's capacity to attempt to answer the second question, but the question should remain as a backdrop against which to contemplate the developments in Indonesian art.

The advent of modern art in Java—the overt emergence of new forms, ideas and attitudes that drastically depart from the traditional Indonesian sphere—seems to have been in the late nineteen-thirties. At that time in Europe pre–World War II tensions had reached a critical stage and could not have failed to affect even such distant regions of the world as the colonial tropics and to foster a general climate conducive to ferment. Intellectual and political ferment had started in Indonesia two decades earlier largely as the result of intensifying Western cultural penetration. In the visual arts, after a mild period of exercises in draftsmanship and naturalistic painting, a breakthrough occurred, as we have seen, with the primary aim of self-assertion.

The unprecedented emergence of the individual in the works of painters during and after the war, is one of the significant phenomena to be noted. In Java, the assertion "I am," followed by the question "Who am I?" is reflected in self-portraits of different styles and moods. Thus Affandi in his expressive sketch "Learning to Paint Myself" (made in 1944) appears as vital and confident as is his calligraphy. Sudibio's frail body and weary face against a desolate background (painted in 1949) is melancholia clad in white. Deaf Tarmizi speaks to us with youth and gentleness from his 1955 self-portrait, his inquiringly attentive eyes attuned to subtle discrimination of shapes and colors.

In Bali stress on the individual is expressed only superficially, not by means of portraits or self-portraits, but mainly through signatures of the artists which are now affixed to paintings and sometimes to woodcarvings—a practice not customary before the thirties. More important, the individuality of outstanding artists can be recognized in certain styles that boldly depart from prevalent fashions. In general, the former anonymity of artists-craftsmen has given way to the recognition of individual painters and sculptors by name and fame.

Drastic change has occurred also in the patronage of the arts. No longer are the princely courts the principal centers of support for the best artists and craftsmen, except to a certain degree in the traditional sphere. Nor are foreign residents and tourists any longer the only buyers of contemporary art. The State and its President have become the chief art patrons, and, in addition to foreigners, Indonesians of the moneyed upper class of urban society have become purchasers and collectors of Indonesian art.

Until the nineteen-thirties palace art and village (or folk) art in Java, though differentiated by quality, were mutually intelligible, and today they remain so in the traditional sphere. Modern urban art, however, though often attracting the attention and interest of visiting villagers, has had little effect on folk art and, except for some modern dancers, the urban artists in Java do not utilize folk art motifs. It is my impression that the opposite is true in India.

In Bali all art is produced within village communities. The distinction there is between traditional temple art and secular art. Although the villagers find it increasingly difficult to subsidize the building and renovation of temples, secular art has become lucrative.

It is worth noting that, when significant changes in art styles occurred in the thirties in Bali and in Java, the situation in each of these islands was very different. In Bali an uninterrupted living tradition could nourish its artists and serve as a basis for innovations and new departures. These departures were of Balinese invention and were stimulated only to a limited degree by

Plate 193. *"Learning to Paint Myself," by Affandi, 1944.*

the presence of certain Western artists and their works. In Java there was no living legacy in painting and sculpture for the artists to perpetuate, alter, or repudiate, except the wayang world. The Javanese modern artists had nothing to lean on but examples of Western art. They could only rebel against the naturalistic landscape painting, the first Western-inspired art which some of the older Indonesian artists had mastered. In the absence of museums where original masterpieces of Western art could be studied, their models, if any, were mainly reproductions; before World War II, the most accessible of these were works of Dutch masters. When I asked painters in Java to name their favorite European artist, Van Gogh was mentioned most frequently. Other names mentioned often were Gauguin and Matisse. Rousseau had made a deep impression on Kartono; the surrealists appealed to Sudibio; a young artist in Jogjakarta, Sukarno Hadian, was enchanted by Klee, but he was an exception, The People's Painters preferred Ben Shahn and Grant Wood. Picasso had no appeal; Mondrian was never mentioned.

In contrast to Japan—where a vigorous modern graphic art has developed, enriched by Western influences but nurtured by Japan's own great traditions—none of the arts in Java could be enriched by, or synthesized with, elements of Western art except such applied arts as the vast and varied field of batik design.

Modern art in Indonesia reflects the groping creativity of artists who are exposed to all art trends, past and present, including schools in the West which, though reflecting and perhaps anticipating the spirit of the times, baffle many members of the society in which they are created. It is questionable to what extent a *Weltgefühl,* arising in a highly developed technological society in the atomic and space age, has penetrated Indonesia.

Plate 195. *"Self-Portrait," by Tarmizi, 1955.*

Plate 194. *"Self-Portrait," by S. Sudibio, 1949.*

Plate 196. *Female figure with mortar and pestle on lid of Toba Batak sarcophagus, North Sumatra.*

No "isms" can serve to characterize the various art styles in Indonesia,[2] not even "Indonesianism." Largely representational in character, Indonesian art of the fifties conveyed a closeness to nature, to people, or to an ideological orientation. The stormy violence of the revolutionary years had subsided. With a few exceptions, such as Affandi's dynamic style or Amrus' violent pathos, there was delicacy and decorativeness in the works, and occasionally idiosyncratic use of color. There was a great deal of talent in evidence. And it was not surprising that, apart from the general diversity of styles, the same artist would paint in several styles at one time or even combine elements of different recognizable styles in a single painting. The search for integration was the ongoing process, not only in the individual artist but in the whole nation.

If some observers denigrate the achievements of Indonesia's contemporary artists by characterizing their works as merely derivative from the West (a criticism I have heard applied not only to Indonesia), they might recall another phase in Southeast Asia's cultural history when influences from India had spread eastward over the continent and the islands. It certainly took more than three, or four, or even ten decades for the impact of ideas, imagery, and art forms stemming from India to be locally digested, adapted, and transmuted into Burmese, Cambodian, Thai, Vietnamese, and Indonesian art. A century is but a brief period in the history of an old civilization. The creativity that goes into the process of learning and assimilation should not be underestimated.

Having come to the end of our inquiry, let us contemplate for a moment a sequence of representations with the eternal theme, fertility, here epitomized in rice. A strong, primitive stone figure—that could be prehistoric—of a woman with mortar and pestle, symbolic of fecundity, is seated on the lid of a Toba Batak sarcophagus in an old cemetery on the island of Samosir in Sumatra; a graceful bronze image of the rice goddess Wasudhara (identified with Dewi Sri, patron-

Plate 197. *The Rice Goddess Wasudhara* (*Sri*), *bronze, Central Java,* c. *9th–10th century.*

Plate 198. *The Rice Goddess Sri on a Balinese palm-leaf altar panel* (lamak).

Plate 199. *"Rice Fields," by Kartono Yudhokusumo, 1955.*

Plate 200. *"Agriculture," mural by Srihadi Sudarsono, 1956.*

ess of fertility and good fortune) was created in Central Java during the Hinduistic era. In the twentieth century the traditional, stylized *tjili* figure of the Rice Goddess adorns the festive palm-leaf altar panels in Bali. Kartono's landscape with the beloved cascading terraces of rice fields and Srihadi's mural "Agriculture" are different examples of the same theme in modern art. From age to age this theme has been embodied in plastic form in the various Indonesian islands in styles that changed in time but also differed from region to region. While the Indonesian state is promoting unity, Indonesia's art will always be richer for its diversity.

Notes

1. Cf. brief surveys on modern art in Indonesia written in English, such as: Kusnadi, "Indonesian Fine Art," in *Indonesian Art,* Art Department, Cultural Office, Ministry of Education and Culture (Jogjakarta, 1955), pp. 55–63; Raden Moerdowo, "Indonesian Painting, Some Contemporary Trends," *The Studio,* CLII, No. 764 (London, 1956), pp. 129–137; Trisno Sumardjo, "The Tendencies in Indonesian Art," in *Perspective of Indonesia; Atlantic Monthly Supplement* (New York, Intercultural Publications, June, 1956), pp. 33–42.

2. Cf. R. M. Sularko, "Exposisi Seni Rupa Asia-Africa, II," *Mimbar Indonesia* (Djakarta, June 11, 1955), no. 24, p. 22. The article appeared in three sections in nos. 23, 24, 25 of *Mimbar Indonesia* (June, 1955).

APPENDIX I

SYNOPSES OF EPICS AND STORIES

A. The Ramayana

THE monumental epic *Ramayana* (story of Rama)* is thought to relate to two North Indian tribes of the late Vedic age (*c.* twelfth to tenth centuries B.C.), the Kosala and the Videha, since in the epic these names are those of the kingdoms allied by the marriage of Rama, prince of Kosala, to the daughter of Videha's illustrious king, Janaka. Of the many extant versions, the oldest is ascribed to the sage Valmiki, supposedly a contemporary of Rama. Research, however, indicates that the epic was written down in its present "Valmiki" form shortly before the beginning of the Christian era. It consists of 24,000 verses (*sloka*) divided into 500 songs.

Like the *Mahabharata,* the *Ramayana* is known throughout Southeast Asia and has inspired much of its art. In Indonesia, the story of Rama was first set down in literary form by a poet named Yogiswara who composed the *Ramayana Kakawin,* probably the oldest Old Javanese (*kawi*) literary work. The time and place of Yogiswara's work is still a matter of scholarly conjecture, but there are strong arguments for assuming that it was done in tenth-century Central Java. Comparison of Yogiswara's poem with different Indian versions of the *Ramayana* revealed that the poet did not follow the so-called Valmiki version, but had as model and inspiration a version from the seventh century A.D. known as *Bhattikavya* ("Bhatti's Poem"), which has only 1,625 stanzas. Yogiswara's poem is far from a mere translation. He has moved away considerably from the Indian prototype, possibly using other sources as well as his own imagination, and composed 2,774 stanzas in elaborate kakawin form. It is thus not only the oldest but also the longest poem in Old Javanese literature.

The magnificent *Ramayana* reliefs on tenth-century Tjandi Prambanan, the "wayang style" series on Majapahit's Tjandi Panataran, and innumerable figures and reliefs with *Ramayana* themes in Bali testify to the uninterrupted popularity of the epic in these two Indonesian islands. Episodes from it continue to be performed in Javanese and Balinese shadow plays (wayang kulit), in classical dance drama (wayang wong), and also in West Java in the theater of round puppets (wayang golek). *Ramayana* wayang wong performances of truly grandiose proportions have been instituted in modern Indonesia. A large amphitheater has been built on the grounds of the Prambanan temples in Central Java to permit thousands of spectators to see during the dry season the story of Rama unfolding under the full moon for seven nights in succession. Hundreds of dancers in gorgeous costumes enact to the sounds of the gamelan episode after episode of the ancient story.

God Wisnu (Vishnu) was once incarnated in the newborn son of a Kosala king of Ayodya, Dasarata by name, whose kingdom lay near the slopes of the Himalaya. In the shape of Rama, the first-born of Dasarata and his wife Kausalya, Wisnu was to fight and conquer the king of demons, Rawana, who ruled Alengka (Langka). While still a youth, Rama displayed amazing prowess and skill in archery. Once he was sent to the hermitage of Wiswamitra to kill the demons who daily despoiled the holy man's offerings. The hermit took the young prince to the court of king Djanaka of the Widehas, where Rama surpassed all his rivals in an archery contest and won the beautiful princess Sita for his bride.

In consultation with his people, the aged king Dasarata has appointed Rama his heir. While preparations for Rama's coronation and attending festivities are begun, however, the king's other wife, Kaikeyi, has reminded him of a vow made to her long ago, in which Dasarata had promised to fulfill anything she might wish. Kaikeyi now demands the banishment of Rama and the coronation of her own son Barata. Heartbroken, the king is forced to keep his vow but dies soon afterward. Rama honors his father's obligation and goes into exile, followed by Sita and his devoted brother

* The synopses of the Indian epics given in this appendix outline their narrative as known in both India and Indonesia. In the transcription of Indian names and words, modern Indonesian usage has been followed.

Laksmana. They wander through the forests and settle at a place called Tjitrakuta. There they are found by Rama's crowned half-brother Barata, who implores Rama to return. Rama refuses but gives his half-brother his sandals to take back to Ayodya, legitimizing Barata's rule in Rama's name.

Thereafter Rama leaves his abode to go deeper into the woods, beyond the reach of his relations and people. With Sita and Laksmana he finds asylum with hermits and saints, including Agastya, who gives him a magic bow. He then settles in the forest of Pantjawati, where with Laksmana's help a cottage is built. Then Sarpakenaka (Surpanakha), the sister of the demon-king Rawana, while wandering in the wood, happens upon Rama, falls in love with him, and tries to win him for herself. Rama repulses her, and when she turns to Laksmana, he mutilates her nose and ears. Seeking vengeance, Sarpakenaka flees to her brother Rawana who orders his servant Maritja to assume the shape of a marvelous golden deer. Sita, enraptured by the sight of the golden deer, begs Rama to capture it for her despite Laksmana's warnings. Rama disappears in pursuit of the deer, leaving Sita in Laksmana's care. But soon they hear Rama's voice calling for help, which is actually Maritja's last cry before he dies, pierced by Rama's arrow. Overcoming Laksmana's protests by unjust accusations, Sita forces him to go to what she believes is Rama's rescue, and she remains alone. Then Rawana himself appears in the disguise of a begging Brahman. After much flattery and an attempt to persuade her to abandon Rama, he grasps Sita and carries her off, soaring into the air as he assumes his own terrible shape of many heads and arms. A brave bird, Djatayu, tries in vain to rescue Sita by attacking Rawana in flight, but is mortally wounded and only manages before dying to tell Rama of Sita's abduction.

The great search begins. Wandering with Laksmana through the dense and dangerous woods and in the Nilgiri mountains, Rama in vain seeks some traces of Sita. Then a white monkey, Hanuman, appears and leads Rama to the king of the monkeys, Sugriwa, who had been deprived of his throne by his brother Subali (Walin, Bali). Rama helps Sugriwa regain his throne by killing Subali with an arrow shot while the monkey brothers are fighting. Out of gratitude, Sugriwa offers Rama his assistance. He orders his monkey armies to search the world for Sita in all four directions. The armies going south are commanded by Hanuman, and Rama and Laksmana join them.

After many adventures and clues obtained from a brother of the bird Djatayu, named Sempati (who lost all his feathers trying to fly to the sun), they reach the shore opposite Alengka. In a daring leap across the sea, Hanuman lands in Alengka for preliminary explorations. He eventually comes to a garden of Rawana's palace, where he discovers Sita. Hidden in the foliage of a tree, he witnesses Sita refusing to yield to Rawana and threatening to commit suicide. After the frustrated king of demons retires, Hanuman sings of Rama and of Rama's coming to Sita's rescue. He is sought out by the captive princess, gives her a token from Rama, and in return receives from her a ring for her husband. Before leaping back to India's coast, Hanuman manages to wreak havoc in Rawana's capital. The demons capture him and set fire to his tail in an attempt to burn him. But Hanuman, freeing himself, jumps from roof to roof and sets houses on fire. His capital aflame, Rawana is alarmed and decides on war. Hanuman then rushes to the sea and leaps back to the mainland.

The monkey armies are then ordered to gather large boulders and rocks which are thown into the sea in order to build a causeway. The armies cross to Alengka, and violent battles ensue. In the end Rawana is slain by Rama with an arrow received from the saint Agastya; Rama and Sita are reunited. But suspicion that she may not have resisted her captor poisons Rama's mind, and Sita is subjected to an ordeal by fire which proves her stainless virtue. Thereupon Rama, Sita, and Laksmana return to Ayodya in an aerial car which had originally been in Rawana's possession.

The triumphant return to Ayodya and Rama's consecration as king, which may originally have concluded the epic, has a melancholy sequel. Sita's captivity in Rawana's palace continues to cast shadows upon her reputation, the previous ordeal notwithsanding. Yielding to public pressure, Rama banishes his devoted wife. She finds shelter in the forest-hermitage of the sage Valmiki. There she gives birth to twins, Lawa and Kusa. The boys grow up under the hermit's care and become his disciples. When, years later, Rama performs the great horse-sacrifice, Valmiki comes to the capital with his two apprentices who day after day chant portions of the *Ramayana* which describe Rama's deeds. Rama recognizes the youths as his sons, and, repentant, he asks Sita to return. But she, having endured too much already, refuses. She appeals to the Goddess of the Earth to receive her and disappears into a cleft in the opening earth. Rama eventually regains heaven in his original shape of Wisnu.

Of all the heroes of the *Ramayana,* apart from Rama and Sita, the white monkey Hanuman probably enjoys the greatest popularity and a favorite lakon is based on his mission to Alengka (See Appendix III). Other favorite characters are: Kumbakarna, the noble giant, wrongly allied with Rawana; and Wibisana, Rawana's brother who courageously objects to the king's evil intentions.

B. The Mahabharata

THE *Mahabharata,* India's other immortal epic and at least as rich a source of mythology as the *Ramayana,* may be based on a historical war between two neighboring tribes, the Kuru and the Panchala, each with their allies, which may have taken place around the ninth century B.C. It is ascribed to the sage Vyasa, the grandfather of the leader of both contending parties, the Pandava and the Kaurava. Through the ages the central tale has been infused with many additions—legendary stories or didactic interludes inserted between or woven into the principal episodes. Thus the epic has assumed truly monumental proportions—90,000 stanzas—and is therefore probably the longest single poem in the world's literature. Its final form became fixed sometime around A.D. 400.

The earliest surviving Indonesian version of the epic is in Old Javanese prose—a highly condensed rendering of eight *parvans* (main subdivisions of the *Mahabharata*). They may have been composed at different times but it is definitely known that three of them were written sometime around A.D. 996 upon order of the reigning East Javanese king, Dharmawangsa. Some thirty years later under King Airlangga, the poet Mpu Kanwa, inspired by one episode in the *Mahabharata,* composed the beautiful kakawin *Ardjuna Wiwaha.* In A.D. 1157 under the celebrated patron of literature, King Jayabhaya of Kediri, Mpu Sedah began and Mpu Panuluh completed the kakawin *Bharatayuddha* ("The War of the Bharatas"), dealing with the climactic eighteen-day battle between the Kaurava and the Pandava of the *Mahabharata.*

Since then, the *Mahabharata* has continued to captivate the minds of the Javanese and Balinese—a constant source of inspiration for their arts and letters. In Java and Bali the epic is performed in the shadow play, wayang kulit (purwa or parwa), in classical dance drama, wayang wong, and, in West Java, in wayang golek.

The tragic conflict between two families of the Kuru clan descended from Bharata—the Pandawa and the Korawa (Kaurava)—is the theme of this epic. The Korawa, ninety-nine in number, are the sons of King Dastarastra (Dhrtarashtra), who was born blind. The five Pandawa brothers are the sons of the King's brother, Pandu. Each of Pandu's sons is of semidivine origin. The eldest, the righteous Yudistira, descended from Dharma, god of virtue; the sanguine and powerful Bima from Bayu (Vayu), god of the wind; the noble Ardjuna from Indra, god of the rains; and the twins, Nakula and Sadewa, from the celestial Aswin twins. Pandu's wife, Kunti (Pritha) had given birth to still another son, Karna, begotten by the sun-god Surya. But Karna, regarded in life as a son of a charioteer, is ignorant of his own origin and eventually joins the camp of the Korawa, becoming a formidable opponent to his half-brother Ardjuna.

Because Dastarastra is blind, his brother Pandu has ruled the kingdom Hastina in his name. Thus the cousins have been raised together and have had the same preceptors, among them their great-uncle Bisma and the wise Brahman, Durna (Drona). In the constant rivalry between the cousins, the Pandawa have always proved superior and incurred the Korawa's jealousy and hatred.

After Pandu's death, the old blind king appoints Yudistira, his eldest nephew, heir to the throne, greatly angering his own sons, headed by the ruthless Duryodana. The Korawa then set out to destroy their cousins. On one occasion the Pandawa are persuaded to visit a distant town, where they must stay in a house made of highly combustible material. At night the house is set afire, and the Pandawa brothers narrowly escape through an underground passage. While they flee through the forests, the indomitable Bima encounters an ogress transformed into a beautiful princess who falls in love with him. She bears him a son, the prodigious Gatutkatja, who inherits from his mother the power to fly and from his father strength and courage. Following this, the Pandawa live in Ekatjakra, disguised as begging Brahmans. Later they are attracted by the announcement of a sayembara (*swayambara*), a contest for the hand of a princess, and they journey to the kingdom of Pantjala ruled by King Drupada. Ardjuna defeats all his rivals in a great archery contest and wins the beautiful princess, Drupadi. According to an ancient custom, Drupadi becomes the wife of all five brothers, although later all had other wives as well. Ardjuna marries Sumbadra, sister of Kresna, with whom he has a son, the gentle and brave Abimanyu. Thereafter, having found powerful allies in King Drupada and in Kresna (Krishna), King of the Yadawa at Dwarawati (and an incarnation of the god Wisnu), the Pandawa return to their land where the Korawa consent to a division of the Hastina kingdom. The Korawa retain the richer eastern portion and its capital Hastinapura, while the Pandawa receive the western part where they build their new capital, Ngamarta (Indraprastha; supposedly it was situated in the vicinity of present-day Delhi).

Not abandoning their designs for the destruction of the Pandawa and the possession of the entire kingdom, the Korawa renew their schemes. With the aid of Sakuni, an expert at loading dice, Duryodana challenges Yudistira, who is a passionate gambler. The outcome is disastrous. Losing game after game, Yudistira forfeits all his wealth, his kingdom, and finally even Drupadi and his own and his brothers' freedom. Through the intercession of the old blind king, a period of exile is substituted for slavery. The Pandawa are to live in hiding for twelve years and then spend one additional year, undiscovered, among the common people. After the twelve years spent in the forests have passed, the Pandawa enter the service of a king, Wirata, under assumed names. Yudistira becomes a Brahman-courtier expert in dice, Bima a cook, Ardjuna a eunuch skilled in music and dance, Nakula a stableboy and Sadewa a cowherd. They remain undiscovered until the end of the year. But despite fulfillment of their part of the bargain, their demand for the return of their kingdom is futile, and, even contrary to the wishes of the old king, Duryodana remains adamant. In council with Kresna, the Pandawa then decide to recapture their kingdom by force.

The climax of the epic is the Great War of the Bharatas. For eighteen days the fields between the two holy rivers, the Ganges and the Yumna, are the scene of terrible carnage. The earth trembles from the furious encounters of warriors mounted on horses and elephants or riding in swift chariots. The famous Bhagavad Gita—which is Ardjuna's dialogue with his mentor and charioteer Kresna, to whom he turns in anguish at the prospect of having to kill his kin—is the prelude to the battle in which the two armies face each other in full battle array. The events of these eighteen days, as described day by day in the epic, are filled with tragic incidents in which the cousins' old venerated preceptors inexorably meet their death, as do many young heroes, including Ardjuna's sons Irawan and Abimanyu and Bima's son Gatutkatja. In the final encounters Ardjuna kills Karna, and Bima slays Duryodana. Funerary rites are then held for all the fallen warriors, the women lamenting their husbands and sons.

Yudistira is crowned king and reigns in Ngastinapura. An epilogue tells of the great horse-sacrifice (*ashwameda*) held by Yudistira upon the advice of the sage Wyasa to expiate the carnage of the war which still haunts the king. His designated heir is Ardjuna's grandson, Pariksit.

Among the favorite heroes of the *Mahabharata* in Java, Ardjuna and Bima are most prominent—the former for his nobility of spirit, irresistible charm in love conquests, and superior power in combat; the latter for his interpidity and physical might. Of Ardjuna's many wives, the amazon Srikandi and the princess Sumbadra appear most frequently in Javanese plays. Bima's son Gatutkatja, as impetuous as his father, is among the most admired heroes of the Pandawa's "younger generation." The sons and grandsons of the five brothers are recurrent participants in plays. Kresna, the deity-king, is almost always present as are, of course, the Korawa headed by Duryodana, with his advisor the perifidious Sakuni (or Sangkuni). The Korawa are depicted in monstrous shapes.

It should be noted that various heroes often have several names. Some are appelations following the Indian pattern, and some are Indonesian inventions. The additional names are connected with: (a) a stage in the hero's life (e.g., Ardjuna is Pamadé in his youth and Djanaka when adult; Bima as a youth is Bratasena, as an adult, Werkudara); (b) a particular activity (e.g., Ardjuna during ascesis is known as Mintaraga); (c) the name of his kingdom or tribe (e.g., Kresna is Dwarawati; Yudistira is Ngamarta; Duryodana is Kurupati); (d) the father's name (e.g., Karna is Suryaputera, son of Surya; Yudistira is Darmaputera, son of Darma). Also, Duryodana, eldest of the Korawa who becomes king of Hastinapura (Astina or Ngastina in Java) is usually called Sujudana.

C. The Ardjuna Wiwaha

THE *Ardjuna Wiwaha,* inspired by the Mahabharata, was composed by Mpu Kanwa in A.D. 1035 during Airlangga's reign. This Old Javanese poem, a kakawin, may be an allusion to Airlangga's own life. The poet's concluding lines read: "Completed is the description of the story of which the name is Ardjuna Wiwaha. This is in fact the first time that Mpu Kanwa has composed a poem and made it public. He is, however, in an anxious frame of mind, since he will accompany the King to battle. Venerated be His Majesty Airlangga, who has doubled the size of the kingdom and who approves of this work." The *Ardjuna Wiwaha* or parts of it are performed in Javanese and Balinese classical dance drama.

Anxiety and confusion reign in Indra's heaven. The demonic king of titans, Niwatakawatja, threatens to destroy the abode of the gods in revenge for their refusal to give him the beautiful nymph Supraba. He is not placated by the gifts of Indra who from time to time sends him other nymphs for his harem. The gods are powerless against Niwatakawatja, since once the highest deity granted him an invulnerability complete except for one secret spot. Although no divine being could slay him, he was forewarned to guard against a man with extraordinary power.

The gods, who had gathered in council, learn that Parta (Ardjuna) has retired to a grotto on Mt. Indrakila, where through ascesis he is accumulating the great power he needs to crush the titan king and save the world. Indra decides to test Ardjuna's steadfastness by subjecting him to the temptation of beautiful celestial nymphs. Were he to resist and prove his steadfastness, the gods would entrust him with the mission of fighting Niwatakawatja.

The gods choose seven heavenly nymphs (*widadari*) experienced in disturbing ascesis to tempt Ardjuna. The most beautiful among them are Tilottama and the lovely Supraba. Followed by a few servant girls, the nymphs descend to the grotto on Mt. Indrakila where Ardjuna sits, deep in meditation. But none of their charms and seductive wiles can divert the meditating recluse. Lovelorn and disheartened, they return to Indra's heaven to report their failure. The gods rejoice in Ardjuna's steadfastness, but now fear that in his complete absorption he will forsake the world, seeking instead his own salvation in ultimate deliverance. Indra then decides to visit Ardjuna himself. He appears before Ardjuna in the guise of an old, weak, half-naked holy man whom at first Ardjuna does not even notice. When Indra finally succeeds in making Ardjuna aware of his presence, a conversation develops in which the god insistently urges Ardjuna, so far advanced in his mystic endeavour, to aim at the highest goal—salvation by entering Nirvana. Ardjuna, however, respectfully insists on fulfilling his duty as a *kshatriya,** on using his power for the benefit of the gods and mankind. Indra then reveals himself in his own divine shape, encourages Ardjuna to persist in his striving, and vanishes.

Meanwhile, rumors of Ardjuna's ascesis have also reached Niwatakawatja, who is alarmed and sends one of his giants, Murka, to decapitate Ardjuna. Unable to find Ardjuna, Murka transforms himself into an enormous wild boar who goes on the rampage, trying to push over Mt. Indrakila; it bursts at the top. Shaken from his meditation, Ardjuna steps out with his bow. At this moment, however, god Shiva, who has descended to earth to observe the doings of men and to ascertain Ardjuna's goals, arrives on the scene, disguised as a king hunting. Simultaneously Ardjuna and the god shoot arrows which pierce the boar at the same spot and then fuse into one. When Ardjuna approaches the boar to extract his arrow, Shiva claims it as his own and challenges Ardjuna in strong and abusive language. A terrible duel ensues with an eruption of the mountain accompanying the battle. Finally, the two begin to wrestle. Thrown down by Shiva, Ardjuna seizes the god's feet, but just as he is ready to topple him over, the feet disappear. A rain of flowers descends with celestial sounds of praise, and the deity becomes a radiant apparition. Ardjuna, kneeling, pays homage to the god and addresses him in a beautiful prayer.

* The second or knightly caste of the Hindu four-caste social system.

Shiva then gives him a magic spear, a fire arrow called Pashupati with a bow, and a war helmet, and instructs Ardjuna in the fine arts of battle.

With his ascesis successfully completed, Ardjuna is summoned to Indra's heaven and asked to help the gods fight the titan king. The gods devise a scheme for discovering Niwatakawatja's vulnerable spot: Supraba, so long coveted by the king of the titans although herself in love with Ardjuna, is to accompany Ardjuna. She must use her seductive charms to try to learn his secret, but without yielding to him. Ardjuna and Supraba journey together to Manimantaka (also Himantaka), the titan's capital.

On Niwatakawatja's palace grounds the two come upon his harem in a crystal pavilion. Some of Supraba's former companions recognize her, while Ardjuna makes himself invisible. Supraba pretends to have come voluntarily, as if recognizing the titan king as the inevitable conqueror of the gods. She begs the nymphs to announce her arrival to Niwatakawatja by saying that she was ready to serve him. Ardjuna remains present invisibly to witness the outcome.

Overjoyed, Niwatakawatja hastens to the pavilion and there, left alone with Supraba, he cradles her in his lap. The nymph repulses his amorous advances with difficulty. While resisting she demands as her "bride price" to know the secret of his power and invulnerability. In his eagerness to possess her, Niwatakawatja boastfully blurts out his secret—that only the tip of his tongue is vulnerable. No sooner has he spoken then Ardjuna produces a terrible concussion which rocks the pavilion. In the ensuing panic, Supraba flies off toward heaven and is soon joined by Ardjuna. While they report to the gods, the enraged Niwatakawatja, who immediately realizes that he has been tricked, gathers his armies of giants and monsters and starts on the warpath. One by one the domains of lesser gods are overrun and destroyed, the demonic forces coming ever nearer Indra's heaven. Indra then mobilizes his hosts and from his chariot leads them against the forces of the titans. During a terrible battle which shakes the world, Ardjuna fights Niwatakawatja. At one point he pretends to have been felled by his foe's spear. When the demon king approaches to mock him, Ardjuna's arrow strikes his tongue through Niwatakawatja's laughing open mouth.

Great celebrations of the victory are then held in Indra's heaven. Ardjuna is made king for seven days (which by heavenly reckoning last seven months). He is crowned, honored by the gods and saints, and sprinkled with the divine water of life. After his initiation, he is given a separate dwelling "excelling the abode of the God of Love," which is surrounded by seven pavilions, one for each the nymphs whose seductive advances he had withstood earlier. Now, however, starting with Supraba and then Tilottama, Ardjuna indulges in all the delights of love. When the seven month-days are over, he begs Indra's permission to return to earth to rejoin his kin. The heartbroken nymphs lament Ardjuna's departure from Indra's heaven. Ardjuna returns to earth where he rejoins his overjoyed brothers.

The title *Ardjuna Wiwaha,* translated literally, means "Celebrations of Ardjuna's Wedding," which may be interpreted as referring to Ardjuna's "weddings" with the seven celestial nymphs who had originally tried to seduce him. In Javanese dance drama, however, the celebrations in Indra's heaven culminate with Ardjuna's wedding to the nymph Supraba. Also the Pandawa and their ally, King Kresna, participate with the gods and Ardjuna in the battle against the titans.

D. A Pandji Romance

THE HERO of an extensive cycle of stories known in different written versions and oral traditions, Pandji is in many ways the East Javanese Ardjuna, the ideal noble prince, unconquerable in battle and irresistible in love. But whereas Ardjuna's strivings are linked with the welfare of the Pandawa clan and their kingdom or the preservation of the divine order, Pandji's goals are narrowly focused on reunion with his elusive bride, the beautiful Tjandra Kirana (Radiant Ray of the Moon), a princess of Daha (Kediri). The stories are full of mysterious disappearances, transformations, disguises and resurrections, and it has been conjectured that the adventures of Pandji in search of Tjandra Kirana reflect an ancient sun and moon myth. On the other hand, the names of certain personages, of the principal kingdoms and some of the events evoke associations with historical East Java. It is thought that the Pandji romances originated there some time in the fifteenth century. From East Java they spread to Malaya, Thailand, and Cambodia where the stories and their heroes are known under many different names and, as in Java and Bali, enjoy great popularity.

In Java, Pandji stories serve as themes for mask plays, wayang topeng, and for the now rare puppet plays known as wayang gedog;* in Bali, where they are known as *Malat*, they are performed in the *Gambuh* plays and in the operatic *Ardja*.

The synopsis below is based on only one of the innumerable versions of the Pandji adventures.

Pandji, prince of Kuripan, is in despair when, on the eve of their wedding, his beautiful bride Tjandra Kirana, the princess of Daha (Kediri), vanishes suddenly from their bridal chamber. Insane with sorrow, he is consoled by the appearance of a princess who claims to be Tjandra Kirana, although outwardly she looks totally different. This princess, in reality an evil demon-princess who wants Pandji for herself, alleges that she had been carried off by the terrible Durga, the goddess of death, and that she will regain her original shape as soon as she and Pandji are married. With new hope Pandji orders preparations for the wedding resumed.

Meanwhile the true Tjandra Kirana finds herself alone in a forest. Her despairing laments are heard by the gods who advise her that in order to be reunited with Pandji she must go to his palace disguised as a man. Tjandra Kirana assumes a male disguise and returns to the palace, where the preparations for Pandji's marriage to the impostor are progressing rapidly. Tjandra Kirana, unable to bear Pandji's attentions to the false bride, writes a letter to the prince in which she reveals the situation. She then vanishes. Pandji, greatly shocked, rushes to search for his true love while his courtiers kill the demonic impostor.

Pandji's long wanderings in search of Tjandra Kirana are filled with adventures in battle as well as in love. He stays in forests with hermits, he works at different palaces as a servant, always and untiringly seeking for traces of his lost bride. Tjandra Kirana, meanwhile, keeps her male disguise, going through her own series of adventures, and eventually becomes the king of Bali—a monarch renowned for his courage as well as for some distinctly feminine skills such as embroidery and lacework. The climax of the story is reached as Pandji and Tjandra Kirana oppose each other on a battle field. All witnesses are ordered to leave, whereupon the princess, ignorant of Pandji's identity, confides to him that she is the bride of Pandji, that her male disguise was assumed because of a command by the gods who said she could win back her beloved prince only in a face-to-face combat in which his blood would flow. Then they fight, first with swords and later with arrows. Tjandra Kirana cannot harm her opponent, however, until finally she slyly resorts to her hairpin as a weapon. Pandji is wounded, reveals his identity, and the two are happily reunited.

The hero of the Pandji romances appears in the different Javanese and Malay versions under various names, including Raden Pandji, Raden Inu, Inu (of) Koripan, Ino (or Hino) Kartapati, Tjekel Wanengpati or Kuda Wanengpati. Tjandra Kirana's other

* See Chapter 5.

name is Sekar Tadji; when she is disguised as a man she is known in some stories as Kuda Narawangsa.

Other prominent personages in Pandji stories and plays are: Klono (Klana), a ferocious king "from overseas" who desires Tjandra Kirana and tries to gain possession of her by threatening the Daha kingdom with destruction; Gunung Sari, Tjandra Kirana's brother; Ragil Kuning (also known as Dewi Onengan), Pandji's sister married to Gunung Sari; Wirun, Kartala, and Andaga, young relatives and companions of Pandji.

E. The Damar Wulan Legend

THE *Damar Wulan* legend is associated with the Majapahit kingdom, when it was ruled by a maiden queen, Dewi Suhita, during whose reign a war arose with the kingdom of Balambangan. The hero's name, "Radiance of the Moon," and that of his foe, Menak Djingga, the "Red Knight" (whose magic weapon is a "yellow iron") have suggested to some writers that the legend contains elements of an older sun and moon myth. It is neither certain when the story was recorded in its present form, nor who wrote it.

In Java the *Damar Wulan* story used to be performed in *wayang kerutjil* (or *klitik*), that is, with flat wooden leather-armed puppets, which, unlike the leather puppets, were not shown as shadows against a screen. On the stage it was performed as Langendriya (a dance-opera with female dancers); today it is part of the *ketoprak* repertory.

The principal persons in the romance of *Damar Wulan* are:

Prabu Kenya, the Maiden Queen of Majapahit (also known as Ratu Kentjana, the Golden Queen), daughter of King Brawidjaya who died without male heirs.

Patih Logender, her prime minister, an ambitious and ruthless man who succeeds his elder brother, Damar Wulan's father, who had retired to a hermitage following King Brawidjaya's death. Logender fails to win the love of his brother's wife, who is pregnant and retires to her father's hermitage where Damar Wulan is born.

Layang Seta and Layang Kumitir, Logender's haughty and envious sons.

Dewi Andjasmara, Logender's beautiful daughter who becomes Damar Wulan's selfless wife.

Damar Wulan, a youth of radiant charm, a nephew of the prime minister, who is raised in the hermitage of his grandfather.

Menak Djingga, the "Red Knight," King of Balambangan (the easternmost part of Java) and vassal of Majapahit, bent on possessing the Maiden Queen; a limping, voluptuous, and cruel prince.

Dewi Wahita and Dewi Puyengan, two princesses held captive at the palace of Menak Djingga. They would rather commit suicide than yield to their captor.

Sabdapalon and Nayagenggong, Damar Wulan's devoted servants and guardians, former retainers of his father.

The trials of Damar Wulan begin when, following the advice of his grandfather, he leaves the hermitage and journeys to the court of Majapahit to seek employment with his uncle, Patih Logender. Even before he can present himself to his uncle, Damar Wulan is mistreated at the gate by his cousins, the prime minister's sons. Patih Logender, attracted by the commotion, learns of Damar Wulan's desire to serve him, but, sensing that his nephew may be a potential rival to his own sons, he assigns Damar Wulan to the lowly service of stableboy and grasscutter. Although stripped of his fine garments and ornaments, the grasscutter's striking beauty nevertheless inspires the intense admiration of the common people. Some market women secretly bring him baskets full of grass for his uncle's horses and food for himself in order to restore his health, badly undermined by near-starvation.

Rumors of the unusual stableboy reach the prime minister's daughter, Andjasmara. Learning that Damar Wulan is her cousin, she seeks him out secretly; they fall in love and are clandestinely married. One night as Andjasmara's brothers pass by their sister's chamber, they hear the lovers' voices. They break in and try to kill Damar Wulan, but he overcomes them and forces them to flee. Badly beaten, the brothers then tell their father what they have seen. In his wrath the prime minister demands that Damar Wulan be executed forthwith, and he is restrained only by his daughter's pleas. Thereupon he imprisons the pair.

At this time danger besets the kingdom of Majapahit. In a letter the king of Balambangan, Menak Djingga, has sought the Maiden Queen's hand. His suit is rejected in a humiliating fashion, and for revenge he declares war. Majapahit's allies have been defeated one by one; the kingdom itself is now threatened by Menak Djingga's forces. In distress the Maiden Queen announces that the man who kills Menak Djingga and brings her his head will become her "brother" (i.e., husband) if he is young, or her "father" if he is old. No potential saviors present themselves, and consternation reigns at the court. Then the queen in a divine revelation learns that a young knight named Damar Wulan can conquer the enemy. Patih Logender, ordered to find Damar Wulan, has to release him from prison and bring him before the queen. She entrusts Damar Wulan with the dangerous mission, but not without falling under the spell of his beauty.

After tenderly taking leave of Andjasmara, Damar Wulan, accompanied by his two faithful servants, makes his way to Balambangan. He arrives at night, penetrates into the gardens of Menak Djingga's palace, and comes upon a pavilion where he overhears a conversation between two captive princesses, who loathe their captor. Damar Wulan enters the pavilion and confides in them, later becoming their lover. The enraptured princesses are ready to follow him to their death. Meanwhile, after heavy feasting, Menak Djingga decides to visit the two princesses. Upon arriving after midnight at their pavilion, he discovers Damar Wulan. A dreadful fight follows, but Menak Djingga proves invulnerable. He taunts and repeatedly wounds Damar Wulan until the youth falls, apparently dead. Menak Djingga withdraws, ordering his servants to guard the corpse. When the servants fall asleep, the two princesses carry Damar Wulan away, revive him, and then disclose to him the secret of Menak Djingga's invulnerability: it is a club of "yellow iron" always kept behind the king's headrest. The king is doomed if hit on his left temple with this club. The princesses, risking their lives, succeed in stealing the "yellow iron" while Menak Djingga is asleep. The second battle is fatal for the Red Knight. Damar Wulan beheads him and, followed by the two princesses and his servants, makes his way back to the court of Majapahit. But as he approaches the capital, he is waylaid by Layang Seta and Layang Kumitir. The brothers kill Damar Wulan and present themselves to the Maiden Queen with Menak Djingga's head. Damar Wulan, however, is miraculously revived by a holy hermit, and before long the greatly disturbed Maiden Queen learns the truth. There is a final battle in which Damar Wulan defeats his two cousins. Eventually he is crowned king of Majapahit and, with the queen's consent, retains Andjasmara as his other wife.

In this legend Damar Wulan's power is a combination of meekness (his nonresistance to evil and his acceptance of suffering, as in his initial submission to Logender' sons and to his servitude), of fiery courage when defending what is sacred to him (his kris and Andjasmara), of strong erotic power and tenderness, and of basic faith.

Some of the most colorful moments in the dramatic presentations of the tale are contributed by Menak Djingga. His obsessive voluptuous dreams of the Maiden Queen, his cunning and malicious temperament, his ravings and mockery all provide great opportunities for expressive acting.

APPENDIX II

THE PERFORMING ARTS IN ANCIENT RECORDS AND LITERATURE

A. Eight Inscriptions from Java, A.D. 840–1358

FOR THE reconstruction of the history of Indonesian performing arts the most valuable sources, after visual representations on the tjandi reliefs, are ancient inscriptions and Old Javanese literature. The earliest references to dance and drama appear in Central Javanese stone or copper plate inscriptions from the eighth and ninth centuries. These inscriptions are mainly royal charters granting freeholds to persons or religious foundations. The text often records the events of the ritual consecration of the grant and the accompanying celebrations, including a variety of performances.

For the selection and translation of pertinent extracts from charters and for guidance to other sources, the author is indebted to the late Dr. Willem F. Stutterheim and to the late Louis-Charles Damais.

The sources (published transcriptions and translations) of all the following inscriptions are listed by Louis-Charles Damais in *Liste des Principales Inscriptions Datées de l'Indonésie; Bulletin de l'Ecole Française d'Extrême-Orient,* XLVI (1952).

1. A.D. 840 (762 Shaka); copper plates from Jaha.

The inscription was issued by Maharaja Sri Lokapala as a charter for the freehold at Kuti. It is of interest because it mentions a number of different officials connected with the performing arts and performers. They are mentioned among other groups upon whom certain restrictions are imposed.

Among those listed are:

pahawuhawu, perhaps officials in charge of amusements or amusement halls
juru jalir, officials in charge of prostitutes
dagang, officials in charge of clowns
atapukan, term not clear but perhaps officials in charge of wayang [or mask-] plays [possibly mask-players]
aringgit, actors [a term frequently encountered in later literature, which may also refer to shadow-play performers]
abanol, clowns [term used to the present day]
halu warak, perhaps persons from the retinue of the king serving as directors of the orchestra, wayang, and other entertainments
winingle, perhaps musicians
pawidu, might refer to performers of dramatic plays [in the light of later research, more likely chanting storytellers, bards]

Interestingly, the *atapukan, aringgit,* and *abanol* are mentioned together with "all sorts of servants of the inner apartments hailing from Champa, Kalinga, Aryya, Ceylon, Cola, Malabar, and Karnataka." This is a good example of material for further elucidation by students of ancient Javanese society; does this arrangement in the listing indicate that the two groups were privileged or unprivileged? May it, on the other hand, indicate that there were foreigners among the performers, especially from India and Ceylon, who thus influenced Indonesian performing arts?

2. A.D. 860 (792 Shaka); copper plates from Gedangan; Rijksmuseum voor Volkenkunde, Leiden.

The charter established the freehold at Kancana in favor of the Buddhist priest, Budhimba, his two children, and the Buddhist temple situated there. Among the classes of professional and tradespeople, *juru barata* are mentioned. Kern thought that these were actors or managers of plays.

3. A.D. 873 (795 Shaka); copper plates from Keboan Pasar; Rijksmuseum voor Volkenkunde, Leiden.

The plates record the foundation of a freehold at Waharu by Sang Hadyan Kuluptiru. It mentions that Kuluptiru held a feast at the founding ceremonies and that performer(s) "went forward (with) paints and flowers" and music was played. The "paints and flowers," by analogy with other more explicit texts, refer to make-up and adornment.

4. A.D. 901 (823 Shaka); copper plates from Panaraga; Djakarta Museum.

The inscription records the grant in freehold of garden lands and *sawah* [irrigated rice fields] to the hermitage of Dewasabha at Taji by favor of King dyah Balitung, Raka (of) Watukura. After defining boundaries, enumerating landowners and their compensation and mentioning the customary distribution of gifts (to 392 persons!) and of food, the text reads:

Now, in this connection, the *tanda rakryans* of Burawan, all together, and the *rāmas* of Taji ate, drank, powdered themselves,* adorned themselves with flowers, joked, danced (and) set the boars and cocks to fighting. At the same time, the *tanda rakryans* exchanged all sorts of jests [with?] . . . the *rāmas*. After the *tanda rakryans* held the cockfight, all *rāmas* danced, turning in a circle [separately]; then the women danced, turning in a circle [separately], [finally] the women stopped dancing.†

This is a rare, explicit reference to circular dancing in Java. The dancing village heads and matrons probably danced around the ritually erected consecration stone.

5. A.D. 902 (824 Shaka); copper plates from Kembang Arum; Djakarta Museum.

The charter in the names of the Rakryan of Wantil, his wife, and three sons, marks out a freehold at Panggumulan for the benefit of the god and goddess of Kinawuhan. Among those who received gifts on this occasion was Si Sru, father of Bukang, hailing from Dihyang (Dieng), who was the sculptor of the *watu sima,* perhaps the consecration stone.

After all had eaten, they removed themselves, made toilette with paints and flowers and sat on the ground in a circle with their faces turned toward Sang Hyang Kudur and the sacred *sima watu kulupang* under the tent,‡ in the middle of the ground. . . .

Then a chicken was sacrificed (crushing the neck), an egg broken, and curses upon potential transgressors pronounced. After paying respects to the stone, the people went "back to their leaves" (i.e., to their food which was served on leaves). "Now there was dancing," the inscription says. Later among the various people who received gifts, a buffoon is favored with four silver pieces.

6. A.D. 907 (829 Shaka); copper plates from central Java; Royal Tropical Institute, Amsterdam.

Issued in the name of King Balitung, the text refers to the village Sangsang, marked as a freehold, the proceeds from which were to go to the god of the cloister at Dalinan. Again, after adorning themselves "with paints and flowers," the participants seated themselves

* Or painted their faces with a colored powder. See Ch. 6, p. 161.

† Translated by Stutterheim and emended by Damais.

‡ This was not a tent made of stretched cloth or skin. It might have been the temporary shelter customarily constructed on festive occasions in Java and Bali, a leaf- or grass-covered roof supported by posts.

in the festive tent facing the Sang Hyang Kudur. There they invoked the gods and prayed. "For the welfare of the sacred foundation and of all subjects," spectacles (*ton-tonan*) were then given.

Sang Tangkil Hyang sang (*mamidu*); si Nalu recited (*macarita*) *Bhima Kumāra* and danced (*mangigal*) as Kiçaka; si Jaluk recited the Rāmayāna; si Mung-muk play-acted (*mamirus*) and clowned (*mabañol*); si Galigi performed wayang (*mawayang*) for the gods, reciting the *Bimmaya Kumāra.**

Thereafter, the dignitaries settled down to gambling, while two persons seem to have engaged in some sort of amusement involving a special (masked?) dress.

The translation of this passage is open to doubt, but only with regard to assignment of roles to the various performers. The text's importance lies in the clear indication that in the beginning of the tenth century, episodes from the *Mahabharata* and the *Ramayana* were recited on ritual occasions. The *Bimmaya Kumara* (presumably a story related to Bima) may have been performed as a shadow play (now, *wayang purwa*).

7. *C.* A.D. 928 (694 Sanjaya); stone of unknown origin; Djakarta Museum.

The inscription in the name of Rakryan Gurumwangi, mentions that the rakryan's players (*memen*) danced (*mangigal*) on the occasion of the founding of a freehold at Taji Gunung. (This inscription is of additional interest because it mentions Sanjaya as conqueror of Bali.)

8. A.D. 1358 (1280 Shaka); copperplate from Trawulan; Modjokerto Museum.

This inscription dates from the regency of Queen Tribhuwana. Her son, Hayam Wuruk, later reigned under the name Rajasanagara. The *Nagarakrtagama,* which will be referred to later in this appendix, was written during his reign. The inscription reads in part:

Sri Hayamwuruk, under the auspices of Her Majesty, Bhatara Sri Tribhuwanottungga, of the coronation name of Rajadewi Jayawisnuwardhani, expert in such qualities as dancing, artistic work, etc. . . .

That this queen was expert in dancing also appears from another inscription in which the Sanskrit word *nrtya* (dance) is used in connection with the queen.

* The author has taken liberties with the translation of this passage. It now deviates from the Dutch translations by Stutterheim and by Van Naerssen.

B. Excerpts from Old Javanese Literature

In Old Javanese literature, both poetry and prose, different forms of the performing arts and a variety of performers are named. Sometimes they are described, as in the *Nagarakrtagama;* at other times they are only mentioned in poetic figures of speech, as in *Ardjuna Wiwaha* and *Sri Tandjung.* Both the direct and indirect references testify to the existence of certain plays in the period between 1000 and 1600.

1. The *Ardjuna Wiwaha* of Mpu Kanwa (*c.* 1030); Canto V, first part of stanza nine. (Translated by the author from the Dutch text, "Arjuna Wiwāha," by Dr. R. Ng. Poerbatjaraka in *BKI,* LXXXII (1926), p. 256.)*

When Indra descends in the guise of an old holy man to probe into Ardjuna's intentions, he speaks provocatively of attachment to the world: "(It is like someone) who looks at the shadow play (*ringgit*) and weeps. . . . Yet he well knows that it is only carved leather made to move and to speak."

2. The *Nagarakrtagama* of Rakawi Prapancha (1365).†

In the *Nagarakrtagama,* the performing arts are frequently mentioned but figure importantly in only two cantos. Although Prapancha's descriptions are insufficient for an unequivocal reconstruction of the spectacles, they are nevertheless valuable. They confirm the existence of certain plays and dances in the fourteenth century which are still alive today and also suggest others which have vanished. The exact nature of some of the plays and dances mentioned remains obscure because, apart from the sketchiness of the descriptions, the Old Javanese text is difficult to translate.

The only existing English translation of the poem is by Th. Pigeaud, published in his *Java in the Fourteenth Century: A Study in Cultural History.* Since this translation is so painstakingly literal that meaning has been sacrificed to an accuracy sometimes resulting in non-English, it needs further interpretation. Therefore, each cited stanza or group of stanzas is accompanied by a commentary or explanation based on Pigeaud's own interpretations. But, when Pigeaud's interpretation of a passage is significantly different from that of other scholars who have translated and/or commented on the poem, their opinions are also mentioned.*

The original 98 cantos of the poem have been grouped into 15 chapters by Pigeaud. Chapter IX is devoted principally to the final post-cremation rites (*shradda*) of the Rajapatni, the reigning king's grandmother. In stanzas 4 and 5 of canto 66 of that chapter, the poet describes the festivities which followed a week-long series of ritual proceedings.

Canto 66, stanza 4:

1. Densely crowded were the onlookers from the ten quarters of the world, thick, noisy, without open space.
2. The order of the place of the *sabha* (durbar) with the honoured ones who offered food there, was looked at by them, pressing (each other), trying to be the foremost.
3. The Illustrious Kings in the *witāna* (great hall) there danced with *binis* (women), *binis* only were the onlookers, entering into the Presence,
4. equally seated, in heaps, in rows, filling up (the space). Some forgot what they were doing, marvelling, looking on.

In this scene, according to Pigeaud, kings, presumably Hayam Wuruk, his father, and his uncles, dance (*mangigel*) with women in a pavilion crowded exclu-

* See Appendix I, pp. 272–273 for synopsis of the poem.
† See Part I, Ch. 3.

* Translations and interpretations of the poem consulted are as follows:

H. Kern, "De Nāgarakrtāgama; Oudjavaansch Lofdicht op Koning Hayam Wuruk," in *Verspreide Geschriften,* VII, VIII, 's-Gravenhage, 1918.

Theodore G. Th. Pigeaud, *Java in the Fourteenth Century: A Study in Cultural History;* The Nāgara-Kĕrtagāma by Rakawi Prapañca of Majapahit, 1365 A.D. (The Hague, 1960–1963), 4 volumes.

Raden Mas Ngabehi Poerbatjaraka, "Aanteekeningen op de Nāgarakretāgama," in *BKI,* LXXX (1924), 219–286.

Slametmuljana, *Nagarakretagama:* diperbaharui kedalam bahasa Indonesia. Djakarta, 1953.

sively with female spectators. The kings' performances cause a state of ecstasy in the women.

This interpretation differs from those of Pigeaud's predecessors in two ways: first, other scholars (Kern and Poerbatjaraka among them) interpreted the passage to mean that only one king danced, Hayam Wuruk himself; and second, that he danced alone, not with a female partner. All readings of the text agree on one point: the king danced and he danced before a group of women—perhaps somewhat like a strutting peacock surrounded by admiring hens?

Canto 66, stanza 5:

1. Whichsoever feast could give pleasure to the common people there was arranged by the Princes, in a word.
2. So the *widus-amancangah* (storytellers), *rakĕts* (dancing players), till all there was of common *gītadas* (singers) every day.
3. Something different were the *bhaṭas mapatra yuddha* (warriors eager for a fight). Natural were the men dancing about, for they were frightening, at the same time causing merriment.
4. In the first place the gifts for all kinds of mendicants without interruption caused delight for all the world.

Of all the performances mentioned in this stanza, the nature of only one is clear; the *bhaṭas mapatra yuddha* obviously were dancing warriors in mock combat. Whether they were wielding clubs (as Kern and Poerbatjaraka thought) or lances (as Pigeaud believes) is open to conjecture, however. Although their performance is described as realistic, or "natural," Pigeaud assures us that "in the ancient dances of two equally armed parties there never was a winner."*

What the other popular entertainments were like is not as certain. Poerbatjaraka translated *widu amancangah* as wayang plays and like Kern he thought *raket* was a mask play. Pigeaud, however, believes that *widu amancangah* was a chanting storyteller. He does not think that the raket was a mask dance but another type of play which will be dealt with in connection with the canto discussed next.

The most extensive description of theatrical performances appears in Chapter 14, the account of the Phalguna-Caitra festival held at Hayam Wuruk's court. Pigeaud believes that this was a kind of harvest festival marking the end of the agricultural cycle and ushering out the West Monsoons season. The festival lasted seven days and it is with the events of the seventh day that we are concerned—the communal banquet and attendant entertainment. After the banquet the assembled nobility and officials were served liquors. The party became very gay and soon singing began.

Canto 90, stanza 6:

1. Pleasant are the *gītadas* (singers), their singing of songs is in turns.
2. The Illustrious Prince's *kirtis* (foundations) are glorified by them, charming.
3. The more content are the honoured drinkers with all imaginable pleasure in their hearts.
4. How long they are competing! At the end there is mockery.

Pigeaud interprets the phrase "their singing of songs is in turns" in connection with "how long they are competing," to mean a kind of singing contest similar to the *pantun* contests still held throughout Indonesia on festive occasions. Kern did not suggest that it was a singing contest but did remark that the singers probably were not professionals but were members of the assembled company.

The next stanza, describing the entertainment following the song contest, has given rise to a number of diverging interpretations. In our chapter on the dance, we have followed Pigeaud's interpretation. His translation of the stanza is as follows.

Canto 91, stanza 1:

1. A *jurw iy angin* (female dancer), witty, in company of *Buyut* (an old man) then causes merriment.
2. She comes on dancing, in the text (of her song, she tells) that she is taking a companion there.
3. All that variegated acting causes laughter, giving pleasure to the onlookers.
4. Therefore she is given clothes by the common *wadanas* (speakers) all.

It is worth noting here, that although he was uncertain, Kern conjectured that *juru i angin* were male buffoons (not female dancers) and that the *buyut* were their chiefs. Slametmuljana, on the other hand, thought that *juru i angin* was a notable from the Angin region who was jesting with village chiefs.

Canto 91, stanza 2:

1. At the end she is ordered to enter into the Presence to join drinking liquor in front (of Royalty).

* Pigeaud, Vol. IV, p. 196.

2. *Mantris* (mandarins) and *upapatties* (assessors-at-law) equally are taken for companion by her, drinking liquor, singing *kidungs* (songs).
3. *Manghuri, Kaṇḍamohi,* their *kidung*-singing is unceasing, and praised.
4. The Illustrious Prince, being expert, joins in, pleasant, (poetically) charming.

Thus after entertaining the commoners and lower-ranking officials the taledek dance girl—Juru i Angin—was invited into the royal pavilion; there she drank and sang songs with high officials. Finally, even the king joined in.

Canto 91, stanza 3:
1. The Prince's singing is moving, causing amazement, touching.
2. A peacock carolling on a tree is the likeness for it in the (poetically) charming (parts).
3. Of the kind of honey and sugar, fluid, mixed, it is in the sweet (parts), agreeable.
4. Grating bamboo is the likeness for it in awe-inspiring (parts), stinging in the heart.

Canto 91, stanza 4:
1. *Ārya* (the Honourable) Ranādhikāra is forgetful that there is a respectful announcement (to be made) to the Princes.
2. *Ārya* (the Honourable) Mahādhikāra now is his companion, together they speak:
3. that the common *handyans* (squires) wish to see Them performing *rakĕts* (musical plays).
4. A [sic]* only is Their word. At once they return (to their places) making provisions.

Thus, after the king's song, two court officials with assonant names, Ranadhikara and Mahadhikara, ceremoniously invite the king and the princes to perform some kind of musical play called *raket.* Although Prapancha devotes the following four stanzas to the raket performance, the precise nature of the play remains open to interpretation. Many scholars (Stutterheim, Poerbatjaraka, Slametmuljana) thought that it was in fact a mask play. Pigeaud, however, does not agree. He sees it as a dance play with singing, in which three stock characters appear; the *gitada,* or singer; the *shori,* or male dancer; and the *tekes,* or female dancer.

Moreover, Pigeaud's reading of the text reveals two discrete raket performances; the first was by a troupe whose patron was the king's father, Prince Krtawardhana; the second was given by the king's troupe. In the stanza below the first performance is described.

After Ranadhikara and Mahadikara's "respectful announcement," all leave the banquet pavilions to make preparations for the raket play. Later in the evening, the court reassembles in the now decorated great hall and the first raket performance begins.

Canto 91, stanza 5:
1. The Illustrious Kĕrtawardhana-Master is *pañjak* (initiator) for Him (the King) first,
2. there is that *witāna* (hall) in the centre, decorated, improvised.
3. His *Shori* here, *Gītada* with His *Tĕkĕses* are beautiful.
4. As it is an act of pleasantry only laughter is aroused then.

Whether Krtawardhana himself participated in the performance of his troupe is uncertain. Almost certainly he did not play one of the three main roles—gitada, shori, or tekes—since they are mentioned separately in the third line of this stanza. Pigeaud thinks he might have played the drum, accompanying the dancers and signaling the changes in pattern to them. Kern, too, thought that Krtawardhana was playing in the gamelan, acting as conductor or director of the performance.

The performance by Krtawardhana's troupe was clearly subordinate, as a kind of comical prologue to the king's raket performance described in stanza 6; Prapancha carefully contrasts the second to the first. Krtawardhana's was "an act of pleasantry, only laughter is aroused then"; but the King's songs "are something different."

Canto 91, stanza 6:
1. Then he disperses (his troupe) at the coming of the Prince, making his appearance.
2. His (the King's) songs are something different, causing the onlookers to be excited.
3. His *Shori* here is doughty, matching, good-looking, skillful.
4. Those songs are insinuating, giving pleasure to the onlookers.

King Radjasanagara himself plays an important part in the second raket, the gitada role, one of the three

* What is probably meant is "aye."

fixed characters described below. The actor who plays the shori is praised for his manliness and beauty, which might point to an erotic element in his role, Pigeaud thinks. It is also possible that the gitada was the priestly mentor of the shori, just as Semar is the mentor of the handsome Ardjuna in contemporary wayang plays.

Canto 91, stanza 7:

1. The Illustrious Prince, not missing the mark is His neatness, completely dressed.
2. Eight are His *Tĕkĕses* here, being *upabhāryas* (companions), beautiful, worthy.
3. Scions of *amātya* (well-born) families, so (they are) discerning, accurate in conduct.
4. Therefore He, *bañol*-playing (joking), letting fall (facetious) sayings, hit the mark.

Thus the third of the three stock roles in the raket is described; we find that the tekes part was taken by no less than eight dancers. Whether these were women or boys playing the female role is open to conjecture. Pigeaud thinks they probably were boys in female attire. In early twentieth-century Central Javanese courts it was still common for young boys to play female roles. "Bañol," or joking, which appears in line 4, has also survived in modern wayang terminology.

Canto 91, stanza 8:

1. So then the *Nawanatya* all was followed by Him and brought to a conclusion.
2. Merriness made the beginning; without interruption was the laughing together in succession,
3. and pity aroused weeping, giving anguish, causing tears.
4. Therefore those who saw it were altogether touched in their minds.

This stanza deals with the content or subject of the raket play. Pigeaud believes the term "nawanatya" which appears in line 1 of the stanza to be a direct reference to the Nawanatya ("Nine Physiognomies," or Countenances), an Old Javanese manual of courtly conduct. The manual lists nine royal amusements (hunting, fishing, drinking, gambling, lovemaking, pleasantries, fighting, sports, enjoying scenery) and the appropriate courtier behavior for each of the nine situations (that is, the courtier's "physiognomies," countenances, or faces). How this manual was adapted to a dramatic play is difficult to establish. Perhaps the gitada sang about the various kingly pastimes and possibly the dancers mimed appropriately. Professor Kern translated nawanatya as "dance of nine," a much less problematic reading since the poet has told us quite clearly that there were nine dancers in the king's troupe—eight tekes and one shori. This in turn led to speculations that the Nawanatya-raket may have been a dramatic precursor of a bedoyo dance in which the leading (female) dancer impersonates a prince and the other eight dancers play a female role.

Still another possibility is that, if the raket was indeed a mask play as Stutterheim, Poerbatjaraka, and Slametmuljana had thought, the nawanatya may have been nine standard dances. The performance of nine basic mask-dances is mentioned in a Javanese treatise on mask-plays written around A.D. 1882.* It is noteworthy that in this text as elsewhere the headdress of mask-dancers is called *tekes*.

3. The *Bhomakawya* (or *Bhomantaka*); Song II, strophe 20. Translated by the author from the Dutch text in *Het Bhomakawya; Een Oudjavaans Gedicht*, by Andries Teeuw. Groningen, 1946, p. 48.

The *Bhomakawya* has not been precisely dated. Kern thought that it might have been written in the fourteenth century, that is, during the heyday of Majapahit power. Perhaps supporting this contention is the fact that scenes from the Bhomakawya appear on the reliefs of Tjandi Kedaton which was built about 1370.

When the three worlds were threatened with destruction by the evil Narakabhoma, Vishnu was incarnated as Krishna, king of Dwarawati. Rshis arrived at Krishna's court to tell him of the danger and appeal to him to rid the gods and humanity of the demons who were dominating the four cardinal points. Krishna agreed to send his son Samba to conquer the followers of Narakabhoma who threatened the rshis in the Himalayas. The prince appeared, paid homage to the king, and met the rshis, who were strongly impressed by his beauty; "should the nuns in those mountains see him, they would all fall under his spell."

Thus the rsi's became acquainted with the Prince and then were feted by the King. Having partaken of everything, they blessed the King and departed (flying) through the air. Leisurely, they sought shade among the clouds, becoming only indistinctly visible, like wayang puppets re-

* Pigeaud, *Javaanese Volksvertoningen*, p. 42.

flected on a white screen. The light of the sun served as the stage lamp.

If indeed the Bhomakawya was written in the fourteenth century, this passage would confirm the existence of the shadow play in the Majapahit period despite the striking absence of any mention of it in the *Nagarakrtagama.*

4. The *Tantu Panggelaran* (written sometime between 1500 and 1635); excerpts from Chapter 6. Translated by the author from the Dutch text, *De Tantu Panggĕlaran; Een Oud-Javaansch Prozageschrift,* by Th. G. Th. Pigeaud. 's-Gravenhage, 1924, p. 170.

Written sometime during the decline of Majapahit power and glory, the *Tantu Panggelaran* is a book about origins. The creation of all sorts of institutions is described, among them two forms of theater art.

In one episode, Lord Guru (Shiva) is enraged by his consort Uma who had cursed and drained the blood and marrow of their son Kumara because he had insulted her. Lord Guru curses Uma whereupon she becomes Durga and withdraws to bury Kumara's blood and marrow.

As for Lord Guru, never before was he seized by wrath, now however, he was overcome with fury; therefore, he cursed himself and became a *rākṣasa* [giant]. Then the Lord Guru took on the shape of a *rākṣasa* with three eyes and four arms; since then he has been called Kāla-Rudra. All the gods were stunned, as was the whole world, when they perceived the shape of the Lord Kāla-Rudra who was bent on devouring everything on earth.

Directly, Içwara, Brahmā, and Wiṣṇu tried to prevent Lord Kala-Rudra from devouring [the world]; they descended to earth and played *wayang;* they told about the true nature of the Lord and the Lady (his consort) on earth. They had a *panggung* [an elevated place] and a *kĕlir* [screen]; their *wayangs* were carved out of leather and were extolled in beautiful *pañjangs.* The Lord Içwara was the *udipan* [*dalang?*], Brahma and Wiṣṇu protected him. They wandered about the earth, making music and playing *wayang,* since then there exists the *baṇḍagina-hawayang;* thus was the origin according to the old tale.

Another means of defense by the Lords Içwara, Brahmā, and Wiṣṇu against the Lord Kāla was they went about the earth and sought out Lord Kāla who, pale-faced, agitated, moved around his *balé* [pavilion], ... Içwara became *sori,* Brahmā became *pederat,* Wiṣṇu *tĕkĕs;* they went around singing songs (*mangidung*) and playing (*hamenamen*); since then there has been the *baṇḍagiṇa-men men.*

Bandagina-hawayang is clearly the *wayang kulit;* we are told that the puppets were made of leather and that the gods "had" a *kelir,* the term still used today for the shadow-play screen. The *bandagina-men men* does not seem to correspond precisely to anything we know today, although the fact that "Icwara became *sori* . . . and Wisnu became *tekes*" strongly suggests that this bandagina refers to a play described in the *Nagarakrtagama* as raket or at least to something very much like it.

Both the shadow play and the play acting with songs (*bandagina-men men*) are clearly designated as "means of defense"—against the destructive wrath of Lord Guru in the shape of Kala-Rudra. To the present day the shadow play retains a propitiating, protective function.

5. The *Tjalon Arang* (from a version dated 1540); excerpts from Chapter II and Chapter III. Translated by the author from the Dutch text, "De Calon Arang," by R. Ng. Poerbatjaraka, in *BKI,* LXXXII (1926), pp. 150, 152.*

During the reign of King Airlangga there lived a widow of Girah named Tjalon Arang who through serving the goddess Durga ("she who is difficult to approach") had acquired demonic powers. She had a beautiful daughter but no suitor dared approach her for fear of acquiring as dangerous a mother-in-law as Tjalon Arang. The widow was angered by the slight to her daughter and decided to appeal to Durga-Bhagawati. She went to the graveyard with her apprentices (*sisia*) in the black arts, danced, made offerings, and asked the goddess' permission to take vengeance on the countryside. Durga granted the widow's request.

The widow . . . making a *sembah* took leave of the goddess Bhagawati. Then, in the middle of the night, Calwanarang with her apprentices went to dance at the crossroads. The *kamanaks* and *kangsis* resounded and they danced together. After they had danced (*mangigel*) they returned, very excited, to (the widow's) home.

Not long afterward people of every village fell ill; there were many deaths. Those who carried away the corpses were in turn carried away.

King Airlangga, told of the fate of his people, sent his soldiers to kill Tjalon Arang. But the widow's black

* See Part I, Ch. 3, p. 67.

magic overpowered them; the soldiers were burned in the flames bursting from her eyes, ears, mouth and nose. Now even more infuriated, Tjalon Arang returned to the cemetery with her apprentices, this time to ask Durga's permission to destroy the keraton as well as the countryside. Putting themselves into the proper state for the occasion, the apprentices danced.

Immediately Guyang began to dance; she danced with outstretched arms, clapped her hands, sat on the ground, and whirled around [holding up] her kain; her eyes bulged and she turned her head to the left and to the right.

Then Larung danced; her movements resembled those of a tiger about to spring; her eyes were reddish in color and she was naked. Her hair hung loose over her face.

Gaṇḍi danced; she danced in leaps; her hair hung loosely sideways. Her eyes were red, (round) like a *ganitri*-fruit.

Lĕnḍĕ danced; she danced on her tiptoes making short jumps, [jerking] her kain. Her eyes gleamed like fire about to flare up. Her hair hung loose.

Wökçirṣa danced; she danced bent forward, constantly glancing backwards; her eyes were torn open and staring. Her hair hung loose to the side and she was naked.

Mahiṣawadana danced with her legs close together; then she ran on her hands, sticking out her trembling tongue; her hands moved as if trying to grasp something.

When all had danced, Calwanarang rejoiced.

The *Tjalon Arang* story offers the only detailed description of dance movements in Old Javanese literature. But these movements do not belong to a dance performance. They are those of dancing witches engaged in the actual practice of their black art. What they are imagined to have been doing must have been contrary to every conception of beauty or appropriateness in the art of dancing at the time the story was written. Their gestures spelled evil. Ominously grotesque, in fact they were unbelievable acts for normal dancers. For, black magic principles and means include the reversal of the normal order, as for example reading a sacred text backwards. Thus the dance of Tjalon Arang's apprentices can be regarded as the reverse of the way women danced in sixteenth-century Java; it is the reverse of the way they dance today.

The "impossible" aspects of their dance—apart from nakedness, eyes glowing, tongues stuck out, and strands of hair hanging loose—were whirling, crouching, leaping, jumping, dancing on tiptoes, bending over forward, and running like an animal on all fours (or, perhaps, even upside down on the hands). Apart from the latter feat, the description of the *sisia's* choreographic exercises may furnish the reader with some inkling of the measure of dismay created in the older generation when Western modern dance techniques were introduced for female Javanese dancers.

6. The *Kidung Sunda** (c. 1550); Song III, strophe 49. Translated by the author from the Dutch text in "Kidung Sunda," by C. C. Berg, in *BKI,* LXXXIII (1927), p. 126.

The *Kidung Sunda,* a semihistorical poem, was composed about two hundred years after the events it recounts had taken place. It is the story of a glorious wedding expedition that ends in an infamous bloodbath. King Hayam Wuruk of Majapahit had sued for the hand of a princess of Sunda (a kingdom in West Java), a renowned beauty. Though initially it may have been a political move, it had soon turned into an infatuation. Thereupon the King of Sunda, accompanied by his wife and their daughter and a large retinue, sailed in a festively decked fleet to East Java for the proposed wedding. In anticipation of a royal reception and escort to the capital, they encamped upon disembarkation at Bubat. At the Majapahi court political intrigue, prompted by the prime minister, produced insulting delays of the reception. Humiliating demands were made that the Sundanese accept Majapahit's suzerainty; the king as vassal would be treated accordingly. Bubat was surrounded by Majapahit's troops. Sunda's king chose to fight against overwhelming odds. He and his men were massacred. His queen and the lovely princess committed suicide and the "Bubat bloodbath" became a dark stain in Majapahit's annals. In the poem, Hayam Wuruk himself is pictured as the victim of passionate love trapped in the mesh of treacherous politics. At the sight of the princess' corpse he mourns: "I have committed a great crime; to live is now the same as being dead. . . . I shall wither under the burden of unsatisfied desires." Disconsolate, he fades and dies.

It is in the description of the death rites held for Majapahit's heartbroken king that we find again an enumeration of a variety of spectacles.

For one month and seven days the funerary celebrations [*titiwanira*] for the king continued. Magnificent was

* In contrast to the Old Javanese kakawins written in meters used in Indian Sanskrit poetry, the *kidungs* were composed in indigenous Javanese meters.

everything that could be beheld [*tinonton*]—all that there was in Majapahit: plays [*men-men*]; beautiful dances [*igel*]; the seven kinds of martial dances [*babarisan*] and especially the "limping" baris; also the dance girls [*ronggeng*], delightful in their movements; splendid wayang performances [*pawayangan*] and mask-plays [*patapelan*].

If we compare this list with the *Nagarakrtagama* description of entertainments held during the *shradda* of the Rajapatni we see that the names of plays and dances are different. Though the story of the *Kidung Sunda* is laid in the fourteenth century, the sixteenth-century poet has apparently mentioned plays current in his own time. Since similar names are used in our time, we feel that we are on much firmer ground. By analogies with a range of contemporary plays and dances, we can get an approximate idea of what the *babarisan, ronggeng, pawayangan,* and *patapelan* might have been like. The *babarisan* has living counterparts in the Balinese martial dances (*baris*), though "limping baris" remains puzzling; it could, of course, mean a baris with a special manner of stepping. The *ronggeng* is now a Javanese street dancer, but in the sixteenth century ronggengs may have been more highly trained dance girls. The *pawayangan* is clearly a shadow play, though we do not know its precise form and content. And *patapelan's* counterpart today is *wayang topeng,* with the root-word *tapel* still meaning "mask" in Bali. *Men-men,* play, and *igel,* dance, remain for us too generalized and hence vague designations, though men-men may well have been the sixteenth-century version of dance drama, *wayang wong.* Thus with the *Kidung Sunda* we have entered into what we know as today's "traditional sphere"—for not only the names become more familiar: one even suspects that in the sixteenth century certain of the theatrical forms may have begun to acquire traits that have gradually crystallized into their present styles.

7. The *Pararaton* (from a manuscript dated 1613); Chapter 9. Translated by the author from the Dutch text in "Pararaton (Ken Arok) of Het Boek der Koningen van Tumapel en van Majapahit," by J. L. A. Brandes, edited by N. J. Krom, in *VBG,* LXII (1920), p. 139.

The *Pararaton,* or The Book of Kings, falls into three parts: the story of Ken Angrok; the romance of Raden Widjaya; and a chronicle of kings with all their titles. In the latter section, among the titles of King Radjasanagara (Hayam Wuruk), we find indications that the King was an actor of various skills. This corroborates the picture we have already formed of him from the *Nagarakrtagama.*

Bhreng Kahuripan, a woman, became king (*prabhu*) in Çaka 1250. She had three children, Bhaṭâra prabhu, also called Çrî Hayam wuruk and Raden Tetep; his nicknames were: when he played *wayang* (*anapuk*), *ḍalang* Tritaraju; vis-à-vis women (?), Pagĕr antimun; while jesting in *wayang* (*awayang bañol*), Gagak katawang. . . .*

That Javanese aristocracy—kings, princes, and nobles—were lovers of the performing arts for many centuries is confirmed in the old literature. It remains true to the present day; the Central Javanese nobility remains the principal patron of the traditional arts, especially of the dance. Before the Indonesian revolution, becoming proficient in martial and dramatic dancing was part of a young prince's education and the young daughters of princes were trained as serimpi dancers.

* Pigeaud, in *Javaanse Volksvertoningen,* (Batavia, 1938), p. 493, translates this passage differently:

The queen of Koripan had three children: born (first) a Baṭara Prabhu (crown prince); his names in youth (?) were Sri Ayamwuruk Radèn Tètèp; his sacral bynames (?) were, when he danced in the mask-dance (*anapuk*), Dalang Tritaradju; when he played a feminine role, Pagĕr-antimun; when he played *wayang* and *banjol* (*awayang banjol*), Gagak-kĕtawang. . . .

APPENDIX III

EIGHT WAYANG LAKONS

A. *Kartawiyoga*

A wayang purwa lakon following a playscript by the dalang Ki Reditanaja.*

The Characters

The kingdom of Mandraka:
King Salya
Queen Setyawati
Burisrawa, Salya's eldest son, crown prince of Mandraka
Rukmarata, Salya's youngest son
Herawati, abducted daughter of Salya
Sutikanti and Banowati, Herawati's younger sisters
Tuhayata, the king's *patih* (vizier or prime minister)

The kingdom of Astina (of the Korawa):
King Kurupati, the young fiancé of Herawati (his adult name will be Suyudana or Duryudana)
The Korawa, Kurupati's ninety-eight brothers
Sakuni, the king's *patih,* and maternal uncle

The underwater kingdom of Tirtakandasan in the River Silugangga:
King Kurandageni
Kartawiyoga, Kurandageni's son, crown prince of Tirtakandasan
Tjantikawerti, a court adviser, expert in black magic
Raksasas (giant-demons), Kurandageni's subjects

The hermitage on Mt. Argasonya:
Djaladara, a hermit of high rank (in reality, Baladewa, son of Mandura's king, Basudewa, and elder brother of Dwarawati's king, Kresna)
Endang Bratadjaya, Djaladara's sister (in reality, Princess Sumbadra)

The kingdom of Amarta (of the Pandawa):
Pamadé (young Ardjuna)
Semar, Gareng, and Petruk, Pamadé's servant-companions (panakawan)
Bratasména (Werkudara or Bima), Pamadé's elder brother, the second Pandawa in youth.

* Ki Reditanaja's *Kartawijoga,* translated into Indonesian by Hardjowirogo (Djakarta, 1951), is a relatively unusual edition of a lakon in that it is complete with dialogue and texts of the dalang's narrations. The scene-by-scene English summary below, prepared by Arlene Lev, is closer in form to the traditional guide-scripts, *pakem,* although it omits directions for chants (*suluk*) and music. The occasional quotations are from the original dialogue. Brief descriptions of the dalang's narrations and some editorial comments are set off within brackets.

The Play

[In his introductory narration,† the dalang recounts that King Salya's daughter, Princess Herawati, was promised in marriage to King Kurupati of Astina but, suddenly one day, she disappeared from the Mandraka palace; her fiancé, Kurupati, has vowed to find her. The dalang then sings a *suluk,* after which the dialogue begins.]

ACT I. *The court of Mandraka. King Salya receives Sakuni, patih of Astina. Present also are Salya's son, Prince Rukmarata, and his vizier, Tuhayata.*

Sakuni reports to the king that his master, the young king Kurupati, questioned the hermits about Herawati's fate, and was told that she had been abducted by a demonic knight who inhabits the depths of the River Silugangga. Kurupati then went with his brothers and his troops to the river, embarked in small boats, and plumbed the depths with all sorts of nets and fishing equipment.

After Sakuni finishes his report, Prince Rukmarata, Herawati's younger brother, speaks up subtly mocking the Korawa's "fishing party." King Salya ponders and in his heart agrees with his son; indeed, he cannot pin his hopes for Herawati's return on the Korawa. He therefore announces to Patih Sakuni that a bridal contest (*sayembara*) will be held: whoever finds the lost princess within forty days, no matter what his rank or estate, will win her as his bride. Sakuni takes his leave, and King Salya instructs his patih, Tuhayata, to spread the news of the forthcoming competition. The patih leaves with Prince Rukmarata.

A commotion outside the palace is heard. Tuhayata and Rukmarata return and tell the king that a man, apparently from the mountains, is approaching the palace; his beauty is so extraordinary that it frightens

† See Part II, pp. 138–139 for excerpts from this narration.

the people. Thereupon, the young knight Pamadé (Ardjuna) enters the throne hall followed by his three servant-companions (panakawan). When King Salya recognizes the newcomer as one of the gallant Pandawa brothers, he tells him of Herawati's disappearance and of the competition to find her. Pamadé declares his intention to join in the search, although he does not wish to be considered a candidate for Herawati's hand.

The king, followed by Pamadé and his servants, leaves the throne hall. [The dalang describes now the beauty of the courtyards and the gates through which the king passes, of the buildings and the bathing places in the royal compound, the king's appearance ("like a groom going to meet his bride"), the way the king walks ("like a hungry lion"), etc.] They enter the harem, and Pamadé pays his respects to Queen Setyawati and her two daughters, Sutikanti and Banowati.

As Pamadé leaves the palace to start on his search for Herawati, he is stopped by her younger sister, Princess Sutikanti. She offers him gifts; he refuses them and she runs off in tears. Then the other princess, Banowati, appears also offering him gifts. After some flirtatious banter, Pamadé accepts. He takes his leave thinking yearningly about Banowati.

Meanwhile, Prince Rukmarata has gone to the apartments of his older brother, the crown prince Burisrawa, and has informed him of King Salya's orders. Burisrawa marshals the army and all leave to search for Herawati.

ACT II. *On the banks of the River Silugangga. King Kurupati consults Sakuni, his vizier.*

Sakuni relates the events of his visit to Mandraka. The king is outraged by the news of the planned contest for the hand of Herawati, *his* fiancée. [The dalang says, "rigid, eyes burning, lips trembling—His Majesty's rage flares like rice straw whipped by fire. He calms himself by chewing betel nut and then directs his suppressed anger toward the river."] He orders his troops to embark and once again to stir up the river with their fishing equipment and fusillade. The noise of the cannons is as earsplitting as during a battle.

ACT III. *In the underwater kingdom of Tirtakandasan. The raksasa king, Kurandageni, is holding court.*

The pampered crown prince, Kartawiyoga, enters and throws himself at his father's feet, weeping. He has abducted Princess Herawati in the hope of making her his wife, but she threatens to kill herself if he should so much as touch her. "If she won't have me," he moans, "my life is finished." Tjantikawerti, a clever raksasa adviser, steps forward and offers to help the prince. He proceeds to teach Kartawiyoga the art of black magic, counseling him first of all to sleep and eat as little as possible. While the raksasa prince assiduously studies, his father, the king, orders his warriors to investigate the cannonballs which have been falling on the aquatic kingdom and causing hardship for his friends the fish. He also commands them to proceed toward Mandraka and ward off any search party looking for Herawati.

ACT IV. [*The indecisive battle* (perang gagal).]

As King Kurandageni's demon warriors emerge from the waters of the River Silugangga, they come upon the Korawa busy shooting their cannon into the river. A battle ensues. The Korawa, suffering many casualties, retreat to the woods pursued by the raksasas.

ACT V. *A pleasure garden in the underwater kingdom. The raksasa crown prince Kartawiyoga visits Herawati.*

Kartawiyoga, hidden from the princess, performs the black magic he has just learned. Suddenly Herawati thinks to herself, "All right, I will do that which will bring happiness to the heart of Kartawiyoga." But, she tells Kartawiyoga, he must first bring her two sisters from Mandraka, for she is very lonely. Kartawiyoga leaves, overjoyed and confident, intending to arrive in Mandraka by nightfall.

ACT VI. *In the midst of the forest.* [Gara-gara *and* perang kembang.]

Pamadé is confused in his heart; he wanders as aimlessly "as a blind dragonfly." His servants, Semar and his sons, try to persuade him to leave the forest. Pamadé replies that he is wandering about with a purpose: to gain the sympathy of the gods who might inspire him with the knowledge of Herawati's whereabouts.

Suddenly the raksasas who have just routed the Korawa [Act IV] appear. After exchanging insults, Pamadé and the demons fight; one after the other, all the raksasas are defeated. The battle over, Pamadé feels very weak and leans against a tree. Semar advises him to rest; he and his sons will search for food.

ACT VII. *At Mt. Argasonya, the hermitage of Djaladara. The hermit's young sister, Endang Bratadjaya, sits conversing with her servants.*

Hearing Semar and his sons outside advertising their skill as jugglers, Endang Bratadjaya invites them into the hermitage. They perform for her and, in payment, are given food which Semar requests be mashed up.*

The three servants bring the food to their master. The fastidious Pamadé, repelled by the mashed food, draws his *kris* (dagger) in fury and marches off to find those responsible.

When he arrives at the hermitage, Endang Bratadjaya, terrified by the strange knight with drawn dagger, runs to her brother the hermit. Djaladara turns to meet the intruder and quietly explains that his young sister meant no insult by mashing the food given to Semar; indeed, Semar himself had asked her to do so. "Is your lack of good manners a source of magical power?" the hermit asks sarcastically. "If so, you have come to a place where your powers might easily be matched; you might even be taught a lesson here." Pamadé understands his mistake, sheathes his kris, and apologizes to the hermit. They introduce themselves. When Pamadé tells Djaladara about his quest for Herawati, Djaladara offers his help. Pamadé explains that whoever finds the princess wins her hand and proposes to introduce Djaladara as a candidate to King Salya. The two young men swear to come to each other's aid in difficulty and in danger and then start out for Mandraka.

ACT VIII. *The court of Mandraka. King Salya discusses preparations for the bridal contest with his son, Prince Rukmarata, and his prime minister, Tuhayata.*

Pamadé, Djaladara, and the three servants enter. Clairvoyant Djaladara warns the king that Herawati's abductor intends to steal the other two princesses as well. He requests that he and Pamadé alone be allowed to guard the keraton that night, and permission is given. All leave the throne hall. Djaladara and Pamadé prepare themselves for their night-long vigil. Djaladara patrols the palace walls, leaving Pamadé behind at the Green South Gate of the harem.

Inside the harem, Banowati is told by her servants that Pamadé has arrived with a mysterious companion who predicted that she and her sister would be kidnapped just as Herawati had been. As night falls she becomes more and more frightened and finally climbs over the harem wall to Pamadé who sits alone before the gate. They go off together into a pavilion which earlier the princess had thoughtfully provided with blankets, pillows, and delicacies. [The dalang tells us that the knight asleep with his princess forgets his duty.]

ACT IX. *The Mandraka palace. The raksasa crown prince, Kartawiyoga, steals into the palace.*

Kartawiyoga magically casts the palace inhabitants into a deep sleep. As he creeps along, he is suddenly grabbed by the wakeful Djaladara but wrenches himself free. The hermit, in pursuit, stumbles over Pamadé's sleeping servants. "Where is your master? He is not living up to his promise to stand by a comrade in trouble." The servants rouse Pamadé and Banowati, and the princess returns to the harem. Djaladara, meanwhile, has caught Kartawiyoga; they fight but the would-be thief escapes into the earth. Djaladara leaps in after him, and Pamadé and the panakawans follow.

ACT X. *Tirtakandasan, the underwater kingdom. The raksasa king, Kurandageni, consults with his patih who reports the death of three soldiers at the hands of Pamadé [Act VI].*

Kartawiyoga arrives breathlessly and tells his father of his unsuccessful second abduction attempt. The king thinks Herawati had intentionally lured Kartawiyoga into a trap and tells his son that, together, they must confront her.

Meanwhile Pamadé and Djaladara have found their way to Herawati in the Tirtakandasan harem; the Pandawa asks her whether she is happy there. Apparently the effects of Kartawiyoga's love-inducing magic have worn off, for Herawati begs Pamadé to take her home to Mandraka as quickly as possible.

Kartawiyoga enters and Djaladara attacks him. The raksasa prince is killed. His father, the king, arrives, fights and is also killed by Djaladara. The hermit escorts Herawati back to Mandraka, while Pamadé returns to the Argasonya hermitage to inform Endang Bratadjaya of Herawati's rescue.

ACT XI. *The hermitage on Mt. Argasonya. Bratadjaya waits for news of her brother.*

[The dalang tells us that she is in fact the youngest child of King Basudewa of Mandura and is ordinarily

* In Java, mashed food is given to invalids; Pamadé, for whom the food is intended, is feeling ill.

called Princess Sumbadra. Thus the audience realizes that the hermit, Djaladara, is actually Baladewa, the older brother of Kresna.] Pamadé arrives and leads the young princess to Mandraka.

ACT XII. *A resting place in the woods. Kurupati, sitting with his patih, brothers, and soldiers, is told that all the wounded have recovered.* [*See Act IV.*]

A lookout reports that a lady and gentleman are making their way through the woods and seem to be in a great hurry. [It is, in fact, Djaladara and Herawati on their way to Mandraka.] Kurupati orders that a sedan chair be prepared. When he meets Djaladara and Herawati, he pretends to be a Mandraka servant under orders to bring a palanquin for the princess. After Herawati enters the palanquin, the Korawa attack and beat Djaladara. "I am not guilty of any crime, gentlemen, why do you attack me?" Djaladara asks. "Because you dared to search for a woman who was already promised to the king of Astina." Djaladara is stabbed and left to die.

Remembering Pamadé's pledge to stand by him in danger, Djaladara weakly calls his name. Bratasénа (Bima), Pamadé's older brother, is by chance traveling through the woods and, hearing Djaladara's cry, goes to him. After Djaladara describes Kurupati's treachery, Bratasénа promises to go on to Mandraka and expose the Korawa's deceit.

Soon Pamadé and Sumbadra arrive and find the badly wounded Djaladara. The hermit describes all that has happened including his meeting with Bratasénа. Sumbadra takes her brother back to their father's kingdom Mandura, and Pamadé hurries on to Mandraka.

ACT XIII. *The kingdom of Mandraka. King Salya and his son, Rukmarata wonder about the results of the search by Pamadé and Djaladara for Herawati.*

The Korawa enter with Herawati, who embraces her weeping father and withdraws into the inner apartments. King Salya asks Kurupati where he found Herawati and is told an obviously ridiculous tale of heroism and rescue. Bratasénа arrives and relates the true story of Herawati's liberation. While Salya ponders silently, Pamadé arrives; like Bratasénа, he claims Herawati for Djaladara. The young hermit, he explains, is really the oldest son of King Basudewa of Mandura and has returned to that country to recover from wounds he received at the hand of the Korawa. When King Salya declares that Herawati shall be Djaladara's wife, the frustrated Korawa become furious and attack the Mandraka forces. Bratasénа goes on the rampage (*amuk*) and the Korawa flee.

The two Pandawa, Bratasénа and Pamadé, return to the audience hall. The king discusses with them plans for the wedding of Djaladara and Princess Herawati.

Tantjeb kayon

B. *Singangembara*

A wayang kulit performance in the Istana Negara (State Palace), Djakarta, on January 19, 1957, by Ki-dalang Gitosuwoko.*

The Characters

The kingdom of Astina (of the Korawa):
King Suyudana
Queen Banowati
Durna, the king's principal spiritual adviser; a Brahman-warrior
Sakuni, the king's vizier and maternal uncle
Djayadrata, a knight allied with the Korawa
Kartamarma, one of the Korawa, Suyudana's ninety-eight brothers

The kingdom of Awangga:
Adipati Karna, a loyal ally of Astina, although he is really the Pandawa's older half-brother
Queen Sutikanti

The kingdom of Amarta (of the Pandawa):
King Yudistira
Werkudara (Bima), Ardjuna, Nakula, Sadéwa — the five Pandawa brothers
Gatutkatja, son of Werkudara and Dewi Arimbi of Pringgadani
Antaredja, son of Werkudara and Dewi Nagagini of Saptabumi
Abimanyu and Irawan, Ardjuna's sons
Semar, Gareng, Petruk, and Bagong, Ardjuna's servant-companions

The kingdom of Dwarawati:
King Kresna, adviser and cousin to the five Pandawa brothers; an incarnation of the god Wisnu, therefore endowed with clairvoyance and wisdom
Samba, the king's son
Sentyaki, the king's loyal companion and brother-in-law

The hermitage of Ganggapratala:
Ganggapramana, a venerable hermit
Ganggiwati, the hermit's daughter and Antaredja's wife; when transformed into a man, she is called Tedjasusena

* This synopsis is a free translation by Arlene Lev of the program (in Indonesian) offered to guests on this occasion.

The Play

ACT I. *The kingdom of Astina. King Suyudana sits in his throne hall conferring with Durna, the priest-counselor; Sakuni, the vizier; Djayadrata; Kartamarma and other Korawa brothers.*

King Suyudana describes the dream he had the previous night: his kingdom was inundated; everybody, all the Korawa, and even he himself, were carried away by the floods. What can this mean? he asks Durna. The Brahman answers that the royal dream portends disaster for the kingdom; Astina will be visited by a dangerous enemy.

Suddenly, a clap of thunder is heard and the floor of the throne hall begins to quake. The courtiers are terrified. The clamor grows louder and louder until the center of the throne hall floor explodes and two figures emerge from the smoke. Everyone, including the king, flees. The two men who have appeared in such a terrifying manner are named Singangembara and Sukmangembara (the younger of the two). Singangembara arrogantly challenges the Astina courtiers to do battle with him, if any are brave enough.

Djayadrata and all the Korawa brothers return and a wild battle ensues. Djayadrata possesses a *pusaka* (magic heirloom) club named Kyai Karawelang. When he strikes Singangembara with it, the force of the blow flings the intruder some distance away, but he rises again now transformed into a tiger, enormous and magically powerful. Everyone at whom he snarls is immediately deprived of all strength. All the Korawa are thus defeated and Singangembara, exultant, enters the keraton.

King Suyudana hurriedly visits Queen Banowati. He has decided to flee to the kingdom of Amarta to ask help from his cousins, the Pandawas. The royal pair leave in a carriage.

Thinking the Korawa have been routed, Singangembara approaches the royal throne to seat himself there as king. But, to his surprise, he cannot sit down even though the seat looks big enough. Final triumph abruptly denied him, he breaks into tears. His mother, Dewi Nagagini, appears and advises him to go to the kingdom of Dwarawati and ask King Kresna's permission to ascend the throne of Astina; only after obtaining Kresna's blessings will he be able to achieve his ends. Singangembara and his younger brother, Sukmangembara, start on their way to Dwarawati.

ACT II. *The kingdom of Awangga. Adipati Karna, Queen Sutikanti, and their two sons watch a serimpi dance performance.*

The Korawa prince Kartamarma arrives breathlessly and describes the disaster which has befallen King Suyudana. Immediately, Karna readies his army to go to the aid of his friend and ally, the King of Astina.

Halfway to Astina, Karna is startled and angered when two men stop his chariot. He orders them to stand aside, threatening them with death if they are not quick about it. Instead the two men kneel in the middle of the road. (They are none other than Singangembara and his brother Sukmangembara who, on their way to Dwarawati, mistake Karna for King Kresna.) Karna orders his charioteer to run them over. Singangembara realizes that the prince is not King Kresna and furiously attacks. When Karna shoots an arrow at him, again he changes into the snarling tiger. Instantly, Karna disappears from sight; the other Awangga soldiers turn on their heels and flee. Singangembara and his younger brother continue on their way to Dwarawati.

ACT III. *The country of Pringgadani. Dewi Arimbi talks with her son, Gatutkatja.*

They discuss the disappearance of Gatutkatja's half-brother, Antaredja, and his cousin, Irawan. Dewi Arimbi orders Gatutkatja to find them. Delighted to have this task, Gatutkaja salutes his mother and takes leave. He arranges his dress, flies up into the sky, and looks down upon the beauty of the earth.

ACT IV. *The hermitage of Ganggapratala. The hermit Ganggapramana comforts his weeping daughter, Ganggiwati.*

The hermit's daughter complains that she hasn't heard from her husband, Prince Antaredja, for a very long time. The hermit urges her to trust her husband who, he explains, is searching for his own happiness. Semar arrives with his three sons, Gareng, Petruk, and Bagong. They have been sent by the Pandawa to inquire after the missing Antaredja. Ganggiwati decides to leave the hermitage to search for her husband. Her father changes her shape into that of a man, names her Tedjasusena, gives her a magic weapon, and instructs her to go to Amarta to serve its king. Tedjasusena may not reveal his origin or true name, but must say that he comes from Ngawu-ngawu and has neither parents nor brothers and sisters. After asking permission, Ganggiwati in the shape of Tedjasusena departs with Semar and his three sons.

ACT V. *In the midst of a dense forest.*

A band of giants (raksasas) led by the demon Kalamenjareng, are wandering in the forests by order of their king, Yagsadjalma; this king is bent on dominating all of Nusantara [the Indonesian archipelago]. Togog and Sarahita, the clownish demon-servants, appear and report that a knight is traveling through the woods nearby. When the raksasas come face to face with the knight [Tedjasusena], a quarrel arises. They come to blows and, although the knight is alone, he fearlessly confronts his numerous adversaries.

Suddenly Gatutkatja swoops down from the sky and destroys all those raksasas who are brave enough to oppose him; the others run away. When the two knights face each other, Gatutkatja is greatly surprised because from a distance the young man looked like his missing cousin Irawan. But, since it is his pleasure to help *all* people, he is not disappointed. Together they go off to Amarta.

ACT VI. *The kingdom of Dwarawati. King Kresna discusses with his son, Prince Samba, and his brother-in-law, Prince Sentyaki, his prospective trip to the Pandawa realm, Amarta.*

Singangembara and Sukmangembara arrive. The elder brother begs Kresna's permission to ascend the Astina throne, but Kresna refuses and there is a quarrel. Without further ado, Prince Sentyaki grabs Singangembara to throw him out. They fight, but Sentyaki and Singangembara are equally matched. Just as Sentyaki strikes his opponent with his magic club, Singangembara again transforms himself into the Tiger, and runs *amuk*. Kresna orders Sentyaki to give way and he himself approaches the Tiger. The king admonishes him, but the Tiger refuses to listen and turns on Kresna himself.

King Kresna does not wish to fight and, instead, rises into the air, his voice trailing behind: "If you are not satisfied with being human, all right, but a god grants the wishes only of human beings." He then disappears in the direction of Amarta. As the King's words reach Singangembara, he finds that he cannot change back into a human being; he has become fixed in the shape of a tiger. In great sorrow, he weeps. He then decides to go to Amarta to seek his death.

ACT VII. *The kingdom of Amarta. King Yudistira confers with his brothers, Werkudara, Ardjuna, Nakula, and Sadéwa.*

King Kresna arrives at the same time as Adipati Karna. They discuss the ominous events that have occurred in Astina. The knight Tedjasusena enters accompanied by Semar and is received with pleasure. Kresna is not, however, deceived as to the true identity of the newcomer. Then King Suyudana and his queen arrive from Astina. Suyudana asks for the Pandawa's help, promising them half his kingdom if the usurper is eliminated. Werkudara observes that King Suyudana's promise is his own responsibility; as for the Pandawa, they are always ready to help someone in distress, even now when they themselves are troubled by the disappearance of two of their sons. All exit to make preparations.

Singangembara, longing for death, continues on his way to Amarta. He meets the Pandawa and a battle ensues. Before attacking, the Tiger kneels in front of Prince Werkudara. Startled and troubled by this seemingly human behavior, the great warrior finds he cannot fight the Tiger and retreats. The same thing happens to Ardjuna. Gatutkatja, Werkudara's son, then advances to meet the Tiger while Abimanyu, Ardjuna's son, engages in a test of strength with Sukmangembara. King Kresna asks Gatutkatja to withdraw and summons the stranger, Tedjasusena. When the latter appears he is asked whether he is brave enough to face the Tiger. He answers that under the orders of His Majesty King Kresna, one cannot feel fear. The Tiger and Tedjasusena confront each other. The knight is clearly at a disadvantage and when he is knocked down near Kresna, the king calls out, "You have forgotten that you possess the *pusaka* Langkap Putih." [This is the magical weapon Tedjasusena received from his father, the hermit Ganggapramana. See Act IV.]

Tedjasusena advances again and strikes the Tiger with the "Langkap Putih." The force of the blow is so great that the Tiger is flung some distance away and is again transformed, this time not into Singangembara but into the long-lost Prince Antaredja. He feels humiliated by his near-defeat and grabs Tedjasusena determined to kill him. How startled he is when, before his eyes, the knight Tedjasusena changes shape and becomes his own wife, Ganggiwati!

King Kresna approaches them, laughing. Antaredja explains why he had assumed the shape of Singangembara and attempted to usurp the Astina throne: it is well known, he says, that rightfully half of the Astina kingdom belongs to the Pandawa; too long have the Korawa been permitted to slander the Pandawa and deprive them of their domain. That is the reason, Antaredja concludes, why he caused all this commotion. King Kresna then expounds the principle that all desires must be pursued only in the proper way and at the proper time. Antaredja understands [that his attempted coup was premature]. He tries to persuade Abimanyu and Sukmangembara to stop fighting, but Abimanyu refuses to withdraw. Then Sukmangembara changes his shape and becomes, to Abimanyu's great surprise, his own brother, Irawan.

King Suyudana and Adipati Karna arrive. They reproach the Pandawa. Understanding that Suyudana intends to break his promise to restore half of Astina to the Pandawa, Werkudara kicks his royal cousin; they join in battle. Eventually Suyudana retreats. Karna challenges Ardjuna and is wounded by the arrow "Wind." When the other Korawa advance, Werkudara goes on the rampage and crushes them all. Then he dances his victory dance, *Tayungan*.

The Pandawa reassemble to celebrate their triumph and are entertained with dances.

Tantjeb kayon

C. *Anuman Duta* (Anuman as Envoy)

A wayang wong lakon performed in honor of the visit of the King and Queen of Siam at the Istana Mangkunagaran, Surakarta, Sept. 5, 1929.*

The Characters

The kingdom of Mount Malyawan:
King Rama, incarnation of the god Wisnu
Dewi Sinta (Sita), Rama's wife who has been abducted
Prince Lesmana (Laksmana), Rama's devoted younger brother

The monkey kingdom of Kiskenda:
King Sugriwa
Queen Tara
Anggada, the red monkey crown prince
Anuman (Hanuman), the white monkey general
Anila, the blue monkey general
Djembawan, another monkey general

The kingdom of the great birds:
King Sempati
Djatayu, the king's younger brother

The giants' kingdom of Alengka:
King Rawana
Prince Kumbakarna, the king's younger brother
Prince Wibisana, another younger brother
Prince Indrajit, Rawana's son, the crown prince
Trisirah, Trikaya, Dewantaka, and Saksadewa, the king's other sons
Dewi Tridjata, daughter of Prince Wibisana
Prahasta, patih
Togog and Sarahita, the clownish servants of the giants

The Play

[Soon after the disappearance of his young wife Sinta (Sita), the prince of Ayodya, Rama, met the monkey king Sugriwa of Kiskenda who had been deprived of both wife and throne by his brother Subali. Rama helps Sugriwa defeat Subali and thus to regain his throne and his consort, Tara. This lakon deals with the monkeys' efforts to repay their king's debt to Rama and find Rama's abducted wife, Sinta.†]

* The following synopsis is a free translation of the program (in Dutch) offered to the guests on this occasion.

† See Appendix I for a synopsis of the *Ramayana.*

ACT I. *The kingdom of Mt. Malyawan. Rama sits with his courtiers in the audience hall of his residence. (This residence had been built for Rama by King Sugriwa's monkey subjects who revere Rama as a deity.)*

SCENE 1: Prince Lesmana [Laksmana], Rama's loyal younger brother, has been sent to remind Sugriwa of his promise that with the advent of the dry season, he would send his armies to help find Rama's missing wife, Dewi Sinta. Rama awaits his brother's return from his mission to Kiskenda.

SCENE 2: Accompanied by Lesmana, King Sugriwa arrives with his generals: his son, Anggada; the white monkey, Anuman; the blue monkey, Anila; and the old monkey general, Djembawan. Sugriwa confesses to Rama that, in his joy at the reunion with his wife, he had indeed forgotten his promise and begs Rama's forgiveness.

Rama had been told by the dying bird-prince Djatayu that Sinta was being held captive by King Rawana of Alengka. Therefore, Sugriwa orders Anuman, Anggada, Anila, and Djembawan, each commanding one hundred thousand monkeys, to march southward to Alengka to discover whether Sinta was indeed held captive by Rawana. Three other monkey commanders are ordered to march, each with one hundred thousand troops, toward the other three cardinal points to search the forests for Sinta.

Rama orders Anuman, the white monkey, to approach, appoints him envoy, and gives him a ring. If indeed Anuman should find Sinta in Alengka, the ring would prove to her that Anuman was truly Rama's messenger. Thereafter, Anuman and the other army generals leave and Rama, Lesmana, and the monkey king Sugriwa withdraw into the inner apartments.

ACT II. *In front of Rama's residence on Mt. Malyawan.*

SCENE 1: The monkey army of Kiskenda awaits the arrival of their officers.

SCENE 2: The army commanders arrive and range their troops according to Sugriwa's orders. Anuman and the three other generals with an army of four hundred thousand apes march off to Alengka, the other commanders toward the three other cardinal points.

ACT III. *In the cave "Windu." Dewi Sayempraba talks with her nymph-servants.*

SCENE 1: (Dewi Sayempraba is the daughter of the princely and magically powerful sage, Wisakrama. This wise man had built himself a palace so magnificent that it threatened to rival the beauty of the gods' own abodes. Angered by this effrontery, the gods transformed the palace into a cold and dank cave.)

One of her servants tells Sayempraba that a new royal seat has arisen on the mountain Malyawan. This kingdom is entirely populated by monkeys, she says, and the king is called Prince Ragawa, or Rama the Victorious, eldest son of King Dasarata of Ayodya. Suddenly, the women hear a roaring in the distance, like the rumbling of thunder.

SCENE 2: The noise signals the approach of the monkey army. Dewi Sayempraba welcomes Anuman and his retinue and offers them fruit as refreshments. In answer to her questions, Anuman reveals to her the aim of his mission. Dewi Sayempraba, herself descended from a buta (monstrous giant) lineage, feels a secret sympathy for her relative, the buta king of Alengka, Rawana; she decides to help him by preventing Anuman from reaching Alengka. She offers to transport the monkeys magically to Alengka; all they have to do is close their eyes. The trusting monkeys do as she says, and Dewi Sayempraba and her attendants instantly disappear.

SCENE 3: The monkeys left behind in the cave realize too late that they have been tricked; all have been struck by blindness. They grope their way out of the cave and, once outside, stumble on the rocks and tumble into ravines. They are completely helpless.

SCENE 4: Suddenly, the featherless bird-king, Sempati, appears. He was attracted to the scene by the loud lamentations of the monkeys, one of whom invoked the name of Djatayu, his brother. Moved by the piteous condition of the monkeys, he cures their blindness by flapping his wings over their faces. He then directs them toward Alengka over the Mahendra and Suwelagiri mountains. The monkeys continue on their way.

ACT IV. *On the seashore near Mt. Mahendra. The monkey army assembles for orders.*

Anuman hopes to avoid arousing Rawana's suspicions and to preserve the secrecy of the expedition. He therefore decides to proceed alone, flying from Mt. Mahendra to Alengka. He rises into the air, leaving behind on the seashore the three other generals with their armies.

ACT V. *In the air above the sea.*

Anuman, flying over the sea, hears a voice calling him from a small mountainous island in the middle of the sea. He descends and asks who is calling his name. The mountain itself answers, saying its name is Mahenaka, and offers him some fruit. Mahenaka gives him further directions for reaching Alengka, whereupon Anuman continues on his flight.

ACT VI. *On the Alengka seashore.*

Kataksini, a buta monster with a dangerously large muzzle who guards the borders of Alengka, is busy with his daily task of fishing on the shore. He eats nothing but fish. Looking up, he suddenly sees something white and shimmering in the air. He opens his mouth wide and sucks the white apparition toward him. So, abruptly, Anuman finds himself falling into the gaping mouth of a buta. Recognizing his peril, he tears the monster's mouth open and again swiftly rises into the air.

ACT VII. *The kingdom of Alengka; the garden, Argasoka, where Sinta is held captive by King Rawana. The garden is situated on the mountain Suwelagiri, which is inhabitated by the sages of the buta lineage.*

SCENE 1: Dewi Sinta seated before her bower chats with Tridjata, her loyal protectrice, the niece of King Rawana. They are attended by ladies-in-waiting.

SCENE 2: Anuman has arrived in Alengka during the night and, at dawn, looking for a secluded hiding place, he stole into the Argasoka garden. Now he quietly nestles in the branches of a Nagasari tree unaware of his proximity to Sinta's bower.

SCENE 3: King Rawana enters the garden and proceeds toward the bower. Only then does Anuman realize that he has landed in the very place where Sinta, whom he seeks, is staying. Rawana begins to woo Sinta but she does not respond to his protestations of love. Infuriated, the demon-king threatens her with his sword, but Tridjata succeeds in calming him so that, although disgruntled, he retires. Anuman, witnessing the scene, can hardly suppress his desire to attack Dewi Sinta's besieger. Much as he would have liked to avenge his beloved queen, the thought that he might worsen Dewi Sinta's precarious situation restrains him. (See Pl. 117.)

SCENE 4: Immediately afterward, four butas arrive in the garden and try to frighten Sinta into submitting to Rawana's will. But Tridjata overwhelms them with abuse and threats and they retreat. At the sight of the butas, Anuman again must suppress his desire to attack.

SCENE 5: In order not to startle Sinta too much by a sudden appearance, Anuman, still seated in the Nagasari tree, begins to sing; he sings of Rama and of his own quest. When his song is finished, he comes down from the tree and offers Sinta the ring sent by Rama to dispel any of her possible doubts. Questioned by Sinta, he describes everything that had happened in Malyawan up to the moment that Rama sent him out to search for her. She then gives the white monkey her hair ornament so that he will be able to prove to Rama that he has fulfilled his mission. Thereupon Anuman takes leave. He intends to set Alengka afire as a memento of his visit and a warning to the butas. Sinta withdraws to her bower.

ACT VIII. *The garden Argasoka.*

SCENE 1: The Argasoka guards wonder at the great number of birds flying up from the garden. Two buta workmen arrive.

SCENE 2: The workmen inform the guards that a large white monkey is in the garden, damaging the shrubbery and alarming the birds. Surprisingly, this monkey can talk like a man.

ACT IX: *The garden Argasoka.*

The guards try to catch Anuman and a fight ensues. The butas are beaten, but one of them escapes to report the incident to King Rawana.

ACT X: *King Rawana's throne hall.*

SCENE 1: King Rawana is holding court. Present are: the giant Prince Kumbakarna; Prince Wibisana; the King's sons, Indradjit, Trisirah, Trikaya, Dewantaka, and Saksadewa; Patih Prahasta and others.

SCENE 2: When the Argasoka guard arrives and reports the event in the garden, Rawana flies into a rage and orders his son Saksadewa with a troupe of warriors to capture Anuman. Saksadewa departs and Rawana withdraws into the inner chambers of his palace.

ACT XI. *The garden Argasoka.*

Anuman and Saksadewa fight. The latter is killed; his warriors carry him away.

ACT XII. *King Rawana's throne hall.*

SCENE 1: Rawana in the company of Prince Kumbakarna, Prince Wibisana, Patih Prahasta, and his sons.

SCENE 2: A warrior arrives and reports the death of Prince Saksadewa. Rawana, wrathful, orders Indradjit and his other sons to capture the monkey. The king withdraws.

ACT XIII. *The garden Argasoka.*

Anuman fights with Trisira, Trikaya, Dewantaka, and Indradjit. At first Anuman is unharmed. When an arrow pierces his left thigh, he ignores the wound. But when Indradjit shoots him with his arrow "Nagapasa," Anuman falls, is captured, and taken to Rawana.

ACT XIV. *King Rawana's throne hall.*

SCENE 1: Rawana sits with Prince Kumbakarna, Prince Wibisana, Patih Prahasta, and a retinue.

SCENE 2: Indradjit arrives with his brothers and followers, dragging the fettered Anuman. At the sight of Rawana, Anuman heaps reproaches upon him for his conduct toward Sinta. Greatly incensed, Rawana wants to kill Anuman, but Prince Wibisana restrains him with the remark that it is not fitting for a king to kill an envoy. Rawana refuses to listen and orders Anuman to be burned alive.

ACT XV. *In the* alun-alun *(plaza) before the Alengka palace.*

Anuman is being burned. Togog and Sarahita (the clownish buta servants) approach out of curiosity and are surprised to see that the fire does not consume the monkey. Upon his request they bring Anuman a drink, whereupon he frees himself, leaps from the pyre and, with his flaming tail, sets fire to Rawana's palace.

ACT XVI. *The palace of Alengka.*

Rawana, seeing his palace afire, hastens to leave it.

ACT XVII. *The garden Argasoka.*

SCENE 1: Dewi Sinta with Tridjata and servants.

SCENE 2: Anuman arrives, announces that he is departing forthwith and takes leave of his queen.

ACT XVIII. *In the air.*

Before leaving Alengka, Anuman, hovering in the heights, lingers to look at the burning palace. Then he proceeds directly to the seashore near Mt. Mahendra.

ACT XIX. *On the seashore near Mt. Mahendra.*

SCENE 1: The generals of the monkey army, Anggada, Anila, Djembawan, and three commanders await Anuman's return from Alengka.

SCENE 2: After a while Anuman indeed appears. The generals inquire about the results of his mission and he describes what has happened. Thereafter, they proceed together to Rama's residence on Mt. Malyawan.

ACT XX. *The kingdom on Mt. Malyawan, in the audience hall of King Rama's abode.*

SCENE 1: Rama with Prince Lesmana, King Sugriwa, and monkey troupes.

SCENE 2: Anuman appears, reports on his mission, and offers Rama the hair ornament sent by Sinta. Rama thanks Anuman for his loyalty and devotion and adopts him as a son under the name of Rama Adayapati.

D. *Pregiwa-Pregiwati*

A wayang wong lakon performed at the Istana Mangkunagaran, Surakarta, on the occasion of the coming of age of Gusti Raden Aju Sekar Kedaton Koestijah, April 6, 1931.*

The Characters

The kingdom of Astina (of the Korawa):
King Suyudana
Queen Banowati
Durna, priest-counselor
Sakuni, vizier
Lesmana, the heir apparent of Astina
Tjitraksi and other Korawa brothers

The kingdom of Mandura:
King Baladewa, older brother of King Kresna but a loyal ally of the Korawa

The hermitage of Handongsumawi:
Sidikwatjana, a venerable holy man
Pregiwa and Pregiwati, the hermit's granddaughters, twin daughters of Prince Ardjuna
Djanaloka, the hermit's apprentice

The kingdom of Dwarawati:
King Kresna
Princess Siti Sundari, Kresna's beautiful daughter

The kingdom of Amarta (of the Pandawa):
Prince Ardjuna, the third of the Pandawa brothers
Angkawidjaya (Abimanyu), Ardjuna's son, Gatutkatja's younger cousin

The kingdom of Pringgadani:
Queen Arimbi, a giantess queen
Gatutkatja, son of Arimbi and Werkudara, the second Pandawa
Giant generals, brothers of Dewa Arimbi

The Play

ACT I. *The kingdom of Astina. In the throne hall, King Suyudana sits with Queen Banowati. Present are Head Priest Durna, Grand Vizier Sakuni, and six of the King's brothers (Korawa).*

King Suyudana has called a council to discuss the marriage of his son, Lesmana Mandrakumara, to Princess Siti Sundari, daughter of King Kresna of Dwarawati. Baladewa, king of Mandura, had been sent to Dwarawati to sue for Siti Sundari's hand on behalf of Lesmana. He has just returned and now reports to the king: Kresna accepts the Astina crown prince as son-in-law, on the condition that Astina provide two exceptionally beautiful bridesmaids for the wedding. Suyudana accepts the condition and orders Sakuni and his royal brothers to find two maids whose beauty should approximate, if not rival, that of the bride, Siti Sundari. Thereupon, King Baladewa, Prime Minister Sakuni, and the Korawa proceed to the plaza (*alun-alun*).

Accompanied by Queen Banowati, Suyudana retires to a chapel to pray for the unhindered consummation of their son's wedding.

ACT II. *Alun-alun of the Astina palace.*

Sakuni takes leave of King Baladewa and departs to execute the orders of King Suyudana.

ACT III. *The hermitage of Handongsumawi. The hermit Sidikwatjana converses with his twin granddaughters, Pregiwa and Pregiwati. Apprentice Djanaloka and other novices are also present.*

Pregiwa and Pregiwati ask Sidikwatjana who their father is; they have never seen him because he left Handongsumawi before they were born. When they are told that they are daughters of the famous ksatriya Ardjuna, they ask permission to go and find him in the kingdom of the Pandawa. The holy man is reluctant to grant his permission, since he knows only too well the dangers of a journey to the Amarta kingdom. Yet, regarding his granddaughters' desire to be justified, he finally blesses them and allows them to leave the hermitage. Djanaloka, the apprentice, is to accompany the two girls and guard them. But, keeping in mind the heavenly beauty of his granddaughters and the

* The following synopsis is a free translation of the program (in Dutch), offered to the guests on that occasion.

weaknesses of human beings in general and of Djanaloka in particular, Sidikwatjana threatens the apprentice with the wrath of the gods should he forget his role of servant and protector and dare to yield to amorous temptation. Djanaloka swears that he will not forget his responsibilities.

ACT IV. *In the forest.*

Pregiwa and Pregiwati wander with Djanaloka through the woods. As Sidikwatjana had feared, the apprentice, completely forgetting his oath, tries to seduce the girls. But they refuse to let him approach and hastily run away into the woods. Djanaloka chases them, but cannot keep pace. Only when he begs them to wait for him and reminds them that after all it is his duty to guard them do they stop. All three sit down to rest under a tree on the shore of a large lake. When Djanaloka continues to address amorous words to the two girls, they regret having heeded his plea and determine to get rid of him. Djanaloka, exhausted, falls asleep. Pregiwa and Pregiwati take the opportunity to slip away.

The servant who has only been dozing awakens with a start; he is overcome by love for his mistresses and resolves, come what may, to marry them. But the consequences of breaking his oath are at hand. At that very moment, a heavy branch breaks from the tree under which he sits and falls on his back. Screaming with pain, he flees but other punishments await him. Suffering from thirst, he seeks a cooling drink from the lake but at his approach the water evaporates.

ACT V. *At the edge of the forest.*

Sakuni and the Korawa have been searching fruitlessly for two girls beautiful enough to be Siti Sundari's bridesmaids. One of the Korawa, Tjitraksi, suddenly appears with the news that he has seen two girls wandering through the woods; they are at least as beautiful as the prospective bride herself. The Korawa decide to stop the girls and to take them to Astina, by force if necessary.

ACT VI. *In the forest.*

Caught between the Korawa and Djanaloka who still pursues them. Pregiwa and Pregiwati pretend to be willing to give in to Djanaloka. Encouraged, the apprentice decides to protect them unto death against the Korawa. Questioned by Sakuni, Djanaloka asserts that he is the husband of the girls; they assure the Korawa that this is true. When Djanaloka refuses to surrender the twins, the Korawa surround and attack him; the girls escape and hide in a ravine. Despite his pleas for forgiveness, Djanaloka is killed, but the beautiful twins have vanished without a trace.

ACT VII. *In the forest.*

Gatutkatja, who had been sent to find his cousin Angkawidjaya, at last discovers him and his three servants, Semar, Petruk, and Gareng, in the woods. Angkawidjaya had left the kingdom of Amarta to roam in the wilderness in order to establish contact with the gods. Gatutkatja tries to persuade him to return to Amarta but Angkawidjaya seems to prefer the soft moss of the woods to the thick carpets of Amarta's palace.

The cousins' conversation is interrupted by what seems to be the voices of women weeping. Angkawidjaya [since he is younger] asks Gatutkatja's permission to investigate. Gatutkatja is unwilling to let his young cousin go alone so he rises into the air to watch over him.

ACT VIII. *At the edge of the forest.*

Pregiwa and Pregiwati, pursued by the Korawa, try to walk as quickly as they can toward Amarta. But time and again, they sink to the ground exhausted. Pregiwati especially can hardly go on, but her elder sister's consoling words renew her strength. Finally they both collapse. Sitting on the ground, leaning on each other and shedding tears, they resign themselves to the inevitable.

Suddenly Angkawidjaya arrives. At the sight of the two girls, he is deeply shaken; their misery makes him feel weak. He asks them who they are and whence they come, and when he learns that they are daughters of Ardjuna, his own father, he sits down next to them unable to restrain his tears. But he is also incensed by the girls' story and eager to fight the evildoers.

Meanwhile, the Korawa arrive. Recognizing Angkawidjaya, they first try to persuade him to relinquish the two princesses. Angkawidjaya answers that the way to the girls is over his dead body. Telling the servants to guard his sisters, he begins to fight the Korawa. Although several of his opponents are felled, Angkawidjaya would have to succumb were it not for Gatutkatja, observing the battle from the heights. Like a falling star, he shoots down from the clouds and throws himself upon the Korawa. They know him only too well and, prizing their necks, they take to their heels.*

When the last enemy has left the battlefield, Gatutkatja notices that his cousin is not alone. At first sight, he falls deeply in love with the beautiful Pregiwa. Angkawidjaya agrees to leave the woods and accompany his sisters to Dwarawati where they will find their father, Ardjuna. Gatutkatja flies off, but before heading toward his own kingdom, Pringgadani, he returns several times pretending either to fear another Korawa attack on Angkawidjaya or that it is difficult to part from his cousin, but actually just to catch another glimpse of Pregiwa. (See Pl. 127.)

ACT IX. *The kingdom of Pringgadani. In her sleeping chamber, Dewi Arimbi, Gatutkatja's mother, discusses with her ladies-in-waiting the protracted absence of her son.*

Gatutkatja descends into the keraton and goes directly to tell his mother about his adventures. He asks her to give him the most beautiful diadems and necklaces she has. He plans, he says, to attend a wedding celebration in Dwarawati. But motherly instinct tells Arimbi that the cause of her son's desire to adorn himself is not the wedding feast.

ACT X. *The alun-alun of the Pringgadani palace.*

The giant army chiefs of Pringgadani, four brothers of Dewi Arimbi, await the arrival of their king, Gatutkatja. He suddenly appears in their midst and, dancing, adorns himself. [He dances the well-known *Kiprah* dance.] Partly because he is exhausted by his obsessive love-dance and partly because he is overcome by his passion, Gatutkatja falls in a faint. The army chiefs revive him, whereupon Gatutkatja, leading his troops, departs for Dwarawati.

ACT XI. *The kingdom of Dwarawati. Pregiwa sits in the pleasure palace behind Kresna's royal residence.*

Pregiwa, transplanted from her forest home to the luxurious milieu of the court, asks her attendants about the layout of the pleasure palace. Then she leaves them to bathe in a beautiful pool in a sheltered part of the garden. Just as she is bathing, Gatutkatja swoops down into the garden close to the pool. Seeing her he hides; he is not able to address the object of his love, but he throws in her direction the garland adorning the handle of his kris. Pregiwa picks up the flowers and is surprised to find that they are strung together. Turning her head, she discovers Gatutkatja half-hidden by a bush. In her innocence and unaware of any impropriety, she asks him to approach. He draws near but cannot utter a single word in response to her welcome. His elemental nature forces him to grope for something as deep in meaning as his love—death—so he draws his kris and tries to kill himself. Pregiwa, frightened by this strange behavior, impulsively grasps Gatutkatja's hand holding the kris. The touch of her hand breaks the spell; he can now express his passion and in Pregiwa, too, love flares up. The two sit down in the garden and declare their devotion to each other.

Palace attendants come out to see why Pregiwa has stayed away so long. When they see her in the company of a man, they hasten to report to King Kresna. Gatutkatja and Pregiwa retire to a bower. (See Pl. 129.)

* Gatutkatja's habit of dealing with enemies is to wrench their necks.

E. *Djaka Pendjaring*

A Pandji lakon performed in wayang topeng.*

The Characters

The kingdom of Kediri:
King Lembu Amidjaya
Queen Maheswara, his wife
Princess Tjandra Kirana
(or Sekar Tadji)
Princess Mindakawati } daughters of the King
Princess Tamiadji }
Prince Gunung Sari, crown prince of Kediri
Djayabadra, vizier of Kediri
Pratama and Pratista, regents

The kingdom of Djenggala:
Prince Pandji Kasatriyan of Tambakbaya
Prince Sinompradapa of Bandjaran Sari, younger brother of Pandji Kasatriyan
Prince Kertala, half-brother and companion of Pandji Kasatriyan
Palet and Sebul, clownish servants of Prince Sinompradapa

The kingdom of Ngurawan:
Princess Kumudaningrat, beloved of Prince Sinompradapa

The kingdom of Nusakembangan:
King Klana Eratnaka (Klono)
Prince Kudarentjaka, younger brother of the king
Buginese warriors

The fishing village of Paminggir:
The widow Sembadil
Djaka Pendjaring, the widow's adopted son (actually Prince Pandji Kasatriyan in disguise)
Ki Djarudi and Prasanta, Djaka Pendjaring's servants

The Play

ACT I. *The kingdom of Kediri. In the throne hall of the palace.*

The king of Kediri, Lembu Amidjaya, holds council. Attending are his son, Prince Gunung Sari, Prime Minister Djayabadra, and the regents, Pratama and Pratista. They talk about a mysterious white elephant who is roaming in the garden of the keraton; none of the princes or warriors dares to approach him. The king orders his prime minister to proclaim that whoever overcomes the elephant will win the princess Tjandra Kirana as his wife.

ACT II. *The kingdom of Kediri. In the apartments of the queen.*

The king retires to the inner apartments where he is received by the queen, Dewi Maheswara, and two of her daughters, Mindakawati and Tamiadji. They discuss what has happened.

ACT III. *The kingdom of Kediri. In the forecourt of the palace.*

The events are discussed by Crown Prince Gunung Sari, the vizier, and two regents. They proceed to make the rounds.

ACT IV. *The kingdom of Nusakembangan. In the throne hall of King Klana Eratnaka's palace.*

King Klana Eratnaka is in council. In waiting are his younger brother, Prince Kudarentjaka, and three servants. The king, passionately in love with the princess of Kediri, Tjandra Kirana, had sent an envoy to sue for her hand. On the way, however, the envoy had met Kediri's army commanders who told him of their king's proclamation that Tjandra Kirana shall belong to him who can overcome the mysterious white elephant. Thus the envoy returned to Nusakembangan, his mission unfulfilled. Klana now orders three of his best Buginese warriors to go to Kediri to fight the elephant.

ACT V. *The kingdom of Kediri. In the throne hall.*

The three Buginese warriors of Nusakembangan appear before the king of Kediri and the regents who

* The following synopsis is a translation of the version appearing in Th. Pigeaud, *Javaanse Volksvertoningen,* pp. 489–491.

had announced the contest, and declare that they have come to fight the elephant [on behalf of their king]. They are led into the garden and begin to fight but are soon overwhelmed and flee.

ACT VI. *In the princely residence at Bandjaransari.*

The young prince of Djenggala, Sinompradapa, informs his servants Palet and Sebul that he is going to Ngurawan. Preparations are made for the departure.

ACT VII. *In the kingdom of Ngurawan. The palace garden.*

Dewi Kumudaningrat, princess of Ngurawan, receives Sinompradapa. After an intimate meeting with the princess, Sinompradapa departs to search for his older brother, Prince Pandji Kasatriyan, who mysteriously disappeared from his residence one night.

On his way, Sinompradapa meets the Buginese warriors of Nusakembangan who are returning home after their defeat in Kediri by the white elephant (Act V). He fights and overwhelms them, then continues on his way.

ACT VIII. *In the fishing village of Paminggir.*

Ki Djarudi and Prasanta sing songs together. Thereafter, they go to join their master, Djaka Pendjaring.

ACT IX. *In the fishing village of Paminggir. The widow Sembadil's house.*

The widow Sembadil wants to marry her adopted son, Djaka Pendjaring the fisherman. But when the young man refuses to consider her proposal, she orders him out of her house. He departs with his two servants.

ACT X. *The kingdom of Kediri. In the throne hall of the keraton.*

The king of Kediri, Lembu Amidjaya, discusses the contest proclamation with his prime minister, Djayabadra. Prince Sinompradapa arrives and asks permission to fight the elephant. The prime minister accompanies him to the garden.

ACT XI. *The kingdom of Kediri. In the palace garden.*

Princess Tjandra Kirana is feeding the white elephant when Prince Sinompradapa arrives in the garden. The prince attacks the beast. In the ensuing battle, the elephant picks up Sinompradapa and hurls him high into the air. Then it lumbers out of the garden and enters the alun-alun.

ACT XII. *In the forest.*

After leaving the fishing village, Djaka Pendjaring and his two servants wander through the woods on the way to Kediri. Suddenly Prince Sinompradapa, who was flung through the air by the elephant, falls before them. After Djaka Pendjaring catches him, Sinompradapa describes his battle with the elephant in the Kediri palace garden. Prince Sinompradapa then adopts Djaka Pendjaring as his brother [not realizing that the stranger is in fact his brother, Pandji Kasatriyan]. The latter undertakes to defeat the elephant.

ACT XIII. *The kingdom of Nusakembangan. In the throne hall of the palace.*

King Klana Eratnaka and his younger brother, Kudarentjaka, are informed that the Buginese warriors they sent to subdue the elephant were unsuccessful, and in addition were beaten by Sinompradapa, prince of Djenggala (Act VII). Frustrated and enraged, the king decides on war with Kediri.

ACT XIV. *The kingdom of Kediri. In the throne hall.*

With the elephant still unconquered, King Lembu Amidjaya and Vizier Djayabadra are at a loss what to do next. King Klana Eratnaka arrives and engages the elephant. During the fight, the elephant suddenly changes his appearance and becomes Kertala, prince of Djenggala. When Djaka Pendjaring arrives, he is disappointed not to be able to confront the elephant, but he gets into a fight with King Klana. During the battle, Djaka Pendjaring acquires his own true shape, Prince Pandji Kasatriyan, brother of princes Kertala and Sinompradapa. He defeats Klana Eratnaka.

F. *Kuda Narawangsa*

A Pandji lakon performed in wayang topeng.*

The Characters

The kingdom of Kediri:
King Lembu Amidjaya
Queen Maheswara
Princess Tjandra Kirana (called Kuda Narawangsa, when transformed into a man), the wife of Pandji Kasatriyan
Crown Prince Gunung Sari
Prince Plabuhan and Prince Wanengsari, other sons of the king
Djayabadra, prime minister
Regents of Kediri

The kingdom of Djenggala:
The King of Djenggala
Prince Pandji Kasatriyan of Tambakbaya, husband of the Kediri princess, Tjandra Kirana (Pl. 122)
Prince Sinompradapa of Bandjaransari, younger brother of Prince Pandji
Princess Ragil Kuning, Pandji's younger sister (Pl. 119)
Bantjak and Doyok, Pandji's servants
Sebul and Palet, servants of Sinompradapa

The kingdom of Ngurawan:
Princess Kumudaningrat, beloved of the Djenggala prince, Sinompradapa
A servant

The kingdom of Bali:
King Klana Suryawibawa (Klono Suryowibowo) (Pl. 121)
Prince Suryapamala, younger brother of the king
Tjiklobo, the king's envoy
Buginese warriors in the king's service

Suralaya (heaven):
Sang Hyang Brahma, a god
Sang Hyang Narada, messenger of the gods

Others:
Prawan Djagalan, the false Tjandra Kirana
Kilisutji, a female recluse

* The following lakon is based on the summary given by Th. Pigeaud in *Javaanse Volksvertoningen*, pp. 491–492, with the addition of occasional explanatory phrases. The story is similar to the synopsis in Appendix I, but differs in details.

The Play

ACT I. *The kingdom of Kediri. The throne hall of the palace.*

The king of Kediri, Lembu Amidjaya, discusses with Prime Minister Djayabadra the anticipated return of his sons, Prince Plabuhan and Prince Wanengsari, from Tambakbaya. He had sent them there to inform his son-in-law, Prince Pandji Kasatriyan, that the princess Tjandra Kirana, who had so mysteriously disappeared from her husband's home, had just as mysteriously reappeared in her father's. Her body was now poisoned and swollen, however, because, as she explained, a raksasa named Badjubaratkrendayana had tried to swallow her. Therefore, if Prince Pandji still wishes to retain her as his wife, she has requested that another wedding feast should be celebrated just like the one in which he had first married her. She also has asked that her husband find a handsome knight from the mountains to serve as her bride's man.

During the conversation between the king and his minister, the two princes return and report that their brother-in-law, Pandji Kasatriyan, has agreed to the celebration of a second wedding and has sent out his servants, Bantjak and Doyok, to search for a handsome, mountain-bred bride's man as requested by the princess.

ACT II. *The kingdom of Kediri. In the inner apartments of the keraton.*

When the king enters from the council hall he meets his queen, Maheswara, and the female recluse of Panggungwetan, Kilisutji. They discuss what has happened.

ACT III. *On the plaza before the Kediri keraton.*

Crown Prince Gunung Sari, Prime Minister Djayabadra, and three regents discuss the prospective wedding celebration. The regents receive orders to [invite the royal families of Ngurawan and Singasari to the forthcoming wedding and to] ready guesthouses for the visiting princes and their retinues.

ACT IV. *The kingdom of Bali. In Klana Suryawibawa's throne hall.*

King Klana Suryawibawa sits in the company of his younger brother, Prince Suryapamala, and three Buginese chiefs. The king has conceived a passionate love for Princess Tjandra Kirana. He orders the Buginese, Tjiklobo, to proceed to Kediri with a letter suing for the hand of the princess. Then the king retires. Tjiklobo with three followers depart.

On the way, they meet the regents of Kediri. There is a conflict and the Buginese are routed. The regents continue to Ngurawan and Singasari [where they are to invite the kings to the forthcoming wedding celebration].

ACT V. *In the princely residence of Bandjarmlati [Bandjaransari].*

Sinompradapa, prince of Djenggala, with Sebul and Palet, his servants, receives a messenger from Princess Kumadaningrat who invites the prince to visit her mistress in Ngurawan. Sinompradapa promises to do so; the messenger then departs and soon after the prince follows.

ACT VI. *The kingdom of Ngurawan. In the palace garden.*

Princess Kumadaningrat first receives the report of her servant and soon afterward Prince Sinompradapa himself appears. After an intimate meeting, Sinompradapa departs for Tambakbaya [the residence of his older brother, Pandji Kasatriyan].

ACT VII. *In the forest.*

On the way, Sinompradapa meets King Klono's Buginese envoys who are fleeing from the Kediri regents [see Act IV], fights with them and defeats them.

ACT VIII. *In another part of the forest.*

Princess Tjandra Kirana awakens in the middle of the woods even though she had gone to sleep in her husband's residence in Tambakbaya. She is confused and despairing and weeps bitterly. This causes a violent upheaval in nature.

ACT IX. *In Suralaya (heaven).*

The gods, Sang Hyang Brahma and Sang Hyang Narada, wonder what has caused the upheaval in nature. Sang Hyang Brahma [descends to earth and] discovers the lost princess. When he tries to approach her, she eludes him, and he is so annoyed that he burns her; the shape of the princess disappears, and she emerges from the flames as a noble youth. Brahma names the young man Kuda Narawangsa and commands him to go to Tambakbaya to serve as a bridal attendant.

"The will of Lord Guru [the highest god] is that you accede to the wishes of Prawan Djagalan, who was able to put herself into your place by having practiced high self-discipline." [Thus we discover that the swollen princess in Kediri is not, as everyone believes, Tjandra Kirana, but an impostor. The request for a second marriage ceremony is now understandable.]

ACT X. *In the forest.*

Bantjak and Doyok [the servants of Prince Pandji, who have been sent to search for a bride's man] sing songs together. Suddenly, they hear a voice calling, "Robbers! I'm being robbed!" Bantjak and Doyok race around wildly and finally come upon Kuda Narawangsa. During the ensuing conversation, they discover that here is the bride's man they seek, so they take him along to Djenggala.

ACT XI. *The kingdom of Djenggala. In the throne hall of the keraton.*

The king of Djenggala discusses with his son Pandji Kasatriyan, his daughter Ragil Kuning, and others the search for the bride's man. Then Bantjak and Doyok arrive with the young knight. Kuda Narawangsa requests Ragil Kuning's help in fulfilling his duties as bride's man. The king agrees [to allow his daughter to assist the young stranger]. Then the bridegroom's procession is organized and starts out to Kediri.

ACT XII. *The keraton of Kediri. In the throne hall.*

The king of Kediri receives the wedding guests, among them the kings of Ngurawan and Singasari. They discuss the mysterious disappearance and return of the swollen Tjandra Kirana. Soon the bridegroom's procession arrives; Pandji Kasatriyan introduces the handsome bride's man, Kuda Narawangsa. The marriage is concluded and Pandji carries the false Tjandra Kirana into the inner apartments of the keraton. The bride's man (the true Tjandra Kirana) follows.

After the wedding night, the newlyweds sit together in the company of Kuda Narawangsa and Ragil Kuning. Kuda Narawangsa asks the bride for a sirih quid:* she gives it to him but Kuda Narawangsa ridicules the bride's manner of wrapping sirih; he rewraps it and returns it. By the artful way the sirih is wrapped, Pandji recognizes the true Tjandra Kirana. The false Tjandra Kirana weeps; Prince Pandji tries to console her. Kuda Narawangsa continues to mock the bride but cannot bear the masquerade any longer. He becomes the true Tjandra Kirana but immediately disappears with Ragil Kuning, leaving behind a letter written on a lontar palm-leaf. Pandji searches for the bride's man but finds only the letter. He calls together his relations, tells them what has happened, and together they go off to search for Tjandra Kirana.

* A quid of betel nut combined with lime and other ingredients wrapped in an astringent sirih leaf.

ACT XIII. *The kingdom of Bali. At the court of King Klana Suryawibawa.*

King Klana in the company of his younger brother, Suryapamala. The king is still burdened by his passionate love for Tjandra Kirana. The prime minister announces that a princess is passing by. The king goes to meet her personally and [to his surprise finds that it is] Tjandra Kirana accompanied by Ragil Kuning. He rushes toward her repeatedly but each time stumbles and falls. Finally, he begs her forgiveness and asks her to settle in Bali so that he might always pay her homage. She agrees [to become queen of Bali and] says: "I demote you to the rank of prime minister and your younger brother will be chamberlain." Klana accepts. Tjandra Kirana then orders him to await and to turn back the Djenggala princes who are pursuing her.

When Pandji and his relatives arrive, a furious battle ensues. The Djenggala forces are kept at bay and they encamp at Kirisgading.

G. *The Wedding of Sekar Tadji and Pandji*

A wayang bèbèr lakon*

The Characters

The kingdom of Kediri:
King Brawidjaya
Ganda Ripa, the king's son [Gunung Sari in the wayang topeng lakons]
Sekar Tadji (also called Tjandra Kirana), the king's daughter
Bok Mindaka, a royal relative
Sedah Rama, commander-in-chief of Kediri
Bok Kili Wanu Saba Nuwa Selamangleng, a holy woman, adviser on religious rite, related in some way to the royal family [Kili Sutji in the wayang topeng lakons]

The kingdom of Djenggala:
Prince Pandji Djaka Kembang Kuning
Tawang Alun and Naladerma, Pandji's servant-companions
Demang Kuning, chamberlain and uncle of Pandji

The kingdom of "Overseas":
King Klana (Klono)
Bok Tigaron, Klana's sister
Kebolorodan, grand vizier

The manor Paluh Ambah:
The venerable Lord (Kyai Tumenggung) Kalamisani, a high official at the Kediri court
Lady Tjonatjani, Kalamisani's wife

The Play

ROLL I, SCENE 1. *The kingdom of Kediri. In the throne hall of the keraton.*

The king of Kediri, Brawidjaya, holds audience. King Klana of Overseas has sent his vizier, Kebolorodan, to sue in his name for the hand of the beautiful Sekar Tadji, Brawidjaya's daughter. Prince Pandji Kembang Kuning, has also come to seek for Sekar Tadji in marriage. King Brawidjaya tells the two suitors that Sekar Tadji has disappeared from the keraton. Whoever finds her shall have her as his wife.

ROLL I, SCENE 2. *In the mountains.*

Pandji, mounted on a white horse and followed by his faithful servants, Tawung Alun and Naladerma, searches for Sekar Tadji. He encounters three retainers of Klana. [Kern's version says that Pandji avoids meeting them and continues on his way.]

ROLL I, SCENE 3. *The Paluh Amba manor of Lord* (Tumenggung) *Kalamisani.*

Princess Sekar Tadji arrives at the manor and explains to Lord Kalamisani and his wife, Lady Tjonatjani, that she has run away from her father's palace because, knowing that King Klana was suing for her hand, she feared lest her father grant Klana's request. She begs them to give her shelter, but the Tumenggung advises her to return to the keraton and submit to the will of her father whatever it might be.

ROLL I, SCENE 4. *The market at Paluh Amba.*

Since Sekar Tadji is unwilling to follow his advice, Kalamisani agrees to let her stay in his compound. Sekar Tadji then goes to the big market place at Paluh Amba. Prince Pandji and his two servants also arrive there. Tawang Alun plays on a tambourine and when Sekar Tadji hears the sounds she turns her head to look at the musician. She recognizes Pandji and quickly turns away, hiding behind the air roots of a big banyan tree. But she is not quick enough and Pandji sees her. Considering his aim attained, Pandji quietly leaves the market place and makes his way to the home of his uncle, the Venerable Chamberlain (Kyai Demang) Kuning.

ROLL II, SCENE 1. *The residence of Chamberlain Kuning.*

Pandji arrives with his two servants. He describes

* This story, depicted on six scrolls, each divided into four scenes, was told to the author in 1937 by the wayang bèbèr dalang of the village of Gedompol, Patjitan regency, south-central Java. In 1909, R. A. Kern had photographed all the scrolls and published the story in "De Wajang Beber van Patjitan," *TBG*, LI (1909), 338–356. His record has been used to supplement the author's notes.

to his uncle all that has happened: that Klana has asked for the hand of Sekar Tadji and is camping with his army at Kedung Rangga; that Sekar Tadji had disappeared and that as a consequence the king had promised her to the one who finds her, and that he himself had discovered her in Paluh Amba and therefore considers that she now should belong to him. After relating all this to the chamberlain, Pandji orders his servant Tawang Alun to go to Kediri and inform the king that Sekar Tadji has been found. Then Pandji orders his other servant Naladerma to take to Bok Mindaka (a high-ranking relative of the Kediri king, perhaps his sister or aunt) beautiful clothing to serve as the bride's price for Sekar Tadji.

ROLL II, SCENE 2. *The kingdom of Kediri. In the women's apartments of the keraton.*

Mindaka and her companions are busy weaving. Bok Tigaron, the sister of Klana, arrives with gifts from her brother intended to serve as his bride's price for Sekar Tadji. Mindaka refuses to accept Klana's gifts.

ROLL II, SCENE 3. *In the women's apartments of the Kediri keraton.*

Bok Tigaron is greatly angered by the rejection of her brother's gifts. She and her companions attack Mindaka and the other Kediri ladies present. In the ensuing battle, the women use household objects as weapons and shields. Tigaron is injured and she and her party flee to Klono's camp at Kedung Rangga.

ROLL II, SCENE 4. *Camp of the Kediri army.*

Prince Ganda Ripa has also been searching for his sister Sekar Tadji. Tawang Alun, on his way to Kediri (see Roll II, scene 1), stops at Ganda Ripa's camp. He informs the Kediri prince and the commander-in-chief, Sedah Rama, that Pandji has already discovered the whereabouts of Sekar Tadji. Ganda Ripa decides to accompany Pandji's emissary to Kediri.

ROLL III, SCENE 1. *The kingdom of Kediri. In the throne hall of the keraton.*

The king is holding an audience when Prince Ganda Ripa and Tawang Alun appear. Tawang Alun gives the king Pandji's message, whereupon the king declares that Pandji has won the hand of Sekar Tadji. Suddenly King Klana arrives to sue in person for the hand of the princess. When he is told that Pandji has won her hand he is furious. King Brawidjaya then agrees to hold another contest for the princess, a hand-to-hand combat. Klana is satisfied and retires.

ROLL III, SCENE 2. *Kedung Rangga, King Klana's encampment.*

Klana asks his giant vizier, Kebolorodan, whether he would dare engage Pandji's servant, Tawang Alun, in battle. Kebolorodan assures his king that he would like nothing better, and Klana appoints him as his representative in the hand-to-hand combat.

ROLL III, SCENE 3. *In the residence of Chamberlain Kuning.*

Naladerma returns from bearing Pandji's gifts to Mbok Mindaka (see Roll II, scene 1) and reports to his master that the gifts have been accepted. Pandji then tells the servant that they must immediately return to Kediri because Tawang Alun has been challenged to a hand-to-hand combat by a vassal of King Klana.

ROLL III, SCENE 4. *The kingdom of Kediri. The tournament grounds on the alun-alun.*

While King Brawidjaya and King Klana and their courtiers look on, Tawang Alun and Kebolorodan fight. Pandji's servant is wounded and forced to acknowledge defeat.

ROLL IV, SCENE 1. *The manor at Paluh Amba.*

Lady Tjonatjani and Sekar Tadji are startled when Naladerma arrives at the manor bearing his wounded friend, Tawang Alun. Naladerma leaves Tawang Alun to recuperate in Paluh Amba and returns to his master, Prince Pandji, who has decided to avenge Tawang Alun's defeat himself.

ROLL IV, SCENE 2. *The kingdom of Kediri. The tournament grounds on the alun-alun.*

There is a fierce battle between Pandji and Kebolorodan and the latter is killed. The kings, Brawidjaya and Klana, and their retinues look on.

ROLL IV, SCENE 3. *The residence of Chamberlain Kuning.*

After the battle with Kebolorodan, Pandji returned to his uncle's home and now sits with his uncle and his servant, Naladerma. Ganda Ripa, crown prince of

Kediri, arrives and orders Pandji in the name of the king to ready himself to kill King Klana.

ROLL IV, SCENE 4. *In the manor of Paluh Amba.*

Lord Kalamisani, Lady Tjonatjani, Princess Sekar Tadji, and Tawang Alun, who has fully recovered from his wounds, are present. Sekar Tadji's brother, Crown Prince Ganda Ripa, arrives with messages from his father, the king: Sekar Tadji must return to the keraton immediately, and Tawang Alun must prepare himself for battle. The king has sent Tawang Alun a special weapon called Kaprabon ing Kasatriyan as a token of his satisfaction with the servant's bravery.

ROLL V, SCENE 1. *In King Klana's encampment at Kedung Rangga.*

King Klana tells his sister, Tigaron, that he plans to disguise himself as Ganda Ripa and enter Sekar Tadji's private apartments in the palace.

ROLL V, SCENE 2. *The kingdom of Kediri; in Sekar Tadji's apartments in the palace.*

Klana, dressed as Ganda Ripa, approaches the seated Sekar Tadji. She recognizes him, draws her dagger [threatening to kill herself?], and turns away her head. The true Ganda Ripa discovers the intruder, and Klana withdraws, shamed and angry.

ROLL V, SCENE 3. *Outside the keraton of Kediri.*

The armies of Klana and Kediri are engaged in a fierce battle. Klana himself is killed by Tawang Alun with the weapons given him by Gandaripa (see Roll IV, scene 4).

ROLL V, SCENE 4. *In the women's apartments of Klana's camp.*

Ganda Ripa, Tawang Alun, and Naladerma penetrate into the apartments of the women and capture them as trophies of war.

ROLL VI, SCENE 1.

Ganda Ripa, followed by Tawang Alun, Naladerma, and Chamberlain Kuning, brings the captured women to Pandji.

ROLL VI, SCENE 2. *The throne hall of the Kediri keraton.*

Pandji escorts the women before King Brawidjaya. The king orders arrangements for the wedding of Prince Pandji and Princess Sekar Tadji to be completed.

ROLL VI, SCENE 3. *In Sekar Tadji's apartments.*

Prince Ganda Ripa informs Sekar Tadji that she is to prepare herself for the wedding. (See Pl. 105.)

ROLL VI, SCENE 4. *In a hall of the keraton of Kediri.*

Prince Pandji Djaka Kembang Kuning is married to Princess Sekar Tadji. Prince Pandji and Sekar Tadji, seated on mats opposite each other, are attended by relations and servants and are being entertained by a dancer (?).

H. *Damar Wulan the Grasscutter*

A Langendriya performance at the Istana Mangkunagaran, Surakarta, Nov. 16 and 17, 1930, on the occasion of the initiation of Gusti Raden Adjeng Siti Nurul Kamaril Ngasarati into the Islamic religious community.*

The Characters

The hermitage of Paluh Amba:
Srenggara-manik, a venerable holy man
Damar Wulan, Srenggara-manik's grandson, son of the former prime minister of Majapahit, Udara, and nephew of the present prime minister, Logender
Sabda Palon and Naya Genggong, Damar Wulan's servants and companions

The prime minister's residence in Majapahit:
Logender, prime minister (patih)
Layang Seta and Layang Kumitir, Logender's sons
Dewi Andjasmara, Logender's daughter
Emban Wasita, Dewi Andjasmara's nurse

Others:
Four market women and their servants

The Play

ACT I. *In the hermitage of Paluh Amba.*

The venerable hermit, Srenggara-manik, deciding that the education of his grandson, Damar Wulan, is now complete, orders the boy to go to the court of Majapahit to serve his ruler and the country as befits a youth of noble birth. He instructs Damar Wulan to report to his uncle, Prime Minister Logender. Damar Wulan is reluctant to leave the hermit but when the old man reminds him of the duty incumbent upon a nobleman, he departs. His servants, Sabda Palon and his son Naya Genggong, follow.

ACT II. *In the forest.*

Damar Wulan and his two followers travel through a forest on the way to Majapahit.

ACT III. *In the reception hall of the prime minister of Majapahit's residence.*

SCENE 1: Patih Logender is told by two officials that young Damar Wulan has arrived in Majapahit and is now at the gate asking to enter into the patih's service. Logender is afraid that should he accept Damar Wulan into his service, the newcomer would overshadow his own sons, Layang Seta and Layang Kumitir. Should he reject his nephew's services, however, the boy might come to the attention of the maiden queen; and this Logender wants to avoid at all cost in view of the plans he cherishes for his own sons. He therefore decides to take Damar Wulan into his service, intending to keep him in obscurity as much as possible and to give him no chance to display his talents. He gives orders to have his nephew shown in.

SCENE 2: Damar Wulan enters and pays his respects to the prime minister. Logender consents to take him into his service and assigns him the duty of cleaning the back courtyard and guarding the rearmost gate of his residential complex.

SCENE 3: Dewi Andjasmara, Logender's daughter, peeping through a small window from her chamber into the hall, has witnessed Damar Wulan's reception. From her attendant, Emban Wasita, she learns that the stranger is her cousin. She immediately feels pity for him and anger toward her father for thus maltreating his only nephew.

SCENE 4: Damar Wulan accepts Logender's orders, even though the work is completely incompatible with his rank.

ACT IV. *At the rear gate of the prime minister's residence.*

SCENE 1: Sabda Palon and his son, Naya Genggong, complain about the heavy work imposed upon Damar Wulan and themselves. Moreover, they are hungry because they have not been given any food.

* The following is a translation from the Dutch-language program offered to the guests on this occasion.

SCENE 2: Emban Wasita arrives, bringing from Dewi Andjasmara *sirih,* cigarettes, and tidbits as tokens of sympathy and welcome. Damar Wulan, suspecting that these gifts signify more than cousinly sympathy and fearing Patih Logender's wrath, dares not accept them despite Emban Wasita's insistence. So, she gives the tidbits to Sabda Palon and Naya Genggong, who promptly begin to quibble over the booty.

ACT V. *At the rear gate of the prime minister's residence.*

SCENE 1: The prime minister's sons, Layang Seta and Layang Kumitir, enter the back courtyard with a follower. Damar Wulan, busy sweeping the yard, does not crouch down as underlings customarily do in the presence of a superior. The two arrogant young men are enraged, demand to know who he is and order him to give them his kris. Damar Wulan refuses to surrender this emblem of his nobility. Thereupon Layang Seta, Layang Kumitir, and their follower attack him.

SCENE 2: Hearing the commotion, Patih Logender and his retinue rush into the courtyard. The prime minister informs his sons that Damar Wulan is their cousin.

SCENE 3: Patih Logender takes this opportunity to impose upon Damar Wulan a still heavier and indeed insurmountable task. (He hopes thereby to goad Damar Wulan into resistance; should his nephew rebel, he would have a pretext for getting him out of the way.) Damar Wulan is charged with the care of twelve horses: every day, he must clean them and their stables and provide them with grass fodder. Damar Wulan accepts this task with his usual gentleness. Also upon the orders of the patih, he divests himself of all his fine garments and dons crudely woven ones; he refuses only to surrender his kris but, again upon the orders of his uncle, he conceals it.

SCENE 4: Logender goes off with his two sons; two of his followers, however, stay behind for a moment; both are painfully affected by the patih's baseness, his degrading treatment of his own nephew.

ACT VI. *On the highway to Majapahit.*

Four market women, each with a servant, meet on the road to the city and after closer acquaintance, they discover that they have a common purpose in going to the city—all are looking for the son of the former patih, Udara, to whom they owe their present prosperity. They hope to be of service to the son out of gratitude to the father. Together they continue on their way.

ACT VII. *In an open field outside the city of Majapahit.*

SCENE 1: Damar Wulan and his two followers are busy cutting grass for Patih Logender's horses. They wear crude clothing. The four market women, passing by and seeing them so heavily loaded with baskets, pity them. Questioning Sabda Palon, they discover that the young grasscutter is precisely the person they are seeking—Damar Wulan, son of Patih Udara. The four women greet him respectfully, tell him that in order to repay his father's beneficence they wish to serve him.

SCENE 2: The women offer Damar Wulan fine clothing but he tells them he cannot accept it because temporarily, for religious reasons, he must abstain from all worldliness. Thus, Sabda Palon receives the gifts. Damar Wulan does, however, accept the four women's offer to provide daily the cut grass for the twelve horses and good food for himself and his followers. After promising to see them again, Damar Wulan returns to the prime minister's residence.

ACT VIII. *In the stable of the prime minister's residence.*

While Damar Wulan and his followers are busy cleaning the stables, Emban Wasita arrives again with gifts from Andjasmara. This time, a letter accompanies the gifts. Again Damar Wulan does not accept the sweetmeats and clothing and again Sabda Palon profits. The latter manages to persuade his master that facing some danger, if necessary even death, for the sake of a beautiful maiden is better than perishing of misery and hunger in a stable. Damar Wulan reaches an understanding with Emban Wasita: at midnight a back gate leading to Andjasmara's garden will be left open for him. Emban Wasita leaves pleased with the success of her mission. Naya Genggong and Sabda Palon quibble over the sweetmeats.

ACT IX. *In the garden of Andjasmara's apartments.*

Andjasmara and Emban Wasita impatiently await Damar Wulan's arrival. In the half-darkness of the setting moon, the young man approaches unobserved and overhears their conversation. Then Damar Wulan declares his love for Andjasmara. They retire together to her chamber.

ACT X. *The back courtyard of the prime minister's residence.*

Layang Seta and Layang Kumitir with their followers are making the nightly rounds. Ordered to do so by their father, they look into the stables to see whether Damar Wulan is there. When they do not find him, they search and discover the open gate leading into Andjasmara's garden; they realize that Damar Wulan has entered into an inadmissible relationship with their sister.

ACT XI. *Within and in front of Andjasmara's apartments.*

SCENE 1: Layang Seta and Layang Kumitir, having entered Andjasmara's garden, knock on her door demanding to be let in. At first she jokes about the unconventionality of such a midnight visit but when they accuse her of admitting Damar Wulan to her room she immediately acknowledges it. Her brothers are naturally furious and challenge Damar Wulan to come out. Meanwhile Andjasmara pelts them with all sorts of household articles. When Damar Wulan emerges there is a terrible fight between him and the brothers. Even though they outnumber Damar Wulan, Layang Seta and Layang Kumitir are beaten.

SCENE 2: Aroused by the turmoil, Patih Logender, his wife, and his followers appear. He commands the three to stop fighting immediately since he realizes that if someone should be killed it could not be kept secret and great difficulties would ensue. He agrees to the marriage of Damar Wulan and Andjasmara since what has happened cannot be undone. But his prime concern is still to keep Damar Wulan in obscurity, so, he has the young couple and their servants locked up in a remote garden pavilion. With his usual gentleness, Damar Wulan submits to this order.

APPENDIX IV

BIOGRAPHICAL SKETCHES

Some Leading Figures in the Development of Indonesian Modern Art

THE relative achievements of an artist in his field or his notable influence as leader dictated the selection below, and yet so many grievous omissions were inevitable for technical reasons.

To avoid confusion, the name by which an artist is commonly known is italicized (*e.g.*, Selamat *Sudibio* or *Kartono* Yudhokusumo), and the biographies are alphabetized accordingly. The artist's place of residence, if known, is given at the right, after the vital statistics.

The names of associations are abbreviated (*e.g.*, Persagi, SIM, BMKN) according to common usage in Indonesia.

ABDULLAH SURIO SUBROTO (Abdullah "The Elder"), 1878–1941

The adopted son of Doctor Wahidin, Abdullah attended medical school in Batavia as a young man. He was sent to the Netherlands to continue his medical education, but instead entered the Academy of Fine Arts to begin his study of painting, where he received a thorough training in Western painting techniques.

After his return to Indonesia, Abdullah became famous for his landscapes of the country surrounding Bandung, his home, in a romantic naturalistic style. His paintings found ready buyers among Dutch residents and he became prosperous. Abdullah trained a number of landscape painters; among them today are some of the commercial landscape painters of Bandung. His son, Basuki Abdullah, is a well-known painter.

AFFANDI (b. 1910, Tjirebon, N. Java) Jogjakarta

Affandi, the third of seven children, was the son of an employee of the Typographical Service. He began to draw as a child and was particularly fascinated by the stylized shadow-play puppets which he re-created from memory. At the age of ten he left Tjirebon for Bandung, where he lived with an elder brother. Affandi attended a Dutch-language continuation school (MULO) in Bandung, where he was the best drawing pupil. He then moved to Djakarta, where he attended a school at the junior-college level (AMS), while living with the Yudhokusumo family. There he met Sudjojono, Yudhokusumo's adopted son, who first introduced him to oil painting.

After graduating from AMS, Affandi taught reading and general subjects in a continuation school for Indonesians (HIS). He was attracted by the poster painting of Tutur, who made billboards for cinemas. Affandi left his teaching position to work with Tutur, and soon moved to Bandung on the same sort of job. There he began painting landscapes with the paint left over from his posters. He entered an exhibit of young painters, where because of his bold style he was awarded the first prize. The judge of the competition, Sumardja, encouraged Affandi to pursue a painting career.

When Persagi was formed in 1938 by Sudjojono in Djakarta, Affandi, Hendra, and Barli established their own small group in Bandung. Affandi visited Persagi when he was in Djakarta.

During the Japanese occupation Affandi worked to perfect his painting technique, although without any formal instruction. Together with Sudjojono, he headed the art department of Putera, an organization left by the Japanese under Indonesian guidance.

With the outbreak of the revolution, Affandi painted anti-Dutch propaganda posters. He moved to Jogjakarta, where he aided in establishing Seni Rupa Masjarakat, which subsequently merged with SIM in 1946. The following year Affandi became a co-founder of Pelukis Rakjat. Returning to Djakarta in 1948, he cooperated in organizing an association there, the GPI.

In 1949 Affandi and his family (his wife and daughter Kartika who is now a painter and sculptress) left Indonesia for a protracted stay abroad. A scholarship from the Government of India made possible his studies and travels in India (1950–1952). Subsequently he went on to Europe. In 1953, together with the painters Kusnadi and Sholihin, Affandi attended the Bienal Art Exhibition in São Paulo, Brazil, and in 1954 he represented Indonesia at the international Biennale shows in Venice, where he was awarded a prize, and in Messina. He returned to Indonesia in September, 1954, rejoined the Pelukis Rakjat then headed by his friend Hendra, and taught at the art academy ASRI, while continuing to work in his studio in Kota Gdé near Jogjakarta and to teach a small group of private students. In 1957–1958 he built his own home and studio in Jogjakarta. He likes to visit Bali and paints there from time to time. Together with four other leading painters, Affandi was nominated in 1955 by the Indonesian Communist Party as a nonparty candidate and subsequently elected to the Constituent Assembly. He held this post from 1956 until the Assembly's dissolution in 1959.

Affandi's works have been acquired by several museums in Europe (Amsterdam, Brussels, and Rome), by the São Paulo museum in Brazil, and the museums of Madras and Santiniketan in India. In 1958 Affandi made a tour of the United States under the sponsorship of USIS and the Asia Foundation, and a collection of his paintings was exhibited in a number of leading American cities. In 1961–1962 he returned to the United States to study techniques of mural painting under the sponsorship of the United States State Department. He is considered one of Indonesia's leading senior artists.

MOCHTAR *APIN* (b. 1923, Bukit Sulungan, Padang Pandjang, W. Sumatra) Bandung

Mochtar Apin was the son of a railroad official. He received extensive education, which in 1948 led to a degree in literature at the University of Indonesia in Djakarta. Although gifted in poetry and writing, painting became his passion while he was still in school (1939–1940). Under the Japanese administration, like so many of his fellow artists, he worked in the Cultural Center. In 1946 he was active as editor of a magazine, *Nusantara,* and in 1947 he worked for the periodicals *Pembangunan* and *Gema Suasana,* while also producing illustrations for the government publishing organization, Balai Pustaka.

With the establishment of the School of Fine Arts in Bandung in 1948, Apin was "discovered" by Admiraal, its first director, and became a close friend and student of "Ries" Mulder, the Dutch painter and principal teacher at Bandung.

In 1951 Apin went to Holland on a STICUSA fellowship where he worked and exhibited for two years. In 1953 he went to Paris to study for the following four years at the École Nationale Supérieure des Beaux-Arts, devoting considerable time to the graphic arts and photography. While working and traveling abroad, he was commissioned to paint murals in the building of the Indonesian Embassy in Paris. In Germany he decorated an Indonesian restaurant in Düsseldorf with murals.

In May, 1958, Mochtar Apin returned to Indonesia, joining the faculty of Bandung's Technological Institute as one of the leading art teachers. In 1966 he was head of the Graphics Division of its Department of Fine Arts.

BAHARUDIN M. S. (b. 1911, Bukittinggi, W. Sumatra) Djakarta

Baharudin, the son of a schoolteacher, graduated from high school in 1928. He then studied graphic arts at several printing firms in Djakarta where he became particularly concerned with the techniques of reproducing illustrations. He began work at the government publishing and printing office, Balai Pustaka, in 1944, and became head of its illustration and lay-out section in 1950. He went to Holland in 1950 under STICUSA sponsorship to study both printing and the fine arts.

Baharudin began to paint actively in 1944. Although he had been greatly attracted by the ideas of Persagi, he had not become a member. He subsequently, however, devoted considerable time to the introduction of modern concepts of art to West Sumatran painters, in opposition to the romantic painters of "beautiful Indonesia." This he accomplished both through lectures on contemporary European and Indonesian art and through making reproductions of modern art works available for study. Together with a young lawyer in Padang, he formed the association Permusjawaratan Kesenian Indonesia, a discussion society for Indonesian arts.

Baharudin's most important contribution has been the introduction of modern ideas into the graphic arts through his work at Balai Pustaka. He has also been occupied with writing a history of European art.

BASUKI ABDULLAH (b. 1915) Djakarta

Basuki Abdullah followed in the footsteps of his father, the accomplished naturalist Abdullah Surio Subroto. In 1933 he went to Holland to study at the Academy of Fine Arts in The Hague, and later studied in both Paris and Rome. His schooling was primarily directed by Dutch artists, as he continued to study under the guidance of the painter Schumacher upon his return to Indonesia. Basuki Abdullah was one of the few well-trained painters in the Indonesian art world of the thirties. He developed competence in portraiture as well as in landscape painting. His portraits are usually idealized, while his free compositions carry a romantic and somewhat flamboyant flavor.

Before World War II Basuki Abdullah had established an art school in Djakarta; it was closed during the Japanese occupation, and he then joined the Cultural Center of the Japanese administration. Since the establishment of the Indonesian Republic, he has been working independently in Djakarta.

Like many of his fellow artists, Basuki Abdullah is gifted in more than one field; he is said to be an excellent dancer in the traditional style, especially in the role of the white monkey-hero of the Ramayana, Hanuman.

Several of Basuki Abdullah's paintings are in the private collection of President Sukarno as well as in other private collections; he is frequently commissioned to paint portraits of personages in high society. From time to time his works are exhibited in one-man shows, as in 1954 when over fifty canvasses were shown at the Duta Indonesia Hotel in Djakarta.

AGUS *DJAJA* (DJAJASUMINTA) (b. 1913, Pandegelang, Bantam, W. Java) Kuta Beach, Bali

Djaja's father, a descendant of an aristocratic Bantam family, was a government employee, who eventually became head of a bank agency and was able to provide a good education for his sons. Following an art education in Djakarta and Amsterdam, Agus started to teach drawing and other subjects in 1934. Three years later he cooperated with Sudojojono in forming Persagi and was chairman of this association for a time, thus becoming one of the initiators of modern Indonesian painting.

During the Japanese occupation he headed the Arts Division of the Cultural Center and later worked in the organization Putera. At this time he also became well-known through numerous exhibitions in which his works appeared with those of Affandi, Hendra, Kartono, and others.

During the revolution he was a colonel in the Indonesian army. In 1947 an exhibition of paintings by Agus Djaja and his younger brother Otto attracted considerable attention in Djakarta. Agus and his brother worked together for some years; their paintings from this time show strong reciprocal influences. The brothers went to Holland together in 1947 with a collection of Indonesian paintings for exhibition in Amsterdam. They remained in Europe for about two years, visiting The Hague, Paris, and Monaco, where exhibitions were also held.

Upon their return to Indonesia in 1950, the brothers opened an art shop and gallery in Djakarta. Subsequently, around 1955, Agus Djaja settled with his wife in Bali, where in his studio at Kuta Beach he painted mainly Balinese subjects in a more naturalistic and commercially appealing style than is found in his earlier works.

OTTO *DJAJA* (DJAJASUNTARA) (b. 1916, Rangkasbitung, Bantam, W. Java) Semarang

Otto Djaja, brother of Agus Djaja, was strongly influenced by the works of the elder Djaja, from whom he also received much of his art education. During the Japanese occupation he worked at the Cultural Center.

Otto Djaja received military training during the Japanese occupation, and in the revolution was a major in the Indonesian army. As a result of his military service, he was sick for some time and is now partially disabled.

In 1947 he and his brother traveled in Europe, where at various exhibitions their works attracted considerable attention as well as winning several prizes and honorable mentions.

Upon his return to Indonesia in 1950, Otto Djaja worked in Djakarta until his marriage in 1952, when he moved to Semarang. Here, in order to support his wife and several children, he had to work in a printing office, and consequently had less time for his painting.

OESMAN *EFFENDI* (b. 1919, Padang, W. Sumatra) Djakarta

Oesman Effendi's father was a cashier at the Netherlands Indies government treasury. Educated at a technical school, Effendi is a self-taught artist who started painting intensively in 1947, inspired by friends who were painters. From 1947 to 1949, he was a member of SIM, first in Solo and later in Jogjakarta. He moved to Djakarta in 1949, where he was a member of GPI from 1949–1951. Effendi was sent to Holland in 1951 for five and a half months by the Bank of Indonesia, where he designed banknotes for the Republic of Indonesia. In December, 1954, he became treasurer of Masjarakat Pelukis Indonesia at the time of its establishment in Djakarta. In 1956 he became a member of the Matahari group. He was also a founding member of Jajasan SD, when that association was begun in 1958.

In addition to painting, Oesman Effendi illustrated books and wrote essays on art and reviews for several Indonesian periodicals. He worked on the editorial board of *Indonesia,* the journal of the BMKN, and after June, 1956, became an active art instructor for BMKN at the Balai Budaya in Djakarta, where 350 students studied painting. He was also the leading design teacher in the Jajasan SD.

HARIJADI SUMODIDJOJO (b. 1921, Ketawang, Kutoardjo, C. Java) Jogjakarta

Harijadi was trained in Djakarta for a business career. He is a self-taught, artist who began to paint in 1941 and has had a difficult time establishing himself. Between 1940 and 1941 he and Suromo worked as commercial artists for a Djakarta firm. During World War II he was a member of the Allied Forces, fighting in Malaya and in

Sumatra. He joined the 17th Brigade of the Indonesian National Army during the revolution, fighting near Jogjakarta while the Dutch occupied that city in 1949.

He joined Seni Rupa Masjarakat, along with Hendra, Rusli, and its founder, Affandi. Shortly thereafter, in 1946, Harijadi joined SIM and became its secretary.

Harijadi has been married twice and has six children.

HENDRA GUNAWAN (b. 1918, Bandung, W. Java) Bandung

Hendra was the son of a low-ranking railroad official. His parents were divorced; he spent his childhood and early adolescence in a dissolute atmosphere created by his gambling, unstable father. After elementary and high school training, he roamed around the villages of West Java, acquiring a reputation as a healer. At the age of 19 he joined a West Javanese theatrical company in which he helped to paint scenery in addition to acting and dancing. After meeting Affandi in 1939 he began to paint seriously. In 1940, together with the painters Barli, Obon, and a few other friends, he established an art club called Pusaka Sunda; at this time he also organized a *reyog* company of costumed entertainers who offered popular comic shows.

During the Japanese occupation Hendra taught painting at the Cultural Center in Djakarta and exhibited his works there. During the revolution Hendra fought with the Indonesian armed forces, was a military judge for a while, and also painted anti-Dutch posters with other members of SIM. He settled in Jogjakarta and in 1947 founded Pelukis Rakjat (with Affandi and Sudarso), which he headed until 1957. From 1950 to 1957 he was also employed as a visiting teacher at ASRI.

Hendra attended the Youth Festival in East Berlin in 1951 and subsequently visited Rumania, the Soviet Union, and the People's Republic of China. This trip had been preceded by a brief visit to Italy. One of Hendra's cherished dreams is a trip to Mexico to study mural painting.

Hendra is considered one of the best and most versatile painters of Indonesia, and, together with Affandi and Sudjojono, he is one of the "fathers" of the modern movement. As well as paintings, he has produced some sculpture. Under his leadership the Pelukis Rakjat undertook sculptural-architectural public projects. He created the monument to General Sudirman now standing in Jogjakarta; his students produced the national monument known as Tugu Muda in Semarang. Under his leadership some labor union buildings and the Djakarta headquarters of the Indonesian Communist Party have been decorated.

A member of the central committee of Lekra, Hendra was also nominated in 1955 by the Indonesian Communist Party as a nonparty candidate for membership in the Constituent Assembly, to which he was elected. Because of his election, Hendra moved to Bandung in 1957, where he has built a house in the *kampung* of his birth. He supplemented his earnings by running a chicken farm. He is married and has one son.

In the early sixties Hendra reportedly devoted time to painting nationalistic subjects, in a more conventional style than in the past. Several of his paintings are in the collection of President Sukarno.

KARTONO YUDHOKUSUMO (b. 1924, Medan, E. Sumatra; d. 1957, Bandung)

Kartono was the son of an art teacher from Central Java, who, at the time of his son's birth, was temporarily employed in Sumatra. As an infant he was taken to Djakarta, where he lived until the end of World War II. Although his father was primarily an art teacher, he also at one time directed a popular theatrical company (*ketoprak*) for which he wrote plays and painted sets, so that the boy grew up in a theatrical atmosphere. In the late fifties his father still taught and wrote prose and poetry; his mother gave English language lessons.

Kartono attended high school in Djakarta, where one of his teachers was Sumardja. His companions included his adopted brother Sudjojono and Affandi who boarded with Kartono's family for about five years.

The Yudhokusumo family photo album shows Kartono, as early as seven years old, painting streetscenes and landscapes. He studied under a number of artists, among them C. Yazaki, W. F. M. Bossardt, B. J. A. Rutgers (1934), T. Akatsuka (1934–1938), E. Dezentjes (1936–1938), and Ch. Sayers (1942–1945). He was influenced by the Swedish artist Maria Ehnborg, who lived at one time in Bandung, as well as by the works of Rousseau. In 1943 Kartono gained prominence from a one-man show sponsored by Putera. He received several prizes for this and other exhibitions during the Japanese occupation.

In 1945 Kartono moved to Jogjakarta, where he married Nurnaningsih, a beautiful and talented film star who also painted. They had one daughter before being divorced in 1952. Kartono joined SIM in 1946, and with other members of SIM he went to Solo, where between 1947 and 1948 he was strongly influenced by the originality and clarity of Sudibio's painting. The association moved back to Jogjakarta in 1948 under the pressure of Dutch military actions. Kartono was in Jogjakarta throughout that city's occupation by the Dutch; in order to make a living at this time, he was forced to peddle wood and charcoal, which left him little time for painting. Subsequently he moved to Madiun for a time, where he became the first leader of Tunas Muda, an association in which Sudibio also participated.

After 1951 he lived and worked in Bandung, teaching painting and heading Sanggar Seniman, a studio which he founded in 1952 with the support of the Cultural Division of the Ministry of Education. In 1955 he remarried and adopted another daughter.

Several of his paintings are to be found in the collection of President Sukarno, his works were also popular among members of the Scandinavian community in Indonesia.

Although Kartono had not traveled abroad, he was under consideration by the Ford Foundation for a fellowship to the United States (he had long wanted to visit Arizona) at the time of his sudden death while he was riding his cherished motorbike near Bandung on July 11, 1957.

The Sanggar Seniman has been taken over by But Muchtar and other members of the Bandung School, who now run it as a free school to honor the memory of Kartono. In 1960 a memorial exhibition of Kartono's works was held in Djakarta.

KUSNADI (b. 1921, Kaliangkrik, Magelang, C. Java) Jogjakarta

Kusnadi was the son of an art lover who collected krisses (Indonesian daggers) and painted shadow-play puppets. He began painting when he was 21, in Purworedjo, Central Java. He is largely self-taught. During the Japanese occupation he went to Djakarta where he was in close contact with Sudjojono and Affandi at Putera; he received technical art training in drawing from Basuki Abdullah at the Japanese-sponsored Cultural Center. One of his first jobs in Djakarta was as a designer at a film studio.

In 1946 Kusnadi moved to Jogjakarta and, shortly thereafter, to Solo as an official of the Indonesian News Film Office (BFI, 1946–1947). He and Luke Abdulrachman edited BFI's monthly publication, *Indonesia,* in Solo. Kusnadi was one of the founders of Pelukis Rakjat in 1947 and subsequently of PI which was organized in 1950. He has been adviser of PI since 1952. In 1950 he became the head of the Fine Arts Section of the Arts Division of the Ministry of Education and Culture; he has been a teacher of esthetics at ASRI since the academy's foundation in 1950. In 1953, together with Sholihin and Affandi, he took a collection of representative Indonesian paintings to the Second Bienal in São Paulo, Brazil. On their way back from São Paulo, he and Sholihin visited Paris to see the collections of the Louvre and of the modern museum. In 1963 Kusnadi made a study trip to the United States to survey art education and museum facilities.

In addition to painting and to his many administrative functions, Kusnadi writes about Indonesian art for several periodicals; he has been on the editorial staff of the journal *Budaya* since 1952, and its chief editor since 1955. He is married to the sculptress Supini, and they have four children.

LEE MAN FONG (b. 1913, Canton, China) Djakarta

At the age of three, Lee Man Fong was taken by his father, who was a trader, to Singapore. Lee was educated there in the Chinese-English school until his father's death in 1929. In 1932, Lee Man Fong went to Indonesia, working in Djakarta as art editor for a Chinese magazine. Later he worked as a designer in the printing department of the publishing firm Kolff and Company; two years later he established an advertising agency and worked in it as a commercial artist.

In 1941 he left the field of commercial art to paint in Bali. After three months he returned to Java, holding his first one-man exhibition in Djakarta in May, 1941, followed by another exhibition in Bandung. During the occupation, he was interned by the Japanese for six months.

As the result of an exhibition in Djakarta, in 1949 the Dutch authorities awarded him a Malino scholarship for three years' study in Holland. There his works were warmly received. During his stay in Europe, he visited England, France, Switzerland, Italy, Luxembourg, and Belgium. He returned to Indonesia at the end of 1952. Shortly thereafter he became art editor of the *Nanyang Post,* a pictorial magazine published in Djakarta. In 1955 he founded the Yin Hua artists' association, of which he is chairman.

In the second half of 1956 he led a delegation of Yin Hua artists on a study-tour of China. On their return to Indonesia an exhibition was held in Djakarta which included more than 80 of Lee Man Fong's works. In 1963 Lee reportedly became curator of the State Art Collection and that of President Sukarno. He is considered the most accomplished Chinese-Indonesian painter. Several of his murals decorate the International Hotel Indonesia in Djakarta.

BUT MUCHTAR (b. 1930, Bandung, W. Java) Bandung

But Muchtar comes from an aristocratic Bantam family. His father, who liked painting, was a railroad official. His family (10 brothers and sisters) have generally pursued technological vocations; intermarriage has occurred between his family and the Djajas.

Following his graduation from high school (SMA) in Jogjakarta, But Muchtar entered the Bandung School of Fine Arts in 1952. In 1957 one of his paintings, "Market Women," won the Stralem Prize at the First Exhibition of Young Asian Artists in Tokyo. After six years of training, primarily with Sumardja and Mulder, But Muchtar graduated from the Bandung School of Fine Arts and became a member of its teaching staff.

In 1960 he received a USIA fellowship for two years' study in the United States. He spent the first year at the Rhode Island School of Design and the second at New York's Art Students League, studying mainly sculpture.

His works include a number of murals, the first done in cooperation with Srihadi and other Bandung students, in the canteen of the University of Indonesia in Djakarta. Subsequently, in 1957, he and Srihadi painted a mural in the Port Building at Tandjung Priok.

As of 1966, But Muchtar combined his creative work with the duties of Secretary of the Department of Fine Arts at the Bandung Institute of Technology.

NASJAH DJAMIN (b. 1924, Perbaungan, Deli, E. Sumatra) Jogjakarta

Nasjah Djamin, a largely self-taught artist, in 1945 aided in the founding of the ASRI association in Medan. During the early days of the revolution the organization made anti-Dutch posters, protesting against the Dutch occupying forces. Nasjah, attracted by reproductions of works by Sudjojono, Affandi, Kartono Yudhokusumo, and others, went to Jogjakarta in 1946, where he studied with Sudjojono and Affandi at SIM. Later in 1947–1948 he joined the Pasukan Obor (Torch Company), which made revolutionary propaganda posters in the Galunggung mountains of West Java.

He lived in Djakarta from 1949 to 1952, where he joined GPI and worked as a book illustrator at Balai Pustaka, the government printing office. In 1952 he returned to Jogjakarta, becoming an official of the Plastic Arts Section of the Ministry of Education and Culture and a member of the editorial staff of the monthly *Budaya.*

Nasjah was sent by the Indonesian government to Singapore with Handrijo and Sumitro to exhibit a collection of Indonesian paintings in 1955. He has been active also in the field of drama, where in addition to painting sets, he has written a number of plays. He was praised as one of the three best writers of one-act plays in 1958, and has been awarded prizes for his writing. In 1957 he was among the founders of the Theater Indonesia, an association of promising dancers, composers, writers, and actors.

HENK *NGANTUNG* (b. 1921, Menado, N. Celebes) Djakarta

Henk Ngantung, son of an official in the Dutch government, was brought up in the aristocratic tradition. He received a Dutch-language education, graduating from continuation school (MULO). Despite his parents' objections to his career as an artist, Ngantung painted from his early youth. He studied first with Bossardt and also in Bandung with the Austrian Rudolf Weinghart. Ngantung developed his techniques rapidly during the Japanese occupation in association with the other painters at the Cultural Center.

In 1954 Ngantung traveled to the Soviet Union and China as the leader of a group of artists from SIM; a year later he went to Czechoslovakia. He was a member of the central body of Lekra; in the 1955 elections he was a Communist Party candidate to Parliament. He was appointed to the National Council by President Sukarno in 1957, where he represented the interests of Indonesian artists.

Ngantung is married and, in the fifties, lived in relative comfort in Djakarta with his wife; frequently he gave art lessons to several nonpaying students. He served as an influential advisor to a number of committees; he participated in the selection of candidates for governmental fellowships abroad, in the organization of cultural missions and art exhibitions, and as a member of a competition jury, and could influence the award of a prize or a commission.

Many of his paintings are of a documentary nature; a number are in the collections of President Sukarno and the Ministry of Information.

In 1961 Ngantung became vice-mayor of Djakarta, a post which presumably curtailed his pursuits as a painter.

MAS *PIRNGADIE* (b. *c.* 1875, d. *c.* 1936)

Pirngadie, one of the old accomplished naturalistic painters of Indonesia, was born into an aristocratic Banjumas family. As a result of his noble birth he came into contact with Dutch residents of Indonesia, among them the painter Du Chattel, who trained the young Indonesian to paint with water colors. Pirngadie mastered the techniques of Western painting; he produced naturalistic landscapes and made paintings of folklife. He trained several younger Indonesian painters, among them Sudjojono and Suromo.

Pirngadie was an extremely skillful and accurate draftsman; he worked for many years for the Royal Batavian Society for Arts and Sciences and the Archaeological Service making intricate reconstruction drawings of ruined monuments; he also made drawings for Jasper to illustrate a large monograph on Indonesian traditional arts and crafts.

BASUKI *RESOBOWO* (b. 1916, Palembang, S. Sumatra) Djakarta

Basuki Resobowo, the son of a surveyor, was educated for a teaching career at the Taman Siswa Teachers' Training School in Djakarta. Although he actually taught for a time, in 1938 he became associated with Persagi. During the occupation he began painting intensively in close association with the leading members of Persagi (Sudjojono, Agus Djaja, and Basuki Abdullah), when he worked in the Japanese-sponsored Cultural Center between 1942 and 1945.

During the revolution he was a member of SIM, both in Solo and in Jogjakarta. For a while he was chairman of SIM. On returning to Djakarta, he joined GPI in 1950 and in 1954 another association, the Masjarakat Seniman Djakarta Raja. He was nominated by the Indonesian Communist Party as a candidate in the 1955 national elections. In the 1960's Resobowo became chairman of Lekra.

His paintings have been acquired by the ministries of Education and Foreign Affairs; he was commissioned by the Government to make a portrait of the nationalist leader Dr. Sutomo, which now hangs in the Presidential Palace.

In addition to painting, Basuki Resobowo worked for a film company, for whom he wrote a very successful satirical scenario entitled "Tamu Agung" ("The Important Visitor," "the VIP"). He has contributed essays on art to various magazines.

RUSLI (b. 1916, Medan, N. Sumatra) Jogjakarta

Rusli was strongly influenced by a prolonged stay in India between 1932 and 1938, where he studied painting, philosophy, literature, dance and music at Santiniketan University founded by Rabindranath Tagore. Upon his return to Indonesia, he taught art for ten years at the Taman Siswa School in Jogjakarta. In 1945 he helped to found the Seni Rupa Masjarakat and became a member of SIM, its successor, until 1949. At one time during the revolution he headed the art and propaganda section of the Ministry of Defense.

Rusli was appointed art instructor at ASRI in 1951. Under the sponsorship of STICUSA, he went to the Netherlands for a study-tour in 1954. Dutch art critics commented on the strong Far Eastern influence they found in Rusli's use of delicate tones and subtle lines. Rusli later visited France and Italy where exhibitions of his work were held.

Rusli returned to Indonesia in 1956.

ACHMAD *SADALI* (b. 1924, Garut, W. Java) Bandung

Sadali was the seventh of thirteen children. His father was an enterprising man who owned a printing press; he was also active in the liberal Islamic movement. Sadali attended schools in his native Garut and in Tasikmalaja; he later graduated from the junior-college level school (AMS) in Jogjakarta. His father had wanted him to become a physician, and in 1945 he enrolled in medical school in Djakarta, where he studied during the last five months of the Japanese occupation. Shortly before the proclamation of independence was made, Sadali returned to Garut, where he became a radio announcer for the revolutionary government. The studio was bombed during the first Dutch "police action," and the Garut population was evacuated into the mountains. His father moved his printing press into hiding, and Sadali helped him print bulletins.

When conditions were temporarily stabilized in 1948, Sadali went to Bandung to enroll in the School of Fine Arts, where his first teacher was the Dutch painter Admiraal. In 1949 Sadali resumed his studies with another Dutch painter, Mulder, with whom he worked until his graduation in 1953. Sadali was then appointed an art instructor at the School of Fine Arts.

Sadali went to Japan in 1954 to attend a Regional Seminar on Arts and Crafts. The following year he received a Rockefeller Foundation fellowship which supported a year of study in the United States.

Sadali's carefully composed, semi-abstract creations, although based on principles learned from Mulder, show his own personal interpretations through his subtle treatment of space and his fine nuances of color. He feels that abstract art is particularly congenial to the Islamic orientation; significantly, one of his long-standing associations has been with the association of Islamic students. Sadali is considered today one of the best younger Indonesian painters. In the early sixties he was appointed head of the Fine Arts Division at the Bandung Institute of Technology.

RADEN *SALEH* BUSTAMAN (1814–1880)

Raden Saleh was born into an aristocratic family, whose members were regents of Semarang and Pekalongan. He was much interested in Western culture, especially in painting, and consequently his uncle sent him to Batavia (Djakarta), the center of Western culture in the Netherlands East Indies. There he came to the attention of the Belgian painter A. Payen, with whom he studied. The Dutch Governor-General, Baron van der Capellen, also became interested in Saleh and arranged for him to continue his studies in Europe.

In Holland, Saleh studied with the portrait painter, C. Kruseman, and the landscape painter, A. Schelfhout. King William I, and later William II, taking interest in the talented young Indonesian, provided him with financial assistance which enabled Saleh to study painting for five years. During the Revolution of 1848 he visited France, and later Italy and Austria; he became a celebrity at various German courts. On his return to Holland, Saleh was given the title of Royal Painter. He later journeyed with the well-known animal painter Horace Vernet to Algiers.

After having lived in Europe for about 20 years, Raden Saleh, married to a wealthy European lady, returned to Java and settled in Weltevreden, Batavia's residential area. He was commissioned to paint a Western-style portrait of the royal family by the Sultan of Jogjakarta, and he consequently lived and worked at the court there for two years, also painting at the court of the Mangkunagara. He finally settled down at Bogor (then Buitenzorg) with his second wife, a Solonese, in a more Westernized atmosphere than that of the traditional Javanese courts.

Raden Saleh was entrusted with the restoration of various portraits and other paintings at the governor-general's palace in Batavia. He also made a series of drawings, mainly landscapes and trees, which were lithographed for use as models in schools.

Near the end of his life Raden Saleh, accompanied by his wife, made a second trip to Europe. Soon after his return to the Dutch East Indies in 1880, he died at Bogor. His epitaph reads:

> Painter to his Royal Highness the King of Holland, Knight of the Order of the Eikenhoorn, Commander with the Star of the Order of Franz Joseph, Knight of the Crown Order of Prussia, Knight of the White Falcon.

For Indonesia, Raden Saleh is an early precursor of modern painting.

S. *SALIM* (b. 1908, Medan, E. Sumatra) Paris, France

Salim was adopted by a well-to-do Dutch family and taken to Europe when he was still a child. In his early twenties he returned to Indonesia hoping to settle there, but found the atmosphere in colonial Batavia (Djakarta) too restrictive and depressing. He struggled to make a living for about four years by painting and installing billboards. Disappointed, he managed to make his way back to Europe, landing penniless in Marseilles.

He managed to reach Paris, where he became Fernand Léger's apprentice and assistant. During this period his own skill and style developed.

The first Indonesian exhibition of his French paintings was held in Djakarta in 1951 under the sponsorship of STICUSA; the same collection was later shown in Bandung and Jogjakarta, where it aroused great interest among local artists.

Although superficially a Parisian, Salim was emotionally an Indonesian nationalist; he was attached to his homeland where he had many friends, among them the Socialist leader Sutan Sjahrir. In 1956 he visited Indonesia and painted for six months in Java and Bali.

SRIHADI SUDARSONO (b. 1932, Solo, C. Java) Bandung

Srihadi's parents live in Solo where they have a small batik business. Srihadi had painted from an early age, although he had no formal instruction as a child. As a senior high school student in Jogjakarta he spent much time sketching; he became associated with the artists working in Jogjakarta during the revolution. He finished his secondary school education in Solo and returned to Jogjakarta after the transfer of sovereignty, where he remained for about a year. At this time he studied with Sudjojono, and for a time became a member of the Communist-sponsored Lekra, which he soon left in disappointment.

He enrolled for a short time in Gadjah Mada University, but soon decided to go to Bandung, where in 1953 he entered the School of Fine Arts. As a student whose talent was immediately recognized he participated in numerous exhibitions; he worked with other Bandung students on the murals for the University of Indonesia's student canteen in Djakarta. He and But Muchtar also painted murals in the port authority building at Tandjung Priok during 1958. Following his graduation from Bandung, he was appointed to its faculty.

In 1960 Srihadi received an ICA fellowship for study in the United States where he spent two years at Ohio State University, obtaining an M.A. there in 1962.

SELAMAT *SUDIBIO* (b. 1912, Madiun, C. Java) Madiun

Sudibio, a sensitive and gifted artist, has been known as an unusual individual since his childhood. Admiring friends describe him during the revolution, when he was a captain in the Indonesian armed forces, as a mild and introverted man who nonetheless could act unexpectedly with reckless courage and with a directness which was both naive and daring.

Between 1947 and 1948, Sudibio associated with the members of SIM when the asscociation was in Solo.

There he strongly influenced the late Kartono Yudhokusumo, who greatly admired Sudibio's painting style.

Sudibio is said to be emotionally disturbed, to be suffering "from a broken heart." His latest paintings have grown more complicated, and his symbolism seems to reflect the inner conflicts and deep frustrations which he has experienced. Sudibio now lives quietly in Madiun with his mother and a sister who take care of him. Together with his friends, the painters Ismono and Sediono, he forms the core of the art association Tunas Muda.

S. SUDJOJONO (b. 1913, Kisaran, E. Sumatra)

Djakarta

Before he was born, Sudjojono's parents had migrated from Java to Sumatra where his father worked as an orderly at the hospital run by the Deli Corporation. At school, Sudjojono's unusual intelligence impressed his headmaster Yudhokusumo, himself a teacher of drawing and the father of the future painter Kartono. He adopted the young Sudjojono when he moved his family to Djakarta. Sudjojono lived as a member of the Yudhokusumo family until he was 28 years old.

Sudjojono completed his high school education in Djakarta, attended a Teachers School in Lembang, West Java, and then enrolled in the Taman Siswa Teachers College in Jogjakarta. He later taught for a while at the Taman Siswa School.

Sudjojono began to draw as a child, when he was fond of sketching soldiers. As a young man he received formal art instruction from Pirngadie and the Japanese painter Yazaki while he was in Djakarta. Deeply impressed by reproductions of Van Gogh, Sudjojono began to paint in an expressionistic style. His scorn for the painters of "the beautiful Indies" developed rapidly; he soon began writing articles critical of the state of Indonesian painting which he signed "S.S. 101." In 1937 Sudjojono gathered a group of artists to form Persagi, an association explicitly devoted to introducing new vitality into Indonesian painting.

During the Japanese occupation, Sudjojono became a prominent figure. At the Cultural Center in Djakarta, he gave painting lessons to a number of young artists. He and Affandi jointly headed the Art Department of Putera.

In the early days of the revolution, Sudjojono gathered a group of artists together in Madiun, where they formed the association SIM, which with Sudjojono as its leader moved first to Solo and finally to Jogjakarta.

By 1950, with the advent of independence, Sudjojono had turned to painting in a naturalistic, meticulous style which he called "realism." These paintings clearly reflected the art policies of the Communist Party, with which he was affiliated. In 1951 Sudjojono attended the Youth Festival in East Berlin; he traveled in Rumania, the USSR, and China with several other members of the Indonesian delegation. Sudjojono was proud of being a Communist and he tried to introduce his concept of "social realism" into the works of younger artists. He worked actively with the Communist-sponsored art federation Lekra with which SIM was affiliated. In the 1955 elections Sudjojono, sponsored by the Communist Party, won a seat in Parliament. He left Parliament in 1958, however, and at the same time was expelled from the Communist Party, reportedly because the Party disapproved of his taking a new young wife. He then settled in Djakarta.

Sudjojono's importance in the art world stems primarily from his role in the thirties, when his efforts stimulated a new approach to art. His paintings are found in the collection of President Sukarno and in other collections, both state and private. He is regarded as one of the "fathers" of modern Indonesian painting.

TRISNO SUMARDJO (b. 1916, Surabaja, E. Java)

Djakarta

Trisno Sumardjo, whose father was an elementary school teacher, was educated in Dutch-language schools; he completed his secondary-school education in 1937.

In 1946, while he was in Madiun, he began to write and to paint. His interest in painting was stimulated by his affiliation with SIM in Solo, when he also directed the publication of its journal *Seniman* (The Artist).

Since 1949 Trisno Sumardjo has lived in Djakarta, where he has been on the Secretariat of the Lembaga Kebudajaan Indonesia, then a member of the board of the cultural federation BMKN, and a member of the editorial staff of its journal, *Indonesia.* Together with Zaini and Oesman Effendi, he established Jajasan SD in 1958.

Trisno Sumardjo is an important figure in the Indonesian art world; he is known for his writing, his translations, and his activities in cultural organizations. A prodigious worker, he has translated many great works into Indonesian, including novels and a number of Shakespeare's plays. He has written novels, plays, essays, poetry, and art criticism. One of his short stories, "Narcissus," appeared in a German anthology entitled *The Most Beautiful Stories of World Literature,* published in Switzerland in 1951.

Trisno Sumardjo traveled in 1952 to America and western Europe for six months; in 1957 he was a member of an Indonesian delegation to China. In 1961 he again visited the United States on a cultural exchange mission.

SUROMO (b. 1919, Solo, C. Java) Jogjakarta

Suromo first studied art with Pirngadie in 1935 when he was in Djakarta. He later worked with the architect Robert Deppe in Djakarta in decorative arts and ceramics. He joined Persagi when the organization was founded in 1938; during 1940–1942 he and Harijadi both worked as commercial artists in a Djakarta firm.

During the Japanese occupation Suromo worked as a free artist. In 1946 he moved to Jogjakarta, where he became a member of Seni Rupa Masjarakat and subsequently of SIM. In 1950 he led the HBS art section in Solo, and in 1951 he was appointed to a teaching position at ASRI. Since 1953 he also taught at SIM's own art school and has been an active member in Lekra.

In addition to painting, Suromo has also been working with woodcuts, a technique which he first began using in 1949.

TRUBUS SUDARSONO (b. 1926, Wates, Jogjakarta, C. Java, d. 1966) Jogjakarta

Trubus was born into a poor family which was unable to provide for more than his elementary schooling. He later remembered that one of the early stimuli to his painting career was his childhood fascination with shadow-play puppets which he cut out and colored. As a youth he worked for a time coloring photographic enlargements for a studio in Solo. In his late teens Trubus made his way to Djakarta, where he found a job working as a servant for the painter Sudarso. He worked part of the time and learned to paint in his free hours.

Trubus studied with Sudjojono and Affandi during the Japanese occupation. He returned to Central Java in the early days of the revolution, where he joined SIM. He left SIM in 1947 when the new association Pelukis Rakjat was founded. During the revolution he worked with other Pelukis Rakjat members producing anti-Dutch political posters, and in 1948, when he attempted to escape abroad, he was imprisoned by the Dutch for his revolutionary activities.

When in 1950, after the transfer of sovereignty, ASRI was established, Trubus was appointed to teach at the academy. In 1954 he was invited to visit Czechoslovakia, a trip which he later described in the February, 1955, issue of *Budaya,* criticizing the art life of that country. Trubus had also made sculptures under the encouragement of Hendra and the PR; his bust of General Sudirman stands in front of the Military Police Corps Museum in Djakarta.

Trubus' home in Pakem, near Jogjakarta, looked out on the volcano Merapi, and the various moods of this "fire mountain" inspired many of his landscape paintings. Some of his best works are portraits of women; several of his paintings are in the collection of President Sukarno. Trubus, who was married and had four children, was essentially a self-made painter. He attained a good reputation as a teacher and was still developing as a creative artist prior to his death during the purges following the coup of October, 1965.

WAKIDI (b. 1889?, Palembang, S. Sumatra) Bukit Tinggi

Wakidi, a member of the older generation of Indonesian painters, went to Bukit Tinggi in 1903 to study at the only teachers training school in Sumatra at that time. There his artistic talent was observed by a Dutch teacher, and he was given the opportunity to go to Semarang, where he studied painting with the Dutch painter Van Dijk.

Wakidi has lived in Bukit Tinggi for the greater part of his life, and his paintings most frequently depict landscapes of this region. During his lifetime he has taught many students, although few have followed his naturalistic style. During his first marriage Wakidi had many children and, following the death of his first wife around 1952, he remarried a much younger woman with whom he has had two children.

Wakidi continued to teach art in Bukit Tinggi in the late fifties and to paint in his free time. He lives quietly, away from the mainstreams of life; he loves music and used to play the violin.

ZAINI (b. 1924, Pariaman, C. Sumatra) Djakarta

Zaini, the son of a trader, received his elementary education at Mohammed Sjafei's school in Kaju Tanam, West Sumatra; he was later sent to Java to continue his education. He was in Djakarta during the Japanese occupation, and he studied painting at the Cultural Center under Sudjojono and Basuki Abdullah and also with Affandi.

During the revolution Zaini moved to Jogjakarta, where he became a member of SIM in 1946. He was also in Solo for a while. In 1949 he returned to Djakarta, where he joined GPI and later Masjarakat Seniman Djakarta Raja. Since 1956 he has been teaching at Balai Budaya in Djakarta, where the BMKN sponsored art courses. In 1958, with Trisno Sumardjo, Oesman Effendi, and others, he helped found the association Jajasan SD and took charge of an art gallery in Kebajoran Baru owned by this association. He also worked as an illustrator.

BIBLIOGRAPHY

BIBLIOGRAPHY

The following abbreviations for periodicals have been used:

BEFEO	*Bulletin de l'Ecole Française d'Extrême Orient*
BKI	*Bijdragen tot de Taal-, Land- en Volkenkunde (van Nederlandsch-Indië), uitgegeven door het Koninklijk Instituut voor Taal-, Land- en Volkenkunde (van Nederlandsch-Indië)*
JAOS	*Journal of the American Oriental Society*
JRASMB	*Journal of the Royal Asiatic Society, Malayan Branch*
TBG	*Tijdschrift voor Indische Taal-, Land- en Volkenkunde uitgegeven door het (Koninklijk) Bataviaasch Genootschap van Kunsten en Wetenschappen*
VBG	*Verhandelingen van het (Koninklijk) Bataviaasch Genootschap van Kunsten en Wetenschappen*
VKI	*Verhandelingen van het Koninklijk Instituut voor de Taal-, Land- en Volkenkunde (van Nederlandsch-Indië)*

A valuable bibliography is the revised edition of Raymond Kennedy, *Bibliography of Indonesian Peoples and Cultures,* Thomas W. Maretzki and H. Th. Fischer, eds., New Haven, Conn. Human Relations Area Files, Inc., 1955, 2 vols.

"Affandi's opinion about painting," *Indonesian Affairs,* III (April–May, 1953), 52–57.

Ali, A., ed. *The Flaming Earth; Poems from Indonesia.* Karachi, New Tide Press, 1949.

Alisjahbana, T. *Indonesia in the Modern World.* Trans. by Benedict Anderson. New Delhi, Congress for Cultural Freedom, 1961.

Almeida, W. B. d'. *Life in Java, with sketches of the Javanese.* 2 vols. London, Hurst and Blackett, 1864.

Archer, R. L. "Muhammadan Mysticism in Sumatra," *JRASMB,* XV (1937), 1–126.

Auboyer, J. "Le Théâtre Classique de l'Inde," in Jean Jacquot, ed., *Les Théâtres d'Asie.* Paris, Centre National de la Recherche Scientifique, 1961, pp. 13–18.

Balsham, A. L. *The Wonder that was India; A Survey of the Culture of the Indian Sub-Continent Before the Coming of the Muslims.* New York, Grove Press, 1959.

Bartlett, H. H. *The Labors of the Datoe.* Reprint from Papers of the Michigan Academy of Science, Arts and Letters, 1930–1931.

Bateson, G., and Mead, M. *Balinese Character; A Photographic Analysis.* New York, New York Academy of Sciences, 1942.

Bedaya Dansen en Zangen; Programma voor het Congres van het Java Instituut te Jogjakarta. 24–27 December 1924.

Belo, J. *Bali: Rangda and Barong.* Monographs of the American Ethnological Society, XVI. New York, J. J. Augustin, 1949.

———. *Bali: Temple Festival.* Monographs of the American Ethnological Society, XXII. New York, J. J. Augustin, 1953.

———. *Trance in Bali.* New York, Columbia University Press, 1960.

Berg, C. C. "Kidung Sunda: Inleiding, Tekst, Vertaling en Aanteekeningen," *BKI,* LXXXIII (1927), 1–161.

———. *Kidung Sundayana.* Soerakarta, "De Bliksem," 1928.

Bernet Kempers, A. J. *Ancient Indonesian Art.* Amsterdam, Van der Peet, 1959.

———. "The Bronzes of Nalanda and Hindu Javanese Art," *BKI,* XC (1933), 1–88.

Bie, C. de. "Verslag van de Ontgraving der Steenen

Kamers in de doesoen Tandjoeng Ara, Pasemah-Hoogvlakte," *TBG,* LXXII (1932), 626–635.

Bloch, S., and Coomaraswamy, A. "The Javanese Theatre," *Asia* (July, 1929), 536–539.

Bonnet, R. "Beeldende Kunst in Gianjar," *Djawa,* XVI (1936), 60 ff.

Bordat, D., and Boucrot, F. *Les Théâtres d'Ombres; Histoire et Techniques.* Paris, l'Arche, 1956.

Bosch, F. D. K. *The Golden Germ; An Introduction to Indian Symbolism.* 's-Gravenhage, Mouton and Co., 1960.

———. "The Oldjavanese Bathing-place Jalatunda," in *Selected Studies in Indonesian Archaeology,* pp. 49–107.

———. *Selected Studies in Indonesian Archaeology.* The Hague, Martinus Nijhoff, 1961.

———. "De Spuierreliefs van Djalatoenda," *Cultureel Indië,* VII (1945), 5–42.

———. "Uit de grensgebieden tussen Indische invloedssfeer en oudinheems volksgeloof op Java," *BKI,* CX (1954), 1–19.

Brandes, J. L. A. *Beschrijving van de ruïne bij de Desa Toempang, genaamd Tjandi Djago, in de residentie Pasoeroean.* 's-Gravenhage, M. Nijhoff, 1904.

———. *Beschrijving van Tjandi Singasari; en de volkentooneelen van Panataran.* 's-Gravenhage, M. Nijhoff, 1909.

———. "Pararaton (Ken Arok) of Het Boek der Koningen van Tumapel en van Majapahit," edited by N. J. Krom, *VBG,* LXII (1920).

Breuil, H. *Four Hundred Centuries of Cave Art.* Montignac, Centre d'Etudes et Documentation Préhistoriques, 1952.

Broderick, A. H. *Prehistoric Painting.* London, Avalon Press, 1948.

Budihardja. "Grepen uit de Wajang," *Djawa,* II (1922), 22–28.

Cammann, S. "Types of Symbols in Chinese Art," in Arthur F. Wright, ed., *Studies in Chinese Thought* (*American Anthropologist,* Memoir no. 75). Chicago, University of Chicago Press, 1953.

Campbell, J. *The Masks of God; Occidental Mythology.* New York, Viking Press, 1964.

———. *The Masks of God; Oriental Mythology.* New York, Viking Press, 1962.

———. *The Masks of God; Primitive Mythology.* New York, Viking Press, 1959.

Casparis, J. G. de. "New Evidence on Cultural Relations between Java and Ceylon in Ancient Times," *Artibus Asiae,* XXIV (1961), 241–248.

———. *Prasasti Indonesia.* Vol. I. Bandung, A. C. Nix, 1950.

———. *Prasasti Indonesia.* Vol. II. Bandung, Masa Buru, 1956.

———. "Short Inscriptions from Tjandi Plaosan-Lor," *Bulletin of the Archaeological Service of the Republic of Indonesia,* no. 4 (1958).

Coedès, G. "Le Culte de la Royauté Divinisée, Source d'Inspiration des Grands Monuments du Cambodge Ancien," *Instituto Italiano per il Medio ed Estremo Oriente, Serie Orientale Roma,* V (1952), 1–23.

———. *Les Etats Hindouisés d'Indochine et d'Indonésie.* Paris, E. de Boccard, 1964.

———. "L'Osmose Indienne en Indochine et en Indonésie," *Cahiers d'Histoire Mondiale,* I (1954), 827–838.

———. "Le Substrat Autochtone et la Superstructure Indienne au Cambodge et à Java," *Cahiers d'Histoire Mondiale,* I (1953), 368–377.

Covarrubias, M. *Island of Bali.* New York, Alfred A. Knopf, 1950.

Cuisinier, Jeanne. *La Danse Sacrée en Indochine et en Indonésie.* Paris, Presses Universitaires de France, 1951.

———. *Le Théâtre d'Ombres à Kelantan.* Paris, Gallimard, 1957.

Damais, L.-C. "Liste des Principales Inscriptions Datées de l'Indonésie," *BEFEO,* XLVI (1952), 1–106.

Dhaninivat, K. B. B., Prince, H. H. *The Nang.* Bangkok, National Culture Institute, 1956.

Dharta, A. S. "Het Cultureel Congress te Solo," *Cultureel Nieuws; Indonesie 1955,* no. 45, 17–18.

Dullah, ed. *Paintings from the Collection of Dr. Sukarno, President of the Republic of Indonesia.* 2 vols. Peking, People's Fine Arts Publishing House, 1956.

Dutt, R. C. *The Ramayana and the Mahabharata.* London and Toronto, J. M. Dent, 1910.

Encyclopaedie van Nederlandsch Indie. 4 vols. 2d ed. The Hague, Nijhoff, 1917–1921.

Esnoul, A.-M. "Les Traités de Dramaturgie Indienne," in Jean Jacquot, ed., *Les Théâtres d'Asie.* Paris, Centre National de la Recherche Scientifique, 1961, pp. 19–27.

Freeman, J. D. "A note on the Gawai Kenyalang, or Hornbill Ritual of the Iban of Sarawak," in B. E. Smythies, *The Birds of Borneo.* London, Oliver and Boyd, 1960, pp. 99–102.

Geertz, C. *The Religion of Java.* Glencoe, Illinois, The Free Press, 1960.

Geertz, Hildred. "Indonesian Cultures and Communities," in Ruth McVey, ed., *Indonesia.* New Haven, HRAF, 1963, pp. 24–97.

Goris, R. *Bali: Cults and Customs*. Djakarta, Ministry of Education and Culture of the Republic of Indonesia, n.d.

———. *Sedjarah Bali Kuna*. Bali, 1948.

Goslings, B. M. *De Wajang op Java en op Bali in het Verleden en het Heden: (Beschouwingen in verband met het vraagstuk van het ontstaan der Javaansche Wajang)*. Amsterdam, Meulenhoff, 1938.

Grader, C. J. "Brajut, de geschiedenis van een Balisch gezin," *Orientatie,* no. 37 (October, 1950), 3–19.

Groeneveldt, W. P. *Historical Notes on Indonesia and Malaya; Compiled from Chinese Sources*. Djakarta, C. V. Bhratara, 1960. Reprint of article in *VBG,* XXXIX (1880).

Groneman, J. *In den Kedaton te Jogjakarta*. Leiden, E. J. Brill, 1888.

Groslier, G. *Danseuses Cambodgiennes; Anciennes et Modernes*. Paris, Augustin, Challamel, 1913.

Gruyter, J. de. "Bataksche Plastiek," *Cultureel Indië,* III (1941), 123–132.

H. O. "Petroek als Vorst," *Djawa,* II (1922), 169–172.

Haan, F. de. *Oud Batavia*. Tweede, Herziene Druk. Bandung, A. C. Nix, 1935.

Hadisoeseno, H. "Wayang and Education," *Education and Culture,* no. 8 (October, 1955).

Hadiwidjojo, P. A. "De Bedojo Ketawang," *Handelingen van het Eerste Congres voor de Taal-, Land- en Volkenkunde van Java*. Weltevreden, Albrecht and Co., 1921, pp. 87–90.

Hall, D. G. E. *A History of South-East Asia*. 2d ed. New York, St. Martin's Press, 1964.

Hall, D. G. E., ed. *Historians of South East Asia*. London, Oxford University Press, 1961.

Harding, S. "The Ramayana Shadow-Play in India," *Asia,* XXV, No. 4 (April, 1935), 234–235.

Hardjowirogo, *Sedjarah Wajang Purwa*. Djakarta, Perpustakaan Perguruan Kementerian P. P. dan K., 1955.

Harrisson, T. "The Caves of Niah: a History of Prehistory," *Sarawak Museum Journal,* VIII (1958), 549–595.

———. "A Living Megalithic in Upland Borneo," *Sarawak Museum Journal,* VIII (1958), 694–702.

———. "New Archaeological and Ethnological Results from Niah Caves, Sarawak," *Man,* LIX (1959), 1–8.

Hazeu, G. A. H. *Bijdrage tot de kennis van het Javaansche tooneel*. Leiden, 1897.

Hedendaagse Kunst van Bali. Centraal Museum, Utrecht, 1962.

Heekeren, H. R. van. *The Bronze-Iron Age of Indonesia*. The Hague, Nijhoff, 1958.

———. *The Stone Age of Indonesia*. 's-Gravenhage, Nijhoff, 1957.

Heine-Geldern, R. von. *Altjavanische Bronzen aus dem Besitze der ethnographischen Sammlung des Naturhistorichen Museums in Wien*. Vienna, C. W. Stern. 1925.

———. "The Archaeology and Art of Sumatra," in Edwin M. Loeb, *Sumatra, its History and People*. Vienna, University of Vienna, 1935, pp. 305–331.

———. *Conceptions of State and Kingship in Southeast Asia*. Revised version. Data Paper no. 18. Ithaca, N. Y., Cornell University Southeast Asia Program, 1956.

———. "Introduction," *Indonesian Art: a loan exhibition from the Royal Indies Institute, Amsterdam*. Baltimore. Baltimore Museum of Art, 1949, pp. 12–20.

———. "Prehistoric Research in Netherlands Indies," *Science and Scientists in the Netherlands Indies*. New York, Board for the Netherlands Indies, Surinam and Curacao of New York City, 1945.

———."Survivance de Motifs de L'Ancien Art Bouddhique de L'Inde dans L'Île de Nias," *Artibus Asiae,* XXIV, 3/4 (1961), 299–306.

Helsdingen, W. H. van, and Hoogenberk, H. *Hecht verbonden in lief en leed*. Amsterdam-New York, Elsevier, 1946.

Helsdingen-Schoevers, B. van. *Het Serimpi Boek*. Weltevreden, Volkslectuur, 1925.

Hoenerbach, W. *Das Nordafrikanische Schattentheater*. Mainz, Rheingold-Verlag, 1959.

Holt, C. *Dance Quest in Celebes*. Paris, Les Archives Internationales de la Danse, 1939.

———. *Théâtre et Danses aux Indes Néerlandaises*. Paris, Les Archives Internationales de la Danse, 1939.

———. "Two Dance Worlds," *Impulse 1958* (San Francisco), 17–28, illus.

Hood, M. *The Nuclear Theme as a Determinant of Patet in Javanese Music*. Groningen and Djakarta, J. B. Wolters, 1954.

Hoop, A. N. J. Th. à Th. van der. *Indonesian Ornamental Design*. Bandoeng, A. C. Nix, 1949.

———. *Megalithic Remains in South Sumatra*. Trans. by W. Shirlaw. Zutphen, Thieme, 1933.

Hooykaas, C. *Āgama Tīrtha, Five Studies in Hindu-Balinese Religion*. Amsterdam, N. V. Noord-Hollandsche Uitgevers Maatschappij, 1964.

———. "The Old-Javanese Rāmāyana Kakawin; With Special Reference to the Problem of Interpolation in Kakawins," *VKI,* XVI (1955).

Hudson, A. B. and J. M. "Telang: A Ma'anjan Village of Central Kalimantan," in Koentjaraningrat, ed., *Villages in Indonesia*. Ithaca, N.Y., Cornell University Press, 1967, pp. 90–114.

Indonesia, Republic of. The Provisional Constitution of the Republic of Indonesia, 1950. Djakarta, Ministry of

Information. Section VI: "Fundamental Principles," Article 40.

"Indonesische Schilders: Affandi," *Het Inzicht,* I, no. 29 (3 August 1946), 4.

Jacob, G., and Jensen, H. "Das Chinesische Schattentheater," no. 3 in G. Jacob and P. Kahle, eds., *Das Orientalische Schattentheater.* Stuttgart, W. Kohlhammer, 1933.

Jacob, G., Jensen, H., and Losch, H. "Das Indische Schattentheater," no. 2 in G. Jacob and P. Kahle, eds., *Das Orientalische Schattentheater.* Stuttgart, W. Kohlhammer, 1931.

Jacquot, J., ed. *Les Théâtres d'Asie.* Paris, Centre National de la Recherche Scientifique, 1961.

Jasper, J. E., and Pirngadie, M. *De Inlandsche Kunstnijverheid in Nederlandsch Indië.* 5 vols. The Hague, Mouton, 1912–1927.

Johns, A. H. "The Genesis of a Modern Literature," in Ruth T. McVey, ed., *Indonesia.* New Haven, HRAF, 1963, pp. 410–437.

Juynboll, H. H. "Wajang Kĕlitik oder Kĕrutjil," *Internationales Archiv für Ethnographie,* XIII (1900), 4–17, 97–119.

Kahin, George McT. *Nationalism and Revolution in Indonesia.* Ithaca, N.Y., Cornell University Press, 1952.

Kahle, Paul. "Der Leuchtturm van Alexandria," no. 1 in G. Jacob and P. Kahle, eds., *Das Orientalische Schattentheater.* Stuttgart, W. Kohlhammer, 1930.

Kalff, S. "Inheemsche Schilderkunst op Java," *Oedaya,* II (1925), 202–203.

Kats, J. *Het Javaansche Tooneel.* 2 vols. Weltevreden, Commissie voor de Volkslectuur, 1923.

———. "Wayang Madya," *Djawa,* (Bijlage, Mangkoe Nagoro-Nummer, September, 1924), 42–44.

———. "Wie is Semar?" *Djawa,* III (1923).

Kaudern, Walter. *Ethnographical Studies in Celebes,* 5 vols. Göteburg, Elandersboktryekeri, 1938.

Kern, H. "De Nāgarakrtāgama; Oudjavaansch Lofdicht op Koning Hayam Wuruk," *Verspreide Geschriften,* VII, VIII. 's-Gravenhage, Martinus Nijhoff, 1918.

Kern, R. A. "De Beteekenis van het Woord Dalang," *BKI,* XCIX (1940), 123–124.

———. "De Wajang Beber van Patjitan," *TBG,* LI (1909), 338–356.

Krom, N. J. *L'art Javanais dans les Musées de Hollande et de Java.* Paris and Brussels, G. van Oest, 1926.

———. *Inleiding tot de Hindoe-Javaansche Kunst.* 3 vols. Rev. ed. The Hague, Nijhoff, 1923.

———. *Lalitavistara. De Levensgeschiedenis van den Buddha op Barabudur.* 's-Gravenhage, M. Nijhoff, 1926.

———. "De Oudste Rijken (Eerste tot Zesde Eeuw)," in F. W. Stapel, *Geschiedenis van Nederlandsch Indië.* Amsterdam, N. V. Uitgeversmaatschappij "Joost ven den Vondel," 1938, I, 119–142.

Krom, N. J., and Erp, Th. van. *Barabudur. Archaeological Description.* The Hague, Nijhoff, 1927.

———. *Beschrijving van Barabudur.* The Hague, Nijhoff, 1920–1931.

De Kunst van Bali, Verleden en Heden. The Hague, Gemeentmuseum, 1961.

Kunst, J. *Music in Java; Its History, Its Theory and Its Technique.* The Hague, M. Nijhoff, 1949.

Kusnadi. "Indonesian Fine Art," *Indonesian Art.* Jogjakarta, Art Department, Cultural Office, Ministry of Education and Culture, 1955.

L., J. de. "Indonesische schilders (Kunstkring te Batavia)," *De Fakkel,* I (1941), 686–688.

Leemans, C. *Bôrô-Boedoer op het Eiland Java, afgebeeld en onder toezigt van F. C. Wilsen.* 4 vols. Leiden, E. J. Brill, 1873.

Legge, J. D. *Indonesia.* Englewood, N.J., Prentice-Hall, 1964.

Lelyveldt, Th. B. van. *De Javaansche Danskunst.* Amsterdam, van Holkema en Warendorf, 1931.

Leur, J. C. van. *Indonesian Trade and Society.* The Hague, van Hoeve, 1955.

Lorm, A. J. de, and Tichelman, G. L. *Beeldende Kunst der Bataks.* Leiden, E. J. Brill, 1941.

Lulius van Goor, M. E. *Korte gids voor de tempelbouwvallen in de Prambananvlakte, het Dieng-plateau en Gedong Sanga.* Weltevreden, Landsdrukkerij, 1919.

Malraux, A. *The Voices of Silence: Man and His Art.* New York, Doubleday, 1953.

Mānasāra Śilpaśāstra, trans. by Prasanna Kumar Acharya in *Architecture and Mānasāra.* London, 1933.

Mangkunagara VII of Surakarta. *On the Wayang Kulit (Purwa) and Its Symbolic and Mystical Elements.* Trans. by C. Holt. Data Paper no. 27. Ithaca, N.Y., Cornell University Southeast Asia Program, 1957.

McPhee, C. "The Balinese Wajang Koelit and Its Music," *Djawa,* XVI (1936), 1–50.

Mellema, R. L. *Wayang Puppets; Carving, Colouring and Symbolism.* Trans. by Mantle Hood. Amsterdam, Royal Tropical Institute, 1954.

Moerdowo, R. "Indonesian Painting, Some Contemporary Trends," *The Studio,* CLII, no. 764 (1956), 129–137.

Muensterberger, Warner. *Sculpture of Primitive Man.* New York, Abrams, 1955.

Mus, P. *Barabudur; Esquisse d'une histoire du Bouddhisme fondée sur la critique archéologique des textes.* Hanoi, Imprimerie d'Extrême Orient, 1935.

Nandikeśvara. *The Mirror of Gesture; Being the Abhinaya Darpana of Nandikeśvara.* Trans. by Ananda K. Coomaraswamy and Duggirāla Gopalakrishnāyya. New York, E. Weyhe, 1936.

Nasroen, M. *Kebudajaan Indonesia* (Indonesian Culture). Djakarta, Bulan Bintang, 1951.

Nieuwenhuis, A. W. *Quer durch Borneo.* Leiden, E. J. Brill, 1904.

Pewarta K.P.P. & K. (Bulletin of the Ministry of Education and Culture.) Djakarta.

Pigeaud, Th. G. Th. *Javaanse Volksvertoningen: Bijdrage Tot de Beschrijving van Land en Volk.* Batavia, Volkslectuur, 1938.

———. *De Tantu Panggelaran; Een Oud-Javaansch Prozageschrift.* 's-Gravenhage, Nedl. Boek en Steendrukkerij voorheen H. L. Smits, 1924.

———. "Wayang Wong," *Djawa,* IX (1929), 7–13.

Pigeaud, Th. G. Th., trans. and ed. *Java in the Fourteenth Century; A Study in Cultural History. The Nagara-Kertagama by Rakawi Prapança of Majapahit, 1365 A.D.* 5 vols. The Hague, Martinus Nijhoff, 1960–1963.

Pikiran Rakjat. Bandung, November, 1960.

Pischel, R. "Das Altindische Schattenspiel," *Sitzungsbericht der Koeniglich Preussischen Akademie der Wissenschaften,* XXIII (1906), 482–502.

Pleyte, C. M. "De Eerste 'Ronggeng'," *TBG,* LVII (1916), 270–272.

Poensen, C. "De Wajang," *Mededelingen van wege het Nederlandsch Zendeling-genootschap,* XVI (1872), 59–116, 204–222, 233–280, 353–367; XVII (1873), 138–164.

Poerbatjaraka, R. Ng. "Aanteekeningen op de Nāgarakrĕtāgama," *BKI,* LXXX (1924), 219–286.

Poerbatjaraka, R. Ng., trans. "Arjuna Wiwaha," *BKI,* LXXXII (1926), 181–305.

———. "De Çalon Arang," *BKI,* LXXXII (1926), 110–180.

Polemik Kebudajaan, ed. by Achdiat K. Mihardja. Djakarta, Balai Pustaka, 1950.

Pott, P. H. "Le Bouddhisme de Java et l'Ancienne Civilisation Javanaise," *Instituto Italiano per il Medio ed Estremo Orientale, Serie Orientale Roma,* V (1952), 109–156.

Prijono. *Sri Tañjung, een oud Javaansch Verhaal.* 's-Gravenhage, H. L. Smits, c1938.

Raffles, T. S. *The History of Java.* 2 vols. London, Black, Parbury and Allen, 1817.

Rajagopalachari, C. *Mahabharata.* Chaupatty and Bombay, Bharatiya Vidya Bhavan, 1958.

Rassers, W. H. *Panji, the Culture Hero; A Structural Study of Religion in Java.* The Hague, Martinus Nijhoff, 1959.

Redfield, R. *The Primitive World and Its Transformations.* Ithaca, N.Y., Cornell University Press, 1953.

Reditanaja, Ki. *Kartawijoga.* Trans. from Javanese into Indonesian by R. Hardjowirogo. Djakarta, Balai Pustaka, 1951.

Resink-Wilkens, A. J. "De Klana-dans," *Djawa,* IV (1924), 99–100, illus.

Rhodius, H., ed. *Schönheit und Reichtum des Lebens Walter Spies.* The Hague, L. J. C. Boucher, 1964.

Röder, J., and Hahn, A. *Felsbilder und Vorgeschichte des MacCluer-Golfes West-Neuguinea.* Darmstadt, Wittich, 1959.

Rouffaer, G. P., and Brandes, J. L. A. *Tjandi Singasari & Panataran.* The Hague, Nijhoff, 1909.

Sachs, C. *Eine Weltgeschichte des Tanzes.* Berlin, Dietrich Reimer/Ernst Vohsen, 1933. *World History of the Dance.* Trans. by Bessie Schönberg. New York, W. W. Norton and Co., 1937.

Scharer, H. *Ngaju Religion: the conception of God among a South Borneo people.* Trans. by R. Needham. Koninklijk Instituut voor Taal-, Land- en Volkenkunde, Translation Series 6. The Hague, M. Nijhoff, 1963.

Schnitger, F. M. *Forgotten Kingdoms in Sumatra.* Leiden, E. J. Brill, 1939.

Schrieke, B. "The End of Classical Hindu-Javanese Culture in Central Java," in his *Indonesian Sociological Studies.* Vol. II. The Hague, van Hoeve, 1957.

———. "Ruler and Realm in Early Java," in his *Indonesian Sociological Studies.* Vol. II. The Hague, van Hoeve, 1957.

———. "Wayang Wong," *Djawa,* IX (1929), 5–6.

Schröder, E. E. W. G. *Nias, Ethnographische, Geographische en Historische Aanteekeningen en Studiën.* Leiden, E. J. Brill, 1917.

Selosoemardjan. *Social Changes in Jogjakarta.* Ithaca, N.Y., Cornell University Press, 1962.

Serrurier, L. *De Wajang Poerwå; Eene Ethnologische Studie.* Leiden, E. J. Brill, 1896.

Slametmuljana, trans. *Nagarakretagama,* trans. into Indonesian. Djakarta, "Siliwangi," 1953.

Soedjatmoko *et al.*, eds. *An Introduction to Indonesian Historiography.* Ithaca, N.Y., Cornell University Press, 1965.

Soedjojono. *Seni Loekis, Kesenian dan Seniman.* Jogjakarta, "Indonesia Sekarang," 1946. "Seni Loekis di Indonesia Sekarang dan Jang Akan Datang," pp. 1–9. "Menoedjoe Tjorak Seni Loekis Persatoean Indonesia Baroe," pp. 10–15.

The Song of God: Bhagavad-Gita. Trans. by Swami Prab-

havananda and Christopher Isherwood. New York, The New American Library/Mentor Books, 1954.
Spies, W. "Das Grosse Fest in Trunjan," *TBG,* LXXIII (1933), 220–256.
Stapel, F. W. *Geschiedenis van Nederlandsch Indië.* 5 vols. Amsterdam, "Joost van den Vondel," 1938–1940.
Staugaard, W. "Koeda Kepang," *Handelingen van het Eerste Congres voor de Taal-, Land- en Volkenkunde van Java.* Weltevreden, Albrecht and Co., 1921, pp. 421–426.
Stutterheim, W. F. "The Exploration of Mount Penanggungan in Eastern Java," *Annual Bibliography of Indian Archaeology for the year 1936,* XI, 25–30.
———. *Gids voor de Oudheden van Soekoeh en Tjeta.* Soerakarta, "De Bliksem," 1930.
———. *Het Hinduisme in de Archipel.* Rev. ed. Cultuurgeschiedenis van Indonesië, II. Djakarta, Groningen, J. B. Wolters, 1951.
———. "Het Zinrijke Waterwerk van Djalatoenda," *TBG,* LXXVII (1937), 212–250.
———. *Indian Influences in Old-Balinese Art.* London, The India Society, 1935.
———. "De Kraton van Madjapahit," *VKI,* VII, 1948.
———. "The Meaning of the Hindu-Javanese Çandi," *JAOS,* LI (1931), 1–15.
———. "Een Nieuwe Loot aan een Ouden Stam," *Elsevier's Geillustreerde Maandschrift* (1934), 391–400.
———. "De Oudheden-Collectie Resink-Wilkens," *Djawa,* XIV (1934), 167–197.
———. "De Oudheden-Collectie van Z. H. Mangkoenagoro VII te Soerakarta," *Djawa,* XVII (1937), 1–111.
———. *Oudheden van Bali.* 2 vols. Singaradja, Bali, De Kirtya Liefrinck- van der Tuuk, 1929.
———. *Rama Legenden und Rama Reliefs in Indonesien.* 2 vols. Munchen, Georg Müller, 1925.
———. *Studies in Indonesian Archaeology. Koninklijk Instituut voor Taal-, Land- en Volkenkunde,* Translation Series. The Hague, Nijhoff, 1956.
Sukmono. "Geomorphology and the Location of Çrivijaya," *Madjalah Ilmu-ilmu Sastra Indonesia,* I (1963), 79–92.
Sulardi, R. M. *Printjèning Gambar Wayang Purwa.* Djakarta, Balai Pustaka, 1953.
Sularko, R. M. "Exposisi Seni Rupa Asia-Africa, II," *Mimbar Indonesia,* nos. 23, 24, 25 (June, 1955).
Sumardjo, T. "The Tendencies in Indonesian Art," *Perspective of Indonesia; Atlantic Monthly Supplement* (1956), 33–42.
Sutaarga, A. "De Wajang Golek in West-Java," *Indonesië,* VIII (1955), 441–456.
Suzuki, P. *The Religious System and Culture of Nias, Indonesia.* Ph.D. thesis at the University of Leiden. The Hague, Excelsior, 1959.
Teeuw, A. *Het Bhomakawya; Een Oudjavaans Gedicht.* Groningen, J. B. Wolters, 1946.
Tichelman, G. L. "Bataksche Sarcofagen," *Cultureel Indië,* IV (1942), 246–261.
Tichelman, G. L., and Gruyter, W. J. de. *New Guineesche Oerkunst.* Deventer, van Hoeve, 1944.
Tjan Tjoe Siem. "Anoman Trigangga," in Koentjaraningrat, ed., *Tari dan Kesusasteraan di Indonesia.* Jogjakarta, Pertjetakan Taman-Siswa, 1959, pp. 30–35.
———. *Hoe Koeroepati zich zijn Vrouw verwerft; Javansche Lakon.* Leiden, Drukkerij "Luctor et Emergo," 1938.

Vogel, J. Ph. *The Relation between the Art of India and Java.* London, The India Society, 1925.
Vogler, E. B. *De Monsterkop uit het Omlijstingsornament van Tempeldoorgangen en -nissen in de Hindoe-Javaanse Bouwkunst.* Leiden, E. J. Brill, 1949.
Vroklage, B. A. G. "De Prauw in Culturen van Flores," *Cultureel Indië,* II (1940), 193–199, 230–234, 263–270.
———. "Das Schiff in den Megalithkulturen Südostasiens und der Südsee," *Anthropos,* XXXI (1936), 712–757.

Wagner, F. A. *Indonesia: the Art of an Island Group.* Art of the World Series. New York, McGraw-Hill, 1959.
Waley, A. *Three Ways of Thought in Ancient China.* New York, Doubleday Anchor Books, 1956.
Wertheim, W. F. *Indonesian Society in Transition.* The Hague, van Hoeve, 1956.
Wilken, G. A. "De Hagedis in het Volksgeloof der Malayo-Polynesiers," *BKI,* XL (1891), 462–492.
Wirz, O. *Nias, die Insel der Götzen.* Zurich, Ornell Füssli Verlag, 1929.
With, K. *Java; Brahmanische, Buddhistiche und Eigenlebige Architektur und Plastik auf Java.* Hagen i. W., Folkwang Verlag, 1920.
Wolters, O. W. *Early Indonesian Commerce; a Study of the Origins of Śrīvijaya.* Ithaca, N.Y., Cornell University Press, 1967.

Zimmer, H. *The Art of Indian Asia, Its Mythology and Transformations.* Compiled and ed. by Joseph Campbell. New York, Pantheon Books, 1955.
———. *Myths and Symbols in Indian Art and Civilization.* Ed. by Joseph Campbell. New York, Pantheon Books, 1953.
Zoete, B. de. *The Other Mind; A Study of Dance and Life in South India.* London, Victor Gollancz, 1953.
Zoete, B. de, and Spies, W. *Dance and Drama in Bali.* London, Faber and Faber, 1952.

INDEX—GLOSSARY

INDEX – GLOSSARY

References to plates, figures, and maps are indicated by the page number on which they appear and are given in italics.